IR35 Defence Strategies:
from Contracts to the Commissioners

IR35 Defence Strategies: from Contracts to the Commissioners

Third edition

David Smith LLB FTII
Accountax

Print on Demand Edition

Tottel
publishing

Published by
Tottel Publishing Ltd
Maxwelton House
41-43 Boltro Road
Haywards Heath
West Sussex
RH16 1BJ

ISBN 13: 978-1-84592-518-5
ISBN 10: 1-84592-518-1

Formerly published by LexisNexis Butterworths

This edition reprinted by Tottel Publishing Ltd 2006

British Library Cataloguing-in-Publication Data.
A catalogue record for this book is available from the British Library.

Typeset by Phoenix Photosetting, Chatham, Kent
Printed and bound in Great Britain by
CPI Antony Rowe, Eastbourne, East Sussex

I dedicate this third edition to my daughters, Hannah and Kate.

Author's foreword

I am delighted to be writing a third edition of this book. IR35 has 'settled down' considerably over the last two years and how cases are argued in practice can be considered in more depth. This edition updates the reader not only on the case law developments but on the emerging tactics of handling IR35 disputes in the real world.

There was some real doubt as to whether IR35 would be around following the 2004 Budget. It is, of course, alive and kicking.

I have included as much extra practical advice as possible, with further case studies and lessons I and others have picked up over the last 18 months since the second edition was published.

Although this book has always aimed to be one of practical advice rather than academic esoterica, I have expanded some of the case law commentary and analysed 'mutuality of obligations' yet further. I am currently researching mutuality for my LL M and the temptation to become distracted by some interesting but rather dry MOO theories is great. I hope I have resisted. Chapter 12 has been expanded, and for this edition I have kept the IR35 specific case law in isolation, so it can be read in context.

Finally, this edition sees expanded commentary on the use of Composite Companies in the IR35 arena and also addresses the possibility of reclaiming IR35 taxes paid in error.

David Smith
Milton Keynes, July 2004

Preface

'What's it all about? Does being caught by IR35 really make that much difference?'

An IT contractor passed away and at the Gates of Heaven was asked if he wanted to spend eternity in Hell or Heaven. Somewhat puzzled he asked for a week's trial in each. Down he went to Hell where, to his surprise, he came across a beautiful Caribbean beach, an enchanting sunset, all his old pals and limitless food, drink and partying. For a whole week he had a wonderful time.

The next week he spent in Heaven playing a harp on a cloud. It was fine, but a bit dull after his week in Hell.

At the end of his week in Heaven he was asked to make his decision, 'where would he prefer to spend eternity?' All things considered he decided Hell was by far the better option and he couldn't wait to get back to the partying.

Down he went to Hell but this time instead of the Caribbean beach party he was greeted by flickering flames, torment and desolation.

Calling out to the Devil he said, 'I don't understand. I was down here last week and it was great. Non-stop partying, beautiful Caribbean sunsets, all my old pals—the lot. This time it's all gone. All there is now is flames, torment and desolation.'

In desperation he shouted at the Devil, 'What's changed?'

'Ah', said the Devil, 'it's really quite simple. You see last week you were *contracting*—but now you're *permanent!*'

(Author's note—while being an old joke, the sentiment remains!)

About the author

David Smith graduated in Law in 1981 and later had legal research published. Following a career in commerce he joined the Inland Revenue as a direct entrant Inspector of Taxes via the Civil Service Commission. He has been in the private sector since 1989 both as the tax partner in two accountancy practices and as a founding director of Accountax in 1996.

For many years David has specialised in status disputes, particularly in the construction industry, though many other self-employed workers have been defended, including supermarket trolley collectors, chicken catchers and even nuns. More recently workers who have been subject to IR35 challenges have been successfully defended.

David has taken many status disputes to the General Commissioners, Special Commissioners and the Secretary of State's Tribunal, and he is well known on the professional lecture circuit. David represented the appellant taxpayers in *Lime IT v Justin* and *Tilbury v Gittins*, the only IR35 appeals to have succeeded at the Special Commissioners. He has contributed many articles on IR35 and status to magazines and websites. David and the Accountax team are available for IR35 and tax status advice and can be contacted at the Milton Keynes office on 01908 277377 or via www.accountax-ltd.com.

Acknowledgements

I would like to thank Lisa and all at LexisNexis for their professional, enthusiastic and courteous support. I would also again like to thank Anne Redston, the PCG and the many practitioners who continue to support and encourage me and Accountax. Thanks to Gordon G at Buckingham for his batch of mutuality discussions.

I should also put on record my appreciation of the whole Accountax team. Debbie, Theresa and Sarah have made substantial contributions to this edition.

Finally my ongoing thanks to Trevor, my business partner, for his support and valued acumen.

Contents

Table of cases

Table of statutes

Appendices in **bold** type indicate where the legislation is set out in part or full.

Table of statutory instruments

Appendices printed in **bold** type indicate where the instrument is set out in part or full.

CHAPTER 1

Introduction to IR35: its consequences and common misunderstandings

The background

1.1 Other than the poll tax no piece of tax legislation has received such orchestrated criticism and lobbying as IR35. Sources close to the Treasury suggest that, if they had the chance again, the government would choose a less contentious approach to this legislation, which had some good arguments going for it. The legislation is poorly worded, creates massive uncertainty and, on reflection, changing the law so national insurance is payable on close company dividends might have been an easier and more successful approach. The 2004 Budget failed to reform IR35 despite widespread rumours that it might do so, or even revoke it completely. The e-Minister Pat Hewitt, in an interview in May 2001, conceded that the original draft legislation was 'much too cumbersome' and that the actual implementation of IR35 was something the government was going to watch very carefully. There is perhaps a glimmer of hope that the enforcement of IR35 may not follow the strict letter of the law, but early experiences do not give much optimism.

IR35 in brief

1.2 In essence, IR35 simply says that if a worker who renders personal service is a disguised employee of his client then he should be subjected to the same tax and national insurance deductions as other regular employees. In principle no reasonable person would have a problem with this. Bogus self-employment should no more work than complex artificial offshore trust schemes.

1.3 However, the government has developed, in recent years, a policy, in several areas of tax, seemingly based on straightforward financial expediency often dressed up as something else. It has been suggested that IR35 is not really an issue about fairness or equity, but is an exercise in improving financial yield for the Treasury. It carries with it the spin of modern politics and was expressed in such emotional language that it was heavily criticised by Mr Justice Burton in the Professional Contractors Group's (PCG's) judicial review application in the Spring of 2001. He said, 'It appears to me to be wholly regrettable and unnecessary that such colourful language was used in the first press release' (*R (on the application of Professional Contractors Groups Ltd and others) v IRC* [2001] EWHC Admin 236, [2001] STC 629 at 640).

The approach is not restricted to the so-called Friday to Monday disguised employees who might be subject to a legitimate IR35 challenge. All manner of skilled consultants who had been running their own businesses for many years are potentially caught by the new rules.

If the Revenue wanted to stamp out national insurance avoidance by the use of dividends taken by close company shareholders (a legal planning strategy) why was it necessary to extend IR35 to partnerships and unincorporated workers who are not able to take dividends?

1.4 Some commentators believe that there was political pressure to 'trickle down' the liability away from the agencies and end-users to the personal service businesses at the bottom of the chain. This avoids traditional status disputes where the putative employer risks the liabilities, interest and penalties.

The history of IR35

1.5 There is limited value in going over the whole history of IR35 in detail. The fact is, it is on the statute book and it has survived the 2004 Budget quite unscathed. The initial judicial review challenge failed and although the right to appeal was eventually given to the PCG in June 2001, the Court of Appeal in late 2001 felt unable to strike out the IR35 legislation. Chapter 2 deals with the judicial review challenge in more depth, but is of historical interest only.

1.6 The initial press release in the Budget of March 1999 was entitled 'IR35' and gave the basic thrust of what was behind the initiative. It was concerned with 'Avoidance of Tax in the Provision of Personal Services'. Yet most personal service businesses are primarily concerned with obtaining work, not avoiding tax or national insurance. In order to obtain work, agencies have often to be used and agencies require contractors and freelancers to incorporate so they, the agencies, can avoid having to operate payroll deductions. Once incorporated a business may pay less tax and NICs, but often that is a by-product of incorporation, not a reason for it at the outset.

1.7 Arguably this was misleading, because the main area of 'avoidance' with so-called personal service businesses is national insurance avoidance by the taking of dividends. Although the Contributions Agency and the Revenue did merge in 1999 it would be going too far to assume that tax avoidance means the same thing as national insurance avoidance. It should also be recognised from the outset that IR35 has always been concerned with 'personal' service. Not only is this word used extensively in the various press releases on the subject it is also used throughout the legislation itself. As will be seen later, one of the principles of defending one's self against IR35 is to show that there is a genuine business to business relationship where 'personal' service is not required. This represents one of the major opportunities in avoiding IR35 and the practitioner should not lose sight of the fact that IR35 has always been aimed at *personal* service for the purpose of a business carried on by a client (ITEPA 2003 s 49(1)(*a*)).

1.8 The Revenue has long accepted, and this has been confirmed in its internal manuals, that where a limited company which in law is a separate third party genuinely enters into a contract, then this will be a contract between that limited company and its client. In other words it is not a contract between the personal service business' controlling shareholder and the clients.

1.9 Many successful individuals, ranging from sportsmen to pop stars, form limited companies in order to exploit their commercial attributes. Putting a limited company between the worker and the client is a perfectly legitimate form of business and the Revenue has been quite happy to accept this so long as the substance matches the form.

1.10 It should be noted that the mere insertion of a company will not divorce the worker from the client where the company is inserted only as an administrative convenience or a sham, and case law both recent and old, shows that in such circumstances the insertion of the company can effectively be ignored. This is discussed in more detail later in this chapter.

1.11 The essential thrust of IR35 is aimed at the so-called one-man band limited company commonly used in the IT, engineering and oil and gas industries. The legislation was extended by FA 2003 s 136 to domestic workers, such as nurses, nannies, chauffeurs and butlers, engaged by service companies. Ironically, one of the main reasons why there are so many personal service limited companies (estimates put the figure in excess of 100,000) is because of the introduction of ITEPA 2003 Pt 2 Ch 7.

1.12 The so-called 'agency rules' found in ITEPA 2003 Pt 2 Ch 7, formally TA 1988 s 134 (and their national insurance equivalent regulations) were introduced originally in F(No 2)A 1975 s 38. In essence, the legislation states that, where a worker contracts with an agency, then the agency will have to make deductions of PAYE and national insurance as if the worker were an employee of the agency even though in law he is not.

1.13 The agency rules do not apply where the worker incorporates into a limited company. This means that, where the worker operates as a limited company, the agency is not obliged to make the PAYE and national insurance deductions that would otherwise have to be made if the worker operated as an individual or as a partner in a firm.

1.14 It is not known for sure why limited companies were excluded from the original agency regulations but the fact is they were. It is for this reason that the overwhelming majority of workers who contract with agencies (with the exception of unskilled or semi-skilled workers, such as warehouse pickers) are effectively forced into incorporating, so that the administrative burdens of operating PAYE and national insurance are lifted from the shoulders of the agency. Indeed, several agencies and accountancy practices specialise in forming limited companies for such workers and then deal with their accounting requirements.

1.15 Had the legislation not given an exception to limited companies there would not now be the need for legislation in respect of the widespread use of them. But use of limited companies within the law is not the same as abuse. It is regrettable that the tone of the IR35 debate has given the impression that contractors who have incorporated, for a variety of commercial reasons other than fiscal, are 'tax cheats'.

1.16 Some commentators have questioned whether IR35 is needed at all. For many years the Revenue has been concerned with establishing correct tax status and the Contributions Agency has been concerned with establishing the correct national insurance status. For example, in recent years there has been a massive targeting of the construction industry. This seems likely to be resurrected again in 2004/05.

1.17 It could be argued that if a worker is a disguised employee of his client there is already a mechanism for challenging his tax status, through the use of determinations under reg 49 of the Income Tax (Employments) Regulations 1993, SI 1993/744. However, there is a fundamental difference with the reg 49 route. If the Revenue were to challenge a worker's tax status under a reg 49 determination and succeed, the liability for paying over the appropriate deductions would rest with the employer *not* with the worker's own personal service company.

1.18 Practitioners will understand that under IR35 any liability to hand over extra tax or national insurance in respect of the disguised employee is a liability of the personal service business itself and not the fictional deemed employer.

1.19 As the IR35 issue became increasingly controversial throughout 1999 it was soon made clear by the end users that they would not want to carry any liability under IR35. At one stage it was considered that the liability to make the appropriate deductions would rest with the agencies used commonly by IR35 at-risk businesses. But again, pressure of one kind or another resulted in the liability falling on the personal service business itself.

1.20 The personal service business worker can find himself in a particularly difficult position. On the one hand his company may be liable (and in certain circumstances he himself may be personally liable—see Chapter 14) to make significant extra tax and national insurance deductions as if the worker were in receipt of a traditional salary. Yet at the same time the worker will not get the benefit of any employee rights from the fictional employer, rights which would be afforded to other regular employees.

This raises the question 'what is the difference between a deemed employee and an actual employee?' and the only way it can be answered is to remember that IR35 creates a fictional salary only for the purposes of extracting PAYE and national insurance. See also 2.10 below.

1.21 Various pressure groups have suggested a so-called 'nuclear option', whereby any worker who is deemed to be caught by IR35 should make his case for employee rights with the client. Indeed, in the judicial review case Mr Justice Burton said that, under the circumstances, the worker's solicitor would be able to send a 'pretty strong letter' claiming employee rights with the client.

1.22 There have already been several court cases where a worker, despite contracting via a limited company, has successfully claimed employment law rights either from the end-user or the agency through whom he contracted. Equally, there are cases where workers have failed in similar circumstances. Having successfully washed their hands of any strict legal liability in respect of IR35 deductions both agencies and end-users should be aware that it is almost certain that claims against them will increase. This trend is evidenced in the Hewlett Packard tribunal case of 2001 discussed in more depth in Appendix 6.

1.23 A further irony is that many of the IR35 at-risk workers were previously employees made redundant in the early 1990s and who have shown the courage and initiative to form their own businesses. The government regularly trumpets its policy of assisting small businesses but in many ways IR35 is a major hindrance for the entrepreneur.

1.24 As stated at the beginning of this chapter, no reasonable person would have serious difficulty in accepting the proposition that a worker who is really a disguised employee should be taxed in the same manner as other genuine employees. During a House of Commons debate the Paymaster General commented that people who were 'the same as an employee' should, as a matter of fairness, pay the same amount of tax as regular employees. It was explicitly stated that IR35 is aimed at relationships which have the 'essential characteristics' of direct employment. The prerequisites of a contract of employment are more fully explained in Chapter 6 where it will be seen that according to the strict letter of the law specific tests have to be met before a worker can be classified as an 'employee'.

1.25 In one sense, this phrase hints at an IR35 defence strategy. To avoid IR35 any worker needs to show, in light of the above statement, that he is not the same as other employees and that his relationship does not have the essential characteristics of employment. This comes down to an examination of his working relationship and his contractual terms and conditions and is considered in Chapter 5, 6 and 8.

1.26 Where a worker is presently acting as a disguised employee he should take advice to change the method by which he operates and the contractual terms and conditions he works to, so that in future he falls outside of IR35.

1.27 The original IR35 press release did not go into extensive detail. Passing reference was made to the so-called Friday to Monday scenario, where a worker who is a direct employee under PAYE on the Friday and comes back on the Monday as a self-employed worker despite the fact that to all intents and purposes he is working for the same people at the same premises doing the same job. But the key here is 'to all intents and purposes'. Tax status is determined by the terms and conditions of the working relationship between the two parties and there are many examples of workers who have changed their tax status 'overnight' but have genuinely done so by entering into different terms and conditions from those that went before.

The courts have made it clear that parties can renegotiate the terms and conditions whenever they wish and the tax and national insurance consequences will then flow from those terms and conditions so long as the new terms are not a sham.

1.28 The approach of the government to IR35 seems to have been more akin to 'once an employee always an employee', but this simply doesn't stand up in law. Furthermore, the Revenue tends not to argue that a person who is self-employed cannot become an employee!

1.29 The original press release indicated that a process of consultation with various representative bodies would proceed, but it has been widely reported that very little change came about as a result of this consultation process. One month after the press release a further paper was produced in April 2001. However, the emphasis on the consultation process changed somewhat and it was made clear that although the April document was up for discussion it was not in fact a 'consultation document'.

1.30 The April paper advanced some principles whereby IR35 would apply. Emphasis was placed on whether the worker was controlled, but a let out clause allowed the client the freedom not to make deductions under PAYE if it knew that 'substantially' all of the monies referable to the work done had in fact been paid to the worker as a salary. This is because salaries are already subject to PAYE and national insurance. This was seen by many, especially the clients, as unworkable.

The April document was roundly criticised from many quarters.

1.31 In September 1999 a further press release advanced matters considerably and formed the basis of the final legislation. It was accepted that the onus to make the appropriate PAYE and national insurance deductions should fall on the shoulders of the personal service business, confusingly called the 'intermediary' in the legislation.

1.32 Just as significantly, the control test described in the April document was dropped in favour of the traditional common-law tests that determine the borderline between Schedule D and Employment Income. The so-called control test, which many years ago had been the single most important criteria in determining status, had been played down over the preceding 25 years or so. All commentators agree that a more comprehensive test, looking at a far wider range of individual factors beyond mere control, must give a more informed and balanced approach to this difficult issue.

1.33 IR35 has resulted in two sets of legislation. The first deals with the national insurance aspects of IR35 and is contained in the Social Security Contributions and Benefits Act 1992 s 4A (as inserted by the Welfare Reform and Pensions Act 1999 s 75). That legislation enabled statutory regulations to be introduced at a later date (namely, the Social Security Contributions (Intermediaries) Regulations 2000, SI 2000/727). The primary legislation, the subject of a very well informed and closely argued debate in the House of Lords, was eventually enacted, although not before the Lords initially rejected it and remitted back to the House of Commons, much to the government's chagrin.

1.34 The tax legislation was initially published in early 2000 and was included in FA 2000 Sch 12 and thereafter superseded by ITEPA 2003 Pt 2 Ch 8. At the time many practitioners noted that Royal Assent would not be granted until the mid-summer of 2000 yet the legislation would be retroactive and apply to services performed from 6 April 2000. Payments received after that date, for services performed before 6 April 2000, were not included within the IR35 provisions. Conversely, any sums received before 6 April 2000 in respect of services performed from 6 April were within the IR35 provisions (FA 2000 Sch 12 para 22, now repealed). This ensured that it was not possible to forestall the legislation by arranging for pre-payments to be made for services to be carried out after the introduction of the IR35 rules.

1.35 The lack of genuine consultation, and the lack of attention to workable detail, in the early forms of IR35 led to fierce criticism of the Revenue. As a public service, and one to be strongly welcomed, the Revenue has now devoted substantial publicity to the whole issue of IR35, including reproducing the press releases, tax bulletin articles and a series of frequently asked questions on its website.

1.36 The Revenue has claimed that IR35 is not as complicated as some people have made out. The author has noted, however, that the Revenue itself has posted a total of 105 frequently asked questions concerning IR35 on its website! This figure was correct at the time the first edition of this book was published. The latest figure has risen to 121, so one can only assume IR35 has become even less complicated.

1.37 Despite this more helpful and informative approach to IR35, many practitioners will not be aware that on occasion the Revenue has had to change its own answers to its own FAQs; worryingly without seeming to notify anyone in the profession, the PCG or the public that it had changed its response, despite the fact that the question asked in one case the author was made aware of was an extremely fundamental one.

1.38 The introduction of IR35 has been controversial and many feel that the Revenue hasn't listened to reasoned and reasonable arguments. In many ways, a lack of proper consideration of the views of genuinely interested parties gave rise to the judicial review challenge of the PCG. When the matter was aired in court under the scrutiny of an independent and highly perspicacious High Court judge the arguments against and the concerns with IR35 were given a fair hearing.

1.39 The Revenue has published many articles on IR35, not all of which are perceived as giving an accurate or up to date analysis of the case law. Tax Bulletins 41, 45, 47 and 51 all contain the Revenue's view of the new legislation. Tax Bulletin 45 is perhaps of most use as it shows, in the celebrated examples of Gordon, Henry and Charlotte, how extraneous business factors and a commercial history and modus operandi can enable a personal service business to escape IR35. Unfortunately some inspectors do not apply the Charlotte 'standing back approach' when they should and this is discussed in more depth in Chapter 12. Tax Bulletin 41 contains useful information on the appeals process and is worth studying. Unfortunately it is not entirely reliable and this is touched on in Chapter 13.

Major consequences of IR35 applying

1.40 This section is not designed to be a detailed analysis of all the consequences, fiscal or otherwise, of being caught by IR35. It is a timely reminder of the principal disadvantages of IR35 and, as such, encouragement to take steps and advance arguments to show IR35 does not apply. Many websites (such as www.contractoruk.co.uk) exist with 'calculator' facilities to show the exact difference in take home pay, where different rates of pay can be entered. The Revenue's website also contains many frequently asked questions in calculating the deductions due under IR35, and can be accessed at www.inland revenue.gov.uk.

1.41 The main fiscal disadvantage of IR35 is that income referable to what is called a 'relevant engagement' will be treated as if it is traditional salary and this deemed salary will therefore be subjected to PAYE and national insurance deductions.

1.42 Typically contractors take a high proportion of their 'drawings' as dividends, which carry no national insurance and can also be tax advantageous, particularly for those who need only draw around £30,000 per annum to live.

The IR35 rules do not prevent the contractor from continuing to take dividends, but he will, at the end of the tax year, have to make a deemed salary calculation in accordance with the rules in ITEPA 2003 s 54 (see Appendix 1) and hand over the deductions by April 19 (by virtue of Income Tax (Employments) Regulations 1993, SI 1993/744, reg 40). This clearly gives very little time, and deductions paid late will usually attract interest (under SI 1993/744, reg 51). Furthermore form P35 will have to be completed by May 19 (in accordance with SI 1993/744, reg 43); this is also not a very generous time limit. Here the contractor will have to decide what to answer in box 6 which asks whether any income is caught by the personal service rules.

As such there is the potential downside of having to pay substantially extra national insurance and, potentially, extra tax, along with there being a tight administrative deadline for completing the forms and making the necessary declarations.

1.43 It is not all bad news. Firstly, the income which is deemed to be in respect of relevant engagements and which must be subject to the IR35 deductions can first be reduced by a flat 5% expense together with a claim for certain other specified extra expenses.

The 5% covers administrative help, marketing costs, certain insurances, professional fees and, among other things, training. The 5% need not be actually expended—it is given automatically.

1.44 Secondly, for those contractors who have only part of their income caught under the IR35 rules (because not all of their work amounts to relevant engagements) they may escape IR35 deductions completely. This is because many contractors already take a traditional salary, either as a tax planning strategy in using up lower rate earned income bands or to 'frank' pension contributions. In fact, out and out so called 'abuse' of dividends is unusual.

This means that a contractor could escape all IR35 deductions. For example, a contractor may have £75,000 of work during a year and one third of it might be caught as a 'relevant engagement'. However, if a salary of £20,000 is already being taken then this, together with the 5% deduction of £1,250 (being 5% of the income from the relevant engagement), has to be deducted. This means that potentially £25,000 less £1,250, ie £23,750, is caught under the IR35 rules but £20,000 is already being taken as a salary. Furthermore, specific extra expenses can also be deducted, including certain professional subscriptions, capital allowances, some forms of pension contributions and employer's national insurance contributions paid for the year in question.

It will be readily appreciated that the IR35 'bill' may well be nil.

1.45 The beauty of the 'deemed salary' is that it can be covered and cancelled by any salary taken, even if the salary taken related to an engagement which was outside of IR35. This is the case even if the salary was paid earlier in the year than when the relevant engagement occurred. For example, a salary drawn in the early part of the tax year, during a period when the income generated by the personal service business was *not* from a relevant engagement, can be off-set as salary in respect of a relevant engagement *later* in the tax year.

1.46 The legislation in respect of the calculation of the deemed salary is contained in nine steps in ITEPA 2003 s 54 (see Appendix 1). The detailed calculations, which are beyond the scope of this book, have been subject to a great deal of debate and it is likely that not all of the wrinkles will be resolved in the immediate future.

It should be noted that the deemed salary calculation is not the same as a corporation tax computation. The latter still has to be completed on normal taxation principles.

1.47 In the corporation tax computation, deductions will be available for salaries paid, employer's national insurance contributions, the deemed salary calculation and the national insurance arising on it and other expenses, including travel, professional indemnity insurance cover, capital allowances and other normal miscellaneous expenses.

The company's actual profit and loss account will be very different to the CT computation. It will show deductions for salaries paid, the employer's national insurance thereon, the employer's national insurance on the deemed salary, the PAYE on the deemed salary, the employee's national insurance on the deemed salary plus capital allowances, travel, professional indemnity insurance cover and any normal miscellaneous expenses.

1.48 It is possible to have a situation where the allowable Employment Income expenses are exceeded by the actual expenses of the company. Where this is the case there may be insufficient funds to pay out a high enough salary to cover the deemed salary. Yet the shortfall would be caught by the rules and tax and national insurance would become payable.

1.49 The exact extent of any greater tax and national insurance take will of course depend on many different factors unique to each personal service business and contractor. The main point is that contractors who have traditionally taken large dividends and low salaries will be hit hard.

There have been suggestions that the extra duties arising on the typical personal service business and contractor is in the region of £7,000 per annum. As there are thought to be in excess of 100,000 small businesses potentially affected by IR35 it is clear why the Revenue is keen to implement it.

1.50 A further consequence of IR35 is that a contractor who wishes to retain substantial funds in his company and shelter them at the lower corporation tax rates will not be able to do so. This is because income from relevant engagements will be treated as a deemed salary (subject to the 5% deduction) and will be deemed to have been paid whether or not this has actually happened.

1.51 For those in the construction industry there is double jeopardy in that an 18% tax deduction under the construction industry scheme may have already been made, in accordance with TA 1988 s 559, yet tax and national insurance still needs to be paid over on a gross deemed salary. Fortunately, an extra-statutory concession (ESC 32) has been introduced to help with this problem.

1.52 The effect of this is that the personal service business will be obliged, assuming IR35 bites, to pay over very significant sums of Schedule E tax and national insurance which could otherwise have been used 'gross' to fund further training or acquisition of equipment.

A note on double taxation and a warning

1.53 Despite the Revenue's assurances to the contrary, it *is* possible to have double taxation under IR35. This arises where a deemed salary is calculated but not drawn. The tax and NIC is paid over and then in the new financial year an *actual* salary is taken in respect of the 'deemed' salary from the previous year. Where an actual salary is taken, the previously paid deemed salary deductions cannot be set off, hence full deductions of PAYE and national insurance have to be made again in respect of the actual salary. Dividends can avoid this.

A warning should also be sounded at this stage. Some practitioners who are not sure whether IR35 applies to their client, advise the contractor to take an actual salary and play safe, and in so doing there cannot be any come-back under IR35. The problem with this is if the contractor later decides the advice he was given was wrong, and he wishes to review whether he really was within IR35, he will have a major problem. This is because if an *actual* salary has been taken this cannot be reversed, even if it is accepted by the Revenue that IR35 did not apply for the period in question.

It would be far better to pay the liabilities on the 'deemed' salary. If the situation was then revisited and IR35 was found not to apply, a supplementary P35 could be submitted and tax/NIC reclaimed.

Dispelling the misunderstandings of IR35

IR35 misunderstanding 1—there is a new status test

1.54 This misunderstanding is an easy one to deal with yet remains misunderstood by many potentially affected by IR35.

Initially there was to be a new statutory 'control' test to determine whether or not a worker was a disguised employee and hence caught by IR35. This was dropped in favour of the existing common law tests developed over the years through the courts.

1.55 The reasons for this volte face are not entirely clear but it is suggested that practical difficulties with a statutory control test had already been encountered in relation to ITEPA 2003 Pt 2 Ch 7 (the agency rules) and the national insurance equivalent regulations.

1.56 Furthermore, it is clear that many specialist contractors are simply *not* controlled, particularly in respect of 'how' they do their work. This is, after all, because they are specialists. Old case law going back to the mid 1960s acknowledged that 'control' can only be an issue where there is scope for it. It might seem a non-starter for the Revenue to devise a 'control' test when, almost by definition, there is very limited scope for it in the case of the typical personal service business expert.

1.57 A new statutory 'control test' could have been extended to 'rights of' rather than de facto control, but this would have been difficult to put into legislative form in any meaningful way. The background to this is that sometimes the Revenue argues that even if there is no actual control the control test might still be satisfied if the client retains a theoretical 'right' to control the worker. It is of course very difficult to prove or disprove a theoretical right of control. Where the Revenue realises there is no actual control they will still sometimes argue that there was a 'right'. If the proposed control test had been extended to a 'right of', as well as actual, control it would have been a formidable line of attack for the Revenue.

For whatever reason the existing case law precedents were found to be preferable.

Case law also gives the opportunity for the law to develop in an organic way by reflecting the ever-changing work place environment.

1.58 The first misunderstanding of IR35 is quite simply clarified by appreciating that no new status test has been brought in. It is no harder now, post-IR35 to escape the status of 'disguised employee' than it was pre-IR35. Self-employment has not become a special or rare category.

Those practitioners who dealt with the Contributions Agency's and Revenue's attacks on self-employment in the construction industry in the late 1990s will remember the impression given by many tax officers to the effect that the 'law on status' had changed. Of course it hadn't changed but many companies went along with it. IR35 is the same. The law on determining self-employment has not changed.

IR35 misunderstanding 2—liability rests with the agency/end-user

1.59 This misunderstanding is still one that many agencies and end-users consider to be fact. This relates to the issue of liability under IR35 and once again shows how fear, uncertainty and doubt have come about from the early draft versions of IR35.

Quite simply the liability for deducting and paying over the appropriate tax and national insurance rests with the personal service business, the so-called 'intermediary' and not with the agency or end-user.

Perhaps the use of the word 'intermediary' was never wise as this, in itself, has caused much confusion. But to this day agencies and end-users still believe that they are somehow liable if they change contractual terms and conditions which allow the worker to escape IR35. They will not be liable and have nothing to fear. More recent experiences suggest that agencies and end-users are getting to grips with IR35 and may have become more flexible when it comes to amending contract terms in order to assist avoiding IR35.

1.60 It should be noted that, in certain limited circumstances, the director of the personal service company may be personally liable for IR35 deductions. This is discussed in greater depth in Chapter 14.

IR35 misunderstanding 3—Booklet IR175 accurately summarises the law

1.61 The third misunderstanding of IR35 is that the Revenue's published guidance is an accurate summary of the legal criteria to be applied in determining whether a worker is a disguised employee—it is not. Booklet IR175 was produced and widely distributed throughout 2000 but failed to give an accurate overview of the new rules or the up to date case law. The author is not aware of any updated version having been published, despite several important judgements having been handed down over the last four years.

1.62 IR175 was published in April 2000 and among other things gave a list of so-called relevant factors to be taken into account when deciding whether IR35 applies. Unfortunately this leaflet, widely read by many accountants and personal service businesses, contains misstatements and inaccuracies.

1.63 Rather than stating tax status depends on the terms and conditions of the working relationship, IR175 picks out certain factors as being important. This would be forgivable if the factors chosen were a fair reflection of the up to date case law.

1.64 The first factor is whether 'set hours' are worked, yet a trawl of all known tax status precedents fails to mention 'set hours' as a matter to be taken into account.

The Revenue knows contractors tend to work 'set hours', so to state 'set hours' indicate IR35 applies is to come at the issue backwards. It is a self-fulfilling prophecy but not one supported by case law.

1.65 'Hiring in a worker' is the leaflet's second factor, but this issue, which is essentially the substitution factor, should have been number one on the list. The question asked in IR175 is slightly skewed. It seems to ask whether a substitute is used in practice, whereas the correct question to ask is, 'Is there a right of substitution?' The courts have identified the right, not the actuality, as being of primary importance.

1.66 The Revenue raises the issue of 'overtime' yet this is not recognised in the tax status law reports as an important criterion.

1.67 It is widely known that the majority of contractors work on the end-user's premises. This is because this is what the job specification necessarily requires due to the practical realities of the nature of the work. Quite simply, an engineer checking air traffic control systems cannot take the control tower home with him. Because there is a large amount of work carried out at the end-user's premises the Revenue has made a fairly desperate attempt in IR175 to revive the 'part and parcel' test.

1.68 The discredited 'part and parcel' test from the 1950s and 1960s indicated direct employment status where the worker was integrated into the employer's premises and organisation. The Revenue is using an out of date 'test' which becomes a self-fulfilling prophecy to show IR35 bites—but it is not supported by current case law. Indeed in the *Synaptek Ltd* General Commissioners Appeal of 2002 the Revenue itself conceded that the 'part and parcel' test had been played down in recent years. It is a pity IR175 fails to acknowledge this.

1.69 IR175 asks whether the contractor works for more than one person at a time. This is an unfair question as most one man limited companies can only work for one person at a time, in that the director can only physically be in one place at a time. Perhaps a fairer question would be to ask whether the personal service business can enter into concurrent contracts and whether it has the freedom to undertake work for other third parties during the subsistence of the contract in question.

1.70 In several places IR175 refers the reader to the earlier status publication IR56. However, the latest print of IR56 was back in April 1999 and it therefore does not take into account the important cases of *Express and Echo Group Publications v Tanton* (heard by the Court of Appeal in 1999, see Appendix 6), *Costain v Smith* (heard in the Employment Appeals Tribunal in 1999, see Appendix 6) and *Carmichael v National Power* (heard by the House of Lords, again in 1999, see Appendix 6).

1.71 An interesting comparison between IR56 and IR175 can be made. IR175 refers to 'set hours' as the number one factor to be taken into account, yet IR56, from only a year earlier, refers to this as factor number four. Could this be because IR56 was used more in the construction industry, where irregular hours are more normal?

Indeed, IR56 does not list, in its factors to be taken into account, whether the worker can work for a number of clients at the same time. It is very surprising that some factors are omitted completely.

1.72 Confusingly IR175 states that the fact that a worker has the final say in how the work is done is a strong indicator of self-employment, whereas the Revenue's Employment Status Manual (at ESM 1024) accepts that specialists cannot be controlled as to the manner in which they do their work. This sounds like good news, but it is suggested that the correct way to phrase the statement is 'without control the worker cannot be an employee (of the client)', rather than 'if the worker is not controlled this indicates self-employment'. The astute practitioner will note that this is not the same thing. In other words, control is part of the irreducible minimum without which the worker cannot be an employee (of the client). Authority for this proposition is found in the *Ready Mixed Concrete* case (see Appendix 6) and the recent *Montgomery* decision (see Appendix 6). For a detailed discussion see Chapter 6.

1.73 One of the major weaknesses with IR175 and other Revenue documents is the issue relating to 'making a loss' on a contract. Again, if a personal service business is selling 'hours' then how can it ever make a loss? There is no cost of manufacturing, or stock, distribution or major overheads.

But in the commercial world it is clear that the concept of loss and financial risk is much wider. A computer consultant may soon find his skills are outdated unless he funds expensive ongoing training. Costs of several thousands of pounds for a two week course are not uncommon. The same consultant may face a financial penalty for not completing a project on time.

He may fail to negotiate effectively or market his skills properly—in short he may be a poor businessman. Few self-employed people will claim never to have made serious mistakes and suffered the consequences. These are all examples of financial risk.

1.74 No guarantee of work after the end of a short term contract, no entitlement to sick pay, holiday pay, special leave or a grievance procedure, are all part of the bigger picture of potential loss and risk. Many personal service businesses can have their contract terminated at short, or with no notice and may also have invested thousands of pounds in equipment.

1.75 The cost and risk of professional indemnity and public liability are classic considerations. The obligation to correct defective work is yet another example and this one is recognised in IR175 and IR56, yet it is often overlooked by the Revenue in practice.

1.76 IR175 refers the reader to IR56 for more information and, on the subject of work arranged with an agency, IR56 not very helpfully states that there are 'special rules' but does not detail them! Considering the vast majority of personal service businesses get their work by contracting with an agency this is disappointing.

1.77 IR175 refers to Tax Bulletin 45 (dated February 2000) (see Appendix 7) for 'more information' but it is suggested that this publication itself does not give an accurate and up to date appraisal of the law. It refers to the so called *Hall v Lorimer* (see Appendix 6) approach of standing back and painting a picture from all the relevant detail, but this approach was played down in the *Express and Echo* case (see Appendix 6). Chapter 6 deals with this in more detail. Furthermore, Tax Bulletin 45 fails to take this case and the House of Lords 1999 decision in *Carmichael* (see Appendix 6) into account.

1.78 Unfortunately IR175 offers little information as to appealing a Revenue decision and the conclusion has to be that this publication, sent to, and read by thousands, is a poor substitute for proper guidance or explanation of the modern law. It should be read with caution.

IR35 misunderstanding 4—having less than 5% of the shares in the intermediary company means that IR35 will not apply

1.79 There is the common misunderstanding that, by having less than 5% of the shares in the intermediary company, the worker cannot be caught by IR35. This is quite wrong and many schemes set up along these lines fail.

1.80 This is because the legislation (ITEPA 2003 s 51, see Appendix 1) employs a much wider test in determining whether the IR35 rules apply in cases where the intermediary is a company. It states that IR35 may apply if the worker has a 'material interest' in the intermediary. Material interest is not determined only by a straight 5% shareholding in the intermediary company. Instead, material interest is, broadly, beneficial ownership or the ability to directly or indirectly control more than 5% of the company's ordinary share capital, possession of or the right to acquire more than 5% of the company's distributions or entitlement to receive more than 5% of the assets available for distribution among participators in a close company. Furthermore, a material interest can be the worker's alone, or the worker's with one or more associates, or an associate's alone, or an associate's with other associates. It should also be noted that an associate is widely defined by ITEPA 2003 s 60 (see Appendix 1).

1.81 However, even where there is no material interest, the worker can still be caught by IR35 if either he or an associate receives (or is entitled to receive) payment or another benefit not chargeable under Employment Income directly from the intermediary company, which can 'reasonably be taken to represent remuneration for services provided by the worker to the client' (ITEPA 2003, s 51(1)(*b*)).

IR35 misunderstanding 5—standard agency contracts fail IR35

1.82 The Revenue has said that standard agency contracts are caught by IR35 (see Tax Bulletin issue 45 dated February 2000). This is too general. It is probably fair to say that the majority of existing standard agency contracts are more likely than not to be caught by IR35, but this is because of their poor drafting in terms of IR35 and the conditions they contain. It is not the fact that they are 'standard' or 'agency contracts' which makes them fail. In fact, a standard contract may fall outside the scope of IR35 if it contains appropriate clauses, which, when agreed and implemented, ensure the worker is not a disguised employee. Most standard agency contracts were drawn up before IR35 was considered although it is fair to say that in recent months agencies and end-users have become more flexible in respect of changing clauses in their standard contracts.

1.83 There is nothing wrong or artificial in both parties agreeing to use a standard form contract. Not only is this practice widespread in other aspects of commercial and domestic life, but it was actively encouraged by Mr Justice Burton in the PCG Judicial Review in the High Court (*R (on the application of Professional Contractors Group Ltd) v IRC*, see Appendix 6). The judge anticipated that the various parties would get together and agree standard terms which would take the relationship out of IR35.

1.84 In fairness to the Revenue, its statement effectively said that standard agency contracts, even if caught by IR35, would tend to be ignored if they were for less than a month in duration. Unfortunately, this has often been misconstrued as meaning that any standard agency contract which lasts for longer than one month is automatically caught. This of course is not the case. It *may* be caught but detailed reference has to be made to the terms and conditions it contains.

IR35 misunderstanding 6—completion of time sheets indicates direct employee status

1.85 The widely promoted Revenue view is that the use of time sheets is a strong indicator of direct employment by the client. This is misleading for two reasons.

1.86 First, the reality is that the overwhelming majority of regular employees do *not* complete time sheets! If completion of a timesheet is so indicative of direct employment status why is it that most employees don't fill them in?

1.87 Secondly, even though some regular employees do complete time sheets, there is no specific reference to 'time sheets' as a relevant factor to be taken into account in any tax status decision made by the courts. In a little-known national insurance case *WHPT Housing Association Ltd v Secretary of State* (1981) (discussed at 6.188 and also see Appendix 6) completion of time sheets was not held against the taxpayer who was found to be self-employed. This case is not in the Revenue manuals. There may be an argument that, at the very most, time sheets are one minor factor in assessing whether the worker is a direct employee of the client, but only in industries where it is the norm for direct employees to complete time sheets. However, there may be other much stronger factors suggesting the worker is not a disguised employee for which there is express judicial authority.

IR35 misunderstanding 7—the mere existence of a limited company ensures that the worker is not a disguised employee of the client

1.88 Case law heard prior to IR35 in the context of determining status for employment law purposes has made it clear that the mere insertion of a limited company as an administrative convenience will not establish self-employed status. If the real contract is between the worker and the client then the company can be ignored.

It has to be emphasised that the inserted company tends to be ignored when the *worker himself* wants to ignore it. This was demonstrated in the 2001 case of *O'Murphy v Hewlett Packard* (see Appendix 6) and the earlier case of *Catamaran Cruisers Ltd v Williams* (see Appendix 6).

1.89 Not all workers who seek to deny the existence of their own company succeed. One notable failure was in the 1978 case of *Winter v Westward Television* (see Appendix 6), heard by the Employment Appeals Tribunal. Mr Winter was represented by a Mr Tony Blair, a former employment lawyer now involved in politics.

Summary

1.90 There are many myths and misunderstandings regarding IR35 and practitioners and their clients should be aware of them. The correct position is as follows:

1 There is no new 'status' test. The existing case law precedents are what matters.

2 The liability under IR35 rests with the personal service business and not the agency or the end-user.
3 IR175 is not a reliable or up to date guide to IR35.
4 Having less than 5% of the shares in the personal service business will not automatically provide an IR35 defence.
5 Standard agency contracts of whatever length do not automatically fail IR35 and many agencies are becoming more flexible.
6 The completion of time sheets is not in itself an indication of direct employment by the client.
7 The mere existence of a limited company does not in itself prevent a worker from being a disguised employee of the client.

CHAPTER 2

IR35 and judicial review: a failed campaign?

2.1 The political campaign against IR35 ultimately failed and FA 2000 (now ITEPA 2003 Pt 2 Ch 8) and the Welfare Reform and Pensions Act 1999 (which inserted the Social Security Contributions and Benefits Act 1992 s 4A) became law. The period of consultation produced little real progress and a judicial review challenge was the last main strategy to achieve a knock out blow.

This also failed, despite a well-orchestrated campaign and fight in the High Court (*R (on the application of Professional Contractors Group Ltd) v IRC*, see Appendix 6). This being the case there is limited merit in going over all the arguments, many concerned with esoteric aspects of European law.

2.2 What should be noted is that the factual arguments advanced by Richard Barling QC on behalf of the Professional Contractors Group (PCG) were accepted by Mr Justice Burton, almost without exception, in the High Court. However, the basis of the judicial review challenge was concerned with specific legal points and, regrettably, the action failed.

2.3 It was argued, among other things, that the new legislation gave 'state aid' to larger corporations not caught by IR35; that it infringed human rights under the European Convention; that 'freedom of movement' into the UK would be impeded; and that, even if the legislation itself was not unlawful, it was 'disproportionate'.

2.4 Despite the loss in the High Court a direct approach was made to the Court of Appeal requesting permission to appeal. This was granted in June 2001. The Court of Appeal heard the application and unanimously rejected it in December 2001.

A further appeal to the House of Lords or Europe has been considered by the PCG, but decided against. Instead it will seek to assist contractors and build up a 'case law strategy' hopefully to develop precedents and roll back the frontiers of IR35.

2.5 In hindsight it was perhaps always likely that a judicial review challenge would fail. IR35 has become a major piece of primary legislation surrounded by controversy. The Paymaster General has on many occasions taken an outspoken and entrenched view about the provisions.

2.6 Other political parties have said they will scrap or modify IR35, which is easy to say when in opposition. If there is a change in government in 2005/6 IR35 will be old news and unlikely to be repealed.

Did any good come of the judicial review?

2.7 Without doubt the High Court hearing gave the PCG an opportunity to air all their arguments to an open-minded and independent third party. In many ways the views expressed in the High Court, always in good humour and with intelligence and insight, represented the consultation process seemingly denied to interested parties in the first place.

2.8 The very process of challenging core legislation by way of judicial review, in the hope that IR35 would be struck off, was a bold and unusual step to take. It sent a very clear message to the government that there was a large group of contractors who were prepared to devote both money and time to organising a professional and serious challenge to legislation which many saw as unfair and riddled with complications. It does no harm to remind the government that interested parties will want to have their say and will prosecute their case when it has merit.

2.9 In future the government may consider carefully any similar legislation. IR35 has become, to a limited extent at least, Labour's poll tax. It has been suggested that the Revenue will be instructed to implement IR35 in a softly, softly fashion without going for a concerted effort to target all those at risk. There is little evidence of this as IR35 compliance works gains pace.

2.10 The judicial review case gave rise to some interesting comments both in argument and in the judgment itself. The Revenue's contract review service, where inconsistent answers were given on the same contract by different officers, was heavily criticised, as was the Revenue's disregard for the concept of mutuality of obligation. The Revenue seemed to accept that mutuality of obligation is part of the irreducible minimum necessary to establish a contract of service. This caused Revenue counsel to run into difficulties when faced with showing the existence of mutuality in an imagined and hypothetical contract.

Mr Justice Burton suggested that while the Revenue has been quick to point out that being caught by IR35 does not confer broader employment law rights to the worker, a contractor's solicitor would be able to write 'a pretty strong letter' to the client claiming such rights. This has become known as the 'nuclear option' in lobbying circles. After all, if there is a 'deemed employee' why should there not be a 'deemed employer'? The government is aware of the massive ramifications of the 'nuclear option' not only for blue chip plcs but also government departments who are the 'end-user'—see 7.10 below. Perhaps for this reason strenuous efforts have been made to clarify that IR35 is a taxation, not employment rights measure. This is despite the fact that one of the Government's early justifications for IR35 was that workers were being denied their employment rights by being forced to contract via their own limited companies.

The judge also suggested that a contractor with multiple clients would be 'home and dry', but it is respectfully submitted that this is not a comment to be relied upon in isolation.

2.11 The case failed to explore other contentious areas of IR35, such as the loose wording of the legislation itself and the massive scope if offers for a challenge based on the principles of statutory interpretation. This is a great pity. The question of who the client is in the personal service business/agency/end-user chain was not explored. These last two issues are analysed in detail in Chapters 4 and 7.

To what extent will the Revenue amend its internal guidance manuals?

2.12 It has been suggested that, in light of Mr Justice Burton's comments, the Revenue would review the guidance it gives to inspectors in its internal manuals, which are of course now in the public domain. Although some minor amendments have usefully been made and there may well be others on the way it is suggested that wholesale changes are unlikely for the following reasons:

1 The old Schedule E Manual was amended, and the new Employment Status Manual (ESM) written, only a few months before the High Court hearing and it is unlikely that the Revenue is going to embark on yet another overhaul. To be fair, the new ESM shows the Revenue making an effort to embrace a more legally accurate and up to date approach to tax status criteria, particularly on the issue of substitution. (For a more detailed discussion on this point, see John Newth's article in *Taxation* magazine, dated 29 March 2001 p 619.) See also Mark Morton's article in the same issue of *Taxation* on p 629.) The Revenue probably feels that it has gone far enough.

2 The section of ESM dealing with a detailed analysis of the case law precedents was released in May 2001, some two months after the judicial review verdict and the critical comments made by Mr Justice Burton. Yet this latest section still puts forward the Revenue's old line on mutuality of obligation, and it fails to mention at all some important case law decisions from the recent past.

   This latest release of the ESM was an opportunity to take a more open approach to, inter alia, mutuality of obligations. The fact that it wasn't taken suggests the Revenue will stick to its old policy. Even where the ESM continues to be updated and improved it should still be read with caution. The ESM is after all, largely the Revenue's opinion and policy interpretation of the law, not the law itself.

3 The judicial review was concerned with technical aspects of complex European law. It was not a case concerning tax status issues or the quality of the Revenue's contract review service. The judge was sitting to decide a matter of European law. Anything else alluded to in his judgment may carry some influence but does not amount to binding legal precedent. In other words there is an argument that, however enlightened the judge's remarks were, they were *obiter dicta*, things said by the way, and as such do not form legal precedent. This is certainly the Revenue's view as expressed in the *FSConsulting Ltd* Special Commissioners Decision in 2002 (see Chapter 12 and Appendix 6).

   Inevitably, different lawyers hold different opinions on the usefulness of the judge's remarks. It is the author's view that the remarks made were helpful—in time they may possibly encourage the Revenue to modify its approach—but in terms of legal precedent the remarks carry no real weight.

4 IR35 is about money. It can be seen as a financial expedient for the Treasury, and accordingly there is a strong financial incentive for the Revenue to leave the IR35 rules unchanged, and for it to interpret case law with whatever 'spin' it sees fit.

A brief reference to the judicial review judgment has now been inserted at ESM 3285 and this is discussed in Chapter 6.

Summary

2.13 The judicial review challenge was a well-organised and focused attempt to have IR35 struck out. It failed, and the prospects of an appeal proceeding and succeeding are limited.

2.14 The comments made by the judge, and certain admissions made by the Revenue's own counsel, can only help the contractor, but it would be unwise to treat remarks said in passing as strict legal precedent. They are not.

2.15 It is necessary to address other strategies of defence against IR35. These are based on carefully analysing the legislation in light of the principles of statutory interpretation to see if it applies at all; considering what contractual arrangements are necessary to demonstrate the contractor is not a disguised employee; and understanding how an appeal is presented to the tax tribunal should a Revenue challenge not be resolved. All these matters are discussed in the following chapters.

CHAPTER 3

Planning to beat IR35: the four basic principles in outline

3.1 Unfortunately, both the political campaign against IR35 and the judicial review (*R (on the application of Professional Contractors Group Ltd) v IRC,* see Appendix 6) have failed. The Labour Party has been returned to government and IR35 is here to stay.

However, although the judicial review floundered, IR35 can still be resisted effectively and this brief chapter outlines the main IR35 defence strategies in principle.

Taking a wider view of the IR35 landscape, there are four main strategies to be considered, all of which can be used either in isolation or as part of a co-ordinated approach to show IR35 may not apply in any particular given circumstance.

1. A critical analysis of the IR35 legislation

3.2 The purpose of this approach is to examine the legislation in fine detail, with the aim of establishing, or at least questioning, whether the legislation applies in principle at all. It has been too readily assumed that the wording of the legislation automatically catches all personal service businesses. However, if it can be shown that this is not the case then IR35 will simply not apply.

3.3 Chapter 4 analyses the primary legislation, ITEPA 2003 Pt 2 Ch 8 together with the Social Security Contributions and Benefits Act 1992 s 4A. It examines the conditions that must be satisfied before IR35 applies, and it suggests some arguments based on the rules of statutory interpretation to defeat the presumed application of IR35.

2. Agreeing and implementing contractual terms which fall outside IR35

3.4 A person's tax status is determined by the terms and conditions of his working relationship. There has been a great deal of commentary about the so-called 'hypothetical' contract IR35 requires to be constructed. The legislation contains no such phrase as 'hypothetical contracts'. It simply asks whether the circumstances are such that, had the contract been entered into directly between the worker and the client, those terms and conditions would amount to disguised employment.

3.5 A detailed understanding of the case law on employment status (explained in Chapter 6) is essential if the practitioner is to demonstrate that a worker is not a disguised employee of the client. Chapter 8 takes this a stage further by considering in detail what terms need to be agreed in the contract in order to help ensure that the contract itself does not fall foul of IR35.

3.6 Tax inspectors, and indeed the Commissioners, will always prefer to see hard physical evidence and proof of contentions being made. It is, therefore, strongly recommended that many small matters, which in themselves will not necessarily win the argument, should be subject to a 'paper trail' or due diligence process. This is also something the PCG advocates.

3.7 If one is attempting to show that contract terms fall outside IR35 and reference is made to, say, professional indemnity insurance or website advertising, then copies of the appropriate certificates and website print out should be retained. Even very well paid contractors may not raise a formal invoice on company stationery but this is exactly the kind of evidence which would indicate a genuine business with a proper business organisation. Accordingly, contractors should always be encouraged to document their business activities thoroughly.

3. Understanding the Revenue's IR35 compliance process

3.8 The third principle of defeating IR35 is to have a clear understanding of what will happen when the Revenue wishes to challenge under IR35. This is dealt with in Chapter 16.

4. Taking an IR35 appeal to the Commissioners

3.9 If a dispute cannot be resolved by argument with the inspector, the only alternative to backing down is taking the case to the tax tribunal. Most practitioners have little experience of conducting contentious appeals, particularly where large sums of money could be involved. Chapters 17 to 19 give a clear step by step guide through the process.

Applying the four principles

3.10 The four principles of defeating IR35 clearly require a comprehensive knowledge and understanding of the legislation, case law, Revenue interview techniques and what is required to mount an effective appeal at the tax tribunal.

3.11 The overwhelming majority of tax practitioners and clients have not been involved in a contentious appeal hearing, with all that that involves, including adducing evidence, cross examining witnesses and making legal submissions. Chapters 17 to 19 contain highly detailed practical guidance on how to take a case to the Commissioners.

3.12 This chapter is deliberately called 'planning' to beat IR35 because a successful defence strategy will not come about by coincidence or apathy. Personal service businesses and their advisers need to take pro-active steps *now* to help ensure that the IR35 rules do not apply. The purpose of this chapter is to help the practitioner focus on the main strategies of beating IR35 and to underline the important message that homework and planning are needed now in order to deal with the challenge, should it come.

3.13 It is suggested that the Revenue is more likely to target easy cases, which tend to be the businesses who have neglected to deal with the essential detail which shows that they fall outside the scope of IR35. The tax courts are littered with the bones of unsuccessful taxpayers who never quite got around to doing what they had to in order to protect themselves. Those who argue that had they organised their tax affairs in a slightly different way they would have received a less harsh tax treatment will receive no sympathy from the inspector, the Commissioners or the courts.

Summary

3.14 Planning a defence against IR35 is all about having an attitude of challenge and a questioning approach. Remaining independent and avoiding the label of 'disguised employee' does not require the worker to fit into some unique category or privileged special case. It should never be forgotten that beating IR35 is not about proving the worker is self-employed; instead, it is about proving the worker is not an employee of the client. The two are not the same.

However, planning to beat IR35 and applying the four basic principles do need careful consideration and forethought. There is a big prize at stake after all. The following chapters will give the open-minded and pro-active practitioner a wealth of arguments, advice and guidance on how the four principles can be used in practice.

CHAPTER 4

Analysing the IR35 legislation for possible escape routes

4.1 It is often assumed, in the author's view far too readily, that the IR35 legislation—to be found in ITEPA 2003 Pt 2 Ch 8, the Social Security Contributions and Benefits Act 1992 s 4A (as inserted by the Welfare Reform and Pensions Act 1999 s 75) and the Social Security Contributions (Intermediaries) Regulations 2000, SI 2000/727—will somehow automatically apply to all personal service businesses.

4.2 It is suggested that a more questioning and critical approach to analysing the legislation will reveal opportunities for demonstrating that IR35 does not apply. In other words, IR35 may be a complete non-starter for certain personal service businesses. In the author's view, the legislation is not well worded; it offers some very arguable points and the tax legislation is worded differently from the national insurance legislation. Yet many advisers and contractors take a fatalistic view of IR35. They see the only argument as one of attempting to show that the terms of their contract take them outside IR35.

4.3 Certainly, IR35 does not apply if it can be shown that the personal service business worker is not a 'disguised employee' of the client, hence the heavy emphasis on contractual terms and conditions and the working relationship. But it would be preferable to avoid the 'disguised employee' argument by showing that the IR35 legislation simply does not apply at all. If it can be shown that, in principle, the intermediaries' legislation does not apply, there will be no need to examine contracts, working relationships or anything else. In a situation where the practitioner is working within the tight financial restraints of limited fee budgets a 'knock out' blow will be preferable to a long and drawn out fight, one which may only result in a narrow win on points and which can be a harrowing process. Quite simply, IR35 may well be a club the personal service business does not have to join.

ITEPA 2003 Pt 2 Ch 8

4.4 The key paragraph in the chapter that defines the engagements to which the IR35 rules apply is ITEPA 2003 s 49. This section sets out three requirements (listed in s 49(1)(*a*), (*b*) and (*c*)), and *all* of these have to be satisfied before the worker can fall within the scope of the rules. Broadly, para 1 requires that there must be three parties: the worker, the intermediary and the client. The worker must personally perform, or be under an obligation to perform, services for the purposes of a business carried on by the client (s 49(1)(*a*)). Those services are performed not under a contract between the worker and the client but under 'arrangements' involving the intermediary (s 49(1)(*b*)). Finally, the circumstances of the arrangements are such that, were there a direct contract between the client and the worker, the worker would for tax purposes be regarded as an employee of the client (s 49(1)(*c*)).

Each of the separate three requirements in para 1 is examined below in turn.

ITEPA 2003 s 49(1)(*a*)

4.5 The first condition for IR35 to apply is covered in ITEPA 2003 s 49(1)(*a*). This requires that:

> 'an individual ("the worker") personally performs, or is under an obligation personally to perform, services for another person ("the client").'

There are two main points here. First, there is a twin test of 'performs' or 'obligation to perform'. Second, the services have to be performed *for a client.*

4.6 The test of 'performs' or 'obligation to perform' is carefully worded. The word 'performs' ensures that the test looks at what actually happens, as opposed to whether there is an unused right of substitution. In other words even if there is a right of substitution but in fact the worker carries out the duties personally then he is still within the scope of s 49(1)(*a*). He may of cause escape IR35 on the 'right of substitution' under s 49(1)(*c*).

4.7 It should be noted that the test in s 49(1)(*a*) requires that it is the worker (and not the personal service business) who must perform or be obliged to perform the services. Therefore, s 49(1)(*a*) would not seem to be met if it can be shown that it is the personal service business (as opposed to the worker) which is under the obligation to perform services. This anomaly could have been avoided if the legislation stated that the Schedule applies when either the worker *or* his intermediary personal service company performs, or is under an obligation to perform, the services. However, s 49(1)(*a*) did not use this wording, and this is potentially to the taxpayer's benefit.

4.8 This raises the question as to what happens in the situation where a substitute is in fact sent to provide the services. The mere fact that a substitute may be sent suggests that the worker is not under an obligation to give personal service (and, indeed, he does not actually perform the services on any occasion when the substitute is sent). It would seem reasonable to interpret this as meaning that the greater the possibility of providing substitutes, the more likely it is that IR35 does not apply.

4.9 Suppose Fred Bloggs, a director/shareholder of Fred Bloggs Computer Services Ltd, sends a substitute for, say, two weeks out of a six month contract. In this situation, it is suggested that there are two possible interpretations of s 49(1)(*a*). The first is that the IR35 rules will still potentially apply to the times when the substitute is not sent. The second possible interpretation is that IR35 will not apply at all to that particular contract because personal service has not always been given. In the author's experience, the Revenue is increasingly willing to exclude from IR35 the income arising under the whole contract when either a substitute is actually sent or where there is a not unreasonably fettered right to send a substitute, although they will often seek third party confirmation of the right.

It should also be noted that the right to send a substitute may also preclude a worker from being viewed as a disguised employee of the client, and thereby not satisfying the test in s 49(1)(*c*), discussed below.

4.10 The second key requirement in s 49(1)(*a*) is that the services must be performed for the purposes of a business carried on by a client. There is no question of IR35 applying to services provided to a client who is not carrying on a business. The legislation defines the term 'business' to mean any trade, profession or vocation, including a Schedule A business (ITEPA 2003 s 61(1)). Furthermore, it is specifically extended in the context of para 1(1)(*a*) to include any activity carried on by a government, public or local authority (in the UK or elsewhere), or any activity by a body corporate, unincorporated body or partnership (ITEPA 2003 s 49(2)). So clearly IR35 may apply if the worker is providing services for the client for the purpose of the client's business under this extended meaning. But IR35 does not apply where a worker is providing services for a client that are unconnected with the client's business. An example of this is where the client is a domestic customer and the worker provides, say, gardening or hairdressing services. Services of this type are clearly outside the scope of IR35 (and in such cases the worker would probably not, in any event, be a disguised employee of the client, as is required by ITEPA 2003 s 49(1)(*c*)). An agency is of course carrying on a business which is relevant to the whole question of 'who is the client' for IR35 purposes and this is discussed in more depth in Chapter 7.

4.11 There is also an argument which concerns the *purpose* of providing the services; namely, that where a worker is providing services to a client, IR35 will not apply if he is not doing so for the purposes of a business carried on by the client (as is required under s 49(1)(*a*)), but is in fact doing so for another reason, such as for the purposes of his own business.

4.12 Let us take an example that many practitioners will recognise in order to put this into context. Brown & Co accountants, instructs a specialist tax firm, Clark & Co, to undertake some work for them as they have a client with a tax problem and Clark & Co are tax experts. Clark & Co undertake the assignment and raise an invoice to Brown & Co for services provided. The Clark & Co employee carries out the work, and a report is typed by the Clark & Co secretary. In this scenario, both the employee who carried out the work and the secretary who typed the report undertake that work in accordance with their duties under their employment contract with Clark & Co, and not for the purposes of the business carried on by the client ie Brown & Co, or indeed Brown & Co's own client.

4.13 This can be put in the context of the typical one-man limited company computer contractor—the typical type of business at risk of falling within the IR35 rules. The company, Fred Bloggs Computer Services Limited, undertakes work for a PLC end-user. It contracts in its own name directly with the end-user to supply computer-programming services. Fred Bloggs is the sole director of the company, and he physically carries out the work. Could it not once again be argued that Fred is merely undertaking that work in accordance with his duties of employment for his employer (which is a separate legal entity), rather than providing the services for the purpose of his client's business? Practitioners should remember that there is no merit in the Revenue simply claiming that it is commonly understood what the legislation was meant to do.

4.14 It is worth considering whether the position would be different if the contract between Fred Bloggs Computer Services Limited and the PLC end-user named 'Fred Bloggs' as the worker. In such a situation, the Revenue might contend that the naming of the worker implies personal service. However, it is submitted that the fact that the worker is named does not, in itself, mean that the worker is more likely to be providing services for the purposes of the client's business. Taking the example above involving Brown & Co and Clark & Co, it may be that Brown & Co specifically requested the services of a particular employee of Clark & Co because they were aware of his reputation and experience in that field. This does not mean that the Clark & Co employee is any more likely to be providing services for the purposes of the client's business. He is still doing nothing more than the duties of his employment with Clark & Co. He cannot realistically be said to be providing services to Brown & Co.

4.15 The naming of the worker may, however, pose a problem in relation to other aspects of IR35 and, in particular, the agency trap in ITEPA 2003 Pt 2 Ch 7 (see Chapter 10).

ITEPA 2003 s 49(1)(*b*)

4.16 Section 49(1)(*b*) provides the second condition that must be met if the legislation is to apply. It requires that:

> 'the services are provided not under a contract directly between the client and the worker but under arrangements involving a third party ("the intermediary")'.

In other words, the services must not be provided directly by the worker to the client, but via an intermediary. IR35 will not apply if there is not at least one intermediary. Obviously, if the worker does not use an intermediary, but simply provides services to the client directly, the worker falls outside the scope of Pt 2 Ch 7. This is possibly the easiest method of escaping IR35, but before the worker gets too excited it must be remembered that he would, in the absence of an intermediary, be then subject to the normal case law in determining whether he is an employee of the client or is self-employed, and would almost certainly be caught by the agency regulations if he contracted with an agency.

It is an interesting moot point to ask what the position would be if the worker entered into a contract personally but on terms which stated he would provide the services via his own limited company. Could it not then be argued that IR35 cannot apply as s 49(1)(*b*) has not been met because the contract *is* directly between the worker and the client? If not why not?

4.17 In the early days of IR35 there was much confusion surrounding the term 'intermediary'. Indeed, it is odd that the legislation does not include a comprehensive definition of that term, when there are definitions for so many other words and phrases for which the meaning is more immediately obvious (such as 'tax year' and 'the Inland Revenue'). What is clear is that the word 'intermediary' does not mean the agency in the classic personal service business/agency/end-user chain. The intermediary is the business that provides the services. Typically, the intermediary is a one-man limited company or a partnership.

4.18 The statutory provision which comes closest to defining the meaning of intermediary is ITEPA 2003 s 49(3); that provision states that the term 'third party' includes 'a partnership or unincorporated body of which the worker is a member'. This phrase is arguably unclear; do the words 'of which the worker is a member' apply to both partnerships and unincorporated bodies? In other words, does s 49(3) mean that an intermediary includes any partnership, or only those partnerships of which the worker is a member? In many ways, this is similar to the debate concerning the interpretation of the phrase 'fixed plant or machinery' in relation to assets qualifying for rollover relief under TCGA 1992 s 155. (In that instance, it was held in *Williams v Evans* [1982] STC 498 that the word 'fixed' qualifies for both plant and machinery). Again, this is arguably another ambiguity in the legislation, and it illustrates the types of issues that can be raised with the Revenue.

4.19 It is interesting that ITEPA 2003 s 49(3) expressly includes partnerships and unincorporated bodies within the meaning of intermediaries, but makes no reference as to bodies corporate. Of course, it is assumed that limited companies are included, and the Revenue would most likely say that there was no need expressly to include bodies corporate within the meaning of a third party. However, it is interesting to note that ITEPA 2003 s 49(2) (in relation to the meaning of business) expressly includes any activity of a body corporate as well activities of an unincorporated body and a partnership, whereas s 49(3) only refers to the latter two.

4.20 Even disregarding these points, not all intermediaries are within the scope of IR35. Specific requirements must be met if Ch 8 is to apply, and these requirements depend on the type of intermediary in question.

4.21 ITEPA 2003 s 51 sets out the requirements where the intermediary is a company. This paragraph is clear evidence, if any were needed, that the legislation is intended to apply to situations where the work is provided by an intermediary company. It provides that an intermediary company will only be within IR35 if the intermediary is not an associated company of the client by reason of them both being under the control of the worker (or the worker and another person) (ITEPA 2003 s 51(1), (2)). Furthermore, the worker must either have a material interest in the intermediary or receive payments or benefits from the intermediary which can reasonably be taken to represent remuneration for services provided by the worker to the client.

4.22 A material interest is, in this context, widely defined as 5% by reference to ordinary share capital, dividend rights, or, in the case of a close company, entitlement to assets (ITEPA 2003 s 51(4)). The interests of associates (defined by ITEPA 2003 s 60; see Appendix 1) can be taken into account for the purpose of the material interest test (ITEPA 2003 s 51(3)).

4.23 Where the intermediary is a partnership, the requirements depend on whether or not the payments or benefits are received (or receivable) by a worker as a member of the partnership. If they are, there are three alternative tests. The first is that the worker and his relatives (ie, spouse, parent or remoter forebear, child or remoter issue, brother or sister) are entitled to at least 60% of the profits of the partnership. This requirement would not therefore be met if at least 60% of the profits went to more remote family members, such as uncles and aunts. The second requirement is that most of the profits of the partnership are derived from services within IR35 provided to a single client (or a single client and his associates). There is no statutory definition of the term 'most' in this context, so it should probably be given its usual meaning of the majority of or over half. The third requirement is that the partnership profit sharing arrangement for any of the partners is based on the amount of income generated by that partner from IR35 services. This requirement is clearly intended to catch partnerships that would not otherwise fall within IR35 which are used as a means of passing income resulting from IR35-type engagements to that worker. If the payments etc are received (or receivable) by a worker who is not a member of the partnership, then the tests are the same as those where the intermediary is an individual (ITEPA 2003 s 52).

4.24 Where the intermediary is an individual, there is a single test: the worker must receive (or be entitled to receive) payment or benefit from the intermediary which can reasonably be said to represent remuneration for services provided by the worker to the client (ITEPA 2003 s 53). The language of that provision (ie 'a payment or benefit . . . received or receivable . . . which can reasonably be taken to represent remuneration for services') is deliberately wide, so that it catches any income other than that which is truly unrelated to the services provided to the client.

4.25 Of course, there may be more than one intermediary. The most common example of this is in the worker/personal service business/agency/client scenario. In such a case, the above rules apply separately to each of the intermediaries in determining whether they are within the scope of IR35 (ITEPA 2003 s 59(3), see Appendix 1).

4.26 IR35 cannot be escaped merely by using a foreign intermediary. However, IR35 does not apply in circumstances where no Employment Income liability would arise if the services were provided directly by the worker to the client (ITEPA 2003 s 56(3)). This could be by reason of any combination of the residence or domicile status of the worker, the residence of the client, or the place in which the service was provided. An example of this is where a non-resident worker performs duties outside the UK. He would not be charged to UK tax under the general principles (as he would be within Schedule E Case II). Therefore, IR35 cannot bring those earnings into the charge to UK tax merely because they are provided via an intermediary.

ITEPA 2003 s 49(1)(*c*)

4.27 Section 49(1)(*c*) is often thought of as the key test. It states that the Schedule applies where:

> 'the circumstances are such that, if the services were provided under a contract directly between the client and the worker, the worker would be regarded for income tax purposes as an employee of the client'.

It requires the circumstances to be considered with a view to seeing if the worker is a disguised employee of the client. As there is no separate test for employment status under IR35, all of the tests for employment in the existing case law are relevant. For a discussion of relevant case law, see Chapter 6, and Chapters 7–9 in the context of who is the client, recommended contract terms and the relevance of the agency/end-user contract.

4.28 The legislation specifically provides that the 'circumstances', in this context, include 'the terms on which the services are provided, having regard to the terms of the contracts forming part of the arrangements under which the services are provided' (ITEPA 2003 s 49(4)). This means that it is necessary to examine the contractual terms under which the services are provided. This is discussed further in Chapter 8.

The national insurance legislation

4.29 The relevant primary legislation is the Social Security Contributions and Benefits Act 1992 s 4A (as inserted by the Welfare Reform and Pensions Act 1999 s 75). The equivalent Northern Ireland legislation is the Social Security Contributions and Benefits (Northern Ireland) Act 1992 s 4A (as inserted by s 76). The detailed regulations are contained in the Social Security Contributions (Intermediaries) Regulations 2000, SI 2000/727; the equivalent Northern Ireland provisions are contained in the Social Security Contributions (Intermediaries) (Northern Ireland) Regulations 2000, SI 2000/728.

4.30 There is a similar point to be raised in relation to the sidenote to SSCBA 1992 s 4A. The sidenote reads: 'Earnings of workers supplied by service companies etc'. It is notable that the sidenote of s 4A specifically includes a reference to personal service companies (unlike the tax legislation in ITEPA 2003 s 49(3)). But in terms of demonstrating that IR35 may not apply, the words 'workers supplied' in the sidenote are potentially very helpful. The extent to which sidenotes are relevant in interpreting the legislation is a reasonably complex issue, and readers are referred to *Bennion: Statutory Interpretation* (Butterworths, 3rd edn, 1997) p 576 (the 4th edition of Bennion is due to be published this year). In general, the sidenote is part of the Act which was passed by Parliament, and may therefore be used in interpreting the legislation. As with headings, sidenotes are necessarily brief and therefore potentially of limited use.

4.31 But there is case law which supports the assertion that modern judges consider it proper to take account of sidenotes, and gather what guidance they can from them. In *Chilcott v IRC*, Vinelott J said ([1982] STC 1 at 23) that the sidenote was 'a permissible . . . [and] useful guide throwing further light on the mischief aimed at'. An example of a case which shows the usefulness of sidenotes is *DPP v Schildkamp* [1971] AC 1, in which the scope of the Companies Act 1948 s 332 was restricted by its sidenote.

4.32 There is, therefore, judicial authority for using the sidenote in interpreting the section. If the national insurance legislation is aimed at 'workers supplied', as the sidenote states, does this not mean that where a worker is not supplied but instead a 'service' is given, then by definition the regulations cannot apply? This would seem to be a very arguable proposition. The national insurance legislation was introduced prior to the tax legislation and it is to be noted that the tax legislation does not have a similar rubric about 'earnings of workers supplied'. One wonders whether the government spotted this, and wanted to avoid it for the purposes of the tax legislation.

4.33 One of the main strategies in defeating IR35 is to show that there exists a genuine business to business relationship to supply services. Not only does this show there is no personal service as required by ITEPA 2003 s 49(1)(*a*) but it also avoids a potential agency problem under ITEPA 2003 Pt 2 Ch 7. Likewise, it is arguable that the national insurance consequences of IR35 can be avoided where it can be shown that the workers are not being supplied but instead services are being undertaken.

4.34 Otherwise, the national insurance legislation is reasonably similar to the tax legislation in relation to determining the scope of IR35. It should be noted, however, that there are one or two discrepancies. Firstly, the tax legislation defines the word 'arrangements' as being those entered into by the intermediary (s 49(4)) whereas the national insurance legislation fails to provide such a definition. Secondly, the hypothetical contract under the national insurance legislation is not defined as a 'direct' contract between the worker and the client, whereas it is so defined in the tax legislation (s 49(1)(*c*)). These differences may prove important when arguing a case as the IR35 'assessments' may be tax, or national insurance, or both.

4.35 Somewhat confusingly, SSCBA s 4A(2) provides a definition of the term 'intermediary', which is also defined in SI 2000/727 reg 5, and which is referred to in reg 6(1)(*b*), whereas the tax legislation defines 'third party' instead (at ITEPA 2003 s 49(3)). It is suggested that this shows, if nothing else, that the legislation is poorly worded.

4.36 There are available to the practitioner other arguments based on statutory interpretation, but in the real world it seems likely that IR35 cases will be won or lost on an examination of the circumstances and arrangements of the hypothetical contract.

Summary

4.37 All too often it is assumed that the IR35 rules automatically apply because it is thought that the situation in question would seem to be one for which the IR35 rules were intended. No assumptions should be made without first looking at the detailed rules. Is the intermediary a relevant one within IR35? If the worker does not actually provide the service, is he (and not the personal service business) the person who is obliged to perform the services? Is the IR35 challenge under the tax or national insurance legislation? The rules are not the same.

4.38 Furthermore, the legislation itself contains a number of ambiguities, particularly, it is suggested, as regards ITEPA 2003 s 49(1)(*a*) and the use of the words 'workers supplied' in the sidenote to SSCBA 1992 s 4A. There are some arguments to be raised on the basis of statutory interpretation—and it is legitimate to raise them. Statutory interpretation is not mere word play or sophistry, and to dismiss it as such is failing to take advantage of the full range of defence strategies available to the practitioner. Indeed, many a court case has turned on the interpretation of seemingly straightforward legislation, let alone these rules, which contain a number of ambiguities.

CHAPTER 5

Why understanding case law is important

5.1 There is no useful definition in the legislation of a contract of service (direct employment) or a contract for services (self-employment).

The Employment Rights Act 1996 s 230(1) says:

> 'an employee means an individual who has entered into or works under (or worked under) a contract of employment'.

And s 230(2) goes on to add:

> 'a contract of employment means a contract of service or apprenticeship whether express or implied and if express oral or in writing'.

The same definition appears in the National Minimum Wage Act 1998 s 54.

5.2 In the absence of a detailed statutory definition of employment and self-employment it is necessary to turn to the court decisions over the years where the status of a person has had to be decided. This is why case law is so important. There is nothing else to go on. Despite this, in an exchange of correspondence with Accountax, a tax inspector declared that case law 'is not relevant to IR35'. Such a lack of understanding is breath-taking. The Revenue will often go on a detailed 'fact finding' initiative, only to discover that the facts they are seeking are not recognised by case law as being relevant. Accountax has witnessed many examples of inspectors who refuse to address case law. By ignorning case law until the last minute they fail to apply the correct tests that, ultimately, the courts will apply.

5.3 It should be noted that many of the court decisions are not directly concerned with income tax or national insurance; some are concerned with employment law rights, such as unfair dismissal or the entitlement to holiday pay or sick pay, and others with industrial accidents. In any event, the court has had to decide whether or not the person concerned was employed or self-employed and a huge body of case law has built up. The Revenue is quite happy to refer to employment law rather than pure tax or national insurance cases where appropriate, as the ESM demonstrates in many places. Without doubt the Revenue has made strenuous efforts to update its internal guidance manuals but as Anne Redston has correctly pointed out on the lecture circuit there are still too many shortcomings.

5.4 When arguing that a client falls outside of IR35 it is too easy to rely on personal opinion or on a sense of what is fair and equitable. When corresponding with the Revenue or representing clients at the Commissioners the mere opinion of the advocate counts for nothing. While it may be possible to put forward a very reasonable view based on common sense this will carry limited weight.

5.5 On the other hand, quotations from the case law decisions give arguments authority and will be convincing. Not only does case law enable points to be made it will also enable the inspector's arguments to be rebutted. A good example of this might be where the inspector claims that the completion of a time sheet is an indicator of direct employment. Yet a search of all tax cases, going back to the nineteenth century, reveals that the phrase 'time sheets' has never been mentioned once. In an attempt to refute the inspector's arguments this would be pointed out. Indeed there is a national insurance case, the *WHPT Housing* case, discussed at 6.19, where it was accepted that completion of time sheets indicated *self-employment.*

5.6 It is important to be able to quote the words the judges have actually used. There are many useful publications which give summaries of the case law judgments (and head-notes of the cases concerning status referred to in this book are included at Appendix 6). Whilst such publications are extremely useful, they rarely quote the actual words the judges have used, and it is that wording which will carry the greatest weight.

The hierarchy of the tribunals and the courts

5.7 Practitioners should be aware of the pecking order of the various tribunals and courts. Quotations from the more senior courts, particularly recent decisions, will carry most weight. One should also be aware of the inspector quoting from a particular case when it was heard in the lower courts despite the fact that the higher courts overturned the decision on appeal. A good example of this is the Revenue's habit of quoting only the High Court judgment in *Hall v Lorimer* (at [1992] STC 599). What the Revenue seems to forget is that the case went on to be heard by the Court of Appeal (see Appendix 6) and it is the judgment of the senior court which is more important and carries more weight. As it is, the Court of Appeal in this case supported the decision of the High Court but Lord Justice Nolan in the Court of Appeal made some extremely important judicial comments that the Revenue often fails to recognise, because in error they concentrate their efforts only on the High Court judgment. They do this because it suits them.

Likewise with *Carmichael v National Power* (see Appendix 6). The Revenue has been known to quote the Court of Appeal decision despite the fact that it was overturned by the House of Lords.

5.8 Although old law is by no means bad law, in fact often the reverse, the employment scene is shifting, and quoting up to date law will be far more impressive than quoting decisions from half a century ago.

An example of this is the 1880 case of *Yewens v Noakes* (see Appendix 6), which introduced the idea of the 'control' test but spoke in terms of the 'master/servant' relationship. This style of language goes back to a time when 'master/servant' had a specific meaning in the social hierarchy and this phrase should not be taken as being synonymous with 'employer/employee'. The phrase 'master/servant' carries a peculiarly Victorian flavour and, bearing in mind the case quoted was heard in 1880, this is hardly surprising. Indeed, the word 'servant' had a technical meaning that would hardly be applicable in the twenty-first century. So old cases must be seen in their historical and social context.

5.9 It is important to quote, wherever possible, up to date case law judgments that have taken into account the modern world and which can be applied easily to present-day circumstances. If the up to date case law quoted is from a senior court then all the better. It should cause no great surprise that the inspector may be unaware of very recent case law. Despite the ready availability of case law judgments on the internet, the Head Office of the Revenue is not always prompt in disseminating new cases to the districts. Various tax inspectors have confirmed this to the author.

5.10 The hierarchy for a tax appeal is as follows. First the case is heard by the General Commissioners or Special Commissioners. The Commissioners are the tribunal of first instance, and from the Commissioners an appeal can be made to the High Court on a point of law or on the basis that no reasonable tribunal could have reached the decision it came to. This is dealt with in greater detail in Chapter 20. From the High Court it is possible to appeal to the Court of Appeal and, ultimately, to the House of Lords, in certain circumstances.

5.11 The House of Lords also hears certain appeals from Commonwealth countries in the Privy Council. An example of this is the *Australian Mutual v Chaplin* case (see Appendix 6) of 1978 which is important in the context of substitution clauses and which is mentioned in the Revenue's internal guidance manuals.

5.12 Prior to the merger of the Contributions Agency with the Revenue a Contributions Agency appeal would be by way of asking the Secretary of State to lay down a question for determination at a Secretary of State's Tribunal, usually presided over by an independent barrister. This appeal process ended in April 1999 when the two departments merged.

5.13 As far as employment law is concerned, the case is initially heard by the Employment Tribunal (formerly called the Industrial Tribunal). This is usually a three person tribunal with a qualified Chairman and two lay members. On appeal the case is referred to the Employment Appeals Tribunal who may hear appeals on a point of law or on the basis that the Employment Tribunal could not have reasonably reached the conclusion it did on the facts. The Employment Tribunal normally consists of three members, including one professional judge and two laymen. On appeal from the Employment Appeals Tribunal the matter is referred to the Court of Appeal and thereafter to the House of Lords.

A good example of this is the *Carmichael v National Power* case of 1999 (see Appendix 6) which started in the Employment Tribunal and finished in the House of Lords. This case is also a good example of why it is important to read the leading judgment of the senior court, as in this case the House of Lords, in a fairly readable 10-page judgment, overturned a 28-page judgment in the Court of Appeal.

Understanding law and fact

5.14 Both practitioners and tax officers may become confused between the facts of the case and the legal precedents they set. It must be understood that the facts will vary from one case to another in 99% of cases. There will be similarities but also differences. It is a mistake to say that *Hall v Lorimer* (see Appendix 6) does not apply to a particular case because that case involved a vision mixer and the present case involves a computer programmer. Yet this mistake is made very commonly.

5.15 The plain truth is that the overwhelming majority of cases can be distinguished on the facts—and this will always be the case. The Revenue also recognises that the courts have consistently stressed that every case must be decided on its own particular facts (see ESM 7009). What is of concern are the legal precedents laid down by the courts and tribunals in the judgments which become the binding precedent for future cases. For example, the important 1999 Court of Appeal case of *Express and Echo* (see Appendix 6) lays down, among other things, that where a substitute can be sent then, as a matter of law, the worker cannot be an employee. It is not relevant that the worker, in that case, was a newspaper delivery man.

5.16 It is important not to compare and contrast facts from one case with those of another as a means of establishing legal precedent. In *Walls v Sinnett* (see Appendix 6) an experienced judge stated that simply comparing facts offers no possibility of assistance. What may be compelling in one case may be less important in another, and this of course is quite correct. What need to be identified are the universal legal principles which can be applied to the facts as established.

5.17 The courts lay down principles through the process of *stare decisis*, that is, abiding by legal precedents set by other, usually superior, courts. Although case law develops over the years and different glosses are placed on earlier decisions it is this emerged trail of legal authority which forms the basis of understanding what the current state of law is.

5.18 A great deal has been written as to whether the process of determining status is one of fact, law or both. Esoteric arguments can be found throughout case law judgments, a prime example being *Carmichael v National Power* (see Appendix 6) where many pages in the Court of Appeal's judgment were devoted to this question.

5.19 The main reason it is so important is that a superior court or tribunal can only interfere when there is an appeal on a point of law or where the conclusion reached by the lower tribunal was so perverse no reasonable tribunal properly conducting itself could possibly have come to that conclusion. Superior courts will not interfere in findings of fact if the finding was within the band of possible conclusions.

5.20 The distinction between law and fact can be seen in the following example. If the tax tribunal establishes as a fact that there is an unfettered right to send a substitute but then decides the worker is an employee, this would be appeallable as a point of law. However, if the tribunal concludes that a substitute could not be sent, that would be a finding of fact and not appeallable (unless totally perverse considering the evidence available).

5.21 So is status fact or law? The answer is probably a bit of both, or, as the courts describe it, a mixed question of fact and law. It is generally accepted that, where a relationship is entirely reflected in a written agreement, then it is a question of law as to what the relationship is. On the other hand, the whole matrix of facts often needs to be considered and this will be the case with IR35, as there is a case for bringing in the broader modus operandi of the contractor and the way he runs, and has run, his business.

5.22 One learned commentator suggests that fine distinctions between fact and law can be substituted with a more common sense approach: was the decision right or wrong? Although one sympathises, the distinction remains important in terms of the prospects of an appeal succeeding in the higher courts, as higher courts do not see their role as one of re-hearing and re-evaluating simple fact.

Summary

5.23 Court decisions remain the single most important source of guidance in demonstrating that a worker is not a disguised employee of the client. Facts will vary from one case to another but binding precedents are principles that remain, and they must be fully understood and quoted when the need arises.

CHAPTER 6

The major case law decisions and status criteria

Introduction

6.1 There are hundreds of cases in the various tribunals and courts that have been concerned with 'status'. The 1968 High Court decision in *Ready Mixed Concrete* (see Appendix 6) is seen by all commentators as the seminal authority for the modern law of status. In an often reaffirmed judgement Mr Justice McKenna said:

> 'I must now consider what is meant by a contract of service. A contract of service exists if the following three conditions are fulfilled: (i) the servant agrees that in consideration of a wage or other remuneration he will provide his own work and skill in the performance of some service for his master. (ii) He agrees, expressly or impliedly, that in the performance of that service he will be subject to the other's control in a sufficient degree to make that other master. (iii) The other provisions of the contract are consistent with its being a contract of service.'

Point (i) covers substitution and mutuality and point (ii) covers control. Arguably, mutuality could also come under point (iii).

It is tempting to concentrate only on the more recent and more senior case law decisions, as such decisions will necessarily carry more weight than old cases which may now be out of favour. It is essential, however, to be aware that the case law regarding tax status is an ever-developing and ever-changing body of law, which often revisits some of the earlier case law decisions. For example, in the Court of Appeal decision in *Montgomery v Johnson Underwood Ltd* (see Appendix 6), March 2001, several references were made to case law going back to the 1960s and, very clearly, the court was strongly influenced by some of those earlier decisions.

6.2 Employment law cases (for example, concerning unfair dismissal or entitlement to holiday or sick pay) may also be relevant in determining status for IR35 purposes. There is a difference in emphasis between cases involving tax and national insurance law and those concerning employment law; the latter are generally brought where the individual is seeking to obtain employee rights, and this may colour the interpretation of them when considered in relation to tax cases. However, employment law cases are still relevant. Indeed, the Revenue itself, where appropriate, refers to employment law cases in the ESM as well as pure tax or national insurance cases. Many employment law cases are important because the tribunal usually has to consider the preliminary issue of the worker's status before the substantive employment law issue (eg unfair dismissal) can be determined.

6.3 It should also be noted that the existing case law largely concerns the distinction between employment and self-employment. In practice, the IR35 debate is usually expressed in similar terms. But, strictly, IR35 is about establishing that the worker is *not* in effect an employee of the client, rather than showing he is self-employed (ITEPA 2003 s 49(1)(*c*)). Indeed, the most common IR35 situation is where a worker is an employee of his own company, and is not, therefore, self-employed. However, the existing case law is essential in showing that the worker is not a disguised employee of the client, as there is no separate test for employment status under IR35.

6.4 Some of the cases mentioned are 'unreported'. This does not mean they are not binding legal precedent. What it does mean is that, for a variety of reasons, the case did not appear in the regular law reports. Firms of court transcribers nonetheless have the judgment typed and these are available and can certainly be used in argument. The professional accountancy bodies should be able to assist practitioners in obtaining transcripts.

6.5 It is therefore necessary to appreciate that although the law changes it is more often than not a question of new glosses or approaches being placed on existing case law, with perhaps more modern attitudes towards the employment scene being taken into account.

6.6 On the other hand, it would be a mistake, in the author's view, simply to take a chronological analysis of all case law in an attempt to see what the current legal approach to tax status might be. There is a mass of case law pulling in decisions from different areas such as employment law, tax and national insurance status, industrial accidents and others, and a study of all relevant decisions going back over the last 100 or so years would be overwhelming.

6.7 The better approach to be taken is to analyse the more important strands or criteria relating to tax status, such as substitution, control, mutuality of obligations, financial risk and intention. It can then be seen, for example, how these significant areas have developed over the years. A similar approach can then be taken with the other criteria, such as mutuality of obligations.

6.8 An analysis of the law using this method will not only lead to a better appreciation of what is important in the early twenty-first century when considering tax status, but will give a clear sense of historical development of the more important criteria.

There have now been a handful of IR35 appeals before the General and Special Commissioners. These are not legally binding precedent but are of interest. They are considered in Chapter 12.

Substitution

6.9 The reason substitution is so important is that when an individual person is directly employed, he is expected to give his personal service. A direct employee works under a contract of service. On the other hand, a self-employed person or a commercial business, be it a limited company or partnership, undertakes to supply services. It is thus said to operate by way of a contract *for* services as opposed to a contract *of* service.

6.10 Substitution is, therefore, crucially important. If a person does not have to give personal service, but can instead send a substitute or delegate in his place, then that person cannot be an employee, as the vital pre-requisite of personal service is missing. This need for personal service is one of the prerequisites of a contract of employment and is discussed in the context of the *Ready Mixed Concrete* case of 1968 at 6.18 below.

External and internal rights of substitution and sub-contracting

6.11 There is, in the author's opinion, a distinction between internal substitution, external substitution and sub-contracting of a contract. In order to defeat IR35 specifically, or a tax status challenge generally, it is important to demonstrate that there is a genuine business to business relationship as opposed to a 'disguised employment' relationship.

6.12 Therefore it follows that, if a one-man limited company computer contractor wants to demonstrate that it is a genuine business, it should be able to show that it has the right to send a substitute on its own behalf to carry out the contract works. This defeats all challenges that personal service is required. It should be remembered that a limited company is a separate legal entity and if the company has the right to send a substitute in its place then that is what can be described as an 'external' right of substitution.

However, where the business has the right to re-allocate or substitute its own internal personnel to carry out the contract works, that is to say it may substitute one of its existing employees for another, then this can be described as an 'internal' right of substitution.

6.13 It is considered that a genuine right to send an external substitute would carry slightly more weight than the right merely to send a different existing employee, that is an internal substitute.

6.14 This view is held for two reasons. The first is that important case law such as *Hall v Lorimer* (see Appendix 6) talks about substitution in the context of 'hiring in' a substitute. Similar phrases have been mentioned in other case law decisions and this type of language leads to the conclusion that the courts anticipate a substitute being called in from outside the business not merely reallocated from the existing internal resources of the business. Why else would the phrase 'hiring in' be used?

Secondly, the issue of substitution often raises arguments about the 'reality' of the right. The plain truth is that the overwhelming majority of personal service limited companies potentially affected by IR35 are one-man band businesses with one director/employee who is the sole fee earner. As such the reality is that an internal substitution clause is quite meaningless because there simply are no other employees who could be sent or re-allocated by way of substitution. The Revenue would quite rightly be suspicious of such a clause.

6.15 Sub-contracting a contract is different from substitution. Substitution is concerned with appointing a third party to stand in the place of the personal service business whereas sub-contracting, or authorised delegation, is concerned with arranging for the obligations to be carried out by a third party. These two approaches are not quite the same, but in all cases the responsibilities under the contract cannot be passed to a third party. As a matter of general contract law it is generally thought that it is not possible to assign contractual liabilities (for a detailed discussion, see Cheshire, Fifoot and Furmston *Law of Contract* (Butterworths, 13th edn, 1996) pp 535–539). Novation is, therefore, the only method by which the contractual responsibilities can be transferred to another party. Under this method, all the parties (say, A, B and C) must make a new contract, which effectively replaces the previous one, in which A releases B from his obligation to provide the services, and C agrees to assume those responsibilities.

6.16 The right to sub-contract the contract works to a third party without the need to seek the client's permission and without other unreasonable constraints is an overwhelmingly strong indicator of self-employment. The court cases have tended to concentrate on the right of substitution, rather than sub-contracting, but the two concepts are closely related. There can be no question that the unqualified right to sub-contract the work would also be an overwhelming indication of a genuine business relationship as opposed to disguised employment. This is simply because in either case personal service is not required.

6.17 As stated above, the law has recognised the need for personal service as a pre-requisite for direct employment status for many years. Although the concept is mentioned in many case law decisions the most important are, in chronological order:

- *Ready Mixed Concrete (South East) Limited v Minister of Pensions and National Insurance* (1968) High Court (see Appendix 6);
- *Global Plant Limited v Secretary of State for Health and Social Security* (1971) High Court (see Appendix 6);
- *Australian Mutual Provident Society v Chaplin* 1978 Privy Council (see Appendix 6);
- *McMenamin v Diggles* (1991) High Court (see Appendix 6);
- *Hall v Lorimer* (1993) Court Of Appeal (see Appendix 6);
- *Express and Echo Publications Limited v Tanton* (1999) Court of Appeal (see Appendix 6); and
- *Macfarlane and Skivington v Glasgow City Council* (2000) Employment Appeals Tribunal (see Appendix 6)

It is interesting to note that the majority of the above seven cases were not concerned with tax status, which is a good example of how relevant case law needs to be drawn from other areas of the law including employment law rights and national insurance matters.

6.18 In the 1968 *Ready Mixed Concrete* case it was stated by McKenna J ([1968] 1 All ER 433 at 440B) that:

> 'freedom to do a job either by one's own hands or another's is inconsistent with a contract of service, though a limited or occasional power of delegation may not be'.

It should be noted that this phrase has been reaffirmed many times in more recent case law, but the final few words relating to a limited or occasional power of delegation have not been approved—a fact often missed by the Revenue.

6.19 The judge also commented that, in order for there to be a contract of service, that is a relationship of direct employment, the worker must provide 'his own work and skill'. The concept of personal service being a pre-requisite to a relationship of direct employment was thus clearly spelt out. Many cases have subsequently reaffirmed this. In a decision which receives little publicity, the *WHPT Housing* case (see Appendix 6), the High Court said 'the principal obligation undertaken by the employee is to provide *himself* to serve' (author's emphasis).

6.20 However, as can be seen from these words, the High Court in *Ready Mixed Concrete* took the view that where the right to send a substitute is 'limited' or where the substitute can only be sent in restricted occasional circumstances, then such a qualified right may not be inconsistent with a direct employment relationship. As stated above, this aspect of McKenna J's quotation has been played down but it has nonetheless given the Revenue the opportunity to resist the right of substitution where such right is fettered, and this has for many years been the Revenue's counter argument to a claimed right of substitution.

6.21 The words of McKenna J deserve closer analysis. He did not say that a limited right to send a substitute would be an indicator of direct employment. He said a limited right *may* not be inconsistent with direct employment. This is a subtle difference and for many years the Revenue's view that a limited right of substitution is ineffective has not been subject to the challenge it deserves. It was noted by Mr Justice Burton in the PCG judicial review challenge in 2001 that this restrictive interpretation of substitution by the Revenue may be difficult to justify.

6.22 The practical difficulties over an unworkable internal right of substitution were stated above and a salutary lesson should be learnt from the 1971 case of *Global Plant.* In this case there was a qualified right to send a substitute, but the High Court had little hesitation in reaching the conclusion that the clause was a sham. Shams do not work, whether in the context of substitution or anything else, and it must be stressed that for a substitution clause to carry any weight it must be genuinely entered into and not simply part of a paper-signing exercise.

6.23 Before looking at the important 1991 case of *McMenamin v Diggles,* the *Australian Mutual v Chaplin* case from 1978 is worth mentioning. This was a case referred to the UK Privy Council from the Australian courts. Lord Fraser referred to substitution by using a different phrase (quoted at ESM 1051) 'the power of unlimited delegation is almost conclusive against the contract being a contract of service'. Interestingly the same court said that where: 'there is nothing in the written contract to prevent (the worker) from delegating the whole performance of the task' this would give an implied right of substitution. This important quotation is generally not known by the average tax inspector and it should be brought to his attention.

6.24 By the late 1970s there was, therefore, a trail of case law starting with *Ready Mixed Concrete* and running through to the *Australian Mutual v Chaplin* case, wherein the courts were increasingly accepting that the right to send a substitute or delegate was so inconsistent with a contract of employment that any worker with such a right would not be deemed to be a direct employee. The important qualification from the *Global Plant* case is that the substitution clause and the right of substitution must be genuine and not a sham and if it is to be relied upon it should not be qualified.

6.25 The 1991 case of *McMenemin v Diggles* (see Appendix 6) developed the concept of substitution somewhat further. This was a High Court case concerned with the income tax status of the worker who operated as a barristers' clerk. He was formerly an employee of many years standing who renegotiated his terms and conditions and claimed thereafter to be self-employed. His tax status was challenged by the Revenue. The main argument run by the Revenue was that the position of barristers' clerk was an 'office' and in accordance with the Taxes Act should automatically trigger PAYE deductions under Employment Income. The court, however, stated that the phrase 'barristers' clerk' was nothing more than a description.

According to his contract the taxpayer had the implied right to send a substitute to fulfil the clerking services he was to provide. This was because he was obliged to provide other less senior clerks and support staff and, by definition, this meant that he was not obliged personally to perform all the services himself. He had the further right to undertake the senior clerking services himself or to provide an alternative head clerk so long as the alternative head clerk had at least ten years' experience. It is understood that the taxpayer conceded that he could not readily supply an alternative head clerk with ten years' experience yet this clause was not held to be a sham. He had the clear contractual right to provide a substitute head clerk and the court accepted that the right was genuine.

6.26 In retrospect it might have been more fruitful for the Revenue to have argued that placing the ten years of experience 'qualification' on the alternative head clerk amounted to such a fettering that it was rendered ineffective under the dictum of McKenna J in the *Ready Mixed Concrete* case. It will be remembered he said that a 'limited' right of substitution may not carry with it the same importance as an unlimited right to send a substitute. Again, perhaps the Revenue could have referred back to the *Australian Mutual v Chaplin* case, where the court referred to the 'power of unlimited delegation'. It seems quite clear that the taxpayer did not have the 'power of unlimited delegation' as the alternative head clerk had to have at least ten years' experience. The Revenue seems not to have picked up on this point but instead concentrated its arguments on the taxpayer having an 'office'. The Revenue lost and did not take the case any further. There were many other factors in this case which were on the taxpayer's side and in some ways it is surprising that the Revenue wanted to take the case as far as the High Court where, having lost, a binding precedent, together with the attendant publicity, was brought to the attention of practitioners.

6.27 In 1993, the Court of Appeal reached an important decision in *Hall v Lorimer*. In that case, the Revenue challenged the tax status of Mr Lorimer but lost the argument at the Special Commissioners. The Revenue appealed but again lost in the High Court. The Revenue appealed once more to the Court of Appeal and lost unanimously. In the context of substitution *Hall v Lorimer* is not, in the author's view a leading case. The case is more important in terms of the general approach to be taken in considering tax status and, in particular, the importance of having multiple clients and the unimportance of the provision of equipment and premises, especially where the taxpayer is merely supplying personal skills and services.

6.28 However, the case did mention the issue of substitution. The taxpayer undertook almost 600 separate engagements and in around six of these sent a substitute. The court took the view that in the context of six occasions out of 600 this would not necessarily have an impact on the remaining engagements where a substitute was not sent. In other words, simply because a substitute was sent for approximately 1% of the total engagements this did not necessarily imply that there was a right of substitution for all the other engagements. Compare this to the *Chaplin* case quotation at 6.23 above in respect of written contracts which are silent on the issue of substitution.

6.29 In the *Lorimer* case substitution was considered more in the context of the actual physical sending of a substitute, whereas the *McMenanin v Diggles* case and later case law tends to concentrate on the right to send a substitute as opposed to the actual sending of one. It should be noted and heavily underlined that the taxpayer in *Hall v Lorimer* did not have a written right of substitution and it is believed that it was for this reason that the court was unwilling to imply that a general right of substitution existed. The lesson here is simple: do not leave these things to chance. If the parties have genuinely agreed a right of substitution this should be clearly spelt out and committed to writing. *Hall v Lorimer*, being a relatively recent Court of Appeal authority, contains many useful hints on how to determine status. Unfortunately it is also a case that can be seen to move away from the fundamental approach of *Ready Mixed Concrete* to a more vague multi-factional approach, whereby a picture is painted from the accumulation of detail. While this offers flexibility, it also produces uncertainty. Case law in the last five years has reverted to a more fundamental approach on substitution as well as other factors.

6.30 The very important case of *Express and Echo Publications Group v Tanton*, heard by the Court of Appeal in 1999 dealt with the issue of substitution in an extremely clear-cut and robust manner.

Practitioners are encouraged to read this fairly brief Court of Appeal judgment given by Lord Justice Peter Gibson. The case concerned a newspaper delivery driver who had previously been treated as a direct employee. He was subsequently re-engaged, doing essentially the same work but in a self-employed capacity. The worker was given a self-employed contract which he never signed. He then questioned his employment status.

6.31 In fact he sought advice from the Revenue, which was so convinced that he was an employee the law report stated the Revenue would 'countenance no other view whatever'. This was a very clear pronouncement by the Revenue which was unanimously rejected by the Court of Appeal.

6.32 Interestingly, however, the Revenue did not challenge the putative employer on the grounds that they were employing Mr Tanton, and instead Mr Tanton took Express and Echo Group through the employment tribunals and the case ended up in the Court of Appeal. Despite many indications of direct employment the court held Mr Tanton was in fact *not* an employee.

6.33 Lord Justice Peter Gibson said that, in establishing employment status, the first question to be asked is whether or not there are any terms of the engagement which are inherently inconsistent with a contract of service. If there are, the question of status is concluded at that point and there is no need to consider the whole range of other factors usually taken into account in status decisions. This simple and fundamental approach is to be welcomed, and reaffirmed the *Ready Mixed Concrete* approach.

6.34 This is, in the view of the author, an important shift in the approach to determining status. In previous cases throughout the 1980s, culminating in *Hall v Lorimer* in 1993, the common approach was to gather all the relevant facts, with no one fact being conclusive on its own, with a view to painting a picture and coming to a balanced conclusion. However, *Express and Echo* reverts to a more fundamental approach. Put simply, any terms which are inherently inconsistent with a direct employment relationship will rule out any possibility that the contract as a whole is one of direct employment.

The author's interpretation of this return to a more fundamental approach is also recognised by Deakin and Morris, professors of law, in their respected text *Labour Law* (Butterworths, 3rd edn, 2001, p 168).

On analysis this approach must be correct. If there are any terms which are so at odds with a direct employment relationship it stands to reason that direct employment cannot be appropriate. This approach continues the much more clear cut line of reasoning from the *Ready Mixed Concrete* case, which took a fundamental view of status criteria.

6.35 In the *Express and Echo* case what was inherently inconsistent with a contract of service was that Mr Tanton had the right to send a 'suitable' substitute. In the words of Lord Justice Peter Gibson ([1999] IRLR 367 at 370):

> '... it is in my judgment, established on the authorities that where, as here, a person who works for another is not required to perform his services personally, then as a matter of law the relationship between the worker and the person for whom he works is not that of employee and employer'.

This is a classic example of a succinct and helpful quotation with real legal authority. Note how clear this quotation is. It does not say that a right to send a suitable substitute is an important factor—it is a determinative factor.

6.36 Two further points emerge from the *Express and Echo* case. Firstly, Mr Tanton did in fact send a substitute on a couple of occasions although the court referred to the importance of the *right* not the actuality of sending a substitute. Secondly, and quite rightly, the judge said that if a clause is a sham it should be exposed as such and discredited.

6.37 What is interesting is that the right to send a substitute was fettered in the *Express and Echo* case to the extent that the substitute had to be 'suitable'. One might argue that any right to substitute, delegate, or sub-contract carries with it an implied term that the substitute is competent or 'suitable' to do the work. But by putting the word 'suitable' into the equation is this not a fettering of the 'unlimited power of delegation' referred to in the *Australian Mutual v Chaplin* case? Perhaps it is, but it is a fettering which the court clearly found to be *reasonable*. In other words, the restriction to being able to send only a suitable substitute did not weaken the right of substitution. It should be remembered that in the *Ready Mixed Concrete* case of 1968 the judge said that a limited power of delegation *may*, and only may, weaken the personal service argument.

6.38 The question as to how far a substitution clause has to be fettered before it loses its value is amply demonstrated in the *MacFarlane and Skivington* case of 2000. Here some gym instructors had a substitution right which Glasgow City Council claimed prevented them being employees on the authority of *Express and Echo*. However, once the substitution clause was analysed carefully it was clear that it was so fettered and qualified that in truth it did not amount to a right of substitution at all. The clause in question restricted the right to send a substitute to those occasions when the worker was 'unable' (not merely unwilling) to work; any substitute to be sent had to come from a pre-approved list maintained by the Council; when a substitute was required the Council themselves would organise this; and the Council (not the original worker) would pay the substitute. On examination this was not a sufficiently open-ended substitution clause and the Council could not rely on it to defeat the workers' claim that they were direct employees.

In a witty observation the tribunal pointed out that the best that could be said about the substitution clause in this case was that if the worker did send a substitute she probably wouldn't have been in breach of contract but that was as good as it got!

An unfettered right of substitution will defeat IR35 as will a right of substitution which is fettered only to the extent that the substitute must be reasonably suitable. So much is clear.

Substitution clauses which merely allow the personal service business to 'offer' a substitute are not reliable. No doubt it is open for any worker to approach his client and suggest or 'offer' a substitute, but such a stance would be totally speculative. The client, clearly, could refuse the offer. So the right to 'offer' a substitute is of little value. What is needed is a right to send one.

It is not uncommon to see substitution clauses where the original worker must work alongside the substitute during the hand-over period. One would naturally expect the original worker to liaise with his substitute as a matter of praticality, but to impose a hand-over period might appear to be too restrictive a fettering. However, the 2002 Special Commissioners judgement in *Lime-IT Ltd v Justin* (see Appendix 6) dealt with this specific issue. Dr Avery Jones placed great emphasis on the substitution clause, which contained a hand over period, and the clause was one of the major factors that helped defeat IR35 in that case.

6.39 A further case law gloss on substitution came in the March 2001 judicial review challenge to IR35 initiated by the Professional Contractors Group (in *R (on the application of Professional Contractors Group Ltd) v IRC*, see Appendix 6). Mr Justice Burton, delivering the High Court judgment, criticised the Revenue's largely strict and narrow interpretation of substitution. The Revenue's view that a restricted right, or the need first to obtain the client's permission would necessarily prove fatal to a substitution clause was not accepted by the judge. He felt a too narrow approach was unwise.

However, it should be remembered that his remarks, while very interesting were arguably obiter dicta. This means they were remarks said in passing only and as they were not directly connected to the European Law he was considering such remarks do not amount to binding legal precedent. It is likely that the Revenue will see it this way and early IR35 appeals have shown this—see Chapter 12.

The Revenue's view of substitution

6.40 The reader should perhaps concentrate on the law rather than being overly concerned with the Revenue's views, but when dealing with an IR35 challenge substitution is one of the most significant aspects and, whether the Revenue's approach is right or wrong, its view of this issue will have to be dealt with. Furthermore, knowing in advance how the Revenue views substitution will give the practitioner forewarning of what he is dealing with.

6.41 To be fair to the Revenue, it significantly modified its view of substitution by taking a less narrow view of the issue. In late 2000 the Revenue made some major changes to its Schedule E Manual and the newly written Employment Status Manual contains some very notable changes in the way the Revenue is now approaching the issue of substitution.

6.42 That having been said, evidence both anecdotal and actual suggests that the Revenue's revised view of substitution has not yet trickled down to all officers at ground level, many of whom seem to be unaware of their new internal guidance in the Employment Status Manual. As such they often operate in accordance with the Revenue's earlier approach to substitution, which to say the least was narrow and restrictive. The author has noted a worrying trend for the Revenue to ask for written confirmation of the substitution right, usually from the end-user, before accepting it. This is despite the fact that ESM 1056 discussed at 6.55 below makes it clear that unless there is reason to doubt the claimed right of substitution it 'may normally be accepted at face value'. In practice the Revenue will not accept a substitution right at face value without speaking to the client. The Revenue should be challenged when it fails to follow ESM 1056 without good reason. A further practical difficulty is that the person at the end-user who is approached for confirmation of the substitution right might be (and indeed is likely to be) completely unaware of what the actual contractual position is between the end-user and agency on the one hand and the agency and personal service business on the other. If the end-user via the human resources department or department manager merely offers their personal opinion, perhaps in a brief telephone conversation, what use is that in terms of reliable legal evidence?It is submitted very little.

6.43 The Revenue has now acknowledged the important case of *Express and Echo Publications Group v Tanton*, heard in the Court of Appeal in 1999. It has publicly stated that, according to the *Express* case, where a substitute can be sent this would 'probably' indicate that the worker was not an employee. The specific words of Lord Justice Peter Gibson should be remembered, as he said something quite different. In his judgment the right to send a substitute would 'as a matter of law' preclude the worker from being an employee. Practitioners will note the difference between 'probably' and 'as a matter of law' and may conclude that the Revenue was loath to embrace the full impact of the *Express* decision on the important subject of substitution.

6.44 Being generous to the Revenue it perhaps made its comments in the context that not all substitution clauses necessarily preclude direct employment, as the substitution clause may be significantly fettered or qualified. But if this is what it meant to say then it should have said it unequivocally. The Revenue's view that a right of substitution would 'probably' preclude direct employment is clearly not a fair precis of what the judge said.

6.45 This important observation once again underlines the importance of reading what the judges say rather than taking at face value an interpretation devised by a third-party with its own self interests to protect.

6.46 The Revenue has now gone into much greater detail in addressing the substitution issue in its internal manuals. The Revenue accepts (at ESM 510) that: 'an essential element of an employment is that the worker provides personal service'.

Unfortunately, it then goes on to say that if the worker is free to utilise a third-party to do the work or to help him then it is 'unlikely' that the worker is an employee. The words of the judgment in the *Express* case must be borne in mind because the Revenue has played down the significance of personal service and substitution in this extract.

6.47 In the more detailed guidance in ESM 1000 onwards the Revenue makes reference to the *Ready Mixed Concrete* case, *Australian Mutual v Chaplin* and the *Express and Echo* case and at last this important topic is given the technical analysis it deserves. The Revenue now accepts (at ESM 1051) that it is 'most unlikely' that any worker who has the right to send a substitute will be an employee.

6.48 The Revenue finally gives a fair precis of the *Express and Echo* judgment (in ESM 1052) where it accepts that:

> 'where a worker does not have to perform the work personally and can hire a substitute to carry out the work, that is inconsistent with employment and the worker will be self-employed regardless of other factors such as control etc'.

The important phrase to bear in mind here is 'regardless of other factors'. In the past the Revenue would accept substitution only as one factor to be taken into account but here it is clearly accepted that the substitution issue alone can conclude the status and IR35 argument.

6.49 The Revenue qualifies this bold and helpful statement by pointing out that in its view the right to provide a substitute must be genuine, the engager (by which it means the client of the personal service business) must not have an unreasonable right of veto over the substitute and that the worker must himself engage and pay the substitute. The author considers this approach to be both reasonable and in line with the *MacFarlane and Skivington* case heard in 2000.

6.50 The Revenue devotes some detailed analysis in asking whether the right of substitution is genuine and whether the right to reject a substitute effectively renders the right worthless. It is quite correct to do so. Helpfully, the Revenue's guidance (at ESM 1054) advises that:

> 'you should therefore accept that a worker is self-employed where a genuine right of substitution exists even if the engager has the right to reject an unsuitable substitute'.

This is an extremely clear and unequivocal statement by the Revenue, and in the author's experience many inspectors and compliance officers are unaware of it. It should be quoted to the Revenue without hesitation.

6.51 Not only has the Revenue spelt out what is a very fair summary of the current law relating to substitution it has in fact gone one stage further. Again at ESM 1054 the Revenue states that, where the client can reject the substitute in one of three circumstances, the right of substitution will *not* be treated as being fettered and will still safeguard self-employment. The three special circumstances given by the Revenue are:

1 Rejection of the substitute because of his inability to do the work effectively or within a reasonable timescale.
2 Rejection of the substitute if he is a known troublemaker.
3 Rejection of the substitute because other workers refuse to work with the person in question.

In other words, the Revenue accepts that where there is a right to send a substitute but that substitute can be rejected if he is not suitable for any of the three reasons mentioned above, the right to send a substitute in these circumstances will still be treated as effectively unfettered and will, therefore, safeguard self-employment.

6.52 There is a major risk in relying too heavily on ESM 1054. If anything, the Revenue is being over generous in its concession regarding the above three special circumstances. The case law itself does not recognise trouble makers or bad team players as being substitutes who can be excluded with no detriment to the right generally. There is always the chance that the Revenue will adopt a stricter approach once again and personal service businesses that have deliberately used a Revenue 'approved' watered down substitution clause may well find themselves in trouble. It may be embarrassing for the Revenue to back track but it is quite capable of doing this. The internal instructions are, after all, only the Revenue's policy. They are not law.

As such, it is strongly recommended that an unfettered right is agreed, or one which is restricted only to the extent that the substitute has to be suitably qualified or experienced.

6.53 Although the Revenue is alert to the possibility of sham substitution clauses being put into contracts, they also accept (at ESM 1056) that unless there is good reason to doubt the bona fides of the substitution clause it should be accepted at face value.

6.54 ESM 1055 points out that the onus is on the Revenue to demonstrate that a substitution clause is a sham. They accept that it is the *right* of substitution which is important and that even where a substitute has not been sent in practice this does not necessarily mean 'that there is no real right of substitution'.

6.55 Paragraph 1056 of the ESM acknowledges that:

> 'disproving a claim to rights of substitution can be difficult. Unless there is reason to doubt a claimed right of substitution it may normally be accepted at face value'.

This represents a sea change in the Revenue's attitude towards substitution. In the past, where a right of substitution was claimed, the usual Revenue response was to ask how many times a substitute had been sent in practice. It is comforting to note that the Revenue has moved on from this incorrect interpretation of the law. Unfortunately, despite the clear guidance at ESM 1056 too many tax officers are far too reluctant to acknowledge that genuine substitution rights exist, and attempt to put the contractor to some trouble by making him prove the right. This is in spite of the clear guidance at ESM 1055 which places the onus on the Revenue to show the substitution right is a sham, and not on the contractor to show it is not.

6.56 Unfortunately the Revenue reverts to its earlier harder line on substitution in ESM 1057. Here they suggest that even where there is a genuine right of substitution but other clauses indicate a contract of employment, the tax officer should take advice from Personal Tax Division (PT5) but this really flies in the face of the clear comments made by Lord Justice Peter Gibson in the *Express and Echo* case and the preceding paragraphs in ESM. These ESM contradictions should be addressed.

6.57 ESM 1058 advises the tax officer that if he wishes to ignore a claimed right of substitution he must find the evidence to show that the claimed right does not exist. In such cases the tax officer is advised that he should 'always speak to the engager and the worker', yet the Revenue has no legal authority to require either party to attend a personal interview—a point not understood by many practitioners.

6.58 It is a pity that the manuals go on to give the tax officer proactive advice to justify ignoring a claimed right of substitution while at the same time advising that a right of substitution should normally be accepted at face value. It all seems to be rather inconsistent and the Revenue should be challenged.

In the author's view this is a straightforward matter of tactics on the Revenue's part. It knows in law that the right to send a substitute (so long as it is not unreasonably fettered) will preclude direct employment as per the *Express and Echo* judgment. The Revenue must, therefore, go out of its way (contrary to the official guidance, whereby a right of substitution should normally be accepted at face value) to try to disprove the right, because, should an IR35 or tax status appeal turn on the issue of substitution, the Revenue knows that the law is against it. In cases handled by the author this has been apparent.

6.59 Sometimes the Revenue will argue that a worker is necessarily employed because he has no *obligation* to send a substitute. But this is to twist the case law into something at odds with the leading cases. A reasonable substitution clause is a silver bullet but the lack of one is not a fatal flaw.

More recently the Revenue's approach to the substitution issue has once again hardened. Following the *Synaptek* High Court appeal (see Chapter 12 and App 6), the Revenue now argues that a fettered substitution clause must be put into practice before it can be seen as effective. This is not quite what *Synaptek* said and it is submitted that *Express Echo* remains a more accurate statement of the law and as a Court of Appeal authority takes precedence.

Hiring helpers

6.60 It almost goes without saying that the right to hire helpers is an overwhelming indicator of self-employment, as the need for personal service would no longer be present. The 1991 case of *McMenamin v Diggles* (see Appendix 6) is a good example of this.

6.61 Furthermore, if a worker (or in the strict context of IR35 the personal service business) has the right to hire and/or actually hires other workers as employees or self-employed consultants then this would also indicate a business modus operandi, with the attendant risks and costs. Any genuine and not unreasonably fettered right to send a substitute or hire help, by definition breaks the personal service obligation and defeats IR35.

Contracts which are silent on substitution

6.62 Where there is no written right to send a substitute, the personal service business is faced with the difficult task of proving, on the balance of probabilities, that the right to send a substitute exists, despite the useful extract from *Chaplin*'s case noted at 6.23 above.

Without question it is possible to have an oral right to send a substitute, but a clear written term provides much better evidence and is open to less cross-examination. For the purposes of clarity all important terms should be recorded in a signed, dated contract.

6.63 It should be remembered that where there is no right to send a substitute at all, or where the right is significantly fettered, this does not mean of itself that the worker is a disguised employee. A properly worded genuine right to send a substitute precludes direct employee status, but a lack of such a right does not in itself mean that the worker is a disguised employee of the client. Where there is no right other factors have to be considered and in particular mutuality of obligations, control and financial risk.

The simple fact that a substitute cannot be sent does not mean IR35 bites, it merely means that IR35 has not been automatically defeated ab initio.

Summary

6.64 The case law shows, and the Revenue (perhaps reluctantly) accepts, that where there is a genuine right to send a substitute, so long as the right is not unreasonably fettered, then as a matter of law the worker will not be an employee of the engager. As such, the right of substitution is a very effective factor in demonstrating that the worker is not a disguised employee of the client. However, attempts by the Revenue to seek third-party confirmation when there is no good reason to doubt the substitution right should be pointed out as being contrary to ESM 1056. Don't hold your breath.

Mutuality of obligation

6.65 To many practitioners and tax officers alike, no other aspect of employment status causes as much difficulty and confusion as mutuality of obligation. This is further evidenced by the many academic articles written on this subject.

The author has researched mutuality of obligations extensively, including interviewing leading academics. Where relevant the results of this research will be brought out in the following paragraphs.

Why is mutuality of obligations so important?

6.66 Mutuality is such an important fundamental that without it there cannot be a contract of employment. Current case law looks to see if the 'irreducible minimum' to create a contract of employment is present. If it is not there the contract cannot be a relationship of direct employment. The irreducible minimum includes mutuality of obligation. The case law discussion below looks at this in more depth.

6.67 Like the issue of substitution, mutuality of obligations has developed through various court cases over the years. At times mutuality of obligations has been very much the single most important factor in determining status, not least during the early and mid-1980s. Yet at other times, particularly in the mid-1990s, the concept was given less importance.

6.68 Current legal precedents, and in particular the *Carmichael* House of Lords case in 1999 (see Appendix 6) and the *Montgomery* Court of Appeal case in 2001 (see Appendix 6), again indicate that mutuality of obligation is an extremely important factor in status disputes generally and potentially IR35 in particular.

Understanding what mutuality of obligations means

6.69 There seems to be ongoing confusion when similar sounding terminology is used. This can usefully be cleared up:

Mutuality of Obligations—this relates to the ongoing relationship between the parties and involves a high level of commitment to each other. This is fully explained below at 6.70–6.75.

Mutual Intention—this is what relationship the parties to a contract wish and intend to create and this could be either a relationship of direct employment or self-employment. It is quite different from mutuality of obligations. The parties' intention is important, see 6.155 et seq below.

The Essentials to Create Any Contract—this is the three attributes that all arrangements need before they can harden into a formal contract and are discussed below.

The Irreducible Minimum to Create a Contract of Service—this is the whole basis of creating a contract of employment as originally developed by McKenna J in the 1968 *Ready Mixed Concrete* case and centres on the trinity of personal service, control and, more recently, mutuality of obligations. This is discussed at 6.90 below, having been reaffirmed in the *Montgomery v Johnson Underwood* case of 2001. Thus it can be seen that these terms are both important and different.

For a binding contract to exist both parties must have the intention of entering into legal relations with each other, there must be an offer and an acceptance and valuable consideration must pass between the parties. However, the mere offer and acceptance of a specific piece of work does not amount to mutuality of obligations in the context of employment status.

This important point has been underlined in the obiter comments made by Burton J in the PCG judicial review hearing at the High Court (see 6.102 below) and also in the 2001 *Hewlett Packard* Employment Appeal Tribunal decision (see Appendix 6).

Mr Justice Burton said that the obligation of the client 'to pay the money' is not enough to establish mutuality of obligations, and this was confirmed in *O'Murphy v Hewlett Packard* (2001).

More recently, in *Propertycare Ltd v Gower* (EAT 547/03,[2004] All ER (D) 16 (Jan); see Appendix 6). His Honour Judge Peter Clark said

> 'the cases, starting with *Ready Mixed Concrete* show that mutuality of obligations means more than a simple obligation on the employer to pay for work done; there must generally be an obligation on the employer to provide work and the employee to do the work. That is how we understand the first of McKenna J's tests in *Ready Mixed Concrete*.'

6.70 In the sense of establishing employment status, mutuality of obligations is concerned with a deeper degree of commitment, trust and confidence between the parties, such that they have a higher plane of obligations beyond the mere offer and acceptance of work.

6.71 Mutuality is not a concept liked by the Revenue and wherever possible it plays down the importance of this factor. Tax officers may point out that employment status is not necessarily the same thing as tax status, although practitioners will note that the Revenue will quote employment law cases when it suits them. When arguing IR35 cases practitioners will constantly come across inspectors who insist that mutuality of obligations is necessarily established by the simple giving and doing of work. While Revenue head office specialists concede the position is more complex than this, the message seems not to have filtered down to district level.

6.72 As pointed out in *Labour Law* (Deakin and Morris, Butterworths, 2nd edn, 1998), at p 162, mutuality of obligations in the context of employment contracts has a specific meaning 'which refers to the presence of mutual commitments to maintain the *employment relationship* in being over a period of time' (author's emphasis). Some commentators believe that this ongoing commitment must extend to a situation where there is no work available and the 1999 *Carmichael* case suggested this. If work runs out but the worker nonetheless receives a retainer payment then it could be argued that the higher plane of obligations has been at least partially met and mutuality of obligations established. This would perhaps also be the case where the worker is obliged to give up work elsewhere and be 'on call' and give his time to a particular paymaster when required to do so, or where the 'employer' is under an ongoing duty to find work for the worker.

As Deakin and Morris point out, every type of contract contains binding promises but a contract of employment requires the 'second tier of obligation consisting of mutual promises of future performance'. They neatly précis the whole concept of mutuality of obligations by saying that'at the first level there is an exchange of work for remuneration. At the second level there is an exchange of mutual promises of future performance. The second level—the promise to employ and to be employed—provides the arrangement with its stability and with its continuity as a contract'.

This two tier approach to mutuality develops an earlier theory of Professor Mark Freedland of Oxford in his 1976 *The Contract of Employment*. This book has recently gone into its second edition and is re-titled *The Personal Employment Contract* (Oxford Monographs on Labour Law).

The author has exchanged emails with Dr Deakin of Cambridge who concedes that the 'two tier' test is one of 'impression' rather than strict case law. The author has also interviewed Dr Brodie of Edinburgh University who reviewed Freedland's book in the *Industrial Law Journal* (March 2004). Dr Brodie believes that mutuality is either in the nature of simple payment in return for work or it requires a higher plane of obligations! As he accurately recognises, case law has described mutuality in many different ways and there is no absolutely clear definition. Arguably Freedland's 'two tier' approach of mutuality was ahead of its time, as the *O'Kelly* case some seven years later referred to mutuality in the context of an obligation to maintain the employment relationship in the future—see 6.79 below.

6.73 The case of *Wickens v Champion Employment* (see Appendix 6) in 1984 described the employment relationship as requiring care and continuity ([1984] ICR 365 at 371E). The *Express and Echo* decision (see Appendix 6) in 1999 referred to 'trust and confidence' ([1999] IRLR 367 at 370), both being inherently required in a contract of service as established by the House of Lords in *Malik v BCCI* (see Appendix 6), and this idea of a higher plane of obligations can be readily recognised. Indeed, in the old case of *Robb v Green* [1895] 2 QB 315 the court recognised that a master/

servant, relationship required the worker to 'serve with faith and fidelity'. Quaint language perhaps, but the point is made.

For mutuality of obligations to be present the bilateral element of the obligations should not be overlooked. If a work provider is obliged to offer work but the work doer is not obliged to do it, or if the work provider is not obliged to offer work but the work doer is obliged to accept it when offered, then there will be no mutuality of obligations, just unilateral obligations, and this is fundamentally not the same thing.

6.74 If either the work provider is not obliged to offer work or the work doer is not obliged to undertake work offered there is no mutuality of obligations even though there may be unilateral obligations.

This does *not* mean to say that the worker is necessarily self-employed and certain workers fall into a no man's land where the courts have held that they have a contract *sui generis* (of its own kind). In other words it is neither a contract of employment nor a contract for services (self-employment).

6.75 Some tax officers consider that mutuality of obligations is the same thing as a mutual intention to create self-employment. It is not and this is a basic error. The Revenue has long held the view that the intentions of the parties as to what type of relationship they have created is not a factor to be taken into account unless the overall position is ambiguous and finely balanced. However, the intention of the parties as to whether they have created employment or self-employment is not the same thing as mutuality of obligations. The parties' intention is important—see below.

6.76 It must be remembered that defeating IR35 is not about proving self-employment. It is simply a question of showing that the worker is not an employee.

There are four further areas of mutuality of obligations worth commenting on.

The first is often overlooked but could prove useful. If the personal service business is entitled to no notice (or very little notice) of termination of its contract then it can be argued that the higher plane of care and continuity inherent in mutuality of obligations is by definition missing and many contracts do have zero termination periods. On the other hand if a long period of notice has to be given to the personal service business then it could be argued that this indicates some element of 'care and continuity'. Often the personal service business itself has to give quite a long period of notice, but this is normally for the protection of the agency's interests. Chapter 12 notes the comments of Mr Justice Hart in this respect in *Synaptek Ltd v Young (HMIT)* (2003) (see Appendix 6)—the only IR35 case to have reached the High Court. In essence the point was made that if there is no mutuality in the sense that this means an obligation to offer work, then why would a period of notice be needed? Turning this around, does the existence of a period of notice imply mutuality. In pure legal theory the answer is probably 'yes', but notice periods are often inserted for practical and commercial reasons and not as oblique evidence of a lack of mutuality.

Secondly, some commentators have suggested that mutuality of obligations can exist *during* an individual contract and as such the presence of mutuality of obligations will be established within the relationship. As such, they argue, the IR35 defence of 'lack of mutuality' is not available. It is submitted that this is incorrect and such an approach fails to appreciate the true meaning of mutuality, that is to say the *ongoing commitments to maintain* the employment relationship. A huge difficulty is that if mutuality amounts to an obligation to offer/do work at what point in time is the 'obligation' to be identified? Before a contract is offered there is no obligation to offer it. This suggests no mutuality. Once the contract is offered and accepted then clearly there is an obligation to complete the contract. Is mutuality established at this point? What if once the contract is offered and accepted either party can unilaterally withdraw within the contract? These questions can only be answered once a definition of mutuality can be devised.

There are 4 possible definitions of mutuality.

1 Mutuality as mere consideration, ie payment in respect of work.
2 An obligation to offer/accept work throughout a contract.
3 An obligation to offer/accept future work.
4 The higher plane test of trust and confidence.

Case law suggests that 1 and 3 are at the extremes and 4 is less reliable. Perhaps 2 is the correct middle ground.

Furthermore, if all mutuality of obligations means is the bundle of contractual rights and promises (as opposed to the higher plane of commitments identified earlier) then the whole concept of mutuality becomes meaningless as every contract, be it of service, for services or just getting on a bus, will have 'mutuality' and the doctrine of mutuality of obligations and its special meaning in status would be rendered nugatory. As will be seen below the Court of Appeal and House of Lords have identified mutuality in the context of status as being an area of prime importance and to suggest that there is mutuality of obligations during the subsistence of every contract where work is undertaken is plainly wrong. The mistake made is one of confusing mutuality of obligations (in the proper sense) with mere contractual rights and obligations which all contracts have.

The third area concerns the impact on mutuality of obligations of the length of the contract, where the contract is for a *fixed* period. Is it correct to assume that a contract fixed for a period of say one week has any less mutuality than a contract fixed for say three years? One's gut instinct might say 'yes' but it is submitted that this again misunderstands what mutuality, in the context of employment status, is all about. As stated above, it is not concerned with the contractual rights and promises that subsist during a specific contract, because all contracts of every kind contain rights and promises, or obligations. Mutuality of obligations in its proper employment status context means a high degree of commitment to maintain an ongoing relationship of employment. However, there is a real argument to say that only once a contract of employment is established does mutuality become an issue. In other words, mutuality in the context of the higher plane of trust and committment is the result of a contract of service, not a determinant of such a contract.

So back to the two fixed term contracts: one for a week, one for three years. If these contracts were entered into as fixed term contracts it is suggested that the length of the engagement *itself* does not impact on mutuality of obligations.

It might be that the three-year contract carries with it other terms which may more readily imply mutuality, for example a long period of notice, the right to enjoy other aspects of 'care and continuity' afforded to regular employees, but these issues are separate from the length of the contract per se. Indeed, the Revenue now accepts that the length of an individual contract is a neutral factor.

It is also suggested that if the one-week contract was automatically renewed or extended week in, week out for a period of three years then this would be more likely to create or imply mutuality than a one-off fixed three-year contract. This concept of mutuality of obligations being capable of slowly crystallising over a period of time is discussed at 6.78 et seq below.

Whenever possible, new negotiated distinct and project leased contracts should be entered into rather than extentions or rolling renewals of existing contracts. This will make it harder for the Revenue to establish mutuality.

Fourthly, if mutuality of obligations, as properly defined, is a prerequsite for a contract of employment, does this means that a supermarket checkout operator doing a temporary job over Christmas will not be an employee? And if not why not? Again one's gut instinct might be to say it is obvious the checkout operator is an employee. Such a worker surely has all the hallmarks of a regular employee. There is control, no financial risk, no rights of substitution, the intention to be an employee, provision of a uniform, etc, but is there mutuality of obligation? Arguably not, if mutuality, correctly defined, falls within 3 or 4 as described above. This is a one off temporary assignment for a few weeks' work with absolutely no ongoing mutual commitments. And before the idea of a non-employed checkout operator is dismissed the true nature of mutuality of obligations should be considered carefully and the landmark *O'Kelly* case, discussed at 6.79 below, explored, where the court came to what is to many an unusual decision.

6.77 The leading case law on mutuality is, in chronological order

- *Airfix Footwear Ltd v Cope* 1978 (see Appendix 6) decided by the Employment Appeals Tribunal
- *O'Kelly v Trust House Forte* 1983 (see Appendix 6) Court of Appeal
- *Nethermere (St Neots) Ltd v Gardiner* 1984 (see Appendix 6) Court of Appeal
- *McLeod v Hellyer Bros* 1987 (see Appendix 6) Court of Appeal
- *Clark v Oxfordshire Health Authority* 1997 (see Appendix 6) Court of Appeal

- *McMeechan v Secretary of State for Employment* 1997 (see Appendix 6) Court of Appeal
- *Carmichael v National Power* 1999 (see Appendix 6) House of Lords
- *Montgomery v Johnson Underwood Ltd* 2001 (see Appendix 6) Court of Appeal
- *R (on the application of Professional Contractors Group and others v IRC* 2001(see Appendix 6) High Court
- *O'Murphy v Hewlett Packard* 2001 (see Appendix 6) decided by the Employment Appeals Tribunal
- *Property Care Ltd v Gower* 2003 (see Appendix 6) decided by the Employment Appeals Tribunal
- *Stuncroft v Havelock* 2001 (see Appendix 6) decided by the Employment Appeals Tribunal
- *Stevedoring and Haulage Services Ltd v Fuller* 2001 (see Appendix 6)
- *Synaptek Ltd v Young* (HMIT) 2003 (see Appendix 6)

There are other mutuality cases but the above are the leading authorities and will now be examined.

The case law

6.78 In the 1978 case of *Airfix Footwear v Cope*, it was established that despite there being no formal legal obligation to offer and accept work, such obligations may crystallise over the passage of a long period of time.

In this case the worker carried out work, usually for five days per week for over seven years. Despite this long period of almost constant work the decision was not clear cut and the tribunal was split. Indeed, there were many factors pointing to self-employment.

It is arguable that mutuality of obligations was misapplied in this case in that its presence was held to indicate direct employment status whereas it is submitted that the correct approach is that a lack of mutuality of obligations precludes direct employment. This is certainly the line later cases took. The *Airfix* case did not go beyond the employment tribunals unlike many of the mutuality cases of later years, which went to the Court of Appeal or indeed the House of Lords.

The work undertaken was essentially unskilled, and part of the reasoning for the decision was that the worker had no technical skill to exploit in the market place. This can be readily contrasted with the typical personal service business worker, who may well be an expert or specialist.

Needless to say, the Revenue is quite keen to quote the *Airfix* case but it should be seen in the context of an unskilled worker. The *O'Kelly* case, heard in the Court of Appeal five years later took a different and much more extreme view.

6.79 *O'Kelly* was something of a landmark decision and is still considered to be a leading precedent on mutuality despite being nearly 20 years old. That case concerned unskilled and semi-skilled workers who attended large hotel functions and acted as wine waiters etc on a 'regular casual' basis. Despite their many hallmarks of direct employment status the workers were held to be self-employed. This was because there was no *legal* obligation on the hotel to offer them work nor on them to accept it. The fact that work was regularly accepted, sometimes in excess of 50 hours per week did not alter the position. There was no *obligation.*

The court described the regular offering and accepting of work as nothing more than 'market forces', which should not be confused with legal obligations.

The original employment tribunal found, and the Court of Appeal agreed, that 'it was a purely commercial transaction for the supply and purchase of services for specific events because there was no obligations for the company to provide work and no obligation for the applicants to offer their "*further*" services' (author's italics—[1983] ICR 728 at 744).

6.80 The *O'Kelly* case is also notable in that it established that the mere supply of semi-skilled labour, with few if any of the trappings of being in business, was nonetheless a perfectly legitimate form of self-employment. The court noted that, although there was no great financial risk on the workers, this did not preclude them from being independent contractors.

It also rejected the idea that there was an umbrella or global contract which subsisted throughout the arrangements.

6.81 The case has been criticised by those who seek to establish employment law rights for unskilled or semi-skilled workers, but the precedent is very clear and the Revenue does not like it. The author has interviewed several academics who hold the view that *O'Kelly* was mutuality's 'low point', in that it made a lack of mutuality easy to establish and hence employment rights difficult to establish. Many also feel the waiters were badly advised and that an astute lawyer should have given them some sound advice 'over the soup'.

6.82 The case of *Nethermere (St Neots) Ltd v Gardiner* should also be considered. In that case, the tribunal found, albeit by only a majority decision, that an apparent lack of mutuality can crystallise into true mutuality, as in the *Airfix* case. The tribunal identified such obligations as coming into force perhaps after one year of the giving and taking of work. However, in the Court of Appeal Lord Justice Kerr ([1984] ICR 612 at 630E) could *not* accept that:

> 'even a lengthy course of dealing can somehow convert itself into a contractually binding obligation.'

The decision in *Nethermere* was a narrow one and the appeal tribunal felt unable to interfere in the findings of the lower tribunal. The period of one year of work giving rise to employment was rejected in the *Montgomery v Johnson Underwood* case (see 6.88–6.92 below) where the worker was in situ for two and a half years and was held not to be an employee. It was *Nethermere* that first developed the concept of the 'irreducible minimum' needed to create a contract of service. The phrase was developed from the earlier dicta of McKenna J in *Ready Mixed Concrete*. The irreducible minimum contains mutuality and the worker 'must be obliged to provide his own work and skill'. If the empahsis is placed on the word 'must' it can be seen that mutuality amounts to an absolute obligation to do the work. On the other hand if the emphasis is placed on the words 'his own' then it seems that the issue of personal service and substitution is being addressed, not mutuality as such.

The author's view is that mutuality, personal service and control are effectively all part of the irreducible minimum needed to create a master/servant relationship, or a contract of employment. In some ways mutuality encapsulates personal service just as it might be argued that control encapsulates personal service. If a worker is obliged to work is this another possible aspect of control?

In any event the 'irreducible minimum' was born in *Nethermere* and it included mutuality of obligations, although no definition was given as such.

6.83 In the important Court of Appeal case of *McLeod v Hellyer Bros* in 1987 Hull-based trawlermen had worked for many years for the same party. Their claim for employee rights was rejected, as mutual obligations did not subsist over the entire duration of the period. This again highlights the essential characteristic of mutuality of obligations: an ongoing commitment of continuity. See Chapter 12 for how the High Court in *Synaptek v Young* developed this in the context of IR35.

6.84 The next notable mutuality decision (*Clark v Oxfordshire Health Authority*) was heard in 1997 by the Court of Appeal and concerned a nurse who was part of a nursing bank. Her terms and conditions were highly consistent with a contract of employment and although she did not work continually for the same 'employer' the question was raised as to whether she had a global contract.

6.85 This important case found there was no global contract and underlined that the concept of mutuality of obligations was very important but not crucial to the issue of status. *Clark's* case perhaps reduced the impact of mutuality, and this is an interpretation which can be placed on the decision in *McMeechan v Secretary of State for Employment* (see Appendix 6) also heard in 1997. However, mutuality became a more prominent factor as a result of the decision of the House of Lords in the 1999 case of *Carmichael v National Power*, which reversed the Court of Appeal ruling. Indeed, in that case Lord Irvine stated ([1999] 4 All ER 897 at 902a) that the workers' claim to be employees 'foundered on the rock of absence of mutuality'.

Rarely is such an unequivocal statement made. This very important recent and senior case once again reaffirmed the importance of the 'irreducible minimum' required to establish a contract of service. Mutuality of obligations was seen as very much part of that minimum.

6.86 It was noted by the court that the workers were not necessarily self-employed. Again practitioners should remember that defeating IR35 is not about proving self-employment—it is about proving the worker is not an employee of the client, which may be somewhat easier.

6.87 The Revenue is unhappy that mutuality is being given such importance but even more recent case law again underlines the relevance of this concept.

6.88 In the 2001 case of *Montgomery v Johnson Underwood Ltd*, the Court of Appeal again referred to the 'irreducible minimum' necessary to create a contract of employment and referred in depth to the importance of mutuality as part of the equation. Earlier cases such as *McMeechan*, which appeared to play down mutuality, were distinguished and the *Montgomery* case provides many strong quotations.

6.89 This case concerned a receptionist who contracted with an agency and carried out her duties at the end-user's premises. She worked at the same place for over two and a half years. She was found *not* to be either an employee of the agency or an employee of the end-user.

This was because she was not sufficiently controlled to be a servant and there was a lack of mutuality. The *Ready Mixed Concrete* case (see Appendix 6) of 1968 was quoted with approval. This laid down the principle that, as well as having to give personal service (not in issue in the *Montgomery* case itself) and being under the control of the 'master', it was important to establish that the other terms were not inconsistent with a contract of service. A lack of mutuality is such an inconsistent term.

6.90 Lord Justice Brooke ([2001] IRLR 269 at 274) said:

> 'the concept of an irreducible minimum of obligations was expressly applied by Lord Irvine . . . in *Carmichael v National Power*, and there is a consistent line of authority contained in decisions of this court, binding both on this court and inferior tribunals, to the effect that the three elements of a contract of service identified by McKenna J in *Ready Mixed Concrete*, must be present before a contract of service can be identified, *whatever other elements there may be which point one way or another*' (author's emphasis).

6.91 Brooke LJ also pointed out ([2001] IRLR 269 at 275) that this trinity of personal service, control and mutuality had first to be considered before the other general factors. It is only necessary to go to the 'second stage' of considering all the other status criteria if personal service, control and mutuality are first established. If they are not, the status will not be one of employee and the argument need go no further.

6.92 Because part of the 'irreducible minimum' of a contract of service was missing Buckley J said 'whatever contractual arrangements were enjoyed . . . she cannot have been an employee'.

This important precedent has been cited in more recent cases heard by the Employment Appeals Tribunal. The case of *Electronic Data Systems v*

Hanbury and Brook Street Bureau ([2001] All ER (D) 369 (Mar), EAT 128/00) involved an agency worker claiming, inter alia, unfair dismissal. The Employment Tribunal decided at a preliminary hearing that there was no contract of service, and the EAT had no hesitation in endorsing that conclusion, stating (at para 10) that it was 'plainly permissible' as there was 'no mutuality of obligation . . . regardless of the contractual position' between the parties.

The case of *Stuncroft Ltd v Havelock* (EAT 1017/00, [2002] All ER (D) 292 (Jan)) involved a claim for redundancy pay. The EAT overturned the Employment Tribunal's decision, explaining at para 8, that 'want of mutual obligation was a knock out blow'. Strong words indeed.

The EAT allowed the appeal of *Propertycare Ltd v Gower* (EAT 547/03, [2004] All ER (D) 16 (Jan)), an unfair dismissal case.

6.93 The judicial review case brought by the PCG (*R (on the application of Professional Contractors Group v IRC*, see Appendix 6) contains some helpful, if obiter, remarks by Mr Justice Burton on the issue of mutuality that were made at the same time the Court of Appeal was deciding the *Montgomery* case. He criticised the Revenue's policy of ignoring mutuality wherever it can and said ([2001] STC 629 at 651):

> 'It cannot be right for the Revenue simply to conclude that mutuality of obligation is not a relevant issue . . . it has now recently been emphasised by the House of Lords in *Carmichael v National Power*'.

The Carmichael decision has also been followed in the little publicised Court of Appeal judgment in *Stevedoring & Haulage Services Ltd v AM Fuller and others* [2001] EWCA Civ 651. This case confirmed that where there is a contractual clause negativing mutuality this cannot be overridden by what happens in practice, even if work is offered and accepted on an ongoing basis. The court said at paragraph 11 of the judgement

> 'the implied terms flatly contradict the express terms contained in the documents: a positive implied obligation to offer and accept a reasonable amount of work (whatever that means) cannot be reconciled with express terms that neither party is obliged to offer or accept any work)

None of the conventional routes for the implication of contractual terms will work. Neither business efficacy nor necessity require the implication of implied terms which are entirely inconsistent with a supposed contract's express terms. This tells us that the lack of mutuality should be committed to writing and not left to chance. In the cases where mutuality crystallised over a period of time (*Airfix; Nethermere*) there was no clause negativing MOD as there was no written contract at all.

Mutuality of obligations, affectionately known as 'MOO', is a powerful IR35 defence strategy simply because most agencies, end-users and contractors are happy to contract away any such obligations. Practitioners should be arguing it until the cows come home. In *Stuncroft Ltd v Havelock* His Honour Judge Wilkie QC said, at para 8, that a lack of mutuality is a 'knock out blow'. Not merely a persuasive factor but a determinitive issue, as it is part of the irreducible minimum. This judgement endorsed the arguements of Clive Sheldon, barrister, who appeared on behalf of the Revenue in the *Synaptek* appeal!

Synaptek v Young is analysed in Chapter 12 as it is an IR35 case. However, it can be usefully underlined that that case established that in an IR35 context for there to be sufficient mutuality of obligation, the obligations must endure for the entire period of the notional contract, not merely in isolation.

The Revenue's view of mutuality of obligations

6.94 Whereas in the past the Revenue has sometimes been suspicious of claimed rights of substitution and have tended to play down the importance of such rights, it has been out and out dismissive of the importance and relevance of mutuality. However, the law is simply not on their side, and it should not be forgotten just how critical of the Revenue's view of mutuality Mr Justice Burton was in the judicial review case (see above 6.93).

6.95 If the fundamental importance of mutuality is acknowledged, that is to say it is a pre-requisite of a contract of employment, being as it is part of the 'irreducible minimum' to create a contract of service, then direct employment status can be defeated by ensuring that, in practice and in terms of contractual conditions, mutuality is not implied or created. In general, work providers are quite happy to contract with the work doer on the basis that there is no obligation to provide work to the work doer and equally the work doer is happy to contract with the work provider that he will not make himself available for work in the future.

6.96 In the real world, work cannot be guaranteed and in the context of project based contracts in particular it would be quite unwise for the work provider, in particular, to guarantee ongoing work.

6.97 One of the main reasons that IT and engineering agencies have thrived over the last ten years is simply because there is a requirement for workers to be engaged and released as work flow dictates. Putting to one side the technical legal arguments regarding mutuality of obligations, the Revenue could make a greater effort to understand the relevance of ongoing mutual commitments and their general undesirability in the real commercial world.

6.98 The Revenue has so little time for the relevance of mutuality that, in both the old Schedule E Manual and the new Employment Status Manual they say the concept 'is rarely of practical use . . . and can confuse the issue' (ESM 514, a view repeated at ESM 1071). In the Schedule

E Manual (at SE 663) the Revenue goes one stage further and says, surprisingly, 'do not consider it (mutuality of obligations) unless the engager or worker raises the subject'.

Practitioners may well question the motives for such a statement which is plainly at odds with the case law.

6.99 The Tax Law Review Committee, part of The Institute of Fiscal Studies, released a detailed paper in January 2001 (entitled 'Employed or self-employed? Tax classification of workers and the changing labour market') which described the above quoted Revenue statement as 'a little unhelpful' and suggests that, as the Revenue has a Service Commitment to help get taxpayers' affairs right, this might include a discussion of the important topic of mutuality. The Tax Law Review Committee also considered the Revenue's approach to be 'a little surprising', as by attempting to ignore mutuality as a concept it could be hindering itself in respect of long term engagements where it will want to argue that there *is* mutuality in order to establish employed status.

6.100 The Revenue's approach to mutuality was also criticised by Mr Justice Burton in the PCG case, see para 6.93.

Quite confusingly the Revenue does accept in ESM 508 that mutuality of obligations *is* a consideration to be taken into account. This is all very inconsistent. Interestingly, the quotation at para 6.98 was also in an earlier version of ESM 514 but appears to have been dropped from later prints.

6.101 The truth is mutuality is a very important topic and, despite dismissing it as essentially irrelevant to tax status, the Revenue goes into some considerable detail in its manuals, analysing all the case law and attempting to draw fine distinctions between the various decisions and individual judgments. Needless to say it can't have it both ways. It is suggested that the importance of mutuality is clearly established in numerous senior court cases, and it is more for reasons of policy than as a result of objective legal analysis that the Revenue seeks to play it down. The author acknowledges the sterling efforts of Anne Redston who has successfully convinced the Revenue to change various paragraphs of the ESM on mutuality and certain other key areas. To this day the Revenue tries to play down *O'Kelly* and play up *McMeechan*. They have even argued at the Special Commissioners that *Montgomery* was wrongly decided, but it has got them nowhere.

6.102 A twist on mutuality comes out from the judicial review case brought by the PCG. During an exchange before the judgment was delivered the Revenue's counsel confirmed that mutuality of obligations was indeed a necessary pre-requisite for a contract of service.

When considering the so-called 'hypothetical' contract between the worker and the client, the Revenue's counsel seemed to accept, during discussion in open court, that there could be no mutuality of obligation in an entirely hypothetical contract. Indeed, how can there be? The Revenue will now have to argue that there can be mutual obligations in an imaginary contract. Is it going to have to show that there is hypothetical mutuality within a hypothetical contract? If so, it would seem that the Revenue has a significant burden in demonstrating that this exists. As Mr Justice Burton pointed out, how can one arrive at the required 'irreducible minimum of obligation from someone who doesn't employ you . . . when there isn't any obligation at all? What is the obligation of the employer? . . . *the obligation [of the client] to pay the money is not enough*' (author's emphasis).

In the April 1997 Tax Bulletin the Revenue acknowledged (in the context of a builder) that regularly accepting work from the same client might simply be a function of the worker managing his business well and he could hardly be criticised for regularly accepting well-paid contracts. Even in the context of IR35 the Revenue should be reminded of these comments.

As the new ESM 3285 says, before there can be a contract of service there must be an irreducible minimum which includes mutual obligation. The Revenue confirms that even in the context of a notional contract 'you must be able to point to an irreducible minimum which would have existed'. This would seem to present the Revenue with a massive challenge where contracts are properly worded.

Summary

6.103 Mutuality is so important in establishing a contract of employment. It requires more than a mere offer and acceptance of work. Arguably, a higher plane of legal obligations is required including continuity and care, trust and confidence as well as the desire to maintain the relationship even during periods when there is no work. At the very least there must be an obligation to offer and accept work for the entire period of the notional IR35 contract. Often this will not exist.

Mutuality of obligations is very much part of the 'irreducible minimum' required to establish direct employment. Quite simply, without it a contract of service cannot exist.

The Revenue's view and interpretation of mutuality is at odds with current case law, and its approach has been criticised by the High Court itself.

Control

6.104 Whereas mutuality of obligations has been afforded varying levels of importance over recent years, the issue of control has, if anything, experienced more fluctuating credence over an even longer period. The Revenue is very fond of the so-called control test and it still appears as the lead item in many Revenue pamphlets, which purport to explain the criteria to be taken into account in determining status.

6.105 Traditionally, and certainly in the author's experience, the Revenue has taken a fairly simplistic approach to the control test. It has often expressed the view that if A can tell B what to do then A is the master of B who is a servant and is, therefore, the employee of A.

6.106 In the construction industry, where the skill level of some workers is at a lower level than, say, IT contractors and engineers, the Revenue has been able to push for direct employee status, on the basis that if someone is told what to do or reports to a foreman he is 'controlled'. The control test alone has become a fertile ground for Revenue status challenges, yet this approach, in the author's opinion, seriously misunderstands the law. It is submitted that control is a pre-requisite for a contract of employment but its existence per se does *not* automatically create direct employment status.

6.107 The reason control is important stems from the Victorian concept that a master would control his servant. It should be noted that the word 'servant' had a specific meaning in Victorian legislation and was not synonymous with the word 'worker'. A servant would always be a worker but a worker would not necessarily be a servant. The idea was that a servant was subject to his master's control and therefore by definition if a person controlled another he would be his employer in the context of status, as he would be his master. The very words master and servant carry with them an old fashioned feel, which is not surprising in the context of the origin of the phrase. Indeed, in eighteenth and nineteenth century Britain (and going back to Roman times) a person's 'status' in society would automatically put him under the command of another superior person.

6.108 Throughout the mid-twentieth century the courts tended to concentrate on the issue of control as the single most important factor in determining status. Indeed, there are precedents going back as far as the nineteenth century which stressed this single issue, such as *Yewens v Noakes* (see Appendix 6) where Lord Justice Bramwell gave the leading judgment. It has, however, been said that the dictum of Bramwell LJ on control has been misapplied almost from the moment of its emergence.

6.109 This is because the word 'servant' designated a specific category of employees who were subject to the Master and Servant Acts and the Employers' and Workmen Act of 1875. Furthermore, under the Workers' Compensation Acts different categories of workers enjoyed specific entitlements. This was the context in which 'servants' had to be identified—*not* in the context of tax status generally.

6.110 The so-called 'control test' was used extensively until it was considered that the test had severe limitations. For example, a ship's captain who would be an employee would nonetheless be quite uncontrolled when he was captaining a ship on the high seas. To put this into a more modern context a brain surgeon within the National Health Service who is regarded as an employee is nonetheless not controlled by the hospital, certainly not as to the manner in which he performs his operations. The Revenue is very keen to compare typical IR35 at risk workers with ships' captains and brain surgeons. This is flawed. The true IR35 test is to compare IT contractors with IT employees, oil engineers with oil engineers and not with unrelated professions.

6.111 It was eventually realised that the control test was not a single criterion which could accurately predict or establish status. Although the concept was still regarded as important up to the late 1960s, its importance appeared to diminish in the 1980s and 1990s. Only in the most recent case law, such as the *Montgomery* Court of Appeal case (see Appendix 6) in 2001, has the control factor again become a much more significant indicator as to status. It should be remembered that control is important as a pre-requisite of a contract of service. It is *not* a factor which on its own establishes a contract of service and in this sense the law has certainly moved on. It is only one part of the irreducible minimum required. As MacKenna J said in the *Ready Mixed Concrete* case ([1968] 1 All ER 433 at 441A), 'An obligation to do work subject to the other party's control is a necessary . . . condition of a contract of service.'

6.112 Case law indicates that control can have relevance in respect of the what, how, where and when work is executed but for there to be sufficient control to indicate a master/servant relationship, there has to be a significant degree of interference in the manner in which the work is carried out. The *Narich* case (see Appendix 6) in 1984 found the worker to be an employee because, in fact, she was 'tied hand and foot' in the way she did her work. It would be unwise to turn this round and say that control only exists where a worker is tied hand and foot, but use of this kind of language implies that control is not satisfied in the context of master/servant relationships at a superficial or low level.

6.113 This latter point should be clearly understood. Control is not synonymous with mere supervision or direction. These latter two are weakened, less intrusive versions of control. The ability of a client to require a worker to report to him or sign in and out of a building may amount to nothing more than a proper regard for health and safety considerations, which is not the same thing as true control.

6.114 Perhaps in recognition of the changing realities of the modern working arena, or for other reasons not fully understood, the courts moved away from the strict control test. It was seen as unworkable and unreliable as a simple fool proof test.

6.115 As an alternative to the discredited control test, the so called 'part and parcel' or 'integration' test was popularised in the 1950s and 1960s. This concentrated on establishing whether the worker had become part and parcel of the putative employer's business. This test, to some extent developed by the maverick judge Lord Denning, itself became discredited when it was realised that many genuinely self-employed workers were part and parcel of the 'employer's' business, while workers who were clearly direct employees were not part and parcel of the 'employer's' business. MacKenna J in *Ready Mixed Concrete (South East) Ltd v Minister of Pensions and National Insurance* ([1968] 1 All ER 433 at 445F) commented that the test raised more questions than he knew how to answer.

6.116 Hence, two single and fairly strict tests (control and integration) were discredited and subsequently the courts tended to take a more holistic approach by looking at the whole balance of factors, with a view to seeing whether the worker was in 'business on his own account'. This also became known as the 'economic reality' test. This approach was popular throughout the 1970s, 1980s and early 1990s, and moved away from the more fundamental approach to status developed by McKenna J in *Ready Mixed Concrete*. Subsequently, the 'in business on own account' test has been downgraded to 'useful' rather than 'fundamental', and more recent case law has reverted to the stricter *Ready Mixed Concrete* approach.

6.117 At the present time it is suggested that the correct approach to status is as laid down in the *Express and Echo* (see Appendix 6) case heard in the Court of Appeal 1999 and is to ask whether there any terms of the contract which are inherently inconsistent with direct employment. This builds precisely upon McKenna J's 'trinity' in *Ready Mixed Concrete*. If there are, the status debate is concluded and the worker will not be an employee of the client. If there are no such inherently inconsistent terms, then all other factors have to be put in the melting pot and a balanced picture painted from the accumulation of detail available. When considering the whole melting pot of factors control will always be a consideration and, following *Montgomery*, a very important one.

6.118 To show just how far the control test per se was played down in the 1980s one need only consider the judgment of Mr Justice McCullogh in the *Swan Hellenic* case (see Appendix 6) in 1983. He said (at page 34H of the judgment):

> 'it is now also well recognised that men who are subject to a very considerable degree of control may nevertheless be independent contractors'.

He went on to say that the best example of this would be a labour only subcontractor in the building industry—a comment to be remembered when dealing with construction industry status challenges.

6.119 It is submitted that, although the issue of control is a wide topic, the most important aspect of control is the 'how'. Often the Revenue will say that having to perform the task at a particular place or at a particular time are equally important aspects of control indicating a master/servant relationship. In the author's view this is faulty reasoning. If an IT contractor is engaged to attend a bank's premises to service computers in the

Directors' Suite on the 10th floor it is quite clear that he will have to carry out the work on the 10th floor where the computers are situated, and may have to carry out the work outside of normal office hours when the computers can be more readily accessed. The reason he works within these 'constraints' is because of the practical realities and requirements of the job specification, not because he is an 'employee'.

6.120 This point was taken in the House of Lords when the Welfare Reform and Pensions Act 1999 was debated at length. One of their Lordships suggested that if a householder instructs a plumber where to fit a new radiator and the plumber complies with this he is doing so not because he is the employee of the householder but because the radiator needs putting in a particular place. It is essential not to allow the Revenue to confuse a job specification with actual detailed control as to how the job is completed. The Revenue's ESM at para 1019 acknowledges that where the nature of the work dictates where the services are to be provided this is not a determining factor. As such, the argument that a contractor is controlled because he has to work at a client's premises can be readily refuted where he has to work there because, for example, that is where the main frame computer is located.

6.121 Again, the important 'how' aspect of control can be seen in the unreported *Staples* case of 1983 (see Appendix 6) when the Department of Health and Social Security challenged the status of a relief chef who worked via an agency in a restaurant. It was accepted as a fact that the chef was controlled, in as much as the hotel dictated particular menus for which the chef had to cook the appropriate food. However, the control the hotel had over the chef went one stage further: not only could they tell him the broad theme of the food but it could dictate the precise dishes the chef had to cook. In these circumstances the DHSS argued that the chef was 'controlled'. The High Court rejected this argument on the basis that the chef could not be told 'how' to cook the food. The importance of the 'how' aspect of control was also highlighted in the *Market Investigations* case and *MacManus v Griffiths* (see Appendix 6), and indeed goes all the way back to *Yewens v Noakes* in the nineteenth century.

6.122 An earlier case, the *Morren* decision (see Appendix 6) from 1965, however, acknowledged that, where a person of some specific professional or technical skill is involved, in that case an engineer, then the possibility of control would be restricted, as by definition there would be little scope for it. In such circumstances the court said that other factors beyond control would have to be taken into account. A consideration of both of these cases suggests a very attractive anti-IR35 argument. The *Staples* case says unless a worker can be told 'how' to do his work he is not controlled, and *Morren* tells us that there is no scope to control an expert. This raises the interesting possibility that an expert is much less likely to be an employee because there is no scope for the prerequisite of control. Interestingly, the Revenue accepts the full force of this logic and is happy to relegate control to a very insignificant factor in respect of specialists (see ESM 1024, 1025). This might sound like 'heads I win, tails you lose'. The Revenue emphasises the importance and impact of the control test when it suits it, yet dismisses the concept when it can be shown the worker is very much left to his own devices, but *Ready Mixed Concrete* should not be ignored so readily.

6.123 If the two cases of *Staples* and *Morren* are considered together it can be seen that a specialist cannot be controlled and is, therefore, less likely to be an employee. It is then tempting to move on from control and consider other factors—an approach advocated by the Revenue. But they are forgetting that control sufficient to render a worker the servant of his master is a *prerequisite* in establishing a contract of service according not only to the *Ready Mixed Concrete* case (see Appendix 6) in 1968 but the more recent and authoritative decision in *Montgomery v Johnson Underwood Ltd* (see Appendix 6), decided by the Court of Appeal 2001. That case underlined the 'irreducible minimum' for direct employment, part of which is control. This really should cause the Revenue major difficulties in the context of highly skilled workers and needs to be explored. *Morren* is not bad law but it has been superceded by *Ready Mixed Concrete* and *Montgomery*.

6.124 To this day many tax officers at district level maintain that if a worker can be told what to do then he will be a servant of his master and an employee for tax purposes. The importance of the 'how' is overlooked as is the requirement that the control must be so strict that it must amount to a significant interference with the worker. A job spec should not be confused with true 'control', whereby a master/servant relationship is created.

6.125 Control was stated to be a prerequisite of direct employment in the *Ready Mixed Concrete* case of 1968. What the High Court did *not* say was that a person who is controlled is necessarily an employee. To suggest otherwise is to twist the words of McKenna J into something quite different. This tactic is sometimes used by the Revenue and should be resisted.

6.126 Practitioners should remember that, before a worker can be an employee, the trinity of a high degree of control, the requirement to give personal service and the other terms not being inconsistent with a direct employment relationship (such as the lack of mutuality of obligations), must *all* be present.

6.127 Despite a general fall from grace, the control factor has remained a factor to consider, but one which carries less influence than it did 30 years ago. However, in the *North West Ceilings* case (see Appendix 6 and 6.132 below) discussed below, a different emphasis was placed on the relevance of control; control was to some extent seen as an indicator of employment, rather than a lack of it as a contra-indicator of employment. This approach seems to be more common in employment law cases where the tribunals tend to lean in favour of the worker.

6.128 The *Montgomery* case (see Appendix 6) was not concerned with substitution and personal service; these were simply not issues on the facts. Instead the court referred in detail to the 'irreducible minimum' required to establish a contract of employment as being mutuality of obligations and sufficient control to render the worker a servant of the master. Despite the worker (an agency supplied receptionist) being under the supervision of an end-user for a period of well over two years the court found that there was no mutuality, actual or implied, nor was there sufficient control over the worker to make her an employee of either the end-user or the agency.

6.129 A lack of mutuality or lack of control are fundamental factors either of which preclude direct employment status on the clear legal precedents laid down by the courts.

6.130 In the past the Revenue has argued that, even if there is no actual control, there may well be a right of control, but it seems that the tribunals and courts are increasingly concerned with actual interference and an actual exercising of control rather than the remote theoretical possibility of it. Practitioners should never lose sight of the fact that in the context of status there must be, in the author's opinion, a significant degree of control, whereby one person is subjugated to the position of being a servant of his master, and without this there can be no contract of service.

6.131 The Court of Appeal was influenced by the control factor in March 2001 in the *Interlink Express v Night Trunkers Ltd* case [2001] EWCA Civ 360, although in the context of IR35 and status generally the case carries little weight. This is because that case was peculiar to the provisions of the road haulage industry (in particular the operation of the Goods Vehicles (Operators Licences) Act 1995), and was concerned with whether a contract can be declared void on the grounds of illegality.

6.132 The latest case on control is *North West Ceilings Ltd v Reid* (see Appendix 6) where in April 2001 the Court of Appeal found the worker to be an employee, despite the fact that previously he had been content to be treated as a self-employed subcontractor. The Revenue had issued a 714 Certificate and he had also had income subjected to SC60 deductions. Mr Reid had been on a self-employed basis for around four years before he went on the payroll in March 1998.

This was an unfair dismissal case where the worker himself wanted to establish direct employee status (for his own financial gain), and it does not sit well with Lord Denning's comment in *Massey v Crown Life Assurance* [1978] 2 All ER 576 at 581d that a person who makes his self-employed bed should have to 'lie in it'. It is further evidence that tribunals often lean in favour of the claimant worker.

6.133 The Court of Appeal in the *North West Ceilings* case felt that Mr Reid was an employee throughout his entire period with North West

Ceilings, and it had no hesitation in reaching such a conclusion. The court was influenced by the control that was exercised over Mr Reid and the fact that he was a 'supervisor'. The evidence also showed that there were other employees doing the same kind of work as Mr Reid and they had always been treated as PAYE employees.

Arguably this case shows that control is an influential factor and not just a contraindicator of self-employment, but the tax treatment of similar workers and Mr Reid's own stance in this case were also very strong factors and even the Revenue tends not to cite this case as a mainstream authority.

Can control be implied?

6.134 In *Addison's* case (see Appendix 6), it was argued that as the musicians had to follow the directions and co-ordination of the conductor this implied control. This was rejected by the court and it was noted that the deceased composer himself could be said to have control over the performance as he had written the music in the first place! This equally was not considered sufficient to create control in the sense of a master and servant relationship.

6.135 Sometimes the courts arrive at surprising conclusions. In the 1988 case of *Bhadra v Ellam* (see Appendix 6), concerning an agency-supplied doctor, the question arose as to whether the doctor was controlled within the terms of the agency legislation. It was common ground that the doctor was professionally qualified and it was argued by him that he was not controlled. It should be noted that in the High Court the doctor represented himself and was up against experienced Revenue counsel.

The court decided as a fact that the doctor was 'accountable' up the chain of hospital command and as such there must have been a right of 'control' coming down the chain and, therefore, the control factor was satisfied. If the control factor is present it is almost impossible to escape the agency regulations on any other arguments.

6.136 Although *Bhadra v Ellam* is not a case that is often relied upon, it illustrates that the courts may be willing to imply a right of control. It should be specifically noted that the Revenue's own counsel accepted that merely telling a worker what task to do next would *not* amount to control.

Summary

6.137 The control test used to be considered fool-proof as a determinant of employee status, but its significance was played down in the 1980s and its whole historical background has been misunderstood. However, the 2001 *Montgomery* case puts it back in vogue and reaffirms the *Ready Mixed Concrete* approach that control is a pre-requisite of employee status but not proof of employee status. It now rejoins personal service and mutuality of obligations in the trinity of essential prerequisites to create a direct contract of employment. And even where it does exist this does not prove of itself that the worker is an employee.

6.138 A significant degree of control is required before a worker can be an employee yet many personal service business workers are beyond control, particularly in respect of how they do their work, as evidenced by their often unique and specialist skills. As such the re-emergence of the control test pre-requisite can only be a fillip to IR35 defence strategies and arguments. No doubt the Revenue will try to dismiss control in the context of highly skilled workers, but such an approach should be resisted. The *Morren* case has been superceded.

Other factors case law recognises as important

6.139 The essential trinity of personal service (no rights of substitution), control and mutuality of obligations have now been considered in depth and according to the case law if there is a not unreasonably fettered and genuine right to send a substitute; *or* insufficient control to make the worker a servant of his master; *or* a lack of mutuality of obligations, then there cannot be a contract of service, or direct employment.

6.140 This is not to say that the worker will be necessarily self-employed. Often the case law, especially employment law decisions, merely say the worker is not an employee or he falls into the category of having a contract *sui generis*. But this is good enough to defeat IR35, which merely requires the worker to demonstrate that he is not a disguised employee.

6.141 Of course the best way to show that the worker is not a disguised employee of the client is to demonstrate that the personal service business is operating independently in a business to business relationship. The trinity of substitution, control and mutuality are without doubt the most essential points to consider but there are others. These other points fall into what can be described as important factors and minor factors.

Important factors

In business on own account

6.142 This is not so much a single factor as a general test. It was first alluded to in the *Market Investigations* case (see Appendix 6) of 1969 and came from earlier US precedents. It was put forward as a fundamental test and asked whether the worker could be regarded as being in business on his own account? This has become known as the 'economic reality' test.

6.143 Mr Justice Cooke said ([1968] 3 All ER 732 at 737I):

> 'Is the person who has engaged himself to perform these services performing them as a person in business on his own account? If the answer to that question is "yes" then the contract is a contract for services. If the answer is "no" then the contract is a contract of service'.

This 'in business on own account' test or approach has been revisited and alluded to many times in the last 30 years but it has been recognised that it has its limitations, as the Revenue itself seems to accept in its internal manuals.

Indeed, the test is a little curious in that in one sense it simply says that if a person is 'in business' that is, self-employed, then he is self-employed!

6.144 As explained in the *Market Investigations* case, the test asked questions relating to the supply of equipment, the method of pay and the level of financial risk. It was also acknowledged that where work was undertaken as part of an existing business then that would help to establish self-employment. Mr Justice Cooke said ([1968] 3 All ER 732 at 738B):

> 'The application of the general test may be easier in a case where the person who engages himself to perform the services does so in the course of an already established business of his own'.

This could be particularly useful for IR35 at-risk businesses which have traded for many years.

6.145 Cooke J added ([1968] 3 All ER 732 at 738C) that an existing business is not *necessary* to establish self-employment:

> '... and a person who engages himself to perform services for another may well be an independent contractor even though he has not entered into the contract in the course of an existing business carried on by him'.

This latter extract should give some comfort to personal service businesses entering into their first contract.

6.146 However, as soon as an approach to status is developed its weaknesses are exposed. What if a person does not have the traditional trappings of being in business, ie he has no stock, premises, staff, etc. Can he still be self-employed? The answer is a resounding 'yes'. There are many examples of self-employed persons who show few if any of the traditional self-employment badges identified in the late 1960s and 1970s. An actor, management consultant, or swimming coach may well have no stock or staff and little apparent financial risk yet they can be self-employed.

6.147 The 'in business on own account test' has been played down in cases such as *O'Kelly v Trust House Forte* (see Appendix 6), heard by the Court of

Appeal in 1983. Here the court took the view that the supply of the 'commodity' of semi-skilled labour was a legitimate form of self-employment.

A similar approach was taken in the case of *Addison v London Philharmonic Ltd* (see Appendix 6). Mr Justice Waterhouse asked ([1981] ICR 261 at 273A):

> 'were the applicants performing their services at the relevant time as persons in business on their own account? We have no hesitation in answering "yes".'

This was despite the fact the workers concerned were part time orchestra musicians with *very little* to substantiate that they were running a 'business'. The court commented ([1981] ICR 261 at 273C) that the musicians: 'contributed their own skills and interpretative powers to the orchestra's performances as independent contractors', and the 'in business' approach was played down.

6.148 In the author's view, the business on own account test is, however, still important because it represents not so much a strict test as more of an attitude or mindset. It raises legitimate questions of whether the worker has a business organisation which could include in the early twenty-first century having an office at home, a website presence or a marketing strategy and business plan. These 'personal factors' which may demonstrate a commercial modus operandi were accepted as being important in the 1993 Court of Appeal decision in *Hall v Lorimer* (see Appendix 6). The Revenue have also accepted in the 'Charlotte' example that personal and business factors might take the taxpayer out of IR35 (see Tax Bulletin 45 at Appendix 7). Personal business factors helped the taxpayer in the IR35 case of *Lime-IT Ltd v Justin* (see Chapter 12 and Appendix 6).

6.149 It is not unreasonable that a person who claims to be running an independent business can demonstrate that he is doing so, by providing examples of his actions which are consistent with his claims, such as being VAT-registered, raising invoices on business stationery, holding insurances and appointing an accountant to draw up accounts in relation to that business. These actions may not, in themselves, prove that he is not a disguised employee of the client, but they do show an approach wholly inconsistent with one who is a regular employee. These differences are important when an appeal is being presented, or arguments are being put to the inspector.

6.150 It will be appreciated that the relevant considerations often start to overlap. Being an independent businessman might equate to a lack of control; having assumed financial risk might be said to be akin with independence and a general 'in business' attitude.

6.151 The 'in business' approach remains an important consideration but it is not to be too slavishly followed. It is more of an indicator of attitude rather than a strict test.

An alternative approach: are engagements an incident of a continuing 'profession'?

6.152 The general approach to beating IR35 is one of understanding the law, agreeing terms and conditions which are outside IR35 and demonstrating a general commercial business approach. Some lobby groups and commentators have, however, suggested that there might be a case law short cut based on an old decision.

The 1931 case of *Davies v Braithwaite* [1931] KB 628 heard in the High Court by Rowlatt J (see Appendix 6) concerned the correct schedule of charge for an actress. She had enjoyed at least ten different contracts for the three-year period in question, including theatre work, making films and radio appearances.

Some of her earnings were fromAmerica. The taxpayer argued that she should be taxed as an *employee* as this would mean her American income escaped UK tax under the then present rules. On the other hand the Revenue argued that she should be taxed as a *self-employed* person under Schedule D and that her American income should be taxed in the UK.

The Revenue's justification was that she was not controlled sufficiently to be in a master/servant relationship and hence was self-employed. This is another case where principles were sacrificed for expediency.

Rowlatt J held all her income was proper to Schedule D, overturning the Commissioners' decision on the basis that

> 'where one finds a method of earning a livelihood which does not consist of the obtaining of a post and staying in it but consists of a series of engagements and moving from one to the other . . . then each of those engagements cannot be considered an employment, but is a mere engagement in the course of exercising a profession . . .' (p 635).

6.153 The parallels with the IT contractor, a professional person moving from one engagement to another seem invitingly easy to make. The author's view is, however, much less optimistic. First, this case was heard when there was a general re-classification of what was to be included in Employment Income, with the historical emphasis being on 'offices' and 'posts' which had a degree of permanency about them. Secondly, the decision is now over 70 years old and its relevance to the modern world can be questioned. Thirdly, and perhaps most importantly, the case has been distinguished, ie not applied in subsequent case law decisions. There is also perhaps a question mark over whether IT contractors really do move from 'engagement to engagement' with the frequency envisaged in *Davies v Braithwaite.*

In the *Davies v Braithwaite* case itself Rowlatt J said: 'It seems to me quite clear that a man can have both an employment and a profession at the same time, in different categories' (page 635). This then was picked up in a much more recent High Court case, *Fall v Hitchen* [1973] 1 All ER

368 which concerned a professional dancer/actor who argued, on the authority of *Davies v Braithwaite* that he was self-employed. He lost. The *Fall v Hitchen* case approached the status test more from a 'business on own account approach (this new 'test' had been recently developed in the *Market Investigations* case of a few years earlier) instead of the 'in a profession on own account' approach. The court said, quite simply and logically, that if a professional person undertakes a contract that is in fact a contract of employment, it will remain a contract of employment 'notwithstanding that he is at the same time carrying on his profession' (p 376e).

The judge in *Fall v Hitchen*, Pennycuick V-C, quotes extensively from *Davies v Braithwaite*. It seems he was concerned that people were getting the wrong end of the stick with *Davies v Braithwaite*. He said:

> 'I have read those passages partly because they contain an accurate exposition of what Rowlatt J really did decide . . . and partly because they show that a person carrying on a profession may perfectly well hold an office and also, plainly, an employment in the same sphere as that in which he carries on his profession' (p 378d).

Other cases have confirmed this approach, including the Court of Appeal in *Hall v Lorimer* (1993). It seems that having a professional existence proves nothing per se. The terms of the actual contracts entered into need analysing before a status decision can be reached. Those who rely on a pure *Davies v Braithwaite* 'in a profession on own account' approach are skating on very thin ice.

6.154 More recent unpublished Special Commissioners' decisions concerning actors in the early 1990s have shown that standard Equity contracts are not caught under Employment Income. It has been rightly suggested that if the word 'actor' in the standard Equity contract was replaced with 'contractor' and the contract then submitted to the Revenue for an IR35 review the Revenue would almost certainly fail it. This anomaly has been pointed out by Anne Redston (to whom thanks), but in the author's view this is nothing more than an anomaly. Only the Revenue knows why they did not appeal to the High Court—and they are not telling. As the Special Commissioners' judgment is unreported and unpublished it will not significantly influence the Revenue or Commissioners in an IR35 dispute. In the ESM the Revenue mentions these cases but plays up the factor that the actors engaged in many different professional activities (unlike the dancer in *Fall v Hitchen*). The Revenue says all cases have to be dealt with on their own facts. Although there is nothing to be lost in arguing for the 'in a profession on own account' approach à la *Braithwaite*, it would seem far more likely that an argument based on substitution, lack of control and lack of mutuality of obligations, backed by modern case law, will succeed. Accountax has seen the *McGowan and West* judgment and on the facts it was reasonable that the taxpayers won. It is submitted there is nothing ground breaking in the decision.

Intention of the parties

6.155 In relation to IR35, this factor refers to whether or not the parties to the contract (ie the client and the personal service business) intend that the worker is to be a direct employee of the client. Identifying what the parties' wished to create is sometimes called their 'mutual intention'.

It is worth noting that the established case law concerns whether the parties intended that the worker is employed or self-employed. Clearly, the most common situation in an IR35 context is where the worker is an employee of his own company, so the distinction here is not strictly between employment and self-employment. However, the case law remains relevant because, as with case law concerning other factors, it goes towards determining whether the worker is a disguised employee of the client (and therefore potentially within IR35 in accordance with ITEPA 2003 s 49(1)(*c*)) or whether he is running a genuine independent business.

6.156 The intention of the parties is often underplayed by the Revenue, but the correct legal position is that it must always be taken into account. That is not to say the parties' intention is always a highly influential factor, but it does have to be taken into account from the outset in all cases.

6.157 The Revenue now seems to accept this view. In its internal guidance on intention, it starts off by saying that (at ESM 1101):

> 'What the parties call their relationship, or what they consider it to be, is not conclusive. It is the reality of the relationship that matters. *Nevertheless the intention of the parties has to be taken into account.* The intention can be decisive where the relationship is ambiguous and where the other factors are neutral.' (Author's emphasis.)

However, it goes on to state that (ESM 1101):

> 'When you have gathered all the facts, you should stand back and look at the bigger picture. *If you consider that the case is borderline, you should then, and only then, look at the intention of the parties.* Where there is mutual intention for a contract of employment or for a contract for services, that will determine the status of the worker.' (Author's emphasis.)

This would seem to be somewhat contradictory. If the intention of the parties has to be taken into account, surely it should be considered in all cases, not merely borderline ones. In the author's experience, the Revenue's approach in practice is to try to play down or even ignore completely the parties' intention. This approach should be resisted.

The ESM has recently been revised (ESM 3286) and now gives a clearer Revenue interpretation. It says that where a case is borderline the intention of the parties 'will remove any ambiguity'. It goes on to say 'you should assume that there was a mutual intention for a contract for services. Therefore, in borderline cases the opinion should be that IR35 does not apply'.

6.158 The relevance of intention is demonstrated by two different approaches. Firstly, and this is an area often not considered by the Revenue when disputing status issues, in order for there to be a valid contract there must be an offer and acceptance, consideration and an intention to enter into a legally binding relationship.

Clearly if one party offers work on a self-employed basis and the work is accepted on that basis, and this is coupled with the fact that the intention of the parties was to enter into a legal relationship based on this, then it can be appreciated just how fundamental the whole issue of intention is. This is not just in the context of tax status but in the whole area of contract law generally. This was noted by Webster J in the 1981 case of *WHPT Housing Association Ltd v Secretary of State* (see Appendix 6). He said:

> 'There also seems to me to be considerable force in [the] argument that the original offer and acceptance was to provide services, not service, and that there is no evidence that the nature of the contract changed after its inception.'

The only way the Revenue can play down intention is effectively to say the parties' desires to offer and accept work on a business to business basis and enter into a legally binding agreement on that basis can be completely ignored. This is not only absurd but no panel of Commissioners would want to ride rough shod over the parties' intentions. This was underlined very recently by Lord Johnston in the case of *Stoddart v Cawder Golf Club* (EAT 873/00, 19 February 2001), heard in the EAT. Although the Tribunal found many factors pointing to employment and the workers had been engaged by the golf club for almost 20 years, this did not allow them to override the stated intention of the parties, which was to have a self-employment relationship. Lord Johnston said (at para 8):

> 'Where persons intend to create a self-employed situation and the ingredients of such can be found, such as method of payment, potential exposure to VAT and a lack of consent to be an employee, it is very difficult for any Tribunal to conclude that the contrary to what the parties intended to achieve had resulted.'

The concept of freedom of contract cannot be ignored so easily.

6.159 Secondly, the established case law recognises that the intention of the parties has to be taken into account in all status disputes, not merely in finely balanced cases as the Revenue often claims. Most commentators would perhaps say that it is another relevant and important factor but no more than that. It is less important than, say, substitution or mutuality of obligations but more important than, say, sick pay and holiday pay. Until the *Express and Echo* case (see Appendix 6) of 1999 this would probably be a reasonable approach, but since that decision it is suggested that the intention of the parties must now be given more weight. Indeed, in that case Lord Justice Gibson said ([1999] IRLR 367 at 370) that in a status dispute 'one starts with the common intention of the parties'.

In ambiguous cases the intention will be the deciding factor. An important case on this point is *Massey v Crown Life Assurance* (see Appendix 6), decided by the Court of Appeal in 1977. Lord Denning said ([1978] 2 All ER 576 at 580a):

> 'It seems to me on the authorities, that, when it is a situation which is in doubt, it is open to the parties by agreement to stipulate what the legal situation between them shall be.'

He also said ([1978] 2 All ER 576 at 580a):

> '. . . if their relationship is ambiguous and is capable of being one or the other, then the parties can remove that ambiguity, by the very agreement itself which they make with one another'.

He went on to say ([1978] 2 All ER 576 at 581c) that if the parties deliberately arrange to be self-employed even to obtain tax benefits, that is strong evidence that that is the real relationship. This was also approved in the High Court *Swan Hellenic* case of 1983 (see Appendix 6). At page 40 Mr Justice McCullough described the intention of the parties in what was a borderline case, as a 'factor of major significance'.

This is why it is important to have a clear intention clause in any contract that is used to demonstrate that IR35 does not apply (as discussed in Chapter 8).

6.160 An example of another case in which the parties' intention was a key factor in determining status is *Calder v Kitson Vickers and Sons Ltd* (see Appendix 6). In that case it was held that when parties deliberately agree for the worker to be self-employed, it might afford strong evidence that that was their real relationship. Furthermore, Lord Justice Gibson stated that ([1988] ICR 232 at 250E):

> 'A man is without question free under the law to contract to carry out certain work for another without entering into a contract of service'.

6.161 There are limitations to the relevance of the intention of the parties. Status cannot be determined merely by applying an artificial label to a relationship. A person who on the terms of his relationship is clearly an employee cannot suddenly become self-employed merely because he is described as such. Nor can a sham relationship of self-employment be legitimised by the use of a label.

Again the *Massey* case illustrates this where Lord Denning said ([1978] 2 All ER 576 at 579i):

> 'The law, as I see it is this: if the true relationship of the parties is master and servant under a contract of service, the parties cannot alter the truth of that relationship by putting a different label on it'.

6.162 The following year a High Court case (*BSM 1257 Ltd v Secretary of State For Social Services*, see Appendix 6) also clarified that the contract could be ignored if 'in practice the relationship is other than that stated in the contract'.

This was supported in a Court of Appeal case (*Young and Woods Ltd v West*, see Appendix 6) in 1980.

6.163 It is therefore clear that false labels and sham contracts do not work and must be avoided. But perhaps the Revenue should be more concerned with bogus contracts and labels of self-employment which have been 'forced' onto the worker rather than trying to undermine the *genuine* intentions of parties who are very clear as to what kind of relationship they wish to enter into.

6.164 Bogus labelling of a relationship does not change it, nor should it. However, it is suggested that the intention of the parties is considerably more important than the Revenue likes to acknowledge, and in finely balanced cases it will become the determining factor. In the context of the IR35 notional or hypothetical contract it is no silver bullet defence to say that just because there was no intention to have a contract of service then by definition there cannot be one. However, when inferring the terms and conditions of the hypothetical contract the original intentions of the parties must be a factor to be taken into account.

Financial risk and chance of profit

6.165 This is not an easy area to pin down because financial risk can incorporate so many different factors.

6.166 From the author's experience, the Revenue's view seems to be that financial risk is nothing beyond giving a fixed price for a job. Clearly if an IT contractor gives a fixed price for writing some software the job might take much longer than anticipated thus resulting in a poorer overall financial return even though an actual 'loss' would still not have been made. It is very difficult for a person supplying his skill to make a 'loss' as such.

But risk comes in many different guises, including the obligation to correct defective work, no guarantee of work or no compensation for work cancelled at short notice, a limited or non-existent period of notice etc.

6.167 Lord Justice Nolan in the 1993 Court of Appeal case of *Hall v Lorimer* (see Appendix 6) specifically noted ([1994] IRLR 171 at 174) that self-employment is characterised by running the risk of bad debts and a lack of work. Dr Avery Jones said in the *Lime-IT* case that the mere fact of invoicing indicates self-employment. This seems to have been overlooked by the Revenue.

6.168 In the earlier *Midland Sinfonia* case (see Appendix 6), the court stated that the question of risk of profit or loss had to be seen in the context of the nature of the work being undertaken. Here the court held that in the context of musicians who merely turned up and performed (like so many IR35 at-risk personal service businesses) the question of profit and loss was 'not particularly appropriate'.

6.169 In the *O'Kelly* case (see Appendix 6), the court accepted that ([1983] 3 All ER 456 at 465b) in the context of the provision of semi-skilled labour: 'it is not to be expected that there would be a financial investment or participation in the profits or losses of the business'.

So far as provision of equipment is relevant to 'financial risk' see 6.180 below.

Freedom to offer services

6.170 A person running a business should have the freedom to undertake work and exploit his available skills in the market place as he sees fit. He should be able to make business decisions and benefit from the sound management of his business.

6.171 One aspect of this is the freedom to contract elsewhere or undertake other work, perhaps in the evenings and the weekends. Mr Justice Burton went so far as to suggest, in the PCG judicial review case (*R (on the application of the Professional Contractors Group and others) v IRC* (see Appendix 6), that where this happens the contractor would be 'home and dry'. This seems a little optimistic but the point is still made. Having a number of different income streams, particularly where they are running coterminously can clearly help the general 'business on own account' approach to be demonstrated.

6.172 In the *Global Plant* case (see Appendix 6) one of the reasons the worker was found to be an employee was that there was a contractual condition which specifically *prohibited* the worker from carrying out work for other parties without the consent of Global Plant.

6.173 In *Hall v Lorimer* (see Appendix 6) the Court of Appeal determined that ([1994] IRLR 171 at 174) the taxpayer was self-employed because he exploited 'his abilities in the market place . . . [and] the more efficient he is at running the business of providing his services, the greater is his prospect of profit'.

6.174 However, if a worker is at the beck and call of a client and has to work for that client when work is available then such a restriction of freedom will be a strong pointer towards a relationship of direct employment.

It will also demonstrate at least one half of the ingredients of mutuality of obligations, that is the worker's obligation to accept offered work. It will also indicate an aspect of control.

This was demonstrated in the Hong Kong case of *Lee Ting Sang v Chung Chi-Keung* (see Appendix 6) where the client (employer) had 'first call' on the worker's time. This case came to the UK Privy Council as the ultimate court of appeal for Hong Kong cases. Both the *Lee Ting Sang* decision and the 1995 Court of Appeal decision in *Lane v Shire Roofing* (see Appendix 6) were concerned with compensation claims for personal injuries which could only be awarded to employees, not the self-employed. It seems clear from the judgments and the comments subsequently made by legal academics that an element of 'public policy' was very much to the fore when the decisions were handed down and the workers were found to be employees. The facts of the *Lane* decision certainly suggest the worker was a genuine self-employed sub-contractor.

It should be noted that in both cases the workers *wanted* to be treated as employees so they could obtain financial compensation for personal injuries. It is assumed that in IR35 cases the worker will be denying he is an employee.

Previous Revenue determinations

6.175 In the 1996 case of *Barnett v Brabyn* (see Appendix 6), the Revenue argued the worker was *self-employed* when he worked for his father's partnership. The worker disagreed and claimed he was an employee. The case ended in the High Court and the Revenue advanced three main reasons why the worker was self-employed. These were that he had input as to the hours he worked, he had expressed an intention to be self-employed and that the Revenue had determined his previous years' tax liabilities on the basis that he was self-employed. This was despite the fact that there was a whole raft of direct employment indicators. These are powerful arguments to put to the Revenue in any status dispute, including IR35.

The court accepted the worker was self-employed despite him having many hallmarks of direct employment. The court accepted as 'cogent evidence' the previous determinations on a self-employed basis.

6.176 For over four years this case was not included in the Revenue's Schedule E manual. To this day many tax officers are unaware of it. The Revenue has tried to play this case down on the basis that it had 'special facts' and that there was an unusual family relationship between the worker and the putative employer (father/son). This may have been the case, but it cannot take away the very forceful arguments in favour of self-employment that the Revenue persuaded the court to accept. Such arguments can be used in an IR35 context to help demonstrate that the worker is not a disguised employee of the client. The law report ([1996] STC 716 at page 139) confirms that the *Revenue* argued:

'It is quite possible for a person to be in business on his own account when all he supplied was his own services without providing any equipment or having any risk of loss of prospective profit'.

This is a devastating passage to quote back to the Revenue or the Commissioners. It rather seems that the Revenue can be very keen to embrace many of the themes of case law, but only when it suits it.

Of course, *Barnett v Brabyn* came before IR35 legislation. Just because the Revenue has previously accepted the personal service business as an independent contractor does not mean that new legislation, ie IR35, will not move the goal posts, but this decision remains highly relevant in looking at how the Revenue tried to prove self-employment and it can certainly be used to good effect in argument.

Minor factors

Provision of equipment

6.177 Practitioners may be surprised to see this listed as only a minor factor but in the context of labour only specialists the 'equipment' criterion is something of a red herring. An IT contractor who writes software is not engaged to provide materials. That is simply not the nature of his work. Just as a bricklayer lays bricks and does not necessarily supply them. A window cleaner cleans windows, he does not supply the windows.

6.178 For many years the Revenue has insisted in placing the provision of equipment at or near the top of the list of status determinants. It is suggested that the correct question to be asked is 'what is the worker there to do?' If this is to supply his specialist skills, that is only his labour, then it is not an issue of fundamental importance to ask if he also happens to supply equipment. He is not there to do that.

6.179 This was amply illustrated in the 1993 Court of Appeal decision in *Hall v Lorimer* (see Appendix 6). Lord Justice Nolan ([1994] IRLR 171 at 174) noted that the taxpayer provided no premises, tools, equipment or workshop. He then went on to deliver a masterpiece of common sense. He said, 'No; he does not. But that is not his business'. The Revenue conveniently tend to quote only from the High Court in the *Lorimer* case as has been pointed out many times by Accountax and other commentators such as Anne Redston.

6.180 If expensive equipment *is* provided then that will show a greater financial risk because of the capital outlay, but this cannot be turned around by saying that where equipment is not provided the worker is automatically an employee.

The court will take into account the reasons why the client/employer provided the equipment. In the *BSM* case of 1978 (see Appendix 6) driving instructors who had been treated as employees but who converted to self-employed status still had the vehicle provided to them. Despite a High Court challenge by the DSS, the decision was that the drivers were self-employed and the court held the provision of the vehicles did not indicate employee status as they had been provided for 'good practical reasons'.

6.181 In the *Midland Sinfonia* case (see Appendix 6) the musicians were accepted as self-employed despite the fact that they were merely 'hiring out their skills as occasion arose'. In that case the musicians did provide their own instruments, but the point is they were not providing consumable materials or large pieces of equipment. One violin would last perhaps a lifetime. The parallel is that the IT contractors do not usually provide large computer systems, just their labour. As an attractive alternative it might be pointed out that the contractor provides his brain—perhaps the most crucial piece of 'equipment' a specialist can provide.

6.182 The provision of equipment is, therefore, something of a red herring where skills are being provided and it seems that there is a hint that the Revenue might be finally accepting the force of this argument—see ESM 511 and, more significantly, ESM 1061 and 1062.

6.183 In the later case of *McManus v Griffiths* (see Appendix 6) in 1997 the Revenue itself contended that the worker was self-employed. The worker argued that as she had not supplied the premises or equipment to do the job she was an employee. The Revenue refuted this and the court agreed that the worker was self-employed. Mr Justice Lightman ([1997] STC 1089 at 1099) said, 'This position is not affected by the fact that the club provided the premises, equipment and services.' See also 6.176.

Employee style benefits

6.184 Cause and effect should not be confused. An employee is entitled to certain benefits because he is an employee in law; a person does not become self-employed simply because he does not receive such benefits.

However, where the parties agree that benefits such as sick pay, holiday pay, partaking in a grievance procedure etc will not apply, such factors will be taken into account as status indicators, albeit minor ones.

This is apparent from the case of *Alpine (Double Glazing) Co Ltd v Secretary of State for Social Services* 1982 (unreported, see Appendix 6)—a case quoted at ESM 1046. More significantly, similar comments were made by Gibson LJ in *Express and Echo Publications Group v Tanton* (see Appendix 6) decided by the Court of Appeal in 1999 ([1999] IRLR 367 at 370).

Perhaps the very contracting away of such benefits also indicates that the parties do not want to have a relationship of direct employment.

Basis of payment

6.185 Traditionally, the Revenue has argued that an hourly or daily rate indicates a relationship of direct employment but this approach is not backed up by the case law or commercial reality.

Many self-employed persons charge by the hour. Why should a computer consultant not do the same? On the other hand, many workers get paid by the 'piece' but are regarded as employees.

6.186 In the ESM (at ESM 513 onwards) the Revenue does accept that the basis of payment may not be conclusive, but this is an approach not often taken by tax officers in the field.

6.187 In the 1983 Court of Appeal case of *O'Kelly v Trust House Forte* (see Appendix 6), it was clearly stated that the method by which remuneration is calculated is not one of the crucial indicators of status.

6.188 In the slightly earlier 1981 case of *WHPT Housing Association Ltd v Secretary of State for Social Services* (see Appendix 6) it was held that being paid by the hour indicated self-employed status as regular employees were paid a salary irrespective of the actual hours they worked. The taxpayer architect however was only paid for the actual hours he worked.

The *WHPT* case is not mentioned in the ESM.

Recognised custom and practice

6.189 In *O'Kelly v Trust House Forte* (see Appendix 6) one of the factors taken into account was that traditionally similar workers had been treated as self-employed. Indeed, the Court of Appeal ([1983] 3 All ER 456 at 465) acknowledged that disregarding the accepted custom and practice of the industry could have 'widespread damaging repercussions throughout the whole industry'.

This extract could be useful in the context of highly skilled consultants, many of whom have been regarded as self-employed for years (and of course in the context of the construction industry also).

Summary

6.190 The factors discussed above carry some weight but the thrust of any case law-based IR35 or general status argument has to be centred on the *Ready Mixed Concrete* and the trinity 'irreducible minimum' without which a contract of service cannot be established. These are personal service, control and mutuality of obligations.

6.191 The overwhelming majority of workers who wish to preserve self-employment have been successful in the courts. The Revenue has not won a traditional tax status case in the courts since 1987 (*Sidey v Phillips*, see Appendix 6) and the Contributions Agency since 1983 (*Warner Holidays Ltd v Secretary of State for Social Services*, see Appendix 6). The case law is on the side of those seeking to establish or preserve self-employment, and this should not be forgotten in an IR35 context, where the worker is hoping to demonstrate that he is not a disguised employee of the client.

CHAPTER 7

Crucial question 1: who is the client?

7.1 This may seem something of an odd question but it is one of the most important questions to ask. In a situation where the personal service business contracts direct with a typical end-user plc (for example, a bank or an oil company), the client of the personal service business will clearly be that plc.

In determining whether there is a disguised employment it is necessary to examine the terms and conditions of the contract signed between the personal service business and the end-user.

7.2 But what if there is an agency? In the author's experience most IT and engineering contractors provide their services to an agency rather than directly to an end-user. There are many sound commercial reasons for doing so.

7.3 Does the existence of an agency make any difference? In the view of the author, it is the agency itself which may be the client of the personal service business. This is for the following reasons.

Where does the contractual relationship lie?

7.4 Although it is possible to find tripartite contractual arrangements which are entered into by the personal service business, agency and end-user, these are very rare. The plain reality is that in 99% of cases involving an agency, the personal service business enters into only one written contract—and that is with the agency.

7.5 It is possible in law to have a situation where two third parties, A and B, can enter into an agreement whereby C benefits despite not being a party to the A/B agreement (for example, certain trusts), but such agreements are rare in normal commercial contracts. As such it is felt that the client of the personal service business is the party with whom it has entered into contractual arrangements, ie the agency.

7.6 Regrettably, this was not explored fully in the judicial review brought by the PCG (*R (on the application of the Professional Contractors Group) v IRC,* see Appendix 6).

Where is the financial relationship?

7.7 Where an agency is involved it is the agency which pays fees to the personal service business. The end-user does not pay fees to the personal service business. In normal commercial terms a business is paid by the customer or client to whom it has provided services. The personal service business provides services to the agency and in return receives consideration under its contract with the agency. Normal business and commercial practice would therefore regard the agency as the client of the personal service business.

The agency is not acting as a mere introducer

7.8 Some agencies exist only to make an initial introduction, as between the worker, or his business, and the end-user. In these circumstances it is possible, and indeed likely, for the agency to 'fall out' of the commercial chain, as following the initial introduction it has no ongoing role to play. An example of this argument (which failed on the facts) can be seen in the 1985 tax case of *Brady v Hart* (see Appendix 6).

7.9 However, in the typical IR35 at risk scenario, there is a personal service business, agency and end-user and once the initial introduction is made the agency does *not* disappear from the scene. It has an ongoing relationship. It continues to charge fees to the end-user for the provision of supplied workers/businesses, it takes its margin and then pays out a fee for services provided by the personal service business. In the 2001 EAT decision in *O'Murphy v Hewlett Packard,* the tribunal accepted the agency was acting as principal on its own behalf. The Revenue's FAQ also admits of the possibility of this, at Agency FAQ 5.

For these three reasons it is felt that commercial common sense and the plain reality of the situation is that, where the personal service business contracts with an agency, it is the agency which may be the client of the personal service business and the end-user, one removed up the 'chain' is not the client.

The end-user will be the client of the agency but that is another matter and not one relevant to the personal service business.

Commercial contracts with many parties

7.10 To suggest that the agency's client is in fact also the personal service business' client leads to potentially ridiculous situations. It is not unknown for a small agency to contract with a larger agency which in turn may contract with a company which contracts with a subsidiary of a plc group. Is the Revenue now suggesting that the personal service business' client is a remote party, five times removed up the commercial chain?

In the author's opinion the Commissioners would find such a proposition preposterous and far removed from the reality of the situation.

In the recent High Court case of *Synaptek Ltd v Young* (2003), Synaptek Ltd, Mr Stutchbury's personal service business contracted with an agency, the agency in turn contracted with EDS and EDS contracted to the Benefits Agency, the 'end-user'. Both before the Commissioners appeal and during it the Revenue asked whether Mr Stutchbury was a disguised employee of EDS, not the Benefits Agency. Why is not at all clear.

If the Revenue maintains the 'end-user' is the client why did the Revenue not treat the Benefits Agency as the client? There are two likely alternatives. The first is that the Revenue was concerned that if the Benefits Agency became the 'deemed' employer this might encourage contractors to take out employment law claims against it. Politically this could be damaging. Second, the Revenue has suggested that they will stop going up the chain of parties once it becomes clear that a person is no long being supplied but where anonymised services are being supplied. As the EDS/Benefits Agency did not mention Mr Stutchbury the Revenue 'stopped' at EDS as he had been named in the agency/EDS contract. A more worrying interpretation is that the Revenue picks the 'client' on the basis of no real logic at all.

In *Tilbury Consulting Ltd v Gittins (HMIT)*, an IR35 appeal heard at the Special Commissioners in 2003, the agency Compuware was deemed to be acting as principal, not agent. The Revenue had identified Ford, who appeared to be the end-user, as the deemed employer, but as Ford had outsourced much of its requirements to Compuware they could never have been the deemed employer. That the Revenue could make such a basic error after a two year enquiry is somewhat worrying. The taxpayer won the appeal. A detailed article, 'Tom, Dick or Roger', on this case appeared in Taxation (Vol 152, Issue 3935, 27 November 2003) by Theresa Naylor of Accountax.

Unfortunately, all IR35 cases to have been heard so far have assumed that the 'client' is the end-user. However, both *Synaptek* and *Tilbury* show that this is not always the case.

ITEPA 2003 Pt 2 Ch 8

7.11 ITEPA 2003 s 49(1)(*a*) (and SI 2000/727 reg 6(1)(*a*)) makes it clear that, for IR35 to apply, services have to be provided 'for the purposes of a business carried on by another person (the client)'. The business referred to can be *any* activity carried on by a body corporate, partnership or unincorporated body (by virtue of ITEPA 2003 s 49(2)). It seems quite clear that the agency is a business carrying out an activity.

7.12 Could it be argued, playing devil's advocate, that the personal service business could be supplying services to two clients, that is the agency *and* the end-user, at the same time? This is simply not possible. There is either a contract with the agency or there is a contract with the end-user.

There cannot be both at the same time in respect of the same work. In any event how can a worker have two so-called hypothetical contracts in respect of one piece of work?

7.13 The legislation requires the existing contractual terms to be recognised (ITEPA 2003 s 49(1)(*c*) and (4)) so the only hypothetical feature is that the worker is deemed to stand in the shoes of the personal service business.

Summary

7.14 Where the contractual and financial relationship is with an agency it is submitted that the agency may be the client of the personal service business. ITEPA 2003 allows this, and commercial and common sense require it. If the Revenue has any legislative, case law, commercial or logical authority to assert that the agency is not the client of the personal service business perhaps it should publish it.

Although the author acknowledges there are other opinions on this specific issue it would seem beneficial to have them argued comprehensively in court where the Revenue's somewhat assumptive view of the end-user (however far removed) as client can be challenged. The Revenue's lack of consistency on treating the non end-user as client in a four party chain should also be explored.

CHAPTER 8

Crucial question 2: what contractual arrangements are needed to defeat IR35?

8.1 Ensuring that IR35 does not apply is not a mere paper-signing exercise. It cannot be emphasised strongly enough that entering into a sham contract for services will never defeat IR35. It may lead to accusations of dishonesty and will be exposed in any robust cross-examination from a tax inspector should the case go to the tax Commissioners on appeal.

8.2 Once the law is properly understood it is then a matter of entering into a genuine commercial business to business arrangement, whereby the contractual terms and conditions take into account the case law precedents, with a view to ensuring one is not a disguised employee.

8.3 In some ways this might be considered by some to be a cynical exercise. But so might the IR35 legislation itself. Practitioners should be aware that in the judicial review brought by the Professional Contractors Group (*R (on the application of the Professional Contractors Group) v IRC*, see Appendix 6) in the High Court, Mr Justice Burton himself suggested ([2001] STC 629 at 651) that it would be wise for the parties to get together and agree terms and conditions which would take them outside IR35. However, any clauses drafted should be genuine, workable and reasonable. Extreme clauses may give the impression that the contract is an exercise in presentation rather than the true terms of the agreement.

8.4 Parties to a contract are free to enter into whatever terms and conditions they wish and it is not open to the Revenue or any other government department to dictate what these terms and conditions should be. If the contractual terms and conditions entered into represent the true agreement between the parties then the motivation behind the agreement is not relevant.

If, however, the agreement is a sham and nothing more than a paper-signing exercise then it will be exposed, and deserve to be exposed, and as such be rendered ineffective.

Mindsets and modus operandi

8.5 Many IR35 personal service businesses genuinely agreeing and entering into terms and conditions which help ensure that IR35 does not apply may require a significant change in both the mindset and modus operandi of the contractor. Despite the massive publicity surrounding IR35 and the disastrous fiscal consequences it brings to the contractor, some personal service businesses tend to operate not so much as disguised employees but actual out and out employees.

8.6 In simple terms, in order to ensure that IR35 does not apply, the personal service business and its directors have to stop acting and thinking and contracting as an IR35 caught business and start acting, thinking and contracting as an IR35 exempt business. If this requires a change of attitude and a change of contractual terms and conditions then so be it.

8.7 An example of contractor apathy is the personal service business director who cannot be bothered to raise an invoice on his business stationery because he has already completed a time sheet and believes a formal invoice is unnecessary. He may have a point, but so long as the tax tribunals and courts takc into account whether or not the worker has a proper business organisation he would be unwise to ignore such formalities. In brief, contractors must help themselves.

The bigger picture

8.8 Factors outside the signed contract can have a significant influence in determining whether a worker is caught under IR35. An individual contract may not be particularly well worded in respect of IR35 but it might be clear from the 'big picture' that the personal service business is indeed a genuine business and not subject to the intermediaries' legislation. Case law recognises that where there is an existing business it will usually be easier to establish on-going self-employment as part of that business (see 6.144). This was also recognised in the PCG judicial review case. In the example of 'Charlotte' the Revenue also recognises that other factors beyond the terms of the contract in isolation, can have a significant impact on an IR35 appraisal.

This might be demonstrated by the fact that the personal service business concerned might employ several fee earning individuals, operate from established business premises with a multitude of different clients, have made substantial investment in equipment and training and perhaps have a web site advertising its services. Few if any of these factors will be apparent from examining a contract is isolation.

It should be understood that an absence of these factors will not mean that the personal service business is caught by IR35 but their presence will undoubtedly help establish IR35 exempt status.

The way forward and looking beyond the contract

8.9 Ensuring that IR35 does not apply should, therefore, be seen as a combination strategy. The contractual terms of the genuine working relationship should wherever possible reflect criteria which the courts have accepted as giving rise to self-employment and the contractor should operate in a true business to business manner, with a demonstrable commercial approach. The Revenue has previously given the example of Charlotte whose overall circumstances take her outside of IR35 (see Appendix 7) and while this is only general guidance it helps establish the principle that the Revenue will consider outside factors beyond the strict terms of the contract. Arguably, this is all part of the 'business on own account' approach.

8.10 However, the Revenue may wish to satisfy itself that the written terms and conditions of the contract truly reflect the reality of the working relationship between the parties. The extent to which they are entitled to do this is somewhat limited.

8.11 In the *Narich* case (see Appendix 6) in 1984 the court made it quite clear ([1984] ICR 286 at 291A) that, with one exception (described below), it is not possible to look beyond the strict terms of the contract as to the manner in which the parties subsequently acted:

> 'The first principle, is that, subject to one exception, where there is a written contract between the parties whose relationship is in issue, a court is confined, in determining the nature of that relationship, to a consideration of the terms, express or implied, of that contract in the light of the circumstances surrounding the making of it; and it is not entitled to consider also the manner in which the parties subsequently acted in pursuance of such contract.
>
> The one exception to that rule is that, where the subsequent conduct of the parties can be shown to have amounted to an agreed addition to, or modification of the original written contract, such conduct may be considered and taken into account by the court'.

This begs a rather difficult question. How can the Revenue satisfy its curiosity as to whether the parties have subsequently varied the original contract if it is precluded from examining the reality beyond the strict contract terms? If the parties to the contract state categorically that the terms remain as per the written contract how can the Revenue force them to discuss the issue? This question is not easily answered but the courts have made their position quite clear and even the Revenue accepts that contract terms should be taken at face value, unless there are already good reasons to suggest that they do not represent the reality of the situation. See ESM 1056 on this in the context of substitution clauses. In practice the Revenue is increasingly treating the personal service business/agency contract merely as the starting point in an IR35 investigation. It will be happy to decide IR35 applies on the basis of the lower contract but if challenged will seek to interview the end-user.

Even if a contract term is not enforced this may be because the parties have agreed temporarily to waive that clause. This might seem thin but this is precisely what Peter Gibson LJ suggested in the *Express Echo* case (see Appendix 6). In the *Stevedoring and Haulage Services v Fuller* case (see Appendix 6) it was stated that a specific contractual clause cannot be negatived by what happens in practice. It seems that, in non-IR35 cases at least, the contract is king so long as it is genuine. More should be made of this when arguing IR35.

It has been noted by the author, when defending non-IR35 status, that the Revenue is keen to accept at face value, and quote back to the contractor, clauses in a contract which suggest the worker is caught. In these circumstances they tend not to look beyond the words.

In *Smith (IR) v Hewitson*, a national minimum wage case heard in the EAT in late 2001 it was held that the issue to focus on was the contractual obligations between the parties and not what actually occurred or how the company treated other workers. It is of course the Revenue that polices the national minimum wage laws.

The contracting market weakened noticeably in 2001/02 and as such the contractor held a poorer negotiating position. There are now a few signs of recovery and the stronger the market the more flexible clients will be when it comes to agreeing new terms. Agencies are becoming more flexible in what terms and conditions they will agree.

It should be noted that the courts are reluctant to imply further terms into a contract if such implied terms directly contradict express terms that already exist. This is discussed in *Cheshire, Fifoot and Furmston's Law of Contract* (14 edn, 2001) Butterworths at pages 154–155.

The Revenue may well try to imply terms that are contrary to the actual written agreement, but the courts may well reject this approach 'where the parties have entered into a carefully drafted written contract containing detailed terms agreed between them' (*Shell UK Ltd v Lostock Garages Ltd* [1976] 1 WLR 1187, 1200).

Also, in *Lynch v Thorne* [1956] 1 WLR 303 the Court of Appeal said it could not imply a term which would 'create an inconsistency with the express language of the bargain'. As such any Revenue attempt to ignore an express written term in favour of a Revenue instigated implied term should be resisted.

Important contract terms and conditions

8.12 Chapter 6 detailed the more important case law precedents. Bearing these in mind it then becomes necessary to incorporate as many business to business clauses into the contract as possible and to ensure that they are implemented in practice.

8.13 This section concentrates on the trinity of personal service, lack of mutuality of obligations and lack of control. Suggested clauses are given and it is a matter of negotiation between the parties as to whether they are agreed in practice. However, it must be emphasised that such clauses should reflect the reality of the relationship in order to be effective.

Personal service, mutuality and control

Services not personnel

8.14 As a fundamental strategy, to help ensure that IR35 does not apply, the following cannot be stressed enough. IR35 is aimed at personal service not the provision of services. Wherever possible the contract should be written in terms which show that a person is *not* being supplied (whether named or not) but that a service is being provided.

This should be clearly spelt out in the contract, any schedules and other correspondence relating to the contract. A genuine business to business relationship to supply services will also have the effect of defeating an 'agency' challenge by the Revenue (see Chapter 10).

Personal service and substitution

8.15 A recommended substitution clause would read as follows:

> 'The company may use a suitably qualified and experienced substitute or delegate to perform the contract works. The company will notify the client where it intends to substitute or delegate all or part of the contract works. Where a substitute or delegate is used by the company, the client shall have no contractual, financial or legal relationship with the substitute or delegate. The company is solely responsible for arranging payments to the substitute or delegate and the substitute or delegate is answerable only to the company.'

8.16 A generally acceptable but perhaps less robust substitution clause might read:

> 'The company may send a substitute but such substitute may be rejected by the client if the client is reasonably satisfied that the substitute does not possess the necessary skills and experience required.'

8.17 These two clauses are both external substitution clauses and a further internal clause is recommended as follows:

> 'The company may use suitably qualified directors, employees or self-employed persons in order to perform the contract works at its own discretion and may also utilise the services of employees or self-

employed persons in an administration capacity. Such persons will be answerable solely to the company and the client shall have no contractual, financial or legal relationship with the hired assistance. Payments to the above persons will be the sole responsibility of the company.'

8.18 A recommended sub-contract clause would read as follows:

'The whole or part of this contract for services may be assigned or sub-contracted to any third party provided that the sub-contractor is suitably experienced and qualified. The company will notify the client if any part of the contract works is sub-contracted or assigned. If this occurs the third party will be bound by terms identical to those in this contract.'

8.19 References to the company are of course references to the personal service business.

8.20 Finally, it is important to show that the contract represents a business to business relationship to undertake services and not provide workers. Simply providing workers plays into the first leg of the intermediaries' legislation in that there is a requirement for personal service and it triggers a potential agency problem (see Chapter 10). Contracts should, therefore, avoid the naming of consultants to be provided and concentrate instead on the nature of the services to be provided. It is just arguable that, if the consultants are not named, there is no need for a specific substitution clause on the basis that substitution is somehow implied. However, a clear written right should always be spelt out to avoid any confusion, and to provide good contractual evidence which may usefully be adduced at an appeal.

8.21 A business to business relationship for the provision of services should clearly be headed 'Contract for Services' and headings such as 'Contract for the Supply of Consultants' are unhelpful. Indeed, the author has seen contracts which have been held out as being 'IR35 proof' headed 'Contract of Employment For the Supply of Temporary Workers'. Although a reasonable tax tribunal or court may be reluctant to read too much into the headings in a contract such phraseology does not help get the IR35 defence off to a good start!

Phrases in a genuine contract for services which are worth avoiding include 'authorised personnel' and 'named consultant'. It is not fatal, however, to name an individual in the personal service business who is to be treated as a point of contact.

Mutuality of obligations

8.22 A suitable clause showing there is a lack of mutual obligations would read as follows:

'The client is not obliged to offer work or contracts to the company nor is the company obliged to accept such contracts if offered. The company is not obliged to make its services available. Specifically both parties declare that they do not wish to create or imply any mutuality of obligations whatsoever either during the course of this contract for services or during any period when contract works are not available'.

Generally, the two parties to a commercial contract have no difficulty in confirming in writing that ongoing work does not need to be offered nor that the personal service business needs to make its services available. Unfortunately, many contracts are at risk from IR35 because they remain silent on fundamental issues, such as a lack of mutuality. This is a great pity because, in practice, agreeing such a clause seldom causes a problem.

8.23 When such fundamental issues are not addressed in writing the possibility of awkward cross-examination with inconsistent answers before a tax tribunal is a real possibility. As such, contractors should help themselves by ensuring a clear lack of mutuality clause is in the contract terms and conditions.

8.24 Clauses which imply that there is mutuality of obligations are very unhelpful and are not that uncommon. Contracts which have no designated end date and are said to 'continue until either party gives notice to terminate' imply actual mutual obligations and if the contract rolls on from one year to the next there may come a time when a tribunal or court may say that the course of dealings between the parties has hardened into mutual obligations. Clauses which say 'work will be allocated' to the contractor also imply mutuality, as in *Synaptek Ltd v Young (HMIT)* (2003) (see Chapter 12 and Appendix 6). This does not of itself mean the personal service business falls foul of IR35, but a golden opportunity to demonstrate that IR35 does not apply has been lost.

Control

8.25 Which party has the right of control is determined by the express terms of the contract, and if the contract terms 'deal fully with the matter one may look no further' (MacKenna J in *Ready Mixed Concrete (South East) Ltd v Minister of Pensions and National Insurance* [1968] 1 All ER 433 at 440E). This passage can usefully be quoted to the Revenue when they try to ignore a contract. It is therefore important to ensure the 'control' aspect is committed to writing. The most important aspect of control is the 'how' and the following clause is suggested:

'The client shall not control, or have any right of control as to how the company is to perform the contract works.'

8.26 Less fundamental aspects of control are dealt with in the following clauses:

> 'How the company fulfils its contractual obligations is a matter for the company.'
>
> 'The company will use its own initiative in how the contract works are to be completed and will have flexibility as to the hours worked on location but will nonetheless assist the client by making all reasonable attempts to work within an overall agreed deadline, will observe health and safety regulations and will comply with all reasonable operational requirements relating to working hours and security.'
>
> 'Start and finish times are at the discretion of the company within an overall programme of contract works which will be verbally agreed from time to time and the company, its directors, employees or consultants are not obliged to seek permission from the client to leave a location at any time.'

8.27 Quite understandably, clients will want to ensure that the services provided meet the required and expected standards. The addition of a clause which makes it expressly clear that 'the company agrees to undertake services in a professional manner at all times and undertakes the services in the capacity of a specialist' may add some comfort for the client.

Such a clause may be strengthened by the additional words, 'The company undertakes that it will devote such time attention skills and ability as the contract works require'. Assurances as to correcting defective work might make a lack of control clause more acceptable to the client.

The single most important aspect is to show that there is a clause which clearly gives the contractor freedom to undertake services in the manner which he feels is appropriate so as to show that he is not controlled by the client as to 'how' the contract works are executed.

Summary

8.28 In light of the *Ready Mixed Concrete* case (see Appendix 6 and Chapter 6) in 1968 and subsequent senior court decisions, the three issues of personal service and substitution, a lack of mutuality of obligations and a lack of control, must be regarded as the essential trinity and pre-requisites of a contract of employment. These are the three issues that must be addressed when drafting contracts with IR35 in mind.

8.29 It must be remembered at all times that if the contract does not deal with substitution, mutuality and control this does not mean that the worker is a disguised employee. What it means is that the worker has not automatically escaped IR35 from the outset and that he will have to rely on other factors to establish a genuine business to business relationship, which may prove difficult.

Other important contract terms and conditions

8.30 Having considered the trinity of personal service, mutuality and control the remaining important contractual factors need to be considered.

Not all will carry the same weight in every case but there are clear legal precedents to suggest that they indicate a self-employed relationship. As such they should be spelt out clearly in a written contract for services, and of course implemented.

They fall into two categories: terms which are of primary importance in establishing self-employment and those of secondary importance.

- Primary importance: financial risk, business organisation, freedom and flexibility and intention.
- Secondary importance: lack of employee benefits, provision of equipment and basis of payment.

Financial risk

8.31 Traditionally the Revenue takes a very narrow view of financial risk and, in the author's opinion, this does not reflect the reality of the commercial world. The Revenue sees financial risk as giving a fixed price for a job. Clearly, if a contract gives a fixed price for a job and there is the chance that the worker overruns then he is potentially suffering risk, but the concept goes considerably further than this.

8.32 The following suggested clauses are all indicative of financial risk to a greater or lesser extent.

8.33 'The company will negotiate the price for the contract works and is obliged to honour any such agreed price'. In other words once a price has been agreed, be it for the whole project or a daily or hourly rate, then that price remains fixed.

Of course, the price is often contained in the contract itself (usually in a Schedule), but here we are making it clear that once a price is agreed, the personal service business cannot go back and ask for more. This merely serves to underline that a commercial business decision is being made by the PSB which has to be honoured and which carries an element of risk.

8.34 'Defective work by the company its directors employees consultants substitutes or hired assistants will be corrected by the company at its own cost or in its own time'. In certain areas this can represent significant financial risk.

The Revenue often (erroneously) argues that the risk of correcting defective work is equally indicative of employed status but this is simply not supported by law. If an employee carries out defective work it is corrected within the normal working day without any form of deduction being made. Tax officers often forget that the doctrine of vicarious liability means that the employer is generally accountable and responsible for any acts of negligence of his employee. Including defective work.

The author has seen defective work clauses imposing massive potential financial risk on the contractor and this important factor should not be underplayed.

8.35 'The company will not be entitled to receive payment for cancelled contract works'. Many IT and engineering contractors who work for an agency have to sign a clause stating that if the agency loses the contract with the end-user then the agency will have no financial liability for cancelling the contract with the personal service business. Quite clearly this represents risk.

However, if a bona fide employer fails to win a contract with a client it will still be obliged to offer continuing work or wages to its employees, subject to the normal redundancy rules. Self-employed contractors working via the personal service business do not enjoy such safeguards.

8.36 'The company accepts it has legal risk in respect of public liability and professional indemnity and will therefore pay the costs of such insurance premiums and maintain adequate cover at all times. During the term of this contract for services and for the following six-years the company will maintain adequate insurance cover in respect of professional indemnity with cover up to at least £1 million'.

Employees do not maintain such insurance because they are not liable. Self-employed people do because they are so liable.

8.37 Other suggested clauses are:

> 'The client reserves the right to offset any losses sustained as a result of the company's actions breach or unsatisfactory performance, from the company's fees.'
>
> 'The company acknowledges the volatility of the (IT/engineering sector) and accepts that there is the financial risk of bad debts when operating as an independent business on its own account.'
>
> 'This contract for services can be immediately terminated by the client for any reason whatever and no notice is required to be given'.

8.38 Contractors will of course want to weigh the benefits of implementing IR35 proof clauses on the one hand with commercial considerations on the other. The final suggested clause is an extreme example of financial risk with which the personal service business may not feel comfortable. It has also been suggested that if a contract can be terminated without notice, that this represents an element of control over the worker. It is suggested that this is not really the case, as control in an employment sense is concerned with interference in how the work is executed not whether a contract can be terminated.

8.39 It is not unknown for personal service businesses to be extremely reluctant to commit to some of the above terms and conditions because they fear it leaves them exposed. It does. But this is part and parcel of being in business, taking risks and demonstrating significant potential financial liabilities.

8.40 It will therefore be a matter of negotiation as to how far the personal service business wants to take on financial risk, but the narrow Revenue view, that financial risk amounts to giving a fixed price for a job, does not come anywhere near a true evaluation of the concept.

8.41 A further element of financial risk, which generally cannot be gleaned from the wording of a contract alone, concerns what might be a very extensive investment on the part of the personal service business into training and equipment. The Inland Revenue has acknowledged that a significant capital investment in training and equipment incurs an element of financial risk and will be taken into account when reviewing tax status—see ESM 1031.

Business organisation

8.42 Personal service businesses wanting to ensure that IR35 does not apply should already be acting in a commercial business to business manner, but several clauses can be agreed which will help underline this. Arguably none of these clauses is particularly significant in itself but when considered together they show a mindset indicative of an independent contractor as opposed to an employee of a client.

8.43 The following clauses are suggested.

> 'The company will prepare VAT invoices for contract works undertaken.'
>
> 'The company being in business on its own account will have its own business stationery and business cards and will if requested by the client supply a specimen for the client's records.'
>
> 'The company will at all times represent itself as an independent business and will in no circumstances represent itself or hold itself

> out as a representative, servant or employee of the client. The company hereby acknowledges it is in business on its own account and is not part and parcel of the client's business, or any other business.'
>
> 'The company will maintain at its own cost appropriate independent office accommodation, telephone system, mobile telephone, fax facility and e-mail facility.'

This final clause may refer to nothing more sophisticated than using a spare bedroom or a study as an office but it is all additional *evidence* that the personal service business is operating as an independent contractor as opposed to a mere employee.

8.44 'The company may advertise its services and may use a business trading name.' Again, this is a further indication of a general business modus operandi.

Freedom and flexibility

8.45 The following clauses are suggested.

> 'The company is free to undertake other contracts for services for other parties at any time, either before, after, or concurrently with this contract for services, providing that the provision of services does not create a conflict of interest or prevent the company from providing services to the client.'
>
> 'The client acknowledges and agrees that it does not have first call on the services of the company and cannot require the company to give the client any priority over another client.'

It may be remembered from Chapter 6 that a significant factor indicating direct employment status in the *Lee Ting Sang* case was that the employer had the right to insist that the worker gave him first priority when he had work available for him.

Intention

8.46 Some practitioners may be surprised to see 'intention' in the list of the more important factors in establishing self-employment.

However, as is explained in Chapter 6, the intention of the parties is always something to be taken into account, despite the Revenue's best efforts over the years. Indeed, in the 1999 Court of Appeal *Express and Echo* case (see Appendix 6) Lord Justice Peter Gibson ([1999] IRLR 367 at 370) went so far as to say that when determining status one 'starts with the common intention of the parties'.

As such, although many personal service businesses and the clients may feel it does not need to be said, it is the Accountax view that a clear intention clause must be helpful in establishing genuine independence. The following clause is recommended:

> 'Both parties agree and intend that this legal relationship is one of giving and accepting independent specialist services and specifically is not a relationship of master and servant or employer and employee.'

Summary

8.47 Before looking at factors of secondary importance it is worth reminding practitioners that many contracts potentially fall foul of IR35, not because they are badly written but because they are silent on the fundamental aspects of establishing self-employment (and, therefore, failing to demonstrate that the worker is not a disguised employee of the client). Silent contracts do not amount to good evidence.

8.48 It will not always be possible for the two parties to a contract to agree to all of the above clauses but every effort should be made to agree to as many as possible.

In committing to the suggested clauses, again strictly on the basis that they represent the true agreement between the parties, this will make the personal service business extremely difficult to attack.

8.49 IR35 is no different from any other aspect of Revenue compliance work. There has to be a realistic yield for the money and man hours spent in collecting it and the Revenue will without question pick on the weaker cases as part of this process.

Contractors should, therefore, make themselves difficult to attack by ensuring that the contractual terms and conditions agreed reflect a genuine business to business relationship.

8.50 If, however, the contract as written does not reflect the true arrangements between the parties then one of the parties to the 'agreement' may ask the tribunal to establish the true relationship. This was seen in *Maurice v Betterware UK Ltd* (see Appendix 6) in the Employment Appeals Tribunal in 2000. Here the workers sought to overturn a signed self-employed contract on the basis that it did not reflect the true arrangements. Mr Justice Keene accepted the argument, and the case was remitted to the Employment Tribunal so the full and correct position could be established. It should be noted that in this case the workers themselves wanted to establish a relationship of direct employment which, one assumes, the personal service business will not want to do.

Factors of secondary importance

Lack of employee benefits

8.51 The Revenue has traditionally taken the view that a lack of employee benefits is not a factor to be taken into account in determining status. It holds the view that employee benefits flow from employment status, not the reverse.

There is certainly a logic to this, but the line of reasoning is not entirely supported by the courts and it is understood that the Revenue itself will now take into account a lack of employee style benefits as being indicative of a genuine business to business self-employed relationship.

8.52 Chapter 6 analyses the relevant case law on employee benefits and bearing this analysis in mind the following clauses are suggested.

> 'The company, its directors, employees and consultants will not be entitled to receive holiday pay or bank holiday pay or special absence paid in any circumstances.'

> 'The company, its directors, employees and consultants will not be entitled to receive sick pay in any circumstances from the client. The company will bear the cost of any health insurance which it may arrange at its own discretion.'

> 'The company, its directors, employees and consultants are not entitled to partake in any grievance procedure offered to employees of the client and as an independent business are not entitled to any employment law rights.'

> 'The company, its directors, employees and consultants are not entitled to receive any company benefits or partake in any pension scheme run by the client. Pension provision may be made by the company at its own discretion for its directors or employees.'

The four clauses above prohibit the company itself from receiving various benefits. Clearly a company cannot receive sick pay etc but it is worth making this expressly clear in the contract as it can only help strengthen the case that IR35 does not apply.

While not being factors of major significance, it is generally easy to agree such terms and conditions and for the sake of clarity they should be committed to writing.

Provision of equipment

8.53 The reality of most personal service business contracts is that the majority of equipment will be supplied by the end-user. Contractors tend not to carry mainframes around in their rucksacks! On the basis that the personal service company is contracted to provide skills rather than equipment, as more fully explained in Chapter 6, it is not considered that provision of equipment is particularly relevant. As stated above, if a personal service business does make a significant investment in equipment then that can only help to indicate a financial outlay, which in turn indicates a potential financial risk, but it is certainly not essential to defeating IR35.

8.54 In terms of contractual conditions it is suggested that where the personal service business does supply computer equipment it warrants that it is technically capable of fulfilling its function and is virus free.

Basis of payment

8.55 It is suggested that attached to the contract for services there is a Schedule which clarifies the basis of payment and invoicing frequency. This is mentioned here only for the purposes of administrative clarity. As explained in Chapter 6, the basis of payment itself is not one of the more important factors in determining status and this is a fact accepted by the Revenue.

General considerations

8.56 Practitioners are urged to note that the suggested clauses are not meant to be an all encompassing blueprint contract for services. They represent example clauses relating to the more important aspects of a genuine contract for services.

8.57 The final version of a contract for services will contain many other clauses relating to the commencement and termination date, the actual services to be provided, aspects of intellectual property rights and confidentiality and specific technical legal clauses relating to the construction of the contract.

Practitioners should, therefore, seek further professional assistance in drawing up self-employed contracts, either from a suitably experienced lawyer or specialist tax advisers.

8.58 If a contract is signed but not understood, or not even read, there is good contract law precedent in the 1934 case of *L'Estrange v F Graucob Ltd* ([1934] 2 KB 394) to say that the contract still stands. However, it would be better all round if contracts are carefully considered before they are entered into.

8.59 It is recommended that fresh contracts are entered into as often as is practicably possible. This is not the same as merely adding a further Schedule to an old contract. Such 'rolling' contracts are generally to be avoided as they imply ongoing commitments. It is recommended that quarterly or six-monthly contracts would show that the parties are re-committing themselves to the terms the contract contains, and if some of the terms are re-negotiated from one contract to the next, then so much the better.

Summary

8.60 The contractual terms and conditions of the working relationship between the two parties are the single most important piece of evidence to be adduced in an IR35 defence.

Care should be taken in ensuring that not only are the contract terms understood but that they represent the reality of the relationship. Shams do not work.

The suggested clauses detailed above do not purport to take into account other highly important considerations in commercial contracts. The clauses have been designed as a strategy to ensure that the worker is not a disguised employee of the client. As such, personal service businesses may want to take advice on other contractual matters, which in themselves have no real relevance to the IR35 position.

8.61 Non-contractual matters which support a genuine business approach, such as advertising, maintaining an office or website, etc, should all be documented and evidence retained. This 'paper trail' is quite rightly advocated by the PCG as one of those things a contractor can do to help himself.

8.62 Hopelessly unworkable and totally impractical clauses of an extreme nature should be avoided. They add nothing and weaken otherwise credible and realistic contracts.

CHAPTER 9

Crucial question 3: is the agency/end-user contract relevant?

9.1 In the majority of contracting relationships the personal service business does not contract with an end-user but with an agency. Where this is the case, the Revenue has, from day one, taken the view that in the common commercial chain of personal service business/agency/end-user the contract, as between the agency and end-user, is as relevant as the contract between the personal service business and the agency. It states (at Frequently asked Questions, Contract 2, on its website at http://www.inlandrevenue.gov.uk/ir35) that:

> 'The Inland Revenue will take account of all relevant contracts in order to discover whether the relationship between a worker and a client would have been one of employment, if there had been no intermediary. This would include any contracts between the client and an agency, and between the agency and the worker's service company.'

But is this approach valid? Some commentators suggest that it is, but in the author's view it is questionable, and it might be resisted. The reasons are fully explored below but, as a preliminary discussion, it is worth bearing in mind the following recent and real life application of the Revenue's official line on taking into account the agency/end-user contract.

Case study

Accountax represented an IR35 at-risk contractor who was subject to an IR35 challenge from a nominated status inspector. Her personal service business contracted with an agency and a bank was the end-user. The Revenue requested sight of the agency/bank contract as this was in its view relevant to the 'circumstances' of the 'arrangements' as per ITEPA 2003 s 49(1)(*c*) and (4).

The Revenue was not given access to this contract, not least because the personal service business did not itself have access to it. In similar situations the Revenue has been known to decline to give an IR35 opinion leaving the personal service business in no-man's land.

However, in a telephone conversation with the author, the status inspector accepted that while she would ideally *like* to see the agency/end-user contract she was in fact able to offer an IR35 opinion without it. For the technical and logical reasons explored below this makes sense, but what is important is that the Revenue confirmed this approach in writing.

A letter is on file from the status inspector saying that an IR35 opinion can be given on the basis of the personal service business/agency contract alone. There is nothing to suggest this was a rogue decision as the inspector had taken head office advice. This decision arguably demonstrates that the Revenue really knows that the personal service business/agency contract is the most important one.

Practitioners should note that the letter was not written with caveats about taking into account the agency/end-user contract should it ever be produced. A clear opinion was given by the nominated status inspector. Quite simply the agency/end-user contract was not needed.

9.2 It is accepted that the approach of this status inspector may be uncommon but, with head office eyes watching how IR35 disputes are unfolding at district level very carefully, it perhaps indicates that the Revenue does not always follow its own official line.

9.3 This was a case which the personal service business was prepared to defend on appeal at the Commissioners—perhaps the Revenue preferred to settle the matter to avoid a possible early defeat at the tax tribunal and the publicity which would ensue. The lesson to be learnt is not to give in at the first hurdle when the Revenue asks for the agency/end-user contract.

9.4 The Revenue is also on record as saying that, where it seems from the personal service business/agency contract that the worker is caught by IR35, it is not necessary for it to examine the agency/end-user contract. But where it appears that the worker escapes IR35 based on the personal service business/agency contract then it will be necessary to examine the agency/end-user contract. This apparent 'heads the Revenue wins, tails the contractor loses' approach should be seen for what it is—an exercise in double standards. The Revenue should have a consistent approach; it should maintain that either both contracts are relevant or that only the lower contract is.

In the 2003 High Court case of *Synaptek Ltd v Young*, the chain of parties was: personal service business/agency/EDS/Benefits Agency.

In that case the Revenue did *not* rely on or even adduce the EDS/BA contract. If they maintain all contracts are relevant then surely they should have done so as the BA was the end-user. Again, an example of, at best, inconsistency.

Secondly, why did the Revenue not argue that the director of Synaptek Ltd was not a disguised employee of the BA?

Why the agency/end-user contract may not be relevant

9.5 It is suggested that there are four main reasons:

- ITEPA 2003 Pt 2 Ch 8
- The doctrine of privity of contract
- Common sense and equity
- Existing case law.

ITEPA 2003 Pt 2 Ch 8

9.6 The legislation does not seem specifically to deal with the common situation where there is an agency. Despite much commentary on the so-called 'hypothetical' contract alluded to in ITEPA 2003 s 49(1)(*c*)—incidentally the phrase 'hypothetical contract' does not appear in the legislation and should, therefore, be used with extreme caution—there is a very convincing argument in favour of not taking into account the agency/end-user contract at all when considering whether IR35 applies. Revenue efforts to imply extra terms that have the effect of overriding existing express terms should be resisted (see 8.13).

9.7 The reasoning is as follows: ITEPA 2003 s 49(4) states that

> 'the circumstances referred to in ITEPA 2003 s 49(1)(*b*) include the terms on which the services are provided, having regard to the terms of the contracts forming part of the arrangements under which the services are provided'.

9.8 This needs analysing carefully. It is clear from the wording of ITEPA 2003 s 49(4) that 'the circumstances' in s 49(1)(*c*) refer to contracts forming part of the 'arrangements'. Crucially, and this is often overlooked, the word 'arrangements' is detailed at s 49(1)(*b*) as being 'arrangements *involving* a third party (the intermediary)' (author's emphasis). In the author's view, this can only mean the contractual arrangements entered into by the personal service business (the intermediary) and in the personal service business/agency/end-user commercial chain the only contract entered into by the personal service business is the one with the *agency.* The contract between the agency and the end-user is not an arrangement involving the personal service business itself, and the worker's day-to-day method of operating at a client's premises, that is, the practical and mundane aspects of the relationship, are equally not arrangements involving the intermediary. They are merely practical day-to-day considerations. The two are quite separate and distinct so it should not be forgotten that s 49(1)(*b*) refers only to arrangements involving the personal service business.

9.9 If there was a tripartite agreement (which is rare but not impossible) then it might seem reasonable to assume that such an arrangement would have to be considered, as clearly it would be an arrangement involving a third party.

9.10 It could just be conceivable that, where an agency contracts with an end-user to supply a specifically named person, it might be considered that this also is an arrangement involving a third party, particularly if the named worker also signs the contract qua worker, not merely qua director of the business. But even this concession to the Revenue's approach is unjustified. This is because the arrangement in this scenario would involve the *worker* not the intermediary personal service business and IR35 is aimed, as the Act says, at intermediaries.

9.11 Indeed, s 49(1)(*b*) specifically points out that the rules are *not* aimed at contracts the worker has directly with a client but only where contracts are entered into under arrangements via a personal service business. In these circumstances the Revenue cannot argue that a contract is relevant to the arrangements if it names the individual, when at the same time the Revenue acknowledges that the contract is not entered into by the personal service business, and hence is not relevant.

9.12 It is the personal service business' contract with the agency which forms the 'arrangements' included in the 'circumstances'.

9.13 The legislation is not easy to read and it is unhelpful that it is necessary to go back and forth to gain the true meaning of the word 'circumstances'. But, taken a step at a time, it is suggested that the correct conclusion is that it is the contract entered into by the personal service business which is relevant.

9.14 Furthermore, s 49(4) does not mention hypothetical contracts or imaginary contracts. On the contrary, the wording is very much concerned with *the provision of the actual services.* The phrase 'the terms on which the services are provided' seems, if anything, to imply that a set of hypothetical terms is not in issue. It is the terms of the contract under which the services are provided that are relevant and it is submitted that the only hypothetical aspect is that the worker stands in the shoes of the personal service business. It is this substitution of the worker for the personal service business which is the hypothesis (s 49(1)(*c*) refers) and this is discussed below in greater detail.

9.15 In simple terms, unless the personal service business is party to the contract either in its own right or within a tripartite agreement, then any other contracts are not relevant, as they are not arrangements involving the personal service business.

9.16 It is often suggested that the word 'arrangements' has a broader meaning than strict contractual agreements. In determining whether or not matters are 'arrangements' and should, therefore, be taken into account, it is interesting to note that the IR35 rules in Pt 2 Ch 7 do *not* employ a wide definition of that term (whereby arrangements 'include any scheme, agreement, undertaking or understanding, whether or not legally enforceable') that is used in four separate occasions elsewhere in that Act (at ITEPA 2003 Sch 2 para 12(2) (in relation to employee share ownership plans), Sch 5 para 58 (enterprise management incentives), Sch 15 para 102(1) (the corporate venturing scheme) and Sch 20 para 21(3) (tax relief for expenditure on research and development)). As such there is no need to give the word 'arrangements' an extended meaning to that laid down in s 49(1)(*b*).

The hypothetical contract—the myth

9.17 As stated earlier, there is no reference in the Act to a hypothetical contract as such. ITEPA 2003 s 49(1)(*c*) asks whether:

> 'the circumstances are such that *if* the services were provided under a contract directly between the client and the worker, the worker *would be* regarded for income tax purposes as an employee of the client' (author's emphasis).

9.18 It is submitted that on its true construction there is no need to construct a hypothetical contract at all. There is, however, a need to construct a fiction as to *who* the parties to the contract are. In other words, the hypothetical aspect relates to the supposed parties to the contract not the hypothetical terms they are meant to have agreed.

9.19 The fiction created by IR35 is to stand the worker in the shoes of his business to see whether the agreed terms would render him an employee of the client. It is not necessary to construct a new set of terms and conditions.

Regrettably this point was not highlighted in the PCG case (*R (on the application of the Professional Contractors Group) v IRC*, see Appendix 6) as that case was concerned with European law, not a detailed interpretation of the Schedule itself.

9.20 It has been readily assumed that an imaginary contract has to be devised. This is not the case. All that is required, by hypothesis, is to ask what the legal relationship would have been if the worker had made the contract himself. There is some logic to this argument, because IR35 is aimed at the artificial insertion of an intermediary (usually a limited company), hence it makes sense to ask what the position would be if the intermediary is simply removed. Clearly this does not require the invention of any new terms and conditions—the worker merely assumes those which his personal business has entered into. However, the comments of the Special Commissioner in the *F S Consulting* appeal and *Usetech Ltd v Young (HMIT)* discussed in Chapter 12 need to be borne in mind.

9.21 This approach of putting the worker in the shoes of his business vis a vis the contract with the client will therefore have the benefit of taking into account the actual terms of a real commercial contract as required by s 49(1)(*c*).

9.22 ITEPA 2003 s 49(1)(*c*) refers to the actual circumstances, not hypothetical circumstances, of the services provided. It can be seen from the full text of s 49(1)(*c*) that the so called hypothetical aspect is the reference '. . . if the services were provided . . . under a contract . . . (between) the worker and the client . . .'. The Act is envisaging the contract terms remaining constant in respect of the services. It is only the parties to it who are changing. This is the IR35 hypothesis.

9.23 Not only does the Act of itself, on a careful analysis, support this approach, but it has the advantage of avoiding the absurd situation where the contractor, his representative, the inspector, the Commissioners and the courts all have to try to guess the detailed terms and conditions of a non-existent contract not entered into by anyone.

9.24 A further and important justification for putting the worker in the shoes of his personal service business as opposed to inventing hypothetical contract terms can be found in the Revenue's own standard contract review letter. This clearly states what the employment relationship would be *if the contract was made directly by the worker*. It does not refer to hypothetical contract terms at all.

The use of 'contracts' (plural) in ITEPA 2003 s 49(4)

9.25 Some commentators and the Revenue have suggested that the use of plural 'contracts' in s 49(4) requires a consideration of both the personal service business/agency contract and the agency/end-user contract. Why else, they argue, is the word used in its plural if the only contract to be considered is the one between the personal service business and the agency? As a preliminary issue those who suggest all the contracts in the chain need to be considered should first address the s 49(1)(*b*) issue at 9.8 above.

9.26 It is submitted that there are two reasons why the use of the plural does not mean that the two different contracts referred to above have both to be considered.

Firstly, the whole language of Pt 2 Ch 8 is written in the plural. It refers to 'engagements', 'services', 'arrangements', and 'circumstances' and therefore the use of 'contracts' (plural) merely continues the same style.

Secondly, in deciding whether IR35 applies and to see if the worker is a disguised employee, all the contracts entered into by the personal service business need to be considered. That is, if a personal service business enters into four quarterly contracts during a given year then all four must be considered to see whether IR35 applies to any of them or to the total bigger picture. The Revenue has accepted, in the illustration of Charlotte (see Appendix 7), that it is possible to stand back and look at a contractor's whole business history and not just the terms of an individual contract. As such it is quite reasonable, even essential, to look at all contracts entered into by the business to come to the right conclusion. If the Schedule merely referred to the 'contract' (singular) this would cause potential difficulties over exactly which contract was being referred to.

9.27 The use of 'contracts' (plural) is quite deliberate and this enables all contracts entered into by the personal service business to be taken into account, both in respect of the deemed salary calculation for the year in question and in order to look at the bigger picture. As further support for this argument, the legislation has been interpreted by Mr Justice Burton as requiring consideration on an individual engagement by engagement basis (*R (on the application of PCG Ltd) v IRC*, see Appendix 6), which may well mean consideration of several contracts (plural).

9.28 In any event, it should never be forgotten that s 49(1)(*c*), read in conjunction with s 49(1)(*b*) and (4), limits the contracts to be considered strictly to those that the personal service business is a party to.

The doctrine of privity of contract

9.29 The second justification to show that the agency/end-user contract is not relevant is the doctrine of privity. This says that A and B cannot make a contract whereby C is obliged to do something or refrain from doing something. A and B cannot enforce obligations on C by agreeing something between themselves.

9.30 An example of this might be where A agrees with B that C has to buy some goods. Such an agreement has no force because C is not a party or privy to the A/B contract. The idea here is that the end-user and agency are represented by A and B and the contractor, C, is not a party to their agreement, and his tax and national insurance obligations should not be influenced by it. It has to be remembered that seldom will the contractor ever get to see the agency/end-user contract and nor will he have any influence over its terms.

9.31 It is fair to say that the doctrine of privity has many exceptions and whole chapters of detailed contract law text books are devoted to the topic. But in principle it is straight-forward. A person cannot be bound by a contract to which he is not a party.

Not only is the agency/end-user contract not within the scope of s 49(1)(*b*), it is not a contract the personal service business has signed.

In this context the doctrine of privity is not eroded by the Contracts (Rights of Third Parties) Act 1999.

Common sense and equity

9.32 Many of the points raised earlier in this chapter show why the agency/end-user contract, if it is brought into the IR35 equation, can lead to some difficult, if not absurd, situations.

Case study

In an IR35 defence worked by Accountax, the personal service business was unable to obtain a copy of the agency/end-user contract. The inspector obtained a copy and claimed it contained clauses that showed IR35 applied. The personal service business wished to refute this and asked for copies of the clauses in question. The inspector refused on the grounds that the agency/end-user contract was confidential and he could not release it! The ability to complete form P35 accurately would seem to depend, at least in part, on the contractor's psychic powers. Absurd.

9.33 But there are other factors. Whenever an IR35 challenge is defended, it is wise, even at an early stage, to consider what the likely arguments will be if the case goes to the Commissioners on appeal.

9.34 It is the author's view that the Commissioners tend to apply a good dose of common sense and try to avoid absurd conclusions where they have an option to do so. This is particularly the case where losing the appeal would result in substantial extra tax or national insurance. In brief it is not impossible to get the benefit of the doubt when a plausible and robust argument is presented, particularly at the General Commissioners.

9.35 Why indeed should a worker have his tax and national insurance liabilities determined by a contract he has never seen or had any influence over and one that he has not signed? It is likely to be perceived as grossly unfair that the worker's own position can be influenced by such a contract. To add insult to injury, IR35 liabilities will be determined after the year has finished and hence any deductions required to be paid over will be retroactive.

9.36 Although it is commonly accepted that there is no equity in tax it is submitted that the Revenue would be going too far if it attempts to impose fiscal liabilities on the contractor by primary reference to the agency/end-user contract.

9.37 To make matters even worse, what would happen where the personal service business did in fact see the agency/end-user contract and tried but failed to have certain clauses improved, removed or clarified? Perhaps the personal service business formally lodges its concerns and objections with the contract to the agency and end-user but to no avail. Not only is the personal service business not a party to the contract but it is now on record as saying that it objects to some of the clauses it contains. Are the Commissioners still going to suggest that the worker is bound by this agency/end-user contract? It is thought not.

9.38 To extend the argument let it be assumed that both personal service business/agency and agency/end-user contracts are to be taken into account. What if the personal service business/agency contract deals with, say, the correction of defective work but the agency/end-user contract is silent on this issue? Which contract carries more weight and why?

9.39 If the personal service business/agency contract says that the worker will have freedom as to how the contract works are carried out, ie there is a lack of control, but the agency/end-user contract says the worker will be under the control of the end-user (a commonly encountered clause) then again, which contract is to take precedence and why?

9.40 All these impossible questions can be neatly avoided if the agency/end-user contract is disregarded as it should be. There is the added complication that there may be as many as five or six parties in the chain, not just three. If the Revenue maintains all contracts in the chain are relevant should they not be examining all the contracts? They seldom do.

Again if all the contracts in the chain are relevant why does the Revenue not ask to see any contract the worker (usually a director) has with his own personal service business?They almost never do.

9.41 The Revenue's view seems to be that, where there are inconsistencies, then what happens 'in reality' takes precedence, but this flies in the face of its hypothetical contract approach. In any event, contracts (real or even imaginary) are concerned with rights and obligations and not just with whether those rights and obligations are called upon in practice. For example, the right to send in a substitute may never be put into practice but the right can still exist; the obligation to correct defective work may never be tested in practice because no defective work is actually carried out, but the obligation still remains. So there could now be an absurd situation where the Revenue would be asking the Commissioners to appraise contradictory terms, some of which the personal service business has not even signed up to. Presumably the Commissioners would also be asked by the Revenue to second guess what rights and obligations might or might not exist in an imaginary contract, not based purely on reality and practice but also on what could be quite untested and theoretical. Surely this is an impossible task. In other words, the hypothetical terms are so open to interpretation and assumption that no one can prove that their view of the hypothetical terms is any more sound than the next person's. The fact that the Revenue has indicated (in its illustration in Charlotte, see Appendix 6) that the broader business background will be taken into account is a different point altogether, and has nothing to do with hypothetical terms, but is concerned with real life incidencies of being 'in business'.

Existing case law

9.42 There already exists a number of cases where an individual has claimed rights (usually employment law rights) against a third party end-user with whom he or his service company did *not* have a contract. The decisions have not all gone the same way.

The main cases can be split between workers who had a limited company and those who did not.

9.43 In the 1978 case of *Winter v Westward TV Ltd* (see Appendix 6) the worker tried to claim he was really an employee of the client despite the use of his own limited company to contract himself out. He failed. The Employment Appeals Tribunal described as 'almost impossible' the suggestion that in a three party chain a hypothetical relationship between the worker and the end-user could be implied. They said any such hypothesis would be 'invalid'.

9.44 The Court of Appeal in the *Tansell v Abbey Life* case (see Appendix 6) in 1999 confirmed that the director of a personal service business which contracted via an agency to an end-user was within the definition of 'worker' for the purposes of the Disability Discrimination Act 1995, but said it was going too far to imagine that there was a hypothetical contract of employment between the worker and the end-user.

9.45 In 2001 the case of *O'Murphy v Hewlett Packard* (see Appendix 6) was heard in the employment tribunal. This case decided that the worker, who was a director of his own service company, was to be treated as an employee of the end-user. It was clear on the facts that the company owned by the worker had been inserted as an administrative convenience and that the contract it had entered had few, if any, hallmarks of a genuine contract for services.

However, the decision in this case was appealed and a hearing took place in the Employment Appeal Tribunal in 2002 and the original decision was reversed. This case still serves to remind practitioners that it is certainly not beyond Tribunals to 'ignore' the personal service company and consider a direct relationship between the client and the worker, even without taking into account the IR35 legislation.

9.46 Turning to cases where workers who did not have their own personal service businesses, a trend can be seen. In the 1998 case of *Serco v Blair* (see Appendix 6), the Employment Appeal Tribunal decided that a contract with the end-user could not be implied, and this was followed in *Costain v Smith* (see Appendix 6) in 1999. A contrary decision was reached in *Motorola Ltd v Davidson* (see Appendix 6) in 2000, where the worker was held to be an employee of the end-user.

9.47 This latter case is unusual in that the main argument put forward by Motorola was the control criterion, yet it was easily established on the facts that Motorola controlled Davidson. The judgment makes for some interesting reading and it is very difficult to understand why Motorola did not argue the *Costain* and *Serco* principle, that is to say, they simply did not have a contract with the worker. In the *Motorola* case, the tribunal felt restricted to consider the one status test advanced, ie control, but may well have come to a different conclusion had the case been argued more comprehensively.

9.48 A recent agency case for a non-incorporated worker is *Montgomery v Johnson Underwood* (see Appendix 6), which was heard by the Court of Appeal in 2001. In this case the worker, a receptionist, worked for an agency at an end-user's premises. She was there for over two years. Having been dismissed for making private telephone calls in the office she took out an action against both the agency and the end-user. As a preliminary point her status had to be determined. The conclusion was that she was not employed by either the agency or the end-user because she was not sufficiently controlled nor was there mutuality of obligations.

9.49 What can be gathered from these cases? Firstly, it must be remembered that in all of these cases the workers themselves wanted to be treated as an employee of the end-user, and one assumes that IR35 at-risk workers will want to resist such an outcome at all costs—at least in the first instance.

Secondly, it is arguable that the *Motorola* case was badly argued and may yet go to appeal, and in the *O'Murphy* case the contract was very poorly drafted and the worker was clearly controlled.

9.50 Nothing can be taken for certain in tribunal proceedings, but overall it seems the tribunals are generally unwilling to imply contractual relations between third parties, whether the worker is incorporated or not. Where sound contractual relations are entered into with the agency, particularly where it can be demonstrated that there is little control or mutuality, the Revenue will take no comfort from the above cases.

9.51 Although the case law has not always been consistent there are several decisions that state that implying hypothetical contract terms is, as in the *Winter v Westward TV* case, 'almost impossible' and an 'invalid' approach. This can only help to underline the fact that, so far as IR35 is concerned, the contract to concentrate on is the one the personal service business enters into. Of course these cases were decided before IR35 came into force and they cannot overrule statutes which came after them. However, if the Revenue is going to argue that there is a disguised employee situation, this case law can only help to show that the courts are generally reluctant to make such a finding. Unfortunately, IR35 requires a hypothetical contract to be inferred from the circumstances and arrangements and this is inescapable. Non-IR35 case law shows how difficult it can be implying hypothetical contracts and this perhaps underlines once again that IR35 as written is at best difficult to apply with any certainty.

Summary

9.52 There are many technical and common sense justifications to disregard the agency/end-user contract and to reject the Revenue's interpretation of the legislation and the need to see the agency/end-user contract. However, in practice all contracts in the chain tend to be considered by the courts.

The Revenue, in FAQs, Agency, 2, and Contract, 2 and 8 (available on the Revenue's website at http://www.inlandrevenue.gov.uk/ir35) expresses the view that all the contracts in the commercial chain need to be taken into account but the detailed arguments in this chapter demonstrate the weaknesses with this approach.

The relevance of the agency/end-user contract was brought up in the *F S Consulting Ltd* Special Commissioners' decision of 2002 and *Usetech Ltd v Young* in 2004. These decisions are considered in Chapter 12 below.

CHAPTER 10

Crucial question 4: is the personal service business an agency within ITEPA 2003 Pt 2 Ch 7?

10.1 There is a further threat. This is found in ITEPA 2003 ss 44–47 (formerly TA 1988 s 134). There are equivalent provisions for national insurance found in the Social Security (Categorisation of Earners) Regulations 1978, SI 1978/1689.

If this legislation applies the consequences can be as devastating in terms of tax and national insurance as they would be under IR35.

Some advisers have been unaware of the potential application of the agency rules to the personal service sector and this chapter explains what the problem is and how it should be addressed and avoided.

The agency trap

10.2 In essence ITEPA 2003 s 44 says that if business A supplies worker B to a client C, then business A will be acting as an agency. There are very few escape strategies.

10.3 Under ITEPA 2003 s 47(3), all forms of payment made by company A to worker B in these circumstances will have to suffer PAYE and national insurance deductions under the NIC regs unless the payments have already been treated as Employment Income, in which case the appropriate deductions should already have been made.

10.4 It does not matter if company A is not registered as an agency or that it does not consider itself to be an agency. It is a question of fact as to whether it has supplied a worker. Nor does it matter whether or not the worker is personally named.

10.5 In the author's extensive practical experience of contract reviews in the context of IR35, it is quite clear that many personal service businesses are doing nothing more than supplying the director to the next party in the commercial chain. Often the director is named as the 'authorised personnel' or 'nominated consultant'. It is even often stated at the outset of the contract that the personal service business will supply personnel.

The personal service business is thus acting as an agency *itself* and falls within the agency regulations. The exemption for incorporated workers at Pt 2 Ch 7 is of no assistance because the agency 'trap' has merely trickled down from the legitimate agency to the personal service business.

10.6 Partners and staff at Accountax have personally handled cases where both the Inland Revenue and former Contributions Agency officers have tried this precise line of attack. During the last year since the first edition of this book was published there has been a noticeable increase in the use of the agency legislation by the Revenue. It is being increasingly applied to composite companies who do not realise they are effectively acting as agencies.

10.7 Although the agency regulations are not the easiest legislation to understand it can certainly be interpreted in such a way so as to justify its application to personal service businesses.

The Revenue clearly believes that this is a technically legitimate argument.

10.8 Furthermore, the flow chart in the internal manuals at ESM (ESM 3032, available only on the version on the Revenue's website) directs tax officers to consider the agency argument where the straight IR35 challenge cannot succeed. In other words, tax officers are having their specific attention drawn to the possibility of an agency challenge. The author understands a specialist unit has been set up within the Revenue to focus on the agency regulations.

10.9 A little known case from 1992, called Revenue Decision Four (RD4) (which was briefly mentioned in past Tax Bulletins and is included in the *Yellow Tax Handbook 2003–04* (2003)), states that a challenge was made to a director of a company who was attempting to extract funds from his company via consultancy fees. This in itself should not overly concern practitioners in the context of IR35 as it is a fairly common place technical argument. What is disturbing is that the Revenue's challenge was not that the consultancy fees were really disguised director's remuneration but that the company was acting as an agency *itself* within the agency regulations. The Revenue's interpretation was upheld.

10.10 The agency trap is a very real threat to tens of thousands of small personal service businesses who merely supply a consultant (usually the director—the worker) to a client. When coupled with the Revenue's new focus on Pt 2 Ch 7 and the success it has had with RD4 it would be an unwise practitioner who fails to address this issue.

It seems s 47(3) could apply to dividends, as 'remuneration' includes all forms of payment. Certainly, the Revenue will consider this line of attack (although it should be noted that TA 1988 s 20 ensures that dividends are chargeable first under Schedule F before Employment Income).

How can the agency trap be avoided?

10.11 There are really only two possibilities of avoiding the agency trap.

Demonstrate that the strict terms of ITEPA 2003 Pt 2 Ch 7 have not been met

10.12 In essence ITEPA 2003 s 44 merely says that if company A supplies worker B to client C then company A will be acting as an agency, and PAYE and national insurance deductions will have to be made from all forms of payment made to the worker. It is, however, first necessary to consider carefully ITEPA 2003 s 44 as these provisions lay down certain criteria which must be satisfied before the section applies.

10.13 Section 44(1)(*a*) provides that the worker must render, or be under an obligation to render, personal services to a client. Unfortunately, even where there is an unfettered substitution clause, this subsection can still be satisfied because it includes de facto personal service as an alternative to an obligation to provide personal service.

10.14 In other words, the existence of a right of substitution will not defeat this subsection where personal service is in fact given. Internal and former contributions agency instructions and guidance state that even where a former substitute is sent, in practice this should not defeat s 44(1)(*a*) in itself, particularly where a substitute is sent only very occasionally. Another argument open to the authorities is that those occasions when a substitute is sent can be severed from occasions when personal service was given and the latter will still be caught by the agency rules and the national insurance regulations equivalent.

10.15 Section 44(1)(*a*) goes on to say that the worker must be 'subject to, or to the right of, supervision, direction or control as to the manner in which he renders those services'. This subsection, it should be noted, concentrates on the 'how' by referring to the 'manner' in which the services are rendered.

10.16 It should be carefully observed that the subsection is worded in such a way that supervision, direction and control are all alternatives to each other. Control is generally accepted as having the quality of a significant degree of interference, whereas mere supervision and direction operates at a lower level. As such, the subsection can be applied in cases were the interference of the agency does not amount to full control but still amounts to supervision or direction.

10.17 In the case of traditional labour agencies (as opposed to personal service business deemed agencies) the Revenue does accept that it is possible for an agency supplied worker not to be under the supervision, direction or control of another person, but practitioners can expect strong resistance, particularly in the case of unskilled or semi-skilled workers.

10.18 Unfortunately, s 44(1)(*c*) does not state that the supervision, direction or control has to be exercised by the agency or any other specific named party. As such, it may apply irrespective of the identity of the person or business which supervises, directs or controls or who has the right to supervise, direct or control the worker.

10.19 In the context of IR35 workers, the scope for control is likely to be limited, but mere supervision or direction may well be present and difficult to resist. This is especially so in light of contract clauses which refer to the worker having to 'comply with all rules and regulations in operation' etc.

10.20 So the first strategy to defeat the agency rules is to show that the worker is not subject either to supervision, direction or control or the right of supervision, direction or control by any third-party 'as to the manner' in which the services are provided. This, quite simply, will be a straight question of fact by reference to the contract terms and practical arrangements if different.

Demonstrate that 'services' and not 'personnel' are being supplied

10.21 It may be possible to show on the facts that s 44(1)(*a*) does not apply because the personal service business is not acting as an agency because it is undertaking services as opposed to supplying mere workers. Again, this will be a question of fact.

10.22 Accountax has reviewed many contracts in respect of IR35 only to find that the contract quite clearly spells out that a person or consultant or authorised personnel, often named in a schedule, is being provided, as opposed to commercial services being undertaken. To put this into context, it is the difference between Fred Bloggs Computer Services Limited contracting to 'supply a consultant at £50 per hour', which would indicate a potential agency position, and contracting to 'undertake Oracle DBA programming at a rate of £50 per hour', which would be the provision of a service, and not caught by the agency rules.

In the late 2001 Court of Appeal decision in *Jobsin.co.uk plc v Department of Health* (see Appendix 6) the court drew the distinction between providing computer services and providing personnel. This was not an IR35 case—it was concerned with tendering regulations in public service contracts but the point is still made. The crucial question to be asked, said the court, was 'what is being provided?'. This very neatly highlights the importance of the contractual obligation to provide 'services' or 'personnel'.

10.23 Sometimes contracts are not quite clear on exactly what is being provided and, even with highly paid specialist IT and engineering contractors, it is not uncommon for there to be no written contract at all.

10.24 In these circumstances reference to the invoices raised may lead to clarification of precisely what is being supplied. If an invoice reads, 'To professional fees in respect of Oracle DBA programming for a total of 35 hours at £50 per hour' then it is fair to say that such wording indicates the undertaking of a service. If, however, the invoice reads, 'To professional fees for the supply of Fred Bloggs for 35 hours at £50 per hour' then such wording would indicate an agency relationship.

10.25 Although the strict contractual terms should carry most weight, other correspondence or invoices which indicate that a worker only is being supplied, as opposed to the undertaking of commercial services, at best muddy the waters and could at worst be used as hard evidence that in truth the personal service business is a deemed agency under ITEPA 2003 Pt 2 Ch 7, with all the disastrous fiscal ramifications which follow on from such a conclusion, courtesy of s 47(3).

A further minor complication is that if the agency rules are deemed to apply (as opposed to IR35) there may well be ramifications for claiming travelling expenses as the rules relating to 'agency workers' and 'temporary work places' are interpreted narrowly by the Revenue.

Summary

10.26 There is a potential trap for personal service businesses in ITEPA 2003 Pt 2 Ch 7. In the past the Revenue has tended not to pursue the agency argument, but it is certainly open for it to do so and, furthermore, the latest on-line print of the Employment Status Manual (at ESM 3032) encourages tax officers to consider the application of the agency rules.

10.27 It can be demonstrated that the agency rules do not apply by showing that the strict criteria laid down in subsection (1) are not met, but this may not be an easy task. The only certain way to avoid an agency challenge is to show that, both contractually and in respect of supporting paperwork and invoices, a worker is not being supplied but that the personal service business is undertaking commercial services.

10.28 The Revenue may not pursue the agency argument to the bitter end but if they can show a requirement for personal service then they have at the same time demonstrated that the first criteria of IR35 has been met.

As IR35 cases unfold it seems that the Revenue is not pursuing the 'agency trap' but practitioners should be aware of it in both IR35 and non-IR35 scenarios.

The agency trap is something those using composite or umbrella companies should be particularly aware of (See Chapter 11).

CHAPTER 11

Crucial question 5: do composite companies defeat IR35?

11.1 This new but short chapter has been inserted because many contractors have worked via composite company structures over the last few years. Such structures are seen as controversial by the Revenue and a special Revenue Unit in Sheffield has been set up to look into such schemes.

11.2 The basic structure of a composite company is one where there are multiple shareholders who often are not directors. A number of shareholders band together and form a composite company. Effectively, an administration company or the scheme's promoter will form the company, provide corporate director and company secretarial functions and prepare business accounts, board minutes, dividend vouchers, etc. The administration company will charge a fee on the basis of so much per worker per week.

11.3 The composite company is usually inserted between the worker and the agency. It is not uncommon for the composite companies and administration company to be set up by the agency. Composite companies appeal to workers who do not want the burden of running their own limited company.

11.4 Initially composite companies were promoted as being IR35 proof, on the basis that if each shareholder had less than 5% of the shares he would not have a material interest and hence would be outside of IR35. However, this was incorrect and 1.79–1.81 above deal with this aspect. It was also felt that if the composite company and the agency were working closely together (often with the administration company coordinating) then IR35 proof contracts could be readily agreed. Sometimes such contracts were shams. The administration company, whose role it was to offer tax advice, would often fail to get any form of contract signed between the agency and the composite company, or where the agency insisted on using its own contract it too would either remain unsigned or ignored. It seemed that so long as the administration company was making a profit by running composite companies little attention was being paid to IR35 or to other important and helpful 'in business' factors, such as insurances and invoicing.

11.5 The extent to which the upper contract, as between the agency and end-user, was taken into account was very limited. Although there are many arguments to justify little if any importance being placed on the upper contract, administration companies would often simply ignore what happened in reality, knowing that reality contradicted the terms of the composite/agency contract. This approach led to some composite companies gaining a reputation for, at best, a lack of care. Some went out of business.

11.6 However, many composite companies thrive. They are properly advised on IR35 issues and offer, to those who want an easy life, a valuable and workable alternative. The key to defeating IR35 is to understand the legislation and case law and to enter into a genuine contract that contains fundamentally anti-IR35 terms and conditions. Successful composite companies also exist in other sectors, such as construction and haulage.

11.7 Some administration companies offer an alternative to the traditional composite company structure—these are umbrella companies, where each worker has his own one-man limited company. The advantage of this structure is that the worker's 'identity' is not lost among numerous other shareholders, although it can be a slightly more expensive option than taking the composite route. Again, often insufficient attention is paid to agreeing and implementing anti-IR35 clauses and promoting other 'in business' traits.

11.8 As well as failing to understand and address IR35 properly those running composites and umbrellas often fail in other areas. The Revenue's Sheffield Unit is kept very busy investigating composites and umbrellas. The main problem areas are: incorrect payment of tax free expenses; incorrect application of the national minimum wage rules; a failure to understand that the composite/umbrella company may be itself acting as an agency (see Chapter 10); associated company problems and s 660A settlements complications.

Summary

11.9 Composite and umbrella structures can work to defeat IR35, but only if those running them understand and apply the law correctly. Contractors should choose very carefully.

CHAPTER 12

Analysing the early IR35 Commissioner's cases

IR35—the first cases

12.1 IR35 has been with us now for over four years and several have been heard by the Commissioners. The first two cases went in favour of the Revenue, the next two in favour of the taxpayer. More are in the pipeline.

Battersby v Campbell (2001) Special Commissioner Dr N Brice Ref SPC 189

12.2 The taxpayer was a computer analyst and programmer. In 1988 he established a limited company of which he and his wife were sole directors. In 1994 the company obtained a contract through an agency with a bank. In 1999 the bank consolidated all of its self-employed contractors through a limited company who then paid the contractors.

12.3 The agreement included the clear intention that this was not an employer/employee relationship. It also stated that the service company was responsible for all sickness, disability and pension arrangements; absence had to be notified to the bank in advance; responsibility for the quality, quantity and performance of the work rested with the bank; normal hours of work were seven hours a day, five days a week and that the taxpayer had to use the bank's mainframe computer system situated at the bank's premises. In April 2001 the taxpayer accepted a position with the bank as an employee.

12.4 The issue to be decided was whether the taxpayer would have been regarded as an employed earner if his contract had been with the bank and not with the service company. The relevant authorities had established the principle that the question of whether a person was employed under a contract of service or a contract for services was a question of fact. The factors pointing towards a contract of service were stronger than those pointing to a contract for services and, therefore, it was held that if the taxpayer's contract had been with the bank, he would have been regarded for the purposes of the 1992 Act as employed by the bank. IR35 applied.

12.5 The appellant defended himself in this case. That is he had no professional advocate speaking on his behalf. His defence was that it was common in the computer industry for enhancement work to be undertaken by self-employed contractors; he took the risks of a self-employed person; the bank could reduce his earnings without notice; his company was not part of an 'umbrella' company and that he was a director of his own company; and finally, that people who supplied their services through service companies were not 'tax fraudsters'.

12.6 In making her decision, Dr Brice, the presiding Special Commissioner, said that she had sympathy with Mr Battersby's assertions that he was not a tax fraudster but the fact that he was running his business correctly did not mean that the IR35 regulations did not apply.

12.7 Unfortunately, the rest of Mr Battersby's defence was not very strong. The appellant did not present any case law nor did he challenge any of the Revenue's case law. Although there were factors which indicated self-employment, in that he had the right to send a substitute, there was no control over the methods he used and there was a clear intention that it was a contract for services, these arguments were not put forward and, therefore, the Special Commissioner had to make a decision based on the facts and legal submissions presented.

F S Consulting v McCaul (Inspector of Taxes) (2002) Special Commissioner Dr N Brice SpC 138

12.8 The taxpayer S was a computer consultant conversion specialist and the sole director and shareholder of a limited company. The company and an agency T Ltd entered into a contract for the company to supply services to a client, B plc. S was the named consultant. A substitute could be proposed but B plc would have to approve the substitute. The contract could be terminated without notice on the grounds that S was incompetent or by T Ltd with four weeks' notice. Between April 2000 and June 2001 the taxpayer provided his services to his company who provided them to B plc. S worked in a project team of seven, five of whom were employees of B plc. S did not act as a team leader and could not decide which employees formed the project team. He could advise the employees but could not tell them what to do. His working hours were flexible and he recorded his time on a timesheet which had to be signed by a representative of B plc. S had to give notice and get permission for leave.

12.9 It was held that: (1) the phrase 'arrangements involving an intermediary' to be found in section 1 of the legislation was wide enough to include arrangements involving both an intermediary and a non-intermediary; the phrase was not 'arrangements with an intermediary' which would exclude arrangements with a non-intermediary; and (2) the principle had been established that the question of whether a person was employed under a contract of service or a contract for services was a question of fact, in each case to be determined having regard to all the relevant factors. In this case, the factors pointing towards a contract of service were stronger than those pointing to a contract for services. Focusing on the actual contractual arrangements rather than their form, had the arrangements taken the form of a contract between S and B plc, S would have been regarded as an employee of B plc.

12.10 In this case the appellant *was* represented. The arguments put forward were that firstly, according to the legislation, the end-user contract could not be taken into account; secondly, as the contract was between T Ltd and the company, S could not be held to be an employee of B plc because B plc paid T Ltd and not S or his company; and thirdly, that as T Ltd did not exercise supervision, direction or control over S, he could not be an employee of T Ltd.

12.11 The Special Commissioner dismissed the third argument on the basis that neither S nor T Ltd was making the appeal.

12.12 Dr Brice then decided that the legislation did allow her to take the end-user relationship into account and said that reference to arrangements involving 'an intermediary' was wide enough to include arrangements involving a 'non-intermediary'. It is thought that this is because Dr Brice's remarks have been misinterpreted (including by the author in the previous edition of this book).

One explanation is that reference had to be made to the non-intermediary, as a contract necessarily requires two parties, and one of those parties must be a non-intermediary. The personal service company (the intermediary) cannot contract with itself and so the arrangements with the non-intermediary have to be taken into account. Perhaps this is all Dr Brice was saying. She did not refer to arrangements with the client or deemed employer, and in fact, according to the judgment, she did not go on to consider the upper contract.

The relevance of the upper contract was also called into question in *Usetech Ltd v Young (HMIT)*—see later.

12.13 This case could arguably have been disputed more comprehensively. The Revenue relied to some extent on out of date case law, but this was not challenged. There were also factors pointing to this being a contract for services as neither B plc nor T Ltd had any right of control over the methods S used in doing the work, S had the right to send a substitute, albeit that this right was fettered by the need to get B plc's permission and there was a clear intention that this was to be a contract for services.

12.14 However, it appears from the published decision that, as none of these points were raised by S or his representative and the Revenue's arguments were not successfully refuted, the Special Commissioner had to make her decision based on the evidence and legal arguments presented.

Synaptek Ltd v Roe (2002) General Commissioners—unpublished decision (see also the High Court decision below)

12.15 The taxpayer was a computer consultant whose company, Synaptek Ltd, contracted with an agency, NESComputer Services, who in turn contracted with another agency, EDS, who contracted to supply services to the Benefits Agency. The taxpayer carried out all of the work at the Benefits Agency's premises. The taxpayer had made substantial investment into Synaptek Ltd, a substitute could be sent with the permission of EDS and Synaptek Ltd had undertaken other contracts concurrently. It was up to the taxpayer to decide on the methods used in carrying out the work.

12.16 It was held that if there had been a contract between the taxpayer and EDS it would have been a contract of service. IR35 applied.

12.17 Again in this case the taxpayer represented himself, being an ex-police officer he did have experience in court hearings. He produced good quality Bundles and gave his evidence clearly and well. Unfortunately, he relied too heavily on comments made by Burton J during *R (on the application of Professional Contractors Group Ltd and Others) v IRC* (2001) which, as they were not made in connection with the actual case in hand, do not form legal precedent. The taxpayer also produced a list of over 40 differences between himself and permanent employees of EDS.

12.18 Some of the case law relied upon by the Revenue was out of date. They argued that the taxpayer did not have to be in the same position as that of a normal employee but as he was in the same position of a temporary employee of EDS then IR35 applied. There were also some fundamental indicators that this was a contract for services, such as the right of substitution and lack of control.

12.19 It is interesting to note that in this case the Revenue did not argue that the 'end-user' (the Benefits Agency) was the client, which would seem to contradict their usual thinking on this matter. The case went on appeal to the High Court and again the Revenue succeeded.

12.20 However, it is worth remembering that, although previous Commissioners' decisions may be persuasive evidence in later cases, they do not form legal precedent and that these early cases are noteworthy for examples of lines of argument which are unlikely to persuade the Commissioners.

12.21 Accountax are very much of the opinion that a taxpayer with a case that is well presented, argued on the main legal principles of status and backed up with relevant case law need not be overly concerned with these outcomes.

G S Ltd v Gregory (2002) Special Commissioner Mr Sadler SpC—unpublished preliminary hearing

12.22 In August 2002 Accountax represented a design engineer contractor who had been subject to an IR35 enquiry.

At a preliminary hearing it was argued by Accountax that the section 8 Notice of Decision (NICIR35 assessment) should be discharged on the basis that it did not refer to a specific time period and was therefore invalid. The defect in the assessment could not be corrected under TMA 1970 s 114 on the Court of Appeal authority of *Baylis v Gregory* (1987). The Special Commissioner accepted the argument. If the Revenue wanted to pursue IR35 it would have to do so on the basis of correctly worded assessments. This technical victory appears to be the first win for a contractor at the Specials and should remind all practitioners to check assessments very carefully.

The name of G S Ltd is anonymised.

Synaptek Ltd v Young (Inspector of Taxes) [2003] EWHC 645 (Ch) [2003] STC 543

12.23 *Synaptek Ltd v Young* was heard on appeal in the High Court in February 2003. The appeal originated from a decision made by the General Commissioners.

12.24 Synaptek Ltd, a company which had traded since 1990, had contracted through an agency to perform IT services which were ultimately for the benefit of the Benefits Agency in Longbenton. In this case the chain consisted of Synaptek Ltd who contracted with NESCO (an agency) who in turn contracted with EDS who had a contract to supply services to the Benefits agency. It is interesting to note that the 'end-user' in this case was found to be EDS and not the Benefits agency.

12.25 Synaptek Ltd had many factors which pointed to it being 'in business on its own account' and had, in fact, won a small-business award. At the hearing the director represented the company himself and put forward evidence to show that the company was being run as a genuine business, that he was not controlled and that the company could send a substitute to do the work. However, the General Commissioners found that the particular contract in question, on balance, was caught by IR35.

12.26 The taxpayer appealed on the following grounds.

- That the fact that Synaptek was in business on its own account was a very strong indicator of the contract being one for services on the authority of *Davies (Inspector of Taxes) v Braithwaite* [1931] 2 KB 628 and that this factor had not been given sufficient weight by the General Commissioners.
- That the General Commissioners had misdirected themselves in law when they considered whether there was sufficient mutuality of obligation for a contract of service to exist.
- That there was a right of substitution and again the General Commissioners had misdirected themselves in law in not considering this to be incompatible with a contract of service.
- That the General Commissioners had misplaced reliance on the case of *F S Consulting Ltd v McCaul* [2002] STC (SCD) 138.

12.27 Mr Justice Hart decided that there was not sufficient reason to interfere in the decision made by the General Commissioners and dismissed the appeal. He had the following to say on the four pertinent points.

In business on own account

12.28 Mr Justice Hart did not see anything in the judgment of *Davies (Inspector of Taxes) v Braithwaite* which suggested that, where a person was in business on his or her own account, any contract entered into by them would automatically be a contract for services. Therefore, although it was an important contextual factor, it was up to the General Commissioners to assess how much weight should be attributed to it.

Mutuality of obligation

12.29 Although the appeal was not successful on these grounds some interesting points were brought out. Firstly, the Inland Revenue agreed that if there was no obligation on the agency to provide work for the entire period of the notional contract there was not sufficient mutuality of obligation for a contract of services to exist. This is a departure from their usual stance that there must simply be work and payment for mutuality to be present.

12.30 Secondly, the judge distinguished between mutuality beyond the contract and mutuality within it, making the point that when considering a particular contract one looks at whether there is mutuality of obligation for the duration of the contract and not simply whether there is an obligation to offer and accept work when the contract is over.

12.31 In the case of *Synaptek Ltd* there was a clause in the contract which stated that there was an obligation on the client to 'allocate work' to Synaptek for the duration of the contract. Mr Justice Hart felt that this, together with a four week notice period (which he argued would serve no purpose were mutuality of obligation not to be present), meant that there was sufficient mutuality of obligation.

Right of substitution

12.32 There was a clause in the contract with Synaptek Ltd which stated that:

> 'In the interests of continuity the Company shall use its best endeavours to procure that the Services are provided by the Company Employee personally but may with the consent of the Client substitute alternative personnel subject to procuring that such alternative personnel are bound by the terms of this agreement'.

It was argued on behalf of the taxpayer that this gave Synaptek Ltd the right to send a substitute which would, in itself, mean that the contract was outside of IR35.

12.33 Mr Justice Hart considered the clause together with the authority in *Express and Echo Publications Ltd v Tanton* [1999] IRLR 367, which is the leading pronouncement on substitution and concluded that:

> 'In the present case the provision in question (cl 9A of the NESCO agreement) does not give Synaptek any *right* to perform the services by anyone other than Mr Stutchbury. The effect of the contract is that, unless and until agreed otherwise, the services do have to be performed personally by Mr Stutchbury'.

Essentially this means that the clause amounted to a limited right of delegation more akin to that in *McFarlane v Glasgow City Council* [2001] IRLR 7. Therefore, it was for the General Commissioners to decide how much weight to attach to this factor.

Misplaced reliance on F S Consulting Ltd v McCaul [2002] STC (SCD) 138

12.34 It was argued on behalf of the appellant that the General Commissioners had placed too much reliance on the case of *F S Consulting Ltd v McCaul* and had therefore misdirected themselves.

12.35 In the stated case the General Commissioners did make the point that the facts in the case bore 'a close similarity' to *F S Consulting Ltd v McCaul* and that the legal principles in that case were a useful guide in deciding *Synaptek*.

12.36 It was argued on behalf of the appellant that the facts of the present case were substantially different and it was therefore a misdirection to apply the principles as set out in *F S Consulting Ltd v McCaul*.

12.37 Mr Justice Hart concluded that the General Commissioners had not misdirected themselves and had not placed too much reliance on *F S Consulting*. He said that had the stated case suggested that the General Commissioners believed the facts of *Synaptek* to be indistinguishable from those in *F S Consulting*, there may well have been a powerful argument for saying that the Commissioners had misdirected themselves, but that this argument did not have the same force where, as was the case here, the Commissioners had merely referred to a 'close similarity' in the facts of the two cases.

12.38 The Revenue has taken the view that this case weakens the substitution argument in IR35 and, following the case, have started to suggest that, for IR35 purposes, a right of substitution can only be of more weight than the other factors where it is in fact utilised. However, it is worth remembering that Mr Justice Hart said that the clause in the contract did not actually equate to a true right of substitution and it was this that made it possible for the General Commissioners to regard it as simply one of many factors to be considered. It should also be noted that, in the stated case, the General Commissioners themselves stated that the clause was a strong indication of self-employment.

12.39 The Revenue has also taken the view that, following this case, any contract which has a termination period must have the pre-requisite amount of mutuality of obligation. There is a certain amount of logic to this argument and it seems fair that where there is a significant period of notice, any argument that there is a total lack of mutuality of obligation would be weakened. It should be noted, however, that the Revenue has been very slow to acknowledge the fact that their barrister conceded that there had to be an obligation to offer work for the entire period of the notional contract for mutuality of obligation to exist, not merely work which is done for payment.

12.40 One final point regarding this case was that it raised awareness of a very fundamental difference between the General Commissioners and the Special Commissioners. When the Special Commissioners give their decision they are required under SI 1994/1811 reg 18 to provide a statement of facts found and the reasons for the determination. The General Commissioners, on the other hand, merely have to give a decision. This makes it much harder to try and show that they have misdirected themselves, especially in an area as grey as IR35.

12.41 It should also be noted that, as in *Battersby v Campbell* [2001] STC (SCD) 189, the director of Synaptek Ltd represented the company at the initial appeal. This would seem to suggest that professional representation is valuable from the outset in these cases as it is the Commissioners who find the facts and make the decision, the higher courts can merely review the decision.

Lime-IT Ltd v Justin (Officer of the Board of Inland Revenue) [2002] Special Commissioner Dr John F Avery Jones CBE SpC 342

12.42 Accountax represented the taxpayer in this case and it was the first IR35 case to be won by the taxpayer at the Special Commissioners.

12.43 F was the sole shareholder and director of L Ltd, an information technology company, formed on 4 April 2000. On 17 April 2000 L Ltd entered into a contract with an agency, E, to provide IT services to M Ltd, the end-user. The contract was for the provision of specific projects, such as introducing a new e-mail system, organising remote access, etc, and had an estimated completion date of 10 April 2001. It was estimated that L Ltd would need to provide a consultant for around 37 hours per week in order to complete the services on time; however, the hours actually worked varied considerably from this. The terms of the contract allowed for L Ltd to send a substitute consultant. This clause was specifically negotiated by F so that should she wish to work on other contracts she could. The clause did allow for M Ltd to reject the substitute but only on reasonable grounds. The agreement between E and M Ltd was drawn up to reflect the terms of the agreement between L Ltd and E. During the term of the contract to provide services to M Ltd, L Ltd provided services to four other clients. The services were carried out from one of M Ltd's offices and partly from F's home, where she had an office containing four computers dedicated to the business of L Ltd.

12.44 The Revenue was of the opinion that IR35 applied and accordingly raised a formal decision which was appealed by the taxpayer. The standard IR35 issue under appeal was whether, had the arrangements in the instant case taken the form of a contract between F and M Ltd, she would be regarded as employed under a contract of service.

12.45 It was held that: the basic test of whether someone was employed or self-employed was to ask whether a person was 'in business on his own account' and three conditions had to be satisfied in order for a contract of service to exist. First, the servant must have agreed that in consideration of a wage or other remuneration he would provide his own work and skill in the performance of some service for his master. Second, the servant must have agreed, expressly or impliedly, that in the performance of that service he would be subject to the other's control in a sufficient degree to make that other master. Third, the other provisions of the contract must be consistent with its being a contract of service. In the instant case, there was very little evidence to suggest an employment relationship. In essence M Ltd was contracting for a particular IT job from a small business in the way one would expect an IT consultant to be engaged. Accordingly, on the hypothesis that F had contracted directly with M Ltd, she would not have been employed under a contract of service; she would have been in business on her own account and IR35 did not apply.

12.46 Obtaining evidence from the end-user is something the Revenue has always been keen to do, but it is believed that it is only necessary if the terms of the contract are varied from the day to day arrangements. In this particular case there was no evidence from the end-user, and the Special Commissioner, Dr Avery Jones, said 'in future cases on this legislation (and its income tax equivalent) the Special Commissioners will wish to explore at a preliminary hearing whether it is possible to obtain evidence from the client'. The Revenue has interpreted this to mean that they must obtain evidence from the end-user in every IR35 case before they can give an opinion. This is clearly not what Dr Avery Jones said.

12.47 There were several factors in this case which pointed to F being in business on her own account. She had a dedicated office containing four computers which were used specifically for the services provided to M Ltd. L Ltd advertised its services via its website and undertook four other contracts during the M Ltd contract. Travel between M Ltd's sites was at the expense of the appellant. In this case these factors were important in helping the Special Commissioner reach his decision.

12.48 There was no control by M Ltd as to the manner in which F carried out her activities. While this was accepted by the Special Commissioner, he agreed with Mr Williams' (brought in from the London Regional Advocacy Unit to represent the Revenue) contention that 'control may not be particularly important when dealing with an expert'.

12.49 While the Special Commissioner did not see liability insurance as a particularly important factor he did highlight the financial risk resulting from invoicing as a pointer towards self-employment. He said 'the fact of invoicing and the 30 day (or even 10 day, if that is what was subsequently agreed) terms for payment, even ignoring the actual delays in payment, seem to me to point towards self-employment'. Unfortunately, the Revenue still fail to accept this argument.

12.50 The Revenue tried to play down the fact that F supplied her own equipment as she was not contractually obliged to do so and even suggested that the desk and telephone provided by M Ltd were slight pointers towards employment. Of this Dr Avery Jones said 'an employee does not normally provide a laptop but a self-employed person may do so if it makes the work easier to do, regardless of any contractual requirement. I do not regard the provision of a desk and telephone at M Ltd as particularly significant'.

12.51 F had specifically negotiated a substitution clause in the contract between L Ltd and E and even though this right had never been exercised, Dr Avery Jones said that 'it is a strong indicator of self-employment' and then went on to quote Lord Justice Peter Gibson in the 1999 Court of Appeal case, *Express and Echo Publications Ltd v Tanton.*

12.52 The contract stated that F was obliged to work a 37 hour week and it was the Revenue's argument that this obligation was the same as any employee of M Ltd. In reality F worked varied hours and Dr Avery Jones said 'the variations in the number of hours actually worked is more indicative of self-employment'. He went on to say, in situations such as this where what happens in reality differs from the contractual terms, one should look beyond the terms of the contract.

12.53 It is also worth pointing out that at the beginning of the hearing the inspector who had been handling the case handed over a two page written apology saying that he was not happy with the way he had handled the case and with the guidance currently available he would have tackled the situation differently. Although the handling of the case is not relevant to the appeal and has no influence on the decision, it does reflect badly on the Revenue. The taxpayer has received financial compensation from the Revenue in this case.

12.54 *Lime-IT* remains an important IR35 case. For the first time the taxpayer was represented by specialists, and in his judgment Dr Avery Jones made it clear that taking an overview there was 'very little to suggest an employment relationship'.

12.55 Regrettably, the Revenue has continued to make formal decisions and force the inconvenience and expense of a contentious appeal on taxpayers when the Revenue's case is, at best, weak.

12.56 When faced with a high profile Commissioners hearing many taxpayers back down and there is evidence, both empirical and anecdotal, that the Revenue play on this. *Lime-IT Ltd v Justin* stopped the rot and reversed the trend.

Tilbury Consulting Ltd v Margaret Gittins (2003)

12.57 *Tilbury Consulting Ltd v Margaret Gittins* was heard in October 2003 and was the fourth IR35 case to be heard at the Special Commissioners. Accountax represented the taxpayer. A preliminary point was heard by Dr Nuala Brice and the substantive issue was heard by His Honour Stephen Oliver QC.

The background

12.58 This case originated from request by the director of Tilbury Consulting Limited for an opinion on his contract from the Revenue. Mr Tilbury sent in copies of his contract and explained that Ford had outsourced part of its IT function to an agency. It was with this agency that Tilbury Consulting Limited had contracted. The local tax office replied explaining that they would need to ask Ford some questions before they gave an opinion and Mr Tilbury gave his permission for it to do this.

12.59 The answers to these questions showed that there was no control by Ford over how the work was done and that they would accept a substitute but only via the agency, because this is where their contract actually lay. There was a corresponding clause in the contract between Tilbury Consulting Limited and the agency which allowed a substitute to be sent by Tilbury Consulting Limited.

12.60 The Inspector, Mrs Gittins, then issued the opinion that this contract did indeed fall within the IR35 legislation and that, in effect, Mr Tilbury was a disguised employee of Ford. The taxpayer was told that he could either accept this opinion, reject it or request a formal decision against which he could appeal.

12.61 In the meantime the Inspector wrote again to Ford, without informing the director that she was doing so, and challenged some of the information provided in the initial responses. The response she received backed up the original statements.

12.62 The director decided that he wanted some certainty and asked for a formal notice of decision to allow him to appeal. This was issued and an appeal was made with an election that the appeal be heard by the Special Commissioners.

The preliminary issue

12.63 A preliminary hearing was held in this case to decide whether the Revenue should be allowed to summons the person at Ford, who had already answered two sets of questions, to give evidence at the substantive hearing.

12.64 The application for a witness summons is usually ex-parte, which means that the other side do not have the right to make representations. However, in this case the taxpayer was permitted to make representations.

12.65 The taxpayer objected on two grounds. Firstly, that the Revenue had already obtained sufficient evidence, and secondly, that by forcing a witness to attend, the Revenue was jeopardising the delicate commercial relationship between the company and Ford. The Revenue argued that having the witness at the hearing meant that the Special Commissioner could ask questions to obtain the facts.

12.66 The Special Commissioner considered both arguments and decided that, in the interests of natural justice, the Revenue should be allowed to call the witness. It is interesting to note that, having gone through this process, the Revenue subsequently decided to call two different people as witnesses.

12.67 Unusually for a preliminary hearing, the judgment was published, as it was felt that this was an area where guidance would be helpful. It is important to remember, however, that the guidance provided was in connection with the calling of witnesses at an appeal hearing and not, as the Revenue has subsequently tried to claim, that in an IR35 case the Inspector should be allowed to interview the end client.

The substantive appeal

12.68 The main arguments for the appellant (Tilbury Consulting Limited) were that there was a right of substitution which flowed through the chain of contracts, there was a lack of control over the manner in which the services were provided, there was an element of financial risk from invoicing and an instance of an invoice which was paid late and there were many differences between Mr Tilbury and an employee of Ford.

12.69 The Revenue was represented by one of the Inspectors from the new Regional Appeals Units. These are an extension of the London Appeals Unit (which represented the Revenue in *Lime-IT v Justin*) and are made up of Inspectors who have been specifically trained to take cases to the Commissioners. The appellant was represented by Accountax.

Construction of the contract

12.70 The Revenue argued that the first step in establishing whether IR35 applied was to assume that Ford had taken Mr Tilbury on directly. The second step would be to establish what the terms would have been had they done this. This meant that they could ignore the terms in the written contracts and the day to day arrangements and construct a completely new hypothetical contract.

12.71 The Revenue's argument, that one starts with the assumption that the worker is taken on directly and then works out what the contract terms would have been, may seem untenable on first hearing but looking at the legislation, which has long been felt to be badly worked, it is actually perfectly possible. FA 2000 Sch 12 says that IR35 will apply where there is personal service and:

> '(b) The services are provided not under a contract directly between the client and the worker but under arrangements involving a third party ('the intermediary'), and

(c) the circumstances are such that, if the services were provided under a contract directly between the client and the worker, the worker would be regarded for income tax purposes as an employee of the client'.

12.72 It had always been assumed by those in practice that this meant one had a look at the terms that were actually in place at the time and then remove the intermediary (service company) and possibly the agency. This creates a hypothetical contract but the terms of that contract are the real terms that were in place.

12.73 Looking at the legislation it is possible to see how the Revenue had come to its opinion. However, had the Revenue been correct it would make it almost impossible for anyone to decide whether they were outside of IR35 or not.

12.74 Fortunately, the impossible situation that this would place taxpayers in was not lost on His Honour Stephen Oliver QC the Presiding Special Commissioner. During the hearing he remarked that this interpretation would lead to a 'sea of unreality' where the Revenue could invent terms which supported an employer/employee relationship.

12.75 This comment did not make it into the judgment, but Mr Oliver has made his view very clear by stating that the legislation calls for a two stage exercise:

1 find the facts as they existed during the period covered by the decision; and
2 then assume that the worker was contracted to perform services to the client and to determine whether *in light of the facts found* the worker would be regarded as an employee of the client.

In other words, the hypothesis of IR35 is to place the worker in the shoes of the intermediary; it is not to invent a whole new set of terms and conditions. The author has maintained this is the correct approach since 2000 when the legislation was passed—and this has now been judicially confirmed.

Substitution

12.76 The Revenue put forward two arguments as to why substitution was not effective in this case. The first was that Ford would only accept a substitute from the agency and not directly from Tilbury Consulting Limited and therefore, as it was the hypothetical relationship between Tilbury Consulting and Ford that one was concerned with, there was no right of substitution in that relationship. The Inspector claimed repeatedly that Ford were only interested in the personal service of Mr Tilbury.

12.77 However, under cross-examination, the Revenue's witness from Ford agreed that so long as the work was done, Ford did not mind whether it was done by 'Tom, Dick or Harry'.

12.78 This case also provided the Revenue with an opportunity to test their new theory on substitution and IR35, which has been borne out of the decision in *Synaptek Ltd v Young* [2003] STC 543. The Revenue interpretation of this case is that, where there is a qualified right of substitution in an IR35 case but this right is not exercised, it is not the knockout blow that it would usually be but it is simply one of the factors to be considered.

12.79 Both of these arguments would seem to have been rejected by the Special Commissioner who found as a fact that Tilbury Consulting Limited could send a substitute to the agency and that the agency could send a substitute to Ford. This fact was then among the most important in his conclusion which he found to be inconsistent with an employment relationship.

Other factors

12.80 There were other factors which were put forward by both sides, including the fact that the director's pass was a different colour to that of an employee and that he was unable to use the staff gymnasium.

12.81 The Revenue also brought out evidence that had he fallen ill whilst on Ford's premises, the director would have received first aid from the Ford medical team, as would any employee of Ford. However, it was brought out in evidence that this would have been the case had the director simply been a visitor to the offices and therefore this point seemed of limited value to the argument.

12.82 The issue of mutuality of obligation was brought up but was not part of the main argument for either side. It is worth mentioning, however, that when the case of *Montogmery v Johnson Underwood Ltd* [2001] EWCA Civ 318 was referred to by the appellant's advocate, the Inspector dismissed the whole case on the grounds that the judges in the Court of Appeal had clearly got mutuality of obligation wrong and had been confused about the points made in *Ready Mixed Concrete (South East) Ltd v Minister of Pensions and National Insurance* [1968] 2 QB 497. This argument did not seem to carry much weight with the Special Commissioner.

The judgment

12.83 It is hard to see from the judgment how much weight has been attributed to these various minor factors, because with this judgment there was a shift away from the 'picture painting' balancing exercise favoured by the Revenue and a return to the purist approach which asks whether any of the terms are fundamentally inconsistent with a contract of employment. This is one of the most important features of this case.

12.84 In these situations, if it were simply a matter of weighing up the number of factors for and the number against, the contractor will often lose. However, the return to the principles as outlined in the *Ready Mixed Concrete* case, that for there to be a contract of employment there must be an irreducible minimum, means that far more contracts would be found to be outside of IR35.

The Revenue's view

12.85 The Revenue has largely sought to disregard this decision for various reasons.

12.86 One of the problems that they had at the appeal was that it quickly became apparent that the agency in this case were not merely supplying bodies but had actually taken over part of Ford's IT function and had project management responsibilities. Essentially this meant that in making their decision the Revenue had arguably picked the wrong 'client'.

12.87 This is borne out by the judgment, and early indications are that the Revenue will claim that this was a simple case of mistaken identity and, therefore, the case has very little to add to the question of IR35.

12.88 However, this is clearly not the case. The fact that the wrong client was picked is part of the reason why the appeal succeeded, in so far as it meant that Ford did not have the necessary control over Mr Tilbury. This in itself is a very important point as it reinforces the argument that, even in IR35 situations, there must be the required control present in order for the relationship to be caught.

12.89 The judgment also points to substitution being a factor 'inconsistent with an employer/employee relationship'. This has nothing to do with who was selected as the client but is a fundamental point in status law and it is pleasing to see it reaffirmed.

12.90 It should be noted that when the issue of who was client was raised at the hearing the Revenue admitted that, knowing what they knew now, perhaps the wrong party had been selected. The Inspector then went on to say that had the client cooperated more and allowed the Revenue access to the end-use, this mistake could have been avoided.

12.91 During the hearing the Inspector suggested that the taxpayer had somehow misled the Revenue as to the identity of the end-user and therefore contributed to the mistake. However, the appellant's advisors pointed out that in one of the very early letters to the Inspector, the representatives of the appellant explained that the function had been outsourced to the agency. As such the Special Commissioner saw little in the Revenue's arguments and they were rejected.

12.92 *Tilbury* is an important IR35 case. It re-emphasised the fundamental approach to status issues and exposed the weakness of several of the Revenue's interpretations of the legislation.

Future Online v S K Faulds (Inspector of Taxes) (2004) Special Commissioner His Honour Stephen Oliver QC SpC 406

12.93 In this case the taxpayer was represented by JSA Services Ltd a well known firm in the contracting world. The Revneue was represented by the Regional Appeal Unit.

12.94 R was a joint shareholder and director of FOL, a company which provided computer consultancy services. From July 2000 through until the end of May 2003 FOL had a contract with ECL (agency) to provide services to EDS. The job had been advertised on the internet and R sent his details. He was contacted by ECL and attended an interview the next day with an EDS contractor where he was offered a contract.

12.95 EDS had an agreement with the Department of Work and Pensions (DWP) to install the Child Support Reform (CSR) programme.

12.96 The contract between FOL and ECL was to provide the services of R (or such other consultant of FOL that FOL may provide in accordance with a 'substitution' clause at 1.4) to EDS and was initially for three months.

12.97 Clause 1.4 of the FOL/ECL contract allowed FOL to provide a substitute consultant with the written consent of EDS. Hours worked in excess of 37.5 per week were to be agreed in advance by EDS. There was a four week notice period on the contract between FOL and ECL.

12.98 The agreement between ECL and EDS was in the form of a Purchase Order issued by EDS which set out the relevant details, eg payment, job description, location, duration, line of reporting, etc. It also made it clear that ECL undertook to require that the contractor to 'comply with any reasonable terms and conditions specified in relation to any particular purchase order'.

12.99 The Purchase Order dated 21 July 2000 was for the 'Professional services of R to work as a systems engineer' and the purchase order dated 12 December 2000 was for the 'Professional services of R to act as a systems test team leader based at EDS Longbenton'. It also stated that 'any hours worked over the standard 7.5 hours a day must be with the prior agreement and authorisation of the EDS project manager' and that 'all work to be carried out in accordance with the instructions from Simon Young or nominee'. Later Purchase Orders contained the same requirements, although the Purchase Order dated 5 June 2001 differed slightly in that the services were described as 'Build Manager'.

12.100 After a few weeks R was 'promoted' (to use his own words) to 'Build Manager', with responsibility for a specific phase of the project for which R was given no specific guidance as to the carrying out of the work.

12.101 R assembled a team and interviewed some 160 staff members on behalf of EDS. R allocated work between team members and ensured the objectives were met.

12.102 R was part of the organisational structure of EDS and His Honour Stephen Oliver QC was satisfied that throughout the period that R worked for EDS, he was part and parcel of the organisation.

12.103 The EDS project line manager allocated work to R and his team following meetings. R attended weekly meetings to report on progress and each night and each morning R reported to the EDS programme manager.

12.104 It was argued on behalf of R that the agreement/purchase orders between ECL and EDS were nothing to do with him as he was not party to them. It was also argued that, despite the contract between FOL and ECL requiring authorisation to work more than 37.5 hours a week, R regularly did so without prior authorisation. The Special Commissioner accepted that while there was a strict legal obligation on R to obtain prior approval, it was not EDS's practice to require this of him and that had EDS wished to insist on the strict position, they could have done so but on giving reasonable notice to R.

12.105 R did carry out some of the work from his home using his own laptop and 'remote access' to the EDS local network. R understood he was the only person on the CSR project to have remote access from home.

12.106 The Special Commissioner said that neither R nor FOL had any *right* to send a substitute, all they could do was offer, but EDS was not obliged to accept. The purchase orders from EDS specifically requested the services of R and, as EDS had to give written consent for FOL to send a substitute, it was fairly clear that personal services was required.

12.107 His Honour Stephen Oliver QC accepted that R had a large measure of control over how he conducted the testing procedure; but there was a Test Manager with overall direction and responsibility for testing procedures. That is, there was a right of control. He found that in law, although not in practice, there was control over the work, as the purchase order required R to carry out work in accordance with instructions. It was also in the FOL/ECL agreement that R had to obtain permission to work additional hours and that R was required to adhere to EDS's rules and regulations.

12.108 It was also found that, although R's work involved an especially high level of skill and independence of judgment, EDS were able to control how the work was to be done through their organisational structure. It was the Special Commissioners conclusion that there was sufficient control to make EDS 'master' and that had there been a contract between R and EDS the contract would have been one of service.

12.109 It was argued by Mr Allen that the actual obligations between EDS and R were so limited that they fell short of the 'irreducible minimum of obligation on each side' required to create a contract of service. His Honour Stephen Oliver QC referred to *Nethermere (St Neots) Ltd v Gardiner* [1984] ICR 612; however, I do not believe he has followed that slavish approach. He found in this case that, until termination of the agreement by EDS, there was an obligation to EDS to provide paid work at a place of work and corresponding obligation on EDS for the provision of R's services to the end-user. That, coupled with R's obligation to conform with EDS's rules and working practices, was enough to show that mutuality of obligations did exist between R and EDS and that they were well above the irreducible minimum. He found that there was an obligation on EDS to provide work; there was an obligation on R to provide his services personally and that there was an obligation on R to conform with EDS's rules and working practices; therefore, there was mutuality of obligations. He has not given a specific definition of what mutuality of obligations is, he has just said that because these factors were present there was mutuality of obligations sufficient to create a contract of service.

12.110 On the facts there seems little if any doubt that not only was this the right decision but all Special Commissioners hearing the case would very likely come to the same conclusion. R was in effect a manager at EDS with few real trappings of self-employment. The author has been advised, unofficially, that an appeal to the High Court is being seriously considered.

12.111 This case illustrates the importance of considering how a contractor acts in practice as well as what his contract says. There was nothing in his contract saying he would recruit 160 people on behalf of EDS yet this is what happened in reality. Accountax reviewed this file a year ago and suggested the contractor was caught by IR35. I regret to note that we were correct.

The London Region Advocacy Unit

12.112 Finally, it is worth mentioning a department in the Inland Revenue called the London Region Advocacy Unit. This department has been set up specifically to take appeals to the Special Commissioners, although they will take some General Commissioners cases, and is based in London. At the time of writing it is staffed by only two Inspectors, who are both experienced in Commissioners' cases. They have been involved in four of the above IR35 cases, but it is worth remembering that they have also lost other cases on non-IR35 matters.

12.113 Readers who have had cases referred to the London Region Advocacy Unit need not be overly concerned but should as a precautionary measure take specialist tax consultancy advice. A number of Regional Advocacy Units have now been set up and increasingly they are taking IR35 appeals forward. The London Unit seems to be taking fewer IR35 cases than in the past.

Summary

12.114 After a disappointing start in *Battersby v Campbell* and *F S Consulting v McCaul* the taxpayer scored two important victories in *Lime-IT v Justin* and *Tilbury Consulting v Gittins. Synaptek* remains the only IR35 case to have reached the High Court and was useful in developing some aspects of IR35, in particularly mutuality of obligations. More recently the *Usetech* appeal failed but is to be appealed to the High Court, and the decision in *Ansell* is at the Special Commissioners awaited. These decisions show that IR35 appeals can and do succeed but nothing can be taken for granted.

CHAPTER 13

Should a Revenue contract review be requested?

13.1 In its press release of February 2000 the Revenue announced that it was offering a service to taxpayers whereby they could obtain a formal Revenue review of the IR35 status of their contract. The Revenue stated that it would reply within 28 days and would give an opinion as to whether the contract was caught by, or escaped from, IR35. The Revenue has assured the taxpaying public time and again that they are not attempting to impose any particular status and will offer a contract review in a neutral customer service led manner. Practitioners' experience and certainly those of the author do not bear this out.

13.2 Under this service, the Revenue undertakes to review signed contracts only, rather than hypothetical drafts (but it is noted that it will be happy to consider hypothetical contracts when it comes to enforcing IR35). Contracts should be submitted to a central Revenue IR35 Unit (LP10, IR35 Unit—first floor, Tyne Bridge Tower, Church Street, Gateshead, Tyne & Wear, NE8 2DT) or by e-mail to IR35@inlandrevenue.gov.uk.

13.3 This service remains available for those who wish to use it, but would it be wise? The first published figures (June 2000) from the Revenue show that 53% of the contracts supplied were within IR35 and the balance were not. To some extent this has removed some of the fears within the industry that the Revenue would automatically apply IR35 to as many contracts as possible. The author's latest information is that the Revenue is now 'passing' around only 40% of contracts. This seems low. Not only are contracts becoming more IR35-proof as time goes by, contracts reviewed by Accountax enjoy a pass rate of around 65%. The gap between 40% and 65% causes concern. In common with many other advisers, the author's view is that there is little point in sending a contract to the Revenue for review for several reasons.

13.4 IR35 was introduced as a financial expedient by the Treasury; it is estimated that almost half a billion pounds will be raised through extra tax and national insurance once IR35 takes effect. It seems at least questionable whether the Revenue will be entirely neutral or objective in implementing this review service as they have much to gain from IR35. While this may seem a little cynical, evidence, both anecdotal and actual, bears out this concern. Many practitioners will readily recall the Revenue's and Contribution Agency's attack on self-employment in the construction industry during the late 1990s. This was rarely conducted in a true spirit of neutral fact finding and application of the correct law. Several websites contain examples of contracts submitted to the Revenue for review which resulted in something of a knee-jerk reaction, with the Revenue stating the contracts were caught by IR35. When challenged with robust argument the Revenue has changed its mind on many of these initial judgments. It should be noted, however, that had the taxpayer accepted the initial judgment then the Revenue would have been happy to have treated the contract as caught by the legislation. This is disturbing.

13.5 Submitting a contract to the Revenue for its opinion arguably sends a message of weakness. Unwittingly the message may be interpreted as a lack of conviction and such a course of action could be interpreted as showing a lack of real confidence or certainty in the case.

13.6 The Revenue has failed time and again to turn contract reviews around within its published 28-day target. Accountax dealt with one particular case where the client submitted a contract to the Revenue for review in March 2000 but did not receive an initial response until September 2000. In this case the Revenue could not meet a 28 week target let alone 28 days and in the meantime the client felt that she was left in limbo and in a very invidious position. Without any explanation the same client then received a second opinion from a quite different tax office, leaving her with the belief that the Revenue's contract review service was a farce, with the left hand not knowing what the right hand was doing.

13.7 There are undoubtedly highly skilled technical experts within the Revenue and former Contributions Agency, who have a valuable role to play in respect of tax status generally and IR35 in particular. However, the reality is that the overwhelming majority of contract reviews are carried out at district level by local status inspectors and their Employer Compliance teams who may not necessarily share the same depth of technical understanding as their head office colleagues. This leads to Revenue opinions often based on a misunderstanding of case law and often in ignorance of the more recent legal precedents. The Revenue's internal guidance is still selective in respect of the case law it cites, with several important cases from the last five years having been omitted completely. This results in superficial decisions that are often based on an outdated interpretation of the law. The author has received many comments from inspectors around the country who claim they have not received proper support and training in the more technical aspects of status. It is also commonly accepted that the Revenue publication IR175 fails to explain the correct criteria which determines whether IR35 applies. Indeed one tax inspector recently commented to the author that

IR35 was unfair to the Revenue! This is, he said, because well-briefed practitioners have all the up-to-date case law and specialist advice at their fingertips and have the technical advantage over the Revenue foot soldiers who have been burdened with IR35. The inspector concerned has been supplied with a free copy of this book. He has confirmed in writing that it is very useful and helpful.

13.8 The standard of contract reviews is also extremely variable across the country. When giving evidence in the judicial review case brought by the Professional Contractors Group in March 2001 (*R (on the application of the PCG) v IRC*, see Appendix 6), the PCG's leading barrister Geoffrey Barling QC, in open court, pointed out that two Revenue offices in different parts of the country had reviewed an identical contract but had come to opposite conclusions as to whether the contract was caught by IR35. This might suggest to some that the fate of a contract review will be determined by which inspector happens to be given the file in which particular tax office, and this cannot be satisfactory. Indeed, Mr Justice Burton in the High Court found such inconsistencies to be 'deeply alarming', although some inconsistency is probably inevitable in the real world.

13.9 The Revenue's standard contract review report letter is written in a stencilled format, whereby it is *already assumed* that certain direct employment factors have been established. A note at the end of the relevant instruction reminds inspectors to send such a standard letter only if it actually fits the facts! There are instances of so called contract reviews where the Revenue has not read the contracts properly, their response letters referring to clauses in the contracts which do not exist. Sham contract reviews are no better than sham contracts.

13.10 Incidentally, it has been suggested that the Revenue selects cases for compliance reviews because contracts have been submitted to them for their opinion. The Revenue has categorically stated that this is not the case (see Frequently Asked Questions, compliance, 2, on their website at http://www.inlandrevenue.gov.uk/ir35). It might seem too obvious to state that a contract submitted for a Revenue review which is deemed to be caught by IR35 leads inevitably from a contract review to an IR35 compliance investigation. This is happening more and more. When this happens it is of course open to the taxpayer to inform the Revenue that he no longer wants a Revenue opinion and that he will complete form P35 as he sees fit. The Revenue has now confirmed, in writing, that where a contract review is requested by the taxpayer then if the Revenue's 'caught' opinion is not accepted and the filing date for completion of form P35 passes, the Revenue will treat the matter as a compliance issue. In other words an innocent customer service contract review will transform into an enquiry. This is a very disturbing development.

It can clearly be seen that there are many disadvantages both practical and technical, in submitting a contract for a Revenue IR35 review. The consensus is to avoid contract reviews.

13.11 As stated above, the Revenue's contract review system is still in place and following submission of the contract and any supporting background information the Revenue will offer an opinion. On the basis that the Revenue's opinion is accepted, that is the end of the matter. The Revenue's standard letter offers the applicant an opportunity to disagree with its opinion, whereby the taxpayer is invited to submit further information or arguments in support of his claim that the contract falls outside IR35. This further information may convince the Revenue to change its mind, but if a stalemate is reached then, subject to one important exception, the Revenue will issue a formal decision stating that the contract is caught by IR35. Again, there will be an opportunity to try to convince the inspector to change his mind through technical correspondence but it is unlikely that he will do so at this stage.

13.12 If the practitioner is determined to continue disputing the Revenue's view it will be necessary to obtain from the inspector a Section 8 Notice of Assessment. This will give a formal charge to national insurance, effectively stating that the contractor is caught by IR35, against which an appeal can be made. This appeal can then be taken to the Commissioners for a contentious hearing and this is dealt with in Chapters 16–19.

13.13 The one exception mentioned above is the quite bizarre situation where the Revenue may request specific additional information from the taxpayer which he cannot obtain. Typically this is found in the classic personal service business/agency/end-user chain where the inspector wishes to see the contract between the agency and the end-user. Much more often than not the personal service business will not have access to, nor will it be able to obtain this contract. After all it contains confidential commercial information between other third parties.

In these circumstances inspectors have refused to give a formal decision, leaving the taxpayer in a quite unsatisfactory position. In one case dealt with by Accountax not only did the inspector refuse to make a formal decision, he went so far as to withdraw his earlier informal opinion. It is understood that head office advice is that a formal decision should not be given unless the inspector has seen all contracts in the chain. However, there is evidence that at district level status inspectors are prepared to make a decision on the information placed before them. See 9.1. The mechanics of obtaining a formal decision are also considered in Chapter 17 below.

13.14 It should be noted that, where a Revenue opinion on a contract is sought, due pressure should be kept on the Revenue should it fail to comply with its published target of 28 days for the review turnaround. The average overworked status inspector, who may not particularly enjoy IR35 work will be happy to let a contract review dispute drag on until such time as he has the time and resources to address the case. As a strategic consideration, wherever possible it is wise to make the Revenue work to the contractor's timetable, or at least to its own published targets. There is an element of 'he who shouts loudest' here and, as with construction industry status disputes in the late 1990s, there will many a case won by the simple expedient of continuing to put the inspector under pressure to account for his actions and opinions.

In short, and as discussed elsewhere in this book, the name of the game is to avoid a drawn out dispute with the Revenue. If by pushing and probing, the inspector drops the case then the client has been represented well.

13.15 It is necessary to read critically the actual wording of a Revenue opinion. In a case Accountax dealt with in Spring 2001 the inspector said that having reviewed the contract and surrounding background information the whole picture 'suggested' the client escaped IR35. Experienced practitioners will at once spot the danger. Use of the word 'suggested' rather than something less equivocal perhaps leaves the door open for a Revenue challenge by a different inspector or a change of mind by the first. This woolly wording leaves the client in a very difficult position.

On speaking to the inspector on the telephone it was immediately acknowledged that the wording from the client's point of view would be unsatisfactory but that the letter was written on the basis of standard wording encouraged by head office. It was agreed that a further exchange of correspondence would be necessary to clarify that, in the inspector's opinion, the IR35 legislation did not apply. This exchange of correspondence was swiftly carried out and the client now has a much more satisfactory and straightforward letter saying she escapes IR35.

There is an important lesson to be learnt here: even where it is possible to obtain a favourable contract review one should ensure that the wording leaves no room for subsequent argument.

Summary

13.16 There seems little worth, both strategically and practically, of going to the time, fees and trouble of obtaining a Revenue contract review. Requests for a Revenue contract review can lead to drawn out correspondence and, effectively, a quasi-investigation. Readers may wish to refer to www.lime-it.com/ir35.shtml to study just how difficult it can sometimes be to get a prompt and sensible response from a Revenue contract reviewer.

IR35 is a financial expedient. It is not concerned with 'employment rights' for disguised employees or anything else. When tax inspectors are asked to provide a contract review opinion they sometimes take head office advice. But this advice is not necessarily focused on providing a neutral customer service. It is concerned with advising the inspector whether the Revenue can win a contentious appeal if the contract in question ends up at the Commissioners.

Most, if not all, commentators agree that seeking a Revenue contract review has little to commend it.

CHAPTER 14

Appraising a case, interest penalties and directors' personal liability and can IR35 be reversed?

14.1 Perhaps the hardest task for the practitioner is to take a wider view of his client's position, particularly where the client has been with the practitioner for many years. A full and objective appraisal of the terms of the working relationship and in particular the contract will now become necessary. It is time to stand back and judge the merits of the case as a whole and whether there is a realistic chance of success at the Commissioners.

14.2 The emphasis will of course be on the trinity of substitution, control and mutuality of obligations, together with an appraisal of the worker's 'bigger picture' and modus operandi. Even at this stage the astute practitioner will be weighing up other relevant factors: will the contractor be a strong witness, will the inspector be a strong witness, is the paperwork and documentation in order?

14.3 Each case will have its own nuances and peculiar features. Few cases are the same on the facts. Ultimately a subjective weighing up of the case has to be made in conjunction with the contractor.

It needs to be decided whether the contractor wants to play safe and embrace IR35 or would rather put his arguments forward if challenged and take his chances. If it is decided that there are no relevant engagements then the 'no' box is ticked on the P35. If a challenge comes and the Revenue's view prevails the consequences for the worker and his business are as follows.

Interest and penalties

14.4 Interest will be charged from the date the deductions should have been handed over, under SI 1993/744 reg 51(1), and is nothing more than commercial restitution for the Revenue. If agreement cannot be reached on the interest payable the collector may issue a certificate of interest payable under SI 1993/744 reg 51(4) which will be evidence that interest is due.

14.5 Penalties are less clear cut and although in theory there could be a penalty equal to a maximum of the duties at stake (under TMA 1970 s 98A(4)) this would never be implemented.

14.6 In court, at the judicial review hearing (*R (on the application of the PCG) v IRC,* see Appendix 6), the Revenue's leading barrister confirmed, in open court, that if 'all reasonable steps' had been taken the Revenue would not seek penalties. This is consistent with its view stated in Revenue leaflet IR109. This helped clarify the Revenue's earlier statement on penalties issued in March 2001.

14.7 There is no definition of what 'all reasonable steps' means, but no doubt a robust argument can be advanced for the personal service business which has taken professional advice, attended courses and genuinely made an effort to fall outside the rules. Certainly, doing nothing and ignoring IR35 is not reasonable. The Revenue have confirmed that taking 'all reasonable steps' does not require the contractor to seek a Revenue contract review. They have issued a helpful 'penalty statement' available on their website.

14.8 Penalties can always be mitigated, and even if they are exigible they are unlikely to be more than 15–25% of the duties at stake. Penalties are abated by reference to the extent that any irregularity is disclosed, the extent to which the taxpayer co-operates with the Revenue, and the overall size and gravity of the case. Whether the penalty ends up at nothing, 10% or 20% will also be down to the skills and experience of the contractor's representative. In any event, rumours of 100% penalty loadings are fantasy, and personal service businesses with a good case should not back down simply because there might be a small penalty if the case is eventually lost.

14.9 Finally, it is considered that any formal penalty determination the inspector makes (if agreement on the level of penalty cannot be reached) has to be proved on appeal at the Commissioners to a *criminal* level; that is, beyond a reasonable doubt. This is because, under European law, a financial penalty is seen as punitive and hence carries a higher burden on the Crown. Normally the burden of proof at the Commissioners is a mere balance of probabilities.

Personal liability

14.10 Some personal service businesses may be tempted to ignore IR35, and, should a liability eventually materialise, ensure the company is without assets whereby the Revenue goes begging; the contractor then starts another limited company the next day. This will not work and, indeed, it probably amounts to evasion. Accordingly, such a course of action should never be attempted or advised.

14.11 While the liability is initially that of the business, not the contractor personally, the director can be held personally responsible. This is because there are powers to serve a Notice of Personal Liability on a 'culpable officer' (in accordance with Social Security Administration Act 1992 s 121C) where he knowingly failed to make the necessary deductions.

14.12 There is a right of appeal and the onus is on the Revenue to prove its case (SSAA 1992 s 121D(4)). If the Revenue does so there is a real risk of imprisonment as well as a fine.

14.13 While it is considered unlikely that many directors will be pursued it is not impossible, and contractors who intend to abuse companies may be in for a big shock. Indeed criminal proceedings may be instigated in accordance with SSAA 1992 s 115.

There is also a new criminal offence of fraudulently evading NICs (introduced by the Social Security Act 1998 and incorporated into SSAA 1992 s 114A). These provisions were not designed with IR35 in mind but are drawn widely enough to apply to service companies.

Can IR35 be 'reversed'?

14.14 What if, on the basis of poor advice, or no advice at all, the taxpayer accepts IR35 applies and pays the duties on the 'deemed salary'. Can the amounts paid be reclaimed?

Subject to one important condition the answer is 'yes'. This condition is that only where a 'deemed salary' has been calculated can there be a possible payment. Where an actual salary has been paid this cannot be reversed.

14.15 There are two methods of reclaiming IR35 tax and national insurance paid in error. The first is to make an 'error or mistake' relief claim under TMA 1970 s 33. This method requires the Revenue to agree that a mistake was made and only if it is satisfied will it make a repayment. If it does not accept the mistake the matter must be referred to the Special Commissioners for adjudication. This can be a very lengthy process.

14.16 The alternative method is for the taxpayer to submit a revised or supplementary form P35 showing no liabilities due. He is, in effect, reassessing his position under a self-assessment regime. The repayment should automatically follow even if the Revenue want to take issue with the claim. This second method should avoid the lengthy delays likely to be encountered in the first method.

14.17 Re-claiming the IR35 duties will have a knock on effect as corporation tax will increase, as there is no longer a deduction for the deemed salary. Most contractors, if not all, will be better off with a reclaim, but professional advice should be taken in all cases.

Summary

14.18 Individual cases need to be weighed up and clients need to be aware that penalties may become due if no action is taken in consideration of IR35. Personal liability for the director of the personal service business cannot be ruled out. Re-claiming IR35 duties paid in error on a deemed salary is also possible under the s 33 route or the supplementary P35 route.

CHAPTER 15

How the Revenue will target IR35 cases

15.1 There are several possible ways in which an IR35 challenge may arise.

1. Ticking box 6 on Form P35

15.2 If a contractor admits to having had personal service income within IR35 by ticking box 6 he is clearly alerting the Revenue to the fact that he should be paying the appropriate deductions from the deemed salary. It is an easy exercise for the Revenue to link the P35 with the contractor's personal tax return in order to see that the correct deductions have been made.

15.3 On the other hand, by ticking 'no' in box 6 particularly where the contractor's personal service business operates in an IR35 at-risk area, for example, computer consulting, the Revenue may wish to satisfy itself that the intermediaries' legislation does not apply.

15.4 Whether or not the Revenue wishes to devote the necessary resources to linking such documents in all cases is doubtful. However, the Revenue has invested heavily in IT in recent years and the benefits of this will no doubt trickle through to compliance activities before too long.

2. Examination of the taxpayer's self-assessment return

15.5 The Revenue operates a sophisticated system of risk assessment when processing tax returns. If it is shown that a personal service business is paying a high level of dividends to its shareholders together with a low salary then it is almost certain that such a scenario will present a possible and worthwhile IR35 challenge for the Revenue.

15.6 Again, whether the Revenue wishes to devote sufficient time and resources to linking personal tax returns to possible personal service companies is doubtful, but, without question, the computer technology is available to do this.

3. Routine compliance visits

15.7 As part of its normal compliance routine the Revenue will send out PAYE auditors to examine the books and records of businesses. Tax officers have now been alerted to look for IR35 type situations and this will become just another aspect of routine compliance.

15.8 The Revenue adopted a similar approach during its status attack on the construction industry in the late 1990s and what was ostensibly a routine books and record review often became very focused on the issue of tax status. It is understood that tax officers have been told to pay particular attention to IR35. Practical advice on how to deal with an actual challenge is given in Chapter 15.

4. Submission of a contract review to the Revenue

15.9 Chapter 13 deals with the issue of submitting a contract to the Revenue for review. It is the consensus of many professional advisers that submission of a contract to the Revenue can only increase the chances of an IR35 challenge. However, the Revenue has categorically stated that cases are selected for compliance reviews using a number of criteria, but whether or not the Revenue is approached for an opinion on a contract is not one of them (see Frequently Asked Questions, compliance, 2, on the Revenue website at http://www.inlandrevenue.gov.uk/ir35). Unfortunately real life experience shows that a request for a contract review can, where the Revenue's view is disputed, slowly slide into what can only be described as quasi IR35 investigation. This has now been acknowledged by the Revenue.

5. Powers under TMA 1970 s 16

15.10 Under TMA 1970 s 16 the Revenue has powers to serve a notice on agencies requiring the agency to give full details of all payments made to personal service businesses.

15.11 This is an extremely effective power as it would enable the Revenue to go direct to the larger agencies and in one fell swoop require the agency to reveal details of hundreds, possibly thousands of personal service businesses.

15.12 The Revenue will then take the appropriate files and cross check the details given to see which entries have been filled in on the P35 and also cross check with the tax returns, which will show the extent to which salary is being sacrificed for dividends.

15.13 It is believed that the larger agencies will be the primary targets of this approach and this will be an extremely successful strategy for the Revenue. Section 16 letters have already been issued to certain agencies.

6. Informants

15.14 Practitioners and personal service businesses alike should never underestimate the sheer volume of anonymous letters received by the Revenue on an almost daily basis in which one taxpayer attempts to spill the beans on another. This was very noticeable during the construction industry status challenge in the late 1990s where a contractor who had decided to operate PAYE would complain to the Revenue via the Business Anti-Fraud Hotline about a competitor who was not operating PAYE.

15.15 While the IR35 sector is not the same as the construction industry it is still expected that informants' letters will trigger a certain number of Revenue investigations.

7. Random enquiries

15.16 These will trigger very few IR35 challenges, but the possibility of a challenge remains.

8. Research teams

15.17 The last Annual Report of the Revenue revealed some poor results in certain areas of compliance. Concerns with yield are widespread and this has lead to more focused campaigns based on risk-assessed analysis. This can only increase the chances of an IR35 challenge.

9. Schemes advertised as 'Avoiding IR35'

15.18 The Revenue's Special Compliance Office has become involved in IR35 cases. The SCO looks at schemes which present themselves as a means to evade or avoid tax. The Revenue has confirmed that 'it is likely that schemes advertised to "Avoid IR35" will consequently attract their attention, and may lead to an investigation' (see General Frequently Asked Questions, compliance, 4, on the Revenue's website at http://www.inlandrevenue.gov.uk/ir35). As a result, taxpayers involved in offshore umbrella company schemes, for example, are probably running a higher risk of challenge. This is not to say that such schemes are illegal or ineffective but they will attract Revenue attention.

Summary

15.19 Not a lot can be done about these sources of an IR35 challenge. Forms P35 should always be filled in correctly as should tax returns.

15.20 One way or another there is a realistic possibility that an IR35 challenge will be at least *considered* by the Revenue for perhaps 3 or 4% of all personal service business per year. Whether it then decides to take the challenge any further will depend on its risk assessment, workloads and other factors.

15.21 If a challenge arises it should be remembered that there is absolutely no legal obligation whatsoever on a personal service business or its directors or shareholders to attend a compliance visit and answer verbal questions put to it by the Revenue. Refusing to attend a meeting is not a lack of co-operation by the taxpayer—it is his right. This is a very commonly misunderstood aspect of tax investigations, and the personal service business is entirely at liberty to insist that any questions are put to it in writing. Attending meetings with professional assistance is a very time-consuming and expensive process. In the heat of the moment questions and answers can easily be misunderstood. Even sophisticated experienced contractors may misunderstand questions being put to them and, in a bid to end a Revenue interview as soon as possible, sometimes say the first thing that comes into their head. This is a perfectly natural reaction, particularly from those who are a little nervous or inexperienced in dealing with the authorities. These considerations are dealt with in Chapter 15.

15.22 If, on the other hand clear, written questions are put to the taxpayer and clear written answers given in return there is a greater possibility that the questions will be better understood and given proper consideration and that the replies will be more reliable and detailed. This makes for a better quality of evidence should the dispute proceed on appeal to the Commissioners.

CHAPTER 16

Inland Revenue interviews and IR35 strategies

16.1 The Revenue envisages that the majority of compliance activity on IR35 will be undertaken by the staff in employer compliance units. Following the Contributions Agency merger, these units contain a mixture of compliance cultures. On the one hand there are the former staff of an agency charged with protecting the interests of the contributor; on the other the tax inspector redressing loss to the Exchequer. Within the Revenue itself, there have been various forms of employer compliance staff: PAYE-only auditors, staff specialising in dealing with benefits-in-kind, Construction Industry Scheme auditors and staff carrying out full reviews in all areas.

16.2 In terms of a compliance visit to inspect the records of a personal service business, the approach may vary depending upon the experience and background of the inspector. To its credit, the Revenue has now standardised the format and scope of employer compliance reviews, and a review now encompasses all the relevant areas of PAYE, national insurance, benefits-in-kind, statutory sick pay, statutory maternity pay, working families' tax credit, disabled persons' tax credit, student loan deductions and the Construction Industry Scheme. And now IR35, of course. A visit can be exhaustive, and exhausting.

16.3 This chapter assumes that the personal service business has been selected for an employer compliance review as above.

The start of the review

16.4 The first indication will be a standard letter (commonly form ECR105) indicating the name of the employer compliance unit (usually, but not always, located where the PAYE scheme is dealt with) and the officer who wishes to call to inspect the client's records. Included with this letter there should be a copy of the Revenue's Code of Practice 3, setting out certain of the rights and obligations taxpayers under review have, and indicating how the review will take place.

16.5 The Revenue does not need to give a reason for undertaking this review, and generally speaking it will not. However, the reason for the review may be evident from the information sought (see, for example, 16.10 below). It will also be reluctant to cancel the review unless there is a good reason to do so, for example, the business is going into liquidation with little chance of any dividend to preferential creditors. If the personal service business has ceased trading, or is insolvent, the Revenue should be informed immediately, otherwise the next step is to decide how the review can be best handled.

16.6 Depending upon the volume of paperwork, it may be quite convenient to provide the Revenue with the records, rather than have them visit to carry out a review. Code of Practice 3 provides for the records to be reviewed at a mutually convenient time and place, which could be the Tax Office. Generally, they will want to see a complete tax year for which a P35 has been submitted (as they will be checking the accuracy of the return), but they may only request a 12-month sample period. The advantages of this approach will become more evident throughout this chapter. A disadvantage is that the inspector will be under far less pressure than he would be if attending the client's premises to carry out a full review in one day, the records will be thoroughly analysed and every discrepancy or uncertainty picked up and queried.

If mutual agreement cannot be reached, the Revenue are entitled to inspect the records at the place where they are normally kept.

16.7 If a visit is acceptable, the compliance officer will have suggested a date, or range of dates, within which the visit can take place. Typically a review will take a half to a full day, perhaps slightly less for the average 'one-man service company' as the records will not be complex. If the business operates from home, and this is where the review takes place, two officers are likely to attend, for reasons of Health and Safety . Even if not, it is becoming more common for a review to be conducted by an employer compliance officer and one administrative assistant, who will carry out the more basic compliance checks.

16.8 Regarding the authority these officers have, generally speaking they are 'authorised officers of the Board' as specified by reg 55 of the Income Tax (Employments) Regulations 1993, SI 1993/744, and should be trained and experienced in dealing with this type of work. There are corresponding powers within the Social Security (Contributions) Regulations 2001, SI 2001/1004 at para 26 of Sch 4, which apply for national insurance purposes. The officer should carry some confirmation of this fact, and all Revenue employees carry identity cards. It is unlikely that any assistant will be an authorised officer, and so will have no power alone to require the production of documents.

16.9 The powers conferred by reg 55 are limited to records relating to the calculation or payment of 'emoluments'. Specifically, they do not cover the following:

- Purchase invoices, although these are sometimes requested during a review. These need only be provided if they relate directly to 'emoluments' (which includes benefits-in-kind). The officer should be politely asked whether he is authorised to request these documents, and a note made of his response.
- Sales invoices, which may be requested to determine fees received by the service company.
- Contracts between the service company and the agency, or any other party
- Self-assessment returns. An officer should not question an entry on the director's self-assessment return without first opening a formal section 9A enquiry. This does not preclude him from investigating a matter that has an implication for both the self-assessment return and the client as an employer. For example, during an employer compliance review, the officer states that a taxpayer has submitted a P11D return for his company car, but has not returned the benefit on his SA return, and asks why this is so. The officer is effectively making enquiries into the taxpayer's return, despite not having followed the necessary formalities. Even if an enquiry is opened in this informal manner, it is still open to the taxpayer to ask the General Commissioners to direct that the enquiry be closed. This is something of significant concern within the Revenue, as a direction to issue a closure notice would preclude the Revenue making any more enquiries into the return in question.
- CTSA returns. Similarly, the officer's enquiries must be focused on the area under review—the employer's statutory obligations, and he must not stray into querying items in the accounts.

16.10 Although there is no explicit power under reg 55 to inspect the company's sales invoices, or the contracts between the service company and the agency or client, it is becoming increasingly common practice for the Revenue to ask that this information is provided when sending the first notification of a review. Clearly, this early request would indicate that the service company is, in the Revenue's eyes, an IR35 target from the outset.

16.11 Although there is no obligation to attend a meeting with the Inland Revenue, many Revenue officers are unaware of this, having met little resistance to a meeting request in the past. It is sometimes found that an officer will become insistent, and develop a strident attitude when a meeting request is refused.

As an example, during a recent contentious dispute handled by Accountax, the inspector threatened verbally to obtain directions from the Commissioners to compel the client to meet with the inspector. A swift written response to the inspector pointing out that he could not seek directions to force a meeting made him realise the irrational and futile stance he was taking. Meetings cost money in lost income and professional fees. Off the cuff knee-jerk answers rarely provide reliable evidence. This has all been explained to the Revenue, for example in the Accountax meeting of September 2003. Still the Revenue persues personal meetings, but these should be avoided as a general rule.

16.12 As mentioned above, the Revenue has standardised the procedural aspects of a review, bringing together the various facets of employer compliance activities into a common approach. There is now a standard questionnaire completed at each review that directs the officer through an interview with the client. This is usually how each review commences. It directs the officer to areas of potential problems. In a face-to-face meeting, the Revenue will expect these questions to be answered. However, there is no obligation to attend a meeting or answer verbal questions put by the Revenue.

16.13 The Revenue will see a meeting as an opportunity to gather background information, to understand the operation of the business, and plan effectively how they will undertake the review of the business records. In reality, this is one of the likely points at which IR35 issues will first emerge, and an alert officer will already be taking note of salient points that can, and will, be used later in argument.

16.14 As is human nature, the officer will be looking for pieces of the jigsaw to complete the picture that the Risk Analyst has already begun. This person is a 'disguised employee'. That is why the case has been selected for review. Make no mistake that the intention of the officer, unless the contrary is strongly argued, will be to bring the company within IR35.

At the risk of criticising the Revenue it should be asked how many times the Revenue has reviewed a PAYE workforce and strongly argued that the workers should be *self*-employed? Probably never. That is not their job. The officer's remit is to ensure compliance with the legislation. If a company can be brought within IR35, it is his duty to do so.

16.15 The innocuous questionnaire can provide the compliance officer with entirely the wrong impression, and all the ammunition needed for an IR35 argument. There is a real danger, particularly with the layman, that questions will be misinterpreted, answers will carry thoughtless connotations with employment and the compliance officer's mindset will gradually and irreversibly be established. And this is before a single contract is reviewed.

16.16 It is imperative that the interviewee is not drawn into the compliance officer's world. The compliance officer will not be communicating on the same level; the representative being interviewed will not be controlling the interview; the pressure of being interviewed in this manner may lead to misleading, even wrong answers against the favour of the business, particularly if the questions are leading; and the compliance officer is likely to be looking only for evidence of 'disguised employment'.

16.17 There is a strong argument to be made that no discussion at all should be had with the Revenue, and that the Revenue should be asked to put all matters in writing; this is any taxpayer's entitlement. It is easy to imagine how difficult this might be when faced with two Revenue officers in one's home, feeling under pressure to act cooperatively. But there is nothing uncooperative in establishing the officers in a suitable room, with the records, and respectfully requesting any questions be put in writing at the end of a review. The Revenue's burden to act with courtesy and not to overstep the mark is more conspicuous when officers are imposing upon a taxpayer's home.

Leaflet IR109

16.18 The Revenue will usually start with recent periods, say, 12 months or so. If earlier records are subsequently requested, this is the first sign that there may be a problem, and the officers may be quantifying the liability going back over a number of years. Similarly, if the officer pounces upon a particular contract, or asks for information relating to a specific item outside the usual extent of the review, he already has his target in mind, and alarm bells should be ringing. The clear indicator that the officer believes that the regulations have not been complied with is the issue of leaflet IR109.

16.19 The Inland Revenue's instructions to its staff on the issue of leaflet IR109 were public until recently, when the Revenue decided to cloak them in a shroud of secrecy. The previous evidence was as follows.

> **'Issue Of Leaflet IR109**
> When you discover irregularity likely to lead to a recovery you must, except in the circumstances indicated below,
>
> - issue leaflet IR109 to the employer/contractor (unless one has been issued earlier on request)
> - record the date of issue on the working papers.
>
> It is important that
>
> - the employer/contractor is given the opportunity to maximise the penalty abatements described in the IR109, but that
> - the IR109 is not issued before irregularity is discovered (except on request) as this may antagonise the employer/contractor whose PAYE/SC performance is satisfactory.
>
> Do not issue leaflet IR109 where
>
> - you suspect fraud (follow the procedures at ECM 23000 onwards and only issue leaflet IR109 where SCO do not take over the case)
> - the only irregularity involves income from which tax cannot be deducted (ECM 13004)
> - the employer has diplomatic immunity (ECM 8008).

> Note. Where fraud is discovered after the issue of leaflet IR109 and the case is taken over by Special Compliance Office, SCO will advise on the withdrawal of the leaflet where appropriate.'

It is understood that the policy has not changed substantially, although this is now officially 'restricted information'.

16.20 The issuing of leaflet IR109 is a useful indicator, as it will be the first thing that occurs when an irregularity is suspected, before questioning takes place. This is an important point for the Revenue, as every taxpayer should be given the opportunity to maximise the penalty abatements. From the point of view of a business under investigation it also indicates that answers to the subsequent questions need to be measured and carefully thought through. Moreover, it can serve as the point at which an unrepresented client can say to the Revenue: 'I would now like to seek professional advice before proceeding, please put any questions to my accountant in writing', thus avoiding the pitfalls identified above.

16.21 Another important development in this area is the Revenue's recent concern that some of their tax-geared penalties may be found to be 'criminal' for the purposes of Article 6 of the ECHR.

As a public body, the Revenue is under a duty to comply with the Human Rights Act 1998. Eventually, this means that the taxpayer is entitled to a 'fair trial'—including the right not to self-incriminate and the right to silence.

The officer may issue a standard letter to the service company inviting cooperation with his review, but drawing attention to the above rights. If he does, this indicates that the officer has not only a loss of tax and NIC in mind, but possibly the addition of a penalty as well. If this occurs, the cautious advice at 16.20 above is particularly important.

16.22 If the leaflet is not issued, or is issued after the event (which is not uncommon), there is a justifiable argument on customer service grounds that the Revenue has failed to comply with its own guidance.

Contracts

16.23 The Revenue officer is bound to request sight of the contract(s) in considering whether IR35 applies. Although the Revenue is giving written opinions elsewhere based solely on what is in the contract, it has always favoured a full fact finding exercise when considering employment status issues. In terms of IR35, ESM 3286 states:

> 'When deciding what the employment status would have been in a direct engagement, you should therefore take into account all of the relevant features of the relationship, including all contracts in the chain between the worker and the client.'

16.24 The officer will want to ask some questions about the contracts, not only for the reason of taking into account all relevant features, but also to determine whether any of the clauses are a sham. More on this later. The information sought at this stage is likely to be fairly minimal, and will be just enough for the officer to make the broadest of judgments.

If the officer then feels that he has enough information to form an opinion that the contract is caught by IR35, he will say so. The aim is to gain agreement, to negotiate the additional tax and national insurance due and to collect the money. The whole process remains informal, and, in the interest of administrative convenience for both parties, the Revenue prefers to deal on this basis.

16.25 In accepting the informal opinion of the officer, a taxpayer is effectively bowing to his superior knowledge of IR35 and employment status issues. However, the taxpayer should not be surprised if the officer has had little or no formal training in the area of employment status.

Employment and special status inspectors

16.26 Employment status training in the Revenue ('categorisation' as the Contributions Agency used to call it), has only recently been given anywhere near the priority it deserves. It is a complex area; a wrong decision can cost hundreds of thousands of pounds, even for a moderately sized company. The decision making process is also technically involved and can only be effectively conducted by standing back and looking at each case from a position of neutrality. The Revenue has a dedicated internal guidance manual on virtually every subject imaginable, from the conduct of the officer himself through to how to deal with a complaint against him. However, the dedicated manual on employment status was not produced until October 2000. Prior to this, guidance was only deemed to warrant several paragraphs in other manuals.

16.27 The Revenue, to its credit, has now put resources into dedicated employment status teams, and provided training and the above mentioned guidance manual to the staff of these teams. However, this technical knowledge is taking time to filter through to the front-line staff, who may have been dealing with status for many years.

16.28 In the case of a routine compliance review, it is unlikely that the officer will be a member of one of the employment status teams. In recognising employment status as a specialism, the specialist knowledge has been invested in specific Revenue staff, those that are usually called upon only when a dispute arises or an issue is beyond the ability of the officer dealing with a particular case. The officer conducting a routine review may not have the knowledge and training to make accurately a contentious or borderline decision.

16.29 In terms of IR35, referring to staff dealing with Schedule E matters, Company Accounts Inspectors *and* employer compliance staff, the Revenue's own internal instructions admit:

> 'Members of staff may not have a comprehensive knowledge of all aspects relating to a particular issue or query. It is therefore important that you consult the appropriate person where necessary.' (ESM 3001)

An adverse decision should therefore be challenged, and the compliance officer will seek a more experienced opinion.

16.30 The next step is typically for the specialist status team to become involved. It is these teams who are undertaking the contract opinions, and they are much more experienced in their field than the average compliance officer. There will undoubtedly be a request for a further meeting, unless the original officer has undertaken a very thorough fact finding exercise and the status inspector can make an immediate judgment based on those facts.

16.31 It is an interesting point that when the Revenue used to give an opinion on the status of a worker, it was called a 'decision'. Similarly, the Contributions Agency used to make 'rulings'. This is despite the fact that neither opinion was binding, nor did it have any force in law and it carried no right of appeal. But it is easy to see how there was a compulsion to accept an opinion, if it were given as a 'ruling'. Thankfully this presumption is discontinued, and the Revenue recognises (at ESM 3285) that taxpayers are 'at liberty to adopt their own alternative view' to the Revenue's when considering status.

This has lead to greater impartiality of approach by the Revenue, as an obviously biased opinion would rightly be ignored, and the status inspector will usually describe the next meeting as an impartial fact gathering exercise.

16.32 Again, the best course of action here is for matters to be put in writing, but the Revenue will want to resist this approach, claiming that this prolongs matters, that meetings are more effective and so on. It should be pointed out to the inspector that a written dialogue ensures that questions are properly understood, thoughtfully and accurately answered, and the matter is properly recorded for both parties to rely on as evidence.

16.33 When conducting a meeting with a status inspector, it is usually found that there is little in the way of contentious argument during the meeting. The Revenue's preferred approach is to take all the information away from the meeting, and come to a considered opinion after weighing up the whole picture. A good status inspector may challenge answers to questions if he feels they are unrealistic or conflict with other information held, but essentially he is conducting the initial interview to establish fact, not argue a case.

16.34 In 'ordinary' (ie non-IR35) status issues there are two sides to the argument. The engager and the worker both have a story to tell, and both stand to gain or lose by the decision made. It is therefore important that both sides are party to the debate, as either party may appeal against a formal assessment.

This is not so with IR35. Only the personal service business is in the frame. This means that the status inspector may have only one side to the argument, and not exactly a neutral side, and he will need to take extra care to make sure he is getting the correct information. This extra care is already hinted at in the Revenue's IR35 chapters of the Employment Status Manual. ESM 3293 reads:

> 'Many contracts submitted for written opinions contain clauses that appear to give a right of substitution. It seems likely that many of these clauses have only been inserted to try and break the requirement for personal service and change the contract from one of service to one for services. Normally a client requires the services of a particular worker and a substitute would not be acceptable so there must be doubts about the validity of such clauses.
>
> Where a contract that has been submitted for a written opinion contains a substitution clause it is important to ensure that there is a genuine right. You should only accept that such a right exists where:
>
> - there is an explicit right for a substitute to be sent, and
> - someone other than a specific worker would be acceptable.
>
> You should not accept that a right of substitution exists just because the contract is in the name of the service company. A right of substitution is only likely to exist where the client does not care from one day to the next for the duration of the contract who turns up to carry out the work, provided that whoever does so is suitably qualified and experienced.'

The same instruction goes on to say:

> 'Where the service company's contract is not with the client and there is a claimed right of substitution, we have said that we will require further evidence that such a right exists. This would normally be a copy of the written contract between the agency and the client. If the service company claims that it cannot get access to that contract then it should be asked to provide alternative evidence. This could be a letter from the client confirming that:
>
> - it has agreed to the service company providing a substitute, and
> - over the course of the contract it does not matter which worker is provided on a day to day basis.'

Effectively this starts with the premise that all substitution clauses are a sham, unless it can be proved otherwise. This is a departure from the

Revenue's usual approach, but it is indicative of the extra vigilance it is exercising over IR35 as a status issue.

16.35 The Revenue's approach to status used to involve completing a green pamphlet known as the Status Fact Finder (AF301). Although still favoured by some, the 'newer generation' of status inspectors, particularly former Contributions Agency staff prefer the more fluid approach of a less regimented discussion in order to gain an insight into the business and the terms on which the worker has been engaged.

16.36 It may be found that, underlying the claimed neutral approach, the status officer gives away his true attitude to the engagement with the words he uses. Many fact finding exercises are riddled with bias, as the object of the exercise is to police the frontier of employment/self-employment and bring as many over the border into employment as possible.

Look out for the status officer calling the client 'the employer' and the worker 'the employee' (of the client). It may sound unlikely but this often happens. 'Who do you work for?' is a question commonly asked by the status inspector. 'The personal service business', the worker should reply!

Throughout the interview the status inspector will, subconsciously or otherwise, focus on the factors indicating employment and not on those indicating self-employment. The balance needs to be redressed by bringing *all* the factors to the forefront of his attention and making sure appropriate weight is given to them.

Factors the inspector will consider

16.37 There is a suggested Fact Finding Questionnaire at ESM 525.

What is the client's business?

16.38 Initially the inspector will want to get a background to the business engaging the worker, to determine how the worker fits into the organisation. This not only provides the inspector with a useful insight into the likely relationship between both parties, it also provides the foundation for a 'part and parcel' argument. Although this test has become discredited in more recent case law, the Revenue still considers it to be a factor, although it does recognise it has limitations.

Endeavour to shift the focus to the business relationship with the client (usually the agency), and make sure the inspector gives as much attention to the features that disassociate the businesses.

In the unlikely case that this argument forms the basis of a challenge by the Revenue, draw the inspector's attention to his own instructions at ESM 1081:

> '. . . another example might be a mechanic, with a contract to maintain a firm's office equipment, who was called in by the firm from a base elsewhere when repairs were needed. In both cases those concerned provide services for the firm yet they are not an integral part of it.'

This example can be compared quite effectively with many IR35 computer consultants.

The instructions add:

> 'But it can be very difficult to decide whether a person works as an integral part of an organisation. Hence this test is usually unhelpful when cases on the border are at issue.'

Are other workers doing the same job?

16.39 The Revenue may ask whether a comparison can be made to other workers doing the same job who are employees of the client. This line of questioning is outside the scope of the personal service business' reasonable knowledge as an independent contractor, who has not seen the employment contracts of his client's employees! Remember it is the terms and conditions that decide the status, not the job title or even the duties. It should be borne in mind that ESM 501 states that:

> '. . . where there is a dispute the Revenue cannot simply assert that individuals are employees because of their job description.'

16.40 The Revenue may also ask whether the worker was formerly an employee of the client. The justification for the IR35 legislation has always been that an employee could leave work on a Friday and return on Monday carrying out the same job through a service company, paying less tax and national insurance. Make sure that the inspector fully appreciates the changes in terms and conditions that come about as a result of working through a service company. If these terms and conditions demonstrate the worker is not a disguised employee of the client, it is irrelevant what the previous terms and conditions might have been.

How did the worker get the job?

16.41 The inspector will be looking for the typical employment scenario of a prospective employee responding to an employer's advertisement or offer of work. Make the inspector aware of any advertising undertaken, and any training needed to undertake the contract.

Is the worker in business on his own account?

16.42 The Revenue sees this as one of the fundamental tests of self-employment. It is also likely to be highly relevant in the case of a service company. In setting up a service company and engaging an accountant, the first steps towards being in business have been taken. Most service companies go beyond this, setting up office facilities at home, buying a computer or other expensive equipment, possibly giving up a company car and buying a private car—a significant investment. Then there are VAT registrations, liability insurances, stationery, advertising etc.

It will be very tempting for the status inspector, in looking 'behind' the service company to the interface between the worker and the engager, to overlook all of these factors. Make sure that they are forcefully advanced. As the Revenue status manual reads at ESM 1011 regarding the 'in business on own account test': 'This goes to the heart of the matter'.

Control

16.43 Control over the work done has always been top of the Revenue's list of factors pointing towards employment. The inspector will be seeking to establish the extent to which control has been exerted over the worker. His instructions direct him to consider:

- control over what work is done;
- control over where the work is done;
- control over when the work is done; and
- control over how the work is done.

If the contract is specific on this point, and there is no right of control over the worker, make sure this is pointed out to the inspector.

In reality what, where and when are usually dictated by the nature of the job itself. Do not let the inspector make the mistake of assuming that because the personal service business is contracted to perform a particular task when the office is open at the client's premises, there is control.

16.44 The Revenue's usual tack in discussing this point is to ask hypothetical questions, and a common example is:

> 'If you were asked to stop doing the work you are currently undertaking and do something else, would you do so?'

Particular caution should be taken with this type of question. Remember that it is the right of control that is important, not how accommodating the personal service business is when fulfilling the contract. The personal service business may well be willing to oblige certain requests, but if ultimately there is a right to refuse to do so, this is the crux of the matter.

It is generally better to avoid such hypotheses altogether. Direct the status inspector back to the terms and conditions of the contract where necessary. Remember also the fundamental test in *Staples v Secretary of State for Social Services* (see Appendix 6) as covered in 6.121.

16.45 The status inspector will place great emphasis on the administrative side of the contract, such as the requirement to report to a manager and complete timesheets, and will view these as an indicator of control. On the contrary, the fact that regular progress reports have to be made and accurate time sheets completed may be a result of the *lack* of control exerted over the personal service business. The fact is that most employees do not complete timesheets, because of the inherent trust in their relationship with their employer and the control that they are under. Be sure to point this out, and emphasise the business efficacy of progress reports. This is an important point because the completion of countersigned timesheets often tops the Revenue's list of factors indicating a contract is caught by IR35 and features predominantly in their published guidance.

Personal service

16.46 At long last the Revenue has recognised that the requirement for personal service is fundamental to a contract of employment. If the worker is not required to carry out the work personally, he is not an employee. Substitution clauses present the Revenue's biggest problem in terms of IR35, and it will seek to break as many of them as possible.

The internal instructions on IR35 form part of the Employment Status Manual. The manual (at ESM 3012) confirms that IR35 does not introduce any new tests, and the normal guidance concerning employment status in the other parts of the manual should be applied. The guidance does not therefore comment on aspects of deciding employment status, with one very notable exception at ESM 3293—substitution clauses. The guidance has already been reproduced earlier in the chapter, and directs the status inspector to put the onus back onto the personal service business to prove that the substitution clause is *not* a sham.

16.47 Unfortunately for the Revenue, it is not incumbent upon the personal service business to prove the contract is a genuine one, it is up to the Revenue to prove that it is not. Authorities are reluctant to start overturning contractual arrangements without very good reason. If the status inspector asks for proof that the right is genuine, and this can be easily done by reference to other documentation, then do so. Otherwise, if the Revenue has reason to challenge the validity of a clause, it is up to it to do so on its evidence, not a preformed assumption.

Another common attitude adopted by the status inspector when faced with a right of substitution is to ask how many times a substitute has actually been sent. Of course, if a substitute has been used, this is undeniable evidence that the right is genuine. If substitution has not taken place, the inspector may place less weight on the clause in forming an opinion. This is wrong. The client has only to establish that a right exists, not to show that the right has ever been exercised. Make sure the inspector appreciates this.

Yet another attack on the clause is to ask who would actually be sent if the right of substitution were to be exercised. Again, it is suggested that this point is irrelevant, and the inspector should be referred to the case of *McMenamin v Diggles* (see Chapter 6 and Appendix 6).

Finally, the status inspector will be looking for a fetter on the substitution right, either within the contract or otherwise. Does the client realistically expect that anybody could turn up to do the work? As the Revenue's internal guidance (at ESM 3293) says:

> 'A right of substitution is only likely to exist where the client does not care from one day to the next for the duration of the contract who turns up to carry out the work.'

This statement has been roundly criticised as not reflecting the current case law.

Whether or not the client (ie the engager in this context) has this carefree attitude to the substitution clause does not supersede any actual right to send a substitute, if it is in the contract. Remember also that a reasonable degree of prescription on the grounds of skills and experience is acceptable.

16.48 The above are some examples from the author's experience of the Revenue's attempts to undermine the right of substitution. Other lines of argument will undoubtedly emerge. At all times the status inspector should be brought back round to whether the contract obliges personal service. If does not, it cannot be a contract of service.

Provision of equipment

16.49 In the scenario of a typical one person computer consultancy carrying out IT work on the client's premises using the client's equipment, the status inspector will probably think he is going to have a field day. The Revenue's interpretation is that the provision of equipment points to a contract of employment, and he will see the engager as supplying the necessary tools to do the job. The status officer's questions will be focused on the IT equipment used, the office facilities available, and any other items provided by the engager.

In the wider sense of the IT contractor's business, he may have his own office facilities at home, a car used to travel between the site of the contract and his base (a significant piece of machinery!), a laptop, mobile telephone and various other items of equipment that are essential to his ability to operate. And let us not forget the main tool of the trade that our imaginary IT contractor possesses, in which he has invested, and on which his business stands or falls—his brain. As we have seen earlier, the provision of labour or skills is an acceptable form of self-employment, and this was underlined firmly in *Hall v Lorimer* (see Appendix 5). The cost of training and keeping up to date can be substantial, and investment in this area funded by the personal service business must be made clear to the inspector.

16.50 The Revenue will want to focus in on the day-to-day work done on the engager's premises—but it must be made aware of the wider picture of the whole business.

16.51 Another point worth making, if it is relevant, is that the nature of the work often dictates the equipment, location and facilities that can be used. For example, an IT contractor working on a bank's secure systems is sometimes confined to the equipment that can be used.

Financial risk

16.52 This is another topic where a biased slant can lead a status inspector to overlook whole areas of financial risk. The inspector will ask if money could be lost on the contract. Usually, this will only happen if the engager or agency does not pay the fees, with the inspector then getting the answer he predicted.

16.53 The reality is that stepping into the world of the personal service business involves losing much of the financial security associated with employment. Here is a list of possible elements of financial risk, most of which apply to the average personal service business.

- No rights to statutory payments such as any sick pay, holiday pay or redundancy.
- Investment in assets (car, computer) that may or may not yield a return depending on the success of the personal service business.
- Advertising costs.
- Faulty work may have to be corrected at the cost of the personal service business.
- Risks of having no contract.
- Unpaid invoices.
- Meeting costs of own travel arrangements.
- Accountancy costs.
- Professional liability indemnity insurance costs.
- Training costs.
- Administrative costs.
- Short notice of termination without compensation.

These are just some examples, there are many more costs incurred by service businesses that the inspector will probably overlook. It is not just a case of whether the client wins or loses on a particular contract without considering all the risk that has been undertaken in gaining the contract in the first place. Draw these costs and financial risks to the inspector's attention and ask for them to be taken into consideration.

In the recent case of *Lime-IT Ltd v Justin* SpC 2002. Dr Avery Jones said 'the fact of invoicing and the 30 day (or even 10 day), if that is what was subsequently agreed) terms for payment, even ignoring the actual delays in payment, seem to me to point towards self-employment'.

Opportunity to profit

16.54 The flipside of financial risk is the opportunity to profit from the sound management of the personal service business. The Revenue believes that the courts interpret this in 'a rather special way' (ESM 1035).

16.55 The average status inspector will interpret the opportunity to profit as representing the dividing line between being paid hourly (for example) and being quoted a fixed price for a job. As many personal service businesses charge by the hour, the status inspector will equate this with employment, and this again features prominently in many IR35 decisions by the Revenue.

If the business is paying by the hour, the inspector will question how profits can possibly be increased. Thankfully, *Hall v Lorimer* provides a ready-made answer. Regarding Mr Lorimer ([1994] IRLR 171 at 174 para 13, Nolan LJ quoting Special Commissioner's judgment):

> 'He has the opportunity of profiting from being good at being a vision mixer. According to his reputation, so there will be a demand for his services for which he will be able to charge accordingly. The more efficient he is at running the business of providing his services, the greater is his prospect of profit.'

The same will be true of any consultant working in any industry. The success, and therefore the profit, of his business is dependent on the demand for his services, which in turn will depend upon the skill and ability with which he fulfils his contracts.

16.56 There is no case law to support the Revenue's contention that hourly paid workers are likely to be employees. If you are a professional adviser it is possible that you charge by the hour yourself, and this is a useful point which the inspector will have to consider.

Mutuality of obligation

16.57 The status inspector will not raise the issue of mutuality of obligation, and the extent of his knowledge is likely to be that it is irrelevant anyway. He may be able to quote from the Revenue's internal guidance at

ESM 1074 which reflects on Waite LJ's comments in *McMeechan* ([1997] IRLR 353 at 360 para 41; see also Appendix 6):

> 'When it comes to considering the terms of an individual, self-contained, engagement, the fact that the parties are not to be obliged in future to offer—or to accept—another engagement . . . is neither here nor there.'

However, the *McMeechan* interpretation of mutuality was criticised in the more recent 2001 Court of Appeal decision in *Montgomery v Johnson Underwood Ltd* (see Appendix 6).

16.58 This is such an important and fundamental point that the status inspector cannot be allowed to gloss over the matter without ensuring that the facts are at least recorded and agreed, even if the significance is not appreciated. The status inspector may not fully comprehend the importance of the facts, as internal Revenue guidance has in the past instructed that mutuality of obligation can 'confuse the issue'.

This view can be rebutted, especially if supported by the above quote, by explaining that the Court of Appeal has directly undermined this in the more recent case of *Montgomery v Johnson Underwood Ltd.* In that case Brooke LJ referred to Waite LJ's comments ([2001] IRLR 269 at 275), and decided that the concept of a minimum of mutual obligations could not be dispensed with:

> 'If, therefore, Waite LJ's judgment in McMeechan is being interpreted as meaning that this line of authority has lost its potency today, that interpretation of it should not be followed.'

Reference should also be made to Mr Justice Burton's criticism of the Revenue's position on mutuality of obligation in the Judicial Review of IR35 (*R (on the application of Professional Contractors Group) v IRC* [2001] STC 629 at 651; as to the case itself, see Appendix 6). In the EAT case of *Stuncroft Ltd v Havelock,* Judge Wilkie agreed that the absence of mutuality of obligations was 'a knockout blow'.

16.59 It is unlikely that the status officer will be willing or able to entertain any debate on this particular subject, other than to play down its significance. But it should be ensured that any lack of mutuality, especially if explicitly written into the contract, is noted by the status inspector.

Entitlement to holiday pay, sick pay etc

16.60 The Revenue, in its internal instructions, quite rightly points out that entitlement to statutory benefits follows employment status, not the other way round. In terms of IR35 of course there will be no statutory benefits from the engager, and the Revenue may be tempted to skirt over this issue.

However, the lack of holiday pay, sick pay and the other trappings of employment has been taken into account by the courts in the past, and is further evidence of the risk associated with operating a personal service business. Again, make sure that the status inspector includes this as a factor in his appraisal of the engagement.

Termination

16.61 The status inspector will be looking for a right of 'dismissal' with a period of notice, which can be found in many employment contracts, as evidence that a 'disguised employment' exists. If he does not find such a right exists, he will determine this factor to be non-conclusive (in accordance with ESM 1085).

16.62 The Revenue's instructions do not give any weight to the financial risk inherent in cases where the contract can be terminated at short notice, or even with no notice at all. Unless there is breach of contract, this is inconsistent with employment, and could be further evidence of a lack of mutuality of obligation.

16.63 In each of the above cases, ensure that the status inspector notes and appreciates the alternative points of view, or no significance at all will be attached to the matter.

Exclusivity

16.64 The nature of the work undertaken by many personal service businesses involves working for one client at a time. Many contracts allow freedom to undertake other work, providing this does not interfere with the performance of the contractual obligations.

16.65 The status inspector will view a requirement for exclusive services as an indicator of employment, although the actual Revenue instructions are far from conclusive. If there are exclusivity clauses within the contract, draw the status inspector's attention to his own instructions at ESM 1105:

> 'However, exclusive services clauses are not only found in contracts of employment. They may also appear in contracts for services. A self-employed individual running an agency for an insurance company may be precluded from selling any other company's policies. Similarly an author may agree to write for only one publisher.'

Parallels can be drawn between the insurance agent in the Revenue's example and the personal service company, particularly where intellectual property rights rest with the engager, or a conflict of interests can arise in the competitive IT industry.

16.66 Also, do not let the status inspector confuse rights with practicalities. He may ask whether other contracts could feasibly be undertaken, and the response may be that they could not. But underlying the answer may be practical considerations—perhaps the current contract is lucrative, or conveniently local. The relevant point is whether there is a right to take other contracts. If there is no mutuality of obligation, or if there is a right to terminate a contract without notice, the personal service business is at liberty to move to another contract at will. Sensible business management may make this unlikely, but that is not the point.

16.67 Ensure that the status inspector is also aware of successive contracts with different clients, as this points away from employment.

Intention of the parties

16.68 The Revenue accepts (as stated at ESM 1101) that in borderline cases, the intention of the parties may be decisive:

> 'When you have gathered all the facts, you should stand back and look at the bigger picture. If you consider that the case is borderline, you should then, and only then, look at the intention of the parties. Where there is mutual intention for a contract of employment or for a contract for services, that will determine the status of the worker.'

In the 1999 Court of Appeal case of *Express Echo Publications Ltd v Tanten*, Peter Gibson LJ said 'One starts with the common intention of the parties that Mr Tanten should not be an employee but should be self-employed'.

This is a vital point, and a very useful argument to use against the status inspector. If a good debate is made against employee status, you will often hear the status inspector admit that this is 'a very difficult decision' or 'a very narrow case'.

Bearing in mind the above instruction, if a good enough argument can be formulated to get the status inspector to concede his opinion is borderline, the intention of the parties is decisive. It almost goes without saying that both parties intend to avoid an employer/employee relationship—that is one of the main reasons for the existence of a personal service business, and more often than not this can be found explicitly stated within the contract.

Notes of interview

16.69 Following any meeting with the Revenue, it is important to request a copy of the Revenue's notes of the meeting. These should be drafted by the interviewer as soon as practicable after the meeting, so there should be no delay in providing them.

16.70 The meeting record will provide an insight into how the status inspector has perceived and interpreted the information given to him. If there are factual inaccuracies, it is obviously imperative that the officer is put right immediately. If any aspect of the notes imply a bias towards IR35 which is unreasonable or does not hold with the facts, again, the officer should be put straight and the fact that a neutral position is advocated by the Revenue should be pointed out.

If the case becomes contentious and ends up before the Commissioners, the Revenue will use the original notes of the meeting as evidence, and if these have been disagreed and challenged at an early stage rather than waiting until the hearing, this lends more weight to the challenge.

Developments in Revenue tactics

Section 20 notices

16.71 Practitioners have noted that the Revenue has shown a marked increase in its willingness to use its statutory powers under TMA 1970 s 20 in IR35 cases.

16.72 This can be seen in cases where information is needed from the end-user client but the end-user is reluctant or unable to provide that information. This may also be the case where the taxpayer or its director (because strictly speaking it is the company that is the appellant) refuses or is unable to provide information.

16.73 Subject to certain limitations and conditions s 20 allows the Revenue to seek information and particulars both from the taxpayer and third parties. A Section 20 Notice is not the same as the old style 'Commissioners' Precepts' practitioners will be familiar with. A Section 20 Notice is an inspector's notice that merely requires ratification by a Commissioner. Because the application for ratification is a private matter between the Revenue and the Commissioner it is ex parte and the taxpayer and his agent have no right to attend or make verbal representations.

16.74 Clearly, in cases of large investigations involving fraud, one can understand the merits and sense in making the application ex parte, but in the run of the mill IR35 case it does nothing other than deny the taxpayer the right to put forward his side of the story. Arguably, this is contrary to natural justice and may amount to a breach of human rights. Section 20 Notices do not require an assessment to be under appeal.

16.75 The Revenue has confirmed in its manuals that any written representations the practitioner wished to give to the inspector will be read out by the inspector at the meeting. There is little doubt that some inspectors will present such written representations with limited vigour.

16.76 Under the precept system an inspector may raise an assessment which, once appealed, could then be subject to a directions hearing where the Commissioners would consider requiring the production of information. Such a hearing would be in open court and the practitioner could make verbal representations and see that fair play was done.

16.77 Given a choice between raising formal assessments, where the taxpayer can then dictate or at least influence the conduct of the case, or pursuing a Section 20 Notice, which in some ways freezes out the agent, it is disappointing, but of little surprise, that inspectors increasingly seem to prefer to go the Section 20 route.

16.78 Although the Revenue seeks the taxpayer's 'co-operation' it is using its statutory powers under Section 20 where it does not get the co-operation it wants. This is the case even in cases of contract reviews, not full compliance enquiries.

End-user evidence

16.79 Following Revenue defeats in *Lime-IT Ltd v Justin* and *Tilbury Consulting Ltd v Gittins* there has been a noticeable shift in the way the Revenue approach IR35 cases. Information and statements will be sought from representatives of the end-user. Unfortunately, this information may be given by Human Resources rather than Procurement and might often muddy, rather than clarify, matters. Of even greater significance is the fact that the Revenue will tend to obtain this information after formal assessments have been issued. From a self-assessment perspective this is very unsatisfactory, as the evidence or views of the end-user might well be highly relevant in deciding whether IR35 applies or not. Yet the taxpayer never gets to see this information unless the case is about to be heard by the Commissioners! The court commented on the virtually impossible position of the taxpayer in the most recent IR35 appeal to be heard at the Special Commissioners, *Ansell Computer Services Ltd v Richardson (HMIT)*. The judgment in this case is still awaited.

Customer service or compliance enquiry

16.80 The Revenue has previously given categoric assurances that where a taxpayer requests a contract review under the customer service initiative, if the Revenue's 'caught by IR35' opinion is not accepted by the taxpayer, that will not lead to the taxpayer being enquired into. However, the Revenue has now changed its policy, despite the FAQs not telling the full story. If a taxpayer now rejects the Revenue's 'caught' opinion, once the filing date for form P35 has passed the Revenue will treat the refusal to accept its opinion as an act justifying a compliance enquiry. The old assurance has gone. When challenged on this the Revenue have responded that 'the position has moved on and an enquiry is justified'. When again challenged as to how the position has moved on the Revenue have responded by saying that the taxpayer has not accepted their 'caught' opinion! Practitioners beware.

A new approach to substitution

16.81 Despite case law that clearly states a substitution clause will be effective in defeating employed status, for example the *Express Echo* case, the Revenue seems to have adopted its own approach.

16.82 Revenue specialists have confirmed to Accountax that substitution is merely another factor to be taken into account. As such they will try to play it down, but the law is not on their side.

16.83 The Revenue will often attempt (and succeed) in getting the end-user to concede that the contractor could not decide 'from one day to the next' to send any substitute he wished. Most end-users will confirm this, but this is not the test.

16.84 As substitution is a central factor (and the Revenue knows this) they will increasingly focus on either playing it down or will present unrealistic scenarios to the end-user in a bid to get confirmation that a substitute could not be sent.

Changing priorities?

16.85 The 2004 Budget did nothing to appeal or amend IR35 despite the many rumours that it would. What has been confirmed by the Revenue is a further review of status in the construction industry following the early campaign in the mid and late 1990s. It has been reported in the press that the number of inspectors working in compliance in the construction industry will double during 2004/05. There are only so many Revenue staff to go around and it would seem likely that there will be fewer taking up new IR35 cases in the coming months, although current IR35 enquiries will be worked to a conclusion.

16.86 Without question, Accountax noticed fewer cases being taken up in early 2004 as well as a willingness to concede IR35 cases that were in progress.

Summary

16.87 Handling an IR35 enquiry, particularly a face to face meeting, is a major aspect of defending a client. Practitioners should note an increased preference for the Revenue to use its statutory powers under section 20. Where the Revenue has obtained statements or information from a third party this should be requested at an early stage to appraise the evidence.

Summary

16.88 To be forewarned is to be forearmed. Compliance officers will concentrate on the above areas, many of which are fundamental to IR35 'disguised employee' status. But they must operate within the law at all times.

Questions on IR35 disguised employee status should be answered in writing and the contractor should not get involved in a technical verbal argument with the officer.

Areas which are important, such as mutuality of obligations may not even be raised by the officer. If the contractor is represented by his accountant this and other factors which are relevant but which have not been raised should be discussed and included in any notes of meeting.

CHAPTER 17

Appeal formalities and strategies in an unresolved IR35 dispute

Making an appeal

17.1 It would be hoped that a robust presentation of the available arguments in Chapters 4, 8 and 9 will result in the Revenue backing down but this will not always be the case. Despite cogent technical argument and possibly attendance at meetings with the Revenue the practitioner may find that the dispute cannot be agreed. As was seen in the last chapter, there is ample evidence that the Revenue will doggedly pursue cases that are either very weak (*Lime-IT Ltd v Justin*) or misconceived (*Tilbury Consulting Ltd v Gittins*).

In these circumstances the Revenue will, or may have already raised formal IR35 decisions to force the matter to the next stage. That is not to say that the raising of such formal decisions necessarily means further arguments cannot be advanced; indeed, formal decisions (and Regulation 49 Determinations under the Income Tax (Employments) Regulations 1993, SI 1993/744) are sometimes raised at an early stage. But it now has to be assumed that deadlock has been reached and despite the best efforts of all concerned agreement cannot be secured.

17.2 If it has not yet done so the Revenue will issue a formal Section 8 Notice or, in the case of a traditional status dispute, a Regulation 49 Determination. Strictly, both Section 8 Notices and Regulation 49 Determinations should be raised if the Revenue wishes to pursue both national insurance and tax. It is therefore necessary to lodge an appeal if the Revenue's view is to be disputed.

17.3 In ESM 3296 the whole focus of the procedure is via a Section 8 Notice with little mention of a Regulation 49 Determination. It seems the Revenue may only raise the Section 8 Notice but then treat any Commissioners' decision as binding for tax purposes also. However, this is unwise. Firstly, the NIC legislation in respect of IR35 is worded differently from the tax legislation so it is difficult to see how an NIC decision could be binding from a tax point of view. Secondly, the appellant taxpayer may *not* accept an NIC determination as binding for tax purposes whatever the Revenue might think is expedient.

17.4 As such a second hearing could be forced. This can be avoided if a Regulation 49 Determination is made at the same time as the Section 8 Notice, whereby appeals can be lodged against both and heard at the same time by the same Commissioners. This appeal must be in writing and must state the grounds of appeal. In a typical case this might be:

> Dear Sir,
>
> Re F Bloggs Computer Services Ltd
>
> We are in receipt of your Section 8 Notice/Reg 49 Determination relating to the above client for the year 2001/02 and wish to appeal.
>
> Our grounds of appeal are that you have failed to apply the correct law to the full facts of this case and as such it is our view that our client is not caught by the intermediaries' legislation and that IR35 does not apply.
>
> Please ensure that all duties are immediately postponed, and please acknowledge safe receipt of this appeal
>
> We will write further in due course explaining our client's further arguments.
>
> Yours faithfully

17.5 Practitioners should note that an appeal must be made within 30 days of the date of the notice of assessment. However, many practitioners are unaware that if they fail to make a timely appeal they have a right to lodge a late appeal under TMA 1970 s 49. Where a late appeal is necessary it should state both the reason the appeal is being made late and that it has not been delayed unreasonably thereafter. For example, a serious illness would normally be accepted as reasonable grounds for lodging a late appeal but if following recovery from the illness the delay continues unreasonably thereafter the benefit of the late appeal provisions will probably not be given.

It should be noted that where the inspector refuses to accept the late appeal on the grounds that the excuse is not reasonable or that the delay continued unreasonably thereafter, he must refer the late appeal to the Commissioners in order that they may consider whether or not to accept it. In other words, the inspector himself does not have the last word on refusing a late appeal. In the author's experience many inspectors seem unaware that if they reject a late appeal they must refer the matter to the Commissioners.

17.6 When listening to a late appeal application the Commissioners are only determining whether or not the late appeal itself should be accepted.

They are not hearing and determining the main subject matter of the appeal, ie whether IR35 applies or not. The overwhelming majority of Commissioners are anxious to have a full and fair hearing and it is unusual for them to reject an application for a late appeal. In most cases the inspector himself will accept the late appeal and will tend to refer only the most extreme cases of delay to the Commissioners.

In truth the inspector knows that the Commissioners are more likely than not to accept the late appeal if it goes before them and as such he will tend to accept the late appeal in order to avoid an unnecessary and expensive hearing before the Commissioners. The Commissioners would not thank the inspector for 'forcing' late appeal hearings when common sense would indicate the General Commissioners would allow it. The General Commissioners are unpaid laymen giving up their personal time and they do not welcome unnecessary hearings. The Special Commissioners probably have better things to hear.

17.7 However, practitioners should also note that it tends to be the same accountants who regularly fail to get their appeals in on time and it is strategically unwise to get a reputation, both with the inspector and local Commissioners, of being the accountant who is always chasing his tail and leaving everything to the last minute. Interestingly, the author has noted on many occasions that it is mysteriously the same accountants who always manage to suffer postal delays, letters not delivered and a history of weak and desperate excuses. Practitioners should ensure they do not get this kind of reputation.

17.8 At the time of making the appeal it is necessary to advise the inspector that any duties charged need postponing. Many accountants lodge the appeal but fail to lodge a postponement application. If a postponement application is omitted the normal collection procedures will continue and the client will wonder what is going on. The suggested letter above illustrates a postponement application as well as the appeal. It is of course not possible to have a postponement application without an appeal. Postponing the duties will not stop the Revenue charging interest if duties are ultimately payable. A Section 8 Notice itself does not bring any duties into charge (unlike a Reg 49 Determination). This is because a Section 8 Notice is a formal decision not an actual assessment. A postponement application is essential where a Reg 49 Determination has been issued.

Which body of Commissioners?

17.9 Most appeals are heard by the General Commissioners who sit on a regular basis at a local district level. They are unpaid men and women who generally have experience of commerce and know the local community well.

They are guided on procedural matters by the Clerk to the General

Commissioners who is paid and who is often, but certainly not always, a local solicitor. The author has dealt with clerks who are professionally qualified coroners or clerks to the local magistrates.

The General Commissioners are not legal or tax experts and many of them will not have sat on an IR35 dispute or even a traditional status dispute.

17.10 The commonly held rule of thumb is that because of their relatively modest level of formal legal and technical experience it is better to take a dispute to the local General Commissioners if it does not turn on fine legal or esoteric arguments. Instead, it would be strategically wise to concentrate on straightforward facts and the credibility of the taxpayer. Some practitioners hold the view that their client would be more likely to get the 'sympathy vote' or the 'benefit of the doubt' from the Generals rather than the Specials.

17.11 The Special Commissioners are legally trained, but they sit in very limited locations, usually London and occasionally in the provinces. Accountax have recently represented a taxpayer who was seriously ill and as a result the Special Commissioners decided to hold the hearing in the taxpayer's living room. As they sit in very limited locations there can be a long delay before the client's case is listed for a hearing. It is argued that the Specials are much better suited to hearing long and complex disputes involving difficult legal and taxation matters, disputes which may last several days. This is the received wisdom and is, in many ways, true.

17.12 The taxpayer has the right to choose which body of Commissioners he wants to hear his appeal, but the election for the Specials should be made at the time the appeal is lodged. If no election is made the appeal will be heard by the Generals. If it turns out that the case is going to be particularly lengthy and complex (as in most IR35 cases) one can apply for a Transfer of Jurisdiction under TMA 1970 s 44(3). It is worth asking the inspector handling the case whether or not he will object. However, be warned that not opposing the application is not the same as supporting it. The General Commissioners will decide whether or not they want to hear the appeal at a hearing, where the taxpayer puts forward his reasons for wanting a transfer. It should be noted that the Generals can refuse a transfer of Jurisdiction and the Specials can refuse to take over a case the Generals want to transfer to them.

17.13 A clear way to think of it is to regard the Generals as being like the local unpaid lay magistrates and the Specials as the professional stipendiary magistrates. Without doubt there is likely to be less left to chance at the Specials. They are on the whole far less likely to make mistakes in law than the Generals or to misinterpret complex facts.

The author has experienced both first and third hand instances where the Generals came to what can only be described as perverse decisions. The General Commissioners rarely hear cases which last more than half a day and in a complex factual and legal dispute which may last perhaps into a second day there is no doubt that their ability to focus on the minutiae of case law and fine legal argument is tested to the full.

17.14 The final decision may be made by reference to other factors. For example, it is more likely that the Revenue will be represented by a barrister or a specialist Revenue advocate if the case goes to the Specials. The Specials alone have the power to award costs against either side if they feel the inspector or the taxpayer has acted wholly unreasonably (see *Scott (t/a Farthings Steak House) v MacDonald* [1996] STC (SCD) 381 for an instance of costs being awarded against the Revenue).

17.15 Most IR35/status disputes are more 'legal' than the inspector realises. The inspector tends to say it is all about establishing 'facts', which it is, but once the facts have been established the law has to be applied to those facts. In most status disputes conducted by Accountax reference has been made to around 15 case law decisions. In every case that Accountax has argued the inspector has relied upon considerably less case law and has often been caught out by not being able to refer to up to date legal decisions. In the author's experience a well prepared and carefully presented argument, even including many case law references can be readily understood by the average General Commissioners, but on balance it is probably better to take IR35 appeals to the Specials.

17.16 General Commissioners hearings can be organised relatively quickly, are quite informal and the Revenue is unlikely to appoint a lawyer to take its case. On the other hand Special Commissioners' hearings are more formal, and are likely to have 'directions' hearings as a preliminary formality in order to lay down a timetable for the exchange of documents, etc. This rarely happens with a General Commissioners' appeal hearing. The advantage of having directions agreed in advance is that there will be no surprises 'on the day'. It is usually possible to agree directions with the Revenue in a standard format that are acceptable to both sides.

Getting the appeal listed for hearing

17.17 It is very commonly misunderstood that only the inspector is entitled to approach the Commissioners to have a case laid down for an appeal hearing. But this is not the case; even before the General Commissioners (Jurisdiction and Procedure) Regulations 1994, SI 1994/1812 (and the Special Commissioners equivalent, SI 1994/1811), came into force it was always open for the taxpayer, or his representative, to have the case listed. See Appendices 4 and 5 for the full Special and General Commissioners' Regulations. Traditionally, however, the vast majority of all listings are instigated by the inspector, not the accountant or taxpayer. There are several reasons for this.

'Delay' hearings

17.18 Firstly, many listings to date have been concerned with what used to be called 'delay' hearings. In the pre-self-assessment era taxpayers would often be behind with their accounts, often by several years. There would typically be several years' assessments, the subject of estimated assessments, which were under appeal. Eventually (and often the Revenue could only be accused of excessive patience) the Revenue would become anxious to bring matters up to date and list the open appeals, along with many other similar cases, at a regular meeting of the Commissioners. This would be called a delay hearing.

17.19 Often the outstanding accounts would come in prior to the date of the hearing and the inspector would then consider the accounts and either agree them and determine the profits under TMA 1970 s 54 or would raise queries on the accounts. Cases where the accounts had arrived would either be removed completely from the list of cases to be considered by the Commissioners or the inspector would tell the Commissioners the accounts had been received and would request the Commissioners to adjourn the appeal 'sine die' (without day). In other words remove the appeal from any future listings.

In such cases there was little point in the taxpayer's accountant turning up at the hearing as the listing had either already been removed or would be adjourned as a mere formality.

17.20 However, the effect of this system was that the accountants rarely appeared at the Commissioners and as such they would fail to develop any familiarity or experience of the tribunal, even in the context of simple matters. On the other hand, the Revenue would appear at the Commissioners on a very regular basis, seeing the same Commissioners and liaising with the Clerk. A competent well organised inspector would have had many opportunities to make his mark with the Commissioners.

It should be stressed immediately that the Commissioners are entirely independent of the Revenue. Yet the party who appears regularly before the Commissioners and who has a long history of performing professionally in front of them must have some kind of advantage.

17.21 Sometimes accounts would not be sent in on time or the extra time the Commissioners gave to the accountant to produce the accounts may have lapsed. In these circumstances the accountant would have to turn up at the hearing and explain to the Commissioners why he or his client needed yet more time to submit the accounts and he would be in the unenviable position of having to ask for the Commissioners' 'indulgence' yet again.

17.22 The majority of practitioners therefore have little experience of the Commissioners and when they do have some experience it is normally when they have been asking for more time because they, or their clients, haven't done what they should have done. It is little wonder the profession does not enjoy a tremendous reputation for advocacy. The conclusion from all of the above is that it is generally the inspector who tends to force the issue by making the listing of an open appeal.

Taking the initiative

17.23 Taking the initiative and contacting the Clerk to the Commissioners to have an appeal listed is effective for three reasons. Firstly, it shows to the client that the practitioner is being pro-active.

Secondly, it sends an extraordinarily strong message to the inspector that the accountant is prepared not only to turn up at the Commissioners but willing to instigate the whole process. Not only does this show the inspector that the taxpayer means business it can also result in the inspector having to respond to the accountant's moves and, to some extent at least, work to his timetable.

Thirdly, because it is so unusual for the taxpayer or accountant to have a case listed (usually because the accountant is trying desperately to avoid a hearing or at least buy time before one goes ahead) it must send a very strong message of confidence to the Clerk and the Commissioners. This fact can usually be brought out at the hearing to stress yet again the proactive approach taken. This is particularly the case when listing an appeal at the Generals.

How a case is listed

17.24 The many Clerks to the Commissioners are listed in *Tolley's Tax Office Directory* and on Tolley's Tax Link. Alternatively, a call to the inspector who 'deals with' Commissioners' hearings with the direct question 'who is the Clerk for this division?' will usually get the information needed. It might also take the inspector by surprise. The Clerk to the Special Commissioners can be contacted on 020 7612 9656 or by post at The Court Service, 15–19 Bedford Avenue, London WC1B 3AS.

17.25 Under the Commissioners (Jurisdiction and Procedure) Regulations 1994, SI 1994/1812 and SI 1994/1811, either the Revenue or the taxpayer can require an open appeal to be listed. Listing a case, although usually instigated by the inspector, is not solely his right. It has to be said that some Clerks to the General Commissioners still feel that a case can only be listed once the inspector makes the request, but this is incorrect. (Both the General and Special Commissioners' Regulations are reproduced in full at Appendices 4 and 5).

17.26 A suggested letter to have a case listed might read as follows:

> Dear Sirs,
>
> Re Fred Bloggs Computer Services Ltd   Tax District ref: XYZ
>
> Our client has under appeal an assessment on his income under Section 8 of the 1992 Social Security Contributions (Transfer of Functions etc) Act. The Revenue alleges our client's income is that of a disguised employee under the IR35 intermediaries' legislation. Our client maintains the intermediaries' legislation does not apply and that he is running a genuine independent business.
>
> Following a long technical argument we have not been able to reach a settlement with the Revenue. Our client has instructed us to contact you in order to request a contentious appeal hearing as soon as possible.
>
> We have asked the Revenue to draw up a draft Statement of Agreed Facts which will no doubt assist the Commissioners on the day.
>
> Please note it is our normal practice to provide the Commissioners with copies of all the case law and statute upon which we rely. We will furnish you with a list of case law references well before the hearing.
>
> At this stage we anticipate calling two witnesses but will confirm this nearer the hearing. We anticipate our client's case will take around two hours to present.
>
> As our client is the appellant and with the burden of proof being on him, we respectfully request that we address the Commissioners first on the day.
>
> We now look forward to hearing from you with a couple of alternative dates for the hearing. Our client is anxious to have the matter laid down as soon as possible.
>
> Yours faithfully

When listing a case at the Specials it will be necessary to enclose a copy of the Notices/Determinations and the appeal, as this will show a valid election for the Specials has been made.

Clerks to the Generals tend to be solicitors, sometimes coroners or other experienced legal personnel and as such careful attention to names, references, etc, should always be a priority. One doesn't, as the saying goes, get a second chance to make a first impression.

What does the above letter to the Clerk say? Firstly, it sends a clear signal that the taxpayer is taking the initiative, and that a prompt hearing is requested. This in turn will put pressure on the inspector and is, therefore, strategically worthwhile.

Secondly, the essence of the dispute has been explained to the Clerk and it has been confirmed that an effort to resolve the dispute has been made but has failed. What is being demonstrated is 'reasonableness'.

By implication the Clerk now knows that the Commissioners' Regulations are understood by the taxpayer's representative, which can only increase the credibility of the practitioner. The references to witnesses, case law etc show a full understanding of the procedures in a contentious case and in particular with reference to the statement of facts.

The letter specifically states 'It is our usual practice . . .'. Clearly this can only be stated when it is true. Where this is the case, a very powerful message is being sent to the inspector that the practitioner is experienced. The purpose of the letter is not merely to request a listing of the client's appeals. It is to send a message of clarity and confidence to all concerned.

Finally, the right to address the Commissioners first on the day has been requested. There are very sound procedural reasons for doing this as will be explained later. For the time being it need only be noted that again the initiative is being taken on behalf of the taxpayer. As any hearing before the Specials will be more formal the appellant will automatically be expected to speak first.

A copy of the listing letter should be sent to the Revenue for its information and action on the draft statement of agreed facts. If directions are agreed this will usually require the Revenue to draft the statement.

Using wording similar to the above will result in a letter far more professional and effective than those produced by many practitioners. This stencil establishes a pro-active attitude and demonstrates an understanding of the basic procedures and considerations involved in a contentious appeal.

17.27 At this stage it is not unknown for the Revenue to request a further meeting to discuss the case and sort out details relating to witnesses and documents. Unless there is a clear indication that the inspector is about to concede and wants to reach a face-saving compromise of some kind, such meetings should be resisted. It is also possible that the inspector might seek a preliminary hearing with a view to seeking a precept in order that documentation he should have sought earlier can now be reviewed! A preliminary hearing for 'directions' is more common in the formal setting of the Special Commissioners but is often a time-buying exercise by the Revenue in cases going to the Generals, and should be resisted in most cases.

The more astute inspector will see this pre-hearing meeting as an opportunity to probe the taxpayer and his accountant with a view to obtaining details of their precise arguments, witnesses and the case law they will use on the day. As the finer details of case law references etc are exchanged only seven days before the hearing the inspector could be trying to get advance knowledge of the strengths of the taxpayer's case and indeed the advocacy skills of the practitioner. In short, the unwary practitioner might end up giving his hand away well in advance of the time he has to, and this will probably be to the detriment of the taxpayer, his client, whom he is meant to be representing.

It might be thought that a genuine attempt to resolve the dispute without the need to go to the Commissioners is a good thing, and so it is. But practitioners should be wary of the inspector who offers a last minute meeting, ostensibly to see if the case can be settled. They may find that in the process the client's detailed case has been given away in advance with the inspector pressing ahead with the appeal hearing anyway. Be warned.

Resistance in achieving a listing

17.28 Although Commissioners Regulations are quite clear in that either the inspector or the taxpayer may request a listing, it is not unknown for Clerks to the Generals to prefer to wait until they get the go-ahead from the Revenue. This is either because they do not fully appreciate that either side may have the matter laid down or, more likely, because it is the custom and practice of the Clerk when organising a listing to wait for the Revenue's official communication first.

This, however, must be resisted. If necessary, write to the Clerk and remind him that, under the General Commissioners Regulations, the taxpayer has the right to have the matter listed. It is sometimes worthwhile having a word with the inspector, who may be prepared to confirm to the Clerk that a listing is required. This should not be necessary, but it may speed up the process.

17.29 Ultimately, if an appeal is not listed, it is possible to complain to the Lord Chancellor's Department, which has overall responsibility for the Clerks to the General Commissioners. They will refer the matter to the Commissioners in the first instance. In one extreme case, the author threatened to apply to the High Court for an order of mandamus, which is a decree forcing a civil servant to do his job. Needless to say, the Clerk then took the matter seriously and arranged the listing.

17.30 A lack of co-operation in arranging a listing should not, however, be confused with genuine logistical difficulties, which can often arise. The suggested draft letter above makes it clear that several alternative dates are put forward because the date of the hearing has to be convenient to all parties including the inspector, the taxpayer, the practitioner, the Clerk, the witnesses and not least the Commissioners.

It can be difficult to arrange a contentious appeal hearing when the movements of all of these persons have to be taken into account and it can be exacerbated by hearings during busy holiday periods etc. Indeed, it is sometimes necessary to organise a contentious hearing three or four months in advance.

Where a case is particularly complicated or where the number of witnesses to be called is excessive it is possible that the hearing will spill over into a second day. In these circumstances it may prove even more difficult to arrange two consecutive days when the General Commissioners, let alone the other people involved in the hearing, will be available. It should always be remembered that the General Commissioners are giving up their time voluntarily.

17.31 As explained earlier in this chapter, there is a choice as to whether the General Commissioners or Special Commissioners hear the appeal; this choice is initially in the hands of the taxpayer who may elect for the case to be heard by the Special Commissioners at the time of making the appeal.

It is still envisaged that the majority of tax status and IR35 appeals will be heard by the Special Commissioners as this is the more appropriate tribunal. So far around eight IR35 appeals have been heard by the Specials.

A note on calling the Revenue's bluff

17.32 During a long and complex technical argument it is easy for both sides to become entrenched in their views and arguments, and, it has to be said, personalities sometimes come into play. The practitioner may feel that he is on a slippery slope that will inevitably lead to a contentious hearing. In some cases both sides will take a very assertive approach where an early hearing is threatened, despite the fact that the case could, with a bit more willing on both sides, be settled amicably.

17.33 In other cases, despite providing the inspector with the facts, relevant case law and reasoned arguments, it is simply impossible to make progress. In this type of situation the practitioner has to take the initiative and proceed to a Commissioners hearing. However, this should not be threatened unless there is the resolve to see the matter through.

Case study

In a recent case the Revenue pulled out of an IR35 appeal very shortly before the hearing. They then wrote to the Clerk saying the dispute had been settled by 'agreement'. We pointed out that the case had been conceded by the Revenue, not agreed.

17.34 Although many cases which are laid down for a hearing are settled shortly before the case goes ahead, it would be very unwise to call the Revenue's bluff. A listing of a case should only be sought where the taxpayer and his representative are prepared to turn up on the day.

17.35 Tactically, pushing for a hearing may result in the Revenue backing down, but this is not something to be relied upon. If the practitioner develops a reputation with the local tax office or the local Clerk that he is constantly requesting and then pulling out of contentious appeal hearings, this cannot enhance his reputation. On the other hand, if it is made clear that there is a real willingness to go to the Commissioners, then without question the inspector will know that he is dealing with somebody who is serious, and not someone merely calling the Inland Revenue's bluff.

Doing the pre-hearing homework

17.36 Having written to the Clerk to have the appeals laid down it is very important at this stage to stand back and again reconsider the strengths and weaknesses of the case as a whole. During the course of the inquiries the practitioner may have taken a very pro-active approach but it now has to be accepted that for whatever reasons, the arguments have failed and it has not been possible to convince the inspector of the merits of the taxpayer's arguments. The challenge now is to convince the Commissioners, on a balance of probabilities, that the appeal should be upheld. Particular attention should be given to the available evidence and, where available, witness statements (these are usually available under directions for a hearing at the Specials).

17.37 Convincing the Commissioners is not the same as trying to win the argument with the Revenue. Many inspectors still like to be completely satisfied before they will concede. Indeed, practitioners may know of instances of inspectors who are 95% 'satisfied' but who still decline to accept the explanations and arguments put forward.

17.38 However, it must be stressed that at the Commissioners the burden of proof is nothing more than the balance of probabilities. In numerical terms this means 51%. If the arguments and explanations are probably correct the appeal should succeed. There are generally three General Commissioners involved in a contentious appeal hearing and it is therefore necessary only to convince two out of the three to the tune of 51% to win the case. This is a standard of proof which falls far short of the inspector's own subjective 'being satisfied'. Generally only one Special Commissioner will hear an IR35 appeal.

17.39 Where a hearing has been laid down it is perhaps worth reminding the inspector that the standard of proof at the Commissioners is nothing more than convincing a majority of them on the balance of probabilities. The author has experienced long drawn out disputes with the Revenue and as the date of the hearing approached, the inspector, often in conjunction with his senior line manager (who may well be taking the case for the Revenue), looks again at the arguments. It is then realised that although the inspector may still not be satisfied himself, the Commissioners may very well be. In these circumstances the senior officer may intervene with a view to closing the case down or coming to some kind of compromise settlement.

The practitioner is far more likely to achieve this result where he has taken the initiative in having the matter listed in the first place and has forced the pace.

17.40 It goes without saying that the case should never have come this far unless there is real confidence that on the balance of probabilities it is felt the appeal can be sustained. In the author's experience, it is in the few weeks leading up to the hearing itself when a great deal of extra detail can be gleaned from the file. As preparation of the detailed appeal presentation gets underway there will undoubtedly be discovered minutiae which may prove very helpful, and sometimes unhelpful, to the contractor's case.

Summary

17.41 At this stage it is vitally important to revisit the entire history of the arguments so that the appeal can be prepared and presented properly. This requires very careful attention to detail, particularly in respect of documentation, witnesses and briefing of the client. These topics are covered in detail in Chapter 18 'Preparing for a Contentious Appeal Hearing at the Commissioners'.

CHAPTER 18

Preparing for a contentious appeal hearing at the Commissioners

Introduction

18.1 Without question the overwhelming majority of practitioners will be nervous when taking a contentious appeal to the Commissioners; particularly for the first time. Indeed, they will be nervous or at least galvanised even if they have taken many such cases. This is normal and perfectly rational, and it should not in itself dissuade a conscientious practitioner from representing his client (and thereby avoiding the higher fees that are likely to be charged by a specialist tax consultant with experience of presenting appeals to the Commissioners). Indeed, there is a school of thought which says that if the advocate is not at least a little anxious about the 'big day' then he is probably not taking it seriously enough.

18.2 Some of the advice on preparing for a contentious appeal offered in this section might seem not worth worrying about, but in the author's experience every extra point is worth scoring. Bearing in mind the onus on the taxpayer is a mere balance of probabilities, anything which can get one step nearer the winning line has to be worth taking. The advice offered is based on the author's practical experience of conducting contentious appeals in the real world.

18.3 Despite the high stakes and the prospect of either an outright win or an outright loss (in status/IR35 cases there is rarely a middle ground) the good news is that the proceedings on the day will be generally slow-paced, quite informal and, if proper preparation has been carried out, an enjoyable and educational experience.

Case study

At a recent IR35 appeal, after both sides had finished, the Special Commissioner said 'This is where I stand and imperiously leave the court . . . but I have too much to carry so leave in your own time'. Such informality makes for an enjoyable experience at the tribunal.

The most important of these factors is the slow-paced nature of the proceedings. There will be plenty of time to 'think on your feet' while the Commissioners are making notes or reading from the bundles of evidence. If an assistant is taken by the practitioner, which is highly recommended, the assistant can organise the paperwork, which will take even more pressure away.

18.4 In short, the whole process, while demanding, is well within the skills range of the ordinarily competent professional adviser. The key is preparation and understanding the rules, then having the courage to proceed in a confident manner.

Before the hearing

18.5 It is normal practice before a contentious appeal that certain administrative formalities are attended to. These are designed simply to make the case run more smoothly on the day and are to the benefit of the Revenue, taxpayer and Commissioners alike. Where a hearing is before the Special Commissioners these pre-hearing formalities are more likely to be laid down by way of a 'directions' order, where a formal timetable is ordered in respect of statements of facts, documents, witness details etc.

Agreed statement of facts

18.6 The statement of facts is an agreed declaration between the Revenue and taxpayer that certain facts are not 'in dispute'. Although there is no obligation on either the Revenue or taxpayer to come to such an agreed statement, indeed it is sometimes impossible, in the majority of cases an agreed statement is expected by the Commissioners.

18.7 The reason why such a statement of facts is important and desirable is that it will speed matters up considerably on the day of the appeal hearing. This is because facts have to be 'proved' and if it is necessary to prove every fact by formal evidence to the Commissioners it makes for a very long hearing indeed. Although some panels of Commissioners are prepared to admit 'facts' relatively informally it will be appreciated that it would be a drawn out and quite unnecessary process to go through matters which are not in dispute in the first place.

18.8 At its simplest a statement of facts consists of the name of the taxpayer and the assessments under appeal. This, however, is exiguous to say the least. A more detailed statement of facts would state, for example, when the taxpayer started trading, what he does, what correspondence has been entered into and what meetings have been attended. In the case of tax status disputes generally, detail might be given regarding the terms and conditions in the contract, the rates of pay etc. In an IR35 dispute agreed facts could include what salary or dividends have been taken or what money has been invested in training or equipment.

It will be appreciated that a statement of facts can vary from the brief bare bones to a fully detailed account of facts established and agreed throughout the course of the Revenue's enquiries leading up to the appeal hearing.

18.9 The advantage of such a statement is obvious—matters are clarified and agreed in advance saving time on the day of the hearing. But there are some potential disadvantages in agreeing a statement of facts. For both the Revenue and the taxpayer once a statement of facts is formally agreed it cannot be resiled from at a later stage.

If, for example, it is agreed that all the terms and conditions of a working relationship were contained in the written contract the Revenue would not be able to go behind this agreed fact at the hearing and seek to establish if there were any other oral terms. Likewise, if the taxpayer concedes in a meeting that he has never funded any training courses, it would not be open to him to come up later with details of courses he claims he funded himself.

Whether there is a legal case to say that a fact has been agreed in 'error' and should therefore be ignored is not something either side would want to put to the Commissioners, as their patience would be severely tested. The danger is in agreeing as a fact something which cannot later be disputed, because both sides are prohibited from doing so. If in doubt don't agree a fact. If it is felt that there is something to add or explain about a 'fact' don't agree it.

Quite simply, having agreed a fact the practitioner will be denied the opportunity to adopt a different view later. This is not to say that the taxpayer should be reserving his right to change his position on a whim. It is more a case of ensuring he is not restricting himself from arguing what the real facts are on the day.

Facts which are not in dispute should be agreed in a written statement in advance. Facts which are in dispute should never be agreed in advance. Instead the determination of the Commissioners should be sought on the day, by evidence.

18.10 A statement of facts is not a list of arguments or contentions. Practitioners should be very cautious about agreeing as a fact something the Revenue is merely alleging. Statements of agreed facts should be just that—agreed facts and nothing else. Any contentious interpretations or arguments are to be aired on the day, backed up by evidence, and either accepted or rejected by the Commissioners.

Case study

The inspector drafted a 120 paragraph statement of facts, about 100 of which were not facts at all. Accountax responded by trimming the statement to 22 facts. This upset the inspector, who then trimmed it further to just 6 facts. The Special Commissioner noted in court that it took him less than 30 seconds to read. In the end, the statement was virtually useless but it would have been harmful to agree as fact what was no more than Revenue contention.

18.11 In the author's experience, the inspector will sometimes try to put a fact into a statement which would not be strictly relevant to the appeal, even though it is still a fact. For example, the taxpayer may have a history of poor tax compliance or may have been investigated by the Revenue in the past, where irregularities were found in the accounts or tax return. If this is the case then although such detail is 'fact' it is not relevant to the proceedings under appeal and it should not be put in the statement.

If it was agreed in the statement of facts that the taxpayer was previously investigated and irregularities were discovered this would undoubtedly be unhelpful to the taxpayer and would be referred to by the inspector in an effort to discredit the taxpayer.

If, on the other hand, such a fact is not agreed in a statement of agreed facts then the inspector would find it much harder to introduce and use against the taxpayer. It might look as if he was being perhaps 'petty' in dragging up the past. Indeed, the practitioner would explain to the Commissioners that the past is not germane to the proceedings under appeal. But without doubt it will be harder to argue this if the taxpayer's fiscal history has been incorporated into the statement of agreed facts. Facts should only be included if they are relevant to the appeal and if there is no wish to dispute them.

Who should prepare the statement of facts?

18.12 The author's view is that the initial draft should be prepared by the Revenue. Although the taxpayer is the appellant and therefore carries the onus of proof, it is nonetheless the Revenue who is trying to challenge the status quo. If the Revenue feels the IR35 intermediaries' legislation applies then it is not unreasonable for the Revenue to take on the initial task of preparing the draft statement of facts. Usually this is a task the Revenue will tend to deal with in any event. This is because traditionally they take the initiative as the taxpayer and his professional representative will have little if any experience of such matters.

An inexperienced practitioner might agree a statement of facts not entirely to his clients' advantage, if the statement is presented to him as a *fait accomplis*. It must be remembered that it takes both parties to agree a statement. It is not a question of imposing a statement on the other side—it has to be agreed through a process of amendment, re-drafting and possible further amendment before it can be signed off by both parties.

There is an interesting possible strategic advantage in actually requesting the Revenue to draft a statement of facts for the taxpayer's approval. This is that the Revenue inspector will not want to be told what to do or when he should be doing it.

Case study

The author advised a practitioner in a status dispute and when it was clear the matter was going to go to hearing the Revenue was asked to produce an initial draft statement of facts. The inspector, who no doubt had countless other files to worry about was reluctant to draft a statement. A reminder was sent to the inspector pointing out that an agreed statement would speed matters up on the day and would in any event be expected by the Commissioners. A copy of the letter was sent to the Clerk.

The inspector was unhappy at being chased and dug in deep and again refused to issue the draft statement. A second reminder was sent and copied to the Clerk who was by now concerned that the inspector seemed to be unco-operative.

Shortly before the hearing the Revenue backed down from the appeal and a statement of facts never was produced. In a telephone conversation with the Clerk, it was made clear to the author that the Clerk, and one can only assume the Commissioners, were unimpressed with the Revenues' dilatoriness and apparent lack of co-operation.

18.13 The lesson to be learned is that by putting the Revenue under pressure to draft a statement of facts, which can be a difficult time-consuming matter if done thoroughly, the inspector may well drag his feet. Part of the reason for this is that inspectors do not like taxpayers' representative suggesting to them what they should be doing. Inspectors like working to their own timetable and may therefore become entrenched in their unwillingness to draft a statement. If this gets back to the Clerk and Commissioners they will not be impressed. A small point perhaps but one which can only help the taxpayer. At the Special Commissioners it is likely that the Directions will require the Revenue to produce the draft statement of agreed facts.

18.14 In the above case study practitioners should imagine what the reaction of the Commissioners would have been had the case gone ahead without a statement of facts? They would not have been pleased with the situation. If correspondence could then be adduced to show that the taxpayer had requested a statement of facts several times but the inspector had refused to co-operate this would tend to work against the inspector.

Of course it doesn't mean that the taxpayer will automatically win just because the inspector has dragged his feet over a statement of facts. It will, however, register in the minds of the Commissioners, who expect very high levels of professionalism and efficiency from the Revenue at all times.

The question for determination

18.15 Although it is not strictly a 'fact' it is common for the question the Commissioners are being asked to determine to be added to the statement, or provided separately. It has to be remembered that the General Commissioners will have no prior knowledge of the case, except perhaps for an advance sight of the agreed statement of facts. They are coming to what could be a highly technical appeal and may not fully understand what it is that they are being asked to determine.

This is not a criticism of the Commissioners nor of their Clerk—it is in fact a criticism of the parties to the appeal, that is the Revenue and the taxpayer, for not making it clear. Failing to make clear exactly what the point at issue is, and the determination being sought, is a typical failing of the accountant advocate.

It therefore makes sense to give *advance* warning to the Commissioners, via the Clerk, as to precisely what they are being asked to determine. The question for determination can be usefully appended to the statement of facts. With the Specials, skeleton arguments will be exchanged before the hearing. This is a fairly detailed summary of each side's case, legal authority, etc, and the skeletons are given to the Special Commissioner usually one to two weeks before the hearing.

18.16 In an IR35 dispute the question to be determined could be along the lines of

> 'Whether the intermediaries' legislation in ITEPA 2003 Ch 8 ss 48–61 applies to the engagements entered into by Fred Bloggs Computer Services Ltd for the year 2000/2001.'

In the more traditional status dispute the question to be determined might be phrased

> 'Whether XYZ Construction Ltd was engaging workers under a contract of services or a contract for services for the year 2000/2001.'

Having the question for determination clearly spelt out can only help, especially for hearings at the Generals.

Administrative procedures

18.17 It is customary and courteous to supply to the Clerk and the inspector, at least seven days prior to the hearing, a list of case law references, statute, documents and details of witnesses. This is a good time for the practitioner to remind the Clerk that he wishes to speak first at the hearing. This should already have been indicated in earlier correspondence with the Clerk and is referred to in Chapter 17. Again, at the Specials, formal directions will deal with this.

18.18 The Clerk to the Generals should also be reminded that on the day of the appeal hearing full copies of all relevant documents and case law decisions will be supplied to the Commissioners. There is nothing more irritating for the Commissioners than finding that insufficient copies of documents have been prepared for all concerned. Surprisingly, this is an error the inspector often makes and it shows a lack of care in preparation, which can only harm one's case.

Case study

At a General Commissioners' hearing on a tax status dispute in late 2001, Accountax prepared documentation running to 234 pages. Copies were available for all persons present. On the other hand the inspector's documents ran to only 4 pages and he had not prepared copies for anyone, not even the Commissioners. He had to read his own documents then hand them to the Commissioners who had to look over each other's shoulders.This is a prime example of bad preparation. The Revenue lost.

So far as the inspector is concerned it is again customary, and indeed wise, to give him a list of case law references, statute, documents not already in the inspector's possession and witness details at least seven days prior to the hearing. If it is not already clear he should be reminded what the taxpayer's main contentions are, but the practitioner is not obliged to go into detail nor is he required to give away all his evidence in advance. Special Commissioner appeals will cater for this via formal directions.

18.19 The reason it is wise to give this information, especially documentation, to the inspector seven days prior to the hearing is that there should be no surprises at the hearing.

If there are any such surprises (by either side) the other side would be entitled to ask for either a brief adjournment to look at the new evidence or, in the case of substantial documentary evidence, an adjournment to another day. The Commissioners will not grant this lightly and if they do they will not be impressed by the party who introduced the new evidence. It is difficult enough arranging a full day appeal hearing without the extra aggravation of having to re-arrange it because one party has tried to deny the other side access to a document.

18.20 It should be noted that, in the case of employment tribunals and Special Commissioners' appeals the chairman will usually issue clear instructions that both sides have to exchange all documentary evidence upon which they seek to rely, including witness statements. It is thought that this approach will be introduced to all tax tribunals and is one of the matters presently being considered as part of the review of the tax tribunal system.

18.21 Practitioners should note that producing a document in advance as an 'agreed' document does *not* mean that its *contents* are agreed. See the Commissioners' Regulations in Appendices 4 and 5.

18.22 It must be stressed that different tax inspectors, Clerks and certainly the different divisions of Commissioners will take their own approach to these administrative formalities and what they expect of the practitioner. For example, the author has dealt both with Clerks who by profession are coroners and who generally demand a higher degree of formality as well as with Clerks who adopt a more informal approach.

A wise practitioner will therefore consider the specific Clerk he is dealing with and adapt his approach accordingly. There is no merit in insisting on a particularly formal or informal approach when it is clear that it is contrary to what the Clerk and the Commissioners expect.

18.23 Dealing with these formalities in an efficient and professional manner will not win the case for the appellant but his credibility will be enhanced from the outset. If this gets him 1% nearer to the magical 51% then it would be foolish not to take it.

18.24 It may be found that once the extensive case law has been detailed and witnesses to be called have been confirmed the inspector may start to feel a little uncomfortable, particularly if this information is revealed only shortly before the hearing. It is clearly better to win the argument without the need of going to the tax tribunal if at all possible, but it has to be said that many inexperienced tax officers may not have given proper attention to the case law and may end up in the unenviable position of having to carry out substantial research when the hearing is only a few days away.

Case study

In a tax status case the inspector was telephoned by the author. It was explained that as deadlock had been reached the best way to proceed would be by having formal assessment that could be appealed. The author explained he would then contact 'Beryl'. This confused the inspector. He was told Beryl was one of the listing clerks at the Special Commissioners. The inspector expressed concern that the case would go to the Specials. He conceded the case shortly afterwards without issuing any assessments. It is interesting to note that a search of the case law database revealed that the inspector concerned had never been to the Specials as either an advocate or witness.

18.25 It should be noted that when presenting the Revenue with a list of case law references the practitioner is *not* obliged to provide details of the specific passages to be quoted nor is he obliged to give the inspector copies of the case law. Essentially, both sides should be aware of the court judgments and the Revenue certainly has the technical resources to obtain copy judgments.

In other words, it is not the practitioner's job to make life easy for the

Revenue by doing the Revenue's homework for it. By the practitioner playing fair but hard, the Revenue may be forced into a situation where it would rather drop the case than proceed.

Case study

In a technical tax dispute the Revenue alleged that an associate dentist had ceased one profession and commenced another when she started her own surgery. This resulted in a significant extra tax charge. The only justification the inspector put forward was that her internal instructions made it clear that in these circumstances the cessation and commencement rules applied. Accountax argued that, in the particular circumstances of the case, there was no cessation and commencement and advised the inspector that witnesses would be called and further case law would be adduced at the contentious appeal hearing which had been arranged.

Accountax made it clear that further details of witnesses, contentions and case law etc would not be given to the inspector until seven days prior to the hearing. The inspector explained that she was part time and this would not give her much time to prepare her case and that she would have to seek an adjournment. Accountax reminded the inspector that this was a contentious appeal hearing, not a mere 'delay' hearing and that any application for an adjournment would be vigorously opposed.

One week later Accountax received a letter from the inspector confirming that she now felt the matter was not clear cut and would therefore drop her arguments.

It should be noted that this case was won, not simply because of the technical arguments *but because the inspector was put under pressure* and had to work to a very tight timetable. This assertive approach, without doubt, helped get the case closed down.

It is of course a judgement in each case as to whether all evidence, case law, witness statements and documents should be given to the inspector well in advance of the appeal hearing. On the one hand the inspector may review his opinion and concede. On the other hand the practitioner may be doing his client a massive disservice by giving away all his evidence in advance.

What needs to be done

18.26 The most important thing to remember is that the onus of proof lies with the taxpayer and hence with the practitioner as his representative.

To show that the appeal should be upheld, facts have to be established and legal argument advanced. Facts are 'proved' in a variety of ways.

Firstly, there may already be an agreed statement of facts, whereby certain issues are not in dispute and are taken as read.

Secondly, the practitioner will have to establish facts by evidencing them and this can be done either through documentary evidence or oral evidence. Having established the facts it is then a matter of showing *precisely how* the law applies to those facts by detailed reference to case law judgments. Chapter 6 deals with the major case law decisions. Essentially the practitioner has to show why his arguments are preferable, on the balance of probabilities, to the inspector's.

Opinions count for nothing

18.27 Although the Commissioners have a very well developed sense of fair play and justice they can only uphold the appeal on the basis of evidence. Clear evidence of fact and legal precedent taken from case law decisions are the two most important factors the Commissioners will take into account.

It is no use the taxpayer complaining about the legislation being 'unfair' any more than the practitioner making vague submissions that, in his opinion, the taxpayer is not a disguised employee. This kind of assertion will carry no weight.

The practitioner must focus on establishing facts by reference to evidence and then refer to detailed case law to support his case. Quoting precis or one paragraph summaries of case law decisions is a waste of time. Quoting the words that judges have actually used is the most devastating weapon in the practitioner's armoury.

For example, simply suggesting that having the right to send a substitute is an important indication of self-employment is nothing more than an opinion. On the other hand, supporting this assertion with the celebrated quotation from Lord Justice Peter Gibson in the *Express and Echo* case ([1999] IRLR 367 at 370 para 31—'where, as here, a person who works for another is not required to perform his services personally, then as a matter of law the relationship between the worker and the person for whom he works is not that of employer and employee'; will result in an important legal point being made effectively.

Case study

In a contentious appeal in the West Country concerning tax status of construction workers the inspector relied heavily on the Revenue publication IR56. This document explains the Revenue's approach, in a rather simplistic manner, to tax status. It is also out of date. At the hearing one of the Commissioners asked the inspector whether the booklet IR56 carried any force of law. The inspector confirmed that it did not. The Commissioner made the point that simply reading out IR56 did not advance the inspector's argument because the publication was nothing more than the Revenue's opinion and, therefore, had no legal weight. On the other hand, every legal submission made by Accountax was backed up with a quotation from a leading case law authority. The Revenue lost.

Documentation

18.28 At this stage it would be hoped that a statement of facts has been finalised and copied to the Clerk.

18.29 It is recommended that the practitioner now prepares two bundles of documents to be called Bundle A and Bundle B. These bundles will contain all of the necessary paperwork to be presented to the Commissioners at the hearing.

Bundle A

18.30 This Bundle will contain all of the non-legal paperwork, including relevant correspondence, copies of the assessments under appeal and any other documentary evidence to be put forward, for example, copies of invoices raised and notes of meetings or telephone conversations.

Each Bundle should have a clear and attractively designed header sheet detailing the names of the parties, the date of the hearing and the assessments under appeal. The practitioner should put in the effort to make sure the header sheets look professional.

At the front of Bundle A there should be a clear index and it is imperative that all pages are clearly numbered. Some documents may be photocopied landscape rather than portrait style and as such they will need numbering in a different corner. Do not overlook these administrative formalities.

18.31 The contents of a typical Bundle A might read as follows:

	Folio
Correspondence to HM Inspector of Taxes dated 14 July 2002 requesting contract review	1–2
Response from HM Inspector of Taxes dated 17 December 2002	3–4
Further correspondence to HM Inspector of Taxes dated 22 December 2002	5–6
Further correspondence from HM Inspector of Taxes dated 6 February 2003	7
Section 8 Assessment dated 1 April 2003	8–9
Appeal against the Section 8 Assessment dated 20 April 2003	10–11
Further correspondence from HM Inspector of Taxes dated 16 May 2003	12
Further correspondence to HM Inspector of Taxes dated 28 May 2003	13

Note of Telephone Conversation dated 1 June 2003	14
Notes of Meeting dated 7 June 2003	15–19
Further correspondence to HM Inspector of Taxes dated 18 June 2003	20–21
Correspondence to Clerk to the General Commissioners dated 29 June 2003	22
Contract for Services dated 31 March 2002	23–27
Copies of earlier contracts	28–38
Copy Invoices	39–41
Copy Public Liability and Professional Indemnity Insurance Certificates	42–47
Copy Business Stationery	48–49
Copy letter from Computer Agency	50–51
Copy web site print out and advertisements	52–57

Bundle B

18.32 This bundle will contain all of the case law authorities to be brought to the attention of the Commissioners together with copies of the relevant statutes or statutory instruments relating to the appeal. Once again it is important that a clear index is prepared and all pages are clearly numbered. It is also recommended that after the index page there is a further sheet giving a separate list of the relevant case law and the years in which the cases were heard. Again, a header page should be included, as with Bundle A.

18.33 A typical Bundle B would contain the following:

	Folio
Full index of case law decisions with references	1
Finance Act 2000 Schedule 12	2–8
Section 8 Notice of Decision	9–10
Case law decisions in full	11–216

Practitioners will appreciate this is only an example of a typical Bundle B in a tax status or IR35 dispute.

18.34 The importance of numbering the bundles in a clear fashion cannot be over-estimated and the General Commissioners will not appreciate badly photocopied paperwork. Careful preparation must not be skipped. There is only one chance at the Commissioners to present the case effectively.

Case study

Several years ago Accountax was involved in a contentious Commissioners appeal, where the inspector had not produced sufficient copies of his own bundle of documents nor checked the quality of the photocopies contained in the bundle. A remarkably similar failing is noted at 18.18 above. The General Commissioners had difficulty not only reading over each other's shoulders but could not decipher a particular enclosure because it was badly photocopied. Accountax had prepared ample copies of its own bundles and the document that was difficult to read was common both to the inspector's bundle and that of Accountax. Accountax pointed this out to the Commissioners who then referred to the Accountax bundle and expressed dissatisfaction with the paperwork produced by the inspector.

18.35 Preparing the paperwork properly will not on its own win the case but it will aid presentation and create a good impression. Once again, if careful preparation of documents gets the taxpayer just 1% nearer to the winning line then it is something that should be undertaken without hesitation.

18.36 It is not always clear which documents should go in one bundle or the other. For example, the inspector's decision and notice under Section 8 could perhaps go in both bundles, as could the basic legislation. As far as is possible it is wise to separate the general correspondence from the more legal documentation to be found in Bundle B.

18.37 It is unhelpful to include in Bundle A copies of documentation which add nothing to the proceedings. As it may be necessary to go through each of these documents and formally admit them in evidence anything which is genuinely superfluous should be left out. The process of introducing documents and other evidence is explained in Chapter 19.

18.38 So far as Bundle B is concerned, this should contain the case law to be relied on. In a typical IR35 or traditional tax status dispute it may be necessary to refer to between 10 and 15 case law decisions. On average each case is perhaps 20 pages long and therefore Bundle B can be over 200 pages long, and that is without taking into account the other enclosures such as the statutes and statutory instruments.

18.39 It is not particularly difficult to prepare the bundles but care must be taken and sufficient time must be allowed to do the job properly. The majority of practitioners will delegate the photocopying of the bundles to a junior member of staff but it is worth checking that everything is correctly numbered and that there are sufficient copies for everybody.

18.40 Although there is no hard and fast rule, in the author's experience the best way to collate bundles is by the use of extra long treasury tags. This is more effective and convenient than paper clips, staples or loose sheets. As many as 8–10 sets of Bundles A and B will be required for the hearing, as every person present should have one.

It might be suggested by the Revenue, that one agreed master Bundle containing both side's documents is collated and paginated.This no doubt makes the paperwork a little easier to handle on the day. The Special Commissioners may formally direct this.

The practitioner's own documents

18.41 As well as having the bundles mentioned above, the practitioner will also have his own set of notes. These documents will contain arguments and various bullet points to act as an aide memoire during the proceedings as well as being a list of the questions to be asked of the witnesses. If an assistant is taken, he can hand out the bundles and this will take away some pressure from the practitioner leaving him free to concentrate on the appeal itself.

18.42 These notes will contain the opening address to the Commissioners, and should be nothing more than a short summary of what the case is about, together with a copy of the questions to be put to the various witnesses, questions to be put to the Revenue's witnesses in cross-examination, legal submissions and a final summary. (The actual presentation of the case is discussed in considerable detail in Chapter 19.)

Clarifying what determination is being sought

18.43 It is very important not to lose sight of what it is the Commissioners are being asked to determine. During the course of an appeal the Commissioners may become overwhelmed with potentially hundreds of pages of photocopied documents and it is recommended that occasional reference is made to the point to be determined. This is particularly important at the Generals.

Witnesses

18.44 Long before the case gets to the Commissioners stock should have been taken of the reliability and quality of the witnesses to be called on behalf of the taxpayer, including the taxpayer himself. Indeed, in many ways the most important witness will be the client. It will also be necessary to consider the Revenue's witnesses and plan ahead for their cross-examination. The actual process of examination of witnesses and the cross-examination of the Revenue's witnesses is explored in greater depth in Chapter 19. It is possible to serve a potential witness with a witness summons under the Commissioners Regulations (see Appendices 4 and 5) thus ensuring attendance at the hearing, see 18.53 below.

18.45 There tends to be two kinds of witness. The first type of witness can be relied upon to turn up on time at the Commissioners, wear smart clothes, treat the Commissioners and Clerk, as well as the inspector, with respect. This witness will consider questions carefully and will answer slowly and clearly. He will not start an argument with the Revenue nor will he ramble when answering questions. This is a good witness.

The second kind of witness is determined to have his 'day in court' and 'give a piece of his mind'. He cannot be relied upon to remain calm or to show the necessary respect to the tribunal. Such witnesses tend not to take on board guidance they are given and often become their own worst enemy.

18.46 If a witness is likely to be a poor witness the practitioner should think very carefully about calling him at all. Not only will a bad witness fail to advance the practitioner's case but, more importantly, after he has been examined by the practitioner the inspector will have the opportunity to cross-examine him. The 'bad' witness can easily be discredited and provoked by an experienced inspector, potentially damaging the taxpayer's case.

18.47 Of course this goes both ways. The inspector who is presenting the case on behalf of the Revenue may be painfully aware that the technical skills of the investigating officer or inspector are limited. The officer may have little or no experience of taking part in contentious appeals with the prospect of being closely cross-examined. Coupled with this if the officer has not handled the case particularly well and there is a risk that any shortcomings would be exposed in front of the Commissioners it is not unheard of for the Revenue to refuse to call the officer as a witness. This can be the case even where the officer concerned has been involved with the case from the outset.

Case study

In a contentious Commissioners appeal the inspector taking the case refused to call the officer who, from the outset, had handled the case. The officer had made many fundamental mistakes and was likely to be given a robust cross-examination. In the circumstances the Inspector taking the case was left without his major witness, but wanted to protect the officer from being shown in a poor light. The Commissioners were unimpressed that the Revenue had failed to call the inspector who had dealt with the case from the beginning and this helped Accountax in winning the appeal hearing.

18.48 Having decided, hopefully, that the witnesses to be called on behalf of the taxpayer will be credible and punctual two things must be clearly explained to them. The first is the general order of proceedings: the layout of the room where the hearing will take place and an idea as to who the various personnel are and what their function is. For those practitioners who are not familiar with this Chapter 19 gives the necessary information.

Having given the client some general guidance as to what happens on the day attention should be turned to the questions that he will be asked when he is examined, that is to say when he is called as a witness. It is perfectly permissible to go through this process before the hearing, and the practitioner can rest assured that the inspector representing the Revenue will go through the same process with any other inspector or person he intends to call as his witnesses.

18.49 What must not happen is the putting of words into the mouth of the witness, either before the hearing or by the process of asking leading questions, during the hearing. There is also a danger that over-rehearsed questions and answer sessions will appear stilted and artificial and will not impress the Commissioners. The questions asked should be open, in order that the client can effectively 'tell his story' in his own words.

It is important to remind the client, several times, and once shortly before the hearing, that he should answer the question but then remain silent.

Case study

In a recent appeal it became very clear that one of the Revenue's witnesses was unhappy with the draft witness statement the Revenue had prepared on his behalf. Words had been attributed to the witness which he had not said. This reflected badly on the Revenue. Witness Statements are living documents and they will be drafted and changed but the starting point should be an accurate record of what the witness actually said when interviewed not what the Revenue wished he had said.

18.50 In the event that any answer is too brief then either the practitioner or indeed the Commissioners themselves may ask the witness to expand upon the information he has given. This is particularly the case in cross-examination, where an experienced advocate will ask the witness an awkward question and will then remain silent after the witness has given his initial response. This is in the hope that the 'pregnant pause' will lead the witness into saying something else beyond his initial answer which may be incriminating.

18.51 In preparing the witness it is important that all the questions he will be asked are fully understood. If he does not understand the wording of the questions, the time to clarify this is before the hearing.

18.52 The full procedures of a Commissioners hearing are explained in Chapter 19 but it is worth mentioning at this stage that after the examination of the taxpayer's witnesses has finished the inspector will have the opportunity to cross-examine them to test the accuracy and truth of the information given. Cross-examination can be very testing. Whereas the examination of the witness can be a fairly pedestrian and gentle conversation, cross-examination will be more focused on inconsistencies or weaknesses in the evidence given, and a competent inspector will wish to expose any such weaknesses. Cross-examination can sometimes border on the hostile and can certainly be very brusque in nature. In cross-examination leading questions are allowed.

Briefing of the witness must include a warning that cross-examination can be difficult but that the key to dealing with this successfully is to listen to the question carefully and to answer slowly and clearly and not to rush into a confrontation with the inspector.

Case study

In 2000 the author appeared as a witness for the plaintiff in a High Court libel action. He was cross-examined by the shadow Attorney-General Sir Edward Garnier QC who suggested that the evidence given was not credible. In an exchange a question was put along the lines of 'are you seriously trying to suggest that . . .'. The answer given was a straightforward unequivocal and calm 'yes'. Nothing more, nothing less. The barrister had nowhere to go and ran out of steam. The plaintiff won and received substantial damages.

Witness summons

18.53 Any person can be called as a witness if it is felt that the person's evidence will be helpful. But what happens if the practitioner wishes to have the opportunity of cross-examining the inspector who has worked the case and the Revenue refuses to call him as a witness?

18.54 Under the Commissioners (Jurisdiction and Procedure) Regulations 1994, SI 1994/1812 and SI 1994/1811, it is possible to serve a witness summons on any person and this includes tax officers and inspectors. The procedure is clearly spelt out in the regulations and a full copy of the regulations is reproduced in the appendices. It is necessary to write to the Clerk explaining why it is necessary to serve a witness summons and the Commissioners will, if satisfied, sign the witness summons and return it via the Clerk. It should be noted that it is now the responsibility of the party who obtained the summons to physically serve it on the witness and also to undertake to reimburse the witness his travelling costs to the hearing. This power of the Commissioners to issue a witness summons should not be underestimated.

Case study

At a contentious tax status dispute in 2001 Accountax served a witness summons on a tax officer who had carried out the initial PAYE compliance review. In examination he was forced to concede that he had not even examined the contract terms and conditions and that in fact he had 'not carried out the review thoroughly or properly'. This evidence was very damaging to the Revenue. Accountax won the appeal.

18.55 The usual justification for a witness summons is that the person concerned has been heavily involved in the case and may have important evidence to give. If a witness fails to comply with a witness summons without good cause he can be fined a maximum of £1,000.

Case study

In the IR35 appeal *Tilbury Consulting Ltd v Gittins* (2003), Accountax tried to argue against a witness from Ford being called as a witness or summonsed, on the basis that it would cause commercial harm to the contractor. Dr Brice decided the summons should be issued in the interests of justice. In the event the Revenue called a different witness from Ford and lost at the substantive hearing. The lesson is: if you want a witness summons you are likely to get one.

18.56 The only witness the practitioner is likely to want to summons will be an inspector who has been involved in the case and whose evidence may be beneficial to the client's appeal. It should go without saying that most reasonable inspectors are prepared to give evidence voluntarily and the Commissioners may raise their eyebrows where an inspector has refused to do so other than for the fact that a witness summons was issued to him. Equally, a witness summons can be issued against the client, although it would be a foolish client who refuses to give evidence on a voluntary basis at his own appeal, unless he would be a very poor witness indeed.

Case study

In a tax status case heard by the General Commissioners in 2000 the initial inspector of taxes had formed the view that the worker was self-employed. His colleague who took the case over adopted a different view and came to the conclusion that the worker was employed. Several years earlier Customs and Excise had visited the worker, who had his own established business, and concluded that the services he provided to the putative employer were part and parcel of his normal business trading activities and VAT should have been charged. The Revenue refused to call the second inspector to give evidence. Accountax applied for and served a General Commissioners witness summons on the VAT inspector and the original inspector voluntarily gave evidence. It was left too late to serve a witness summons on the second inspector, who refused to give evidence.

The refusal by the second inspector to give evidence was extraordinary and must have had some influence on the General

Commissioners appraisal of the Revenue's case. The initial inspector explained in a very straightforward and honest manner why he felt the worker was indeed self-employed and the VAT inspector did the same. In an unusually long written decision the General Commissioners explained that they had found unanimously in favour of self-employment and made several references to the quality of the witnesses called and the evidence given.

18.57 It will not have escaped the attention of the sharper practitioner that although a witness summons can be used very effectively against the Revenue, sometimes there is more to be gained by letting the Revenue withhold one of its main or most obvious witnesses. The Commissioners will draw their own conclusions from such an unusual, and arguably unprofessional, stance.

18.58 The Commissioners Regulations make it clear that a person who attends a hearing in obedience of a witness summons will be the witness of the person who issued the summons. As such that witness cannot be cross-examined by the party who served the summons unless it can be shown the witness is a hostile witness. This is dealt with in Chapter 19.

The reader may wish to refer to an article in Taxation 14 February 2002 where the author comments on the procedural complications of calling witnesses.

Summary

18.59 The key to a successful Commissioners hearing is preparation, preparation and more preparation. Having taken the initiative in getting the case listed (see Chapter 17) the biggest danger facing the practitioner is not a lack of familiarity with appeal hearings but the giving of insufficient time and resources to the preparation of the case. This should never be underestimated. In the author's experience 7–10 working days are required, and the work must start well in advance of the hearing.

18.60 Bundles of documents must be carefully prepared, indexed and numbered. Full case reports are available from most university libraries or from the various professional accountancy bodies or the internet.

18.61 Witnesses have to be considered carefully and fully briefed but not over-prepared. Although the taxpayer has probably never been to the Commissioners before and will almost inevitably be nervous a great deal can be done to calm his nerves by going through the procedures in advance. In this respect Chapter 19 will be particularly useful.

18.62 Witness summons should always be considered where a key witness, often a tax officer, is reluctant to give evidence voluntarily. There can, however, also be a tactical advantage to be gained in letting the Revenue *not* call an obvious witness.

18.63 The Commissioners (Jurisdiction and Procedure) Regulations 1994, SI 1994/1812 and SI 1994/1811, contain a wealth of procedural information and should be read in full from beginning to end. These Regulations are reproduced in full in Appendices 4 and 5.

18.64 In summary, it must be remembered that preparation is all.

CHAPTER 19
Presenting an appeal at the Commissioners

19.1 This chapter gives guidance on what to expect at the appeal hearing in order to assist the practitioner who is not familiar with such proceedings. It is also very important to explain to the client what will happen on the day. Those practitioners who have never been to a Commissioners hearing should learn a great deal from this chapter.

Location

19.2 The division of General Commissioners who will hear the client's appeal is laid down in TMA 1970 Sch 3. This will usually be the General Commissioners for the tax district which deals with the client's PAYE affairs but where this is a remote office the taxpayer may request that a local division of Commissioners hears his appeal. This may be the division where the client resides or works and the inspector will normally be flexible on this. It is important to liaise with the correct Clerk for the division of Commissioners that will hear the appeal, and this should have been clarified at an early stage.

19.3 More often than not the hearing will take place in a public building such as civic offices, a meeting room in a library or something similar. Occasionally, the hearing will take place in the Clerk's office, the Clerk quite often being a solicitor, or the appeal may be heard in a magistrates court.

19.4 The proceedings are heard in public. Other than the parties to the appeal, the Clerk and the General Commissioners, other persons entitled to attend are Special Commissioners and members of the Council on Tribunals or the Scottish Committee of the Council on Tribunals or a member of the Judicial Studies Board or one of its committees, as well as the public.

19.5 Regulations 3(1)–(3) lay down the administrative formalities pertaining to the listing of a hearing at the Generals. The most important points to note here are that either party may request a date for the hearing to be fixed and that unless the parties agree otherwise 28 days' notice must be given of the hearing.

Hearings at the Specials are usually heard in Bedford Square, London, but occasionally in Edinburgh, Manchester and elsewhere.

Representation

19.6 In accordance with SI 1994/1812, reg 12(*a*), a lawyer or qualified accountant can represent the taxpayer, but in practice the General Commissioners will allow any representative to speak so long as they are satisfied that he is competent. The actual regulations state that the General Commissioners may refuse to hear any person if there are 'good and sufficient reasons for doing so'. In the author's experience the General Commissioners have never refused to hear the taxpayer's representative. The Specials adopt a similar approach.

19.7 The Revenue will usually be represented by a senior officer from the local district, particularly when the case is heard by the General Commissioners. Exceptionally, the Revenue will be represented by either a barrister or a solicitor or a member of the Revenue's specialist advocacy unit, but this is much more likely when a case goes to the Special Commissioners.

19.8 The inspector representing the Revenue may have an assistant with him to help with the paperwork. No objection should be made to this. Just as the practitioner will question his own client to draw out the evidence the inspector will question the officer who has dealt with the file, again to draw out the evidence.

19.9 One of the advantages of the Revenue being represented by a senior inspector is that the inspector may not be familiar with all of the detail of the file's history. Although one would think that very careful preparation goes without saying, the author has been involved in contentious hearings where the inspector leading for the Revenue was not as familiar with the file as he should have been.

The Clerk

19.10 The Clerk's function at the Generals is to make sure the hearing runs smoothly from a procedural point of view. He will have been involved in the pre-hearing formalities, such as arranging suitable dates for the hearing and the venue. He will be concerned that both parties have the appropriate paperwork to hand out at the hearing and, where necessary, he will give the General Commissioners legal guidance. The

Clerk will not, however, take part in the actual determination of the facts or the outcome of the appeal.

Quite often the Clerk is a practising solicitor, but may also be professionally qualified in a different field, or not all.

At the Specials the Clerk's staff often do not sit in on the hearing. They deal with the administrative formalities before the case. Occasionally court stenographers will attend, whereby a transcript can be prepared to assist the Special Commissioner.

The General Commissioners

19.11 The General Commissioners are members of the public who are chosen on the basis of their experience of business matters and affairs generally. In many ways they are similar to magistrates. In the author's experience the majority of General Commissioners are male and middle-aged but this generalisation is meant to give nothing more than a typical feel. There are many female General Commissioners and, increasingly, the average age of the typical General Commissioner is falling.

19.12 The General Commissioners are entirely independent of the Revenue. They are reasonable people who will listen to the taxpayer's arguments and, if the evidence is good enough, will be persuaded by them. They have a very well-developed sense of fair play and expect high standards from both clients and their representatives, but even more so from the Revenue, whom they expect to know the ropes.

19.13 The General Commissioners do not suffer fools gladly and they have a broad definition of the fools whom they decline to suffer. They become understandably irritated and frustrated by poor presentation skills, such as mumbling or an inability to provide the appropriate paperwork. They do not welcome presentations made at breakneck speed. It is often forgotten that the General Commissioners come to the appeal hearing knowing virtually nothing about the case perhaps other than having had sight of the statement of agreed facts.

How many Commissioners?

19.14 Traditionally three General Commissioners will hear a contentious appeal. The minimum number for a valid quorum is two, with a maximum of five. In the event that only two Commissioners are available to listen to the appeal the Chairman will have the casting vote. See SI 1994/1812 reg 11(1)–(2).

19.15 Commissioners will withdraw from an appeal hearing where there is a conflict of interest, for example, a Commissioner could be a director of a computer business which supplies the taxpayer with products.

It may pay dividends to do a little research on the division of Commissioners that will hear the appeal:

Case Study

The author took a contentious appeal hearing and shortly beforehand carried out a search on *Tolley's Case Link* to see if the division of Commissioners concerned had been involved in any recent cases which had gone on to the High Court. The search revealed that the Commissioners concerned had dealt with *McManus v Griffiths* (see Appendix 6), a tax status case in 1997. The Commissioners had determined the worker was self-employed.

At the hearing the *McManus* case was quoted and the Commissioners, unsurprisingly, took a real interest in it. The author commented that the Commissioners would be no doubt be familiar with the case yet the inspector seemed oblivious to its relevance. This just added some topical interest and showed that the background to the case was fully appreciated. Not a winning factor per se but a small point in the client's favour perhaps.

The Special Commissioners

19.16 These are legally qualified professionals, including several QCs and academic Drs, who all have at least 10 years post-qualification experience.

They tend to sit singly. The presiding Special Commissioner is His Honour Stephen Oliver QC (who heard the *Tilbury* and *Future Online* appeals).

The inspector

19.17 It should be borne in mind that once at the hearing the inspector will be there in the role of advocate, not negotiator, and the practitioner should be aware that the inspector will do whatever he reasonably can to win the case. The Revenue does not like losing at the Commissioners anymore than the taxpayer, not least because it can affect their credibility with the local Commissioners, particularly if several cases are lost in a short period of time.

The layout of the meeting room

19.18 Although it will vary, the traditional layout will typically comprise a top table, where the General Commissioners sit, with the Clerk to one side. Looking towards the top table from the back of the room there will usually be a table on the left where the taxpayer and his representative will sit and a table on the right where the inspector will sit.

Occasionally the tables will be arranged whereby the taxpayer and his representative sit immediately in front of the Commissioners with the inspector sitting to one side. Unfortunately, such an arrangement is a little off-putting and the taxpayer and his representative may feel that they have been summoned to the headmaster's study to explain themselves! Thankfully, this type of arrangement is unusual and most Commissioners are sensitive to the propriety of a symmetrical layout.

At the Special Commissioners formal courts are the norm. In the author's experience they are small and a lack of air-conditioning is inconvenient. The top table or 'bench' is raised and a horse-shoe shape is not used. Both taxpayer and Revenue sit in front of the bench and next to each other, with the public behind.

19.19 A contentious appeal hearing relating to IR35 or tax status generally can be a drawn-out affair. A well-organised Clerk will already have made arrangements for drinking water to be available for the representatives and the witnesses but this cannot be taken as read. Presenting a client's case may take two to three hours and it would be a wise precaution to take some bottled water just in case none is provided. This is not an issue at the Specials.

The order of proceedings

19.20 It should always be remembered that the taxpayer is the appellant and the onus of proof is with him. He has made an appeal against an assessment or notice of decision and, in order for his appeal to succeed, he must show that on the balance of probabilities the assessment should be discharged.

19.21 SI 1994/1812 reg 15 states that, at the beginning of the hearing, the General Commissioners shall explain the order of proceedings unless it is unnecessary to do so. Certainly the Commissioners will explain the proceedings to an unrepresented taxpayer, but unless the taxpayer's representative appears to be lost it is unlikely that the proceedings will be explained to him. The purpose of this section is to give the practitioner a clear understanding of the order of the proceedings so he in turn can explain this to his client in advance.

19.22 It should be noted in reg 15(2) that the tribunal conducts the hearing in such manner as it considers most suitable and shall seek to avoid formality. Strictly speaking this means that the Commissioners may ask the inspector to address them first, but this should be resisted at all costs. This is because the basic rule of procedure in a tribunal is that he who speaks first also speaks last.

19.23 Not only does it make sense that the appellant speaks first, because the burden of proof is on him, but tactically it must help his case to do so. By speaking first as well as last an advantage will be gained, if only in being able to emphasise one's arguments at the outset and at the conclusion of the proceedings. Furthermore, if the appellant speaks first the Revenue not only has to worry about making its own presentation after the practitioner has made some forceful points, but will have to try to incorporate some of the issues already raised. In other words, the Revenue will have to think on its feet under pressure.

Case Study

At a Special Commissioners 'directions' hearing in 2002 the inspector forgot that because he had applied for the directions he was obliged to speak first. This completely threw him as he was expecting to speak second, as he would at a full hearing. He was thus unprepared and struggled. The Special Commissioner subsequently accepted Accountax's arguments and refused the inspector's proposed directions.

19.24 Despite the advantages of speaking first and last, many inexperienced practitioners will allow the inspector to go first. This is usually because the practitioner is unsure of the procedures and he feels he may be able to ease his way into the proceedings by sitting back and letting the Revenue take the initiative. This would be a major tactical mistake.

19.25 It was explained in Chapter 17 that the practitioner should take the initiative in having the matter listed and, when writing to the Clerk, should specifically request that he addresses the Commissioners first on the day of the hearing.

19.26 Not only does this show initiative and confidence, it also avoids a potentially awkward situation. It is not uncommon for the General Commissioners to *assume* that the Revenue will speak first and they may even encourage this. Typically they might say, 'We have no real detail as to what this appeal is all about so perhaps the inspector could start by explaining the point at issue'.

It will then be very difficult to interrupt and insist on speaking first. That is why it is so important to clearly make the request to speak first when writing to the Clerk. It is suggested that a reminder to the Clerk is sent a few days before the hearing. In these circumstances, even if the Chairman of the General Commissioners suggests the Revenue should start first, the Clerk himself will advise the Chairman that a request has been made for the taxpayer's representative to speak first. This way a potentially awkward situation can be avoided. It would be extraordinary for the General Commissioners to ignore the practitioner's request to speak first.

At the Specials the appellant will be expected to speak first, as more formal procedures are generally adopted.

19.27 Having agreed that the practitioner will speak first, the usual order of proceedings is as follows:

1. The practitioner addresses the Commissioners and introduces himself and his client.
2. The practitioner offers a very brief summary of the appeal under consideration, and hands out Bundle A only. (The Specials will already have this.)
3. The practitioner calls his client and any other witnesses to give evidence. This is called the examination in chief. Documents will be referred to such as witness statements, contracts, letters, etc.
4. The inspector has the right to cross-examine the taxpayer and witnesses called on behalf of the taxpayer to test the truth and completeness of their evidence.
5. The practitioner then has a further opportunity to re-examine his witnesses.
6. The Commissioners themselves may well want to ask the witnesses some questions and may do so at any stage.
7. Having established the facts, either by calling evidence from the witnesses or by referring to documentation, the practitioner will then hand out Bundle B and make his legal submissions to show why the case law supports his point of view and why the appeal should succeed. Increasingly, legal submissions are made after all witnesses (including the Revenue's) are dealt with.
8. The practitioner then summarises his case.
9. The inspector responds and again establishes facts by reference to documents and the evidence of his witnesses.
10. The practitioner has the opportunity to cross-examine the Revenue's witnesses.
11. The inspector has the opportunity to re-examine his witnesses.
12. The Commissioners may ask the Revenue's witnesses any questions.
13. Having dealt with their witnesses the Revenue will now make its case law submissions to show why the appeal should be rejected. If the appellant has not yet made legal submissions he will do so at this stage, immediately before the Revenue.
14. The inspector will summarise his case.
15. On the taxpayer's behalf the practitioner has a final summary.
16. The Commissioners then retire to make the decision and all other parties leave the room. The decision of the Commissioners may be given later the same day, when the decision will be announced to

the parties to the appeal. Alternatively, the Commissioners may wish to take longer considering their decision and will then write to the taxpayer and the inspector notifying them of the determination in due course. Specials rarely announce the decision on the day. A wait of 2–4 weeks is normal.

The whole process is fairly straightforward and logical. There is absolutely nothing to be worried about so long as the case has been prepared carefully.

This summary of the order of proceedings and the various stages is examined in more depth below.

1. Addressing the Commissioners and introducing the client

19.28 Many practitioners do not know what to call the Commissioners. This point of etiquette is fairly straightforward but is worth learning and committing to memory. The Commissioners should be called either 'Sir' or 'Madam'. The Chair can be called 'Mr Chairman' or 'Madam Chairman'.

The Clerk should preferably simply be called 'the Clerk' although his actual surname could be used.

The client should be called 'my client' or 'the taxpayer' or referred to by his surname. Overuse of the word 'appellant' may lead to the further use of formal legalese, which is not necessary.

The Revenue representative should be referred to as 'the inspector' or by his surname. It is also permissible to say 'the Revenue' when referring to actions taken by the inspector, for example, 'the Revenue wrote to our client on 14 July'. It should be remembered that the inspector is not a policeman. The author has heard references to 'Inspector Black of the Inland Revenue said . . .', which is quite inappropriate.

19.29 Throughout the entire hearing, with the exception of asking direct questions of the witnesses, the practitioner should direct his remarks *to the Chairman.* It is equally important to remind the client before the hearing that he should address his answers, including those given in cross-examination, not to the person who asks the question but to the Chairman. It is vitally important to make sure that the Commissioners clearly hear what is being said.

19.30 It goes without saying that the taxpayer and his representative should never engage in a verbal battle across the room with the inspector. There is a great deal to be said for keeping within kicking distance of one's client!

This will not be possible at the Specials where the witnesses give evidence from behind a bullet proof glass partition—no, not really—from a witness stand.

19.31 The General Commissioners may be acquainted with the inspector and it will therefore be obvious who is the taxpayer's representative. However, as a courtesy it is important that the practitioner introduces himself and his client.

19.32 It is strongly recommended that before the Commissioners are addressed the practitioner makes the effort to stand up and show respect to the tribunal. Showing 'respect' to the tribunal also touches on what clothes should be worn. It is strongly recommended that a sober business suit and tie is appropriate for men and a business suit for women. Turning up without a jacket or wearing an absurd tie will not lose the case but it might suggest to the Commissioners that the proceedings are not being taken seriously.

Case study

The author represented a taxpayer in a very important capital gains tax appeal at the General Commissioners. It was a very warm summer's day and the author left the office without taking his suit jacket. Turning up in mere shirt sleeves even in hot weather is not recommended as it gives the appearance of being rather casual. Fortunately the author had with him an assistant who was wearing a suit. Unfortunately, it was not the same colour as the author's trousers. The view was taken that it wouldn't be too bad if the assistant turned up without a jacket but it would look bad if the taxpayer's main representative was not wearing one. The author entered the hearing carrying boxes of documents wearing a blue jacket with black trousers, said hello to the Commissioners, commented on what a hot day it was and asked if the Commissioners objected to jackets being removed. The Commissioners did not object and the non-matching jacket was hastily dispatched to the back of the chair!

19.33 When standing to address the Commissioners it is very likely that the Chairman will give immediate permission to sit down, on the basis that the proceedings are informal. In these circumstances unless the practitioner particularly wishes to stand (which could be for a very long time) he is then at liberty to sit. By initially standing the practitioner has registered his respect for the Commissioners, which cannot harm his credibility. Interestingly, it is *rare* for the inspector to stand when he first addresses the Commissioners and the contrast in the two approaches will be self-evident.

19.34 Having stood to address the Commissioners the following opening words are suggested:

'Good morning. My name is John Brown and I am a partner in Brown and Green Chartered Accountants. I represent the appellant taxpayer here on my right, Mr Fred Bloggs who is a director of Fred Bloggs Computer Services Limited'.

19.35 It is recommended that the practitioner sit *between* his client and the General Commissioners. The reason for this is that when the client is asked questions whereby he can give his evidence, it is important that the answers are directed to the Chairman. If the client is sitting between his representative and the General Commissioners it will be very awkward for him to look at his representative and pay attention to the question being asked and then turn around 180 degrees and give his answer to the Chairman. This will not be possible at the Specials, where witnesses speak at a witness stand.

It is also recommended that the practitioner's own assistant sits between the practitioner and the General Commissioners so he does not get in the way of any questions being asked of the witness.

It is far better to deal with the seating arrangements at the beginning of the meeting rather than playing musical chairs half way through.

(See diagrams below and overleaf for typical seating arrangements.)

2. Presenting a brief summary

19.36 It is very tempting to launch into a detailed submission without first giving the Commissioners an overview of what the appeal is about.

Typical General Commissioners Layout

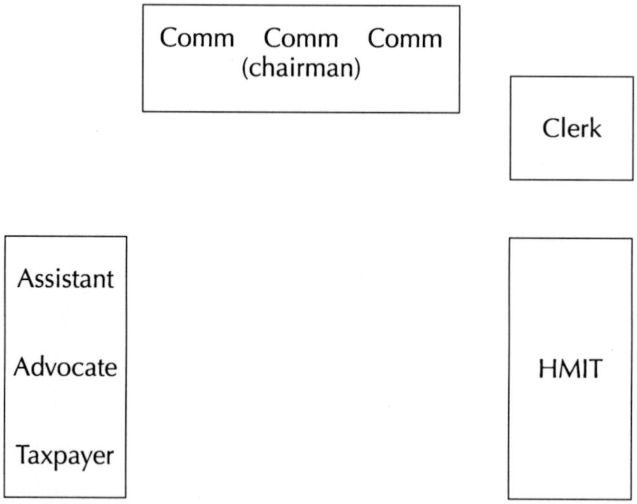

Typical Special Commissioners Layout

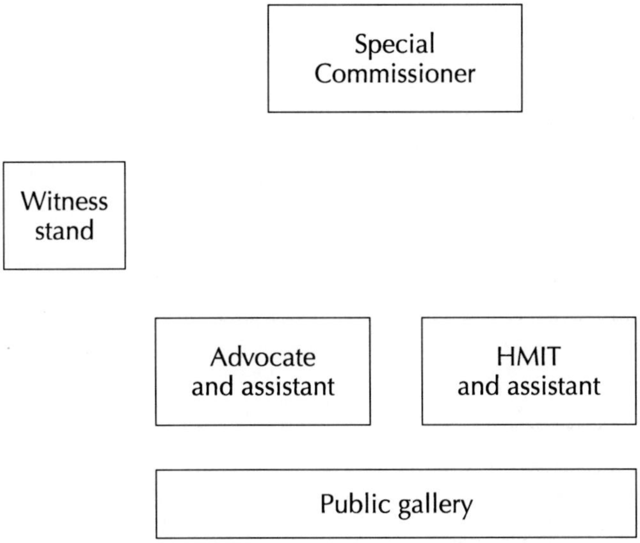

Just as it is important to offer a concise conclusion when wrapping up a case it is equally important to offer a succinct summary at the outset. The Commissioners need to be given a true idea of the substance of the appeal before witnesses are called or legal arguments started. Following on from the introductions the following summary might be used:

> 'Before going into the detail of this appeal it might assist the Commissioners to have a brief summary of what this case is all about. (Pause) My client has appealed against what is known as a Section 8 Notice issued by the Inland Revenue for the tax year 2000/01. (Pause) In essence the Section 8 Notice assesses my client as if he were a disguised employee under what are commonly called the IR35 rules. (Pause) This appeal is made on the basis that the taxpayer is not a disguised employee and that he is in fact running a genuine business and is not caught by the IR35 rules. (Pause) I hope to demonstrate to the Commissioners that the Section 8 Notice should, on the balance of probabilities, be discharged. I will call witnesses and in due course adduce detailed case law in support of this appeal.'

19.37 At this point the practitioners assistant should hand out Bundle A to the Clerk (unless the hearing is at the Specials where it will already have been handed in previously), making sure beforehand that there are sufficient copies for everybody, including the Revenue. The Clerk will then distribute the bundles to those present. Tactically, at this stage it would be *unwise* to distribute Bundle B. Instead the Chairman should be informed that the bundle of case law extracts will be handed out when the legal submissions are made. The following case study shows how it can be tactically disadvantageous to hand out Bundle B too early:

Case study

In the run-up to a contentious appeal hearing at the General Commissioners it became obvious that the Revenue was not particularly familiar with the case law precedents relevant to the point at issue. Although a list of case law references had been provided to the inspector seven days prior to the hearing the list was particularly long and it was quite likely that the inspector did not have the time to read the full judgments. This placed him at a distinct disadvantage as he would have to try to counter the case law arguments put forward by Accountax as they developed on the day. The author made the mistake of handing out both Bundles A and B at the beginning of the hearing. An early lunch break was called by the Chairman, which lasted for one and a quarter hours. At this stage witnesses were still being called and the legal submissions had not started.

During the lunch break the inspector had ample opportunity to go through Bundle B, where all of the relevant case law extracts Accountax was going to cite and rely upon had been clearly asterisked and highlighted! This gave the inspector a last minute opportunity to revise his own legal submissions as he now knew in advance what passages would be quoted from the judgments. The Revenue still lost but there is a lesson to be learnt. Do not give away information and arguments until you need to.

19.38 The above opening summary will take no more than 60 seconds but it neatly encapsulates what is the essence of the issue. Note the regular pauses, they are very important. At all times the Commissioners must be given ample opportunity to make their notes and to take in what is being said. If they are not given enough time it cannot be assumed that they will ask for a slower pace or to go over something again. Instead, there is the serious risk of simply failing to make the point, and the practitioner cannot afford to do this. The Commissioners will soon tire of asking the speaker to slow down and vital points may be lost.

By getting into the habit of making regular pauses this early in the presentation it will be that much easier to carry on in the same manner throughout the course of the hearing.

3. Calling and examining witnesses

19.39 It is important to realise that one of the most powerful forms of evidence is that given by the taxpayer himself. A credible, calm and articulate taxpayer can do himself a great deal of good when asked to give evidence.

The Regulations state that the Commissioners, when assessing the truth and weight of any evidence, may take into account its nature and source and the manner in which it is given. It is therefore preferable for the taxpayer to give oral evidence, attending the hearing rather than simply sending in a letter although documentary evidence from witnesses who cannot attend can be useful, particularly if a sworn statement is produced.

19.40 The Regulations make it clear that the Commissioners will take into account *any* form of evidence, despite the fact that such evidence would be inadmissible in proceedings before a court of law. In other words, the witness may offer hearsay evidence and the Commissioners are entitled to take it into account, although of course they may not attach much weight to it.

However, 'without prejudice' evidence *cannot* be adduced. Using the phrase 'without prejudice' on a letter or document means that it cannot be used against the person who wrote it. It might be that the practitioner makes a last ditch effort to avoid a hearing by making an offer in settlement. If this is headed 'without prejudice' then the letter cannot be adduced by the inspector at the hearing (to show the taxpayer's doubts in his own case) should negotiations break down.

Case study

At a contentious appeal the inspector, who was badly prepared generally, attempted to put a without prejudice letter, sent by Accountax, in evidence. Virtually before he had referred to it his senior colleague apologised to all present for the inspector's mistake. The Commissioners were not impressed. The Revenue lost and its lack of understanding of the rules of evidence must have played a part.

19.41 It should be remembered that the Commissioners have the power to require any witness to give evidence on oath or affirmation. In the author's experience this is rare, except at the Specials, but where the taxpayer is prepared to give evidence on oath this may be worth pointing out to the Commissioners, as it underlines the bona fides of the taxpayer.

19.42 The taxpayer himself, although a witness, will be present throughout the entire proceedings. He would be called by addressing the Commissioners along the following lines:

> 'I would now like to ask my client Mr Fred Bloggs to give evidence to the Commissioners. (Turning to the client.) Please give your name and address to the Clerk'.

This is a fairly simple formality which should be gone through with every witness called. He can then be given a copy of his witness statement and asked if it is his signature and whether he is still happy with the statement.

19.43 The best way to elicit oral evidence from the client, and indeed any other witness, is to ask him a series of questions which he can in broad terms be made aware of earlier. There is no point in over-rehearsing the questions and answers. It is important that your client gives his evidence in his own words. Putting words into the mouth of the client is very unwise.

19.44 The practitioner must not ask his own witnesses what are called 'leading questions'. A leading question is one which anticipates and suggests the required reply. An extreme example might be:

> 'Isn't it correct that you had a *written* contract?'.

The question should be:

> 'Did you have a contract?'

This may be followed up with:

> 'What form did the contract take?'.

It should be noted that when cross-examining a Revenue witness leading questions *can* be asked just as the Revenue can ask the taxpayer and his witnesses leading questions during cross-examination.

19.45 It is now a matter of asking the questions in a clear and methodical manner so that the client's evidence unfolds as a natural conversation. In a typical IR35 or tax status dispute this will work towards establishing what the working terms and conditions of the relationship are. If there are other factors which may help the case, for example, the extent to which the client has invested in equipment or training courses, he should also be asked questions on these points.

19.46 By the time the taxpayer has been examined he should have given convincing, clear and confident evidence on all the major issues. In an IR35 or tax status dispute the practitioner will want to concentrate on the more important factors, such as the right of substitution, mutuality of obligations, financial risk, control and the client's business organisation and general modus operandi.

19.47 The client's oral evidence should be cross-referenced to documentation in Bundle A wherever possible. For example, the client might give evidence to the effect that he has professional indemnity insurance in place and raises invoices on a business letterhead. Once this point is made the Commissioners should then be referred to the appropriate enclosures in Bundle A.

19.48 Hopefully by now, the client through responding to questions asked has painted a picture of the facts the practitioner is hoping to establish, in a measured and clear manner.

19.49 It is important to suggest to the Commissioners that they formally *find* or accept certain facts. This is because, unless the tribunal reaches a completely perverse conclusion, its factual findings cannot be overturned by a superior court. An astute advocate will always be looking to the Commissioners to accept as *fact* certain contentions and to document them accordingly.

19.50 It is tempting only to draw out the evidence which helps the client's case and to try to ignore those factors which do not assist. This is generally unwise because a well-prepared inspector will expose weaknesses in the taxpayer's case when he has his chance to cross-examine the client. Tactically it is often better to address weaknesses in the client's arguments and try to play them down rather than to pretend that they don't exist in the first place.

4. Cross-examination of the taxpayer and the appellant's witnesses

19.51 The inspector will now try to test the accuracy and truth of the client's evidence by putting to him a series of questions in cross-examination. Cross-examination will generally be less polite than the examination in chief. The client's integrity and cool will be tested as cross-examination can be quite hostile.

19.52 It is important that the client remains calm and listens carefully to the question that is being put to him. If he does not understand the question then he should say so. He should answer the question and say no more. Sometimes the inspector will ask the same question in several different ways until he tries to get the answer that he is looking for. Your client must be steadfast. If he has answered the question he is quite at liberty to point this out to the Commissioners.

19.53 There are different techniques of cross-examination. The first is to increase the pace and hostility of the questions being asked in the hope that the witness will become flustered and may then contradict himself or lose his composure. The author has witnessed this at first hand where an inspector was particularly effective in his very assertive style of cross-examination.

The second technique is to take a far more measured and calm approach whereby the witness can be lulled into a false sense of security only to find that he has contradicted something he has said earlier.

It cannot be stressed strongly enough that in either case the witness must listen carefully to the question and think carefully before answering. He should direct his answers to the Chairman not to the inspector asking him the questions even during hostile cross-examination.

19.54 An example of cross-examination is where the inspector mounts an out and out challenge to the earlier evidence given by the witness. If, for example, the witness stated earlier that the entire terms and conditions of his working relationship were contained in a written contract then the inspector might try to show that there were other oral or implied arrangements. If he can establish this, he will then attack the credibility of the witness time and again by referring to his earlier incomplete evidence. This is cruel but fair.

19.55 Another technique of cross-examination is to lessen the weight to be attached to evidence given earlier by the witness. For example, it may have been established that the client invested money from his own pocket in attending training courses. This sounds like helpful evidence of financial investment and being in business. But if the question 'How much did the training course cost?' is asked by the inspector, and the answer is 'Only £30', then the importance of the training course will be diluted considerably. Remember the inspector's role, just the same as the accountant's, is that of an advocate who wants to win. On cross-examination and re-examination it is necessary, more than ever, to be able to remain calm and think on your feet.

5. Re-examination of the taxpayer and his witnesses

19.56 During cross-examination careful notes should be taken of anything the client is saying which is *unhelpful* to his case. This is because, after the inspector has finished cross-examining the witness, there will be a final opportunity for his representative to re-examine him. New evidence cannot be adduced at this stage but matters dealt with earlier can be re-visited. For example, referring back to the inexpensive training course it may be possible to establish the fact that the client funded *several* of these courses. The purpose of re-examination is to undo, wherever possible, any damage inflicted by the inspector during cross-examination.

19.57 This process of calling witnesses, examining them, the inspector cross-examining them followed by a final re-examination is carried out for all witnesses called by the taxpayer's representative and the inspector. The taxpayer's representative will of course have his own opportunity to cross-examine the inspector's witnesses in due course.

19.58 The key to a successful examination of the client is preparation. All of the questions need to be written out and the client needs to be aware of the questions he is going to be asked. If the case has been prepared properly there should be no real surprises and there should be an appreciation of the weaknesses in the case, which will give a good idea of the questions the inspector is likely to raise in cross-examination. The key to dealing successfully with cross-examination is to back up the oral evidence wherever possible by reference to documentary evidence and to ensure at all times that the plain truth is told.

19.59 Where the cross-examination of the client has resulted in little or no damage this should be pointed out to the Commissioners as it underlines the fact that the client's evidence and credibility have not been dented by the inspector.

19.60 The client as the appellant will remain in the hearing throughout the entire process. Other witnesses who have been called may have other engagements and it is customary to ask the Chairman if the witnesses can leave the proceedings once they have given their evidence.

It should be noted that once the client has been cross-examined, unless the Commissioners themselves wish to raise any further questions, the inspector is not at liberty to re-question the client at a later stage.

6. Questions asked by the Commissioners

19.61 It should be noted that the Commissioners may ask questions of the taxpayer at any time but they will usually only do this where a point needs clarifying. Just as a witness may not fully understand the question being put to him by the inspector so the Commissioners may not fully understand the information given in reply. The witness is most likely to be asked questions after he has been examined and cross-examined. One's sympathy must be with the Commissioners as they are coming to a case cold and are being asked to take in a great deal of factual information as well as considering many pages of photocopied documents placed before them. It is for this reason that it should be remembered that replies to questions must be given clearly and slowly in order that the Commissioners may take notes and ask any relevant questions.

7. Legal submissions by the practitioner (possibly given later)

19.62 Winning the appeal hearing is a two part process. First, the facts must be established by bringing out evidence, either oral or documentary. Second, legal precedents as established by the courts must be advanced and shown how they apply to the facts. Chapter 6 contains all the major case law decisions. Reference should be made to the skeleton arguments submitted earlier (particularly relevant for hearings at the Specials).

This is relatively straight forward if the practitioner has a thorough understanding of what the current case law says. If, for example, it has been established as fact that the client has the right to send a substitute, then attention would be drawn to the *Express and Echo* Court of Appeal case of 1999 (see Appendix 6) and a quotation from the judgment of Lord Justice Peter Gibson would be read out to the Commissioners. It will be remembered from Chapter 6 that his Lordship made the very clear statement that where a substitute can be sent then 'as a matter of law the relationship will not be one of employer and employee'.

Another example might be where a lack of mutuality of obligations has been established. Here the practitioner may refer to the judgment of Lord Irvine in the 1999 House of Lords *Carmichael* case (see Appendix 6), when the workers' claim to employed status foundered on the 'rock of absence of mutuality'.

19.63 It is important not merely to recite a long list of case law decisions but to show their *relevance* to the facts established. The practitioner must constantly refer back to the evidence given, particularly where it was not challenged successfully in cross-examination. For example, reference might be made to the recent Court of Appeal decision in *Montgomery v Johnson Underwood Ltd* (see Appendix 6) where, inter alia, the court stressed the need for the 'irreducible minimum' which needs to be in place before there can be a contract of service. One of the components of the irreducible minimum was control of the worker sufficient to render her a servant of her master. The relevant passage from the case judgment would be quoted to the Commissioners whereafter they would be reminded that it had already been established in evidence that the worker had freedom as to how and where the job was carried out.

19.64 The practitioner must always highlight the relevance of the case law precedents to the facts as established. The law and the facts need marrying up so their combined worth can be applied in support of the appeal.

19.65 Remember, opinions count for nothing. The Revenue booklets contain subjective interpretation which do not carry the force of law. The most effective way of making a point is to quote the words of the judges, preferably from senior courts in well established and recent case law precedents.

19.66 Do not over-burden the Commissioners with lengthy case law extracts unless it is absolutely necessary.

Case study

At a contentious tax status appeal the inspector insisted not only in referring to an overwhelming amount of case law, much of which was not relevant, but made the mistake of reading out page after page verbatim. Despite the protests of the Chairman he continued to read great extracts aloud. Eventually the inspector was told in no uncertain terms that he was to stop and that the Commissioners would read the judgments for themselves. They then proceeded to do so but it was obvious that they skipped over it. The inspector had made the mistake of not heeding the Commissioners' wishes and also failed to maintain their attention. The Revenue lost.

8. Summarising the taxpayer's case

19.67 This summary should not be too brief as it is meant to pull all the evidence and legal submissions in support of the appeal together. It will be unwise to go over everything in what might already be becoming a long hearing, but all pertinent points should be re-visited.

The emphasis must be on the facts established and those not weakened in cross-examination and the application of the law to those facts as supported by appropriate quotations from the actual judgments.

At this stage it is worth reminding the Commissioners that the burden of proof is nothing more than the balance of probabilities.

Finally, a separate sheet which clearly reminds the Commissioners what decision is being sought may be handed out via the Clerk, unless it has been incorporated in Bundle A. The Commissioners should be thanked for their attention.

9. The inspector responds

19.68 Most of the hard work has been done by this stage. The facts have been established on the basis of oral and documentary evidence and legal submissions in support of the appeal have been made. Hopefully, the Revenue has not exposed too many weaknesses in the client's case during cross-examination.

19.69 The inspector is now likely to make a minor tactical error. As it is traditional for the Revenue to speak first (because the accountant is happy for him to do so and because this is often the assumption of the General but not the Special Commissioners) inspectors tend to prepare their appeal brief on this basis. This can have a damaging effect on the inspector's case if he fails to adapt his presentation to the practitioner having spoken first.

Case study

Accountax addressed the Commissioners first in a very long contentious hearing with many witnesses being called. The inspector had prepared his presentation in a style more appropriate to him speaking *first*. The result of this was that when he addressed the Commissioners he effectively trawled over the entire history of the file including many aspects which had already been dealt with exhaustively earlier in the day.

The inspector was soon testing the patience of the Commissioners, who on more than one occasion asked him to move on and to stop repeating the background facts which had already been established. This caused the inspector difficulty as he was effectively reading out a prepared speech from longhand notes. He missed his chance to hold the attention of the Commissioners by offering fresh arguments and the Revenue lost the appeal.

As the inspector has already had an opportunity to cross-examine the main witnesses, ie the taxpayer, he may have little more to add. He is of course at liberty to call his own witnesses (usually other Revenue officers who have been involved in the case). But at this stage there may not be many more facts to establish. In IR35 cases the Revenue may call witnesses from the end-user.

10. Cross-examining the inspector's witnesses

19.70 The rule here is not to be afraid of taking an assertive approach. If the Revenue's witnesses and their evidence can be legitimately discredited then it is in the client's interests to do so. Cross-examination need not be overly polite, though out and out aggression is not recommended.

19.71 It is an old adage from the legal profession that one should never ask a question in cross-examination unless the answer is known. This is because a successful cross-examination is about controlling the *pace* and *direction* of the questioning and not being taken by surprise.

19.72 A fertile area of cross-examination is often to be found in a careful look through the file. Any errors by the Revenue have to be exposed and exploited. The Revenue will exploit any inconsistencies or anomalies in the client's case and the practitioner has to be prepared to do the same.

Furthermore, there must be a willingness to make a point even if this causes the witness some embarrassment. Remember, representing a client at an appeal hearing requires the approach of an advocate. The practitioner is his best hope of success. In an attempt to save the client's business and house the practitioner must represent the client to the best of his ability and if that means making a few waves so be it. It can work to the client's advantage if handled properly.

Case study

A tax officer involved in a status case had expressed the view on the telephone that in his opinion the workers were 'probably self-employed'. His line manager disagreed and the case eventually proceeded to a contentious appeal hearing. The original officer was called to give evidence and then cross-examined. He was persistently asked why he felt the men were 'probably self-employed'. This was extremely awkward for him, and he tried to avoid answering the question. By the time the question was put to him a third time the Commissioners were clearly expecting an answer. In a fit of pique the officer said:

> 'It's obvious they are self-employed.'

No more questions. This was the time to remain silent and let the point register with the Commissioners. It subsequently did and the taxpayer's appeal was successful.

It would have been easy to ease off, but then nothing would have been gained.

19.73 Experienced tax inspectors will expect robust cross-examination, but both before and after the hearing a professional but friendly attitude should be the order of the day.

19.74 It is of course the Commissioners who will decide the worth of the evidence brought out in examination, cross-examination and re-examination.

Case study

When being cross-examined by the author at a contentious appeal hearing a junior tax inspector was being prompted by his senior colleague who was sat next to him. This happened several times and a complaint to the Chairman was made. The Commissioners were singularly unimpressed with the inspector's behaviour and in no uncertain terms told the senior inspector this was quite unacceptable. This is exactly the kind of procedural error that can help the taxpayer's case.

19.75 Practitioners should note that in accordance with the Regulations it is not permissible, with one exception, to cross-examine a witness who has been summoned. This is because, if a person attends in obedience to a witness summons that person is the witness of the person who summoned him and it is not possible to cross-examine one's own witness. The one exception is where the Commissioners may give permission to cross-examine where they are satisfied that the person summoned is a 'hostile witness'. A hostile witness is a person whose mind discloses a bias adverse to the party examining him (see the author's article on this point in Taxation, 14 February 2002).

19.76 If a witness summons is applied for, any questioning of the witness must be carefully worded, as cross-examination will not be permitted unless it can be shown he is a hostile witness. The mere fact that a witness summons has been served does not necessarily mean that the person is hostile.

If, on the other hand, it is possible to have the Revenue call the witness in question as a *Revenue* witness then he can be cross-examined in the normal way.

Case study

In a contentious General Commissioners appeal the Revenue were reluctant to call a tax officer to give evidence. However, it was agreed by the Revenue that a witness summons was unnecessarily formal and might cause the officer some distress. The Revenue therefore agreed to call the witness as their own witness. This involved the inspector who was leading for the Revenue simply asking the witness his name and confirmation of his job title in the Revenue. There were no more questions and the witness was then cross-examined robustly.

19.77 It should be noted that sometimes a person might actually prefer to be served with a witness summons as this will give him protection from breach of confidentiality. A real life example of this was when Accountax served a witness summons on a VAT inspector who was concerned that if she disclosed confidential information in evidence on a 'voluntary' basis she could be at risk from an interested party.

19.78 There are other niceties in applying for a witness summons, such as giving seven days' notice of the hearing, applying for a summons only in respect of a UK based person and other formalities which are detailed the Regulations.

19.79 In the final analysis, cross-examination is about exposing weaknesses and inconsistency in the other side's evidence. This attacks the credibility of the Revenue's witnesses and in so doing enhances the value of one's own witnesses' evidence. Like everyone else, Revenue officers make errors. In the recent past Accountax has been sent a Head Office memo in error (it was meant to go to Milton Keynes Tax Office but was faxed to Accountax); an entire file destined for Head Office was sent to Accountax in error (the file contained some unprofessional comments on an Accountax employee, which resulted in a written apology from the Chairman of the Board of Inland Revenue); and for several years the Complaints Handbook has been in the public domain yet an Accountax employee was virtually accused of stealing it (this resulted in a written apology from the Revenue's Solicitor's Office). Where errors are made they should be exposed where this can help the client, and this can most usefully be achieved in cross examination of the inspector, and other witnesses called by the Revenue.

11. Re-examination by the Revenue

19.80 Here the Revenue will try to undo any damage caused during cross-examination or will try to clarify issues to the advantage of its own case. It should be remembered that re-examination should not introduce any new areas of questioning. If it does there will be a further opportunity to cross-examine the witness on those new questions.

12. Questions by the Commissioners

19.81 It should not be assumed that the Commissioners will only want to test the quality of the evidence or ask questions of the taxpayer or any witnesses called by him. They are quite prepared to question the

Revenue's witnesses in a robust manner where appropriate. Tactically, if it is felt that the Commissioners are picking up on a particular strand of the argument then it would be wise to re-emphasise such a point in the final summary.

19.82 If, during the Commissioners' questions, anomalies or inconsistencies are exposed the astute practitioner should again remind them of this at the end of the hearing.

Case study

At a contentious appeal evidence was extracted in cross-examination that the Revenue had handled the taxpayer's affairs very inefficiently. The Commissioners picked up on this and went so far as to observe that the Revenue had seriously messed the taxpayer around.

To make matters worse the inspector then conceded there had been several 'Revenue cock-ups'. The author won the appeal on behalf of the taxpayer and the Revenue were determined to take the matter on appeal to the High Court. When a transcript of the hearing was produced the inspector's use of the phrase 'Revenue cock-ups' was recorded verbatim by the Clerk. The Revenue decided not to proceed to the High Court and substantial financial compensation was recovered for the taxpayer on the basis that the matter should never have got as far as the Commissioners in the first place.

13. The Revenue makes its legal submissions (possibly immediately after the appellant's legal submissions)

19.83 Just as the taxpayer makes legal submissions so the Revenue has its opportunity. Any submissions made by the Revenue which are not backed up by case law quotations should be noted and if the Revenue is unable to offer much by way of legal submissions to back up its opinions a note of this should be made for the appellant's final summary.

19.84 The quality of legal submissions varies considerably and it will be quickly noted if the inspector is seeking to rely on out of date or superseded case law. If the inspector fails to apply the most up to date legal precedents this should be pointed out to the Commissioners in the final summary. Chapter 6 contains details of the major case law decisions. The Revenue will probably cross-refer their submissions to an earlier submitted skeleton argument, especially at the Specials.

14. The Revenue summarises its case

19.85 This is the last chance the Revenue has to underline the facts it feels it has established and the application of the law to those facts. The summary is not meant to be a wholesale repetition of everything that has been said before. It is meant to be a reasonably detailed but concise reiteration of the most salient points. An overly detailed summary with needless repetition can suggest desperation and should be avoided by both parties.

Case study

In a recent case the Revenue read out what was clearly a pre-written summary. It had little relevance to the evidence heard earlier and sounded more like a 'wish list'. As this was the Revenue's last chance to speak it was a wasted opportunity.

15. The taxpayer's final summary

19.86 This should be not much longer than the opening two minute summary. The practitioner should remind the Commissioners of the more pertinent facts that have been established, and the most important legal authorities submitted, to show that, on the balance of probabilities, the appeal should succeed. The Commissioners should be reminded of exactly what it is the taxpayer is requesting them to determine and, where appropriate, that the client's evidence has not been weakened by cross-examination and that the case law quoted is more up to date than the Revenue's. Again reference can be made to the practitioner's appeal summary, either as a separate page or as part of Bundle A, as it will contain a note of what determination is being sought. Final cross-references to the skeleton arguments may be made.

16. The decision

19.87 Having listened to both sides the Commissioners will want to retire and consider the evidence. In fact it is usually a question of the Commissioners staying in the room and the taxpayer and inspector leaving.

At no stage should the inspector or the taxpayer be left alone with the Commissioners. Either both sides should be in the room or both should be out.

19.88 At this stage, whilst waiting for the decision, it is customary for the two sides to adopt a more informal approach to each other.

Case study

Accountax represented a taxpayer in a contentious tax status dispute at the General Commissioners. After the hearing a less formal approach was adopted. The inspector told Accountax that it was the best appeal presentation he had ever seen. The author confirmed the inspector's presentation was the worst he had ever seen!

The inspector claimed the Revenue knew it was likely to lose. In other words everyone's time and money had been wasted. Accountax made a claim for reimbursement of all its fees and this was subsequently paid by the Revenue.

19.89 The General Commissioners may decide the case quickly, that is to say in less than half an hour, though it could be an hour or more. Although they will discuss the case among themselves they may well have already come to their own individual conclusions. The decision does not have to be unanimous. Special Commissioners decisions are rarely given on the day. A wait of 2–4 weeks is common.

19.90 Where it seems likely that the General Commissioners will be considering their decision for a protracted period of time they will probably excuse the parties and write with their decision in due course. The author has experienced this several times, both at the General Commissioners and the Secretary of State's Tribunal (the former Contributions Agency appeal tribunal). The reserved decision may take a week or so to come through the post but in one extreme case a client had to wait nearly two months.

19.91 On the basis that the General Commissioners give their decision on the day of the hearing, the Clerk will call in the parties and the Chairman will announce the decision. This can be a rather brief and indeed disappointing formality out of all proportion to the lengthy case which preceded it.

Typically the Chairman will say something along the lines of:

> 'The Commissioners would like to thank both parties for their detailed and clear arguments today. Having carefully considered the evidence put before them it is the determination of the Commissioners that this appeal should be upheld and, therefore, the Section 8 Notice of Assessment for 2000/01 will be discharged. Thank you and good day'.

19.92 The Commissioners will not explain their reasoning or what they felt was particularly influential in their decision making process. The parties may never know whether it is a unanimous decision or a majority decision. In fact, by the time the decision has been written down the Commissioners will be packing their briefcases and getting ready to leave. Unless a Stated Case is requested, as a precursor to going to the High Court on appeal, neither side will have any real idea as to how the evidence was perceived or regarded. Indeed, even a Stated Case may not give any real insight as to what impressed the Commissioners. General Commissioners are not required to give any reasons for their decision which can make it difficult when appealing to the High Court. With the Special Commissioners a detailed written judgement, often running to many pages, is provided. This may be in an anonymised form, but at least there is some detail to go on.

In one case where the General Commissioners reserved their decision and wrote to the parties later they did go into some considerable detail as to whose evidence they considered to be influential and they confirmed that they found in favour of the taxpayer unanimously but this level of disclosure is unusual.

19.93 The only other formality following the announcement of the decision may be a reminder by the Clerk that, if unhappy with the decision, either party can express dissatisfaction and in due course request a Stated Case for the opinion of the High Court. This is dealt with in Chapter 20. A letter confirming the decision is sent to all parties, but again this will generally say very little in terms of detail, unless the case has been heard by the Special.

Notes on presentation style

19.94 An over-theatrical style or the use of formal and pompous language should be avoided. Do not offer 'humble submissions'; instead say 'it is my view'. Do not use 'if it pleases the Commissioners' or other such phrases. Just use straightforward everyday language.

19.95 The key to an effective presentation at the Commissioners is clarity and a modest pace. Give them time to assimilate the points being made. If the Commissioners are making notes, which is inevitable, give them plenty of time. Wait until the Chairman has stopped writing before the next point is made.

19.96 If a good point is made, perhaps when examining the client or when cross-examining the Revenue's witness, be quite prepared to look directly at the Commissioners and remain silent, so as to emphasise the gravity of the particular point. Indeed, repeat the point to underline it.

For example, the client may have had to correct faulty work in his own time or at his own expense. Let this point sink in and then find some way of repeating it.

19.97 Do not distract the attention of the Commissioners with *very* fine points of dubious worth. It is a well accepted fact that very little of what is heard is remembered, so concentrate at all times on the important points that will weigh heavily in the client's favour. Establish facts by evidence, make authoritative legal points and link the law to the facts as established.

Case study

The Special or General Commissioners will not thank you for pushing unrealistic arguments. At one stage in the *Tilbury* IR35 appeal the Special Commissioner accused the Revenue of 'entering a sea of unreality'. Possible arguments are worth pursing, but desperate arguments should be dropped.

A mistake to avoid

19.98 Do not indicate to the Commissioners during the case that if they find for the Revenue the client will express dissatisfaction and appeal to the High Court. This kind of thinly veiled threat is unprofessional and will do the client's case no favours.

Case Study

In a recent General Commissioners Appeal concerning the issuing of a CIS certificate the inspector made the mistake of telling the Commissioners that if they didn't find for the Revenue, the Revenue would be very unhappy and would go to the High Court. The Commissioners were very put out by this outburst and found for Accountax. The case did not go further.

19.99 Other aspects of procedure at the Commissioners are also covered by the Regulations. Rules relating to agreement of documents, joining of additional parties, postponements, expert evidence and the case stated procedures can all be found in the Regulations, reproduced in Appendices 4 and 5.

Summary

19.100 The key to a successful presentation is preparation, preparation and preparation. Careful attention must be given to compiling and numbering Bundles A and B, briefing the client and any other witnesses as to what they can expect and finally to speak clearly, confidently, slowly and avoid an over theatrical presentation. Be prepared to cross-examine the inspector and his witnesses in a robust manner and to expose inconsistencies, doubts or errors in the way the case has been handled and the actual facts of the case.

19.101 The practitioner must be constantly aware of the need to link the relevance of the case law with the established facts. Do not assume the Commissioners will automatically do this. This is your job!

19.102 Finally, and this cannot be underestimated, make it clear at the beginning and the end exactly what it is the Commissioners are meant to be determining and what decision is being sought.

A blueprint for an IR35 defence and appeal

19.103 It is suggested that a focused approach is made. Where appropriate:

1 Argue that the legislation does not apply *at all* because, for example, the client is not giving 'personal service'.
2 Argue that statutory interpretation requires not a hypothetical contract but the placing of the worker in the shoes of the personal service business. Expose the many difficulties of the Revenue's interpretation of the hypothetical contract.
3 Establish the full terms and conditions of the personal service business contract with *its* client, usually an agency. Don't allow the Revenue to imply terms that are contrary to the contract. Where possible get 'end-user' confirmation on the important areas of substitution, control and mutuality.
4 Establish all broader factors which show the client has a business mindset and history.
5 Quote from case law in support of all contentions made.

Points 1–5 above need to be followed throughout the technical argument with the Revenue during an IR35 challenge. If the dispute cannot be resolved it will be necessary to proceed to a contentious appeal hearing at the Commissioners.

(a) Be wary of attending last minute meetings with the Revenue, where it may attempt to extract in advance the evidence likely to be presented by the taxpayer.
(b) At the Commissioners always *link* the case law to the established facts.
(c) Vigorously cross-examine the Revenue's witnesses and expose all weaknesses in the Revenue's case, either technical or procedural.
(d) At the Commissioners make sure all documentation is properly prepared and checked and that the client and witnesses know what to expect on the day.

CHAPTER 20

What happens after the appeal hearing

If the taxpayer has won

20.1 During the course of the hearing the practitioner, the inspector and the Clerk would have made detailed notes, in particular in relation to the examination and cross-examination of witnesses. If the appeal has been upheld the onus will be on the inspector to mount a challenge and he will do this initially by 'expressing dissatisfaction' with the Commissioners' decision. He may then require the Clerk to produce a Stated Case, which is essentially a record of the entire appeal hearing. This is the Generals' way to proceed. For this time-consuming and difficult task the Clerk will receive the princely sum of £25. Requesting a draft Stated Case places upon the Clerk a tremendous administrative burden and neither the inspector nor the practitioner should make the request lightly.

20.2 Prior to the introduction of the General Commissioners (Jurisdiction and Procedure) Regulations 1994, SI 1994/1812, it was not unknown for Clerks to take an inordinate amount of time in preparing the draft Stated Case. In one particular instance the author had to threaten the issue of an application for an Order of Mandamus which is a High Court precept requiring a person to complete a task within his official capacity. Since the introduction of the Regulations there are strict statutory time limits within which the Clerk must produce the draft and, if the taxpayer has won the appeal, the onus will be on the inspector to request this and pay the fee.

20.3 It should be noted that the Clerk to the Generals has the right to challenge the application for the Stated Case by requiring the applicant to make clear what is the point of law that may be in issue. In extreme circumstances, if the Commissioners are not satisfied that there is a valid point of law upon which application to the High Court can be made, they may refuse to state a case.

20.4 The Commissioners Regulations contain timescales within which the draft Stated Case has to be produced—see Appendices 4 and 5.

20.5 On receipt of the draft Stated Case both parties have a statutory time period within which they can offer amendments or comments on the draft as produced.

20.6 Practitioners should remember that there are only two bases for going on appeal to the High Court. The first and most common is that the Commissioners have made an error in law. The second is that the Commissioners reached a conclusion which, based on the facts, was so perverse that no reasonable tribunal could have reached that conclusion.

20.7 Getting all sides to agree the draft Stated Case can be a time consuming process, with a great deal of nitpicking correspondence going backwards and forwards between the parties. However, where the inspector has requested a Stated Case the practitioner should not readily agree it without robust scrutiny, as once it has been agreed and signed off the client will not be able to challenge it later. It is important not to lose sight of the fact that the Stated Case is meant to be nothing more than a record of what was said and what was produced in evidence at the appeal hearing.

20.8 Having agreed the Stated Case it is then open to the inspector to make a final decision as to whether the case is put before the High Court, and inevitably he will only do this after having taken Head Office advice. In the author's experience inspectors may threaten to go to the High Court, even before the Commissioner's case has been heard, but more often than not this is nothing more than bluff.

Case study

In a specific contentious appeal in which the author was involved relatively recently the inspector made the mistake of advising the Commissioners, half way through his presentation, that if they did not reach the determination the inspector was seeking he would be going to the High Court. This was a major error on the inspector's part as it did nothing to endear him or his case to the Commissioners, who felt that they were being unduly pressured. In the event the Revenue lost the appeal, the inspector asked for a Stated Case but, after taking further Head Office advice, dropped the matter.

20.9 When the Commissioners complete the Stated Case the question for the High Court is often framed in non-specific terms such as: 'Were we the Commissioners entitled in law to reach the determination made?'

In the case of an appeal from the Special Commissioners it is not necessary to ask for a stated case. TMA 1970 s 56 gives the appellant 56 days to lodge an appeal in the High Court. The Special Commissioners' decision is effectively the stated case.

It is not open to the High Court to establish or challenge facts previously found and that is why it is so important that any findings of fact made by the Commissioners during the course of the hearing are accurately recorded. It is common for experienced inspectors and practitioners, during the course of a hearing, to request that the Commissioners 'find' and record a specific fact which they consider to be highly relevant.

20.10 In the High Court the matter will be heard by one professional judge. It is common for both sides to be represented by Counsel, although taxpayers may represent themselves or have an assistant who must be unpaid. The costs of going to the High Court are substantial and it is likely that the losing side will have to pay the other side's costs. Although this may not be a major factor for the Revenue to consider it will no doubt play heavily on the mind of the practitioner and his client. In exceptional cases, where an important principle of law is involved which needs to be aired and decided for the good of the general tax paying public, the Revenue may agree to cover all costs or not to seek its costs should it win.

20.11 It is possible to appeal from the High Court to the Court of Appeal, and ultimately to the House of Lords, on a point of law.

20.12 The hierarchy for non-tax cases such as employment disputes, where status may be the principle preliminary point in issue, is somewhat different. A case will proceed from the Employment Tribunal to the Employment Appeals Tribunal and then on to the Court of Appeal and ultimately the House of Lords.

20.13 Where the taxpayer has won it is of course the Revenue's task to have the Commissioner's decision overturned, but just as the onus of proof at the original hearing was the balance of probabilities so it is in the High Court and beyond.

If the taxpayer has lost

20.14 Exactly the same procedural considerations apply and again it is important to emphasise that it is too easy for the bitter taxpayer to request a Stated Case on the grounds that he has 'nothing to lose'. Unless specific points of law can be identified where, on the balance of probabilities, there is a clear chance of making a successful appeal to the High Court one's losses should be cut.

20.15 Having lost at the Commissioners the inspector has not established a binding legal precedent, other than in respect of the specific appeal for the named taxpayer involved in the hearing. General Commissioner's appeals are heard in private and even Special Commissioners' decisions, which are generally reported and which carry influence, are not strict legal precedent.

20.16 It should also be remembered that, win or lose at the General Commissioners, neither side can recover their costs from the other and only in exceptional circumstances can hearings before the Special Commissioners lead to the award of costs. Costs can only be given under SI 1994/1811 reg 21 in respect of the 'conduct of the appeal'. As such, any pre-appeal misdemeanours by the inspector or appellant are not relevant to an award of costs. If costs are being sought early reference should be made to this. The Special Commissioners are not interested in hearing complaints unless an award for costs is in point. It is open to the taxpayer to make a compensation claim to the Revenue, effectively a 'complaint' (see 19.88 above), but this is not a costs 'order' issued by the Commissioners. Despite the often heard bravura of the losing party the best advice is to call it a day unless there are very substantial resources and strong legal arguments to present to the High Court. Occasionally funds for a High Court appeal may be offered by the PCG or subject to a fighting fund appeal publicised in Taxation Magazine.

What lessons can be learnt

20.17 Whether the client wins or loses at the Commissioners the decision will relate only to the years under appeal and as such there will be important lessons to learn. If successful there may nonetheless be lessons to be learned from the weaknesses in the client's arguments, exposed by the inspector perhaps in cross-examination. There may be factors not previously considered and from this there may be scope to re-negotiate clauses in the contract, whereby the client's position will be further strengthened. Such lessons can be applied for the benefit of other clients.

Case study

At the first day of the *Ansell* IR35 appeal (the decision is awaited at the time of publication of this third edition) a total of eight Revenue personnel attended the hearing. One assumes this was some kind of training exercise for them.

On the other hand, if the taxpayer loses the practitioner will be painfully aware of the strong points put forward by the Revenue that resulted in the defeat. Bearing in mind that contracts can be re-negotiated at any stage the Revenue's successful arguments may well give some very strong clues as to what areas of the contract need to be tightened up when the client next comes to re-negotiate his terms and conditions.

20.18 Winning or losing at the Commissioners will also give valuable practical experience to the practitioner, which will stand him in good stead for the next appeal hearing.

Case study

Accountax has lost three appeal hearings. The first concerned a business which used a very poorly worded home-made contract for services, which even misdescribed the workers' trades. Even so, it was a tight decision and the inspector privately conceded that he thought he had lost. In the second case everything went according to plan yet the Commissioners found for the Revenue. The taxpayer considered this decision to be quite perverse but a lack of funds prevented a High Court appeal. The third was the IR35 *Usetech* appeal, and this case may go to the High Court on appeal.

These decisions underline the fact that the outcome at the Commissioners is never guaranteed.

Summary

20.19 The real issue is what to do if the taxpayer has lost the appeal. It is a major decision to go on appeal to the High Court, in terms of costs for both the personal service business itself and those of the Revenue if victory in the High Court is not achieved.

This also assumes there is a point of law on which an appeal can be made.

20.20 Contract terms can always be re-negotiated for the future and lessons can be learnt from the whole appeal process which might well stand the practitioner and his other clients in good stead in the future.

CHAPTER 21

The advice clients need now

1. Agree and implement a sound written contract

21.1 When the Revenue carried out its status challenge on the construction industry in the late 1990s it had most success with the taxpayers who had become, by their actions, or lack of them, 'easy targets'. For example, where there was no written contract (still frighteningly common even in the specialist knowledge-based sector) it was easy for the Revenue to say that the whole situation needed to be established by asking questions of both the engager and the worker. This would often lead to uncertainty, simply because many of the issues raised by the Revenue in its questions had not been specifically considered by the parties previously.

21.2 In truth, even if there is no written contract there must still be a contract of some kind as there has been an offer and acceptance of work; consideration (value) has passed between the parties and there has been an intention to create a legal relationship. In other words, the three basic requisites for a binding contract are in place.

21.3 The problem with contracts which are not written is that they may lead to a very real uncertainty as to what the verbal or implied terms are. That is not to say that a written contract is not open to interpretation, but it is far more *certain* than a verbal contract. In terms of evidence, at a possible appeal hearing before the Commissioners it is clearly advantageous to start with a comprehensive and well written contract. A contract which is signed and dated. A contract must not be back-dated in any circumstances.

21.4 Even when advising clients at the early stages of a dispute it is important to have in the back of one's mind the quality of the evidence to be adduced, and one of the most important pieces of evidence in an IR35 dispute will be the contract. So the first task of any practitioner who is trying to defend his clients from the effects of IR35 is to ensure that a comprehensive and competently worded contract for services is committed to writing and that it is signed, dated and implemented.

2. Maintain due diligence records to show the contract is implemented

21.5 There is an interesting legal debate as to whether the terms of a written contract are the only means by which the IR35 relationship can be examined. The Revenue traditionally argues that the contract wording is irrelevant if it does not reflect the reality of the working relationship. Unquestionably there comes a point when a sham contract will be exposed as such and it will carry little if any weight. But does the Revenue have the right to disregard the written contract on the assumption that it *may* not fully reflect the true terms and conditions of the working relationship?

21.6 The case law makes it quite clear that, where the terms and conditions governing the relationship of the parties are laid down entirely in a written contract, the Revenue is restricted to an examination of those terms only. This is accepted in the Revenue's internal guidance manuals. There is one exception to this rule and that is where the subsequent actions of the parties are such that they have effectively amended or varied the terms of their original contract. The *Narich* case (see Appendix 6) discussed in Chapter 6 confirms this.

If there is a subsequent variation to the contract then those varied terms have to be considered on their own merits. However, there is a significant difference between parties genuinely varying their terms and parties not implementing them.

21.7 Notwithstanding the approach in *Narich*, it is still desirable to be able to show the inspector that the contract is implemented in practice. The client should be able to hand over to the Revenue a copy of the comprehensive written contract for services and at the same time provide a series of mini due diligence reports showing that the contract has been implemented and re-visited. For example, any sensible anti-IR35 contract will have a requirement that the contracting company maintains a business organisation and goes about its work in a business-like manner. This may include the simple requirement to maintain adequate public and professional insurances and to raise invoices on a proper business letterhead.

21.8 The IR35 defence will be made much easier if the various insurance certificates etc can be produced and shown to the inspector at a moment's notice. The inspector can then be provided with not only a comprehensive anti-IR35 contract but with hard proof that its terms are being implemented in practice.

A simple due diligence checklist which can be carried out perhaps twice a year should be a more than adequate way of demonstrating that the contract is being lived and breathed.

21.9 It should of course be remembered that contracts are concerned with rights and obligations and sometimes these are not easy to 'prove'.

For example, if there is a liability on the contracting company to correct defective work without receiving further fees then this is a burdensome risk. If the contracting company never commits defective work this does not take away its liability—it is just that it has never been called upon.

In these situations inspectors have been known to dismiss the defective work clause as ineffective but this misses the point. If the risk and liability is there then it stands, notwithstanding the fact that the client has not had to implement the clause. Of course the due diligence record will make a note of any instances of defective work and its correction.

3. Educate the client

21.10 Having helped the client agree and implement a sound anti-IR35 contract for services it is important to ensure he knows exactly what is expected of him if he is to be able to resist a Revenue challenge. He should be encouraged to take professional advice at an early stage if a challenge arises, and absolutely must be briefed on what happens at a contentious appeal hearing should he end up going to one. Preparation is all.

It is vital that the contractor realises that the evidence his end-user will give is extremely important at any appeal. So even at an early stage the 'long view' has to be taken, and contractors should recognise this.

CHAPTER 22

Closing remarks

22.1 *IR35 Defence Strategies: From Contracts to the Commissioners* is not a book about tax compliance. In fact in many ways it is quite the opposite. The book offers various strategies and ideas to the pro-active practitioner who is *trying* to keep his clients out of IR35 or who needs to go on appeal to the Commissioners. And if all else fails it explains how to win at the Commissioners.

Since the Second Edition we have had our first High Court case on IR35, *Synaptek v Young,* which the taxpayer lost. Accountax have also had success at the Special Commissioners with two IR35 cases, *Lime-IT Ltd v Justin* (2002), and more recently *Tilbury Consulting Ltd v Margaret Gittins* (2003).

22.2 There are many aspects of IR35 deliberately not covered in this book. Partnerships have not been considered for the simple reason that the overwhelming majority of personal service businesses operate as limited companies. It will be these very same limited companies the Revenue will target as it seeks national insurance lost to the dividend route. Equally, overseas considerations have been left out, again because most personal service businesses operate in the UK with UK registered companies.

22.3 Not all of the arguments in this book will work in every situation but it is hoped that practitioners will, at least, now have a much better understanding of the arguments which are potentially available to them. This is also a good time to stand back and think about the style of language that has become common currency in IR35. Should phrases such as 'personal service business' be so readily used? Do not these words automatically imply an admission that personal service is being given as opposed to the undertaking of a commercial service? One has to be careful.

22.4 There are other more complicated routes which may show that IR35 does not apply, such as the use of composite and umbrella companies or convoluted off-shore schemes. These *may* work for some personal service businesses in certain circumstances, but many practitioners are highly suspicious of such arrangements and tend to shy away from them. Such schemes are often shrouded in controversy and based on questionable off-shore arrangements. Indeed, the Revenue has confirmed that its Special Compliance Office and Sheffield Unit are taking an active interest in schemes that present themselves as a means to evade or avoid tax (see General Frequently Asked Questions, Compliance, 4, on the Revenue's website at http://www.inlandrevenue.gov.uk/ir35). A much easier approach is to operate as a true business and agree and implement contract terms which are clearly outside IR35.

22.5 The importance of understanding and applying current case law with a view to assisting contractors to negotiate anti-IR35 clauses in their contracts must not be underestimated. IR35-proof contracts are not that difficult to agree but they must not be shams.

22.6 The Revenue can only investigate a very small number of personal service businesses and it will want to pick on the weaker cases or contractors who offer little resistance.

22.7 If technical argument fails and a contentious Commissioners appeal becomes necessary most practitioners have the necessary skills to make a good job of representing their clients. The practitioner should establish the facts, apply the case law and have the courage and confidence to go to the Commissioners and win.

APPENDIX 1

ITEPA 2003 Pt 2 Ch 8

Income Tax (Earnings and Pensions) Act 2003 Part 2 Chapter 8: Application of Provisions to Workers Under Arrangements made by Intermediaries

Application of this Chapter

Scope of this Chapter

48—(1) This Chapter has effect with respect to the provision of services through an intermediary.

(2) Nothing in this Chapter—

(*a*) affects the operation of Chapter 7 of this Part, or

(*b*) applies to payments subject to deduction of tax under section 555 of ICTA (payments to non-resident entertainers and sportsmen).

GENERAL NOTE

This Chapter replaces FA 2000 Sch 12 and relates to services provided through an intermediary. This legislation became known as 'IR35' following the original Revenue announcement. Payments to foreign entertainers and sportsmen subject to the withholding tax regime operated by the Revenue's 'Foreign Entertainers Unit' are excluded from these provisions.

Engagements to which this Chapter applies

49—(1) This Chapter applies where—

(*a*) an individual ('the worker') personally performs, or is under an obligation personally to perform, services [for another person][1] ('the client'),

(*b*) the services are provided not under a contract directly between the client and the worker but under arrangements involving a third party ('the intermediary'), and (*c*) the circumstances are such that, if the services were provided under a contract directly between the client and the worker, the worker would be regarded for income tax purposes as an employee of the client.

(2) . . .[2]

(3) The reference in subsection (1)(*b*) to a 'third party' includes a partnership or unincorporated body of which the worker is a member.

(4) The circumstances referred to in subsection (1)(*c*) include the terms on which the services are provided, having regard to the terms of the contracts forming part of the arrangements under which the services are provided.

(5) In this Chapter 'engagement to which this Chapter applies' means any such provision of services as is mentioned in subsection (1).

Amendments— [1] Words substituted by FA 2003 s 136(1), (2) with effect in relation to services performed or due to be performed on or after 10 April 2003.

[2] Repealed by the FA 2003 ss 216, 136(1), (3)(*a*), Sch 43, Pt 3(1) with effect in relation to services performed or due to be performed on or after 10 April 2003.

General note

This Chapter introduces the personal service company rules outlined in the IR35 Budget Press Release of 9 March 1999. From 6 April 2000 a person working for a personal service company who provides services for clients through his company has to pay tax and National Insurance as if he were a direct employee subject to a minor exemption for costs, if in the absence of the company, the arrangements would have amounted to an employment rather than a self-employment individual providing freelance services.

These are also supplemented by the Social Security Contributions (Intermediaries) Regulations 2000, SI 2000/727, and the Social Security Contributions (Intermediaries) (Northern Ireland) Regulations 2000, SI 2000/728, dealing with the National Insurance charge. The schedule applies where the employee of the service company (known as the worker) personally provides his services to a business client not as a direct employee of the client but through the service company (known as the intermediary) in such circumstances that if there was a direct contract between the worker and the client for the provision of those services it would amount to a contract of employment. Although the third party would normally be a personal services company it could be a partnership or an unincorporated body. The arrangements must take account of the contractual terms and the fact that the worker is an officer of the client is ignored.

Worker treated as receiving earnings from employment

50—(1) If, in the case of an engagement to which this Chapter applies, in any tax year—

(*a*) the conditions specified in section 51, 52 or 53 are met in relation to the intermediary, and

(*b*) the worker, or an associate of the worker—

 (i) receives from the intermediary, directly or indirectly, a payment or benefit that is not employment income, or

 (ii) has rights which entitle, or which in any circumstances would entitle, the worker or associate to receive from the intermediary, directly or indirectly, any such payment or benefit,

the intermediary is treated as making to the worker, and the worker is treated as receiving, in that year a payment which is to be treated as earnings from an employment ('the deemed employment payment').

(2) A single payment is treated as made in respect of all engagements in relation to which the intermediary is treated as making a payment to the worker in the tax year.

(3) The deemed employment payment is treated as made at the end of the tax year, unless section 57 applies (earlier date of deemed payment in certain cases).

(4) In this Chapter 'the relevant engagements', in relation to a deemed employment payment, means the engagements mentioned in subsection (2).

General note

Where there is a relevant engagement under this Chapter, the intermediary is deemed to have paid to the worker a payment of employment earnings if the intermediary meets the criteria set out in ITEPA 2003 s 51, 52 or 53 below and the worker, or an associate, receives the payment or other benefit from the intermediary not as employment income, but in the form of a dividend or other non-employment income. The deemed 'employment payment' is treated as made on 5 April in each tax year, subject to ITEPA 2003 s 57 below, and there is only one such deemed payment irrespective of the number of engagements during the year.

Conditions of liability where intermediary is a company

51—(1) Where the intermediary is a company the conditions are that the intermediary is not an associated company of the client that falls within subsection (2) and either—

(*a*) the worker has a material interest in the intermediary, or

(*b*) the payment or benefit mentioned in section 50(1)(*b*)—

(i) is received or receivable by the worker directly from the intermediary, and
(ii) can reasonably be taken to represent remuneration for services provided by the worker to the client.

(2) An associated company of the client falls within this subsection if it is such a company by reason of the intermediary and the client being under the control—
(*a*) of the worker, or
(*b*) of the worker and other persons.

(3) A worker is treated as having a material interest in a company if—
(*a*) the worker, alone or with one or more associates of the worker, or
(*b*) an associate of the worker, with or without other such associates,
has a material interest in the company.

(4) For this purpose a material interest means—
(*a*) beneficial ownership of, or the ability to control, directly or through the medium of other companies or by any other indirect means, more than 5% of the ordinary share capital of the company; or
(*b*) possession of, or entitlement to acquire, rights entitling the holder to receive more than 5% of any distributions that may be made by the company; or
(*c*) where the company is a close company, possession of, or entitlement to acquire, rights that would in the event of the winding up of the company, or in any other circumstances, entitle the holder to receive more than 5% of the assets that would then be available for distribution among the participators.

(5) In subsection (4)(*c*) 'participator' has the meaning given by section 417(1) of ICTA.

GENERAL NOTE

The liability outlined in ITEPA 2003 s 50 above will only apply where the intermediary is not an associated company of the client, ie where both the intermediary and the client are under the control of the worker either alone or with another person/other persons. The meaning of 'associate' and 'associated company' is provided in ITEPA 2003 s 61.

Conditions of liability where intermediary is a partnership

52—(1) Where the intermediary is a partnership the conditions are as follows.

(2) In relation to any payment or benefit received or receivable by the worker as a member of the partnership the conditions are—

(*a*) that the worker, alone or with one or more relatives, is entitled to 60% or more of the profits of the partnership; or

(*b*) that most of the profits of the partnership concerned derive from the provision of services under engagements to which this Chapter applies—

(i) to a single client, or

(ii) to a single client together with associates of that client; or

(*c*) that under the profit sharing arrangements the income of any of the partners is based on the amount of income generated by that partner by the provision of services under engagements to which this Chapter applies.

In paragraph (a) 'relative' means husband or wife, parent or child or remoter relation in the direct line, or brother or sister.

(3) In relation to any payment or benefit received or receivable by the worker otherwise than as a member of the partnership, the conditions are that the payment or benefit—

(a) is received or receivable by the worker directly from the intermediary, and

(b) can reasonably be taken to represent remuneration for services provided by the worker to the client.

GENERAL NOTE

The arrangement is caught where:

(*a*) the services are provided to the client by a partnership of which the worker, alone or with one of more relatives (ie spouse, direct ancestor, issue or sibling) is entitled to 60 per cent or more of the profits of the partnership;

(*b*) most of the partnership profits arise from engagements with a single client and its associates; or

(*c*) the profit sharing arrangements are such that the partners' income is based on the income generated personally from relevant engagements.

A payment received by the worker other than as a member of the partnership is within the provisions if received directly from the partnership and the payment or benefit can reasonably be taken to represent remuneration for services provided by the worker for the client.

In determining a spouse, ITEPA 2003 s 61(4) provides that a man and woman living together as husband and wife are treated as if they were married.

Conditions of liability where intermediary is an individual

53—Where the intermediary is an individual the conditions are that the payment or benefit—

(*a*) is received or receivable by the worker directly from the intermediary, and
(*b*) can reasonably be taken to represent remuneration for services provided by the worker to the client.

GENERAL NOTE

This applies where the worker receives a payment or benefit directly from the intermediary and it is such that it can be reasonably taken to represent the worker's earnings from a relevant engagement for services provided to the client.

The deemed employment payment

Calculation of deemed employment payment

54—(1) The amount of the deemed employment payment for a tax year ('the year') is the amount resulting from the following steps—

Step 1
Find (applying section 55) the total amount of all payments and benefits received by the intermediary in the year in respect of the relevant engagements, and reduce that amount by 5%.

Step 2
Add (applying that section) the amount of any payments and benefits received by the worker in the year in respect of the relevant engagements, otherwise than from the intermediary, that—
(*a*) are not chargeable to income tax as employment income, and
(*b*) would be so chargeable if the worker were employed by the client.

Step 3
Deduct (applying Chapters 1 to 5 of Part 5) the amount of any expenses met in the year by the intermediary that would have been deductible from the taxable earnings from the employment if—
(*a*) the worker had been employed by the client, and
(*b*) the expenses had been met by the worker out of those earnings.
If the result at this or any later point is nil or a negative amount, there is no deemed employment payment.

Step 4
Deduct the amount of any capital allowances in respect of expenditure incurred by the intermediary that could have been deducted from employment income under section 262 of CAA 2001 (employments and offices) if the worker had been employed by the client and had incurred the expenditure.

Step 5
Deduct any contributions made in the year for the benefit of the worker by the intermediary to a scheme approved under Chapter 1 or 4 of Part 14 of ICTA that if made by an employer for the benefit of an employee would not be chargeable to income tax as income of the employee.

This does not apply to excess contributions made and later repaid.

Step 6
Deduct the amount of any employer's national insurance contributions paid by the intermediary for the year in respect of the worker.

Step 7
Deduct the amount of any payments and benefits received in the year by the worker from the intermediary—

(*a*) in respect of which the worker is chargeable to income tax as employment income, and
(*b*) which do not represent items in respect of which a deduction was made under step 3.

Step 8
Assume that the result of step 7 represents an amount together with employer's national insurance contributions on it, and deduct what (on that assumption) would be the amount of those contributions.

The result is the deemed employment payment.

(2) If section 559 of ICTA applies (sub-contractors in the construction industry: payments to be made under deduction), the intermediary is treated for the purposes of step 1 of subsection (1) as receiving the amount that would have been received had no deduction been made under that section.

(3) In step 3 of subsection (1), the reference to expenses met by the intermediary includes—

(*a*) expenses met by the worker and reimbursed by the intermediary, and
(*b*) where the intermediary is a partnership and the worker is a member of the partnership, expenses met by the worker for and on behalf of the partnership.

(4) In step 3 of subsection (1), the expenses deductible include the amount of any mileage allowance relief for the year which the worker would have been entitled to in respect of the use of a vehicle falling within subsection (5) if—

(*a*) the worker had been employed by the client, and
(*b*) the vehicle had not been a company vehicle (within the meaning of Chapter 2 of Part 4).

(5) A vehicle falls within this subsection if—

(*a*) it is provided by the intermediary for the worker, or

(*b*) where the intermediary is a partnership and the worker is a member of the partnership, it is provided by the worker for the purposes of the business of the partnership.

(6) Where, on the assumptions mentioned in paragraphs (*a*) and (*b*) of step 3 of subsection (1), the deductibility of the expenses is determined under sections 337 to 342 (travel expenses), the duties performed under the relevant engagements are treated as duties of a continuous employment with the intermediary.

(7) In step 7 of subsection (1), the amounts deductible include any payments received in the year from the intermediary that—

(*a*) are exempt from income tax by virtue of section 229 or 233 (mileage allowance payments and passenger payments), and

(*b*) do not represent items in respect of which a deduction was made under step 3.

(8) For the purposes of subsection (1) any necessary apportionment is to be made on a just and reasonable basis of amounts received by the intermediary that are referable—

(*a*) to the services of more than one worker, or

(*b*) partly to the services of the worker and partly to other matters.

GENERAL NOTE

There is a multi-step calculation as follows:

Step 1 is the total amount received by the intermediary during the tax year from all relevant engagements, including any benefits provided to the intermediary. The calculation is made on a tax year basis irrespective of the accounting date of the intermediary. The total amount received is reduced by five per cent as a notional allowance for the running costs of the intermediary.

Step 2 includes any payments or benefits received by the worker in respect of any relevant engagements from anyone other than the intermediary which are not otherwise chargeable to tax as employment income, but which would have been if the worker had been employed by the client.

Step 3 allows a deduction for any expenses which would have been allowed if the worker had paid for them and had been an employee of the client.

Step 4 also allows as a deduction any capital allowances that would have been claimable had the worker been an employee of the client.

Step 5 allows as a deduction any contributions paid by the intermediary to an approved pension scheme for the benefit of the worker.

Step 6 deducts any employer's NIC paid by the intermediary in respect of salary or benefits provided to the worker during the year as employee of the intermediary.

Step 7 deducts the salary and benefits provided to the worker by the intermediary during the year which have already been taxed as employment income and subjected to NIC.

If Step 7 results in a nil or negative figure there is no deemed employment payment under these provisions.

Step 8 allows a deduction in respect of the amount resulting from Step 7 inclusive of employer's NIC. The resulting figure is the deemed employment payment.

The provisions in sub-ss (3) to (7) were first amended by FA 2002 and allow reimbursed expenses and mileage allowances, in order to put the employee of the personal service company or partnership on the same footing as if he had been employed by the client directly and incurred the costs which the client had reimbursed or had the use of a car.

Where the personal service company ceased to trade this is the date on which a deemed employment payment may be treated as paid, so that the company can claim credit for the relief in its final accounts. Where the intermediary is a partnership the expenses rules are modified accordingly.

If the worker is subject to the construction industry scheme under TA 1988 s 559 it is the gross receipt which is brought into account at Step 1. However, it appears that the amount withheld under the construction industry scheme cannot be set against the amount due on the deemed employment payment and therefore will have to be recovered at the end of the intermediary's tax year as an overpayment. This would appear to present the worker with considerable cash flow problems.

Any just and reasonable apportionment may be made where an intermediary receives a single payment covering the services of more than one worker or includes something else, such as the provision of materials.

Application of rules relating to earnings from employment

55—(1) The following provisions apply in relation to the calculation of the deemed employment payment.

(2) A 'payment or benefit' means anything that, if received by an employee for performing the duties of an employment, would be earnings from the employment.

(3) The amount of a payment or benefit is taken to be—

(*a*) in the case of a payment or cash benefit, the amount received, and

(*b*) in the case of a non-cash benefit, the cash equivalent of the benefit.

(4) The cash equivalent of a non-cash benefit is taken to be—

(*a*) the amount that would be earnings if the benefit were earnings from an employment, or

(*b*) in the case of living accommodation, whichever is the greater of that amount and the cash equivalent determined in accordance with section 398(2).

(5) A payment or benefit is treated as received—

(*a*) in the case of a payment or cash benefit, when payment is made of or on account of the payment or benefit;

(*b*) in the case of a non-cash benefit that is calculated by reference to a period within the tax year, at the end of that period;

(*c*) in the case of a non-cash benefit that is not so calculated, when it would have been treated as received for the purposes of Chapter 4 or 5 of this Part (see section 19 or 32) if—

(i) the worker had been an employee, and

(ii) the benefit had been provided by reason of the employment.

GENERAL NOTE

A payment or other benefit is defined as anything which would have been taxable as income or a benefit if the worker had been an employee of the client. A payment or cash benefit is treated as received when payment is made. A non-cash benefit is treated as received:

(*a*) if it is calculated by reference to a period within the tax year, at the end of that period;

(*b*) if it is not so calculated, when it would have been treated as earnings if the worker had been an employee and the benefit had been provided by reason of the employment.

Application of Income Tax Acts in relation to deemed employment

56—(1) The Income Tax Acts (in particular, the PAYE provisions) apply in relation to the deemed employment payment as follows.

(2) They apply as if—

(*a*) the worker were employed by the intermediary, and

(*b*) the relevant engagements were undertaken by the worker in the course of performing the duties of that employment.

(3) The deemed employment payment is treated in particular—

(*a*) as taxable earnings from the employment for the purpose of securing that any deductions under Chapters 2 to 6 of Part 5 do not exceed the deemed employment payment; and

(*b*) as taxable earnings from the employment for the purposes of section 232.

(4) The worker is not chargeable to tax in respect of the deemed employment payment if, or to the extent that, by reason of any combination of the factors mentioned in subsection (5), the worker would not be chargeable to tax if—

(*a*) the client employed the worker,

(*b*) the worker performed the services in the course of that employment, and (*c*) the deemed employment payment were a payment by the client of earnings from that employment.

(5) The factors are—

(*a*) the worker being resident, ordinarily resident or domiciled outside the United Kingdom,

(*b*) the client being resident or ordinarily resident outside the United Kingdom, and

(*c*) the services in question being provided outside the United Kingdom.

(6) Where the intermediary is a partnership or unincorporated association, the deemed employment payment is treated as received by the worker in the worker's personal capacity and not as income of the partnership or association.

(7) Where—

(*a*) the worker is resident in the United Kingdom, [and][1]

(*b*) the services in question are provided in the United Kingdom, . . . [2]

(*c*) . . . [2]

the intermediary is treated as having a place of business in the United Kingdom, whether or not it in fact does so.

(8) The deemed employment payment is treated as relevant earnings of the worker for the purposes of section 644 of ICTA (relevant earnings for purposes of permissible pension contributions).

Amendments— [1] Word inserted by the FA 2003 s 136(1), (3)(*b*)(i) with effect in relation to services performed or due to be performed on or after 10 April 2003.

[2] Para (c) and word immediately preceding it repealed by the FA 2003 ss 136(1), (3)(*b*)(ii), 216, Sch 43, Pt 3(1) with effect in relation to services performed or due to be performed on or after 10 April 2003.

General Note

The ordinary employment income rules and PAYE provisions apply to deemed employment payments in the same way as ordinary payments of salary or benefit, ie as if the worker was employed by the intermediary and engagements were carried out as part of his employment with the intermediary rather than as if he were employed direct by the client.

Where there would be no tax charge if the worker was a direct employee of the client because of his non-residence, non-ordinary residence or non-UK domicile, and the services were proved outside the UK again for a non-resident client, the deemed employment payment is not subject to tax. The deemed employment payment is treated as employment income from the intermediary for the purposes of determining benefits in kind and expenses wholly, exclusively and necessarily incurred for that employment.

Where the intermediary is a partnership or an unincorporated association the deemed employment income payment is treated as paid by the worker in his personal capacity and not as income of the partnership.

Where the worker is resident in the United Kingdom, providing services in the UK to a client carrying on business in the UK, the intermediary is treated as having a place of business in the UK whether or not it in fact does so, which prevents employment by a non-UK company escaping these rules.

The deemed employment payment is treated as relevant earnings of the worker for pension purposes.

Supplementary provisions

Earlier date of deemed employment payment in certain cases

57—(1) If in any tax year—

(*a*) a deemed employment payment is treated as made, and

(*b*) before the date on which the payment would be treated as made under section 50(2) any relevant event (as defined below) occurs in relation to the intermediary,

the deemed employment payment for that year is treated as having been made immediately before that event or, if there is more than one, immediately before the first of them.

(2) Where the intermediary is a company the following are relevant events—

(*a*) the company ceasing to trade;

(*b*) where the worker is a member of the company, the worker ceasing to be such a member;

(*c*) where the worker holds an office with the company, the worker ceasing to hold such an office;

(*d*) where the worker is employed by the company, the worker ceasing to be so employed.

(3) Where the intermediary is a partnership the following are relevant events—

(*a*) the dissolution of the partnership or the partnership ceasing to trade or a partner ceasing to act as such;

(*b*) where the worker is employed by the partnership, the worker ceasing to be so employed.

(4) Where the intermediary is an individual and the worker is employed by the intermediary, it is a relevant event if the worker ceases to be so employed.

(5) The fact that the deemed employment payment is treated as made before the end of the tax year does not affect what receipts and other matters are taken into account in calculating its amount.

General Note

Where the worker ceases to be connected with the intermediary before the end of the tax year, an employment payment is deemed to have been made immediately before such relevant event. Relevant events include ceasing to be a member, officer or employee of the company or a partnership is dissolved or the worker ceases to be an employee of the partnership or individual employer. The calculation proceeds as if the period ending with the relevant event was a fiscal year.

Relief in case of distributions by intermediary

58—(1) A claim for relief may be made under this section where the intermediary—

- (*a*) is a company,
- (*b*) is treated as making a deemed employment payment in any tax year, and
- (*c*) either in that tax year (whether before or after that payment is treated as made), or in a subsequent tax year, makes a distribution (a 'relevant distribution').

(2) A claim for relief under this section must be made—

- (*a*) by the intermediary by notice to the Inland Revenue, and
- (*b*) within 5 years after the 31st January following the tax year in which the distribution is made.

(3) If on a claim being made the Inland Revenue are satisfied that relief should be given in order to avoid a double charge to tax, they must direct the giving of such relief by way of amending any assessment, by discharge or repayment of tax, or otherwise, as appears to them appropriate.

(4) Relief under this section is given by setting the amount of the deemed employment payment against the relevant distribution so as to reduce the distribution.

(5) In the case of more than one relevant distribution, the Inland Revenue must exercise the power conferred by this section so as to secure that so far as practicable relief is given by setting the amount of a deemed employment payment—

- (*a*) against relevant distributions of the same tax year before those of other years,
- (*b*) against relevant distributions received by the worker before those received by another person, and

(*c*) against relevant distributions of earlier years before those of later years.

(6) Where the amount of a relevant distribution is reduced under this section, the amount of any associated tax credit is reduced accordingly.

General note

To prevent double taxation, where the intermediary is a company which is treated as making an employment payment in the tax year and has already paid a dividend during that or any other subsequent year, the intermediary may submit a claim in writing to the Revenue, who, if satisfied with the claim will make any amendment, discharge or repayment of tax to avoid a double charge to tax by whatever method appears relevant to the Revenue. Relief is given by reducing the tax liability or the distribution on the deemed employment payment. Relief is given against earlier distributions first.

Provisions applicable to multiple intermediaries

59—(1) The provisions of this section apply where in the case of an engagement to which this Chapter applies the arrangements involve more than one relevant intermediary.

(2) All relevant intermediaries in relation to the engagement are jointly and severally liable, subject to subsection (3), to account for any amount required under the PAYE provisions to be deducted from a deemed employment payment treated as made by any of them—

(*a*) in respect of that engagement, or
(*b*) in respect of that engagement together with other engagements.

(3) An intermediary is not so liable if it has not received any payment or benefit in respect of that engagement or any such other engagement as is mentioned in subsection (2)(*b*).

(4) Subsection (5) applies where a payment or benefit has been made or provided, directly or indirectly, from one relevant intermediary to another in respect of the engagement.

(5) In that case, the amount taken into account in relation to any intermediary in step 1 or step 2 of section 54(1) is reduced to such extent as is necessary to avoid double-counting having regard to the amount so taken into account in relation to any other intermediary.

(6) Except as provided by subsections (2) to (5), the provisions of this Chapter apply separately in relation to each relevant intermediary.

(7) In this section 'relevant intermediary' means an intermediary in relation to which the conditions specified in section 51, 52 or 53 are met.

GENERAL NOTE

As a consequence of the widely drafted provisions there could be more than one relevant intermediary making a deemed employment payment in respect of the same engagement.

Where one relevant intermediary has made a payment or benefit to another, the amount taken into account in Steps 1 and 2 in ITEPA 2003 s 54 is reduced as necessary to avoid double counting.

All intermediaries involved in the same relevant engagement are joint and severally liable for PAYE on the deemed employment payment made by any of them unless the intermediary can show that it has not received any payment or benefit in respect of that engagement.

Meaning of 'associate'

60—(1) In this Chapter 'associate'—
- (*a*) in relation to an individual, has the meaning given by section 417(3) and (4) of ICTA, subject to the following provisions of this section;
- (*b*) in relation to a company, means a person connected with the company; and
- (*c*) in relation to a partnership, means any associate of a member of the partnership.

(2) Where an individual has an interest in shares or obligations of the company as a beneficiary of an employee benefit trust, the trustees are not regarded as associates of the individual by reason only of that interest except in the following circumstances.

(3) The exception is where—
- (*a*) the individual, either alone or with any one or more associates of the individual, or
- (*b*) any associate of the individual, with or without other such associates,

has at any time on or after 14th March 1989 been the beneficial owner of, or able (directly or through the medium of other companies or by any other indirect means) to control more than 5% of the ordinary share capital of the company.

(4) In subsection (3) 'associate' does not include the trustees of an employee benefit trust as a result only of the individual's having an interest in shares or obligations of the trust.

(5) Sections 549 to 554 (attribution of interests in companies to beneficiaries of employee benefit trusts) apply for the purposes of subsection (3) as they apply for the purposes of the provisions listed in section 549(2).

(6) In this section 'employee benefit trust' has the meaning given by sections 550 and 551.

General note

Associate is defined by reference to TA 1988 s 417, except that trustees of an employee benefit trust are not regarded as associates of a beneficiary unless where an individual with his associates has control of more than five per cent of the ordinary share capital of the company. However, this only applies to employee benefit trusts as applied by ITEPA 2003 s 549(2), ie one where all or most of the employees are eligible to benefit and distributions have only been made to employees or former employees, their spouses, relatives or dependants.

Interpretation

61—(1) In this Chapter—

'associate' has the meaning given by section 60;

'associated company' has the meaning given by section 416 of ICTA;

'business' means any trade, profession or vocation and includes a Schedule A business;

'company' means a body corporate or unincorporated association, and does not include a partnership;

'employer's national insurance contributions' means secondary Class 1 or Class 1A national insurance contributions;

'engagement to which this Chapter applies' has the meaning given by section 49(5);

'national insurance contributions' means contributions under Part 1 of SSCBA 1992 or Part 1 of SSCB(NI)A 1992;

'PAYE provisions' means the provisions of Part 11 or PAYE regulations;

'the relevant engagements' has the meaning given by section 50(4).

(2) References in this Chapter to payments or benefits received or receivable from a partnership or unincorporated association include payments or benefits to which a person is or may be entitled in the person's capacity as a member of the partnership or association.

(3) For the purposes of this Chapter—

(*a*) anything done by or in relation to an associate of an intermediary is treated as done by or in relation to the intermediary, and

(*b*) a payment or other benefit provided to a member of an individual's family or household is treated as provided to the individual.

(4) For the purposes of this Chapter a man and a woman living together as husband and wife are treated as if they were married to each other.

General note

Various terms are defined.

APPENDIX 2

SSCBA 1992 s 4A

Social Security Contributions and Benefits Act 1992

(1992 Chapter 4)

[4A Earnings of workers supplied by service companies etc

(1) Regulations may make provision for securing that where—

(*a*) an individual ('the worker') personally performs, or is under an obligation personally to perform, services [for another person][2] ('the client'),

(*b*) the performance of those services by the worker is (within the meaning of the regulations) referable to arrangements involving a third person (and not referable to any contract between the client and the worker), and

(*c*) the circumstances are such that, were the services to be performed by the worker under a contract between him and the client, he would be regarded for the purposes of the applicable provisions of this Act as employed in employed earner's employment by the client,

relevant payments or benefits are, to the specified extent, to be treated for those purposes as earnings paid to the worker in respect of an employed earner's employment of his.

(2) For the purposes of this section—

(*a*) 'the intermediary' means—

(i) where the third person mentioned in subsection (1)(*b*) above has such a contractual or other relationship with the worker as may be specified, that third person, or

(ii) where that third person does not have such a relationship with the worker, any other person who has both such a relationship with the worker and such a direct or indirect contractual or other relationship with the third person as may be specified; and

(*b*) a person may be the intermediary despite being—

(i) a person with whom the worker holds any office or employment, or

(ii) a body corporate, unincorporated body or partnership of which the worker is a member;

and subsection (1) above applies whether or not the client is a person with whom the worker holds any office or employment.

(3) Regulations under this section may, in particular, make provision—

(*a*) for the worker to be treated for the purposes of the applicable provisions of this Act, in relation to the specified amount of relevant payments or benefits (the worker's 'attributable earnings'), as employed in employed earner's employment by the intermediary;

(*b*) for the intermediary (whether or not he fulfils the conditions prescribed under section 1(6)(*a*) above for secondary contributors) to be treated for those purposes as the secondary contributor in respect of the worker's attributable earnings;

(*c*) for determining—

(i) any deductions to be made, and

(ii) in other respects the manner and basis in and on which the amount of the worker's attributable earnings for any specified period is to be calculated or estimated,

in connection with relevant payments or benefits;

(*d*) for aggregating any such amount, for purposes relating to contributions, with other earnings of the worker during any such period;

(*e*) for determining the date by which contributions payable in respect of the worker's attributable earnings are to be paid and accounted for;

(*f*) for apportioning payments or benefits of any specified description, in such manner or on such basis as may be specified, for the purpose of determining the part of any such payment or benefit which is to be treated as a relevant payment or benefit for the purposes of the regulations;

(*g*) for disregarding for the purposes of the applicable provisions of this Act, in relation to relevant payments or benefits, an employed earner's employment in which the worker is employed (whether by the intermediary or otherwise) to perform the services in question;

(*h*) for otherwise securing that a double liability to pay any amount by way of a contribution of any description does not arise in relation to a particular payment or benefit or (as the case may be) a particular part of a payment or benefit;

(*i*) for securing that, to the specified extent, two or more persons, whether—

(i) connected persons (within the meaning of section 839 of the Income and Corporation Taxes Act 1988), or

(ii) persons of any other specified description,

are treated as a single person for any purposes of the regulations;

(*j*) (without prejudice to paragraph (*i*) above) for securing that a contract made with a person other than the client is to be treated for any such purposes as made with the client;

(*k*) for excluding or modifying the application of the regulations in relation to such cases, or payments or benefits of such description, as may be specified.

(4) Regulations made in pursuance of subsection (3)(*c*) above may, in particular, make provision—

(*a*) for the making of a deduction of a specified amount in respect of general expenses of the intermediary as well as deductions in respect of particular expenses incurred by him;

(*b*) for securing reductions in the amount of the worker's attributable earnings on account of—

(i) any secondary Class 1 contributions already paid by the intermediary in respect of actual earnings of the worker, and

(ii) any such contributions that will be payable by him in respect of the worker's attributable earnings.

(5) Regulations under this section may make provision for securing that, in applying any provisions of the regulations, any term of a contract or other arrangement which appears to be of a description specified in the regulations is to be disregarded.

(6) In this section—

'the applicable provisions of this Act' means this Part of this Act and Parts II to V below;

. . .[3]

'relevant payments or benefits' means payments or benefits of any specified description made or provided (whether to the intermediary or the worker or otherwise) in connection with the performance by the worker of the services in question;

'specified' means prescribed by or determined in accordance with regulations under this section.

(7) Any reference in this section to the performance by the worker of any services includes a reference to any such obligation of his to perform them as is mentioned in subsection (1)(*a*) above.

(8) Regulations under this section shall be made by the Treasury with the concurrence of the Secretary of State.

(9) If, on any modification of the statutory provisions relating to income tax, it appears to the Treasury to be expedient to modify any of the preceding provisions of this section for the purpose of assimilating the law relating to income tax and the law relating to contributions under this Part of this Act, the Treasury may with the concurrence of the Secretary of State by order make such modifications of the preceding provisions of this section as the Treasury think appropriate for that purpose.][1]

Regulations—See the Social Security Contributions (Intermediaries) Regulations 2000, SI 2000/727 and the Social Security Contributions (Intermediaries) (Amendment) Regulations 2002, SI 2002/703.

Amendments—[1] This section inserted by the Welfare Reform and Pensions Act 1999 s 75, with effect from 22 December 1999.
[2] Words substituted by SI 2003/1874 arts 2, 3 with effect from 8 August 2003.
[3] Definition 'business' repealed by SI 2003/1874 arts 2, 4 with effect from 8 August 2003.

APPENDIX 3

SI 2000/727

Social Security Contributions (Intermediaries) Regulations 2000, 2000/727

Made by the Treasury under SSCBA 1992 ss 4A, 122(1), 175(1A), (2)–(4) and the Inland Revenue under SSC(TF)A 1999 s 8(1)(*m*)

Made	13 March 2000
Laid before Parliament	13 March 2000
Coming into force	6 April 2000

Commentary—*Simon's Direct Tax Service* **E4.205**.
Revenue & other press releases—IR Tax Bulletin October 2001 p 819 (Providing services through an intermediary: IR35—what happens next?).

Citation, commencement and effect

1—(1) These Regulations may be cited as the Social Security Contributions (Intermediaries) Regulations 2000 and shall come into force on 6 April 2000.

(2) These Regulations have effect for the tax year 2000/01 and subsequent years and apply in relation to services performed, or to be performed, on or after 6 April 2000.

(3) Payments or other benefits in respect of such services received before that date shall be treated as if received in the tax year 2000/01.

Interpretation

2—(1) In these Regulations unless the context otherwise requires—
'arrangements' means the arrangements referred to in regulation 6(1)(*b*);
'associate' has the meaning given by regulation 3;

'attributable earnings' in relation to a worker shall be construed in accordance with regulation 6(3)(*a*);
'the Board' means the Commissioners of Inland Revenue;
. . .[2]
'Class 1A contributions' has the meaning given by section 10 of the Contributions and Benefits Act;
'client' shall be construed in accordance with regulation 6(1)(*a*);
'company' means any body corporate or unincorporated association, but does not include a partnership;
'the Contributions and Benefits Act' means the Social Security Contributions and Benefits Act 1992;
['the Contributions Regulations' means the Social Security (Contributions) Regulations 2001;][1]
'intermediary' has the meaning given by regulation 5;
'relevant benefit' means any benefit falling within regulation 4 that is provided to the intermediary or to or on behalf of the worker under the arrangements;
'relevant payment' means any payment made to an intermediary or to or on behalf of the worker under the arrangements;
'secondary Class 1 contributions' has the meaning given by section 6 of the Contributions and Benefits Act;
'secondary contributor' has the meaning given by section 7 of the Contributions and Benefits Act;
'the Taxes Act' means the Income and Corporation Taxes Act 1988;
'tax year' means year of assessment;
'worker' means the individual referred to in regulation 6(1)(*a*).

(2) References in these Regulations to payments or benefits received or receivable from a partnership or unincorporated association include payments or benefits to which a person is or may be entitled in his capacity as a member of the partnership or association.

(3) For the purposes of these Regulations—
(*a*) anything done by or in relation to an associate of an intermediary is treated as done by or in relation to the intermediary, and
(*b*) a payment or other benefit provided to a member of an individual's family or household is treated as provided to the individual.

(4) The reference in paragraph (3)(*b*) to an individual's family or household shall be construed in accordance with [sections 721(4) and (5) of ITEPA 2003][3].

(5) For the purposes of these Regulations a man and a woman living together as husband and wife are treated as if they were married to each other.

Amendments—[1] Definition of 'the Contributions Regulations' substituted by the Social Security Contributions (Intermediaries) (Amendment) Regulations 2002, SI 2002/703 reg 3, with effect from 6 April 2002.

[2] Definition ' business' revoked by SI 2003/2079 regs 3, 4 with effect for the tax year 2003–04 and subsequent years and applying in relation to services performed or due to be performed on or after 1 September 2003.
[3] Words substituted by SI 2004/770 reg 35(1), (2) will effect from 6 April 2004.

Meaning of associate

3—(1) In these Regulations 'associate'—
- (*a*) in relation to an individual, has the meaning given by section 417(3) and (4) of the Taxes Act, subject to the following provisions of this regulation;
- (*b*) in relation to a company, means a person connected with the company within the meaning of section 839 of the Taxes Act; and
- (*c*) in relation to a partnership, means any associate of a member of the partnership.

(2) Where an individual has an interest in shares or obligations of the company as a beneficiary of an employee benefit trust, the trustees are not regarded as associates of his by reason only of that interest except in the following circumstances.

(3) The exception is where—
- (*a*) the individual, either on his own or with one or more of his associates, or
- (*b*) any associate of his, with or without other such associates,

has been the beneficial owner of, or able (directly or through the medium of other companies or by any other indirect means) to control, more than 5% of the ordinary share capital of the company.

(4) In paragraph (2) 'employee benefit trust' has the same meaning as in [sections 550 and 551 of ITEPA 2003][1].

Amendment—[1] Words substituted by SI 2004/770 reg 35(1), (3) with effect from 6 April 2004.

Meaning of benefit

4—[(1) For the purposes of these Regulations a 'benefit' means anything that, if received by an employee performing the duties of an employment, would be general earnings of the employment.][1]

(2) The amount of a benefit is taken to be—
- (*a*) in the case of a cash benefit, the amount received, and
- (*b*) in the case of a non-cash benefit, the cash equivalent of the benefit.

(3) The cash equivalent of a non-cash benefit is taken to be whichever is the greater of—

[(*a*) the amount that would, for income tax purposes, be general earnings if the benefit were general earnings from an employment, and

(*b*) the cash equivalent determined in accordance with section 398(2)(b) of ITEPA 2003][2].

(4) For the purposes of these Regulations a benefit is treated as received—

(*a*) in the case of a cash benefit, when payment is made of or on account of the benefit; and

(*b*) in the case of a non-cash benefit, when it is used or enjoyed.

Amendments—[1] Para substituted by SI 2004/770 reg 35(1), (4)(*a*) with effect from 6 April 2004.

[2] Sub-paras substituted by SI 2004/770 reg 35(1), (4)(*b*) with effect from 6 April 2004.

Meaning of intermediary

5—(1) In these Regulations 'intermediary' means any person, including a partnership or unincorporated association of which the worker is a member—

(*a*) whose relationship with the worker in any tax year satisfies the conditions specified in paragraph (2), (6), (7) or (8), and

(*b*) from whom the worker, or an associate of the worker—

(i) receives, directly or indirectly, in that year a payment or benefit that is not chargeable to tax [as employment income under ITEPA 2003][1], or

(ii) is entitled to receive, or in any circumstances would be entitled to receive, directly or indirectly, in that year any such payment or benefit.

(2) Where the intermediary is a company the conditions are that—

(*a*) the intermediary is not an associated company of the client, within the meaning of section 416 of the Taxes Act by reason of the intermediary and the client both being under the control of the worker, or under the control of the worker and another person; and

(*b*) either—

(i) the worker has a material interest in the intermediary, or

(ii) the payment or benefit is received or receivable by the worker directly from the intermediary, and can reasonably be taken to represent remuneration for services provided by the worker to the client.

(3) A worker is treated as having a material interest in a company for the purposes of paragraph (2)(*a*) if—

(*a*) the worker, alone or with one or more associates of his, or (*b*) an associate of the worker, with or without other such associates,

has a material interest in the company.

(4) For this purpose a material interest means—

(*a*) beneficial ownership of, or the ability to control, directly or through the medium of other companies or by any other indirect means, more than 5% of the ordinary share capital of the company; or

(*b*) possession of, or entitlement to acquire, rights entitling the holder to receive more than 5% of any distributions that may be made by the company; or

(*c*) where the company is a close company, possession of, or entitlement to acquire, rights that would in the event of the winding up of the company, or in any other circumstances, entitle the holder to receive more than 5% of the assets that would then be available for distribution among the participators.

In sub-paragraph (*c*) 'close company' has the meaning given by sections 414 and 415 of the Taxes Act, and 'participator' has the meaning given by section 417(1) of that Act.

(5) Where the intermediary is a partnership the conditions are as follows.

(6) In relation to payments or benefits received or receivable by the worker as a member of the partnership, the conditions are—

(*a*) that the worker, alone or with one or more relatives, is entitled to 60% or more of the profits of the partnership; or

(*b*) that most of the profits of the partnership derive from the provision of services under the arrangements—

(i) to a single client, or

(ii) to a single client together with an associate or associates of that client; or

(*c*) that under the profit sharing arrangements the income of any of the partners is based on the amount of income generated by that partner by the provision of services under the arrangements.

In sub-paragraph (*a*) 'relative' means husband or wife, parent or remoter forebear, child or remoter issue, or brother or sister.

(7) In relation to payments or benefits received or receivable by the worker otherwise than as a member of the partnership, the conditions are that the payment or benefit—

(*a*) is received or receivable by the worker directly from the intermediary, and

(*b*) can reasonably be taken to represent remuneration for services provided by the worker to the client.

(8) Where the intermediary is an individual the conditions are that the payment or benefit—

(*a*) is received or receivable by the worker directly from the intermediary, and (*b*) can reasonably be taken to represent remuneration for services provided by the worker to the client.

Amendment—[1] Words substituted by SI 2004/770 reg 35(1), (5) with effect from 6 April 2004.

Provision of services through intermediary

6—(1) These Regulations apply where—

(*a*) an individual ('the worker') personally performs, or is under an obligation personally to perform, services [for another person][1] ('the client'),

(*b*) the performance of those services by the worker is carried out, not under a contract directly between the client and the worker, but under arrangements involving an intermediary, and

(*c*) the circumstances are such that, had the arrangements taken the form of a contract between the worker and the client, the worker would be regarded for the purposes of Parts I to V of the Contributions and Benefits Act as employed in employed earner's employment by the client.

(2) Paragraph (1)(*b*) has effect irrespective of whether or not—

(*a*) there exists a contract between the client and the worker, or

(*b*) the worker is the holder of an office with the client.

(3) Where these Regulations apply—

(*a*) the worker is treated, for the purposes of Parts I to V of the Contributions and Benefits Act, and in relation to the amount deriving from relevant payments and relevant benefits that is calculated in accordance with regulation 7 ('the worker's attributable earnings'), as employed in employed earner's employment by the intermediary, and

(*b*) the intermediary, whether or not he fulfils the conditions prescribed under section 1(6)(*a*) of the Contributions and Benefits Act for secondary contributors, is treated for those purposes as the secondary contributor in respect of the worker's attributable earnings,

and Parts I to V of that Act have effect accordingly.

(4) Any issue whether the circumstances are such as are mentioned in paragraph (1)(*c*) is an issue relating to contributions that is prescribed for the purposes of section 8(1)(*m*) of the Social Security Contributions (Transfer of Functions, etc) Act 1999 (decision by officer of the Board).

Amendment—[1] Words substituted by SI 2003/2079 regs 3, 5 with effect for the tax year 2003–04 and subsequent years in relation to services performed or due to be performed on or after 1 September 2003.

Worker's attributable earnings—calculation

7—(1) For the purposes of regulation 6(3)(*a*) the amount of the worker's attributable earnings for a tax year is calculated as follows—

STEP ONE

Find the total amount of all payments and benefits received by the intermediary in that year under the arrangements, and reduce that amount by 5%.

STEP TWO

Add the amount of any payments and benefits received by the worker in that year under the arrangements, otherwise than from the intermediary, that—

(*a*) are not chargeable to income tax [as employment tax under ITEPA 2003][3], and

(*b*) would be so chargeable if the worker were employed by the client.

STEP THREE

Deduct the amount of any expenses met in that year by the intermediary that under [ITEPA 2003][4] would have been deductible from [taxable earnings of the employment, within the meaning of section 10 of ITEPA 2003, in accordance with section 327(3) to (5) of that Act][5] if the worker had been employed by the client and the expenses had been met by the worker out of [those earnings][6].

STEP FOUR

Deduct the amount of any capital allowances in respect of expenditure incurred by the intermediary in that year that could have been claimed by the worker [under Part 2 of the Capital Allowances Act 2001 (plant and machinery allowances) by virtue of section 15(1)(i) of that Act (which provides that employment is a qualifying activity for the purposes of that Part)][7] if the worker had been employed by the client and had incurred the expenditure.

STEP FIVE

Deduct any contributions made in that year for the benefit of the worker by the intermediary to a scheme approved under Chapter I or Chapter IV of Part XIV of the Taxes Act that if made by an employer for the benefit of an employee would not be chargeable to income tax as income of the employee.

This does not apply to excess contributions made and later repaid.

STEP SIX

Deduct the amount of secondary Class 1 contributions and Class 1A contributions paid by the intermediary for that year in respect of earnings of the worker.

STEP SEVEN

Deduct—

(*a*) the amount of any payments made by the intermediary to the worker in that year that constitute remuneration derived from the worker's employment by that intermediary including, where the intermediary is a body corporate and the worker is a director of that body corporate, payments treated as remuneration derived from that employment by virtue of regulation [22(2)][1] of the Contributions Regulations (payments to directors to be treated as earnings), but excluding payments which represent items in respect of which a deduction was made under Step three, and

(*b*) the amount of any benefits provided by the intermediary to the worker in that year, being benefits that constitute amounts of [general earnings][8] in respect of which Class 1A contributions are payable, but excluding any benefits which represent items in respect of which a deduction was made under Step three.

If the result at this point is nil or a negative amount, there are no worker's attributable earnings for that year.

STEP EIGHT

Find the amount that, together with the amount of secondary Class 1 contributions payable in respect of it, is equal to the amount resulting from Step seven (if that amount is a positive amount).

STEP NINE

The result is the amount of the worker's attributable earnings for that year.

(2) Where section 559 of the Taxes Act applies (sub-contractors in the construction industry—payments to be made under deduction) the intermediary is treated for the purposes of Step one of the calculation in

paragraph (1) as receiving the amount that would have been received had no deduction been made under that section.

(3) For the purpose of calculating the amount of deductible expenses referred to in Step three of the calculation in paragraph (1) it shall be assumed that all engagements of the worker under the arrangements involving the intermediary are undertaken in the course of the same employment.

(4) For the purposes of this regulation any necessary apportionment shall be made on a just and reasonable basis of amounts received by the intermediary that are referable—
- (*a*) to the services of more than one worker, or
- (*b*) partly to the services of the worker and partly to other matters.

(5) For the purposes of this regulation the time when payments are received by the intermediary or the worker under the arrangements shall be found in accordance with the rules contained in [sections 18 and 19 of ITEPA 2003, subject to the qualification that the worker shall not be treated, by virtue of Rule 2 in section 18, as receiving a payment prior to the time of its actual receipt][9].

[(6) The reference in Step Three of the calculation in paragraph (1) to expenses met by the intermediary includes expenses met by the worker and reimbursed by the intermediary.

(7) Where the intermediary is a partnership and the worker is a member of the partnership, expenses met by the worker for and on behalf of the intermediary shall be treated for the purposes of paragraph (6) as expenses met by the worker and reimbursed by the intemediary.

(8) Where—
- (*a*) the intermediary provides a vehicle for the worker, and
- (*b*) the worker would have been entitled to an amount of mileage allowance relief under [section 231 of ITEPA 2003][10] for a tax year in respect of the use of the vehicle if the worker had been employed by the client, or would have been so entitled if the worker had been employed by the client and the vehicle had not been a company vehicle.

Step Three of the calculation in paragraph (1) shall have effect as if that amount were an amount of expenses deductible under that Step.

(9) Where—
- (*a*) the intermediary is a partnership,
- (*b*) the worker is a member of the partnership, and
- (*c*) the worker provides a vehicle for the purposes of the business of the partnership.

then for the purposes of paragraph (8) the vehicle shall be regarded as provided by the intermediary for the worker.

(10) Where the intermediary makes payments to the worker that are exempt from income tax [as employment income under ITEPA 2003][11] by virtue of [section 229 or 233 of ITEPA 2003][12] (mileage allowance payments and passenger payments), paragraph (a) of Step Seven of the calculation in paragraph (1) shall have effect as if the intermediary had made payments to the worker that constituted remuneration derived from the worker's employment by the intermediary.][2]

Amendments—[1] Reference in para (*a*) of step seven substituted by the Social Security (Contributions) (Amendment) Regulations 2002, SI 2002/703 reg 4, with effect from 6 April 2002.

[2] Paras (6)—(10) inserted by the Social Security Contributions (Intermediaries) (Amendment) Regulations 2002, SI 2002/703 reg 5, with effect from 6 April 2002.

[3] Words substituted by SI 2003/2079 regs 3, 6(1), (2)(*a*) with effect for the tax year 2003–04 and subsequent years in relation to services performed or due to be performed on or after 1 September 2003.

[4] Words substituted by SI 2003/2079 regs 3, 6(1), (2)(*b*)(i) with effect for the tax year 2003–04 and subsequent years in relation to services performed or due to be performed on or after 1 September 2003.

[5] Words substituted by SI 2003/2079 regs 3, 6(1), (2)(*b*)(ii) with effect for the tax year 2003–04 and subsequent years in relation to services performed or due to be performed on or after 1 September 2003.

[6] Words substituted by SI 2003/2079 regs 3, 6(1), (2)(*b*)(iii) with effect for the tax year 2003–04 and subsequent years in relation to services performed or due to be performed on or after 1 September 2003.

[7] Words substituted by SI 2003/2079 regs 3, 6(1), (2)(*c*) with effect for the tax year 2003–04 and subsequent years in relation to services performed or due to be performed on or after 1 September 2003.

[8] Words substituted by SI 2004/770 reg 35(1), (6) with effect from 6 April 2004.

[9] Words substituted by SI 2003/2079 regs 3, 6(1), (3) with effect for the tax year 2003–04 and subsequent years in relation to services performed or due to be performed on or after 1 September 2003.

[10] Words substituted by SI 2003/2079 regs 3, 6(1), (4) with effect for the tax year 2003–04 and subsequent years in relation to services performed or due to be performed on or after 1 September 2003.

[11] Words substituted by SI 2003/2079 regs 3, 6(1), (5)(*a*) with effect for the tax year 2003–04 and subsequent years in relation to services performed or due to be performed on or after 1 September 2003.

[12] Words substituted by SI 2003/2079 regs 3, 6(1), (5)(*b*) with effect for the tax year 2003–04 and subsequent years in relation to services performed or due to be performed on or after 1 September 2003.

Worker's attributable earnings—deemed payment

8—(1) The amount referred to in Step nine of the calculation in regulation 7(1) is treated, for the purposes of Parts I to V of the Contributions and Benefits Act, as a single payment of the worker's attributable earnings made by the intermediary on 5 April in the tax year concerned or, as the case may be, on the date found in accordance with paragraphs (4) to (7), and those Parts of that Act shall have effect accordingly.

(2) The worker's attributable earnings shall be aggregated with any other earnings paid to the worker by the intermediary in the year concerned to or for the benefit of the worker in respect of employed earner's employment, and the amount of earnings related contributions payable in respect of that aggregate amount shall be assessed in accordance with the appropriate earnings period specified in regulation [8][1] of the Contributions Regulations (earnings period for directors), whether or not the worker is a director of a company during that year.

(3) Where the intermediary is a partnership or unincorporated association, the amount referred to in Step nine of the calculation in regulation 7(1) is treated, for the purposes of Parts I to V of the Contributions and Benefits Act, as received by the worker in his personal capacity and not as income of the partnership or association.

(4) If in a tax year—

(*a*) an amount of the worker's attributable earnings is treated as made under paragraph (1), and

(*b*) before the date on which the payment would be treated as made under that paragraph any relevant event (as defined below) occurs in relation to the intermediary,

that amount is treated, for the purposes of Parts I to V of the Contributions and Benefits Act, as having been made immediately before that event or, if there is more than one, immediately before the first of them.

(5) Where the intermediary is a company the following are relevant events—

(*a*) where the worker is a member of the company, his ceasing to be such a member;

(*b*) where the worker holds an office with the company, his ceasing to hold such an office;

(*c*) where the worker is employed by the company, his ceasing to be so employed;

[(*d*) the company ceasing to trade][2].

(6) Where the intermediary is a partnership the following are relevant events—

(*a*) the dissolution of the partnership or the partnership ceasing to trade or a partner ceasing to act as such;

(*b*) where the worker is employed by the partnership, his ceasing to be so employed.

(7) Where the intermediary is an individual and the worker is employed by him, it is a relevant event if the worker ceases to be so employed.

(8) The fact that an amount of the worker's attributable earnings is treated as made under paragraph (1) before the end of the tax year concerned does not affect what payments and benefits are taken into account in calculating that amount.

Amendments—[1] Reference to '8' substituted by the Social Security Contibutions (Intermediaries)(Amendment) Regulations 2002, SI 2002/703 reg 6(1)(*a*), with effect from 6 April 2002.

[2] Para (5) sub-para (*d*) inserted by the Social Security Contibutions (Intemediaries) (Amendment) Regulations 2002, SI 2002/703 reg 6(1)(*b*), with effect from 6 April 2002.

Multiple intermediaries—general

9—(1) Regulations 10 and 11 apply where in any tax year the arrangements involve more than one intermediary.

(2) Except as provided by regulations 10 and 11, the provisions of these Regulations apply separately in relation to each intermediary.

Multiple intermediaries—avoidance of double-counting

10—(1) This regulation applies where a payment or benefit has been made or provided, directly or indirectly, from one intermediary to another intermediary under the arrangements.

(2) In that case, the amount taken into account in relation to any intermediary in Step one or Step two of the calculation in regulation 7(1) shall be reduced to such extent as is necessary to avoid double-counting having regard to the amount so taken into account in relation to any other intermediary.

Multiple intermediaries—joint and several liability

11—(1) Where the arrangements involve more than one intermediary, all the intermediaries are jointly and severally liable, subject to paragraph (3), to pay contributions in respect of the amount of the worker's attributable earnings treated in accordance with regulation 8(1) as paid by any of them—

(*a*) under those arrangements, or
(*b*) under those arrangements together with other arrangements.

(2) For the purposes of paragraph (1), each amount of the worker's attributable earnings shall be aggregated, and the aggregate amount shall be treated for the purposes of regulation 8(1) as a single payment of the worker's attributable earnings, but so that the total liability of the intermediaries to pay contributions in respect of that aggregate amount is not less than it would have been if the arrangements had involved a single intermediary and that aggregate amount had been an amount treated as paid in accordance with regulation 8(1) by a single intermediary.

(3) An intermediary is not jointly and severally liable as mentioned in paragraph (1) if the intermediary has not received any payment or benefit under the arrangements concerned or under any such other arrangements as are mentioned in sub-paragraph (*b*) of that paragraph.

Social Security (Categorisation of Earners) Regulations 1978—Saving

12 Nothing in these Regulations affects the operation of regulation 2 of the Social Security (Categorisation of Earners) Regulations 1978 (treatment of earners in one category of earners as falling within another category and disregard of employments) as that regulation applies to employment listed in paragraph 2 in column (A) of Part I of Schedule 1 to those Regulations (earner supplied through a third person treated as employed earner).

APPENDIX 4
SI 1994/1811

Special Commissioners (Jurisdiction and Procedure)Regulations 1994, SI 1994/1811

Made by the Lord Chancellor under TMA 1970 ss 46A, 56B—D

Made	6 July 1994
Laid before Parliament	14 July 1994
Coming into Force	1 September 1994

Commentary—*Simon's Direct Tax Service* Divisions A3.5; I11.3.

Arrangement of regulations

Part III Hearing and determination of proceedings

Part IV Special procedure

Part V Miscellaneous

Part I Introductory

Citation, commencement and application

1—(1) These Regulations may be cited as the General Commissioners (Jurisdiction and Procedure) Regulations 1994 and shall come into force on 1 September 1994.

(2) These Regulations do not apply in relation to any proceedings in respect of which notice of the place, date and time of the hearing was given, or a summons was issued, prior to 1 September 1994.

Interpretation

2 In these Regulations unless the context otherwise requires—
'the Board' means the Commissioners of Inland Revenue;
'the Clerk', in relation to any proceedings, means the Clerk to the Special Commissioners;
'costs' includes fees, charges, disbursements, expenses and remuneration;

['the enactments relating to stamp duty' means section 13(4) of the Stamp Act 1891 and Part II of Schedule 17 to the Finance Act 1999;][1]

'final determination' means the decision finally determining any proceedings before a Tribunal;

'General Commissioners' shall be construed in accordance with section 2(1) of the Management Act;

'inspector' means an inspector of taxes;

'the Management Act' means the Taxes Management Act 1970;

'party' means a party to any proceedings, and for the purposes of these Regulations—

(*a*) where the proceedings relate to an assessment, decision or determination made by the Board, the Board and any inspector or other officer of the Board for the time being concerned with the proceedings shall together constitute a party to those proceedings;

(*b*) where the proceedings relate to an assessment, decision or determination made by an inspector or other officer of the Board, that person and any other inspector or other officer of the Board for the time being concerned with the proceedings shall together constitute a party to those proceedings;

and references to 'the Revenue' are references to a party within paragraph (*a*) or, as the case may be, paragraph (*b*) above;

'proceedings' means—

(*a*) any appeal to the Special Commissioners under the Taxes Acts;

(*b*) any proceedings before the Special Commissioners which under the Taxes Acts are to be heard and determined in the same way as such an appeal;

(*c*) any proceedings before the Special Commissioners which relate to a penalty and are not within paragraph (*a*) or paragraph (*b*) above;

(*d*) any appeal before the Special Commissioners relating to inheritance tax;

(*e*) any appeal to the Special Commissioners relating to stamp duty reserve tax;

(*f*) any appeal to the Special Commissioners relating to petroleum revenue tax;

(*g*) any question in dispute falling to be determined by the Special Commissioners under section 46B or 46C of the Management Act;

(*h*) any appeal which under regulation 19(3) of the General Commissioners (Jurisdiction and Procedure) Regulations 1994 falls to be determined by the Special Commissioners;][2]

[(*i*) any appeal to the Special Commissioners under the enactments relating to stamp duty;][3]

[(*j*) any appeal to the Special Commissioners under Part II of the Transfer Act or Part III of the Transfer Order;

(*k*) any appeal to the Special Commissioners under regulation 14(4) of the Working Tax Regulations;

[(*ka*) any appeal to the Special Commissioners under section 320(1) of the Proceeds of Crime Act 2002;][5]

(*l*) any preliminary hearing held under the provisions of regulation 9;][4]

'proceedings in Northern Ireland' means any proceedings (as defined in this regulation)—

(*a*) which fall within the meaning of that expression as defined in section 58(3) of the Management Act, or

(*b*) as respects which an appeal from the determination of the Special Commissioners under any enactment lies to a court in Northern Ireland;

'proceedings in Scotland' means any proceedings (as defined in this regulation) which fall to be determined by reference to the law of Scotland;

['respondent' means—

(*a*) in relation to an appeal under section 320(1) of the Proceeds of Crime Act 2002, the Director of the Assets Recovery Agency;

(*b*) in relation to an appeal under regulation 16 of the Community Investment Tax Relief (Accreditation of Community Development Finance Institutions) Regulations 2003, the Secretary of State;

(*c*) otherwise, the Revenue;][6]

'Special Commissioners' and 'the Presiding Special Commissioner' shall be construed in accordance with section 4(1) of the Management Act;

'the Taxes Acts' has the meaning given by section 118(1) of the Management Act;

['the Transfer Act' means the Social Security Contributions (Transfer of Functions, etc) Act 1999;

'the Transfer Order' means the Social Security Contributions (Transfer of Functions, etc) (Northern Ireland) Order 1999;][7]

'Tribunal', in relation to any proceedings, means the Special Commissioner or Special Commissioners by whom the proceedings are [heard;][8]

['the Working Tax Regulations' means the Working Tax Credit (Payment by Employers) Regulations 2002.][9]

Amendments—[1] Definition inserted by the Special Commissioners (Jurisdiction and Procedure) (Amendment) Regulations 2000, SI 2000/288 reg 3(*a*), with effect from 1 March 2000.

[2] Paras (*g*) and (*h*) added by the Special Commissioners (Jurisdiction and Procedure) (Amendment) Regulations 1999, SI 1999/3292 reg 3, with effect from 1 January 2000.

[3] Para (*i*) inserted by the Special Commissioner (Jurisdiction and Procedure) (Amendment) Regulations 2000, SI 2000/288 reg 1, with effect from 1 March 2000.

[4] Paras (*j*), (*k*), (*l*) inserted by SI 2002/2976 regs 2, 3(*a*) with effect in relation to proceedings before the Special Commissioners on or after that date).

[5] Para (*ka*) inserted by SI 2003/968 regs 2, 3(*a*) with effect from 22 April 2003.

[6] Definition inserted by SI 2003/968 regs 2, 3(*b*) with effect from 22 April 2003.

[7] Definitions inserted by SI 2002/2976 regs 2, 3(*b*) with effect from 31 December 2002 in relation to proceedings before the Special Commissioners on or after that date.

[8] Word substituted by SI 2002/2976 regs 2, 3(*c*) with effect from 31 December 2002 in relation to proceedings before the Special Commissioners on or after that date.

[9] Definition inserted by SI 2002/2976 regs 2, 3(*d*) with effect from 31 December 2002 in relation to proceedings before the Special Commissioners on or after that date.

Part II Preparation for a hearing

Listing and notice of hearing

3—(1) Except in relation to proceedings under section 100C of the Management Act, or section 249 of the Inheritance Tax Act 1984, any party to proceedings which are to be heard by the Special Commissioners may serve notice on the Clerk that he wishes a date for the hearing to be fixed.

(2) On receipt of a notice under paragraph (1) above and on being satisfied that the Special Commissioners have jurisdiction over the proceedings and that he has sufficient particulars of the proceedings and of the issues for determination, the Clerk shall, unless the Presiding Special Commissioner otherwise directs, send notice to each party of the place, date and time of the hearing.

(3) Unless the parties otherwise agree or the Tribunal otherwise directs, the date of the hearing specified in a notice under paragraph (2) above shall be not earlier than twenty eight days after the date on which the notice is sent to the parties.

General power to give directions

4—(1) A Special Commissioner prior to the hearing of any proceedings, for the purpose of enabling the parties to prepare for the hearing or of assisting a Tribunal to determine any of the issues in those proceedings, may on the application of a party or of his own motion, give such directions as he thinks fit.

(2) A Tribunal hearing any proceedings may, for the purpose of assisting the determination of any of the issues in those proceedings, on the application of a party or of its own motion, give such directions as it thinks fit.

(3) An application by a party for any directions under this Part of these Regulations (otherwise than during a hearing) shall be made in writing to the Clerk and, unless it is accompanied by the written consent of all the parties, shall be served by the Clerk on any other party who might be affected by such directions.

(4) If any such party, by notice to the Special Commissioners and the other party or parties, objects to the directions sought in the application, the Special Commissioner concerned shall consider the objection and, if the application is not one in respect of which the parties are entitled to be heard under these Regulations, shall if he considers it necessary for the determination of the application, give the parties an opportunity to be heard.

Summoning of witnesses

5—(1) Where a party to any proceedings requires the attendance of a person at the hearing of those proceedings to give evidence or to produce any document in his possession, custody or power relevant to the subject matter of the proceedings, a Special Commissioner may, on the application of that party, issue a summons (in this regulation referred to as a 'witness summons') requiring the attendance of that person at the hearing, or the production of the document, wherever that person may be in the United Kingdom.

(2) A witness summons issued under paragraph (1) above shall state the name and address of, or otherwise describe, the person to be served and shall be signed by the Special Commissioner issuing it, and it shall be the responsibility of the party on whose application the summons was issued to serve it on that person.

(3) Service of a witness summons under this regulation shall be effected—
- (*a*) in the case of an individual, by leaving a copy of the summons with him;
- (*b*) in the case of a body corporate registered in the United Kingdom, by leaving a copy of the summons with the secretary or clerk of the body corporate;
- (*c*) in the case of a foreign body corporate with a place of business in the United Kingdom, by leaving a copy of the summons with a person authorised to accept service of process on the body corporate.

(4) A person who in obedience to a witness summons attends the hearing of any proceedings and gives evidence—
- (*a*) is a witness of the party on whose application the summons was issued, and
- (*b*) may not be cross-examined by that party without the leave of the Tribunal hearing the proceedings.

(5) Leave shall not be given by a Tribunal under paragraph (4)(*b*) above unless the Tribunal decides that the witness may be treated as a hostile witness.

(6) No person shall be required to attend in obedience to a witness summons unless it has been served on him at least seven days before the

hearing or, if it has been served on him within that period, he has informed the Clerk that he accepts such service.

(7) No person shall be required to attend and give evidence or to produce any document in obedience to a witness summons unless the party serving the summons either—

(*a*) pays or tenders to that person, at the time when the summons is served on him, a sum sufficient to cover his reasonable expenses of travelling to and from, and his attendance at, the hearing, or

(*b*) has agreed with that person prior to service of the summons, to pay such a sum to him at a different time.

(8) No person shall be compelled in obedience to a witness summons to give any evidence or produce any document that he could not be compelled to give or produce in an action in a court of law in that part of the United Kingdom by reference to the law of which the proceedings are to be determined.

(9) No person who has been appointed as an auditor for the purposes of any enactment or who is a tax adviser within the meaning of section 20B(10) of the Management Act shall be compelled in obedience to a witness summons to produce any document if, having regard to section 20B(9) to (13) of that Act, he would not be obliged to deliver or make available that document in response to a notice under section 20(3) or (8A) of that Act.

(10) Where, in the case of any document, a person could under section 20B(14) of that Act comply with such a notice by delivering a copy of parts of the document and making those parts available for inspection, he shall not be compelled in obedience to a witness summons to do more at the hearing than—

(*a*) produce a photographic or other facsimile copy of those parts of the document, and

(*b*) make those parts of the document available for inspection by the Tribunal.

(11) On the application, by notice served on the Clerk, of a person on whom a witness summons has been served, a Special Commissioner may set aside the summons in whole or in part; and the party on whose application the summons was issued shall be entitled to be heard on such an application.

(12) This regulation shall apply to proceedings in Scotland—

(*a*) with the omission of paragraphs (4) and (5) above;

(*b*) with the substitution for references to issuing a summons and to a witness summons of references to issuing a citation and to a witness citation.

Agreement of documents

6—If a party agrees a document for the purposes of any proceedings he shall be deemed, subject to the terms of the agreement, to admit for the purposes of those proceedings—

(*a*) that the document was written and signed or executed by the person by whom, and on the date on which, it purports to have been, and

(*b*) if it purports to be a copy of another document, that it is a true copy of that document,

but, subject to any enactment or rule of law, in the absence of an express admission or agreement, he shall not be deemed to admit the truth of the contents of that document.

Proceedings to be heard together or in succession

7—(1) Where two or more proceedings have been brought before, but have not yet been heard by, the Special Commissioners or have been brought before, but have not yet been heard by, the Special Commissioners and any General Commissioners and it appears to [a][1] Special Commissioner—

(*a*) that some common issue arises in both or all of them, or

(*b*) that both or all of them are relevant to some common issue,

[a][1] Special Commissioner may, of his own motion or on application by a party to any of those proceedings, direct that those proceedings be heard at the same time or consecutively and by the same Tribunal.

(2) A direction shall not be given under paragraph (1) above except on notice sent to all the parties to the proceedings in question who shall be entitled to be heard before any direction is given.

(3) On the giving of a direction under paragraph (1) above, the Clerk shall send notice of the date and terms of the direction to all the parties to the proceedings and, where one or more of the proceedings in question was pending before the General Commissioners, to the Clerk to the division or, as the case may be, each division of General Commissioners concerned.

(4) References in this regulation to proceedings pending before the General Commissioners are references to proceedings in relation to which the General Commissioners (Jurisdiction and Procedure) Regulations 1994 apply.

Amendment—[1] Word substituted by SI 2002/2976 regs 2, 4 with effect from 31 December 2002 in relation to proceedings before the Special Commissioners on or after that date.

[Lead cases

[**7A**–(1) Where—

(*a*) one or more proceedings under Part II of the Transfer Act or Part III of the Transfer Order have been brought before, but have not yet been heard by, the Special Commissioners; or

(*b*) one or more proceedings under Part II of the Transfer Act or Part III of the Transfer Order have been brought before, but have not yet been heard by, any General Commissioners; and

(*c*) it appears to the Presiding Special Commissioner that those proceedings give rise to common or related issues of fact or law ('same issues proceedings'),

the Presiding Special Commissioner may of his own motion or on application by a party to any of these proceedings direct that one of those proceedings be heard in the first instance as the lead case.

(2) The Presiding Special Commissioner may give such further directions as he also considers appropriate for determination of the lead case and without prejudice to the generality of the foregoing, such further directions may include in particular directions as to—

(*a*) which common or related issues of fact or law ('same issues') are to be determined in the lead case; or

(*b*) which Tribunal is to hear the lead case.

(3) Subject to paragraph 14 the Presiding Special Commissioner may also direct that pending determination of the lead case all other same issues proceedings before the Special Commissioners, or that were pending before the General Commissioners, shall be stayed.

(4) Directions shall not be given under paragraphs (1) to (3) except on notice to all parties to the proceedings in question who shall be entitled to be heard before any directions are given.

(5) Without prejudice generally to the parties' rights of appeal and to paragraphs (8) and (9) as appropriate, the Tribunal's determination of the same issues in the lead case shall be binding on the parties to each of the same issues proceedings unless the Tribunal or the Presiding Special Commissioner directs otherwise.

(6) On the giving of directions under paragraphs (1) to (3) the Clerk shall send a copy of the directions to all the parties to the same issues proceedings.

(7) Upon determination of the same issues in the lead case the Clerk shall send a copy of that determination to all the parties to the same issues proceedings.

(8) Notwithstanding the provisions of paragraph (5) any party to any of the same issues proceedings may within 21 days beginning with the date

on which that party receives notice of the determination of the same issues in the lead case apply to the Presiding Special Commissioner for a direction that the determination as to the same issues in the lead case shall not apply to those proceedings.

(9) Within 28 days beginning with the date of determination of the same issues in the lead case the Presiding Special Commissioner shall—

(*a*) give such further directions as he considers appropriate in relation to the lead case and each of the same issues proceedings stayed pending the determination of the same issues in the lead case; and

(*b*) such directions shall, without prejudice to the generality of the foregoing also include, as appropriate—

(i) directions as to the extent to which the determination of the same issues in the lead case is binding on any subsequent proceedings;

(ii) any further directions required as a result of an application under paragraph (8) which shall include, a direction as to any further hearing required in relation to those proceedings.

(10) On the giving of any further directions under paragraph (9) the Clerk shall send a copy of the relevant directions to each of the parties to the same issues proceedings.

(11) Where one or more of the same issues proceedings or the lead case was pending before the General Commissioners, the Clerk shall also send the notice of the matters specified in paragraphs (1) to (3) and (7) to (9) to the Clerk to the division or, as the case may be, each division of the General Commissioners concerned.

(12) Where a direction has been given for any proceedings to be heard as a lead case and those proceedings are withdrawn or discontinued either before or during the hearing, the Revenue shall—

(*a*) within seven days of withdrawal or discontinuance as the case may be, give notice to—

(i) the Presiding Special Commissioner;

(ii) as appropriate, the Clerk to the relevant division of the General Commissioners;

(iii) all the parties to the same issues proceedings; and

(*b*) the Presiding Special Commissioner may then direct that—

(i) one of the remaining same issues proceedings be substituted as the lead case; and

(ii) may also direct the extent to which any directions made prior to substitution shall be binding in relation to the substituted proceedings.

(13) On the giving of directions under paragraph (12)(*b*) the Clerk shall send a copy of the directions to all the remaining parties to the same issues proceedings and as appropriate, to the Clerks to the relevant divisions of the General Commissioners.

(14) Any same issues proceedings that were pending before the General Commissioners which the Presiding Special Commissioner considers are not appropriate for the lead case procedure shall be remitted to the General Commissioners for determination.

(15) References in this regulation to proceedings pending before the General Commissioners are references to proceedings pending in relation to which the General Commissioners (Jurisdiction and Procedure) Regulations 1994 apply.

(16) References in this regulation to 'proceedings' shall for the avoidance of doubt, include more than one appeal against the same decision to the Special Commissioners or the General Commissioners as the case may be.][1]

Amendment—[1] Inserted by SI 2002/2976 regs 2, 5 with effect from 31 December 2002 in relation to proceedings before the Special Commissioners on or after that date.

Joining of additional parties

8—(1) If it appears to a Special Commissioner, whether on the application of a party or otherwise, that it is desirable that any person other than the [respondent][1] be made a party to any proceedings, he may direct that such person be joined as a party in the proceedings and may give such further directions for giving effect to, or in connection with, the direction as he thinks fit.

(2) Where—

(*a*) pursuant to a direction under paragraph (1) above a person is joined as a party in any proceedings by reason of a question arising in those proceedings which may affect his liability to tax or in which he otherwise has an interest, and

(*b*) pursuant to an application under regulation 15(2) by another party the hearing or, as the case may be, part of the hearing of the proceedings is to take place in private,

he shall not be entitled, unless all the other parties consent, to be present at the hearing of the proceedings or, as the case may be, the part of the hearing which is to take place in private except during such part as relates to that question, and a Tribunal shall, if necessary, hear any such question separately from the rest of the proceedings.

(3) Subject to paragraph (4) below, on the application of a person who has been joined as a party in the circumstances specified in paragraph (2) above, a Special Commissioner may, if he is satisfied that it would be to the convenience of the parties to do so, direct that the proceedings be transferred to the General Commissioners for the division in which the applicant ordinarily resided at the date of the application.

(4) No application may be made under paragraph (3) above in any case where the proceedings in question under any enactment lie only to the Special Commissioners and not to the General Commissioners.

Amendment—[1] Word substituted by SI 2003/968 regs 2, 4 with effect from 22 April 2003.

Preliminary hearing

9—(1) Where it appears to a Special Commissioner that any proceedings would be facilitated by holding a preliminary hearing, he may, on the application of a party or of his own motion, give directions for such a hearing to be held.

(2) The Clerk shall give to the parties not less than fourteen days notice, or such shorter notice as the parties agree or the Special Commissioner sees fit to impose, of the time and place of the preliminary hearing.

(3) On a preliminary hearing the Special Commissioner—

(*a*) shall give all such directions as appear necessary or desirable so as to enable the proceedings to be disposed of expeditiously, effectively and fairly;

(*b*) may, if the parties so agree, determine the proceedings without any further hearing.

Power of Special Commissioners to obtain information

10—(1) A Special Commissioner on a preliminary hearing of any proceedings, or a Tribunal in the course of the hearing of any proceedings, may serve notice on any party . . .[1] directing that party within the time specified in the notice—

(*a*) to deliver to him or, as the case may be, the Tribunal such particulars as he or the Tribunal may consider are required for the purposes of determining any of the issues in the proceedings, and

(*b*) to make available for inspection by him or the Tribunal, or by [any other party ('inspecting party')][2], all such books, accounts or other documents in the party's possession or power as may be specified or described in the notice, being books, accounts or other documents which, in the opinion of the Special Commissioner or Tribunal issuing the notice, contain or may contain information relating to the subject matter of the proceedings.

(2) Any [inspecting party][3] may at all reasonable times inspect and take copies of, or extracts from, any particulars delivered under paragraph (1)(*a*) above, and the Special Commissioner or Tribunal who issued the notice, or any officer of the Board, may take copies of, or extracts from,

any books, accounts or other documents made available for inspection under paragraph (1)(*b*) above.

Amendments— [1] Words omitted revoked by SI 2003/968 regs 2, 5(1)(*a*) with effect from 22 April 2003.
[2] Words substituted by SI 2003/968 regs 2, 5(1)(*b*) with effect from 22 April 2003.
[3] Words substituted by SI 2003/968 regs 2, 5(2) with effect from 22 April 2003.

Postponements and adjournments

11—(1) A Special Commissioner may postpone the hearing of any proceedings, and the Clerk shall send notice to the parties of the place, date and time of the postponed hearing.

(2) A Tribunal may from time to time adjourn the hearing of any proceedings and, subject to paragraph (3) below, the Clerk shall send notice to the parties of the place, date and time of the adjourned hearing.

(3) If the place, date and time of the adjourned hearing are announced before the adjournment in the presence of the parties, no notice need be sent by the Clerk under paragraph (2) above.

(4) When any hearing is adjourned in order that further information or evidence may be obtained, a Tribunal may give directions regarding the disclosure of such information or evidence to the parties prior to the resumption of the hearing.

Expert evidence

12—(1) Unless a Special Commissioner otherwise directs, no expert evidence may be adduced by a party at the hearing of any proceedings unless—

(*a*) he has agreed with the other party or parties that the substance of the evidence shall be disclosed in the form of a written report or opinion in advance of the hearing and not later than such date as is specified in the agreement, and the substance of the evidence has been so disclosed, or

(*b*) where no such agreement has been reached or where the substance of the evidence has not been so disclosed, an application is made to a Special Commissioner under paragraph (2) below by the party seeking to adduce the evidence to determine whether a direction should be given under paragraph (3) below, and the party seeking to adduce the evidence complies with a direction given under that paragraph.

(2) An application under this paragraph—
- (*a*) shall be made not later than twenty one days after the date on which notice is sent by the Clerk under regulation 3(2) or, if the Special Commissioner so permits, at any later time prior to or in the course of the hearing, and
- (*b*) shall state whether the party is willing to disclose the substance of the evidence prior to its being given at the hearing and, if not, the reasons for his objection.

(3) On an application under paragraph (2) above, unless it considers that there are special reasons for not doing so, the Special Commissioner shall direct that the substance of the evidence shall be disclosed in the form of a written report or opinion to such other parties and within such period as it may specify.

(4) This regulation shall not apply to proceedings in Scotland.

[Appeals under Proceeds of Crime Act 2002

12A—(1) This regulation applies to an appeal under section 320(1) of the Proceeds of Crime Act 2002.

(2) Paragraphs (3) to (8) apply where the Presiding Special Commissioner nominates an assessor under section 320(2) of that Act in relation to any proceedings.

(3) The assessor shall take such part in the proceedings as the Tribunal may direct and in particular the Tribunal may—
- (*a*) direct the assessor to prepare a report for the Tribunal on any matter at issue in the proceedings; and
- (*b*) direct the assessor to attend the whole or any part of the hearing or any preliminary hearing.

(4) Not more than 14 days after the nomination of an assessor, the Clerk shall notify each party in writing of the assessor's name.

(5) The Tribunal shall send to the parties a copy of any report prepared by the assessor within 21 days of receiving it.

(6) The parties shall have the opportunity to make observations on the assessor's report within such time and in such manner as the Tribunal shall direct.

(7) The Tribunal shall take any observations made under paragraph (6) into account when making its decision.

(8) The assessor shall not give oral evidence or be open to cross-examination or questioning.][1]

Amendment— [1] Inserted by SI 2003/968 regs 2, 6 with effect from 22 April 2003.

Part III Hearing and determination of proceedings

Constitution and sittings of Tribunal

13—(1) Any one, two or three of the Special Commissioners shall constitute a Tribunal.

(2) Where any proceedings are before a Tribunal which comprises two or three Special Commissioners—

(*a*) if the Presiding Special Commissioner is one of them, he shall preside at the hearing unless he otherwise directs and, if he is not, one of them shall be nominated by him to preside;

(*b*) the proceedings may be continued by any one or more of them if all the parties give their consent and unless the Presiding Special Commissioner otherwise directs.

Representation at hearing

14—At the hearing of any proceedings before a Tribunal—

(*a*) a party other than the [respondent][1] may be represented by any person whether or not legally qualified, except that if in a particular case the Tribunal is satisfied that there are good and sufficient reasons for doing so, it may refuse to permit a particular person, other than one who is legally qualified or who has been admitted a member of an incorporated society of accountants, to represent a party at the hearing;

(*b*) the [respondent][1] may be represented by a barrister, advocate, solicitor or any officer of the Board.

Amendment—[1] Word substituted by SI 2003/968 regs 2, 7 with effect from 22 April 2003.

[Hearings in public

15—(1) Subject to the following paragraphs of this regulation, hearings before a Tribunal shall be in public.

(2) A Tribunal may direct that all or part of a hearing shall be in private—

(*a*) upon the application of all the parties by notice to the Clerk;

(*b*) upon the application of any party by notice to the Clerk;

(*c*) of its own motion,

if in each case, a Tribunal is satisfied that a hearing in private is necessary—
- (i) in the interests of morals, public order, national security, juveniles or for the protection of the private life of the party; or
- (ii) it considers that publicity would prejudice the interests of justice.

(3) Before determining an application under paragraph (2)(*b*), or giving a direction under paragraph (2)(*c*), a Tribunal shall give all other parties to the proceedings an opportunity to make representations.

(4) Before giving a direction under paragraph (2) that the entire hearing be in private, a Tribunal shall consider whether only part of the hearing should be heard in private.

(5) The following persons shall be entitled to be present at the hearing of any proceedings before a Tribunal notwithstanding that the hearing or part of the hearing takes place in private, and those referred to in sub-paragraphs (*b*) to (*e*) only may remain during the deliberations of a Tribunal but shall take no part in those deliberations—
- (*a*) the parties and their representatives;
- [(*aa*) an assessor nominated under section 320(2) of the Proceeds of Crime Act 2002;][2]
- (*b*) the Presiding Special Commissioner and any of the Special Commissioners to the extent that they do not constitute the Tribunal or part of the Tribunal for the purpose of the hearing;
- (*c*) the Clerk and any of the staff of the Special Commissioners;
- (*d*) a member of the Council on Tribunals or of the Scottish Committee of that Council in the capacity of member;
- (*e*) a member of the Judicial Studies Board or of one of its committees in the capacity of member.

(6) A Tribunal, with the consent of the parties, may permit any other person to be present at the hearing of proceedings before it which is to take place, or part of which is to take place, in private.

(7) A Tribunal may exclude from the whole or part of a hearing any person whose conduct, in the opinion of a Tribunal, has disrupted or is likely to disrupt the hearing.

(8) Where all or part of a hearing is held or is to be held in private, a Tribunal may direct that information about the whole or part of the proceedings (including information that might help to identify any person) before a Tribunal shall not be made public.

(9) For the purpose of paragraph (2)(*i*) 'party' shall not include the Revenue.][1]

Amendments—[1] Substituted by SI 2002/2976 regs 2, 6 with effect from 31 December 2002 in relation to proceedings before the Special Commissioners on or after that date.
[2] Sub-para nserted by SI 2003/968 regs 2, 8 with effect from 22 April 2003.

Failure of parties to attend hearing

16—(1) If a party fails to attend or to be represented at a hearing of which he has been duly notified, the Tribunal may—

(*a*) unless it is satisfied that there is good and sufficient reason for such absence, hear and determine the proceedings in the absence of the party or his representative, or

(*b*) postpone or adjourn the hearing.

(2) Before deciding to hear and determine any proceedings in the absence of a party or his representative, the Tribunal shall consider any representations in writing or otherwise submitted by or on behalf of that party in response to the notice of hearing and shall give any party present at the hearing an opportunity to be heard in regard to those representations.

Procedure and evidence at hearing

17—(1) At the beginning of the hearing of any proceedings the Tribunal shall, except where it considers it unnecessary to do so, explain the order of proceeding which it proposes to adopt.

(2) The Tribunal shall conduct the hearing in such manner as it considers most suitable to the clarification and determination of the issues before it and generally to the just handling of the proceedings and, so far as appears to it appropriate, shall seek to avoid formality in its procedure.

(3) The parties shall be heard in such order as the Tribunal shall determine and shall be entitled—

(*a*) to give evidence,

(*b*) to call witnesses,

(*c*) to question any witnesses including other parties who give evidence, and

(*d*) to address the Tribunal both on the evidence and generally on the subject matter of the proceedings.

(4) In assessing the truth and weight of any evidence, the Tribunal may take account of its nature and source, and the manner in which it is given.

(5) Evidence before the Tribunal may be given orally or, if the Tribunal so directs, by affidavit or a statement made or recorded in a document, but at any stage of the hearing the Tribunal may, on the application of any party or of its own motion, require the personal attendance as a witness of—

(*a*) the maker of an affidavit, or

(*b*) the maker of such a statement, or

(*c*) in the case of an oral statement recorded in a document, the person by whom the statement was so recorded.

(6) The Tribunal may receive evidence of any fact which appears to the Tribunal to be relevant to the subject matter of the proceedings notwithstanding that such evidence would be inadmissible in proceedings before a court of law in that part of the United Kingdom by reference to the law of which the proceedings before the Tribunal are to be determined, but, save in cases where claims for privilege are allowed (including, in proceedings in Scotland, claims for protection from disclosure by virtue of any rule of law relating to the confidentiality of communications), it shall not refuse to admit any evidence which would be admissible in such proceedings.

(7) The Tribunal may require any witness to give evidence on oath or affirmation and for that purpose there may be administered an oath or affirmation in due form.

Decisions of Tribunal

18—(1) Where proceedings are before a Tribunal which comprises two or three Special Commissioners, any decision of the Tribunal shall be made by the votes of the Special Commissioners comprising that Tribunal.

(2) Where proceedings are before a Tribunal which comprises two Special Commissioners, in the event of an equality of votes, the Special Commissioner presiding at the hearing shall be entitled to a second or casting vote.

(3) Where proceedings are before a Tribunal which comprises three Special Commissioners, any decision or direction of the tribunal shall be made by the votes of the majority of the Special Commissioners comprising that Tribunal.

(4) The final determination may be given orally by a Tribunal at the end of the hearing or may be reserved and in either event shall be recorded forthwith in a document which, subject to paragraph (7) below, shall contain a statement of the facts found by the Tribunal and the reasons for the determination and shall be signed and dated by the Tribunal.

(5) A Tribunal may, after reserving the final determination—

(*a*) give a written decision in principle on one or more issues arising in the proceedings, and

(*b*) adjourn the making of the final determination until after its decision in principle has been issued and such further questions arising from that decision have been agreed by the parties or, failing agreement, decided by the Tribunal after having heard the parties.

(6) A decision in principle given under paragraph (5)(*a*) above shall contain, in relation to the matters covered by the decision—

(*a*) a statement of the facts found by the Tribunal, and
(*b*) the reasons for the decision.

(7) In any case where a decision in principle has been given under paragraph (5)(*a*) above, the document recording the final determination need not contain a statement of the facts and reasons referred to in paragraph (4) above except in so far as is necessary in order to explain the final determination of the Tribunal on matters not covered in the decision in principle.

(8) The Clerk shall send a copy of the document recording a decision in principle, and a copy of the document recording the final determination, to each party.

(9) Except where the final determination is given at the end of the hearing, it shall be treated as having been made on the date on which a copy of the document recording it is sent to the parties under paragraph (8) above.

(10) Every copy of the document recording the final determination sent to the parties under this regulation[, other than a document recording a final determination made in accordance with regulation 23(2)(*b*),][1] shall be accompanied by a notification of the provisions of—
(*a*) the Management Act,
(*b*) these Regulations, and
(*c*) rule of court,
relating to appeals from the Special Commissioners, and of the time within which, and the manner in which, such appeals shall be made.

Amendments—[1] In para 10 words inserted by the Special Commissioners (Jurisdiction and Procedure) (Amendment) Regulations 1999, SI 1999/3292 reg 4, with effect from 1 January 2000.

Review of Tribunal's final determination

19—(1) If, on the application of a party or of its own motion, a Tribunal is satisfied that—
(*a*) a decision in principle or the final determination was wrongly made as a result of an administrative error on the part of the Clerk or any of the staff of the Special Commissioners or a party, or
(*b*) a party, who was entitled to be heard at a hearing but failed to appear or to be represented, had good and sufficient reason for failing to appear or to be represented, or
(*c*) accounts or other information relevant to a party's case had been sent to the Clerk or to the appropriate inspector or other officer of the Board prior to the hearing of the proceedings but had not been received by the Tribunal until after the hearing,
the Tribunal may review and set aside or vary the decision in principle or final determination (or both the decision in principle and the final determination).

(2) An application for the purposes of paragraph (1) above shall be made to the Tribunal not later than fourteen days after the date on which a copy of the document recording the decision in principle or, as the case may be, the final determination was sent to the parties under regulation 18(8), or by such later time as the Tribunal may allow, and shall be in writing stating the grounds in full.

(3) Where the Tribunal proposes to review of its own motion the decision in principle or final determination, it shall serve notice of that proposal on the parties not later than fourteen days after the date on which a copy of the document recording the decision in principle or, as the case may be, the final determination was sent to the parties under regulation 18(8).

(4) The parties shall have an opportunity to be heard on a review, or in relation to any application or proposal for review, under this regulation and the review shall be determined by the Tribunal which decided the case or, where it is not practicable for it to be heard by that Tribunal, by a Tribunal appointed by the Presiding Special Commissioner; and if, having reviewed the decision in principle or final determination, the Tribunal sets aside that decision or determination, it shall substitute such decision or determination as it thinks fit or order a rehearing before either the same or a differently constituted Tribunal.

(5) Regulation 18 shall apply to a decision by a Tribunal varying a decision in principle or final determination, or substituting a new decision in principle or final determination, as it applies to a decision in principle or final determination.

Publication of decisions in principle or final determinations

20—(1) The Presiding Special Commissioner may make arrangements for the publication of reports of such of the decisions in principle and final determinations given by Tribunals as he considers appropriate.

(2) Where the Presiding Special Commissioner considers it appropriate to publish a report of a decision in principle or final determination pursuant to paragraph (1) above, and that decision or determination relates to proceedings the whole or part of which were heard in private in accordance with regulation 15(2), he shall ensure that the report is in a form which so far as possible prevents the identification of any person whose affairs are dealt with in the decision or determination.

Order for costs

21—(1) Subject to paragraph (2) below, a Tribunal may make an order awarding the costs of, or incidental to, the hearing of any proceedings by it against any party to those proceedings (including a party who has withdrawn his appeal or application) if it is of the opinion that the party has acted wholly unreasonably in connection with the hearing in question.

(2) No order shall be made under paragraph (1) above against a party without first giving that party an opportunity of making representations against the making of the order.

(3) An order under paragraph (1) above may require the party against whom it is made to pay to the other party or parties the whole or part of the costs incurred by the other party or parties of, or incidental to, the hearing of the proceedings, such costs to be taxed if not otherwise agreed.

(4) Any costs required to be taxed pursuant to an order under this regulation shall be taxed in the county court according to such of the scales prescribed by rules of court for proceedings in the county court as may be directed by the order or, in the absence of any such direction, by the county court.

(5) In the application of this regulation to proceedings in Scotland—

(*a*) any reference to costs shall be construed as a reference to expenses;

(*b*) in paragraph (4) above, for the references to the county court there shall be substituted references to the sheriff court and for the reference to proceedings there shall be substituted a reference to civil proceedings.

(6) In the application of this regulation to proceedings in Northern Ireland, for paragraphs (3) and (4) above there shall be substituted—

> '(3) An order under paragraph (1) above may require the party against whom it is made to pay to the other party or parties the whole or part of the costs incurred by that other party or parties of, or incidental to, the hearing of the proceedings, such costs to be taxed in the county court if not determined by the Tribunal or otherwise agreed.
> (4) Any costs which may be determined by the Tribunal under paragraph (3) above shall be determined by reference to the scales prescribed by rules of court for proceedings in the county court and any costs required to be taxed pursuant to an order under this regulation shall be taxed in the same manner as costs in equity suits or proceedings in the county court.

Part IV Special procedure

Proceedings relating to tax on chargeable gains

22—(1) Where the market value of an asset on a particular date or the apportionment of an amount or value is a material question in any proceedings relating to tax on chargeable gains, the Tribunal hearing the proceedings shall, if so required by any party, record in its final determination that market value or apportionment.

(2) The final determination on an appeal of the market value of an asset on a particular date or of the apportionment of any amount or value may be proved in any proceedings relating to tax on chargeable gains by a certificate stating the material particulars signed by—

(*a*) an inspector where the appeal was settled by agreement, or
(*b*) the Clerk where the Special Commissioners determined the appeal, or
(*c*) the Clerk or registrar of another tribunal where the material question was determined by that other tribunal in accordance with section [46D][1] or 47B of the Management Act or section 222(4A) of the Inheritance Tax Act 1984,

and a document purporting to be such a certificate may be received in evidence in any such proceedings without further proof.

(3) In this regulation the expression 'final determination on an appeal' shall be construed in accordance with regulation 11(2) of the Capital Gains Tax Regulations 1967, and the expression 'material question in any proceedings' shall be construed in accordance with regulation 15(*a*) of those Regulations.

Amendments—[1] Reference in para (2)(*c*) substituted by the Special Commissioners (Jurisdiction and Procedure) (Amendment) Regulations 1999, SI 1999/3292 reg 5, with effect from 1 January 2000.

[*References of questions to other tribunals*

23—(1) A question in an appeal which is required to be determined in accordance with section 46D or 47B of the Management Act or section 222(4A) of the Inheritance Tax Act 1984 shall be referred to the appropriate tribunal by the Tribunal before whom the appeal is brought or, if the hearing of the appeal has not yet begun, by an inspector or other officer of the Board.

(2) Where any question in an appeal has been referred to another tribunal in accordance with paragraph (1) above, the Tribunal before whom the appeal is brought—

(*a*) shall finally determine the remaining question or questions in the appeal without awaiting the determination of the question referred to the other tribunal, and
(*b*) shall make a final determination of the appeal (in accordance with regulation 18) once all the questions in the appeal have been finally determined.

(3) The reference in paragraph (2)(*b*) above to all the questions in the appeal having being finally determined is a reference to a time when no further appeals in relation to those questions under any enactment are pending.][1]

Amendments—[1] Para substituted by the Special Commissioners (Jurisdiction and Procedure) (Amendment) Regulations 1999, SI 1999/3292 reg 1, with effect from 1 January 2000.

Penalty for failure to comply with Tribunal direction

24—(1) If any party or other person fails to comply with any direction of a Tribunal under these Regulations including a direction in a notice under regulation 10, the Tribunal may summarily determine a penalty against that party or other person not exceeding £10,000.

(2) Subject to paragraphs (6) to (11) of regulation 5, if a person on whom a summons is served under that regulation—

- (*a*) fails to attend in obedience to the summons, or
- (*b*) attends, but refuses to be sworn or to affirm, or
- (*c*) refuses to answer any lawful question, or
- (*d*) refuses to produce any document which he has been required to produce,

the Tribunal may summarily determine a penalty against him not exceeding £10,000.

(3) Subject to [paragraphs (4) and (5)][1] below, any penalty determined by the Tribunal under paragraph (1) or (2) above shall for all purposes be treated as if it were tax charged in an assessment and due and payable.

(4) Any penalty by the Tribunal under paragraph (1) or (2) above in proceedings relating to—

- (*a*) an appeal under section 222 of the Inheritance Tax Act 1984, or
- (*b*) an appeal under regulation 8 of the Stamp Duty Reserve Tax Regulations 1986,

shall for all purposes be treated as if it were tax determined by the Board and due and payable.

[(5) Any penalty determined by the Tribunal under paragraph (1) or (2) above in proceedings relating to an appeal under the enactments relating to stamp duty shall for all purposes be treated as if it were a penalty, other than a penalty under section 15B of the Stamp Act 1891 (penalty on late stamping), determined by an officer of the Board, and due and payable, under those enactments.][2]

Amendments—[1] Words in para 3 substituted by the Special Commissioners (Jurisdiction and Procedure) (Amendment) Regulations 2000, SI 2000/288 reg 4(*a*), with effect from 1 March 2000.

[2] Para 5 inserted by the Special Commissioners (Jurisdiction and Procedure) (Amendment) Regulations 2000, SI 2000/288 reg 4(b), with effect from 1 March 2000.

Part V Miscellaneous

Irregularities

25—(1) Any irregularity resulting from any failure to comply with any provision of these Regulations or with any direction given by a Tribunal before the Tribunal has reached its decision shall not of itself render the proceedings void.

(2) Where any such irregularity comes to the attention of a Tribunal, the Tribunal, before reaching its decision, may, and if it considers that any person may have been prejudiced by that irregularity shall, give such directions as it thinks just to cure or waive the irregularity.

(3) Clerical mistakes in any document recording a direction or a decision of a Tribunal, or errors arising in such a document from an accidental slip or omission, may be corrected by the Special Commissioner presiding at the hearing or any other of the Special Commissioners comprising the Tribunal, or by the Presiding Special Commissioner if all the Special Commissioners comprising the Tribunal have died or ceased to be Special Commissioners, by certificate under his hand.

Notices

26—Every notice required by these Regulations shall be in writing unless a Tribunal authorises it to be given orally.

Service

27—(1) Any notice or other document (other than a summons under regulation 5) required or authorised by these Regulations to be sent or delivered to, or served on, any person shall be duly sent or delivered to, or served on, that person—

(*a*) if it is sent to him at his proper address by post; or
(*b*) if it is sent to him at that address by facsimile transmission or other similar means which produce a document containing a text of the communication, in which event the document shall be regarded as sent when it is received in a legible form; or
(*c*) if it is delivered to him or left at his proper address.

(2) Any such document may—

(*a*) in the case of a body corporate, be sent or delivered to, or left with, the secretary or clerk of that body;

(*b*) in the case of a foreign body corporate, be sent or delivered to, or left with, the person authorised to accept service of process on it;

(*c*) in the case of a partnership, be sent or delivered to, or left with, any partner;

(*d*) in the case of an unincorporated association other than a partnership, be sent or delivered to, or left with, any member of the governing body of the association.

(3) For the purposes of this regulation, a person's proper address is—

(*a*) in the case of the secretary or clerk of a body corporate registered in the United Kingdom, the address of the registered or principal office of that body corporate;

(*b*) in the case of the person authorised to accept service of process on a foreign body corporate, the address of the principal office or place of business of that body corporate in the United Kingdom;

(*c*) in the case of the Special Commissioners or their Clerk, the address of the Clerk;

(*d*) in the case of any other person, the usual or last known address of that person.

Substituted service

28—If any person to or on whom any notice or other document (other than a summons under regulation 5) is required to be sent, delivered or served for the purposes of these Regulations cannot be found or has died and has no known representative, or is out of the United Kingdom, or if for any other reason service on him cannot be readily effected, a Tribunal may dispense with the requirement that the notice or other document be sent or delivered to, or served on him or may make an order for substituted service on such other person or in such other form (whether by advertisement in a newspaper or otherwise) as the Tribunal may think fit.

APPENDIX 5
SI 1994/1812

General Commissioners (Jurisdiction and Procedure) Regulations 1994, SI 1994/1812

Made by the Lord Chancellor under TMA 1970 ss 46A, 56B

Made	6 July 1994
Laid before Parliament	14 July 1994
Coming into Force	1 September 1994

Commentary—*Simon's Direct Tax Service* Divisions A3.5; A3.7.

Arrangement of regulations

Part IV Special procedure

Part V Miscellaneous

Part I Introductory

Citation, commencement and application

1—(1) These Regulations may be cited as the General Commissioners (Jurisdiction and Procedure) Regulations 1994 and shall come into force on 1 September 1994.

(2) These Regulations do not apply in relation to—

(*a*) any proceedings in respect of which notice of the place, date and time of the hearing was given or, in the case of more than one such notice, first given by the Clerk prior to 1 September 1994, and in respect of which an election is made by any party to the proceedings, by notice served on the Clerk, that these Regulations shall not apply, or

(*b*) any proceedings under section 100C of the Taxes Management Act 1970 in respect of which a summons was issued prior to 1 September 1994 by the General Commissioners to the defendant (or, in Scotland, the defender) to appear before them at a time and place stated in the summons.

(3) Where these Regulations apply in relation to any proceedings in respect of which notice of the place, date and time of the hearing was

given or, as the case may be, first given by the Clerk prior to 1 September 1994, anything done in relation to those proceedings prior to that date which, if the proceedings had been brought before the General Commissioners on or after that date, could have been done pursuant to these Regulations, shall have effect as if done pursuant to these Regulations.

(4) An election under paragraph (2)(*a*) above shall be made prior to the time of commencement of the hearing of the proceedings in question or, in the case of a hearing which commenced before 1 September 1994 but which was adjourned, prior to the time of commencement of the first continuation of the hearing on or after that date, and shall be irrevocable.

Interpretation

2 In these Regulations unless the context otherwise requires—

'the Board' means the Commissioners of Inland Revenue;

'the Clerk', in relation to any proceedings, means the Clerk to the General Commissioners;

'division' shall be construed in accordance with section 2(1) of the Management Act;

'final determination' means the decision finally determining any proceedings before a Tribunal;

'General Commissioners' shall be construed in accordance with section 2(1) of the Management Act, and 'the General Commissioners', in relation to any proceedings, means the General Commissioners for a division before whom the proceedings are brought (and references to a General Commissioner are to be read accordingly);

'inspector' means an inspector of taxes;

'the Management Act' means the Taxes Management Act 1970;

'party' means a party to any proceedings, and for the purposes of these Regulations—

(*a*) where the proceedings relate to an assessment, decision or determination made by the Board, the Board and any inspector or other officer of the Board for the time being concerned with the proceedings shall together constitute a party to those proceedings;

(*b*) where the proceedings relate to an assessment, decision or determination made by an inspector or other officer of the Board, that person and any other inspector or other officer of the Board for the time being concerned with the proceedings shall together constitute a party to those proceedings;

and references to 'the Revenue' are references to a party within paragraph (*a*) or, as the case may be, paragraph (*b*) above;

'proceedings' means—

(*a*) any appeal to the General Commissioners under the Taxes Acts;

(*b*) any proceedings before the General Commissioners which under the Taxes Acts are to be heard and determined in the same way as such an appeal;

(*c*) any proceedings before the General Commissioners which relate to a penalty and are not within paragraph (*a*) or paragraph (*b*) above;

[(*d*) any appeal to the General Commissioners under Part II of the Transfer Act or Part III of the Transfer Order;

(*e*) any appeal to the General Commissioners under regulations 8(6) and 14(4) of the Working Tax Regulations;][1]

'proceedings in Northern Ireland' means any proceedings (as defined in this regulation) which fall within the meaning of that expression as defined in section 58(3) of the Management Act;

'proceedings in Scotland' means any proceedings (as defined in this regulation) which fall to be determined by reference to the law of Scotland;

'Special Commissioners' shall be construed in accordance with section 4(1) of the Management Act;

'the Taxes Acts' has the meaning given by section 118(1) of the Management Act;

['the Transfer Act' means the Social Security Contributions (Transfer of Functions, etc) Act 1999;

'the Transfer Order' means the Social Security Contributions (Transfer of Functions, etc) (Northern Ireland) Order 1999;][2]

'Tribunal', in relation to any proceedings, means, subject to regulation 11(3), two or more, but not more than five, General Commissioners for a division before whom the proceedings are [brought;][3]

['the Working Tax Regulations' means the Working Tax Credit (Payment by Employers) Regulations 2002.][4]

Amendments—[1] Paras (*d*), (*e*) inserted by SI 2002/2976 regs 7, 8(*a*) with effect from 31 December 2002 in relation to proceedings before the General Commissioners on or after that date.

[2] Definitions inserted by SI 2002/2976 regs 7, 8(*b*) with effect from 31 December 2002 in relation to proceedings before the General Commissioners on or after that date).

[3] Word substituted by SI 2002/2976 regs 7, 8(*c*) with effect from 31 December 2002 in relation to proceedings before the General Commissioners on or after that date).

[4] Definition inserted by SI 2002/2976 regs 7, 8(*d*) with effect from 31 December 2002 in relation to proceedings before the General Commissioners on or after that date).

Part II
Preparation for a hearing

Listing and notice of hearing

3—(1) Except in relation to proceedings under section 100C of the Management Act, any party to proceedings which are to be heard by the General Commissioners may serve notice on the Clerk that he wishes a date for the hearing to be fixed.

(2) On receipt of a notice under paragraph (1) above the Clerk shall send notice to each party of the place, date and time of the hearing.

(3) Unless the parties otherwise agree or a Tribunal otherwise directs, the date of the hearing specified in a notice under paragraph (2) above shall be not earlier than twenty eight days after the date on which the notice is sent to the parties.

Summoning of witnesses

4—(1) Where a party to any proceedings requires the attendance of a person at the hearing of those proceedings to give evidence or to produce any document in his possession, custody or power relevant to the subject matter of the proceedings, a General Commissioner may, on the application of that party, issue a summons (in this regulation referred to as a 'witness summons') requiring the attendance of that person at the hearing, or the production of the document, wherever that person may be in the United Kingdom.

(2) A witness summons issued under paragraph (1) above shall state the name and address of, or otherwise describe, the person to be served and shall be signed by the General Commissioner issuing it, and it shall be the responsibility of the party on whose application the summons was issued to serve it on that person.

(3) Service of a witness summons under this regulation shall be effected—

(*a*) in the case of an individual, by leaving a copy of the summons with him;

(*b*) in the case of a body corporate registered in the United Kingdom, by leaving a copy of the summons with the secretary or clerk of the body corporate;

(*c*) in the case of a foreign body corporate with a place of business in the United Kingdom, by leaving a copy of the summons with a person authorised to accept service of process on the body corporate.

(4) A person who in obedience to a witness summons attends the hearing of any proceedings and gives evidence—

(*a*) is a witness of the party on whose application the summons was issued, and

(*b*) may not be cross-examined by that party without the leave of the Tribunal hearing the proceedings.

(5) Leave shall not be given by a Tribunal under paragraph (4)(*b*) above unless the Tribunal decides that the witness may be treated as a hostile witness.

(6) No person shall be required to attend in obedience to a witness summons unless it has been served on him at least seven days before the

hearing or, if it has been served on him within that period, he has informed the Clerk that he accepts such service.

(7) No person shall be required to attend and give evidence or to produce any document in obedience to a witness summons unless the party serving the summons either—

(*a*) pays or tenders to that person, at the time when the summons is served on him, a sum sufficient to cover his reasonable expenses of travelling to and from, and his attendance at, the hearing, or

(*b*) has agreed with that person prior to service of the summons, to pay such a sum to him at a different time.

(8) No person shall be compelled in obedience to a witness summons to give any evidence or produce any document that he could not be compelled to give or produce in an action in a court of law in that part of the United Kingdom by reference to the law of which the proceedings are to be determined.

(9) No person who has been appointed as an auditor for the purposes of any enactment or who is a tax adviser within the meaning of section 20B(10) of the Management Act shall be compelled in obedience to a witness summons to produce any document if, having regard to section 20B(9) to (13) of that Act, he would not be obliged to deliver or make available that document in response to a notice under section 20(3) or (8A) of that Act.

(10) Where, in the case of any document, a person could under section 20B(14) of that Act comply with such a notice by delivering a copy of parts of the document and making those parts available for inspection, he shall not be compelled in obedience to a witness summons to do more at the hearing than—

(*a*) produce a photographic or other facsimile copy of those parts of the document, and

(*b*) make those parts of the document available for inspection by the Tribunal.

(11) On the application, by notice served on the Clerk, of a person on whom a witness summons has been served, a General Commissioner may set aside the summons in whole or in part; and the party on whose application the summons was issued shall be entitled to be heard on such an application.

(12) Subject to paragraphs (6) to (11) above, if a person on whom a witness summons is served—

(*a*) fails to attend in obedience to the summons, or

(*b*) attends, but refuses to be sworn or to affirm, or

(*c*) refuses to answer any lawful question, or

(*d*) refuses to produce any document which he has been required by the summons to produce, the Tribunal hearing the proceedings may summarily determine a penalty against him not exceeding £1,000.

(13) Any penalty determined by a Tribunal under paragraph (12) above shall for all purposes be treated as if it were tax charged in an assessment and due and payable.

(14) This regulation shall apply to proceedings in Scotland—
  (*a*) with the omission of paragraphs (4) and (5) above;
  (*b*) with the substitution for references to issuing a summons and to a witness summons of references to issuing a citation and to a witness citation.

Agreement of documents

5 If a party agrees a document for the purposes of any proceedings he shall be deemed, subject to the terms of the agreement, to admit for the purposes of those proceedings—
  (*a*) that the document was written and signed or executed by the person by whom, and on the date on which, it purports to have been, and
  (*b*) if it purports to be a copy of another document, that it is a true copy of that document,
but, subject to any enactment or rule of law, in the absence of an express admission or agreement, he shall not be deemed to admit the truth of the contents of that document.

Proceedings to be heard together or in succession

6—(1) Where two or more proceedings have been brought before, but have not yet been heard by, the General Commissioners for one or more divisions and it appears to two or more of the General Commissioners for one of those divisions—
  (*a*) that some common issue arises in both or all of them, or
  (*b*) that both or all of them are relevant to some common issue,
those Commissioners may, of their own motion or on an application by a party to any of those proceedings, direct that those proceedings be heard at the same time or consecutively and by the same Tribunal within their division.

(2) A direction shall not be given under paragraph (1) above except on notice sent to all the parties to the proceedings in question who shall be entitled to be heard before any direction is given.

(3) On the giving of a direction under paragraph (1) above, the Clerk to the General Commissioners by whom the direction is given shall send notice of the date and terms of the direction to all the parties to the

proceedings and, except where all the proceedings have been brought before the General Commissioners for the same division, to the Clerk to the other division or, if more than one, each other division of General Commissioners concerned.

[Lead cases

6A—(1) Where—

(*a*) one or more proceedings under Part II of the Transfer Act or Part III of the Transfer Order have been brought before, but have not yet been heard, by General Commissioners for one or more divisions, and

(*b*) those proceedings give rise to common or related issues of fact or law ('same issues proceedings')

the General Commissioners or each of the General Commissioners for each division as the case may be, shall arrange for transfer of those proceedings to the Special Commissioners.

(2) Before transferring any same issues proceedings the appropriate General Commissioners shall give all the parties to the proceedings in question an opportunity to make representations.

(3) For the purpose of this regulation 'proceedings' shall for the avoidance of doubt, include more than one appeal against the same decision to the General Commissioners.][1]

Amendment—[1] Inserted by SI 2002/2976 regs 7, 9 with effect from 31 December 2002 in relation to proceedings before the General Commissioners on or after that date.

Joining of additional parties

7—(1) If it appears to a Tribunal, whether on the application of a party or otherwise, that it is desirable that any person other than the Revenue be made a party to any proceedings, the Tribunal may order such person to be joined as a party in the proceedings and may give such directions for giving effect to, or in connection with, the order as it thinks fit.

(2) Where pursuant to an order under paragraph (1) above a person is joined as a party in any proceedings by reason of a question arising in those proceedings which may affect his liability to tax or in which he otherwise has an interest, he shall not be entitled, unless all the other parties consent, to be present at the hearing of the proceedings except during such part of the hearing as relates to that question, and a Tribunal shall, if necessary, hear any such question separately from the rest of the proceedings.

(3) On the application of a person who has been joined as a party in the circumstances specified in paragraph (2) above, a Tribunal may, if it is satisfied that it would be to the convenience of the parties to do so, transfer the proceedings to the General Commissioners for the division in which the applicant ordinarily resided at the date of the application, or to the Special Commissioners.

Postponements and Adjournments

8—(1) A Tribunal may postpone the hearing of any proceedings, and the Clerk shall send notice to the parties of the place, date and time of the postponed hearing.

(2) A Tribunal may from time to time adjourn the hearing of any proceedings and, subject to paragraph (3) below, the Clerk shall send notice to the parties of the place, date and time of the adjourned hearing.

(3) If the place, date and time of the adjourned hearing are announced before the adjournment in the presence of the parties, no notice need be sent by the Clerk under paragraph (2) above.

(4) When any hearing is adjourned in order that further information or evidence may be obtained, the Tribunal hearing the proceedings may give directions regarding the disclosure of such information or evidence to the parties prior to the resumption of the hearing.

Expert evidence

9—(1) Unless a Tribunal otherwise directs, no expert evidence may be adduced by a party at the hearing of any proceedings unless—

- (*a*) he has agreed with the other party or parties that the substance of the evidence shall be disclosed in the form of a written report or opinion in advance of the hearing and not later than such date as is specified in the agreement, and the substance of the evidence has been so disclosed, or
- (*b*) where no such agreement has been reached or where the substance of the evidence has not been so disclosed, an application is made to a Tribunal under paragraph (2) below by the party seeking to adduce the evidence to determine whether a direction should be given under paragraph (3) below, and the party seeking to adduce the evidence complies with a direction given under that paragraph.

(2) An application under this paragraph—

- (*a*) shall be made not later than twenty one days after the date on which notice is sent by the Clerk under regulation 3(2) or, if the Tribunal so permits, at any later time prior to or in the course of the hearing, and (*b*) shall state whether the party is willing to disclose the substance of the evidence prior to its being given at the hearing and, if not, the reasons for his objection.

(3) On an application under paragraph (2) above, unless it considers that there are special reasons for not doing so, the tribunal shall direct that the substance of the evidence shall be disclosed in the form of a written report or opinion to such other parties and within such period as it may specify.

(4) This regulation shall not apply to proceedings in Scotland.

Part III Hearing and determination of proceedings

Power of Tribunal to obtain information

10—(1) A Tribunal hearing any proceedings may at any time before the final determination of those proceedings serve notice on any party, other than the Revenue, directing him within the time specified in the notice—

(*a*) to deliver to it such particulars as it may require for the purpose of determining any of the issues in the proceedings, and

(*b*) to make available for inspection by it, or by an officer of the Board, all such books, accounts or other documents in his possession or power as may be specified or described in the notice, being books, accounts or other documents which, in the opinion of the Tribunal, contain or may contain information relevant to the subject matter of the proceedings.

(2) Any officer of the Board may at all reasonable times inspect and take copies of, or extracts from, any particulars delivered under paragraph (1)(*a*) above, and the Tribunal or any officer of the Board may take copies of, or extracts from, any books, accounts or other documents made available for inspection under paragraph (1)(*b*) above.

(3) If any person fails to comply with a notice served under this regulation, the Tribunal may summarily determine a penalty against him not exceeding £300 and, if the failure continues after the determination of such penalty, a further penalty or penalties not exceeding £60 for each day on which the failure continues after the day on which the penalty was determined (but excluding any day for which a further penalty has already been determined).

(4) Any penalty determined by the Tribunal under paragraph (3) above shall for all purposes be treated as if it were tax charged in an assessment and due and payable.

Revenue Internal Guidance—Enquiries Handbook EH386 (this regulation will not normally be used where there is an enquiry in progress, since the Revenue will use its powers under TMA 1970 s 19A).

Inspector's Manual IM4982b ('particulars' in para (1)(*a*) is a wide term: Commissioners can obtain trading and profit and loss accounts, balance sheets and supporting computations and details of any entry in accounts or returns, but not the completed return itself).
IM4989 (the Revenue will consider the cost to the taxpayer of compliance with any order to produce particulars).
Simon's Tax Cases—*Phipps v New Forest West General Comrs and IRC* [1997] STC 797.
reg 10(1)(*b*), *Johnson v Blackpool General Comrs and IRC* [1997] STC 1202.
reg 10(3), *Johnson v Blackpool General Comrs and IRC* [1996] STC 277.

Constitution and sittings of Tribunal

11—(1) A Tribunal hearing any proceedings shall, where possible, comprise at least three General Commissioners but the validity of any proceedings before a Tribunal shall not be challenged where the Tribunal in question is comprised of two General Commissioners.

(2) The General Commissioners comprising a Tribunal shall decide which one of them shall preside at the hearing of proceedings before them.

(3) Proceedings before any Tribunal may be continued by any one or more of the General Commissioners comprising that Tribunal if all the parties give their consent.

Representation at hearing

12 At the hearing of any proceedings before a Tribunal—
(*a*) a party other than the Revenue may be represented by any person whether or not legally qualified, except that if in a particular case the Tribunal is satisfied that there are good and sufficient reasons for doing so, it may refuse to permit a particular person, other than one who is legally qualified or who has been admitted a member of an incorporated society of accountants, to represent a party at the hearing;
(*b*) the Revenue may be represented by a barrister, advocate, solicitor or any officer of the Board.

[Hearings in public

13—(1) Subject to the following paragraphs of this regulation, hearings before a Tribunal shall be in public.

(2) A Tribunal may direct that all or part of a hearing shall be in private—
(*a*) upon the application of all the parties by notice to the Clerk;
(*b*) upon the application of any party by notice to the Clerk;
(*c*) of its own motion,

if in each case, a Tribunal is satisfied that a hearing in private is necessary—

(i) in the interests of morals, public order, national security, juveniles or for the protection of the private life of the party; or

(ii) if it considers that publicity would prejudice the interests of justice.

(3) Before determining an application under paragraph (2)(*b*) or giving a direction under (2)(c) a Tribunal shall give all other parties an opportunity to make representations.

(4) Before giving a direction under paragraph (2) that the entire hearing be in private, a Tribunal shall consider whether only part of the hearing should be heard in private.

(5) The following persons shall be entitled to be present at the hearing of any proceedings before a Tribunal notwithstanding that the hearing or part of the hearing takes place in private, and those referred to in sub-paragraphs (*b*) to (*e*) only may remain present during the deliberations of the Tribunal but shall take no part in those deliberations—

(*a*) the parties and their representatives;

(*b*) the Clerk and any of the staff of the General Commissioners;

(*c*) a member of the Council on Tribunals or of the Scottish Committee of that Council in the capacity of member;

(*d*) any of the Special Commissioners;

(*e*) a member of the Judicial Studies Board or of one of its Committees in the capacity of member.

(6) A Tribunal may exclude from the whole or part of a hearing any person whose conduct, in the opinion of a Tribunal, has disrupted or is likely to disrupt the hearing.

(7) A Tribunal, with the consent of the parties, may permit any other person to be present at the hearing of proceedings before it which is to take place, or part of which is to take place, in private.

(8) Where all or part of a hearing is held or is to be held in private, a Tribunal may direct that information about the whole or part of the proceedings (including information that might help to identify any person) before a Tribunal shall not be made public.

(9) For the purposes of paragraph (2)(i) 'party' shall not include the Revenue.][1]

Amendment— [1] Substituted by SI 2002/2976 regs 7, 10 with effect from 31 December 2002 in relation to proceedings before the General Commissioners on or after that date.

Failure of parties to attend hearing

14—(1) If a party fails to attend or to be represented at a hearing of which he has been duly notified, the Tribunal may—

(*a*) unless it is satisfied that there is good and sufficient reason for such absence, hear and determine the proceedings in the absence of the party or his representative, or

(*b*) postpone or adjourn the hearing.

(2) Before deciding to hear and determine any proceedings in the absence of a party or his representative, the Tribunal shall consider any representations in writing or otherwise submitted by or on behalf of that party in response to the notice of hearing and shall give any party present at the hearing an opportunity to be heard in regard to those representations.

Procedure and evidence at hearing

15—(1) At the beginning of the hearing of any proceedings the Tribunal shall, except where it considers it unnecessary to do so, explain the order of proceeding which it proposes to adopt.

(2) The Tribunal shall conduct the hearing in such manner as it considers most suitable to the clarification and determination of the issues before it and generally to the just handling of the proceedings and, so far as appears to it appropriate, shall seek to avoid formality in its procedure.

(3) The parties shall be heard in such order as the Tribunal shall determine and shall be entitled—

(*a*) to give evidence,

(*b*) to call witnesses,

(*c*) to question any witnesses including other parties who give evidence, and

(*d*) to address the Tribunal both on the evidence and generally on the subject matter of the proceedings.

(4) In assessing the truth and weight of any evidence, the Tribunal may take account of its nature and source, and the manner in which it is given.

(5) Evidence before the Tribunal may be given orally or, if the Tribunal so directs, by affidavit or a statement made or recorded in a document, but at any stage of the hearing the Tribunal may, on the application of any party or of its own motion, require the personal attendance as a witness of—

(*a*) the maker of an affidavit, or

(*b*) the maker of such a statement, or

(*c*) in the case of an oral statement recorded in a document, the person by whom the statement was so recorded.

(6) The Tribunal may receive evidence of any fact which appears to the Tribunal to be relevant to the subject matter of the proceedings notwithstanding that such evidence would be inadmissible in proceedings before a court of law in that part of the United Kingdom by reference to the law of which the proceedings before the Tribunal are to be determined, but, save in cases where claims for privilege are allowed (including, in proceedings in Scotland, claims for protection from disclosure by virtue of any rule of law relating to the confidentiality of communications), it shall not refuse to admit any evidence which would be admissible in such proceedings.

(7) The Tribunal may require any witness to give evidence on oath or affirmation and for that purpose there may be administered an oath or affirmation in due form.

Simon's Tax Cases—reg 15(6), *Walker v Smith* [1999] STC 605.

Decisions of Tribunal

16—(1) Any decision of a Tribunal shall be made by the votes of the majority of the General Commissioners comprising that Tribunal and, in the event of an equality of votes, the General Commissioner presiding at the hearing shall be entitled to a second or casting vote.

(2) The final determination may be given orally by a Tribunal at the end of the hearing or may be reserved and in either event shall be recorded in a document which shall be signed and dated by the Tribunal.

(3) The Clerk shall send to each party a notice setting out the final determination recorded under paragraph (2) above.

(4) Except where the final determination is given at the end of the hearing, it shall be treated as having been made on the date on which the notice is sent to the parties under paragraph (3) above.

(5) Every notice sent to the parties under paragraph (3) above[, other than a notice setting out a final determination made in accordance with regulation 19(2)(*b*),][1] shall be accompanied by a notification of the provisions of—

(*a*) the Management Act,
(*b*) these Regulations, and
(*c*) rules of court,

relating to appeals from the General Commissioners and of the time within which, and the manner in which, such appeals shall be made.

Amendments—[1] In sub-s (5) words inserted by the General Commissioners (Jurisdiction and Procedure) (Amendment) Regulations 1999, SI 1999/3293 reg 3, with effect from 1 January 2000.

Review of Tribunal's final determination

17—(1) If, on the application of a party or of its own motion, a Tribunal is satisfied that—

- (*a*) the final determination was wrongly made as a result of an administrative error on the part of the Clerk or any of the staff of the General Commissioners or a party, or
- (*b*) a party, who was entitled to be heard at a hearing but failed to appear or to be represented, had good and sufficient reason for failing to appear or to be represented, or
- (*c*) accounts or other information relevant to a party's case had been sent to the Clerk or to the appropriate inspector or other officer of the Board prior to the hearing of the proceedings but had not been received by the Tribunal until after the hearing,

the Tribunal may review and set aside or vary the final determination.

(2) An application for the purposes of paragraph (1) above shall be made to the Tribunal not later than fourteen days after the date on which notice setting out the final determination was sent to the parties under regulation 16(3), or by such later time as the Tribunal may allow, and shall be in writing stating the grounds in full.

(3) Where the Tribunal proposes to review of its own motion the final determination, it shall serve notice of that proposal on the parties not later than fourteen days after the date on which notice setting out the final determination was sent to the parties under regulation 16(3).

(4) The parties shall have an opportunity to be heard on a review, or in relation to any application or proposal for review, under this regulation and the review shall be determined by the Tribunal which decided the case or, where it is not practicable for it to be heard by that Tribunal, by another Tribunal; and if, having reviewed the final determination, the Tribunal sets aside that determination, it shall substitute such determination as it thinks fit or order a rehearing before either the same or a differently constituted Tribunal.

(5) Regulation 16 shall apply to a decision by a Tribunal varying a final determination or substituting a new final determination, as it applies to a final determination.

Revenue Internal Guidance—Inspector's Manual IM4922 (no appeal against decision of Commissioners to reopen appeal).

Part IV Special procedure

Proceedings relating to tax on chargeable gains

18—(1) Where the market value of an asset on a particular date or the apportionment of an amount or value is a material question in any proceedings relating to tax on chargeable gains, the Tribunal hearing the proceedings shall, if so required by any party, record in its final determination that market value or apportionment.

(2) The final determination on an appeal of the market value of an asset on a particular date or of the apportionment of any amount or value may be proved in any proceedings relating to tax on chargeable gains by a certificate stating the material particulars signed by—

(*a*) an inspector where the appeal was settled by agreement, or

(*b*) the Clerk where the General Commissioners determined the appeal, or

(*c*) the clerk or registrar of another tribunal where the material question was determined by that other tribunal in accordance with section [46D][1] or 47B of the Management Act,

and a document purporting to be such a certificate may be received in evidence in any such proceedings without further proof.

(3) In this regulation the expression 'final determination on an appeal' shall be construed in accordance with regulation 11(2) of the Capital Gains Tax Regulations 1967, and the expression 'material question in any proceedings' shall be construed in accordance with regulation 15(*a*) of those Regulations.

Amendments—[1] In sub-s (2)(*c*) figure substituted by the General Commissioners (Jurisdiction and Procedure) (Amendment) Regulations, SI 1999/3293 reg 4, with effect from 1 January 2000.

[*References of questions to other tribunals*

19—(1) A question in an appeal which is required to be determined in accordance with section 46B, 46C, 46D or 47B of the Management Act shall be referred to the appropriate tribunal by the Tribunal before whom the appeal is brought or, if the hearing of the appeal has not begun, by an inspector or other officer of the Board.

(2) Where any question in an appeal has been referred to another tribunal in accordance with paragraph (1) above, the Tribunal before whom the appeal is brought—

(*a*) shall make a final determination of the remaining question or questions in the appeal, and shall at the request of any party state a case thereon under regulation 22, without awaiting the determination of the question referred to the other tribunal, and (*b*) shall make a final determination of the appeal (in accordance with regulation 16) once all the questions in the appeal have been finally determined.

(3) Where—

(*a*) a question in an appeal has been referred to the Special Commissioners in accordance with paragraph (1) above, and

(*b*) that question is the sole question in dispute in the appeal,

the proceedings shall be transferred to the Special Commissioners by the Tribunal before whom the appeal is brought or, if the hearing of the appeal has not yet begun, shall be brought before the Special Commissioners by an inspector or other officer of the Board.

(4) The reference in paragraph (2)(*b*) above to all questions in the appeal having been finally determined is a reference to a time when no further appeals in relation to those questions, whether by way of case stated under these Regulations or under any other enactment, are pending.][1]

Revenue Internal Guidance—Inspector's Manual IM4919a (appeals to the court on other matters may proceed before the determination of valuations by the Land Tribunal).

Amendments—[1] This regulation substituted by the General Commissioners (Jurisdiction and Procedure) (Amendment) Regulations 1999, SI 1999/3293 reg 5, with effect from 1 January 2000.

Case stated procedure

20—(1) Within thirty days after the final determination of any proceedings falling within paragraph (*a*) or (*b*) of the definition of 'proceedings' in regulation 2 is made by a Tribunal[, other than a final determination to which regulation 19(2)(*b*) refers,][1] or, as the case may be, within thirty days after a decision varying such a final determination or substituting for it a new final determination is made by a Tribunal under regulation 17, any party to the proceedings, if dissatisfied with the determination or decision as being erroneous in point of law, may by notice served on the Clerk require the Tribunal to state and sign a case for the opinion of the High Court.

(2) A case stated pursuant to a requirement under paragraph (1) above shall set forth the facts and the final determination of the Tribunal.

(3) After a party has required a case to be stated under paragraph (1) above, the Tribunal may by notice served on him require him [within a period of time stated in the notice, not being less than twenty eight days,][2] to identify the question of law on which he requires the case to be stated.

(4) If a party fails to comply with a notice served under paragraph (3) above, or if the Tribunal is not satisfied that the question identified is a

question of law, or until the fee specified in section 56(3) of the Management Act has been paid, the Tribunal may refuse to state a case.

(5) Where a final determination of a Tribunal is set aside or varied under regulation 17, a requirement for a case to be stated in respect of that determination shall cease to be valid.

Revenue Internal Guidance—Inspector's Manual IM4916b (where Commissioners make a decision in principle, a final decision is normally required once figures have been determined if the case is to go to court).
Amendments—[1] Words inserted by the General Commissioners (Jurisdiction and Procedure) (Amendment) Regulations 1999, SI 1999/3293 reg 6(*a*), with effect from 1 January 2000.
[2] Words substituted by SI 1999/3293 reg 6(*b*), with effect from 1 January 2000.

Consideration of draft case

21—(1) Within fifty six days after the receipt of a notice served under regulation 20(1) requiring a case to be stated or, if a notice is served under regulation 20(3), within fifty six days after the day on which a question of law is identified to the satisfaction of the Tribunal, the Clerk shall send a draft of the case to the party who required the case to be stated and to the other party or parties.

(2) Within fifty six days after the draft case is sent to the parties under paragraph (1) above, any party may make representations on the draft to the Clerk in writing and shall at the same time send a copy of any representations so made to the other party or parties.

(3) Within twenty eight days after the latest date on which representations may be made under paragraph (2) above, any party may make further representations on the draft to the Clerk in writing in response to any representations made under paragraph (2) above, and shall at the same time send a copy of such further representations to the other party or parties.

(4) A failure by the Clerk to send a draft case within the time specified in paragraph (1) above, or a failure by a party to make representations within the time specified in paragraph (2) or (3) above, or to send a copy of representations under either of those paragraphs to the other party or parties, shall not affect the validity of the case after it has been stated and signed pursuant to regulation 22, or of any subsequent proceedings in relation to the case.

(5) Where a party fails to send a copy of any representations to another party in accordance with paragraph (2) or (3) above, that other party may apply to the Clerk for a copy of the representations.

Preparation and submission of final case

22—(1) Subject to paragraph (2) below, as soon as may be after the latest date on which representations may be made under regulation 21, the Tribunal whose decision is questioned, after taking into account any representations made under that regulation, shall state and sign the case.

(2) If a member of the Tribunal has died or ceased to be a General Commissioner, then the case shall be stated and signed by the continuing Commissioner or Commissioners or, if there is no continuing Commissioner, by the Clerk.

(3) After the case has been stated and signed the Clerk shall send it to the party who required it to be stated, and shall notify the other party or parties that the case has been sent to that party.

(4) The party requiring the case shall—
- (*a*) transmit the case to the High Court within thirty days of receiving it, and
- (*b*) at or before the time when he transmits the case to the High Court, send notice of the fact that the case has been stated on his application, together with a copy of the case, to the other party or parties.

Revenue Internal Guidance—Inspector's Manual IM5041 (date of receipt of case stated by the party concerned in para (4)(*a*) is the date on which it is delivered at the place given as his address at the time of requiring the case, unless in the meantime notice of a change of address has been given to the Clerk to the Commissioners).

Simon's Tax Cases—reg 22(1), *McKinney v Hagans Caravans (Manufacturing) Ltd* [1997] STC 1023.

Case stated procedure—Scotland and Northern Ireland

23—(1) In relation to proceedings in Scotland, references in regulations 20(1) and 22(4) to the High Court shall be taken as references to the Court of Session as the Court of Exchequer.

(2) In relation to proceedings in Northern Ireland—
- (*a*) the reference in regulation 20(1) to the High Court shall be taken as a reference to the Court of Appeal in Northern Ireland;
- (*b*) the procedure relating to the transmission of a case stated under regulation 22 to the Court of Appeal in Northern Ireland shall be that for the time being in force in Northern Ireland as respects cases stated by a county court in exercise of its general jurisdiction, and regulation 22(4) shall not apply.

Part V Miscellaneous

Irregularities

24—(1) Any irregularity resulting from any failure to comply with any provision of these Regulations or with any direction given by a Tribunal before the Tribunal has reached its final determination shall not of itself render the proceedings void.

(2) Where any such irregularity comes to the attention of a Tribunal, the Tribunal before reaching its final determination may, and if it considers that any person may have been prejudiced by that irregularity shall, give such directions as it thinks just to cure or waive the irregularity.

(3) Clerical mistakes in any document recording a direction or a decision of a Tribunal, or errors arising in such a document from an accidental slip or omission, may be corrected by the General Commissioner presiding at the hearing or any other of the General Commissioners comprising the Tribunal, or by the Clerk if all the General Commissioners comprising the Tribunal have died or ceased to be General Commissioners, by certificate under his hand.

Notices

25 Every notice required by these Regulations shall be in writing unless a Tribunal authorises it to be given orally.

Service

26—(1) Any notice or other document (other than a summons under regulation 4) required or authorised by these Regulations to be sent or delivered to, or served on, any person shall be duly sent or delivered to, or served on, that person—

(*a*) if it is sent to him at his proper address by post; or
(*b*) if it is sent to him at that address by facsimile transmission or other similar means which produce a document containing a text of the communication, in which event the document shall be regarded as sent when it is received in a legible form; or
(*c*) if it is delivered to him or left at his proper address.

(2) Any such document may—

(*a*) in the case of a body corporate, be sent or delivered to, or left with, the secretary or clerk of that body;
(*b*) in the case of a foreign body corporate, be sent or delivered to, or left with, the person authorised to accept service of process on it;
(*c*) in the case of a partnership, be sent or delivered to, or left with, any partner;

(*d*) in the case of an unincorporated association other than a partnership, be sent or delivered to, or left with, any member of the governing body of the association.

(3) For the purposes of this regulation, a person's proper address is—

(*a*) in the case of the secretary or clerk of a body corporate registered in the United Kingdom, the address of the registered or principal office of that body corporate;

(*b*) in the case of the person authorised to accept service of process on a foreign body corporate, the address of the principal office or place of business of that body corporate in the United Kingdom;

(*c*) in the case of the General Commissioners for a division or their Clerk, the address of the Clerk;

(*d*) in the case of any other person, the usual or last known address of that person.

Substituted service

27 If any person to or on whom any notice or other document (other than a summons under regulation 4) is required to be sent, delivered or served for the purposes of these Regulations cannot be found or has died and has no known representative, or is out of the United Kingdom, or if for any other reason service on him cannot be readily effected, a Tribunal may dispense with the requirement that the notice or other document be sent or delivered to, or served on him or may make an order for substituted service on such other person or in such other form (whether by advertisement in a newspaper or otherwise) as the Tribunal may think fit.

APPENDIX 6

Case headnotes

Abbey Life Assurance Co Ltd v Tansell

COURT OF APPEAL (CIVIL DIVISION)
STUART-SMITH, WARD AND MUMMERY LJJ
6 APRIL 2000

Disability discrimination—Discrimination by others than employers—principals—Disability Discrimination Act 1995 ss 12(1), (3), (6).

Mr Tansell offered computer skills and services through Intelligents Ltd, a company in which he was sole shareholder and one of four directors. He placed his name with several agencies, including MHC Consulting Services, an employment agency specialising in placing computer personnel with third parties. MHC entered into an agreement with Abbey Life to supply personnel to them. Mr Tansell was interviewed by Abbey Life and a contract was entered into between MHC and Intelligents on 31 October 1997 to supply Mr Tansell's services to Abbey Life. This contract had the effect of putting him under the control of Abbey Life. Fees were paid to MHC, who in turn paid Intelligents. Mr Tansell was paid a salary by Intelligents, but funds were also retained within the company. There was no contract between Abbey Life and either Intelligents or Mr Tansell personally. In February 1998, Mr Tansell was diagnosed as having diabetes. His services with Abbey Life were terminated on 20 March 1998. He sought to complain that he had been discriminated against contrary to the Disability Discrimination Act by Abbey Life and/or MHC on grounds that he had been withdrawn from the site by MHC because Abbey Life rejected his services by reason of his disability. An employment tribunal held a preliminary hearing on whether Mr Tansell was a contract worker within the meaning of s 12 of the Act. Section 12(1) makes it unlawful 'for a principal, in relation to contract work, to discriminate against a disabled person'. Section 12(6) specifies that 'principal' means 'a person ("A") who makes work available for doing by individuals who are employed by another person who supplies them under a contract made with "A"'. Similar provisions are contained in the Sex Discrimination and Race Relations Acts. The employment tribunal took the view that s 12 requires a direct contractual relationship between the employer and the principal. On that basis, the applicant was not a contract worker for Abbey Life. However, the tribunal found that he was a contract worker for MHC. MHC appealed and Mr Tansell cross-appealed against the tribunal's finding that he had no claim against Abbey Life. The EAT [1999] IRLR 677 sub nom *MHC Consulting Services v Tansell* allowed the appeal and the cross-appeal. According to the EAT, where there is an unbroken chain of contracts between an individual and an end-user, the end-user is the 'principal' within the meaning of s 12(6). Such a construction of s 12(6) gave effect to the general principle that the statute should be construed purposively and with a bias towards conferring statutory protection rather than excluding it. Abbey Life was given leave to appeal to the Court of Appeal. On appeal, it was argued that in order to bring a case within s 12, it is necessary for the person who employs the worker to have a direct contractual relationship with the principal who makes the work available.

Held—The EAT had correctly held that the applicant, who was employed by a company which supplied him to an agency, which in turn supplied him to an end-user, the appellants, was a 'contract worker' within the meaning of s 12 of the Disability Discrimination Act who could present a claim against the end-user as being a 'principal'. Section 12(6), which provides that 'principal' means 'a person ("A") who makes work available for doing by individuals who are employed by another person who supplies them under a contract made with "A"', does not require a direct contractual relationship between the employer and the principal. It applies to a case where there is no direct contract between the person making the work available and the employer of the individual who is supplied to do that work. The statutory definition only requires the supply of the individual to be 'under a contract made with "A"'. It does not expressly stipulate who is to be the party who contracts with 'A'. It was more probable that Parliament intended to confer than to deny protection from discrimination in cases where the supply of the employee was made by his company to the principal through an employment agency rather than direct to the principal. In the present case, the applicant's employer supplied him to work for the end-user within the meaning of the statutory definition. The supply of the individual also had to be under a contract made with the principal, and, in the present case, the applicant was supplied under a contract between the agency and the end-user. Although in many cases the contract with the end-user will be made by the employer who supplies the individual, the definition in s 12 does not require that to be the case.

Notes

For equal opportunities: people with disabilities, see *Harvey on Industrial Relations and Employment Law* Division L.3.

For the Disability Discrimination Act 1995 s 12, see ibid, Division Q.

Cases referred to in judgments

Duport Steels v Sirs [1980] IRLR 116, HL.
Ealing Hammersmith and Hounslow FHSA v Shukla [1993] ICR 710, EAT.
Harrods Ltd v Remick [1997] IRLR 583 CA.
Inco Europe Ltd v First Choice Distribution [2000] 1 WLR 586, HL.
Jones v Tower Boot Co Ltd [1997] IRLR 168, CA.
Lloyd v IBM (UK) Ltd, EAT/642/94.
Mirror Group Newspapers v Gunning [1986] IRLR 27, CA.
Rice v Fon-a-Car [1980] ICR 133, EAT.

Christopher Jeans QC and *John Cavanagh* (instructed by Abbey Life Legal Department) for Abbey Life Assurance Co Ltd.
Brian Langstaff QC (instructed by the *Disability Law Service*) for Mr Tansell.

Addison and others v London Philharmonic Orchestra Ltd

EMPLOYMENT APPEAL TRIBUNAL
WATERHOUSE J, MRS D EWING AND MR T H GOFF
25 SEPTEMBER, 20 OCTOBER 1980

Employment—Contract of service—Distinction between contract for services and contract of service—Musicians performing part-time for orchestra—Whether employees—Whether performing under contract of service.

The applicants were musicians who performed part-time with the respondent's orchestra. They were not full shareholding members of the orchestra. They were paid fees and certain expenses when performing with the orchestra. None was obliged to accept particular engagements. They regarded themselves as self-employed musicians when playing for the respondent; they paid tax and national insurance contributions accordingly. The applicants applied to an industrial tribunal to determine the particulars of their employment on the ground that the respondent had refused to provide them with statements of their terms of employment in accordance with s 1 of the Employment Protection (Consolidation) Act 1978 (the 1978 Act) which provided that an employer should give to an employee a written statement containing, inter alia, particulars of the terms of employment, within 13 weeks of the beginning of the period of employment. The tribunal dismissed the applications, holding: (i) that a contract of employment would require, inter alia, obligations to attend particular engagements and disciplinary provisions and accordingly (ii) that none of the applicants performed with the orchestra as 'employees' within s 153(1) of the 1978 Act which provided that 'employee' meant an individual who worked under a contract of employment. The applicants appealed

Held—The requirements of personal attendance, punctuality, attendance at rehearsals and general self-discipline were not to be regarded as elements pointing decisively to a contract of service. They were simply pre-requisites of a concert artist's work. Considerations as to: the provision of equipment; the incidence of tax and national insurance; the parties' own view of their relationship; the traditional structure of the applicants' profession and arrangements within it; and what the parties intended pointed against a contract of service. It was well settled that the label which the parties chose to use to describe their relationship could not alter or decide their true relationship; but, in deciding what that relationship was, the expression by them of their true intention was relevant but not conclusive. The argument centred on the relevance and importance of: the degree of control exercised by the respondent; whether the applicants' interest in the performance involved any prospect of profit or risk of loss; whether they were properly regarded as part and parcel of the respondent's organisation at the relevant times; and whether at the relevant times they were carrying on business on their own account or carrying on the business of the respondent. The tribunal had found as a fact that there was some degree of control by the respondent while the applicants were actually working but no more than was required by the very nature of the work. Control could not be regarded in any way as a decisive pointer to a contract of service in the light of the tribunal's findings of fact. In the general framework of the year to year relationship, the tribunal had been entitled to accept that the basis of the relationship between the parties was moral and professional rather than contractual. The other elements could be considered together. The fundamental test to be applied was: 'is the person who has engaged himself to perform these services performing them as a person in business on his own account?' Applying the facts of the instant case to that test there was no hesitation in answering: 'yes'. The facts found by the tribunal showed that when playing for the respondent each applicant remained essentially a freelance musician, pursuing his or her own profession, with an individual reputation, and carrying on his or her own business. It might be that they became part and parcel of the respondent's orchestra for specific performances, but not essentially of the respondent's business, and they contributed their own skills and interpretative powers to the orchestra's performances as independent contractors. The fact that the applicants did not risk their own capital in orchestral performances was not a persuasive argument. As for their opportunity of profit in 'their own business', it might not have depended on single performances but, in a more general sense, it depended to a significant degree on the way they 'managed their work'.

Young & Woods Ltd v West [1980] IRLR 201; *Market Investigations Ltd v Minister of Social Security* [1969] 2 QB 173; *Bank voor Handel en Scheepvaart NV v Administrator of Hungarian Property* [1954] AC 584, *Construction Industry Training Board v Labour Force Ltd* [1970] 3 All ER 220 applied.

The applicants' appeal would, accordingly, be dismissed.

Notes

For categories of workers: servants and independent contractors, see *Harvey on Industrial Relations and Employment Law* Division A.1.A and C.

For characteristics of the relationship of master and servant, see ibid Division A.3.

The right to a statement of initial employment particulars is now contained in s 1 of the Employment Rights Act 1996.

For the Employment Rights Act 1996, see ibid Division Q.

Cases referred to in judgment

Bank voor Handel en Scheepvaart NV v Administrator of Hungarian Property [1954] AC 584, [1954] 1 All ER 969, 35 TC 311, HL.
Binding v Great Yarmouth Port and Haven Comrs (1923) 92 LJKB 377.
Construction Industry Training Board v Labour Force Ltd [1970] 3 All ER 220, DC.
Ferguson v John Dawson & Partners (Contractors) Ltd [1976] 3 All ER 817, [1976] 1 WLR 1213, [1976] IRLR 346, CA.
Global Plant Ltd v Secretary of State for Health and Social Security [1971] 3 All ER 385, [1972] 1 QB 139.
Market Investigations Ltd v Minister of Social Security [1968] 3 All ER 732, [1969] 2 QB 173.
Massey v Crown Life Insurance Co [1978] 2 All ER 576, [1978] 1 WLR 676, [1978] ICR 590, [1978] IRLR 31, CA.
Morren v Swinton and Pendlebury Borough Council [1965] 2 All ER 349, [1965] 1 WLR 576.
Winfield v London Philharmonic Orchestra Ltd [1979] ICR 726, EAT.
Young & Woods Ltd v West [1980] IRLR 201, CA.

Appeal

Richard Addison, Geoffrey Downs, Frank Rycroft and Averil Myrna Williams (the applicants) appealed from a decision of the industrial tribunal that the applicants were not employees of the London Philharmonic Orchestra Ltd (the respondent) as defined by s 153 of the Employment Protection (Consolidation) Act 1978.

Michael Spencer (instructed by *Compton Carr*) for the applicants.
Anthony Scrivener QC and *Caroline Moore* (instructed by *Charles Russell*) for the respondent.

Airfix Footwear Ltd v Cope

EMPLOYMENT APPEAL TRIBUNAL
SLYNN J, A L T TAYLOR AND J D HUGHES
28 JUNE 1978

Contracts of employment—Meaning of 'employee'—Unfair dismissal—Exclusions and qualifications—meaning of 'employee'—Trade Union and Labour Relations Act 1974 s 30(1), Sch 1 para 4.

For seven years Mrs Cope had worked at home making heels for the shoes manufactured by the appellant company. When she began, she was given some training and, thereafter, supplied with patterns, gauges, materials, tools and equipment and glue for the purpose of doing her work. Materials and patterns were delivered each day to her home at about 4 pm. She generally worked five days a week, with occasional breaks when demand was low. She worked according to instructions issued by the company. She was also warned that the glues were highly inflammable and that she must ensure that there was adequate ventilation. She was paid what were called 'wages' on a piecework basis. National insurance contributions and income tax were not deducted. On these facts, an industrial tribunal held as a preliminary point that Mrs Cope was employed by the appellants under a contract of employment within the meaning of s 30(1) of the Trade Union and Labour Relations Act and was thus entitled to make a complaint of unfair dismissal. The company appealed against this decision arguing that there was no contract of employment or, alternatively, that if there was, it was not a single contract but a series of contracts, one for each day, which automatically terminated at the end of the day.

Held—The industrial tribunal was entitled to come to the conclusion that the respondent 'outworker' was employed under a contract of employment within the meaning of s 30(1) of the Trade Union and Labour Relations Act. The fact that for seven years, generally five days a week, the appellants had delivered 12 dozen pairs of heels each day to the respondent for her to work on, except when lesser quantities were available, meant that there had grown up between the appellants and the respondent a continuing relationship in the sense of a continuing contract of employment which met the definition set out in s 30(1). The industrial tribunal were thus entitled to conclude that they had jurisdiction to hear the respondent employee's complaint of unfair dismissal. Nor had the industrial tribunal erred in failing to consider whether there was here a series of contracts rather than one contract. In deciding that the overriding contract was a contract of employment, the industrial tribunal must have implicitly decided that there was not, as was argued on behalf of the appellants, a separate contract of employment on each day that heels were delivered to the respondent.

The company's appeal would therefore be dismissed.

Notes

For categories of workers, see *Harvey on Industrial Relations and Employment Law* Division A.1.

For characteristics of the relationship of master and servant, see ibid, Division A.3.

Cases referred to in judgment

Global Plant Ltd v Secretary of State for Health and Social Security [1971] 3 All ER 385, [1972] 1 QB 139.
Mailway (Southern) Ltd v Willsher [1978] ICR 511, [1978] IRLR 322, EAT.
Market Investigations Ltd v Minister of Social Security [1968] 3 All ER 732, [1969] 2 QB 173

Mr R J Walker (instructed by *Malcom C Foy & Co*) for Mrs Cope.
Mr P Turl (instructed by *Walker & Son*) for the company.

Alpine (Double Glazing) Co Ltd v Secretary of State for Social Services

QUEEN'S BENCH DIVISION
SIR DOUGLAS FRANK QC
7 APRIL 1982

Employment—Contract of service—Distinction between contract for services and contract of service—Engineers engaged on 'self-employed' basis by company—Company making out work schedules and providing vans and equipment for use by engineers—Engineers giving priority to company's work—Whether contract of service.

P and W were service engineers working for the company in its business as double glazing specialists. They worked on a 'self-employed' basis. P and W were paid a weekly retainer by the company and a sum for each ordinary visit to the company's customers. They paid class 2 national insurance contributions; their dealings with the Revenue and Customs and Excise were appropriate to persons employed otherwise than under a contract of service. The company's service manager made out daily work schedules a week in advance for them listing each of the company's customers to be visited on each working day at times requested by the customers. P and W met the manager each Friday and were given the next week's work schedule. They discussed any special feature of a call, obtained from the company's depot any of the company's products likely to be needed in connection with the following week's work and loaded it into their vans. The work schedules were made out on the basis that seven or eight calls a day were made. On average P and W worked an eight hour day. Each week P and W handed in their completed work schedules for the past week and received their cheques for their retainers and visits. The company was under no obligation as to the amount of work provided for P and W. They carried out their visits in vans belonging to the company and bearing its insignia. P and W supplied their own basic tools. The company provided them with mastic guns, ladders and rivet guns. There was no day-to-day supervision of quality by the company but if a customer was dissatisfied with the quality of work done the service manager sent P or W back to do the work again without further payment. P and W were expected to telephone in once a day in case there was work for which they were required as a matter of urgency. They received two weeks holiday pa whilst on a retainer from the company. They were not entitled to receive the retainer in the event of sickness although special arrangements could be made. In the event of sickness they were expected to send in a medical certificate. They were expected to give priority to the work scheduled by the company over any other work they might have. Neither side was entitled to notice of termination but P and W and the company regarded themselves as bound in honour to give reasonable notice. The Secretary of State decided that P and W were employed under a contract of service and included in the category of employed earner for the purposes of s 2(1)(a) of the Social Security Act 1975 so that the company was liable as a secondary contributor to pay national insurance contributions in respect of them. The company appealed.

Held—The label which the parties chose to use to describe their relationship could not alter or decide their true relationship but in deciding what that relationship was, the expression by them was relevant but not conclusive. A contract of service existed if three conditions were fulfilled: (i) the servant agreed that, in consideration of a wage or other remuneration, he would provide his own work and skill in the performance of some service for his master; (ii) he agreed expressly or impliedly that in the performance of that service he would be subject to the other's control in a sufficient degree to make that other master; (iii) the other provisions of the contract were consistent with its being a contract of service. In the instant case condition (i) was clearly fulfilled. As to condition (ii), the facts found showed that the control of the company was exercised at a number of points. The company's service managers made out the daily work schedules giving a list of customers to be visited in each day of the week and at the end of the week the men handed in their completed schedules. The men made their visits in vans belonging to the company, which also provided some of the equipment. The service manager sent a man back again if there was a complaint. The men were expected to give priority to the company's work. The company provided any materials, such as glass, likely to be needed. It was apparent that the control which the company had the right to exercise was very extensive indeed, and was so extensive as to be entirely consistent with a contract of service and inconsistent with an independent business. The fact that the men had a limited discretion was to when they would do the work was not inconsistent with a contract of service, nor of their hypothetical freedom to work for others. The degree of control exercised by the company was such as to be more consistent with a contract of service than a contract of services. As to condition (iii), there was nothing in the other findings of fact inconsistent with a contract of service. The informal arrangements relating to sick pay, holidays and notice of termination were not necessarily inconsistent with a contract of service; but such arrangements were not consistent with a man carrying on his own business.

Ready Mixed Concrete (South East) Ltd v Minister of Pensions and National Insurance [1968] 2 QB 497 and *Market Investigations Ltd v Minister of Social Security* [1969] 2 QB 173 applied.

Accordingly, the company's appeal would be dismissed.

Notes

For categories of workers: servants and independent contractors, see *Harvey on Industrial Relations and Employment Law* Division A.1.A and C.

For characteristics of the relationship of master and servant, see ibid Division A.3.

Cases referred to in judgment

Global Plant Ltd v Secretary of State for Health and Social Security [1971] 3 All ER 385, [1972] 1 QB 139.

Market Investigations Ltd v Minister of Social Security [1968] 3 All ER 732, [1969] 2 QB 173.

Ready Mixed Concrete (South East) Ltd v Minister of Pensions and National Insurance [1968] 1 All ER 433, [1968] 2 QB 497.

WHPT Housing Association Ltd v Secretary of State for Social Services [1981] ICR 737.

Young & Woods Ltd v West [1980] IRLR 201, CA.

Appeal

Alpine (Double Glazing) Co Ltd (the company) appealed against the decision of the Secretary of State for Social Services that two of its service engineers were employed under contracts of service and that the company was liable as a secondary contributor to pay national insurance contributions in respect of them.

H de Lotbiniere (instructed by *Paisner & Co,* Leicester) for the company.

J Laws (instructed by the *Solicitor for the Secretary of State for Social Services*) for the Secretary of State.

Australian Mutual Provident Society v Chaplin and another

PRIVY COUNCIL

LORD DIPLOCK, LORD SIMON OF GLAISDALE, LORD FRASER OF TULLYBELTON, LORD RUSSELL OF KILLOWEN AND LORD SCARMAN

14 MARCH 1978

Employment—Contract of service—Distinction between contract for services and contract of service—Written agreement between representative and insurance society stating that relationship between representative and insurance society that of principal and agent not that of master and servant—Whether contract of service—Whether entire contract contained in written agreement—Whether written agreement amended or varied.

The respondent, C, was appointed a representative of the A M P Society (the appellant) in 1967. The terms of the appointment were set out in a detailed written agreement. Clause 3 of the agreement provided that the relationship between the appellant and the respondent was that of principal and agent and not that of master and servant. The agreement also provided, inter alia: in cl 5, that the business of C's agency was to be conducted in a manner approved by the appellant and in accordance with practices laid down by the appellant and advised to C from time to time; in cl 6, that C's appointment as an agent might be terminated by either party to the agreement at any time; and, in cl 12, that the appellant's consent was required before C entered into any partnership in connection with its business or any continuing arrangement which provided for his commission earnings to be shared with another agent. C also had the right to appoint sub-agents and the right to incorporate. C claimed that as the appellant's representative he was employed by the appellant under a contract of service, so falling within the definition of 'worker' in the Long Service Leave (South Australia) Act 1967, and consequently entitled to certain benefits under that Act. The Supreme Court of Australia upheld the finding of the Industrial Court that C was employed under a contract of service. The appellant appealed.

Held—The written agreement was the principal, though not the only, source of information as to the nature of the contractual relationship between the parties. Clearly cl 3 of the agreement, which if it stood alone would be conclusive in favour of the appellant, could not receive effect according to its terms if they contradicted the effect of the agreement as a whole. Nevertheless, cl 3 was important and the correct way in which it could properly be used by the court was that if the true relationship of the parties was that of master and servant under a contract of service, the parties could not alter the truth of that relationship by putting a different label upon it; on the other hand, if their relationship was ambiguous and capable of being one or the other, then the parties could remove that ambiguity, by the very agreement itself which they made with one another. The agreement itself then became the best material from which to gather the true legal relationship between them. In the instant case, where there was no reason to think that the clause was a sham or that it was not a genuine statement of the parties' intentions, it had to be given its proper weight in relation to other clauses in the agreement. If cl 5 stood alone it would be a strong indication of a relationship of master and servant. But the effect of reading the clauses together was that cl 5 was coloured by cl 3 and ought to be read as applying only to such practices as could be laid down by a principal for his agent. Clause 6 did not confer on the appellant a power to dismiss its representatives, but merely provided that the appointment might be terminated by either party without notice. Accordingly, that clause was neutral. There were a number of clauses which pointed clearly to the conclusion that the contract was one for services. The first was cl 12 which recognised that the respondent had a right to enter into a partnership in connection with the appellant's business. An even stronger indication to the same effect was the agent's right to appoint sub-agents. That power of unlimited delegation was almost conclusive against the contract being a contract of service. The unlimited extent of the power of delegation was one consequence of the striking absence of any express obligation upon the respondent to perform any particular duties, or to work any particular hours, or indeed to do any work at all on behalf of the appellant. Payment wholly by commission was not by itself fatal to the respondent's claim, but the absence of an obligation to do any work for the appellant was a strong indication that he was not their servant. A further important indication was the right of the respondent to incorporate himself. It might not be impossible for a body corporate to be a servant but the concept was certainly unfamiliar. Clause 14 referred to employees of the agent and this was an indication against a contract of service. The conclusion to be drawn from a detailed examination of the written agreement was that it was providing for a contract of agency and not of service. However, it was possible that the contract made in 1967 might have been amended or varied by the subsequent actings of the parties, as well as by written amendments. The freedom enjoyed by the respondent to work when and where he chose was to be regarded as indicia in favour of agency. However, his freedom in those respects involved no departure from the terms of the written agreement. There was no importance to be attached to the fact that the respondent described himself in his income tax returns as a consultant. But what did appear to be important was the relatively large amount that he claimed in respect of business expenses which included commission to sub-agents, wages to secretarial staff, depreciation of motor car and office furniture and equipment. Nearly half his gross income and more than half his commission went in expenses. Such a high ratio appeared much more consistent with the view that the taxpayer was carrying on a business of his own than with the view that he was an employee under a contract of service. Accordingly, the effect of the written contract was not varied in any material respect by the subsequent conduct of the parties and the conclusion which necessarily emerged from the facts was that the respondent was not employed under a contract of service.

Notes

For categories of workers: servants, independent contractors and agents, see *Harvey on Industrial Relations and Employment Law* Division A.1.A, C and H.

For characteristics of the relationship of master and servant, see ibid Division A.3.

Cases referred to in judgment

Massey v Crown Life Insurance Co [1978] 2 All ER 576, [1978] 1 WLR 676, [1978] ICR 590, [1978] IRLR 31, CA.
Miller (James) & Partners Ltd v Whitworth Street Estates (Manchester) Ltd [1970] AC 583, [1970] 1 All ER 796, HL.
Montreal v Montreal Locomotive Works Ltd [1947] 1 DLR 161, PC.
Murphy v Ross [1920] 2 IR 199.
Mutual Aid Permanent Benefit Building Society, Re, ex p James (1883) 49 LT 530.
Robinson v Hill [1910] 1 KB 94, DC.
Schuler (L) AG v Wickman Machine Tool Sales Ltd [1974] AC 235, [1973] 2 All ER 39, HL.

Appeal

The Australian Mutual Provident Society appealed against a decision of the Full Court of the Supreme Court of South Australia discharging an order nisi for certiorari made by Hogarth J on 29 April 1977 directed to Judge Allan, a judge of the Industrial Court of South Australia. Judge Allan had found that the respondent, Mr Chaplin, was employed under a contract of service and was therefore a 'worker' within s 3(1) of the Long Service Leave Act (South Australia) 1967.

T R Morling QC, R G Matheson QC and *B A Beaumont* (instructed by *Knox & Hargreave*) for the appellant.
T M McRae and *C M Johnston* (instructed by *Reilly, Ahern & Kerin*) for the respondents.

Barnett v Brabyn (Inspector of Taxes)

CHANCERY DIVISION
LIGHTMAN J
16, 22 MAY 1996

Emoluments from office or employment—Employment—Meaning—Contract of service or contract for services—Taxpayer working under an oral agreement for a partnership carried on by his father and another—Whether contract of service or contract for services.

Appeal—Settlement by agreement—Additional assessment after agreement—Effect of agreement on appeal against additional assessments—Taxpayer assessed as self-employed—Appeals compromised on the basis that taxpayer self-employed—Additional assessments made on the basis that taxpayer self-employed—Whether taxpayer entitled to appeal additional assessments on the ground that not self-employed—Effect of compromise of previous assessments—Taxes Management Act 1970 s 54.

Between 1 December 1988 and 1 November 1990 B worked under an oral agreement for LTV, a partnership carried on by B's father and another. He worked only for LTV and was paid originally weekly and later monthly. B wanted to be a self-employed technician free to exploit alternative interests and LTV agreed. The parties intended and understood that B was to be self-employed and not an employee. The arrangement was that B should receive regular payments for work but that he should be able to nominate his own hours, work times, and absences, and that he, like the partners, should be responsible for the payment of his income tax and national insurance contributions. The parties thereafter acted to implement that agreement. B worked his own hours. A personal account in the books of LTV was opened in his name to which were debited payments of class 2 national insurance contributions and ultimately some Sch D tax. Income tax was not deducted at source from the payments made to B. B notified the Revenue that he was self-employed. He was assessed to tax for 1988–89, 1989–90 and 1990–91 on the basis that he was self-employed. His appeals against those assessments were compromised under s 54 of the Taxes Management Act 1970 on the basis that he was self-employed and the tax was duly paid. Additional assessments were made under Case I of Schedule D for 1989–90 and 1990–91 in respect of additional payments which were discovered to have been made by LTV to B on the basis that those payments were income of B's trade as a video and television technician. The General Commissioners upheld the additional assessments on the ground that B was self-employed. B appealed against the additional assessments contending that, despite the compromise of the previous assessments on the basis that he was self-employed, he was entitled to challenge the additional assessments on the ground that, whatever the intentions of the parties, his relationship with LTV bore all the badges of a contract of employment, and that those were inconsistent with his status being that of an independent contractor.

Held—(1) Although the commissioners' functions no longer included the making of assessments, their decision on an appeal was still not a decision on litigation between parties. Accordingly, a determination of an appeal by commissioners, or an agreement under s 54 which had the same effect as a determination of the appeal to that effect by the commissioners, did not afford scope for the application of the doctrine of res judicata or estoppel in respect of additional assessments for the same year, although a previous determination of a question might be a cogent factor on a subsequent determination of the same question. Otherwise a taxpayer who appealed an assessment and agreed a figure with the Revenue would be in a worse position with respect to an additional assessment than one who had not appealed and had permitted the first assessment to become final. It was therefore open to B to challenge the additional assessments on the ground that he was not self-employed.

(2) There was no one test which was conclusive for determining whether a particular engagement constituted employment or self-employment. The proper course for the court in each case, after first identifying the individual badges of potential significance, was to form an overall view giving due weight to the relative significance of the various badges in the particular case. While reference to authority might be of assistance in determining questions of law, a comparison of the badges to be found in the case in question and previous cases and an analysis of the relative weight afforded to particular badges in previous cases were generally unhelpful. Factors relevant in one situation might be irrelevant or of no weight in another. The relevant factors in the instant case were the fact that B had the right to control the amount of time he worked for LTV to enable him to exploit other interests, and there had been a clear agreement that B should be self-employed. Although such an agreement could not contradict the effect of a contract as a whole and had to be disregarded if inconsistent with the substantive terms or general effect of the contract as a whole, when the terms and general effect of the contract as a whole were consistent with either relationship, the parties' label might be decisive. The determinations of the previous assessments on the basis that B was self-employed were also a cogent factor. The commissioners were plainly correct in their decision that B was self-employed.

B's appeal would therefore be dismissed.

Notes

For the distinction between employment and self-employment, see *Simon's Direct Tax Service* E4.202–211.

For proceedings at a hearing, see ibid, A3.534.

For the Taxes Management Act 1970 s 54, see ibid, Part G2.

Cases referred to in judgment

Caffoor and others (Trustees of the Abdul Gaffoor Trust) v Comr of Income Tax, Colombo [1961] AC 584, [1961] 2 All ER 436, PC.

Edwards (Inspector of Taxes) v Bairstow [1956] AC 14, [1955] 3 All ER 48, 36 TC 207, HL.

Fall (Inspector of Taxes) v Hitchen [1973] STC 66, [1973] 1 WLR 286, [1973] 1 All ER 368, 49 TC 433.

Hall (Inspector of Taxes) v Lorimer [1994] STC 23, [1994] 1 WLR 209, [1994] 1 All ER 250, 66 TC 349, CA; affg [1992] STC 599, [1992] 1 WLR 939.

IRC v Sneath [1932] 2 KB 362, 17 TC 149, CA.

Lee Ting Sang v Chung Chi-Keung [1990] 2 AC 374, PC.
Market Investigations Ltd v Minister of Social Security [1969] 2 QB 173, [1968] 3 All ER 732.
Massey v Crown Life Insurance Co [1978] 1 WLR 676, [1978] 2 All ER 576, CA.
Narich Pty Ltd v Comr of Pay-Roll Tax [1984] ICR 286, PC.
O'Kelly v Trusthouse Forte plc [1984] QB 90, [1983] 3 All ER 456, CA.

Appeal

Spencer Allan Barnett (the taxpayer) appealed by way of case stated from the decision of the General Commissioners for the division of Flitt upholding additional assessments to income tax made under Case I of Sch D in respect of payments held to be income of the trade as a video and television technician.

Battersby v Campbell (Inspector of Taxes)

SPECIAL COMMISSIONER: DR NUALA BRICE
3 AUGUST, 12 SEPTEMBER 2001

National insurance—Earnings of workers supplied by service companies etc—Provision of services through intermediary—Taxpayer establishing personal service company—Company contracting with bank for provision of services—Taxpayer supplying services to bank through company—Whether company liable for national insurance contributions on payments made by bank to company—Whether, if arrangements had taken the form of a contract between taxpayer and bank, taxpayer would have been regarded as gainfully employed by the bank—Social Security Contributions (Intermediaries) Regulations 2000, SI 2000/727, reg 6(1)(c).

The taxpayer was a computer analyst and programmer. In 1988 he established a limited company (the service company) of which he and his wife were the sole directors. In 1994 the service company obtained a contract through an agency with a bank and the taxpayer started supplying his services to the bank through the service company. The bank paid the agency which in turn paid the service company. The taxpayer took his remuneration from the service company in the form of dividends. In 1996 the service company bought out the contract with the agency. Thereafter the taxpayer continued to work for the bank as a self-employed contractor supplying his services to the bank through the service company. In 1999 the bank consolidated the procurement of all its self-employed contractors through a limited company, Staff Agency Ltd. Thereafter the bank paid Staff Agency which paid the service company. The taxpayer continued to receive his remuneration in the form of dividends from the service company. The agreement between Staff Agency and the service company was initially for six months and later for twelve months at a time. Under the agreement the service company agreed that the taxpayer would devote his time, attention, skill and ability in accordance with the requirements of the bank at such location as the bank might reasonably require. The agreement specifically provided that it did not create the relationship of employer/employee between Staff Agency or the bank and the service or the taxpayer. The agreement also provided, inter alia, that the service company remained responsible for the taxpayer's sickness, disability and pension arrangements. Any absence of the taxpayer had to be agreed and approved in advance by the bank. Staff Agency could end the agreement at any time on four weeks' notice or with immediate effect if the taxpayer failed to meet certain professional standards. Responsibility for the quality, quantity and performance of the services rested with the bank at all times. At the bank's premises, the taxpayer managed a small group of people; two of whom were self-employed contractors and the rest of whom were permanent employees of the bank. In April 2001 the taxpayer accepted the bank's offer of a permanent position as an employee. The Social Security Contributions (Intermediaries)Regulations 2000, which came into effect on 4 April 2000, provided that, in certain stated circumstances, payments to service companies were to be treated as earnings paid to a worker in respect of an employment. Under reg 6(1) those regulations applied where:(a) an individual (the worker) personally performed services for the purposes of a business carried on by another person (the client); (b) the performance of those services by the worker was carried out, not under a contract directly between the client and the worker, but under arrangements involving an intermediary; and (c) the circumstances were such that, had the arrangements taken the form of a contract between the worker and the client, the worker would be regarded for the purposes of Pts I to V of the Social Security Contributions and Benefits Act 1992 as employed in employed earner's employment by the client. The Revenue considered that reg 6(1) was satisfied and that accordingly the taxpayer's personal service company was liable to pay primary and secondary Class I national insurance contributions in respect of the payments made to it by the bank during the period from 31 May to 29 November 2000. The taxpayer appealed. It was common ground that paras (a) and (b) of reg 6(1) applied and the sole issue in the appeal was whether the circumstances were such that, had the arrangements taken the form of a contract between the taxpayer and the bank, the taxpayer would be regarded for the purposes of the 1992 Act as employed in earner's employment by the bank within the meaning of reg 6(1)(c).

Held—'Employed earner' was defined in s 2(1)(a) of the 1992 Act as, inter alia, a person who was gainfully employed under a contract of service. Thus the issue to be decided was whether the taxpayer would have been gainfully employed under a contract of service if his contract had been with the bank and not with the service company. The relevant authorities had established the principle that the question as to whether a person was employed under a contract of service, or whether he was self-employed and provided a contract for services, was a question of fact in each case to be determined having regard to all the relevant circumstances. In the instant case, the factors which pointed towards there being a contract of service outweighed those which pointed towards there being a contract for services. Concentrating on the substance of the contractual arrangements rather than on their form, it was clear that, if the taxpayer had been employed under a contract with the bank, he would be regarded as being gainfully employed under a contract of service. Accordingly, if the arrangements had taken the form of a contract between the taxpayer and the bank, the taxpayer would be regarded for the purposes of the 1992 Act as employed in employed earner's employment by the bank and the taxpayer's appeal would therefore be dismissed.

Notes

For national insurance contributions on earnings paid through certain personal service companies, see *Simon's National Insurance Contributions Service* 8.346.

For the Social Security Contributions (Intermediaries)Regulations 2000, SI 2000/727, reg 6(1)(c), see *Simon's National Insurance Contributions Service* Part III.

Cases referred to in judgment

Bank voor Handel en Scheepvaart NV v Administrator of Hungarian Property [1954] AC 584, [1954] 1 All ER 969, 35 TC 311, HL

Carmichael v National Power plc [1999] ICR 1226, [1999] 4 All ER 897, HL.

Express and Echo Publications Ltd v Tanton [1999] ICR 693, CA.

Hall (Inspector of Taxes) v Lorimer [1994] STC 23, [1994] 1 WLR 209, [1994] 1 All ER 250, 66 TC 349, CA.

MacFarlane v Glasgow City Council [2001] IRLR 7, EAT.

Market Investigations Ltd v Minister of Social Security [1969] 2 QB 173, [1968] 3 All ER 732.

Massey v Crown Life Insurance Co [1978] 1 WLR 676, [1978] 2 All ER 576, CA.

McManus v Griffiths (Inspector of Taxes) [1997] STC 1089, 70 TC 218.

Morren v Swinton and Pendlebury BC [1965] 1 WLR 576, [1965] 2 All ER 349, DC.

O'Kelly v Trusthouse Forte plc [1984] QB 90, [1983] 3 All ER 456, CA.

O'Murphy v Hewlett-Packard Ltd (27 March 2001, unreported), ET.

R (on the application of Professional Contractors Group Ltd) v IRC [2001] EWHC Admin 236, [2001] STC 629.

Ready Mixed Concrete (South East) Ltd v Minister of Pensions and National Insurance [1968] 2 QB 497, [1968] 1 All ER 433.

The taxpayer appeared in person.
Barry Williams, Regional Advocacy Adviser, for the Revenue.

Bhadra v Ellam (Inspector of Taxes)

CHANCERY DIVISION
KNOX J
24, 25 NOVEMBER 1987

Emoluments from office or employment—Deduction from emoluments—Expenses necessarily incurred in the performance of duties of office or employment—Remuneration to doctor from agency engagements—Employment at below consultancy grades within hospital system—Whether taxpayer assessable under Sch E—Whether travelling and office expenses qualifying for relief—Finance (No 2) Act 1975 s 38—Income and Corporation Taxes Act 1970 s 189.

The taxpayer was a doctor who obtained several locum jobs at below consultant level through medical agencies. He was assessed under Sch E for the year 1983–84 on his earnings through these agencies on the basis that he satisfied the conditions imposed by s 38 of the Finance (No 2) Act 1975 under which the services a worker rendered a client were treated as duties of an office or employment with remuneration chargeable under Sch E where a worker rendered personal services to a client and was supplied through an agency. The taxpayer appealed to the General Commissioners contending that he should not be assessed under Sch E as he was in reality self-employed and did not fall within the conditions imposed by s 38 of the 1975 Act, and that if he was assessable under Sch E his expenses in respect of his wife's wages for secretarial services, travelling, meals and telephone calls qualified for relief within the terms of s 189 of the Income and Corporation Taxes Act 1970. The commissioners found as a fact, that the taxpayer had been supplied to the hospital authorities through the respective agencies and had rendered services under the terms of a contract made between himself and the agency; that although little supervision was in fact exercised, the hospital authority, through their consultants, had the right to supervise, direct or control the manner in which he carried out his duties; whether or not he was employed through an agency or directly, that the taxpayer, working as a doctor in the NHS had to have insurance cover against negligence claims both for regular and locum posts and also for agency engagements, but that his liability would be the same whatever the status of his employment. The taxpayer was not paid anything toward his travelling expenses between his home and the hospital while he was on an agency engagement and the commissioners found that his duties commenced when he arrived at the hospital. The commissioners found that the taxpayer had been correctly assessed and satisfied the conditions of s 38 of the 1975 Act and that his expenses for secretarial work and travelling were not allowable under s 189 of the 1970 Act. The taxpayer appealed.

Held—(1) The commissioners were entitled to conclude on the facts before them that the requirements imposed by s 38 of the 1975 Act had been satisfied and accordingly by virtue of that section, the services rendered by the taxpayer fell to be treated as if they were the duties of an office or employment and his income derived therefrom was assessable to tax under Sch E.

(2) The taxpayer's travelling and secretarial expenses came within the provisions of s 189 of the 1970 Act. However, since the taxpayer's work did not begin until he arrived at the hospital's premises, they were not deductible as they were not incurred in the performance of the duties of his office. The mere fact that the taxpayer was engaged in a profession which carried with it responsibilities was not sufficient for his expenses incurred in travelling to his work to qualify for relief under s 189 of the 1970 Act.

The appeal would therefore be dismissed.

Mitchell and Edon (Inspector of Taxes) v Ross [1962] AC 813, 40 TC 11 applied; *Pook (Inspector of Taxes) v Owen* [1970] AC 244, 45 TC 571 distinguished.

Cases referred to in judgment

Mitchell and Edon (Inspector of Taxes) v Ross [1962] AC 813, [1961] 3 All ER 49, 40 TC 11, HL.

Pook (Inspector of Taxes) v Owen [1970] AC 244, sub nom *Owen v Pook (Inspector of Taxes)* [1969] 2 All ER 1, 45 TC 571, HL.

Appeal

Dr Tushar Kanti Bhadra (the taxpayer) appealed by way of case stated from the decision of the General Commissioners for Chelmsford in which they upheld a Sch E assessment on emoluments which were earnings of the taxpayer through agencies.

The taxpayer appeared in person.
Alan Moses (instructed by the *Solicitor of Inland Revenue*) for the Crown.

Brady (Inspector of Taxes) v Hart (trading as Jaclyn Model Agency)

CHANCERY DIVISION
HARMAN J
19 MARCH 1985

Emoluments from office or employment—Deduction of tax by employer on payments of income assessable to tax—Failure to deduct tax—Employment agency—Agency supplying workers for sales promotions—Whether contract between agency and worker in respect of work done for third party—Whether agency liable to deduct tax under pay-as-you-earn system from workers' remuneration—Finance (No 2) Act 1975 s 38(1)(b).

The taxpayer, through the Jaclyn Model Agency (the agency), carried on the business of supplying workers for sales promotions. Most of the work was carried out for P Ltd. When P Ltd was engaged in a promotion it sent a form to the agency and when the agency had supplied the names of a number of workers, P Ltd nominated the workers whom it wanted to employ on that promotion. Payment for the workers' services was made by P Ltd to the agency and the agency deducted its fee before remitting the net amount to the worker. On occasion the agency would advance a worker up to a one week's remuneration before a promotion started and deduct that advance from the money it paid to the worker when it was paid by P Ltd. P Ltd exercised day-to-day supervision and control over the workers and, if necessary, dispensed with the services of an unsatisfactory worker and asked the agency for a replacement. In the year 1979–80 payments made by the agency to sales promotion workers totalled £12,343.97 from which tax was not deducted. The Revenue made a determination of the tax which should have been deducted by the agency in the sum of £2,061.05 on the grounds that the services of the workers were supplied under a contract between each worker and the agency; that, by virtue of s 38 of the Finance (No 2) Act 1975, the remuneration received by each worker under such a contract was chargeable to tax under Sch E; and that, under s 204 of the Income and Corporation Taxes Act 1970 the agency was obliged to deduct tax. The taxpayer appealed contending that there was no relevant contract between the agency and the workers for the purposes of s 38(1)(b). The General Commissioners inferred from the primary facts that there was no relevant contract between the agency and the workers because the agency could not be sued by P Ltd for a worker's failure to fulfil her obligations and allowed the taxpayer's appeal. The Crown appealed.

Held—There was a relevant contract between the worker and the agency within the meaning of s 38(1)(b), ie a unilateral oral contract, made when the agency contacted a worker, in terms that, on the worker supplying services to P Ltd, the agency would pay her for that work. It followed that the agency was required to deduct Sch E tax from payments made to the workers. The appeal would therefore be allowed.

Notes

For workers supplied by agencies, see *Simon's Direct Tax Service* E4.204.

Case referred to in judgment

Edwards (Inspector of Taxes) v Bairstow [1956] AC 14, [1955] 3 All ER 48, 36 TC 207, HL.

Appeal

The taxpayer appealed by way of case stated from the decision of the General Commissioners for the Wymondham, Norfolk division that the taxpayer was not obliged to deduct tax as an employer from payments made by it to workers it supplied for sales promotions.

Robert Carnwath (instructed by the *Solicitor of Inland Revenue*) for the Crown.
Geoffrey Jaques (instructed by *Hill & Perks,* Norwich) for the taxpayer.

BSM (1257) Ltd and another v Secretary of State for Social Services

QUEEN'S BENCH DIVISION
SIR DOUGLAS FRANK QC (SITTING AS A DEPUTY JUDGE OF THE QUEEN'S BENCH DIVISION)
14, 15 FEBRUARY, 7 MARCH 1978

Employment—Contract of service—Distinction between contract for services and contract of service—Driving instructor employed by company under contract of service—Company reorganising business and incorporating new companies—Driving instructor and new company entering into new contract providing for driving instructor to work as independent contractor—Whether contract for services—Whether new contract changing status of driving instructor from employed person to independent contractor.

T was employed by BSM Ltd as a driving instructor under its standard conditions of employment. In 1973 BSM Ltd was reorganised and in 1974 T's contract was terminated and he started working for BSM (1257) Ltd (the company) under the terms of a new contract. The purpose of the new contract was to change T's status from an employee under a contract of service to that of an independent contractor working under a contract for services. The new contract, inter alia, provided that T would receive fees and commissions for his work at set rates, stated that T would be an independent contractor and liable as a self-employed person for national insurance and prohibited T from providing driving lessons and advising on driving tuition in competition with the business of the company. T was entitled to give notice of the times when he did not wish to teach and there was no obligation on the company to provide work for T. He gave driving lessons to pupils provided by the company in a car provided by the company. The company applied for a decision of the Secretary of State as to whether T was an employed person for national insurance purposes. The Secretary of State's decision was that T was an employed person. The company and T appealed.

Held—Undoubtedly T was a 'company man' in that he gave instruction in a car owned, maintained and fuelled by the company and his pupils were provided exclusively by the company. On the other hand, T was paid only on commission without any guaranteed amount and without any requirement on his part to work full-time or indeed any specified minimum time for the company. The fact of T being a 'company man' was certainly not conclusive of a contract of service, although in the absence of other factors it would be very persuasive. However, the reality of the matter was that the parties entered into the agreement for the express purpose of changing T's status to that of a self-employed person and what they intended to do clearly was to incorporate only such terms as were consistent with that relationship. It followed that unless it could be shown that there were provisions inconsistent with that relationship or that in practice the relationship was other than that stated in the contract, the label they had put upon it had to be accepted. Although some of the provisions of the contract were more appropriate for an employee than an independent contractor, none of them was inconsistent with the latter relationship. There being nothing in the contract or in practice irreconcilable with the assertion in the contract, that assertion had to be accepted.

Massey v Crown Life Insurance Co [1978] 1 WLR 676 applied.

Accordingly, the appeal of the company and T would be allowed.

Notes

For categories of workers: servants and independent contractors, see *Harvey on Industrial Relations and Employment Law* Division A.1.A and C.

For characteristics of the relationship of master and servant, see ibid Division A.3.

Cases referred to in judgment

Construction Industry Training Board v Labour Force Ltd [1970] 3 All ER 220, DC.

Ferguson v John Dawson & Partners (Contractors) Ltd [1976] 3 All ER 817, [1976] 1 WLR 1213, [1976] IRLR 346, CA.

Graham (Maurice) Ltd v Brunswick (1974) 16 KIR 158, DC.

Massey v Crown Life Insurance Co [1978] 2 All ER 576, [1978] 1 WLR 676, [1978] ICR 590, [1978] IRLR 31, CA.

Ready Mixed Concrete (South East) Ltd v Minister of Pensions and National Insurance [1968] 1 All ER 433, [1968] 2 QB 497.

Smith v General Motor Cab Co Ltd [1911] AC 188, HL.

Appeal

BSM (1257) Ltd (the company) and Barry Thorn appealed from the decision of the Secretary of State for Social Services that Mr Thorn was an employed person and employed in insurable employment after ceasing employment with BSM Ltd under a contract of service and commencing work for the company, after a reorganisation of BSM Ltd into a number of new companies, under a new contract which provided for his status to be an independent contractor.

Gerald Godfrey QC and *Reginald Nock* (instructed by *Titmuss, Sainer & Webb*) for the company and Mr Thorn.
Philip Otton QC and *Harry Woolf* (instructed by the *Solicitor for the Department of Health and Social Security*) for the Secretary of State.

Calder v H Kitson Vickers & Sons Engineering Ltd

COURT OF APPEAL (CIVIL DIVISION)
KERR, RALPH GIBSON AND RUSSELL LJJ
7, 8, 9, 30 JULY 1987

Employment—Contract of service—Distinction between contract for services and contract of service—Worker employed in breaking up ship—Employer supplying equipment—Employer's liability insurance covering employees and labour only sub-contractors—Worker severely injured by faulty equipment—Whether worker employed under contract of service—Whether labour only sub-contractor.

C worked on and off for K V & Sons Ltd for many years, sometimes as an employee and sometimes as a labour only sub-contractor. His two most recent engagements were as an employee, as a lorry driver and as helping to break up a steelworks. C was asked by a director of K V & Sons Ltd if he wanted a job with good money working away from home and went to work at the docks at breaking up a minesweeper and recovering the metal. The breaking of the superstructure of the minesweeper had already been done and C went to replace one member of the three man team working on it. The men were paid on a tonnage recovered basis depending on the amount of metal recovered. The yard manager calculated the amount for the tonnage removed by the work of the team and paid it in cash, usually to C, who collected it and shared it with his mates. K V & Sons Ltd made no deduction for tax or national insurance contributions. The equipment used by the team, which included a dock-side crane and a wrecking ball and trigger arm was provided by K V & Sons Ltd who employed the crane driver. The yard manager and the safety officer would go on their rounds and check on the standards being achieved. If the crane broke down the yard manager would move the wrecking team to do other work. The mechanism of the crane and wrecking ball was in an unsafe state and part of the machinery fell on C, injuring him severely. C claimed damages for personal injury, loss and damage against K V & Sons Ltd. K V & Sons Ltd's insurers were later joined in the proceedings as second defendants. The High Court held that C was an employee of K V & Sons Ltd (whose contract of insurance provided cover for injuries arising to employees and labour only sub-contractors). The judge also held that K

V & Sons Ltd had been negligent, assessing C's contributory negligence at 25%, awarded damages, interest and costs to C and made a declaration that the insurers were liable to indemnify K V & Sons Ltd. K V & Sons Ltd and the insurers appealed contending, inter alia, that C was neither an employee nor a labour only sub-contractor.

Held—(1) (Russell LJ dissenting) The fact that the arrangements under which the team was paid provided for the payment of a lump sum, based on the tonnage recovered in the week and that K V & Sons Ltd were not concerned with the division of that sum was a fact relevant to the determination of the status of C but on the facts the insurers could not show that, because of the terms as to payment of remuneration, a necessary condition for proof of a contract of service was for that reason alone not satisfied. There was no doubt that the remuneration agreed to be paid to a number of workmen could be based upon the results of the work of all of them, and be provided to be paid to them all as a group for division by themselves, without the relationship of the individual workman to the employer being by that fact alone rendered incapable of being that of master and servant. A man was without question free under the law to contract to carry out certain work for another without entering into a contract of service. Since the law looked to the substance and not form, the fact that the parties honestly intended that between themselves the contract should be a contract for services and not of service was not conclusive but it was a relevant fact, and when parties did deliberately agree for the man to be self-employed it might afford strong evidence that that was their real relationship. The court had to have regard to all the relevant factors, which included the nature and degree of control over the work to be done, the methods of doing the work, the hours of work and the selection and provision of tools and equipment. Factors which might be of importance were what degree of financial risk the man took, what degree of responsibility for investment he had, and whether and how far he had an opportunity of profiting from sound management in the performance of his task. In the instant case, first, C had worked for K V & Sons Ltd for many years, sometimes as a self-employed labour only sub-contractor and sometimes as an employee. He worked on the terms which seemed to him the most advantageous and to which the employer would agree. He had been working as a servant driving a lorry. He agreed to do different work on the minesweeper on different terms under a changed status and there was no reason to doubt the genuineness of the intention on either side to change that status. Secondly, C agreed to work on breaking up the minesweeper as a self-employed person. There was no basis for inferring that K V & Sons Ltd could under the contract have required him to do any other work, still less that as a matter of contractual right they could have required him to cease work on the minesweeper on the basis of being paid for tonnage recovered and go to some other work at some other place. Thirdly, C went from the job of driving a lorry to take the well paid job of breaking up the minesweeper. There was no basis for holding that it would have been open to K V & Sons Ltd under the terms agreed to return him to driving a lorry; it was obvious that C could have insisted upon staying to finish the work on the minesweeper and could have recovered damages for any estimated loss of earnings if his work there had been wrongly terminated at an earlier date. Fourthly, the evidence showed that the team was left to decide how to do the work and the hours during which they would work. The way they worked and the hours they worked directly affected the amount they would earn. That relationship of the parties was consistent with the self-employed status of C which the parties intended to establish, and which they thought they had established, being a real relationship and not a mere device. A declaration by the parties that a workman was to be self-employed, or a term having like effect, when agreed, was strong evidence that that was the real relationship. When such a term was agreed by the parties it affected their actions and other obligations, for example with reference to the deduction of tax and, so far as concerned the employer, the nature of the insurance that he would need and the information which he had to give to his insurers. The decision did not depend on the circumstances in which the question was raised. Accordingly, at the material time, C was a self-employed labour only contractor and not an employee on a contract of service.

(2) K V & Sons Ltd had failed in the duty of care owed to C to see that the operation of breaking the minesweeper was reasonably safe and accordingly were liable in negligence.

Ready Mixed Concrete (South East) Ltd v Minister of Pensions and National Insurance [1968] 2 QB 497 and *Massey v Crown Life Insurance Co* [1978] 2 All ER 576 applied. *Ferguson v John Dawson & Partners (Contractors) Ltd* [1976] 3 All ER 817 distinguished.

The appeal of K V & Sons Ltd and the insurers would therefore be dismissed.

Notes

For categories of workers: servants and independent contractors, see *Harvey on Industrial Relations and Employment Law* Division A.1.A and C.

For characteristics of the relationship of master and servant, see ibid Division A.3.

Cases referred to in judgment

Ferguson v John Dawson & Partners (Contractors) Ltd [1976] 3 All ER 817, [1976] 1 WLR 1213, [1976] IRLR 346, CA.

Global Plant Ltd v Secretary of State for Health and Social Security [1971] 3 All ER 385, [1972] 1 QB 139.

Market Investigations Ltd v Minister of Social Security [1968] 3 All ER 732, [1969] 2 QB 173.

Massey v Crown Life Insurance Co [1978] 2 All ER 576, [1978] 1 WLR 676, [1978] ICR 590, [1978] IRLR 31, CA.

Membery v Great Western Rly Co (1889) 14 App Cas 179, HL.

Ready Mixed Concrete (South East) Ltd v Minister of Pensions and National Insurance [1968] 1 All ER 433, [1968] 2 QB 497.

Appeal

H Kitson Vickers & Sons (Engineers) Ltd and Iron Trades Mutual Insurance Co Ltd appealed against an order of French J made on 31 July 1986 awarding damages in negligence for personal injuries suffered by James William Calder in an industrial accident.

Graham Machin and *Stephen Beresford* (instructed by *Whitfield Son & Hallam,* Dewsbury) for Iron Trades Mutual Insurance Co Ltd.
Giles Wingate-Saul QC and *Timothy White* (instructed by *Robert Leach Brooks & Co,* Blackpool) for Mr Calder.

Carmichael and another v National Power plc

HOUSE OF LORDS
LORD IRVINE OF LAIRG LC, LORD GOFF OF CHIEVELEY, LORD JAUNCEY OF TULLICHETTLE, LORD BROWNE-WILKINSON AND LORD HOFFMANN
11, 12 OCTOBER, 18 NOVEMBER 1999

Employment—Contract of service—Written particulars of employment—Appellant's predecessor making written offer of employment to respondents on 'casual as required basis'—Respondents giving written acceptance of offer and working on invitation when available and choosing to work—Respondents claiming to be entitled to written particulars of terms of employment as employees under contracts of employment—Tribunal inferring from documents, surrounding circumstances and parties' conduct that no contractual relationship existed when respondents not working—Whether tribunal entitled to do so—Whether issue to be determined solely by reference to documents.

In 1989 the appellant's predecessor, CEGB, advertised for tour guides to work at its power station on 'a casual as required basis', and subsequently made a written offer of employment to the respondents on that basis. Both respondents signed and returned a pre-typed reply letter stating that they accepted 'the offer of employment . . . on a casual as required basis'. The documents contained no provisions for notice of termination and said nothing about when, how or with what frequency guide work would be offered. The sickness, holiday and pension arrangements for regular staff did not apply; nor did the grievance and disciplinary procedures. After accepting the offers, the respondents worked as guides on invitation when they were available and chose to work, and no disciplinary measures were taken when they were not so available. Subsequently, the respondents claimed that they were employees under contracts of employment and that they were therefore entitled to written particulars of the terms of their employment under s 1(1) of the Employment Protection (Consolidation) Act 1978. The industrial tribunal rejected that contention, holding that the respondents were not in any contractual relationship with CEGB when they were not working. In reaching that conclusion, the tribunal took into account the language of the documentation, the way in which it had been operated and the evidence of the parties as to how it had been understood. The tribunal's decision was upheld by the Employment Appeal Tribunal, but reversed by the Court of Appeal which treated the matter solely as one of construction of the documents and therefore as one of law rather than fact. The appellant appealed to the House of Lords.

Held—Unless it appeared from the terms of documents, or from what was done or said at the time or subsequently, that the parties intended those documents to form an exclusive memorial of their relationship, it was not appropriate to determine the nature of that relationship solely by reference to the documents. Moreover, the question of whether the parties intended a document or documents to be the exclusive record of the terms of their agreement was a question of fact. In the instant case, the tribunal had to be taken to have decided that the documents were not so intended, and that they merely constituted one, albeit important, relevant source of material from which the parties' true intentions were to be inferred, together with the surrounding circumstances and the parties' subsequent conduct. On the basis of that material, the tribunal had been entitled to infer that the parties had not intended in 1989, or subsequently, that their relationship was to be regulated by contract when the respondents were not working as guides. Accordingly, the appeal would be allowed.

Moore v Garwood (1849) 4 Exch 681 applied.

Notes

For the characteristics of the employment relationship and for written particulars of terms of employment, see 16 *Halsbury's Laws* (4th edn reissue) paras 3, 59 respectively.

Section 1 of the Employment Protection (Consolidation) Act 1978 has been replaced by s 1 of the Employment Rights Act 1996. For s 1 of the 1996 Act, see 16 *Halsbury's Statutes* (4th edn) (2000 reissue) 590.

Cases referred to in opinions

Clark v Oxfordshire Health Authority [1998] IRLR 125, CA.
Davies v Presbyterian Church of Wales [1986] 1 All ER 705, [1986] 1 WLR 323, HL.
Miller (James) & Partners Ltd v Whitworth Street Estates (Manchester) Ltd [1970] 1 All ER 796, [1970] AC 583, [1970] 2 WLR 728, HL.
Moore v Garwood (1849) 4 Exch 681, 154 ER 1388, Ex Ch.
Nethermere (St Neots) Ltd v Gardiner [1984] ICR 612, CA.

Appeal

National Power plc, the operator of Blyth Power Stations, Northumberland, appealed with the leave of the House of Lords given on 23 July 1998 from the decision of the Court of Appeal (Ward and Chadwick LJJ; Kennedy LJ dissenting) on 27 March 1998 ([1998] ICR 1167) allowing the appeal of the respondents, Heather Carmichael and Janet Leese, from the decision of the Employment Appeal Tribunal on 24 May 1996 dismissing their appeal against the decision of an industrial tribunal at Newcastle upon Tyne on 19 July 1995 dismissing their applications for written particulars of their terms of employment as tour guides at the power stations.

David Pannick QC and *Sean Wilken* (instructed by *Paisner & Co*) for National Power.
Brian Langstaff QC and *Tess Gill* (instructed by *Andrew Freer*) for Mrs Carmichael and Mrs Leese.

Catamaran Cruisers Ltd v Williams and others

EMPLOYMENT APPEAL TRIBUNAL
TUDOR EVANS J, T S BATHO AND P TURNER
15 FEBRUARY 1994

Contracts of employment—Meaning of 'employee'—Unfair dismissal—Other substantial reason for dismissal—Sufficiency of reason for dismissal—reasonableness in the circumstances—other substantial reason—Employment Protection (Consolidation) Act 1978 ss 57(1)(b), 57(3).

The seven respondents were all employed by the appellant company in connection with its operation of river bus and pleasure cruise services on the river Thames. The company was in a serious financial state when it was purchased by a French company in 1991. The new owners wanted to improve safety and efficiency, and at various meetings with the employees' union, the TGWU, proposals for new contracts of service were put forward. Eventually, new terms and conditions were agreed which were accepted by many of the employees concerned. The respondents, however, considered that the new contracts were unsatisfactory and refused to accept them. As a consequence, they were dismissed. The employers contested the employees' complaints of unfair dismissal on the ground that the change to the new contracts was for a sound business reason, that the dismissals, therefore, were for 'some other substantial reason' within s 57(1)(b) of the Employment Protection (Consolidation) Act and that, in the circumstances, they were fair. According to the industrial tribunal, the principle of law to be applied in such cases is that, 'if the new terms are much less favourable to the employee than were the old terms, then unless the business reasons are so pressing that it is absolutely vital for the survival of the employer's business that the terms be accepted, the employee is not unreasonable in refusing to accept those terms and, consequently, any dismissal of him for a refusal to accept is unfair'. The Tribunal thus embarked upon a comparison of the old and new contracts of employment and the employers' motives for making the changes. It concluded that the new terms were much less favourable to the employees and that the company's financial position was not sufficiently serious to require the imposition of those terms. Accordingly, the dismissals were held to have been unfair. The employers appealed against that decision on the ground that the tribunal had directed itself according to a wrong principle of law. They also appealed against the tribunal's finding that one of the claimants, Mr Williams, was an 'employee' and thus qualified to complain of unfair dismissal, notwithstanding that, in recent years, he had provided his services through a limited company.

Held—The industrial tribunal had erred in holding that the respondent employees had been unfairly dismissed for refusing to accept new terms of employment which were much less favourable than their existing ones, in circumstances in which acceptance of the new terms was not vital for the survival of the employers' business. The basis upon which the tribunal had reached that decision was wrong in principle and unsupported by authority.

There is no principle of law that if the new terms of a contract of employment are much less favourable to an employee than the terms of the old contract, dismissal of the employee for refusing to accept them will be unfair unless the business reasons are so pressing that it is vital for the survival of the employer's business that the new terms are accepted. Such a proposition is not supported by any of the authorities dealing with the need for business reorganisation. It is a principle of law, however, that the tribunal must examine the employer's motives for the changes and satisfy itself that they are not sought to be imposed for arbitrary reasons. What has to be carried out is a balancing process.

The appeal would be allowed and the case remitted to the same industrial tribunal. In reconsidering the reasonableness of the dismissals, the tribunal should not look solely at the advantage or disadvantage of the new contracts from the employees' point of view but should also consider and take into account the benefit to the employers in imposing the changes. It should make an express finding as to whether it accepts the employers' evidence that the reorganisation was partly based on the question of safety and, if so, what effect that has on the reasonableness of the dismissals. An express finding should also be made as to whether the dismissals were reasonable in light of the fact that many employees accepted the new terms. The tribunal should also consider the question of reasonableness in the light of any evidence that the employees' trade union recommended the changes.

The industrial tribunal had not erred in finding that the respondent Mr Williams was an 'employee' of the appellants, and thus entitled to claim unfair dismissal, notwithstanding that in recent years he had provided his services to them through a limited company.

There is no rule of law that the importation of a limited company into the relationship prevents the continuation of a contract of employment. If the true relationship is that of employer and employee, it cannot be changed by putting a different label on it. Whether or not the contract in question is one of service or one for services is a question of fact. The formation of a company may be strong evidence of a change of status but that fact has to be evaluated in the context of all the other facts found.

In the present case, it was clear from the industrial tribunal's findings of fact that, save for the gross payments made to the limited company and described as a 'fee', there was no factual change whatsoever in Mr Williams's employment. In the circumstances, therefore, the tribunal was right to find that he worked for the appellants under a contract of service.

Cases referred to in judgment

Chubb Fire Security Ltd v Harper [1983] IRLR 311, EAT.
Ellis v Brighton Co-operative Society Ltd [1976] IRLR 419, EAT.
Evans v Elemeta Holdings Ltd [1982] IRLR 143, EAT.
Genower v Ealing, Hammersmith and Hounslow Area Health Authority [1980] IRLR 297, EAT.
Hollister v The National Farmers' Union [1979] IRLR 238, CA.
Massey v Crown Life Insurance Co [1978] IRLR 31, CA.
Richmond Precision Engineering Ltd v Pearce [1985] IRLR 179, EAT.
St John of God (Care Services) Ltd v Brooks and others [1992] IRLR 546, EAT.

Notes

For unfair dismissal generally, see *Harvey on Industrial Relations and Employment Law* Division D.1.

For dismissal for 'some other substantial reason', see ibid, Division D.12.

For categories of workers, see ibid, Division A.1.

The provisions relating to unfair dismissal are now contained in the Employment Rights Act 1996, see ibid, Division Q.

Ruth Downing (instructed by *Warner Cranston*) for the appellants.
Mr Williams appeared in person.
Anthony Higgins (instructed by *Wortley Redmayne & Kershaw*) for the other respondents.

Clark v Oxfordshire Health Authority

COURT OF APPEAL (CIVIL DIVISION)
BELDAM, SCHIEMANN LJJ AND SIR CHRISTOPHER SLADE
18 DECEMBER 1997

Contracts of employment—Meaning of 'employee'—Unfair dismissal—Exclusions and qualifications—meaning of 'employee'—Employment Appeal Tribunal—Employment Protection (Consolidation) Act 1978 s 153(1) (Note: The corresponding provision of the Employment Rights Act 1996 is s 230).

Mrs Clark worked for Oxfordshire Health Authority's 'nurse bank' as a staff nurse. As such, she had no fixed or regular hours of work but was offered work as and when an appropriate temporary vacancy occurred at any one of the hospitals within the authority's area. The relevant conditions of service stipulated that bank nurses are not regular employees and have no entitlement to guaranteed or continuous work. When she did work, Mrs Clark was paid an hourly rate calculated on the basis of the applicable Whitley Council scale, which rose by annual increments. Her pay was subject to deductions in respect of PAYE and national insurance and her contributions under the NHS superannuation scheme. She had no entitlement to any pay when she did not work, or to holiday pay and sick leave. The 'statement of employment' which Mrs Clark received when she joined the nurse bank also included provisions relating to discipline and dismissal, an express grievance procedure 'relating to the terms and conditions of your employment', imposed a duty of confidentiality and encouraged union membership. Mrs Clark worked for the nurse bank between 21 January 1991 and 27 January 1994 when, she alleged, she was dismissed. There was a break from 23 August to 25 October 1992 during which she provided no services and had four weeks' leave. She did not work for a week in November 1992, or for three weeks in January and two weeks in April 1993. An industrial tribunal concluded that Mrs Clark worked for the nurse bank on a casual basis, that she was not an 'employee' within the statutory definition and that, therefore, she could not pursue a claim for unfair dismissal. The tribunal found that there was no obligation on the authority to offer her work and no obligation upon her to accept work when it was offered. If she was not offered work there was no action she could take to require the authority to offer her work. She had no entitlement to any pay when she did not work and no entitlement to holiday pay or sick leave. Accordingly, although there were factors which pointed towards a conclusion that she was an employee, the 'mutuality of obligation' which is an essential feature of a contract of employment was missing. The tribunal considered only whether there was a 'global' contract of employment between Mrs Clark and the authority and not whether, at the relevant time, there existed a specific engagement which amounted to a contract of service which could provide the basis for a claim of unfair dismissal. On appeal, the EAT held that the lack of mutuality of obligation was a significant factor but must be seen in the context of the other terms and conditions of the contract. On that basis, the EAT concluded that, properly construed, the contract between Mrs Clark and the authority was a global contract of employment. The appeal was allowed by a majority decision after the majority rejected the authority's argument that the decision of the industrial tribunal was based upon a mixture of fact and law, that there was no misdirection in law and, therefore, the EAT could not interfere.

Held—The EAT had erred in holding that the applicant's relationship with the health authority as a 'bank nurse', who was offered work as and when an appropriate temporary vacancy occurred, was governed by a global contract of employment, notwithstanding a lack of mutuality of obligation during the periods between engagements.

A 'contract of employment' within the meaning of the statutory definition cannot exist in the absence of mutual obligations subsisting over the entire duration of the relevant period. The decisions of the Court of Appeal in *Nethermere (St Neots) Ltd v Gardiner* [1984] IRLR 240 and *McLeod v Hellyer Brothers Ltd* [1987] IRLR 232 are binding authority for that proposition. Although the mutual obligations required to found a global contract of employment need not necessarily and in every case consist of obligations to provide and perform work, some mutuality of obligation is required. For example, an obligation by the one party to accept and do the work if offered and an obligation on the other party to pay a retainer during such periods as work was not offered would be likely to suffice.

In the present case, no such mutuality existed during the periods when the applicant was not occupied in a single engagement. The authority was under no obligation to offer the applicant work nor was she under any obligation to accept it. She had no entitlement to any pay when she did not work and no entitlement to holiday pay or sick leave. Accordingly, no global contract of employment between the authority and the applicant was in existence at any time during the three years that she was a bank nurse. The appeal would therefore be allowed and the matter remitted to the industrial tribunal to consider all other issues relevant to the applicant's contention that she was unfairly dismissed, including whether, at the relevant time, there existed a specific engagement which amounted to a contract of service and could provide the basis for a claim of unfair dismissal.

The majority of the EAT had erred in holding that the issue of whether the applicant worked under a contract of employment was a question of law arising from the construction of documents and that, therefore, it was free to give effect to its own conclusion as to the correct interpretation of those documents, unrestricted by the decision of the industrial tribunal.

In the ordinary case, where the determination of whether a person is 'employed' under a 'contract of employment' depends not only on reference to written documents but also on an investigation and evaluation of the factual circumstances in which the work is performed, the responsibility of determining and evaluating all the relevant admissible evidence is that of the tribunal at first instance.

In the present case, the industrial tribunal reached its decision not merely by reference to written documents but also by reference to findings of fact, reached after hearing oral evidence from both sides. In those circumstances, the EAT was entitled to interfere with the industrial tribunal's decision only if it had misdirected itself in law or its decision was one which no tribunal, properly directing itself, could have reached.

In any event, because of the absence of mutuality of obligation, the tribunal's conclusion that no global contract of employment existed was, as a matter of law, the only one open to it. Accordingly, whether viewed as a mixed question of fact or law, or solely one of law, the EAT had no grounds for interfering with the decision.

The appeal would therefore be allowed and the case remitted to the industrial tribunal.

Cases referred to in judgment

City & East London FHS Authority v Duncan 24 September 1996, EAT.
Clifford v Union of Democratic Mineworkers [1991] IRLR 518, CA.
Davies v Presbyterian Church of Wales [1986] IRLR 194, HL.
Edwards v Bairstow [1956] AC 14, HL.
Ironmonger v Movefield Ltd [1988] IRLR 461, EAT.
Lee v Chung [1990] IRLR 236, PC.
McLeod v Hellyer Brothers Ltd [1987] IRLR 232, CA.
McMeechan v Secretary of State for Employment [1995] IRLR 461, EAT, [1997] IRLR 353, CA.
Nethermere (St Neots) Ltd v Gardiner [1984] IRLR 240, CA.
O'Kelly v Trusthouse Forte plc [1983] IRLR 369, CA.

Jeremy McMullen QC (instructed by the *Legal Services Department, Royal College of Nursing*) for Mrs Clark.
Patrick Elias QC and *C Sheldon* (instructed by *Cole & Cole*) for the health authority.

Costain Building and Civil Engineering Ltd v Smith and another

EMPLOYMENT APPEAL TRIBUNAL
MORISON J, MRS R CHAPMAN, AND MR AC BLYGHTON
25 MAY, 29 NOVEMBER 1999

Employment—Contract of service—Distinction between contract for services and contract of service—Engineer supplied through agency to work for building contractors—Engineer appointed by trade union as health and safety representative on building contractors' site—Whether employed under contract of service—Employment Rights Act 1996 s 100(1)(b).

S was an engineer registered with an agency who supplied labour to building contractors. Through the agency he commenced work for C Ltd (the contractors) in June 1998 at their site. After raising a number of health and safety issues S contacted his trade union representative and after discussion he was appointed the union safety representative at the site. S completed a number of safety reports which were critical of the contractors' management of the site. In July S was informed by the agency that the contractors had indicated that they did not want S to work on the site any more. S claimed that he had been unfairly dismissed contrary to s 100(1)(b) of the Employment Rights Act 1996 (the 1996 Act) which provided that an employee who was dismissed should be regarded as unfairly dismissed if the reason for the dismissal was that, being a representative of workers on matters of health and safety at work, the employee performed any function as such a representative. An employment tribunal, to which he applied for interim relief pending determination of the complain of unfair dismissal, held that S had not been self-employed but was an employee of the contractors. It considered that the facts that S was paid tax-free by the agency and that the dismissal was brought about by the agency as artificial devices designed to foster the image that S was not an employee of the contractors. The contractors appealed.

Held—(1) Defining the status of agency workers, who might be employees or independent contractors, could be a particularly difficult task. There was no doubt that the tribunal had erred in law in finding that S was an employee of the contractors. There were two relevant contracts which governed the responsibilities of the parties to this case: there was a contract between the agency and the contractors, and a contract between the agency and S. There was not, however, any contract of employment between the contractors and S. The essential facts were clear: S chose to operate on a self-employed agent basis, as he was paid tax free and had to submit invoices to the agency, he did not receive holiday or sick pay, had no notice provisions and was provided with no other benefits associated with being an employee. By determining that S's position of self-employment was a device used by the contractors to avoid their statutory duties, the tribunal had lost sight of the facts that clearly indicated that S could not be an employee of the contractors. Proper consideration of the tests and criteria of service also indicated that S was not an employee of the contractors. They sought a site engineer for a temporary period and went to the agency to supply them with a worker. They did not identify S nor did they specifically request him. Although S was required to work site hours and there was an obligation to perform the work, either side could terminate the arrangement without notice without further obligations and the contractors had a supervisory role only, which was inconsistent with S working as an employee.

(2) To come within the protection afforded by s 100 of the 1996 Act, a safety representative had to be an employee. The appointment of S as a safety representative did not mean that he was an employee or elevated to the status of an employee. Accordingly the union's appointment of S was ineffective in law as at the time of the purported appointment S was

not an employee of the contractors. Moreover, the purported appointment did not alter S's status as he did not become an employee of the contractors on the basis that he was a union representative.

The contractors' appeal would therefore be allowed.

Notes

For categories of workers: servants and independent contractors, see *Harvey on Industrial Relations and Employment Law* Division A.1.A and C.

For characteristics of the relationship of master and servant, see ibid Division A.3.

For unfair dismissal on health and safety grounds, see ibid Division N.22.G.3.

For the Employment Rights Act 1996, s 100, see ibid Division Q.

Appeal

Costain Building & Civil Engineering Ltd (C Ltd) appealed against the decision of the employment tribunal that David Smith (S), who had made a claim for unfair dismissal against C Ltd and Chanton Group plc (the agency), was an employee of C Ltd

Ingrid Simler (instructed by the *Solicitor, Costain Group plc*) for C Ltd.
Andrew Hogarth (instructed by *O H Parsons and Partners*) for S.

Davies (Inspector of Taxes) v Braithwaite

KINGS BENCH DIVISION
ROWLATT, FINLAY JJ
10 JUNE 1931, 18 JULY 1933

Emoluments from office or employment—Employment—Meaning—Contract of service or contract for services—Professional actress employed in series of different professional engagements—Whether remuneration from employment—Income Tax Act 1918, Schs D, E—Finance Act 1922 s 18(1).

B was an actress, residing in England, who earned her living by exercising her activities in any way that her professional qualifications fitted her for. During the three years ending on 5 April 1928 she acted in various stage plays in England, and one in America, she performed in films, performed live on the wireless and made recordings for gramophone companies. The Revenue assessed her for that period under Sch D of the Income Tax Act 1918 in respect of the profits from her profession or vocation as an actress. B considered that she had worked under contracts which were contracts of employment, the relation between herself and the various producers being that of master and servant, so that she was in 'employments' within Sch E, even though, in a colloquial sense, carrying on a profession. The General Commissioners allowed B's appeal against the Sch D assessments and discharged them. The Revenue appealed.

Held—It was clear that you could have both an employment and a profession at the same time. Quite clearly you could have it in different categories. A man might have the steadiest employment in the world by day, and he might do something else entirely different in the evening and make some more money by way of a professional vocation. 'Employments' in Sch E were something like offices, which might be expressed as 'posts'. When a person occupied a post resting on a contract, not roughly called something in the nature of a post, and if, then, that was an employment as opposed to a mere engagement in the course of carrying on a profession, that was not a very difficult term of distinction, although in general, it was perhaps a little difficult to apply to all cases, as every distinction was. Where one found a method of earning a livelihood which did not contemplate the obtaining of a post and staying in it, but essentially contemplated a series of engagements and moving from one to the other—and in the case of an actor's or actress's life it certainly involved going from one to the other and not going on playing one part for the rest of his or her life, but in obtaining first one engagement and then another, and a whole series of them—then each of those engagements could not be considered an employment but was mere engagement in the course of exercising a profession, and every profession and every trade did involve the making of successive engagements and successive contracts, and in one sense of the word, employments. That was the line which was to be drawn on that principle. In the instant case it was quite clear that B had to fall under Sch D because she did not make a contract with a producer for a post. She made a contract with a producer for the next things she was going to do, and then with another producer and then with a third, and at any time she might make a gramophone record or act for a film. Essentially whatever she did or whatever contracts she made for the running of a play which might last a long time were nothing but incidents in the conduct of her professional career. Therefore, she was taxable under Sch D.

Notes

The Finance Act 1922 took 'employment' out of Sch D and provided that profits or gains arising or accruing to any person from employment should be chargeable under Sch E.

Cases referred to in judgment

Great Western Rly Co v Bater (Surveyor of Taxes) [1920] 3 KB 266, 8 TC 231; *rvsd* [1921] 2 KB 128, 8 TC 236, CA; *affd* [1922] 2 AC 1, 8 TC 231, HL.
Colquhoun v Brooks (1889) 2 TC 490, HL.

Appeal

The Revenue appealed from a decision of the General Commissioners allowing the appeal of Lilian Braithwaite against assessments made on her under Sch D of the Income Tax Acts in respect of profits from her profession or vocation as an actress.

The Solicitor-General (Sir Stafford Cripps KC) and *RPHills* (instructed by the *Solicitor of Inland Revenue*) for the Crown.
Raymond Needham KC and *JSScrimgeour* (instructed by *Theodore Goddard &Co*) for the taxpayer.

F S Consulting Ltd v McCaul (Inspector of Taxes)

SPECIAL COMMISSIONER: DR NUALA BRICE
3 DECEMBER 2001, 22 JANUARY 2002

National Insurance—Earnings of workers supplied by service companies etc—Provision of services through intermediary—Taxpayer establishing personal service company—Company contracting with agency for provision of services to client of agency—Whether company liable for national insurance contributions on payments made by client to agency and then by agency to company—Whether, if arrangements had taken the form of a contract between taxpayer and client, taxpayer would have been regarded as gainfully employed by the client—Whether arrangements to be considered those involving both personal service company and agency—Social Security Contributions (Intermediaries)Regulations 2000, SI 2000/727, reg 6(1)(b), (c).

S was a computer consultant conversion specialist and the sole director and shareholder of the taxpayer company. The taxpayer company and an agency, T Ltd, entered into a contract in April 2000 which provided that the taxpayer company would provide an individual to perform consultancy services for a client of T Ltd. S was the individual named but the taxpayer company could propose a replacement who would have to be approved by the client. The contract could be terminated immediately if T Ltd's client terminated its agreement with T Ltd because of the individual's incompetence, unsuitability or unprofessional conduct. Otherwise it could be terminated by T Ltd with four weeks' notice. The contract stipulated that it was a contract for the supply of services only and not a contract of employment. Between April 2000 and June 2001 S provided his services to the taxpayer company which provided them to T Ltd, which provided them to B plc where S worked as a member of a project team developing systems to convert one information technology system to another. B plc paid T Ltd; T Ltd paid a lesser sum to the taxpayer company and the taxpayer company paid S. S worked in a project team of seven members. Five of the team members were employees of B plc. S never acted as team leader and had no job title. He could not decide which B plc employees worked in the team; he could advise the employees but could not instruct them what to do. There was little direction or control by B plc over how S did his work. His working hours were flexible and recorded on a time sheet which had to be signed by a representative of B plc. Prior notice of non-attendance was required and permission was required before leave could be taken. S told B plc in advance when he wanted to take time off for holidays. The Social Security Contributions (Intermediaries)Regulations SI 2000/727 (the 2000 regulations) provided that in certain stated circumstances, payments to service companies were to be treated as earnings paid to a worker in respect of an employment. Under reg 6(1) those regulations applied where: (a) an individual (the worker) personally performed services for the purposes of a business carried on by another person (the client); (b) the performance of those services by the worker was carried out, not under a contract directly between the client and the worker would be regarded for the purposes of the Social Security (Contributions and Benefits) Act 1992 Pts I to V as employed in employed earner's employment by the client. Regulation 5 of the 2000 regulations provided, inter alia, that a company was an 'intermediary' where either the worker had a material interest in the intermediary or payment was received by the worker directly from the intermediary and could reasonably be taken to represent remuneration for services provided by the worker to the client. In June 2001 the Revenue notified the taxpayer company of their decision that the circumstances of the arrangements between S and B plc for the performance of services were such that reg 6(1) applied and that the taxpayer company was to be treated as liable to pay primary and secondary class I national insurance contributions in respect of the worker's attributable earnings from that engagement. The taxpayer company appealed contending, inter alia: (i) that the 'arrangements' mentioned in reg 6(1)(b) and (c) were those involving the intermediary (the taxpayer company) but not the arrangements involving the agency, T Ltd, which was not an intermediary; and (ii) that had those arrangements taken the form of a contract between S and B plc, S would not have been regarded as employed by B plc.

Held—The phrase 'arrangements involving an intermediary' was wide enough to include arrangements involving both an intermediary and a non-intermediary; the phrase was not 'arrangements with an intermediary' which would exclude arrangements with a non-intermediary. In the instant case the arrangements mentioned in reg 6(1)(b) and (c) were those involving both the intermediary, the taxpayer company, and the non-intermediary, T Ltd.

(2) The principle was established that the question as to whether a person was employed under a contract of service, or whether he was self-employed and provided a contract for services, was a question of fact in each case to be determined having regard to all the relevant circumstances. In the instant case, the relevant factors which pointed towards

there being a contract of service outweighed the factors which pointed towards there being a contract for services. Concentrating on the substance of the contractual arrangements rather than their form, had the arrangements taken the form of a contract between S and B plc, S would have been regarded as employed in employed earner's employment by B plc.

The taxpayer company's appeal would, accordingly, be dismissed.

Notes

For national insurance contributions on earnings paid through certain personal service companies, see *Simon's National Insurance Contributions Service* 8.346.

For the Social Security Contributions (Intermediaries) Regulations 2000, SI 2000/727, reg 6(1)(b), (c), see *Simon's National Insurance Contributions Service* Part III.

Cases referred to in judgment

Hall (Inspector of Taxes) v Lorimer [1994] STC 23, [1994] 1 WLR 209, [1994] 1 All ER 250, 66 TC 349, CA.

Johnson Underwood Ltd v Montgomery [2001] EWCA Civ 318, [2001] IRLR 269.

Market Investigations Ltd v Minister of Social Security [1969] 2 QB 173, [1968] 3 All ER 732.

McManus v Griffiths (Inspector of Taxes) [1997] STC 1089, 70 TC 218.

Pepper (Inspector of Taxes) v Hart [1992] STC 898, [1993] AC 593, [1993] 1 All ER 42, [1992], 65 TC 421, HL.

R (on the application of Professional Contractors Group Ltd) v IRC [2001] EWHC Admin 236, [2001] STC 629; affd [2001] EWCA Civ 1945, [2002] STC 165.

Ready Mixed Concrete (South East) Ltd v Minister of Pensions and National Insurance [1968] 2 QB 497, [1968] 1 All ER 433.

Staples v Secretary of State for Social Services (15 March 1985, unreported), QBD.

John Antell for the taxpayer company.

I B Mitchell, advocacy of the *London Region Advocacy Unit*, for the Revenue.

Fall (Inspector of Taxes) v Hitchen

CHANCERY DIVISION
PENNYCUICK V-C
29, 30 NOVEMBER 1972

Income tax—Income—Emoluments from office or employment—Employment—Contract of service—Contract an incident in carrying on of profession—Professional dancer—Dancer entering into engagements in the carrying on of his profession—Engagement with theatrical company under standard form contract—Contract amounting to contract of service—Whether earnings from contract constituting emoluments from 'employment'—Income and Corporation Taxes Act 1970 s 181(1) (Sch E).

The taxpayer, a professional ballet dancer, was engaged by Sadler's Wells Trust Ltd ('the company') under a standard form of contract for a minimum period of rehearsals plus 22 weeks and thereafter until the contract was determined by a fortnight's notice on either side. He was to work full time during specified hours for a regular salary. The contract provided that he should work exclusively for the company and should not undertake other work without its consent, which was not to be withheld unreasonably. The company provided the taxpayer with costumes for stage use. The taxpayer was assessed to income tax in respect of his earnings from the company for the year 1969–70 under Sch E in s 181 of the Income and Corporation Taxes Act 1970. The general commissioners discharged the assessment holding, inter alia, that the taxpayer's employment constituted an 'incident' in the carrying on of his profession as a theatrical artiste and the assessment should therefore have been made under Sch D, Case II. The Crown appealed.

Held—The taxpayer, in respect of his engagement with the company, was not a person performing services in business on his own account; all the relevant factors pointed to the relation between the taxpayer and the company as being one of a contract of service. Once it had been established that the emoluments in question arose from a contract of service, it followed that they arose from an 'employment' within Sch E and it was immaterial that the taxpayer was at the same time carrying on his profession. Accordingly in respect of the income derived from his contract with the company, the taxpayer was assessable under Sch E and the appeal would be allowed.

Davies v Braithwaite (1931) 18 TC 198 distinguished).

Notes

For offices and employment within the scope of Sch E, see *Simon's Taxes* C4.113–115. For the Income and Corporation Taxes Act 1970 s 181 *Simon's Taxes*, Part GI.

Cases referred to in judgment

Davies v Braithwaite [1931] 2 KB 628, 18 TC 198, [1931] All ER 792, 100 LJKB 619, 145 LT 693, 28 (1) Digest (Reissue) 241, 746.
Global Plant Ltd v Secretary of State for Social services [1971] 3 All ER 385, [1972] 1 QB 139, [1971] 3 WLR 269.
Great Western Rly Co v Bater [1922] 2 AC 1, 8 TC 231, 1 ATC 104, 91 LJKB 472, 127 LT 170, HL; rvsg CA [1921] 2 KB 128, 90 LJKB 550, 125 LT 321; affg [1920] 3 KB 266, 90 LJKB 41, 124 LT 92, 28 (1) Digest (Reissue) 320, 1132.
Household v Grimshaw (Inspector of Taxes) [1953] 2 All ER 12, 34 TC 366, [1953] 1 WLR 710, 32 ATC 133, [1953] TR 147, 46 R &IT 347, 28 (1) Digest Reissue) 338, 1227.
I R C v Brander &Cruickshank [1971] 1 All ER 36, 46 TC 574, [1971] 1 WLR 212, [1970] TR 353, HL, 28 (1) Digest (Reissue) 46, 193.
Market Investigations Ltd v Minister of Social Security [1968] 3 All ER 732, [1969] 2 QB 173, [1969] 2 WLR 1, Digest (Cont Vol C) 701, 2636b.
Mitchell and another (Inspector of Taxes) v Ross [1961] 3 All ER 49, [1962] AC 813, 40 TC 11, [1961] 3 WLR 411, 40 ATC 199, [1961] TR 191, HL; rvsg CA [1960] 2 All ER 218, [1960] Ch 498, [1960] 2 WLR 766, 39 ATC 52, [1960] TR 79, 53 R &IT 347; affg [1959] 3 All ER 341, [1960] Ch 145, [1959] 3 WLR 550, 38 ATC 422, [1959] TR 225, 53 R &IT 75, 28 (1) Digest (Reissue) 321, 1138.

Leonard Bromley QC and *Patrick Medd* for the Crown.
Barry Pinson for the taxpayer.

Express and Echo Publications Ltd v Tanton

COURT OF APPEAL (CIVIL DIVISION)
HURST, PETER GIBSON AND AULD LJJ
11 MARCH 1999

Contracts of employment—Meaning of 'employee'—Employment Rights Act 1996 s 230.

Mr Tanton originally worked for the appellant company as an employee but was made redundant in 1995. In August of that year, he was re-engaged as a driver on what the company intended, and Mr Tanton initially accepted, to be a self-employed basis. In January 1996, Mr Tanton was sent a copy of a document headed 'An agreement for services'. A clause in the agreement provided that 'In the event that the contractor is unable or unwilling to perform the services personally, he shall arrange at his own expense entirely for another suitable person to perform the services'. Mr Tanton found the agreement unacceptable and refused to sign it. However, he continued to work in accordance with its terms and, from time to time, utilised the right to provide a substitute driver. He subsequently applied to an employment tribunal for a statement of written particulars, asking for his status as an employee to be confirmed. At a preliminary hearing, the tribunal chairman, sitting alone, approached the question of whether Mr Tanton was an employee or a self-employed contractor on the basis of what actually occurred, rather than what the documents recorded as being the obligations of the parties. The chairman also considered that, in a case of this nature, it was necessary to look at the overall position and, whilst it was useful to consider a number of different factors which may be pointers, it was not necessarily the case that any one factor could tip the balance either way. The chairman concluded that the factors pointing to Mr Tanton being an employee outweighed those factors which pointed to contractor status. He was required to follow a set route, wear a uniform provided by the company and drive a vehicle from the company's pool. The chairman regarded those requirements and the degree of control exercised by the company as suggesting a contract of employment. According to the chairman, the provision enabling Mr Tanton to provide a substitute driver which, on his own evidence, he had used from time to time, was only one factor of many and though there might come a point at which the provision of a substitute was so frequent as to change the whole nature of the arrangement, there was no evidence that that point had been approached. The EAT refused the company's appeal against that decision on the grounds that the tribunal chairman had reached a permissible conclusion and no arguable point of law was raised. On appeal to the Court of Appeal, it was submitted for the company that a term enabling provision of a substitute was inherently inconsistent with the existence of a contract of employment.

Held—The employment tribunal chairman had erred in holding that the applicant was an employee of the appellant company, rather than a self-employed contractor, even though the contract under which he worked contained a provision enabling him, at his own expense, to arrange for his duties to be performed by another person when he was unable or unwilling to perform the services personally. The chairman had incorrectly approached the question of whether the applicant was engaged under a contract of employment by concentrating on what actually occurred rather than by seeking to determine the mutual obligations by which the parties were bound.

Where a person who works for another is not required to perform his services personally, as a matter of law, the relationship between the worker and the person for whom he works is not that of employer and employee. A right to provide a substitute is inherently inconsistent with the existence of a contract of employment. A contract of employment must necessarily contain an obligation on the part of the employee to provide his services personally. Without such an irreducible minimum of obligation, it cannot be said that there is a contract of employment. The recognition that a contract of employment involves mutual trust and confidence is consistent with a requirement of personal service.

In determining whether an applicant was engaged under a contract of employment or was a self-employed contractor, the employment tribunal should first establish what were the terms of the agreement between the parties. It should then consider whether any of those terms are inherently inconsistent with the existence of a contract of employment. If there is an inherently inconsistent term, what actually occurred may not be decisive. If a term is not enforced, that does not justify a conclusion that it is not part of the agreement. The obligation could be temporarily waived. If there are no such inherently inconsistent terms, the tribunal should determine whether the contract is a contract of service or a contract for services, having regard to all the terms.

In the present case, the provision in the contract entitling the applicant not to perform any services personally was not a sham and the only conclusion which could properly be reached was that this was a contract for services. The EAT had erred, therefore, in dismissing the company's appeal on the grounds that the tribunal chairman had reached a permissible conclusion and no arguable point of law was raised.

The company's appeal would accordingly be allowed.

Cases referred to in judgment

Clark v Oxfordshire Health Authority [1998] IRLR 125, CA.
Malik v BCCI SA [1997] IRLR 462, HL.
Nethermere (St Neots) Ltd v Gardiner [1984] IRLR 240, CA.
Ready Mixed Concrete (South East) Ltd v Minister of Pensions and National Insurance [1968] 2 QB 497, HC.

Jonathan Swift (instructed by *Foot & Bowden*) for Express Echo Publications Ltd
Mr Tanton appeared in person.

Global Plant Ltd v Secretary of State for Health and Social Security

QUEEN'S BENCH DIVISION
LORD WIDGERY CJ
9 JUNE 1971

National insurance—Appeal—Decision of Minister—'Employed person'—Determination that employee engaged under contract of service—Appeal on question of law to high Court—Question whether person engaged under contract of service or for services mixed question of law and fact—Grounds on which court may interfere with Minister's decision—Driver engaged by company to drive earth moving machines—Features of contract with company pointing both to contract of service and contract for services—Decision of Minister one on which person properly instructed in relevant law could have come—Evidence to support decision—Decision containing no ex facie false proposition of law—No error of law established on appeal—National Insurance Act 1965 ss 1(2)(a), 65.

The appellant company was engaged in the hiring out of industrial plant, including earth moving machines. S worked for the company as a driver of these machines. He was engaged by the company on the basis that he was self-employed and provided his services to them as a sub-contractor. He stamped his own insurance cards at the self-employed person's rate and paid his own income tax under Sch D. Under his contract S was free to work for the company when he chose, and was entitled to send a suitably qualified substitute in his place, but in practice, and as contemplated by the parties, he worked the normal hours of a full-time employee. He was paid at an hourly rate of remuneration on the basis of the number of hours worked. He drove the company's machines on sites selected by them, under the control of the customer's site foreman on the site. He could only go to sites chosen by the company and he had to be there at the time stipulated by the company, as being that required by the customer, before the receipt of the machine. The company appealed under s 65(1) of the National Insurance Act 1965 against a determination of the Secretary of State for Social Services ('the Minister') under s 64(1) of the 1965 Act that S was employed under a contract of service within the meaning of s 1(2)(a) of the 1965 Act and that the company as employers were liable to pay insurance contributions for him under the Act.

Sections 64 and 65, so far as material, provide:

'64.—(1) Subject to the provisions of this Act, any question arising under this Act . . . (c) as to the class of insured persons in which a person is to be included . . . shall be determined by the Minister . . .

65.—(1) Any question of law arising in connection with the determination by the Minister of any question such as is mentioned in section 64(1)(a) to (c) of this Act may, if the Minister thinks fit, be referred for decision to the High Court . . .

(3) Any person aggrieved by the decision of the Minister on any question of law such as is mentioned in subsection (1) of this section which is not referred in accordance with that subsection may appeal from that decision to the High Court . . .'

Held—The question whether a contract was a contract of service or a contract for services was a question of mixed law and fact and therefore, on an appeal under s 65 of the 1965 Act, it was not for the court to balance the arguments for and against the decision which the Minister had reached, giving the separate factors the weight which the court thought they should have; that balancing operation was one for the Minister and the only question for the court was whether the conclusion which the Minister had reached was one which no person properly instructed as to the relevant law could have come; although there were pointers both for and against the Minister's conclusion it was impossible to say that his decision was open to attack on these grounds; furthermore it had not been suggested that the decision contained a false proposition of law ex facie and there was plainly evidence on which the conclusion could be supported; accordingly the company had failed to establish that there was an error of law and the appeal must be dismissed.

Dictum of Lord Radcliffe in *Edwards (Inspector of Taxes) v Bairstow* [1955] 3 All ER at 57 applied.

Morren v Swinton and Pendlebury Borough Council [1965] 2 All ER 349 distinguished.

Notes

For employed earners liable to pay national insurance contributions for the purposes of the Social Security Contributions and Benefits Act 1992 see 44(2) *Halsbury's Laws* (4th Edn) (1997 reissue) para 32.

Cases referred to in judgment

Cassidy v Ministry of Health [1951] 1 All ER 574, [1951] 2 KB 343.
Construction Industry Training Board v Labour Force Ltd [1970] 3 All ER 220.
Edwards (Inspector of Taxes) v Bairstow [1955] 3 All ER 48, [1956] AC 14.
Market Investigations Ltd v Minister of Social Security [1968] 3 All ER 732, [1969] 2 QB 173.
Morren v Swinton and Pendlebury Borough Council [1965] 2 All ER 349, [1965] 1 WLR 576.
Phipps v Minister of National Insurance (30 November 1951) unreported.
Ready Mixed Concrete (South East) Ltd v Minister of Pensions and National Insurance [1968] 1 All ER 433, [1968] 2 QB 497.
Simmons v Heath Laundry Co [1910] 1 KB 543.
Terrar v Minister of Pensions and National Insurance (30 July 1960) unreported.

Case stated

This was an appeal by way of case stated by Global Plant Ltd ('the company') against the decision of the Secretary of State for Social Services ('the Minister') (formerly the Minister of Social Security and subsequently the Secretary of State for Health and Social Services) that Kenneth Summers and Petter Morrissey were, during specified periods in 1968, each employed under a contract of service with the company and were gainfully employed thereunder in Great Britain; by virtue of s 1(2) of the National Insurance Act 1946 and subsequently s 1(2)(a) of the National Insurance Act 1965, Mr Summers and Mr Morrissey were each included in the class for employed persons for the purposes of those Acts; by virtue of s 1 of, and Sch 1 Part I para 1 to, the National Insurance (Industrial Injuries) Act 1965 Mr Summers and Mr Morrissey were each employed in insurable employment within the meaning of that Act; and, by virtue of ss 3 and 11(1) of the National Insurance Act 1965 and ss 2 and 3(1) of the National Insurance (Industrial Injuries) Act 1965, the company were liable as employers to pay contributions for Mr Summers and Mr Morrissey under the Acts.

A P Lester (instructed by *Alan, George & Sacker* agents for *Maurice Putsman & Co*, Birmingham) for the company.
Gordon Slynn (instructed by *the Solicitor, Department of Health and Social Security*) for the Minister.

Hall (Inspector of Taxes) v Lorimer

COURT OF APPEAL, CIVIL DIVISION
DILLON, NOLAN AND ROCH LJJ
2, 3, 5 NOVEMBER 1993

Emoluments from office or employment—Employment—Meaning—Contract of service or contract for services—Taxpayer in receipt of fees for services rendered as vision mixer under short-term contracts with various production companies—Whether contracts with companies contracts of service or contracts for services.

The taxpayer trained as a vision mixer. In 1985, he left full-time employment with a television production company and went free-lance charging more than the union rate for his services. The work of a vision mixer was a skilled editing job. It involved selecting from different camera shots the best and most appropriate shots (in accordance with the director's desired result) to be shown on the viewer's television screen. The taxpayer registered for value added tax and set up an office at home where his wife helped him with the paperwork until their marriage was dissolved. His engagements consisted of short-term contracts lasting one to two days. Between 1985 and 1989, he worked on over 800 days. He did not hire any staff but on six occasions he provided a substitute with the consent of the production company concerned. All his work was conducted at the studios and he would stay there until his work was completed. The equipment was provided by the studios; the taxpayer provided none of his own. He neither contributed to the cost of production nor did he share in the profit or loss made by the production company. However, he could lose money if a client became insolvent or an invoice remained unpaid. The taxpayer appealed to a Special Commissioner against assessments to income tax under Sch E Case I for the years 1984/85 to 1988/89 inclusive, contending that his profits had been earned not under contracts of service but under a series of contracts for services and were properly assessable under Sch D. The Special Commissioner allowed the appeal on the grounds that the activities of the taxpayer bore the hallmarks of a man who was in business on his own account and that the taxpayer's profits had been earned under contracts for services. Mummery J decided that the Special Commissioner had considered all the relevant elements of the taxpayer's work and had applied the proper test and was entitled on the facts found to reach the conclusion that the taxpayer's earnings were assessable to income tax under Sch D. The Crown appealed contending that the taxpayer could not be said to be in business on his own account because: the production company controlled the time, the place and duration of any given engagement; the taxpayer provided no equipment; he hired no staff; he ran no financial risk save those of bad debts and of being unable to find work; he had no responsibility for investment in or management of the work of programme-making; and he had no opportunity of profiting from the manner in which he carried out individual assignments.

Held—In deciding whether or not the contracts from which the taxpayer derived his earnings were contracts of service, there was no single path to a correct decision. An approach which was appropriate to the facts and arguments of one case might not be helpful in another. The question whether an individual was in business on his own account, though often helpful in distinguishing between a contract of service from a contract for services, might be of little assistance in the case of one carrying on a profession or vocation. It did not include factors which were of critical importance in the instant appeal: the duration of the particular engagement or the number of people by whom the individual was engaged. There was much to be said, in deciding cases such as the present one, for bearing in mind the traditional distinction between a servant and an independent contractor where what was significant was the extent to which the individual was dependent on or independent of a particular paymaster for the financial exploitation of his talents. The commissioner's conclusion in the instant case was not inconsistent with the facts found by him. The Crown's appeal would therefore be dismissed.

Market Investigations Ltd v Minister of Social Security [1969] 2 QB 173 considered.

Notes

For the distinction between employment and self-employment, see *Simon's Direct Tax Service* E4.202–203.

Cases referred to in judgment

Davies (Inspector of Taxes) v Braithwaite [1931] 2 KB 628, 18 TC 198.
Fall (Inspector of Taxes) v Hitchen [1973] STC 66, [1973] 1 WLR 286, [1973] 1 All ER 368, 49 TC 433.
Lee Ting Sang v Chung Chi-Keung [1990] 2 AC 374, PC.

Market Investigations Ltd v Minister of Social Security [1969] 2 QB 173, [1968] 3 All ER 732.
O'Kelly v Trusthouse Forte plc [1984] QB 90, [1983] 3 All ER 456, CA.
Walls v Sinnett (Inspector of Taxes) [1987] STC 236, 60 TC 150.

Appeal

The Crown appealed against a decision of Mummery J given on 22 May 1992 (see [1992] STC 599) dismissing the appeal of the Crown against a decision of a Special Commissioner upholding the appeal of Ian Malcolm Lorimer (the taxpayer) against assessments under Case 1 of Sch E on his earnings as a freelance vision mixer for the years 1984–85 to 1988–89 inclusive. The commissioner held, that those earnings were properly assessable not under Sch E but under Sch D.

Peter Goldsmith QC and *Launcelot Henderson* (instructed by *the Solicitor of Inland Revenue*) for the Crown.
Stephen Allcock QC and *Andrew Hitchmough* (instructed by *Simmons & Simmons*) for the taxpayer.

Heydon's Case

EXCHEQUER
SIR ROGER MANWOOD CB AND BARONS OF THE EXCHEQUER
1584

Statutes—Interpretation of statutes—Rules for interpretation of statutes.

In an action against an intrusion into certain lands the court set out guidelines on the general interpretation of all statutes.

Per curiam. For the sure and true interpretation of all statutes in general (be they penal or beneficial), restrictive or enlarging of the common law, four things are to be discerned and considered: (i) what was the common law before the making of the act; (ii) what was the mischief and defect for which the common law did not provide; (iii) what remedy the parliament hath resolved and appointed to cure the disease of the commonwealth; and (iv) the true reason of the remedy.

Notes

For general rules of statutory interpretation see 44(1) *Halsbury's Laws* (4th edn reissue) para 1369.

Jobsin.co.uk plc (trading as Internet Recruitment Solutions) v Department of Health

COURT OF APPEAL (CIVIL DIVISION)
THORPE, DYSON LJJ AND ASTILL J
13 JULY 2001

Contracting authority issuing tender inviting proposals for development of online recruitment service—Whether tender for personnel placement and related services or for computer and related services—Public Services Contracts Regulations 1993, SI 1993/3228.

The Department of Health (the department) issued a briefing document in August 2000 inviting proposals for the development and management of an online recruitment service for the NHS. The website was to display job vacancies throughout the NHS and be the vehicle for applications to fill them in. J plc submitted a tender which was not included on the final short list. The Public Services Contracts Regulations 1993 (the 1993 regulations) governed the tender. The 1993 regulations were intended to implement EC Directive 92/50 (the Services Directive). Part A of Sch 1 to the 1993 regulations included 'Computer and Related Services' and identified the corresponding United Nations Provisional Central Product Classification Series MN077 of 1991 (CPC) reference as 84. Part B of Sch 1 included 'Personnel Placement and Supply Services' and identified the corresponding CPC reference as 872. In March 2001 J commenced proceedings claiming that the tender process had been conducted in breach of the 1993 regulations in that the services for which tenders had been invited were 'computer and related services' within the meaning of Pt A and not 'personnel placement and supply services' within the meaning of Pt B. It was common ground that the tender had not complied with the requirements applicable to computer and related services. On a trial of preliminary issues Blofeld J held, inter alia, that the tender was for computer and related services. The department appealed contending, inter alia, that the 1993 regulations had to be interpreted in the light of the Services Directive which classified contracts according to the services which they had as their 'object', and that the 'object' of the department had been to develop a recruitment service.

Held—The correct classification involved comparing the services which, by the briefing document, the department invited tenderers to provide to it as the contracting authority with the detailed description of services under the relevant CPC heads and deciding whether those services fell under CPC 84 or CPC 872. That exercise of comparison involved an objective analysis of the services described in the briefing document and the services described under the two CPC heads. The 'object' of the contract was the service to be provided to the contracting authority. The use of the word 'object' did not mean that it was permissible for the purposes of classification to investigate the motivation behind the decision to put the contract out to tender, or the wider intentions of the contracting authority in relation to the use to which it intended to put the service that it had requested. The question was simply: what were the tenderers actually being asked to provide to the contracting authority. If the approach of the department to the issue of classification were correct it was difficult to see when a contract involving the provision of computer software would ever be for 'computer services' since software was always required in connection with some other function or activity. By the briefing document tenderers were asked to provide software development and implementation services by designing a website in accordance with the client's needs and also to write the programs to put the website into effect, to maintain and support, and manage and operate the website and database, to work with the NHS, to input the content for the website, to train the NHS staff who would actually post vacancies on the site and to make available documentation for those NHS staff. There was no doubt that those services were not 'personnel placement and supply services'. Most of CPC 872 related to the actual provision of staff; in other words the service provider was asked to provide the contracting authority with staff who were the service provider's employees in return for a fee. That was essentially the role of an employment agency. It was plain from the way those classes of services were worded that what was contemplated was the service provider creating a specific job specification, actually searching for and locating a specific individual, screening, testing and interviewing that individual, investigating references, doing other research, and selecting and referring that individual for a specific job. The briefing document did not ask tenderers to supply it with staff, nor did it ask tenderers to supply executive search or placement services. It was not the tenderer's role to describe the jobs or to search for and identify suitable applicants for particular jobs or to refer or to place candidates. The briefing document contemplated that it would be the NHS, not the service provider, who would put the vacant positions on to the website. Accordingly, the services had been properly classified as entirely for the provision of computer services.

Notes

For the Public Services Contracts Regulations 1993, SI 1993/3228, see 11 *Halsbury's Statutory Instruments* 272.

For EC Council Directive 92/50 relating to the co-ordination of procedures for the award of public services contracts, see the Official Journal L209 24.07.92 p 1.

Cases referred to in judgment

KeyMed (Medical and Industrial Equipment) Ltd v Forest Healthcare NHS Trust [1998] Eu LR 71.
EC Commission v Denmark (Case C-243/89) [1993] ECR 1-3353, ECJ.

G v G [1985] 2 All ER 225, [1985] 1 WLR 647, HL.
R v Warwickshire CC, ex p Collymore [1995] ELR 217.
R v Secretary of State for Trade and Industry, ex p Greenpeace [2000] CMLR 94.
Matra Communication SA v Home Office [1999] 3 All ER 562, [1999] 1 WLR 1646, [1999] 1 CMLR 1454, CA.

Appeal

The Department of Health (the department) appealed against a decision of Blofeld J on a trial of certain preliminary issues, in proceedings brought by Jobsin.co.uk plc (the company) trading as Internet Recruitment Solutions against the department, that a tender issued by the department inviting proposals for an online recruitment service fell within the category of computer and related services for the purposes of the Public Services Contracts Regulations 1993, SI 1993/3228.

A Lewis (instructed by the *Treasury Solicitor*) for the Department of Health.
J Crow (instructed by *DLA*, Birmingham) for the company.

Lane v Shire Roofing Company (Oxford) Ltd

COURT OF APPEAL (CIVIL DIVISION)
NOURSE, HENRY AND AULD LJJ
16 FEBRUARY 1995

Contracts of employment—Meaning of 'employee'—Health and safety at work—Employer's liability—Damages—Contributory negligence—Construction (Working Places) Regulations 1966, reg 7.

Mr Lane was a builder/roofer/carpenter who, in 1982, began trading as a one-man firm, P J Building. He was categorised as 'self-employed' for tax purposes. Initially, he solicited for work through advertisements and was engaged directly by clients. However, that work dried up and he then usually worked for other contractors. Shire Roofing was a newly-established roofing contractor. Not wishing to take on too many long-term employees in its early days of trading, the company's proprietor, Mr Whittaker, hired men for individual jobs. In September 1986, after advertising for men to work on a large roofing sub-contract in Marlow, he hired Mr Lane at a daily rate of £45. When that work was nearing completion, Mr Whittaker asked him to re-roof a porch at a private house. The building contract in relation to that job had been entered into by Mr Whittaker and the householders for an agreed price of £389 plus VAT. Mr Whittaker and Mr Lane then visited the site together, agreed an all-in fee of £200 and discussed what was necessary in terms of plant and equipment. The cost of hiring scaffolding would have made the job unprofitable. According to Mr Whittaker, he offered Mr Lane a trestle-type platform or tower scaffold to work from but Mr Lane declined the offer, saying that he preferred to use his own ladder. Whilst carrying out the work, Mr Lane fell from the ladder and suffered head injuries which caused serious brain damage. He claimed damages from Shire Roofing. Because of the nature of Mr Lane's injuries, he was unable to recollect exactly how the accident had happened and there were no witnesses to the incident. In the High Court, Judge Hutton found that, on the balance of probabilities, Mr Lane had lost his balance whilst cutting a slate when he was at the top of the ladder. The judge went on to hold that the defendants were not liable for the injuries thus sustained because Mr Lane was doing the work as an independent contractor, not as an employee, and that accordingly, the defendants owed him no duty of care. In reaching that decision, the judge took into account the fact that Mr Lane had his own roofing business, that he was recognised as self-employed for tax purposes, he was capable of working without supervision, and there was no guarantee of continuing work with the defendants. The judge also concluded that even if the defendants had owed a duty to Mr Lane as an employee, they were not in breach of that duty because the work in question could have been done safely from a ladder. Moreover, he accepted Mr Whittaker's evidence that the offer of a tower scaffold had been made and rejected.

Held—The High Court judge had erred in holding that the appellant had been engaged by the respondents to re-roof the porch of a house as an independent contractor, not an employee. The judge had erred, therefore, in finding that since the respondents did not owe the appellant a duty of care, they could not be held liable for the injuries he sustained when he lost his balance and fell off a ladder whilst carrying out that work.

In determining whether a worker was an employee or an independent contractor, the element of control will be important: who lays down what is done, the way in which it is to be done, the means by which it is to be done, and the time when it is done? Who provides, ie hires and fires, the team by which it is done, and who provides the material, plant and machinery and tools used?

However, the control test may not be decisive—for instance, in the case of skilled employees with discretion to decide how their work should be done. In such cases, the question is broadened to 'Whose business was it?'—was the workman carrying on his own business, or was he carrying on that of his employers? The answer to this question may cover much of the same ground as the control test, such as whether he provides his own equipment and hires his own helpers, but may involve looking to see where the financial risk lies, and whether and how far the workman has an opportunity of profiting from sound management in the performance of his task.

These questions must be asked in the context of who is responsible for the overall safety of those doing the work in question. In the current employment situation, where there are more self-employed and fewer in employment, and where there are perceived advantages for both workers and employers in avoiding the 'employee' label, there are good policy reasons in the safety at work field to ensure that the law properly categorises between employees and independent contractors and recognises the employer/employee relationship when it exists because of the responsibilities that the common law and statutes place on the employer.

In the present case, although the appellant had his own one-man business and was self-employed for tax purposes, his relationship with the respondents was much closer to the 'lump', where workmen are engaged only for their labour and are clearly employees whatever their tax status might be, than to a specialist sub-contractor engaged to perform some part of a general building contract. In the circumstances, the question 'Whose business was it?' could only be answered by saying that it was the respondents' business and not the appellant's. Accordingly, the appellant was carrying out the work as the respondents' employee and they therefore owed him a duty of care.

The High Court judge had also erred in finding that even if the respondents did owe the appellant a duty of care as his employers, they were not in breach of that duty in allowing him to carry out the work using a ladder, rather than providing scaffolding.

A ladder is not 'appropriate' and 'sufficient and suitable for the purpose' in terms of reg 7 of the Construction (Working Places) Regulations 1966, where the doing of the work from the ladder involves a foreseeable risk.

In the present case, looking at the work as a whole, it was foreseeable that over-reaching and/or some other loss of balance would occur if a ladder was used. The job involved working on the ladder for four days and a fair number of slates required cutting, giving rise to the temptation to cut them while on the ladder itself rather than returning to the ground each time. Since the work could not be done safely from a ladder, the respondents should have provided scaffolding. Although the argument against the use of scaffolding was that it was unnecessarily expensive, that expense was only unnecessary if the work could be done safely from a ladder. The respondents were thus liable for the injuries sustained by the appellant when he lost his balance and fell off the ladder.

The appellant was guilty of contributory negligence in refusing the respondents' offer of a trestle or tower scaffold to work from and in cutting the slates to size while on the ladder. Combining both those acts of contributory negligence against the employers' responsibility to protect their employee from the consequences of momentary acts of carelessness or inattention or the taking of foreseeable shortcuts by the provision of a fail-safe system, the appellant's contribution would be assessed at 50%.

Cases referred to in judgment

Ferguson v John Dawson & Partners (Contractors) Ltd [1976] IRLR 346, CA.

Market Investigations Ltd v Minister of Social Security [1969] 2 QB 173.
Readymix Concrete (South East) Ltd v Minister of Pensions and National Insurance [1968] 2 QB 497.
United States of America v Silk [1946] 331 US 704 US Sup Ct.

Notes

For categories of workers, see *Harvey on Industrial Relations and Employment Law* Division A.1.

For characteristics of the relationship of master and servant, see ibid, Division A.3.

Thomas Saunt (instructed by *D C Kaye & Co*) for Mr Lane.
Julian Matthews (instructed by *Vizards*) for Shire Roofing Co (Oxford) Ltd.

Lee Ting Sang v Chung Chi-Keung and another

PRIVY COUNCIL
LORD BRIDGE OF HARWICH, LORD TEMPLEMAN, LORD GRIFFITHS, LORD GOFF OF CHIEVELEY AND LORD LOWRY
29, 30 JANUARY; 8 MARCH 1990

Employment—Contract of employment—Service, of, or for services—Mason working mainly for one subcontractor—Paid piece rate or daily rate—Not supervised—Claim for compensation for injury at work—Whether mason subcontractor's employee—Employees' Compensation Ordinance (Laws of Hong Kong 1988 rev, c 282) s 2(1).

The applicant, a mason, was working for a subcontractor, at a construction site, chiselling concrete as instructed by the subcontractor. The applicant used tools supplied by the subcontractor and his work was not supervised but was inspected periodically by the main contractor's foreman. Depending upon the nature of the work he had to do the applicant was paid either a piece-work rate or a daily rate for working from 8 am to 5 pm. If he finished his work early he assisted the subcontractor to sharpen tools. He sometimes worked for other contractors but he gave priority to urgent work of the subcontractor telling those for whom he was then working to replace him. During the course of his work at the site he was injured. On his application against both the subcontractor and the main contractor for compensation under the Employees' Compensation Ordinance the judge dismissed the claim holding that the applicant was not an employee within section 2(1) of the Ordinance but an independent contractor. The Court of Appeal of Hong Kong upheld that decision. The applicant appealed.

Held—English common law standards had to be applied in determining whether the applicant was working as an employee of the subcontractor or an independent contractor, the fundamental test being whether or not he was performing services as a person in business on his own account and thus as an independent contractor; that since the factual circumstances in which he performed his work had to be investigated and evaluated in determining the applicant's status it was a question of fact for the trial judge, and an appellate court would not interfere with his finding unless it was unsupported by the evidence or was one which he could not reasonably have reached if he had properly directed himself on the law; but that, although the courts below had concurrently found as a fact that the applicant was an independent contractor, they had been misled in assessing the facts by wrongly relying on two dicta from inapposite cases; that the finding was contrary to the established facts and so unreasonable as to constitute an error of law, so that the Board were justified in reversing their decisions; and that, therefore, the applicant was working as an employee under a contract of service with the subcontractor and was entitled under the Employees' Compensation Ordinance to be compensated by the subcontractor and main contractor for his injury.

The appeal would therefore be allowed.

Market Investigations Ltd v Minister of Social Security [1969] 2 QB 173 applied.

Edwards v Bairstow [1956] AC 14, HL(E) and *O'Kelly v Trusthouse Forte plc* [1984] QB 90, CA considered.

Stevenson Jordan & Harrison Ltd v MacDonald & Evans [1952] 1 TLR 101, CA and *Bank voor Handel en Scheepvaart NV v Slatford* [1953] 1 QB 248, CA distinguished.

Decision of the Court of Appeal of Hong Kong [1988] 2 HKLR 476 reversed.

Cases referred to in judgments

Bank voor Handel en Scheepvaart NV v Slatford [1953] 1 QB 248, [1952] 2 All ER 956, CA.

Bobbey v W M Crosbie & Co Ltd (1915) 114 LT 244, HL.

Davies v Presbyterian Church of Wales [1986] 1 WLR 323, [1986] ICR 280, [1986] 1 All ER 705, HL.

Easdown v Cobb [1940] 1 All ER 49, HL).

Edwards v Bairstow [1956] AC 14, [1955] 3 WLR 410, [1955] 3 All ER 48, HL.

Market Investigations Ltd v Minister of Social Security [1969] 2 QB 173, [1969] 2 WLR 1, [1968] 3 All ER 732.

O'Kelly v Trusthouse Forte Plc [1984] QB 90, [1983] 3 WLR 605, [1983] ICR 728, [1983] 3 All ER 456, CA.

Smith v General Motor Cab Co Ltd [1911] AC 188, HL.

Srimati Bibhabati Devi v Kumar Ramendra Narayan Roy [1946] AC 508, PC.

Stevenson Jordan & Harrison Ltd v MacDonald & Evans [1952] 1 TLR 101, [1952] WN 7, CA.

Appeal

(No 44 of 1989) with special leave by the applicant, Lee Ting Sang, from the judgment of the Court of Appeal of Hong Kong (Cons V-P, Clough and Power JJA) [1988] 2 HKLR 476 given on 26 April 1988 dismissing his appeal from the judgment of Judge Yam in the District Court of Hong Kong (Civil Jurisdiction) at Kowloon on 10 December 1987 dismissing the applicant's claim against the respondents, Chung Chi-Keung and Shun Shing Construction & Engineering Co Ltd, for compensation for injuries suffered in the course of his employment.

Patrick Bennett QC and *Emma Griffiths* (instructed by *Philip Conway Thomas & Co*) for the applicant.
Peter Goldsmith QC and *Nigel Kat* (of the English and Hong Kong Bars) (instructed by *Macfarlanes*) for the respondents.

Lime-IT Ltd v Justin (Officer of the Board of Inland Revenue)

SPECIAL COMMISSIONER: DR JOHN F AVERY JONES CBE
2, 17 OCTOBER 2002

National insurance—Earnings of workers supplied by service companies etc—Provision of services through intermediary—Worker establishing information technology company—Company contracting with agency for provision of information technology services to client of agency—Whether company liable for national insurance contributions on earnings of worker—Whether, if arrangements had taken the form of a contract between worker and client, worker would have been regarded as gainfully employed by the client—Social Security Contributions (Intermediaries) Regulations 2000, SI 2000/727, reg 6(1)(c).

F was the sole shareholder and director of the taxpayer company, an information technology (IT) company formed on 4 April 2000. On 17 April 2000 the taxpayer company contracted with ERS (an agent which provided expert help and assistance to 'end-users') for the provision of certain IT services to M, as end-user. The contract provided for the taxpayer company to work on specific projects, such as organising and managing (rather than providing) a computer support function, introducing a new email system, organising remote access, and changing to Windows 2000. Those projects were expected to take one year to complete and the contract specified an estimated completion date of 10 April 2001. The taxpayer company (with F as its only employee) was expected to work an estimated 37 hours per week or such hours as were reasonably requested by M. F negotiated a non-standard condition to be inserted in the contract whereunder the taxpayer company had the right to substitute another person in place of itself, should it find itself unable to provide the whole or any part of the specified services for whatever reason. M had the right to refuse to accept the substitute on reasonable grounds. ERS, pursuant to the contract, concluded an agreement with M which reflected the terms of the agreement between the taxpayer company and ERS. During the M contract the taxpayer company worked for four other clients. F worked at one of M's offices, and partly from her office at home, where there was a room containing four computers dedicated to the taxpayer company's business. The taxpayer company appealed against a notice of decision dated 11 February 2002 whereby the Revenue determined that the taxpayer company was liable to pay primary and secondary Class 1 national insurance contributions in respect of F's earnings because the Social Security Contributions (Intermediaries) Regulations, which provided that in certain stated circumstances, payments to service companies were to be treated as earnings paid to a worker in respect of an employment, applied. Under reg 6(1) of the 2000 regulations, those regulations applied where: (a) an individual (the worker) personally performed services for the purposes of a business carried on by another person (the client); (b) the performance of those services by the worker was carried out, not under a contract directly between the client and the worker, but under arrangements involving an intermediary; and (c) the circumstances were such that, had the arrangements taken the form of a contract between the worker and the client, the worker would be regarded for the purposes of the Social Security Contributions and Benefits Act 1992 Pts I–V as employed in employed earner's employment by the client. It was common ground that the taxpayer company was an 'intermediary'. 'Employed earner's employment' was defined in s 2(1) of the 1992 Act to include a person who was gainfully employed under a contract of service. The issue in the appeal was whether, had the arrangements in the instant case taken the form of a contract between F and M, she would be regarded as employed under a contract of service.

Held—The basic test of whether someone was employed or self-employed was to ask whether a person was 'in business on his own account'. Three conditions had to be satisfied in order for a contract of service to exist. First, the servant must have agreed that in consideration of a wage or other remuneration he would provide his own work and skill in the performance of some service for his master. Second, the servant must have agreed, expressly or impliedly, that in the performance of that service he would be subject to the other's control in a sufficient degree to make that other master. Third, the other provisions of the contract must be consistent with its being a contract of service. In the instant case, there was very little evidence to suggest an employment relationship. In essence M was contracting for a particular IT job from a small business in the way one would expect an IT consultant to be engaged. Accordingly, on the hypothesis that F had contracted directly with M, she would not have been employed under a contract of service; she would have been in business on her own account. Dicta of Cooke J in *Market Investigations*

Ltd v Minister of Social Security [1969] 2 QB 173 at 184 and of MacKenna J in *Ready Mixed Concrete (South East) Ltd v Minister of Pensions and National Insurance* [1968] 2 QB 497 at 515 applied.

The taxpayer company's appeal would therefore be allowed.

Notes

For national insurance contributions on earnings paid through certain personal service companies, see *Simon's National Insurance Contributions Service* 8.346.

For the Social Security Contributions (Intermediaries) Regulations 2000, SI 2000/727, reg 6(1)(*c*), see *Simon's National Insurance Contributions Service* Part III.

Cases referred to in decision

Express and Echo Publications Ltd v Tanton [1999] ICR 693, [1999] IRLR 367, CA.

Hall (Inspector of Taxes) v Lorimer [1994] STC 23, [1994] 1 WLR 209, [1994] 1 All ER 250, 66 TC 349, CA.

Market Investigations Ltd v Minister of Social Security [1969] 2 QB 173, [1968] 3 All ER 732.

Ready Mixed Concrete (South East) Ltd v Minister of Pensions and National Insurance [1968] 2 QB 497, [1968] 1 All ER 433.

David Smith, of Accountax Consulting Ltd, for the taxpayer company.
Barry Williams, London regional advocacy unit, for the Revenue.

Macfarlane and another v Glasgow City Council

EMPLOYMENT APPEAL TRIBUNAL
LINDSAY J (PRESIDENT), DR A H BRIDGE AND T MARSLAND
25 MAY 2000

Contracts of employment—Meaning of 'employee'—Unfair dismissal—Exclusions and qualifications—meaning of 'employee'.

The applicants were qualified gymnastic instructors working at recreational and sports centres operated by Glasgow City Council. If, for any reason, the applicant was unable to take a class, she would arrange for a replacement from a register of coaches maintained by the council. Occasionally, the council itself organised the replacement. The replacements were paid directly by the council, not by the applicant. In 1998, the applicants were presented with a new form of contractual agreement which, in their view, significantly changed their terms and conditions of employment and had the effect of making them self-employed. They declined to accept the new form and subsequently claimed that they had been constructively and unfairly dismissed. The employers contested the claims on the ground that the applicants had always been self-employed. At a preliminary hearing, the employment tribunal held that the applicants were not employees and, therefore, were not entitled to claim unfair dismissal. The tribunal concluded that although the picture was largely one of the applicants being employees, the fact that they could arrange for substitutes to attend on their behalf was inconsistent with the existence of a contract of employment and, on that basis alone, the applicants' claims were bound to fail. The tribunal relied upon *Express and Echo Publications Ltd v Tanton*, where the Court of Appeal held that a contract of employment must necessarily contain an obligation on the part of the employee to provide his or her services personally. According to the tribunal, the present case could not be distinguished on the ground that the substitutes were paid directly by the council, whereas in Tanton, the worker could employ a substitute at his own expense. On appeal, it was submitted for the applicants that the tribunal had erred in concluding that informal, irregular arrangements for providing cover in the event of sickness indicated the absence of an obligation to perform services personally.

Held—The employment tribunal had erred in law in holding that the fact that the applicant gymnastic instructors could arrange for a replacement from a register maintained by the respondent council if for any reason they were unable to take a class was inconsistent with the existence of a contract of employment. The tribunal had wrongly held that it was bound to reach that conclusion by the decision of the Court of Appeal in *Express and Echo Publications Ltd v Tanton* that a contract of employment must necessarily contain an obligation on the part of the employee to provide his services personally.

A provision allowing for a limited ability to delegate does not inescapably lead to a conclusion that the contract was one for services, not a contract of service. Properly regarded, Tanton does not oblige a tribunal to conclude that under a contract of service the individual has always and in every event, however exceptional, personally to provide his or her services. Tanton indicates that a contract cannot be a contract of service if it contains a provision that the individual need not perform any services personally. The relevant clause in Tanton was extreme and there was nothing in the Court of Appeal's decision to suggest that it was meaning to depart from the observations of MacKenna J in *Ready Mixed Concrete (South East) Ltd v Minister of Pensions and National Insurance* that although freedom to do a job by one's own hands or by another's is inconsistent with a contract of service, a limited or occasional power of delegation may not be.

In the present case, the provision allowing the applicants to arrange for an approved replacement if unable to attend work could not be regarded as having such force that it had to overwhelm the factors pointing the other way and inescapably lead to a conclusion that the applicants were not employees. The present case was distinguishable from Tanton, where the individual, at his own will and his own expense, could perform his contract by sending along someone else. The applicants, however, could not simply choose not to work in person. Only if they were unable to attend could they arrange for another to take their class. Secondly, the applicants could only provide someone from the council's own register. To that extent the council could veto a replacement and could also ensure that such persons as were named on the register were persons in whom the council could repose trust and confidence. Thirdly, the council itself sometimes organised the replacement. Fourthly, the council did not pay the applicants for the time served by a substitute but instead paid the substitute direct.

The appeal would therefore be allowed. Since it could not be said that the only possible proper conclusion was that the applicants were employees, the matter would be remitted to the employment tribunal.

Cases referred to in judgment

Carmichael and another v National Power plc [2000] IRLR 43, HL.
Express and Echo Publications Ltd v Tanton [1999] IRLR 367, CA.
Lee Ting Sang v Chung Chi-Keung and another [1990] IRLR 236, PC.
Ready Mixed Concrete (South East) Ltd v Minister of Pensions and National Insurance [1968] 2 QB 497, HC.

Notes

For categories of workers, see *Harvey on Industrial Relations and Employment Law* Division A.1.

For characteristics of the relationship of master and servant, see ibid, Division A.3.

Rachel Edgar, representative, *Scottish Employment Rights Network* for the appellants.
Ian Truscott QC (instructed by *Glasgow City Council Legal Services*) for Glasgow City Council.

Malik v Bank of Credit and Commerce International SA (in liquidation)

Mahmud v Bank of Credit and Commerce International SA (in liquidation)

HOUSE OF LORDS
LORD GOFF OF CHIEVELEY, LORD MACKAY OF CLASHFERN, LORD MUSTILL, LORD NICHOLLS OF BIRKENHEAD AND LORD STEYN
24, 25, 26 FEBRUARY, 12 JUNE 1997

Employment—Contract of service—Implied term—Implied term in contract of employment that employer would not conduct itself in manner likely to damage relationship of trust and confidence between employer and employee—Bank employees—Bank involved in fraudulent activities—Employees made redundant by liquidators—Employees claiming damages for stigma suffered in search for future employment as former employees of bank—Whether damages recoverable in law.

The two appellants were long-serving employees of a bank which collapsed as the result of a massive and notorious fraud perpetrated by those controlling the bank. The appellants were unaware of and had no part in the fraud. After the bank went into liquidation the appellants were made redundant by the liquidators and thereafter they found difficulty in obtaining employment in the banking field because of their association with the bank. The appellants lodged a claim in the liquidation for 'stigma compensation' arising out of the fact that they had been put at a disadvantage in the employment market. The appellants appealed to the court against the liquidators' rejection of their claim, contending that it was an implied term of their contracts of employment that an employer would not conduct his business in a manner calculated or likely to destroy or seriously damage the relationship of confidence and trust between the employer and employee. The judge held on the trial of a preliminary issue that a claim for stigma compensation did not disclose a reasonable cause of action or a sustainable claim for damages because the term contended for could not be implied in a contract of employment as it was not part of that contract that the employer should prepare an employee for employment with future employers or that he should ensure that employees were not put at a disadvantage in the employment market in the event of their employment being terminated. On appeal, the Court of Appeal held that although the employees had an arguable case that there had been a breach of the implied mutual obligation of trust and confidence the employees had no remedy as damages were not recoverable in contract for damage to or loss of an existing reputation except in certain limited situations which did not apply. The Court of Appeal accordingly dismissed the appeal. The appellants appealed to the House of Lords. The liquidators contended that injury to reputation was protected by the law of defamation, that the implied obligation of trust and confidence was not breached if the employer's dishonest behaviour was directed at defrauding third parties, not the employees, and that the employee had to have been aware of such conduct while he was an employee.

Held—The appeal would be allowed for the following reasons—

(1) In appropriate cases damages could in principle be awarded for loss of reputation caused by breach of contract. Furthermore, provided a relevant breach of contract was established and the requirements of causation, remoteness and mitigation were satisfied, financial loss in respect of damage to reputation caused by breach of contract could be recovered for breach of a contract of employment.

(2) An employer was under an implied obligation that he would not, without reasonable and proper cause, conduct his business in a manner likely to destroy or seriously damage the relationship of confidence and trust between employer and employee, and an employer who breached the trust and confidence term would be liable if he thereby caused continuing financial loss of a nature that was reasonably foreseeable. Thus, if it was reasonably foreseeable that conduct in breach of the trust and confidence term would prejudicially affect employees' future employment prospects and loss of that type was sustained in consequence of a breach, then in principle damages in respect of the loss would be recoverable. The trust-destroying conduct need not be directed at the employee, either individually or as part of a group, in order to attract liability, nor was it necessary that the employee must have been aware of the employer's trust-destroying conduct while he was an employee; *Addis v Gramophone Co Ltd* [1908–10] All ER Rep 1 explained; *Marbe v George Edwardes (Daly's Theatre) Ltd* [1927] All ER Rep 253, approved; *Withers v General Theatre Corp Ltd* [1933] All ER Rep 385 overruled.

(3) Since the bank had promised, in an implied term, not to conduct a dishonest or corrupt business the promised benefit being employment by an honest employer which benefit did not materialise the appellants were entitled to damages if they proved that they were handicapped in the labour market in consequence of the bank's corruption.

Decision of the Court of Appeal [1995] 3 All ER 545 reversed.

Notes

For damages recoverable for breach of contract of employment, see 16 *Halsbury's Laws* (4th edn 2000 reissue) paras 455–456.

Cases referred to in opinions

Addis v Gramophone Co Ltd [1909] AC 488, [1908–10] All ER Rep 1, HL.
Aerial Advertising Co v Batchelors Peas Ltd (Manchester) [1938] 2 All ER 788.

Anglo-Continental Holidays Ltd v Typaldos Lines (London) Ltd [1967] 2 Lloyd's Rep 61, CA.
Brandt v Nixdorf Computer Ltd [1991] 3 NZLR 750, NZ HC.
Clayton (Herbert) & Jack Waller Ltd v Oliver [1930] AC 209, [1930] All ER Rep 414, HL.
Cointax v Myham & Son [1913] 2 KB 220.
Foaminol Laboratories Ltd v British Artid Plastics Ltd [1941] 2 All ER 393.
GKN Centrax Gears Ltd v Matbro Ltd [1976] 2 Lloyd's Rep 555, CA.
Hadley v Baxendale (1854) 9 Exch 341, [1843–60] All ER Rep 461, 156 ER 145.
Imperial Group Pension Trust Ltd v Imperial Tobacco Ltd [1991] 2 All ER 597, [1991] 1 WLR 589.
Lewis v Motorworld Garages Ltd [1986] ICR 157, CA.
Lonrho plc v Fayed (No 5) [1994] 1 All ER 188, [1993] 1 WLR 1489, CA.
Marbe v George Edwardes (Daly's Theatre) Ltd [1928] 1 KB 269, [1927] All ER Rep 253, CA.
Maw v Jones (1890) 25 QBD 107, DC.
Norton Tool Co Ltd v Tewson [1973] 1 All ER 183, [1973] 1 WLR 45, NIRC.
O'Laoire v Jackel International Ltd (No 2) [1991] ICR 718, CA.
Scally v Southern Health and Social Services Board (British Medical Association, third party) [1991] 4 All ER 563, [1992] 1 AC 294, [1991] 3 WLR 778, HL.
Spring v Guardian Assurance plc [1994] 3 All ER 129, [1995] 2 AC 296, [1994] 3 WLR 354, HL
Vivian v Coca-Cola Export Corp [1984] 2 NZLR 289, NZ HC.
Vorvis v Insurance Corp of British Columbia (1989) 58 DLR (4th) 193, Can SC.
Whelan v Waitaki Meats Ltd [1991] 2 NZLR 74, NZ HC.
Withers v General Theatre Corp Ltd [1933] 2 KB 536, [1933] All ER Rep 385, CA.
Woods v WM Car Services (Peterborough) Ltd [1981] ICR 666, EAT; *affd* [1982] ICR 693, CA.

Appeal

Qaiser Mansoor Malik and Raihan Nasir Mahmud appealed with leave granted by the Appeal Committee from the decision of the Court of Appeal (Glidewell, Morritt and Aldous LJJ) ([1995] 3 All ER 545, [1996] ICR 406) delivered on 9 March 1995 dismissing their appeal from the decision of Evans-Lombe J ([1994] TLR 100) delivered on 16 February 1994 whereby, on the trial of a preliminary issue, the judge held that proofs of debt submitted to the respondents, the provisional liquidators of Bank of Credit and Commerce International SA, did not disclose a reasonable cause of action or a sustainable claim for damages and had been properly rejected by the liquidators.

Eldred Tabachnik QC and *Andrew Stafford* (instructed by *Manches & Co*) for the appellants.
Patrick Elias QC and *Christopher Jeans* (instructed by *Lovell White Durrant*) for the liquidators.

Market Investigations v Minister of Social Security

QUEEN'S BENCH DIVISION
COOKE J
24, 29 JULY 1968

National insurance—Employed person—Part-time employment—Series of contracts of employment—Whether contract of service or for services—Interviewer working for market research company—Extent and degree of control—Nature and provisions of contracts—National Insurance Act 1965 (c 51) s 1(2)—National Insurance (Industrial Injuries) Act 1965 (c 52) s 1(2), Sch 1 Pt 1 para 1.

A company engaged in market research employed a number of persons as interviewers for short periods of time. Mrs I was employed by the company on several occasions in this way. Before she was engaged to undertake a particular survey Mrs I agreed with the company, in consideration for a fixed remuneration, to provide her own work and skill in the performance of a service for the company. The company might specify the persons to be interviewed, the questions to be asked, the order in which questions should be asked and recorded, how answers were to be recorded and how she should probe for answers. She might be required to attend the company's office for instructions or might receive these from a supervisor. Within the period specified for completion of a survey, however, she was normally free to work when she wanted, could undertake similar work for other organisations, and could not be moved by the company from the area in which she had agreed to work. Furthermore, when she was working in the field the supervisor would have no means of getting into touch with her, and the company's officers were of the opinion that she could not be dismissed in the middle of a survey. No provision was made in the agreements between Mrs I and the company for time off, sick pay or holidays. On the question whether, whilst working under agreements with the company, Mrs I was included in the class of 'employed persons' (ie, persons employed under a contract of service) for the purposes of the National Insurance Act 1965 s 1(2), and was employed in 'insurable employment' within the meaning of the National Insurance (Industrial Injuries) Act 1965 s 1(2), and para 1 of Pt 1 of Sch 1.

Held—Mrs I had been employed by the company under a series of contracts of service and hence was within the terms 'employed persons' and persons in 'insurable employment' in those Acts, because—

(i) the extent and degree of control exercised by the company, no other factors being taken into account, were consistent with her being employed under a contract of service; and

(ii) in particular, it not having been shown that Mrs I was in business on her own account, the nature and provisions of the contracts as a whole were consistent, rather than inconsistent, with their being contracts of service.

Appeal dismissed.

Notes

For employment under contract see 16 *Halsbury's Laws* 4th edn (2000 reissue) para 1 et seq.

For the distinction between a contract of service and a contract for services, see ibid para 501.

Cases referred to in judgment

Amalgamated Engineering Union v Minister of Pensions and National Insurance [1963] 1 All ER 864, [1963] 1 WLR 441.
Bank Voor Handel en Scheepvaart NV v Slatford [1952] 2 All ER 956, [1953] 1 QB 248, *revsd* sub nom *Bank Voor Handel en Scheepvaart NV v Administrator of Hungarian Property,* [1954] 1 All ER 969, [1954] AC 584.
Cassidy v Ministry of Health [1951] 1 All ER 574, [1951] 2 KB 343.
Collins v Hertfordshire County Council [1947] 1 All ER 633, [1947] KB 598.
Hobbs v Royal Arsenal Co-operative Society Ltd (1930), 23 BWCC 254, 144 LT 10.
Montreal Locomotive Works v Montreal and A-G for Canada [1947] 1 DLR 161.
Morren v Swinton and Pendlebury Borough Council [1965] 2 All ER 349, [1965] 1 WLR 576.
Queensland Stations Pty v Federal Comr of Taxation (1945), 70 CLR 539.
Ready Mixed Concrete (South East) v Minister of Pensions and National Insurance [1968] 1 All ER 433, [1968] 2 QB 497.
Sadler v Henlock (1855), 4 E & B 570, 3 CLR 760.
US v Silk (1946), 331 US 704.
Whittaker v Minister of Pensions and National Insurance [1966] 3 All ER 631, [1967] 1 QB 156.

Case stated

This was an appeal by way of case stated by Market Investigations (the company) against the decision of the Minister of Social Security given on 16 February 1967, under s 64(1) of the National Insurance Act 1965, and s 35(1) of the National Insurance (Industrial Injuries) Act 1965, that Mrs Ann Florence Irving while working as an interviewer in association with the company during certain weeks in 1964 and 1965 was: (i) included in the class of employed persons for the purposes of the National Insurance Acts, 1946 and 1965; and (ii) was employed in insurable employment within the meaning of the National Insurance (Industrial Injuries) Acts, 1946 and 1965.

Peter Pain QC and *K E Evans* (instructed by *P R Kimber*) for the company.
Gordon Slynn (instructed by the *Solicitor*, Ministry of Social Security) for the Minister.

Massey v Crown Life Insurance Co

COURT OF APPEAL, CIVIL DIVISION
LORD DENNING MR, LAWTON AND EVELEIGH LJJ
2, 3, 4 NOVEMBER 1977

Unfair dismissal—Excluded classes of employment—Employment under contract for services—Employer and manager agreeing for tax purposes that manager to be self-employed in the future—Inland Revenue accepting arrangement—Manager operating under firm name rather than own name—Manager continuing to perform same duties as before—Manager dismissed and bringing claim for unfair dismissal—Whether manager an individual who has entered into or worked under a contract of employment—Whether manager an 'employee'—Trade Union and Labour Relations Act 1974 s 30(1) Sch 1 para 4(1).

Master and servant—Contract of service—Distinction between contract of service and contract for services—Declaration of parties—Intention of employer and manager to change manager's status to self-employed for the purposes—Genuine agreement with explicit terms—Whether parties' agreement conclusive in determining status of manager.

The appellant was employed as a branch manager by the respondents, an insurance company, from 1971 until 1973 under two contracts, under one of which he was treated as an employee and under the other as a general agent. Under his contract as an employee the appellant was paid wages by the respondents from which PAYE tax and contributions to the respondents' pension scheme were deducted, and he received a memorandum under the Contracts of Employment Act 1963. Under the general agency contract the appellant was a freelance agent paid on commission only and free to work for other insurance brokers. In 1973 the appellant, who wished to be taxed as a self-employed person, approached the respondents with a view to coming to a new arrangement with them. The respondents agreed and the parties entered into a new agreement whereby the appellant called himself 'John L Massey and Associates', a name which he registered under the Registration of Business Names Act 1916. Under the new agreement John L Massey and Associates were appointed manager of the appellant's branch, the appellant was repaid his contributions from the respondents' pension fund, and was thereafter paid by the respondents without tax or other deductions being made. The appellant arranged with the Inland Revenue to be treated as a self-employed person for tax purposes. Under the agreement John L Massey and Associates were allowed to employ other persons in the course of their work, but the appellant's duties vis-à-vis the respondents remained almost indentical to his previous duties. In 1975 the appellant was dismissed by the respondents with one month's notice. The appellant made a complaint to an industrial tribunal of unfair dismissal. The tribunal considered, as a preliminary issue, whether the appellant was entitled to make a claim for unfair dismissal under the Trade Union and Labour Relations Act 1974, para 4 of Sch 1 to which extended the right not to be unfairly dismissed only to an 'employee', which by s 30(1) was defined as 'an individual who has entered into or [has worked under] a contract of employment'. A contract of employment was further defined as a 'contract of service ... whether it is express or implied and (if it is express) whether it is oral or in writing'. The tribunal held that the work which the appellant performed for the respondents was not performed under a contract of employment. The appellant appealed to the Employment Appeal Tribunal which dismissed his appeal. He appealed to the Court of Appeal contending that his relationship with the respondents had remained throughout that of employer and employee regardless of what he chose to call himself or the way in which he was assessed to tax.

Held—The appellant could not say that for the purpose of claiming tax advantages he was not an employee and then say that for the purpose of claiming compensation for unfair dismissal he was an employee. The 1973 agreement was a genuine transaction which had been aimed to effect, and did in fact effect, a change in the appellant's status from that of an employee to that of a self-employed person, and he was not therefore an 'employee' within the meaning of s 30 of the 1974 Act and could not bring a claim for unfair dismissal under the Act. Accordingly the appeal would be dismissed.

Ferguson v John Dawson & Partners (Contractors) Ltd [1976] 3 All ER 817 distinguished.

Notes

For the right of an employee not to be unfairly dismissed, see 16 *Halsbury's Laws* (4th Edn 2000 reissue) para 471.

For the distinction between a contract of service and a contract for services, see ibid para 501.

For the Trade Union and Labour Relations Act 1974 s 30(1) Sch 1 para 4, see 44 *Halsbury's Statutes* (3rd Edn) 1781, 1787. The legislation is now consolidated in the Trade Union and Labour Relations (Consolidation Act) 1992, see 16 *Halsbury's Statutes* (4th edn) (2000 reissue) 183.

Cases referred to in judgments

Alexander v Rayson [1936] 1 KB 169.
Construction Industry Training Board v Labour Force Ltd [1970] 3 All ER 220, 5 ITR 290, DC.
Davis v New England College of Arundel [1977] ICR 6, EAT.
Ferguson v John Dawson & Partners (Contractors) Ltd [1976] 3 All ER 817,[1976] 1 WLR 1213, CA.
Global Plant Ltd v Secretary of State for Social Services [1971] 3 All ER 385, [1972] 1 QB 139.
Graham (Maurice) Ltd v Brunswick (1974) 16 KIR 158, DC.
Inland Revenue Comrs v Duke of Westminster [1936] AC 1 sub nom *Westminster (Duke) v Inland Revenue Comrs* 19 TC 490, HL.
Ready Mixed Concrete (South East) Ltd v Minister of Pensions and National Insurance [1968] 1 All ER 433, [1968] 2 QB 497.
Stevenson Jordon and Harrison Ltd v MacDonald and Evans [1952] 1 TLR 101, 69 RPC 10, CA.

Appeal

This was an appeal by John Linnell Massey against a decision of the Employment Appeal Tribunal (Kilner Brown J, Mr A C Blyghton and Mr A J Nicol) dated 30 November 1976, dismissing his appeal against a decision of an industrial tribunal (chairman C H A Lewes) whereby the tribunal determined, on a preliminary issue, that the appellant could not pursue a claim for unfair dismissal against the respondents, Crown Life Insurance Co, because he was not 'employed' by them at the date of his dismissal.

Alistair Sharp (instructed by *Rosling, King, Aylett & Co*) for the appellant.
Anthony Boswood (instructed by *Coward Chance*) for the respondents.

Maurice v Betterware UK Ltd

EMPLOYMENT APPEAL TRIBUNAL
KEENE J, MR I EZEKIEL AND MRS T A MARSLAND
3 JULY 2000

Employment—Employment tribunals—Pre-hearing review—Chairman making no order requiring deposit—Second pre-hearing review—Chairman making order requiring deposit—Whether holding second pre-hearing review within powers of tribunal—Whether appeal against chairman's order within time—Whether principles of issue estoppel applicable.

M presented a complaint of unfair dismissal against B Ltd. At a pre-hearing review on 4 December 1998 the chairman made no order under r 7(4) of the Rules of Procedure in Sch 1 to the Employment Tribunals (Constitution and Rules of Procedure) Regulations 1993 (the 1993 Regulations). That provision empowered a tribunal to order a party to pay a deposit of an amount not exceeding £150 as a condition of being permitted to continue to take part in the proceedings. B Ltd requested a second pre-hearing review which took place before a different chairman on 4 August 1999. The chairman concluded that M's case had no reasonable prospect of success and made an order that M pay a deposit of £150 as a condition of proceeding. M appealed by notice dated 13 September 1999 contending: (i) that there was no power in an employment tribunal to reconsider a decision made under r 7; (ii) that the review power which the tribunal possessed under r 11 of the Rules of Procedure in Sch 1 to the 1993 Regulations did not apply to cases dealing with an order under r 7 or a decision not to make an order; and (iii) that the reconsideration of a previous decision under r 7 was restricted by the doctrine of issue estoppel. B Ltd contended that the appeal was out of time under r 3(2) of the Employment Appeal Tribunal Rules 1993 (the 1993 Rules) which provided that the period within which an appeal to the appeal tribunal might be instituted was 42 days from the date of the decision appealed against.

Held—(1) It was clear from r 3(2) of the 1993 Rules that the 42-day time limit simply did not apply to a decision to list a matter for a pre-hearing review, whether the first or any subsequent pre-hearing review. The notice of appeal was lodged within 42 days of the order and the reasons for the order being given by the employment tribunal chairman on 4 August 1999. Therefore, the appeal was within time.

(2) Nothing in either the statutory or the regulatory provisions expressly limited the number of times a pre-hearing review might be held. If a numerical limit had been intended then s 9 of the Employment Tribunals Act 1996 and the 1993 Regulations would have expressly spelled out such a limit. There were good practical reasons why a second pre-hearing review could be very useful, given the purposes to which s 9 of the 1996 Act referred. That might particularly be so in a large complicated case or where there was a considerable time lapse between the lodging of the application initially and the full hearing of that application. But even in cases like the instant one, a second pre-hearing review might have some value.

(3) The review power under r 11 of the Rules of Procedure in Sch 1 to the 1993 Regulations did not apply, because that power only existed according to r 11(1) where there had been a 'decision', and it was clear from reg 2 of the 1993 Regulations that a decision under r 7 did not fall within that definition and did not give rise to the review power under r 11. The review power existed, as was made clear by r 11 read in combination with the definition in reg 2(2), in situations where there had been decisions of a substantive nature, including actual awards made on an application. But it did not follow from that that an employment tribunal could not revisit such interlocutory matters in appropriate cases. By r 16(1) the tribunal had power at any time, on the application of a party or of its own motion, to give directions on any matter arising in

connection with the proceedings. Accordingly, there was a power in an employment tribunal to revisit that matter, whether there had been an order made under r 7 or whether it had been decided to make no such order.

(4) Issue estoppel was not strictly speaking applicable to the situation with which the tribunal had to deal. When an employment tribunal exercised its powers under r 7(4) it was not truly deciding an issue between the parties. It was using its powers to control its own proceedings and to impose conditions on what seemed to be unmeritorious applications. None the less, the principles underlying issue estoppel were not irrelevant. The power to re-visit a r 7 issue was not a power to be used in order to have a second or third or further bite at the same cherry when there had been no material change in facts or in the law, nor was it a procedure to be used to enable a party to go, as it were, chairman shopping, moving from one chairman to another until it could find a chairman who would come up with a decision in its favour. It would be quite wrong for either party to be able simply to make a second or third attempt at getting the outcome which it wanted if there was no material change in the facts or the law. It followed, that if a matter was considered on a second or further occasion, it was incumbent upon the chairman to consider whether or not there had been such a change and that in turn required some consideration to be given as to the basis of the earlier decision which it was being asked to re-visit. On that basis, while there was a power in an employment tribunal to re-visit the matters arising under r 7, it was a power only to be exercised if there were a material change in the factual circumstances or a relevant change in the law. It followed that if a chairman was faced with an application by a party to revisit the issue arising under r 7 the approach should be one of asking whether there had been a material change in the facts or law and whether, as a consequence of that, a different outcome should now obtain. That meant that at such a further hearing a chairman had to consider the basis of the previous decision. In the instant case the chairman declined to be informed about the previous pre-hearing review. That approach was mistaken: the chairman adopted the wrong approach as a matter of law.

The appeal would, accordingly, be allowed.

Notes

For the Employment Tribunals (Constitution and Rules of Procedure) Regulations 1993, SI 1993/2687 and the Employment Appeal Tribunal Rules 1993, SI 1993/2854, see *Harvey on Industrial Relations and Employment Law* Division R.

Cases referred to in judgment

Arnold v National Westminster Bank plc [1991] 2 AC 93, [1991] 3 All ER 41, HL.

Express and Echo Publications Ltd v Tanton [1999] ICR 693, [1999] IRLR 367, CA.
Glossop v Shropshire Community Health Service NHS Trust (27 July 1999 unreported) EAT.
Hunter v Chief Constable of West Midlands Police [1982] AC 529, [1981] 3 All ER 727, HL.
Kuttapan v London Borough of Croydon [1999] IRLR 349, EAT.
Mackie v John Holt Vintners Ltd [1982] ICR 146, [1982] IRLR 236, EAT.
Nikitas v Solihull Metropolitan B C [1986] ICR 291, EAT.

Appeal

Cynthia Maurice appealed from an interlocutory decision of the employment tribunal of 4 August 1999 making an order under r 7(4) of the Rules of Procedure in Sch 1 to the Employment Tribunals (Constitution and Procedure) Regulations 1993 requiring her to pay a deposit of £150 as a condition of continuing her action for unfair dismissal, on the ground that a tribunal had held a previous pre-hearing review without making an order and there was no jurisdiction in the tribunal to hold a further pre-hearing review.

David Curwen (instructed by *DAS Legal Expenses Insurance & Co Ltd*) for M.
Christopher Mordue (instructed by *Pinsent Curtis*, Leeds) for the company.

McLeod and others v Hellyer Brothers Ltd

Wilson and another v Boston Deep Sea Fisheries Ltd

COURT OF APPEAL (CIVIL DIVISION)
SLADE, MUSTILL AND RALPH GIBSON LJJ
25 FEBRUARY 1987

Contracts of employment—Meaning of 'employee'—Continuity of employment—Redundancy payments—Exclusions and qualifications—Meaning of 'employee'—Exclusions and qualifications—Service qualification—Was employee dismissed?—Termination by employer—Was employee dismissed?—Termination by employer—Termination of fixed-term contract—Employment Appeal Tribunal—Court of Appeal—Employment Protection (Consolidation) Act 1978 ss 81, 83(2)(a), 83(2)(b), 101(2), 136, 153(1); Sch 11 para 17; Sch 13 para 9

The five appellants in these two appeals were all trawlermen based on the Port of Hull. Prior to January 1984 they had each worked exclusively for the respective respondent over a long period of time. They had served on the terms of a series of 'crew agreements' which were signed on each engagement on board a fishing vessel. In between sailings they had registered as unemployed and received social security benefits. Their final sailings had all ended some time in 1983 on the basis of what was termed a 'mutual consent discharge' In January 1984 both companies announced that all their vessels were being taken out of commission and that they were ceasing their fishing activities. The trawlermen claimed that they had been dismissed on grounds of redundancy. They argued that at all material times they had been employed under a 'global' contract of employment which had been unilaterally terminated by that announcement, that therefore they had been dismissed within the meaning of s 83(2)(a) of the Employment Protection (Consolidation) Act and that they had sufficient continuous service to qualify for redundancy payments. The two cases were heard separately but by the same industrial tribunal. By a majority decision in each case, the chairman dissenting, the claims were upheld. According to the majority, as at January 1984, each claimant, whilst not currently employed under a subsisting crew agreement, was employed under a continuing contract of employment. The majority found that, in the intervals between the successive crew agreements, 'the reality was that the applicants were on an inactive register and that the respondent had the right to lay off his men for indefinite periods which was accepted by the applicants'. The majority therefore held that each applicant had been dismissed in January 1984 with sufficient continuous service to claim a redundancy payment. The EAT allowed appeals against those decisions. In the second case, the Appeal Tribunal refused leave for a new argument to be raised in answer to the employer's appeal, viz that the trawlermen had been employed on a series of fixed-term contracts, the last of which expired without being renewed at the end of the final sailing in March 1983 so that there was a deemed dismissal under s 83(2)(b).

Held—The industrial tribunal had erred in holding that when the respondent employers announced that they were ceasing fishing operations, each of the appellant trawlermen, whilst not employed under a crew agreement at that time, was employed under a 'global' contract of employment which spanned the intervening periods between crew agreements and which was terminated by that announcement. The tribunal had erred, therefore, in holding that the appellants had been dismissed in law with sufficient service to entitle them to redundancy payments.

In order to create a contract of service there must be mutual legally binding obligations on each side. Although it may be open to an industrial tribunal properly to infer from the parties' conduct (notwithstanding the absence of any evidence as to any express agreement of this nature) the existence of a continuing overriding arrangement which governed the whole of their relationship and itself amounted to a contract of employment, a global contract cannot be brought into existence simply by counting the heads of a series of individual contracts which may have subsisted during its alleged currency. There has to be present the necessary element of continuing mutual contractual obligations.

In the present case it could not be inferred from the facts as found that at the times when there was no subsisting crew agreement, the parties were still subject to mutual contractual obligations sufficient to found a global unbroken contract of employment. It was not possible to infer from the parties' conduct the existence in between crew agreements of a trawlerman's obligation 'to serve' which is part of the 'irreducible minimum of obligation' on the part of an employee required to support the existence of a contract of service. The men had never placed themselves under a legally binding obligation to make themselves available for work for the respective respondents in between crew agreements or to refrain from seeking or accepting employment from another trawler owner during such periods. On the contrary, on the appellants' own admissions, had they wished they could have signed on and worked for other employers in between crew agreements. For their part, the employers could not be said by their conduct to have placed themselves under a contractual obligation to offer employment to any particular individual after the termination of a crew agreement to which he was a party.

Whether at the relevant date the appellants were employed under contracts of employment and therefore enjoyed the status of 'employees' depended partly on the interpretation of various written documents and partly on the inferences to be drawn from the parties' conduct. Therefore, the principle set out in *Edwards v Bairstow* and followed by the majority of the Court of Appeal in *O'Kelly and others v Trusthouse Forte plc* [1983] IRLR 369 applied and an appellate court was entitled to interfere with the decision of the industrial tribunal only if the tribunal had misdirected itself in law or its decision was one which no tribunal properly instructed could have reached.

It could not be accepted that the reasoning of the majority in *O'Kelly's* [1983] IRLR 369 case was overruled by implication by the House of Lords in *Davies v Presbyterian Church of Wales* [1986] IRLR 194. The observation of Lord Templeman as to the inapplicability of *Edwards v Bairstow* was restricted to the case before him, a case which turned entirely upon the construction of a document and thus a pure question of law to which there could be only one correct answer. Since their Lordships made no reference to *O'Kelly's* [1983] IRLR 369 case where, as in the present case, the relevant contractual arrangements were not embodied in a single document but had been concluded (if at all) by a course of conduct, the *Davies* [1986] IRLR 194 decision could not be said necessarily to imply any disapproval of the reasoning of the majority in *O'Kelly* [1983] IRLR 369.

The decision in the present case was one to which no person acting judicially and properly instructed as to the law could have come and, therefore, the EAT was entitled to overrule it. The EAT was also entitled to substitute its own conclusion. Where the EAT finds that the industrial tribunal has misdirected itself in law, the statement in *Dobie v Burns International Security* [1984] IRLR 329 that if a tribunal's decision was wrong or might have been wrong, the case must be remitted to the tribunal, must be read subject to an implicit qualification correctly stated by Waite J in the present case, that where a conclusion reached as a result of a misdirection is plainly and unarguably wrong upon the facts found by the industrial tribunal, and those facts do not require further amplification or reinvestigation, the EAT is bound to substitute its own conclusion as to what those findings require in law. The present case, therefore, was not appropriate for remittance to the industrial tribunal since, on the material before the EAT, the only decision to which as a matter of law they could have come was that, on the relevant date, none of the appellants was employed by the respective respondents under a contract of employment so that none of them was dismissed. There was no reason to disturb the order of the EAT.

The EAT had not erred in refusing the employees in the second case leave to raise in answer to the employer's appeal the new issue of whether they had been employed under a series of fixed-term contracts.

It is within the powers of the EAT to establish rules of practice to control the taking of new points on appeal contrary to the justice of the case. In *Secretary of State for Employment v Newcastle upon Tyne City Council*, the position of respondents to an appeal from an industrial tribunal was rightly treated by the EAT as similar to that of respondents to an appeal from a county court to the Court of Appeal—that, in the absence of special or exceptional circumstances, they cannot be permitted to raise a new point of law in order to retain a judgment in their favour unless it is clear that no new evidence is necessary and that no further relevant evidence or investigation of the evidence given would have been produced or carried out if the new point had been pleaded, and provided further that the point has not been abandoned.

In the present case, the EAT had rightly regarded the point as to fixed-term employment as a new point of law. It had formed no part of the case before the industrial tribunal, the attention of the tribunal had not been directed to it and an appeal on the basis of that new ground could not have been disposed of on the tribunal's findings of fact.

Moreover, there were no grounds for the Court of Appeal to grant the appellants leave to raise a new case which would in substance require, in part at least, a rehearing before the industrial tribunal. The Court could not accept that such leave was required in the interests of justice having regard to similar cases pending. It would be contrary to the settled practice of industrial tribunals and the EAT, which applies equally to those who make claims and those against whom such claims are made, and which is in conformity with the long-established practice of the Court of Appeal, to permit these appellants who have failed in the case which they chose to advance, to present for consideration a new case to the industrial tribunal. There was nothing which in justice required an exceptional course to be taken in the appellants' favour.

Obiter dicta

The rule as stated by Widgery LJ in *Wilson v Liverpool Corporation*, that if a point is not taken in the court of trial it cannot be taken in the Appeal Court unless that court is in possession of all material necessary to dispose of the matter finally, without injustice to the other party and without recourse to a further hearing below, except where justice demands a different view to be taken owing to the special circumstances of the case, was to be preferred to the more stringent test stated in the NIRC in *GKN (Cwmbran) Ltd v Lloyd,* which rules out a new point on appeal which could have been but was not raised before the tribunal, irrespective of whether any further evidence would be necessary.

Cases referred to in judgment

Airfix Footwear Ltd v Cope [1978] IRLR 396.
Central Scotland Water Development Board v Johnston 6 ITR 86.
Chadwick v Pioneer Private Telephone Co Ltd [1941] 1 All ER 522.
Davies v Presbyterian Church of Wales [1986] IRLR 194.
Dixon v BBC [1979] ICR 281.
Dobie v Burns International Security [1984] IRLR 329.
Edwards (Inspector of Taxes) v Bairstow (1956) AC 14, [1955] 3 All ER 48, 36 TC 207.
Flack v Kodak Ltd [1986] IRLR 255.
Ford v Warwickshire CC [1983] IRLR 126.
GKN (Cwmbran) Ltd v Lloyd [1972] ICR 214.
Hereford and Worcester County Council v Tolley [1976] ICR 450.
Hunter v Smith's Dock Co Ltd [1968] 1 WLR 1865.
J Smith Coats (London) Ltd v Rifkin (1970) 5 ITR 188.
Kumchyk v Derby City Council [1978] ICR 1116.
Melon v Hector Powe Ltd [1980] IRLR 477.
Nethermere (St Neots) Ltd v Gardner [1984] IRLR 240.
O'Kelly and others v Trusthouse Forte plc [1983] IRLR 369.
Oscroft v Benabo [1967] 1 WLR 1087.
Pitts v Boyd Lines Ltd [1986] ICR 244.
Puttick v John Wright & Sons (Blackwall) Ltd [1972] ICR 457.
Ready Mixed Concrete (South East) Ltd v Minister of Pensions and National Insurance [1968] 1 All ER 433, [1968] 2 QB 497.
Secretary of State for Employment v Newcastle upon Tyne City Council [1980] ICR 407.
Smith v Baker & Sons [1891] AC 325.
Stewart v Alexander (1969) 4 ITR 234.
Thomas v Marconi's Wireless Telegraph Co Ltd [1965] 1 WLR 850.
UCATT v Brain [1981] IRLR 224.
Wilson v Liverpool Corporation [1971] 1 WLR 302.
Wiltshire CC v NATFHE [1980] IRLR 198.
Woods v WM Car Services (Peterborough) Ltd [1982] IRLR 413.
Young v British Aeroplane Ltd [1944] KB 718.

Notes

For an employee's right to a redundancy payment, see *Harvey on Industrial Relations and Employment Law* Division E.
For categories of workers, see ibid, Division A.1.

Mr J Samuels QC and *Mr P Hamlin* (instructed by *Collyer-Bristow*) for Mr McLeod, Mr Margerison and Mr Kemp.
Mr A Pardoe and *Mr R Wynne-Griffiths* (instructed by *Walter West*) for Mr Wilson and Mr Johnson.
The Hon J Melville Williams QC and *Mr J Perry* (instructed by *Chambers Thomas*) for Hellyer Brothers Ltd.
Mr A Pardoe and *Mr R Wynne-Griffiths* (instructed by *Andrew M Jackson & Co*) for Boston Deep Sea Fisheries Ltd.

McManus v Griffiths (Inspector of Taxes) and related appeal

CHANCERY DIVISION
LIGHTMAN J
10, 18 JULY 1997

Emoluments from office or employment—Employment—Meaning—Contract of service or contract for services—Taxpayer and taxpayer's spouse employed by club—Taxpayer's spouse required to carry on catering business on own account at club's premises—Whether profits from catering business within Sch D or Sch E.

Mr and Mrs M were employed as steward and stewardess of a golf club by a contract of employment dated 4 February 1981, which was not professionally drafted. The duties included the provision of catering services at the club. Mrs M was responsible for the purchase of all food, its preparation and presentation, and the engaging and remuneration of any staff required. The remuneration under the contract of employment was a salary paid jointly plus the profits from the catering service. The club was to provide the necessary equipment and services to enable Mrs M to maintain a suitable catering service. The contract of employment was varied, inter alia, in 1985, when it was provided that the salary was payable to Mr M alone. The contract was further varied in 1987 when Mrs M's duties as stewardess were defined as including the provision of a catering service approved by the house committee at times agreed with the club, and she was to be entitled to holidays by agreement with the club, providing that alternative catering arrangements were made. Under all the contractual documents Mrs M was alone responsible for providing the catering service and was 'responsible for the proceeds of all money received from catering', or 'the catering operation'. She was thereby entitled to such money and accordingly was entitled to the profits and responsible for the losses arising from the provision of such service. Although she had to respect certain requirements of the club as to the times when the catering service was to be available and as to the character of the catering service to be provided, she alone decided the menu and the prices. By virtue of the 1987 contract Mr M was alone responsible for cleaning, and

Mrs M's responsibilities were limited to catering. Mr M also had duties in respect of the bar service which was the club's business. Mr M was assessed under Case I of Sch D for the years 1980–81 to 1989–90 in respect of the profits from the catering business on the basis that during that period a wife's income was aggregated with that of her husband for income tax purposes. Mrs M was assessed under Case I of Sch D for the years 1990–91 to 1991–92 on the basis of separate taxation of husband and wife with effect from 1990–91. Mr and Mrs M respectively appealed against those assessments, contending that Mrs M was carrying on the catering business as an employee by the contract of employment, and that profits of the business constituted emoluments from that employment assessable under Sch E. The General Commissioners upheld the assessments on the ground that Mrs M was self-employed in respect of the provision of the catering services. Mr and Mrs M appealed. The Crown submitted that the commissioners' decision was one of mixed fact and law, which could not be challenged unless it could be shown that they had misdirected themselves in law.

Held—The question whether Mrs M was an employee or self-employed depended solely on the construction of the contractual documents, which set out the full terms of the contract between her and the club, viewed in the matrix of facts in which they were signed. The question was accordingly one of law for the court.

For that purpose it was necessary to concentrate on the substance of the contractual arrangements made rather than their form or the parties' labels. The required exercise was to look at all the terms of each of the contractual documents in turn, to consider all aspects of the relationship between the club and Mrs M, in particular in respect of the catering business, and from the total picture so formed, after giving the weight appropriate in the circumstances to each factor and balancing one factor against another, to form a view as to the status which she occupied. The critical factors were that Mrs M had been in business on her own account (a factor of importance, though not decisive); that she had not been subject to the control of the club in respect of the menu or the prices or indeed (save as to hours and the character of the catering service) how the business was to be conducted; and that she had had a free hand in the employment of staff engaged in the provision of the service and had been the employer and paymaster of such staff. The overwhelming balance was therefore in favour of holding that Mrs M had to provide the catering service in a self-employed capacity. She had had in effect a catering concession at the club. Her employment had given her the opportunity and indeed had required her to trade on her own account (and accordingly was the proximate cause of her earning the profits made); but the profits were the profits of her trading; trading (and not employment) was the the immediate cause of those receipts, and the profits therefore fell within Sch D and were not an emolument of her employment.

Accordingly, Mr and Mrs M's appeals would be dismissed.

Notes

For the distinction between employment and self-employment, see *Simon's Direct Tax Service* E4.202–203.

Cases referred to in judgment

Barnett v Brabyn (Inspector of Taxes) [1996] STC 716.
Calvert (Inspector of Taxes) v Wainwright [1947] KB 526, 26 TC 475.
Edwards (Inspector of Taxes) v Bairstow [1956] AC 14, [1955] 3 All ER 48, 36 TC 207, HL.
Fitzpatrick v IRC (No 2) [1994] STC 237, [1994] 1 WLR 306, [1994] 1 All ER 673, 66 TC 407, HL.
Hall (Inspector of Taxes) v Lorimer [1994] STC 23, [1994] 1 WLR 209, [1994] 1 All ER 250, 66 TC 349, CA.
Hochstrasser (Inspector of Taxes) v Mayes [1960] AC 376, [1959] 3 All ER 817, 38 TC 673, HL.
IRC v Brander and Cruickshank [1971] 1 WLR 212, [1971] 1 All ER 36, 46 TC 574, HL.
Lee Ting Sang v Chung Chi-Keung [1990] 2 AC 374, PC.
Mitchell and Edon (Inspectors of Taxes) v Ross [1962] AC 813, [1961] 3 All ER 49, 40 TC 11, HL.
Shilton v Wilmshurst (Inspector of Taxes) [1991] STC 88, [1991] 1 AC 684, [1991] 3 All ER 148, 64 TC 78, HL.

Cases stated

John Richard McManus and Diane Sandra McManus appealed by way of cases stated from the decision of the General Commissioners for Peterborough upholding assessments under Case I of Sch D in respect of catering income earned by Mrs McManus at the Burghley Park Golf Club where Mr McManus was at all times an employee.

Stephen Silman (instructed by *Aitken Kelly Associates*) for the taxpayers.
Timothy Brennan (instructed by *the Solicitor of Inland Revenue*) for the Crown.

McMeechan v Secretary of State for Employment

COURT OF APPEAL (CIVIL DIVISION)
McCOWN, WAITE AND POTTER LJJ
11 DECEMBER 1996

Contracts of employment—Meaning of 'employee'—Employment rights—Insolvency—Conduct of Employment Agencies and Employment Business Regulations 1976, reg 9(6)(a)—Employment Protection (Consolidation) Act 1978 ss 122, 153(1).

Mr McMeechan was a temporary worker on the books of Noel Employment Ltd, an employment agency. He fulfilled a series of engagements supplied to him by the agency, the final one involving four days' work as a temporary catering assistant for Sutcliffe Catering. There was no master agreement regulating the general terms of engagement. For each assignment, he was issued with a job sheet which included a standard written statement of terms and conditions. The statement specified that he would provide his services 'as a self-employed worker and not under a contract of service'; the agency would offer him the opportunity to work on a self-employed basis where there was a suitable assignment with a client, but reserved the right to offer each assignment to such temporary worker as it elected where the assignment was suitable for one of several temporaries. Mr McMeechan was under no obligation to accept the offer of an assignment but if he did, he would be 'required to fulfil the normal common law duties which an employee would owe to an employer so far as they are applicable'. The agency was not required to provide, and Mr McMeechan was not required to serve, any particular number of hours during any day or a week; he had no entitlement to payment for holidays or absence due to sickness or injury, nor any pension rights. The conditions acknowledged that there could be periods between assignments when no work was available. Under the conditions, the agency would pay Mr McMeechan a weekly wage calculated at a specific hourly rate, subject to deductions for unsatisfactory time-keeping, attendance, job performance, attitude or conduct. The agency undertook responsibility for making the appropriate deductions for income tax and national insurance. The conditions further provided that the agency could instantly dismiss him for improper conduct and could instruct him to end an assignment with a client at any time without giving a reason. Mr McMeechan had the right to request a review of a decision to dispense with his services, and a grievance procedure was set out. When Noel Employment Ltd went into insolvent liquidation, Mr McMeechan applied to the Secretary of State for Employment under what was then s 122 of the Employment Protection (Consolidation) Act, for payment of money owed to him by the company in respect of his last engagement. The application was refused on the ground that he was not an 'employee' of the insolvent company but an independent contractor and, therefore, the Secretary of State had no obligation under s 122 to make the payments claimed. That refusal was upheld by an industrial tribunal which considered itself bound by the decision of the EAT in *Wickens v Champion Employment* to hold that temporaries on the books of employment agencies are not in a relationship of employment with the agency. The EAT allowed an appeal against the tribunal's decision on the grounds that Wickens was not binding and the totality of the written conditions of service did create an employment relationship between Mr McMeechan and the employment agency [1995] IRLR 461.

The Secretary of State appealed against that decision. During the course of proceedings before the Court of Appeal, it became evident that the relief for which Mr McMeechan was really and primarily asking was to be treated as an employee of the agency for the purposes of the single stint served with the particular client in respect of whom the monies claimed had been earned, and it was agreed that he should be permitted to advance an alternative case to that effect. In resisting that claim on its merits, it was submitted for the Secretary of State that, as a matter of law, the specific engagement could not be separated from the general engagement. However, if the individual stint was capable of giving rise to an independent contract of employment, the absence in the conditions of service of mutual obligation to provide work and to do it, and the importation of a term that the worker would fulfil 'the normal common law duties which an employee would owe to an employer' were fatal to such a finding in this case. Support for those submissions was said to derive from the decision of the EAT in *Pertemps Group plc v Nixon*.

Held—The respondent temporary worker was entitled to be treated as an employee of an employment agency for the purposes of the specific contract governing the engagement in respect of which payment was owed to him when the agency went into liquidation.

A temporary worker can have the status of employee of the employment agency in respect of each assignment actually worked, notwithstanding that the same worker may not be entitled to employee status under his general terms of engagement. In determining whether a temporary worker is to be treated as an employee, in a case where the money claimed is related to a single stint served for one individual client, it is logical to relate the claim to employment status to the particular job in respect of which payment is being sought.

Where the agency and the temporary worker have committed themselves to standard terms and conditions which are intended to apply both to the general engagement and to the individual stints worked under it, those conditions have to be interpreted from a different perspective, according to whether they are being considered in the context of the general engagement or in the context of a single assignment. Whilst that will not make the task of industrial tribunals any easier and is liable to lead to the unsatisfactory consequence that the same condition may need to be given a different significance in the one context from that accorded to it in the other, those disadvantages do not supply any valid reason for denying the temporary worker or the contractor the right to have the issue of contractual status judged separately in the two contexts.

In so far as the decision of the EAT in *Pertemps Group plc v Nixon* purported to lay down any principle contrary to those propositions, it should not be followed. The holding in that case that an industrial tribunal is excluded, as a matter of law, from finding that a single engagement had given rise to a contract of employment between the worker and the contractor was not supported by the authorities.

In the present case, construing the conditions of service in the context of a specific engagement, the general impression which emerged was that the engagement in question gave rise, despite the label put on it by the parties, to a contract of service between the respondent and the contractor. On the one side, in support of a contract for services, was the express statement that the worker was to be regarded as self-employed and not to be working under a contract of service; and the liberty reserved to the worker of being able to work on a self-employed basis for a particular client. On the other side, supporting a contract a service, were the reservation of the power of dismissal for misconduct; the power of the contractor to bring any assignment to an end; the provision of a review procedure in the event of such termination; the establishment of a grievance procedure; the stipulation of an hourly rate of pay, which was subject to deductions for unsatisfactory time-keeping, work, attitude, or mis-conduct; and the importation of the normal common law duties of an employee.

The EAT had correctly held, therefore, that the respondent was entitled to recover the unpaid earnings due to him in respect of that engagement from the Secretary of State in accordance with the provisions of s 122 of the Employment Protection (Consolidation) Act.

Notes

For categories of workers, see *Harvey on Industrial Relations and Employment Law* Division A.1.

The relevant provisions are now contained in the Employment Rights Act 1996 ss 182 and 230(1), see ibid, Division Q.

Cases referred to in judgment

Construction Industry Training Board v Labour Force Ltd [1970] 3 AER 220, HC.
Ironmonger v Movefield Ltd [1988] IRLR 461, EAT.
Lee v Chung [1990] IRLR 236, PC.
McLeod v Hellyer Brothers Ltd and Wilson v Boston Deep Sea Fisheries Ltd [1987] IRLR 232, CA.
Nethermere (St Neots) Ltd v Taverna and Gardiner [1984] IRLR 240, CA.
O'Kelly v Trusthouse Forte plc [1983] IRLR 369, CA.
Pertemps Group plc v Nixon 496/91, EAT.
Wickens v Champion Employment [1984] ICR 365, EAT.

Lord Meston QC (instructed by *the Treasury Solicitor*) for the Secretary of State.
The Respondent appeared in person.

McMenamin (Inspector of Taxes) v Diggles

CHANCERY DIVISION AT MANCHESTER
SCOTT J
6, 7 JUNE 1991

Emoluments from office or employment—Office—Head clerk of chambers, previously under contract of employment, entering into new contractual arrangements with members of chambers to provide full clerking service—Whether head clerk holding an 'office'—Income and Corporation Taxes Act 1970 s 181.

The taxpayer, Mr Diggles, was at all material times the senior clerk of a leading set of barristers' chambers in Manchester. It was common ground that for a considerable number of years until 7 October 1985 he was senior clerk under a contract of employment and was assessable to tax under Schedule E as an employee. On 7 October 1985 new contractual arrangements were brought into effect between the taxpayer and each member of the chambers. Under those arrangements, the taxpayer, in return for a specified percentage of the gross income of each member, agreed to provide at his own cost and expense a full clerking service for each member. The agreement held it open to the taxpayer either to act as head clerk himself or to provide some other suitably qualified or experienced person to act as one. In the event, throughout the relevant period he acted as head clerk himself and the services which he supplied in discharging his contractual obligation to provide full clerking services included all the traditional services provided by head clerks to barristers' chambers. The taxpayer appealed to the Special Commissioners against assessments to income tax under Sch E for the years 1985–86, 1986–87 and 1987–88. The questions before the commissioners were (1) whether for the three years the taxpayer was an employee and hence assessable under Sch E and (2) whether the assessments under Sch E could be upheld on the alternative ground that during the relevant years he was the holder of an 'office' within the meaning of that word in s 181 of the Income and Corporation Taxes Act (the 1970 Act). The Special Commissioners concluded that the taxpayer was not an employee and also that he was not an office holder for the purposes of s 181. On appeal, the Crown accepted that the taxpayer was not an employee but contended that the taxpayer was an office-holder for the purposes of s 181.

Held—The Special Commissioners had not misdirected themselves in law and it was open to them on the evidence to conclude that the taxpayer was not the holder of an office for the purposes of s 181 of the Income and Corporation Taxes Act 1970. The appeal would accordingly be dismissed.

Notes

For the meaning of office, see *Simon's Direct Tax Service* E4.201.

For the Income and Corporation Taxes Act 1970 s 181 (now the Income and Corporation Taxes Act 1988 s 19), see ibid, Part G1.

Cases referred to in judgment

Edwards (Inspector of Taxes) v Bairstow [1956] AC 14, [1955] 3 All ER 48, 36 TC 207, HL.

Edwards (Inspector of Taxes) v Clinch [1979] STC 148, [1979] 1 WLR 338, [1979] 1 All ER 648; [1980] STC 438, [1981] Ch 1, [1980] 3 All ER 278, CA; [1981] STC 617, [1982] AC 845, [1981] 3 All ER 543, 56 TC 367, HL.

Great Western Railway Co v Bater (Surveyor of Taxes) [1920] 3 KB 266, 8 TC 231.

Case stated

Stephen John Diggles (the taxpayer) appealed by way of the case stated against the determination of the Special Commissioners that his remuneration as a barrister's clerk was properly taxable under Sch E as emoluments from an office or employment.

Launcelot Henderson (instructed by *the Solicitor of Inland Revenue*) for the Crown.

Stephen Oliver QC and *Timothy Lyons* (instructed by *Bullock Worthington & Jackson*, Manchester).

Midland Sinfonia Concert Society Ltd v Secretary of State for Social Services

QUEEN'S BENCH DIVISION

GLIDEWELL J

3, 4, 7 NOVEMBER 1980

Employment—Contract of service—Distinction between contract for services and contract of service—Musicians performing part-time for orchestra—Whether employees—Whether performing under contract of service.

M Ltd carried on the business of producing performances of orchestral music. It engaged musicians, some more frequently than others, to take part in each performance or sequence of performances. The musicians were paid at a fixed rate without deduction of income tax. The musicians were engaged by being invited to indicate on advance schedules of performances, the dates on which they were free to accept a booking to play. The selected musicians were informed by telephone. About ten days before a performance a final schedule and confirmation was sent out to each musician selected. That was regarded as a firm acceptance. If a musician was unable to attend he was expected to inform the company as soon as possible. P was a freelance oboe player who was registered for value added tax who paid income tax and national insurance contributions on the basis that he was self-employed. M was a violinist and S was a trumpeter. M Ltd applied to the Secretary of State for Social Services for a decision on whether P, M and S (who had been chosen as representative of those who played in the orchestra) were included in the category of employed earners for the purposes of the Social Security Act 1975. After an inquiry the Secretary of State determined that they were so included. M Ltd appealed submitting that the tests to be applied in order to determine whether each contract was or was not a contract of service were: (i) what were the actual arrangements between the parties, including their rights and obligations under the contract; (ii) what degree of control did M Ltd exercise over the musicians engaged to perform; (iii) were the musicians 'part and parcel' of M Ltd's organisation; (iv) did the musicians carry on business on their own account; (v) what chance of profit or risk of loss did each musician have; (vi) who provided the necessary equipment, that was to say, musical instruments; (vii) what were the 'traditional arrangements' between an orchestra and the musicians performing with it; (viii) what was the incidence of tax; and (ix) what did the parties themselves believe to be the position.

Held—On the issue of the degree of control exercised by the company the facts established no more than the minimum arrangement necessary to ensure that the various musicians assembled in the right place at the right time in order to form an orchestra for an engagement, while the control exercised by the conductor was clearly a fundamental part of orchestral playing. Neither amounted to the sort of control of the manner in which an employee carried out his work which was one of the important characteristics of a contract of employment. Further, it was clear that these musicians were not part and parcel of the company's organisation. The facts relating to P made it clear that he carried on business on his own account and there was nothing to suggest in relation to M and S that they were not carrying on business on their own account. The test of 'the chance of profit or risk of loss' was not particularly appropriate and on the remaining tests, the facts all pointed in the same direction. The musicians, except the pianist, provided their own equipment. Traditionally many orchestral players had been freelance performers. The company did not deduct tax from its payment to musicians and P paid income tax under Schedule D. The parties themselves clearly believed that the players were self-employed. Finally, an ordinary person, told the facts, would say, 'I think these musicians were not engaged under contracts of service. They were not employees; they were self-employed, hiring out their skills as occasion arose'. In summary, when applied to the relevant criteria, the facts pointed to the musicians not being employed under contracts of service. The facts found were such that no person acting judicially and properly instructed as to the relevant law could have come to the determination under appeal. Accordingly, the Secretary of State's decision was wrong in law and the company's appeal would be allowed.

Addison v London Philharmonic Orchestra Ltd [1981] ICR 261 considered. Dictum of Lord Radcliffe *Edwards (Inspector of Taxes) v Bairstow* [1956] AC 14 at 36 applied.

Notes

For categories of workers: servants and independent contractors, see *Harvey on Industrial Relations and Employment Law* Division A.1.A and C.

For characteristics of the relationship of master and servant, see ibid Division A.3.

Cases referred to in judgment

Addison v London Philharmonic Orchestra Ltd [1981] ICR 261, EAT.
Cassidy v Ministry of Health [1951] 2 KB 343, [1951] 1 All ER 574, CA.
Edwards (Inspector of Taxes) v Bairstow [1956] AC 14, [1955] 3 All ER 48, 36 TC 207, HL.
Ferguson v John Dawson & Partners (Contractors) Ltd [1976] 3 All ER 817, [1976] 1 WLR 1213, [1976] IRLR 346, CA.
Global Plant Ltd v Secretary of State for Health and Social Security [1971] 3 All ER 385, [1972] 1 QB 139.
Gould v Minister of National Insurance [1951] 1 KB 731, [1951] 1 All ER 368, KBD.
Market Investigations Ltd v Minister of Social Security [1968] 3 All ER 732, [1969] 2 QB 173.
Morren v Swinton and Pendlebury Borough Council [1965] 2 All ER 349, [1965] 1 WLR 576.
Ready Mixed Concrete (South East) Ltd v Minister of Pensions and National Insurance [1968] 1 All ER 433, [1968] 2 QB 497.
Simmons v Heath Laundry Co [1910] 1 KB 543, CA. *Young & Woods Ltd v West* [1980] IRLR 201, CA.

Appeal

The Midland Sinfonia Concert Society Ltd (M Ltd) appealed against the decision of the Secretary of State for Social Services under s 93(1) of the Social Security Act 1975 (the 1975 Act) that Graham Reginald Pfaff, Margaret Betty Mace and William Stokes were included in the category of employed earners for the purposes of the 1975 Act and that M Ltd was consequently liable, as secondary contributor, to pay contributions under s 4 of, and Sch 1 to, the 1975 Act.

Anthony Scrivener QC and *Ian Foster* (instructed by *Woodham Smith* as agents for *Hunt, Dickins & Willatt,* Nottingham) for M Ltd.
David Latham (instructed by the *Solicitor, Department of Health and Social Security*) for the Secretary of State.

Montgomery v Johnson Underwood Ltd

COURT OF APPEAL (CIVIL DIVISION)
BROOKE, LONGMORE LJJ AND BUCKLEY J
9 MARCH 2001

Contracts of employment—Meaning of 'employee'—Identity of employer—Unfair dismissal—Exclusions and qualifications—Meaning of 'employee'—Employment Appeal Tribunal—Employment Relations Act 1999 ss 13, 23.

Mrs Montgomery registered with Johnson Underwood, an employment agency, in early 1995. She was looking for a part-time job as a receptionist/telephonist. On 30 May, she was contacted by the agency and offered a position with a local company. Hours of work were discussed and agreed and on the following day, she received a letter from the agency confirming the appointment, together with their printed terms and conditions. In return, she sent her P45 and bank details. Mrs Montgomery started work at the client company on 1 June 1995 and continued working there for more than two years. She was paid by the agency on the basis of time sheets approved by the client. In November 1997, however, the client became unhappy about her use of its telephone for personal calls and asked the agency to terminate the assignment which it duly did. Mrs Montgomery was offered another position which she did not take up. In her originating application claiming unfair dismissal, Mrs Montgomery named both the employment agency and the client company as her employer. Following a preliminary hearing, the employment tribunal decided that she was an employee of the agency and not of the client company. The tribunal directed itself in accordance with what it understood to be the guidance of Lord Justice Waite in *McMeechan v Secretary of State for Employment.* It considered all aspects of the relationship between Mrs Montgomery and the employment agency, including mutuality of obligation and control, and concluded that, on balance, those factors pointing to the existence of an employment contract outweighed those against. Included in the list of factors against a contract of employment was the finding that there was 'little or no control, direction or supervision'. As regards the absence of mutuality of obligation, the tribunal took the view that, following the reasoning in McMeechan, that appeared to be largely irrelevant. The employment tribunal's decision was upheld on appeal by the majority of the EAT.

Held—The employment tribunal had erred in holding that the applicant was employed by the employment agency through which she had obtained a long-term specific assignment, notwithstanding that was 'little or no control, direction or supervision' of the applicant by the agency.

'Mutuality of obligation' and 'control' are the irreducible minimum legal requirements for the existence of a contract of employment. In determining whether a contract of employment exists, the guidance of McKenna J in *Ready Mixed Concrete (South East) Ltd v Minister of Pensions and National Insurance*, approved by the Lord Chancellor in *Carmichael v National Power plc*, is the best guide and should be followed by tribunals. This requires three conditions to be fulfilled: (i) that the servant agrees that, in consideration for a wage or other remuneration, he will provide his own work and skill in the performance of some service for his master, 'mutuality of obligation'; (ii) he agrees, expressly or impliedly, that in the performance of that service he will be subject to the other's control in a sufficient degree to make that other master; and (iii) the other provisions of the contract are consistent with its being a contract of service. The test set out in *Ready Mixed Concrete* permits tribunals appropriate latitude in considering the nature and extent of 'mutual obligations' in respect of the work in question and the 'control' an employer has over the individual. It does not permit those concepts to be dispensed with altogether. It directs tribunals to consider the whole picture to see whether a contract of employment emerges, although 'mutual obligation' and 'control' must be identified to a sufficient extent before looking at the whole.

If the approach of Lord Justice Waite in *McMeechan v Secretary of State for Employment*, which was applied by the employment tribunal in the present case, was intended to reduce the 'criterion of mutual obligation', and by inference 'control' as well, to no more than matters to be weighed up with all the other factors, it was contrary to *Ready Mixed Concrete* as well as Court of Appeal authority and could not be agreed with.

A contractual relationship concerning work to be carried out in which there is no control cannot sensibly be called a contract of employment. It is not essential that there is control of how the work should be done. In many cases, the employer or controlling management may have no more than a very general idea of how the work is done and no inclination directly to interfere with it. However, some sufficient framework of control must exist.

In certain circumstances, an offer of work by an employment agency, even at another's workplace, accepted by an individual for remuneration to be paid by the agency, could satisfy the requirement of mutual obligation. Whether in any given situation 'sufficient control' exists to constitute the one party an employer is a matter for the tribunal. It could not be said that an assignment provided and paid for by an agency could never, as a matter of law, give rise to 'sufficient control'. In the present case, however, the employment tribunal's clear finding of lack of control was fatal to its decision that the applicant was an employee of the agency and the appeal would be allowed.

Obiter dicta (per Buckley J)

As the EAT suggested, in view of the considerable uncertainty concerning the status of individuals who find work through employment agencies, the power conferred on the Secretary of State for Trade and Industry by s 23 of the Employment Relations Act 1999 to extend the protection of employment legislation to a specified description of individuals might be put to good use in this respect.

Cases referred to in judgment

Carmichael v National Power plc [2000] IRLR 43, HL.
Chadwick v Pioneer Private Telephone Co Ltd [1941] 1 All ER 522.
Clark v Oxfordshire Health Authority [1998] IRLR 125, CA.
Clifford v Union of Democratic Mineworkers [1991] IRLR 518, CA.
Express and Echo Publications Ltd v Tanton [1999] IRLR 367, CA.
Humberstone v Northern Timber Mills (1949) 79 CLR 389.
McMeechan v Secretary of State for Employment [1997] IRLR 353, CA.
Moore v Garwood [1849] 4 Exch 681.
Nethermere (St Neots) Ltd v Taverna and Gardiner [1984] IRLR 240, CA.
Ready Mixed Concrete (South East) Ltd v Minister of Pensions and National Insurance [1968] 2 QB 497.

Notes

For categories of workers, see *Harvey on Industrial Relations and Employment Law* Division A.1.

For characteristics of the relationship of master and servant, see ibid, Division A.1.3.

For the Employment Relations Act 1999 ss 13, 23, see ibid, Division Q.

Ramby De Mello (instructed by *Murria*) for Mrs Montgomery.
Charles Samek (instructed by *Eyton Morris Winfield*) for Johnson Underwood Ltd.

Morren v Swinton and Pendlebury Borough Council

QUEEN'S BENCH DIVISION
LORD PARKER CJ, MARSHALL AND WIDGERY JJ
23, 24 FEBRUARY 1965

Master and Servant—Contract of service—Engineer employed by local authority to work under consultant engineers—Whether contract of service or contract for services—Local Government Superannuation Act 1937 (1 Edw 8 & 1 Geo 6 c 68) ss 3(2)(a), 40(1).

A contract for services, made between a local authority and consultant engineers, provided for the consultant engineers to supervise the execution of sewerage works and that the local authority should appoint and pay a resident engineer, to be approved by the consultants, to supervise the works under the consultants' instructions. The local authority, with the approval of the consultants, appointed the appellant at a salary. The local authority had the right to dismiss the appellant; he was paid subsistence allowance and for holidays, employer's national insurance contributions were paid in regard to him, and there was provision for a month's notice.

Held—The appellant was employed by the local authority under a contract of service, not a contract for services, notwithstanding that he was to work under the instructions of the consultant engineers; accordingly the appellant was within the definition of employee in s 40(1) of the Local Government Superannuation Act 1937.

Indicia quoted by Lord Thankerton in *Short v J & W Henderson Ltd* (1946 SC (HL) at p 33) applied.

Per Curiam. (a) the factor of superintendence and control is of little use as a test whether a contract is or is not a contract of service where the person concerned is a professional man, engaged for his skill and experience.

(b) the terms of a contract are fact, but, once the primary facts are found, then it is a pure question of law what is the reasonable inference, based on the legal interpretation of the contract, that should be drawn with regard to the legal quality of the contract.

Notes

As to the characteristics of a contract of service see 16 *Halsbury's Laws* (4th Edn) (2000 reissue) para 1 et seq.

Cases referred to in judgment

Cassidy v Minister of Health [1951] 1 All ER 574, [1951] 2 KB 343.
Short v J&W Henderson Ltd 1946 SC (HL) 24.
Stevenson, Jordon & Harrison v MacDonald & Evans [1952] 1 TLR 101, 69 RPC 10.

Special case stated

This was a Special Case Stated by the Minister of Housing and Local Government for the opinion of the High Court of Justice, pursuant to s 35 of the Local Government Superannuation Act 1937.

On 4 March 1963, the appellant, Francis Hendry Morren, being dissatisfied with the decision dated 11 February 1963, of the respondents, the borough council of Swinton and Pendlebury, that, for the purposes of the Local Government Superannuation Act 1937 s 40(1), he did not fall within the definition of 'employee' contained in that section and was accordingly not entitled to become a contributory employee for the purposes of the Local Government Superannuation Acts, referred the matter for determination by the Minister of Housing and Local Government under s 35 of the Local Government Superannuation Act 1937. The contention of the appellant was that he was employed by the respondents as an engineer and whole-time officer of the council.

The Minister found the following facts. The respondents were a local authority specified in Pt 1 of Sch 1 to the Act of 1937, a constituent authority of the South East Lancashire (Local Authorities) Superannuation Joint Committee, and were, for the purposes of the Local Government Superannuation Acts 1937 to 1953, and regulations made thereunder, an employing authority. The respondents, on 10 March 1962, entered into an agreement with Messrs J B Kershaw and Kaufman, consulting engineers, covering services in connexion with the execution of certain works of sewerage and sewage disposal. Clause 7 of the agreement stated: 'The [respondents] shall appoint and pay a qualified clerk of works or resident engineer to be approved by the engineer together with such inspectors (not exceeding two in number) as may be necessary properly to supervise the execution of the works under the engineer's instructions.' Sometime before 14 February 1962, the respondents advertised the appointment of resident engineer for the Clifton Drainage—Contract No 4, and the advertisement stated: 'The work will be executed by contract, the resident engineer will be under the direction and control of the [respondent's] consulting engineers, Messrs G B Kershaw and Kaufman. The post is not superannuable.' The appellant applied for the post, and was interviewed by the consulting engineers on a date between 19 February and 28 February 1962, and, on 28 February 1962, the town clerk of the respondents wrote to the appellant offering the post to him and re-iterating that the post was not superannuable. On or about 19 March 1962, the appellant took up the appointment. The appellant was appointed by the respondents, the respondents having the right to dismiss the appellant, the appellant's salary, mileage and subsistence allowance and the national insurance contributions being paid by the respondents. The appellant's holiday entitlement was governed by the respondents' 'Terms of Employment'. The respondents were not responsible for the direction or control of the appellant's work, except that they requested the permission of the consulting engineers for their consent to the appellant carrying out certain supervisory works for the respondents at the beginning of 1963. The consulting engineers gave their consent, and the appellant carried out these works (which were connected with the cleansing of an existing sewer of the respondents) under the control and direction of the respondents for a period of four weeks.

On those findings of fact, the Minister determined that the appointment of the appellant by the respondents did not bring the appellant within the definition of 'employee' contained in s 40(1) of the Act of 1937.

J M Rankin (instructed by *J G Haley*) for the appellant.
R I Threlfall (instructed by *Lees & Co* agents for Town Clerk, Swinton and Pendlebury) for the respondents.

Motorola Ltd v Davidson and Melville Craig Group Ltd

EMPLOYMENT APPEAL TRIBUNAL
LINDSAY J (PRESIDENT), A J RAMSDEN AND T MARSLAND
1 AUGUST 2000

Contracts of employment—Meaning of 'employee'—Identity of employer—Unfair dismissal—Exclusions and qualifications—Meaning of 'employee'.

In November 1996, Mr Davidson responded to an advertisement for jobs as analysers to repair mobile telephones with Motorola at their plant in Bathgate. The recruitment process was carried out by Melville Craig Group Ltd, which had an operating agreement with Motorola for the supply of temporary workers. Mr Davidson was taken on by Melville Craig and assigned to work at Motorola's site. Under the terms of his contract, he was bound to comply with all reasonable instructions and requests made by Motorola. In December 1998, Mr Davidson was suspended by Motorola's regional service manager following a disciplinary hearing. The manager then decided to terminate Mr Davidson's assignment with Motorola. Mr Davidson presented a complaint of unfair dismissal against both Motorola and Melville Craig. Motorola asserted that it had all along regarded Mr Davidson as an employee of Melville Craig and that he had never had a contract of service with Motorola. At a preliminary hearing, the employment tribunal held that Mr Davidson was an employee of Motorola and that his unfair dismissal claim should proceed against Motorola alone. Motorola's appeal against that decision was limited to challenging the tribunal's conclusion that as between Motorola and Mr Davidson, there existed the right of the former to control the latter to a degree sufficient to enable the tribunal properly to regard Mr Davidson as Motorola's employee.

Held—The employment tribunal had not erred in holding that the appellants had a sufficient degree of control over the first respondent that he could properly be regarded as their employee, in circumstances in which, although the appellants had no direct legal right of control over the respondent under a contract they had made with him, he was bound by the terms of his contract with the employment agency who then assigned his services to the appellants to comply with all reasonable instructions and requests made by the appellants and control of what he did on a day-to-day basis lay with them.

In determining whether there is a sufficient degree of control to establish a relationship of employer and employee, there is no good reason to ignore practical aspects of control that fall short of legal rights. Nor is it a necessary component of the type of control exercised by an employer over an employee that it should be exercised only directly between them and not by way of a third party acting upon the directions, or at the request, of the employer. The law has long regarded it as possible in appropriate contexts that an act which

A procures B to do should be regarded as done by A. The existence of a degree of control over a worker consistent with his being an employee of A is not necessarily disproved by showing that B had equal or even greater powers over him.

In the present case, once he was at the appellants' site, the respondent became largely subject to control much as would have been the case had he been an ordinary full-time employee. It was the appellants who, in the words of MacKenna J in *Ready Mixed Concrete (South East) Ltd v Minister of Pensions and National Insurance,* determined 'The thing to be done, the way in which it shall be done, the means to be employed in doing it, the time when and the place where it shall be done'. It was the appellants' manager who suspended him following a disciplinary hearing and decided to terminate his assignment.

Motorola Ltd's appeal would therefore be dismissed.

Cases referred to in judgment

Ready Mixed Concrete (South East) Ltd v Minister of Pensions and National Insurance [1968] 1 All ER 433, [1968] 2 QB 497.
Serco Ltd v Blair and ors 31 August 1998, EAT.

Notes

For categories of workers, see *Harvey on Industrial Relations and Employment Law* Division A.1.

For characteristics of the relationship of master and servant, see ibid, Division A.3.

Stephen Hurley, solicitor (instructed by *Hammond Suddards*) for Motorola Ltd.
Brian Murphy, solicitor (instructed by *A C White*) for Mr Davidson.
Joan Cradden, solicitor (instructed by *Brodies*) for Melville Craig Group Ltd.

Narich Property Ltd v Commissioner of Pay-Roll Tax

PRIVY COUNCIL
LORD KEITH OF KINKEL, LORD ELWYN-JONES, LORDROSKILL, LORD BRANDON OF OAKBROOK AND LORD TEMPLEMAN
31 OCTOBER, 1 NOVEMBER, 5 DECEMBER 1983

Employment—Contract of service—Distinction between contract for services and contract of service—Company in the business of weight control—Company a franchisee—Franchise agreement stipulating fixed and detailed programme—Contracts between company and lecturers teaching programme providing that lecturers teach only fixed and detailed programme—Contracts also providing that lecturers independent contractors—Whether lecturers employed under contracts of service.

N Ltd was a franchisee of Weight Watchers International Inc (WW) whose business was to help people lose excess weight. The franchise agreement stipulated that WW's fixed and detailed programme was not to be departed from. The method of operation by which the business was carried on was by the conducting of classes. The immediate conduct of the classes was in the hands of lecturers who imparted oral instruction and advice in accordance with a detailed programme prescribed by WW. The lecturers were chosen and trained by N Ltd and remunerated by N Ltd for each lecture. The contract used between N Ltd and its lecturers recited that N Ltd had acquired extensive 'weight control skills' and that N Ltd had agreed to hire to the lecturer its WW Lecturer's handbook, containing material for guidance only. It provided: inter alia, in cl 1 that any substitute lecturer had to be approved by N Ltd and that if the lecturer failed to carry out her duties and obligations in a proper manner or exceeded her goal weight her engagement might be terminated without notice; in cl 2 that a fee would be paid per lecture; in cl 3 that the lecturer was not an employee of N Ltd but an independent contractor who would perform her duties free from the direction and control of N Ltd; in cl 4 that the lecturer would teach 'the programme and plateau and maintenance plans'; and in cl 6 that N Ltd would rent the WW handbook to her for the period of her engagement. The Commissioner of Pay-Roll Tax for New South Wales assessed N Ltd for pay-roll tax in reference to the lecturers' remuneration. N Ltd made objection on the basis that the remuneration was not 'wages' as required by the Pay-Roll Tax Act 1971 as it was not paid to employees nor paid by N Ltd as employer. Woodward J dismissed N Ltd's appeal on the basis that the contracts between N Ltd and its lecturers were contracts of service. N Ltd appealed.

Held—The principles of law relating to the determination of the question such as that in the instant case were well settled. The first principle was that, subject to one exception, where there was a written contract between the parties whose relationship was in issue a court was confined, in determining the nature of that relationship, to a consideration of the terms, express or implied, of that contract in the light of the circumstances surrounding the making of it; and was not entitled to consider also the manner in which the parties subsequently acted in pursuance of such contract. The one exception to that rule was that, where the subsequent conduct of the parties could be shown to have amounted to an agreed addition to, or modification of the original written contract, such conduct might be considered and taken into account by the court. The second principle was that, while all relevant terms of the contract had to be regarded, the most important, and in most cases the decisive criterion for determining the relationship between the parties was the extent to which the person, whose status as employee or independent contractor was in issue, was under the direction and control of the other party to the contract with regard to the manner in which he did his work under it. The third principle related to cases where the parties had, as in the instant case, included in their written contract an express provision purporting to define the status of the party engaged under it. If the true relationship of the parties was of master and servant, the parties could not alter the truth of that relationship by putting a different label on it. If their relationship was ambiguous and was capable of being either service or agency, then the parties could remove that ambiguity, by the very agreement itself which they made with one another. The agreement itself then became the best material from which to gather the true legal relationship between them. In the instant case, the franchise agreement formed an important and significant part of the circumstances surrounding the making of the contracts between N Ltd and its lecturers, and its terms were therefore relevant in interpreting the latter. In determining the true nature of the relationship the following terms, apart from cl 3 itself, required particular consideration. First, the elaborate description in the recitals of the 'weight control skills' possessed by N Ltd. Secondly, the arrangement referred to in the recitals for the hire by N Ltd to the lecturer of the WW Lecturers' handbook. Thirdly, cl 1(a) which provided that any substitute lecturer had to be approved by N Ltd and that classes were to be held at such times and places as N Ltd might arrange. Fourthly, cl 4(a) which required the lecturer to teach what was described as 'the programme and plateau and maintenance plans'. Fifthly, cl 4(f) which required the lecturer so to conduct her classes as to advance the principles of WW. And sixthly, cl 1(b) which entitled N Ltd to terminate the engagement of the lecturer, immediately and without notice, either if she failed to carry out her duties and obligations as a lecturer in a proper manner or if her weight exceeded her goal weight. The reference in cl 4(a) was a clear reference to the WW Lecturers' handbook. The body of the handbook contained lengthy, detailed and specific instructions as to how each of 28 subjects was to be taught or handled. It was impossible for a lecturer who was required to teach and act, at or in connection with WW classes, in accordance with that handbook, to use it 'for guidance only'. She either taught and acted in the way prescribed in all its elaborate detail or she did not. If she did teach and act in the manner prescribed, not only the nature and scope of her work, but also the precise manner in which she did it, was closely controlled and directed by N Ltd through the medium of the handbook. Such close direction and control was clearly essential if N Ltd was to comply with its own obligations to WW under the franchise agreement. If on the other hand, a lecturer failed or neglected to teach and act in the manner prescribed by the handbook she was liable to have her engagement terminated immediately without notice. She was liable to undergo the same fate if her weight exceeded her goal weight. The court was in complete agreement with summary of the judge that N Ltd was clearly able to control not only the task allotted to the lecturer but the manner in which the task was performed. It was impossible for cl 3 of the contract to receive effect according to its terms if they contradicted the effect of the agreement as a whole and the effect of the contract as a whole did contradict cl 3. The effect of the contract as a whole was to create between N Ltd and the lecturer the relationship of employer and employee, and in so far as cl 3 purported to provide otherwise it had to be treated as failing in its purpose. That was so even though there had never been any suggestion either that cl 3 was a sham or that the parties did not include it in the contract in good faith and with the desire that it should be effective. The plain situation in law was that a lecturer was tied hand and foot by the contract with regard to the manner in which she performed her work under it. The only possible conclusion was that she was an employee.

Australian Mutual Provident Society v Chaplin (1978) ALR 385 followed.

The appeal, accordingly, would be dismissed.

Notes

For categories of workers: servants and independent contractors, see *Harvey on Industrial Relations and Employment Law* Division A.1.A and C.

For characteristics of the relationship of master and servant, see ibid Division A.3.

Cases referred to in judgment

Australian Mutual Provident Society v Chaplin (1978) 18 ALR 385, PC.
Massey v Crown Life Insurance Co [1978] 2 All ER 576, [1978] 1 WLR 676, [1978] ICR 590, [1978] IRLR 31, CA.

Appeal

Narich Property Ltd (N Ltd) appealed from an order of Woodward J sitting in the Administrative Law Division of the Supreme Court of New South Wales made on 6 November 1981, with leave to appeal granted on 23 February 1982, that the notice of objection to an assessment by the Commissioner of Pay-Roll Tax to pay-roll tax on N Ltd be disallowed. N Ltd had been assessed to pay-roll tax in reference to the remuneration of lecturers paid by N Ltd in connection with the operation of its franchise from Weight Watchers International Inc.

Leolin Price and *John Trew* (instructed by *Baker & McKenzie*) for N Ltd.
Mary Gaudron QC and *John Bryson* (instructed by *Lovell, White & King*) for the commissioner

Nethermere (St Neots) Ltd v Gardiner and Taverna

EMPLOYMENT APPEAL TRIBUNAL
TUDOR EVANS J, J W COLLERSON AND D LANCASTER
12 NOVEMBER 1982

Contracts of employment—Meaning of 'employee'—Unfair dismissal—Exclusions and qualifications—meaning of 'employee'—Employment Protection (Consolidation) Act 1978 s 153(1).

Mrs Taverna and Mrs Gardiner were at one time both employed at the appellants' factory. Mrs Taverna left in 1977 to have a baby. Before leaving, she arranged with the factory manager that when her child was old enough, she would do work at home. She began home work at the beginning of 1978, initially putting pockets on trousers. Later her work was changed to putting artificial flaps on to trousers. The machine she used for the work was provided by the appellants. She had no fixed hours for doing the work and for a number of weeks she did no work at all. She was paid weekly according to the number of garments she did. Mrs Gardiner ceased working at the factory in 1976. In September 1979 the appellants asked if she would do home work and she agreed. At first she used her own machine but after a month or so was supplied with one by the appellants. She normally put 200 pockets on trousers a day. If she wanted less work, she would tell the driver who delivered the work to her. The only stipulation being that it had to be sufficient to make it worthwhile for the driver to call. When these arrangements came to an end in 1981 following a dispute about holiday pay, Mrs Taverna and Mrs Gardiner complained that they had been unfairly dismissed. As a preliminary issue, the Tribunal were asked to decide whether the two women were employees of the company within the meaning of s 153(1) of the Employment Protection (Consolidation) Act or whether they were self-employed under a contract for services. The Tribunal held that the women were employed under a contract of service and were therefore eligible to complain of unfair dismissal.

Held—(Tudor Evans J dissenting) Whether there is a contract of service or a contract for services is a matter of law (per Stephenson LJ in *Young and Woods Ltd v West* [1980] IRLR 201). West's [1980] IRLR 201 case also established that in determining the status of the contract on the facts of a particular case, all the indicia have to be considered with perhaps the fundamental test being whether the applicant was in business on his or her own account. Other than that test, there are no conclusive indicia and no pre-conditions. In the present case, therefore, the test to be adopted was whether or not the respondent homeworkers were in business on their own account, giving consideration to what pointers there were which indicated one direction rather than the other.

The argument advanced on behalf of the appellants that the decision in *Airfix Footwear Ltd v Cope* [1978] IRLR 396 establishes the proposition that before a contract of service can exist there must be continuing mutual obligations on the employer to provide work or pay wages and on the employee to be ready and willing to work could not be accepted. Nor could it be accepted that *Mailway (Southern) Ltd v Willsher* [1978] IRLR 322 is authority for the proposition that once it is found that there was no obligation on either side, it is impossible to conclude that there was a contract of service.

The respondent homeworkers were employed under a contract of service. They were not in business on their own account. Nor could it be said, per Bristow J in *Withers v Flackwell Heath Football Supporters' Club* [1981] IRLR 307, that the respondents were on their own business rather than on the business of the party for whom the work was being done. The industrial tribunal had not erred, therefore, in holding that the respondents were 'employees' within the meaning of s 153(1) of the Employment Protection (Consolidation) Act and eligible to complain of unfair dismissal.

Factors taken into account in reaching this conclusion were that the appellants provided the respondents with a machine to do the work; the respondents were paid at the same rate as those who worked in the factory; the respondents had no freedom to negotiate the rate of remuneration and there was evidence before the industrial tribunal that one of them had had a drop in the rate imposed unilaterally by the appellants; the nature of the work was not negotiable; although the respondents were free to choose their hours of work, once they had accepted the work from the driver they had to do it or they would have been 'sacked'; one respondent was asked to go down to the factory to be shown what to do and was told that if her machine broke down to call the factory and a mechanic would be sent out; looking at the economic realities of the relationship, the respondents were not free to refuse work; this was a settled relationship which had lasted for some considerable time; although the respondents could decide how much work to do, it had to be sufficient to make it worthwhile for the driver to call; the work done by the respondents was similar to that done in the factory; and though the respondents were not running any economic risk, they had no opportunity to profit from sound management.

Cases referred to in judgment

Airfix Footwear Ltd v Cope [1978] IRLR 396.
Bullock v Merseyside County Council [1979] IRLR 33.
Ferguson v John Dawson and Partners (Contractors) Ltd [1976] IRLR 346.
Mailway (Southern) Ltd v Willsher [1978] IRLR 322.
Ready Mixed Concrete (South East) Ltd v Minister of Pensions and National Insurance [1968] 1 All ER 433, (1968) 2 QB 497.
Withers v Flackwell Heath Football Supporters' Club [1981] IRLR 307.
Young and Woods Ltd v West [1980] IRLR 201.

Notes

For categories of workers, see *Harvey on Industrial Relations and Employment Law* Division A.1.

For characteristics of the relationship of master and servant, see ibid, Division A.3.

A Blair (instructed by *Messrs Polden, Bishop & Gale*) for Nethermere (St Neots) Ltd.

Mr G Jones (instructed by *Messrs Wilkinson & Butler*) for Mrs Gardiner and Mrs Taverna.

O'Kelly and others v Trusthouse Forte plc

COURT OF APPEAL, CIVIL DIVISION
SIR JOHN DONALDSON MR, ACKNER AND FOX LJJ
20, 21 JUNE, 20 JULY 1983

Master and servant—Contract of service—Distinction between contract of service and contract for services—Whether issue of law or mixed fact and law—Jurisdiction of Employment Appeal Tribunal—Employment Protection (Consolidation) Act 1978 ss 136(1), 153(1).

The employers carried on a banqueting business at their hotel. Only a few of the banqueting staff were employed permanently under contracts of employment, the rest of the banqueting staff being casual workers engaged for each function, that being the usual practice in the catering industry. However a large number of the casual staff were so-called 'regular casuals', ie they were engaged on a regular basis by the employers to such an extent that some of them had no other regular work. Regular casuals were given priority of engagement over other casual workers. The applicants, who were three regular casuals, sought, through their union, recognition by the employers that regular casuals were permanent employees working under contracts of employment because of the length and continuity of their service and the manner in which they were paid. Thereupon the employers dismissed the applicants, who then complained to an industrial tribunal, pursuant to the Employment Protection (Consolidation) Act 1978, that they had been unfairly dismissed for taking part in trade union activities. On the question whether the applicants were working under a contract of employment within s 153(1) of the 1978 Act and were thus entitled to complain of wrongful dismissal, the industrial tribunal concluded that there was no overall contract between the parties and that the applicants were in business on their own account as independent contractors supplying services. The applicants appealed to the Employment Appeal Tribunal, which held that the question whether a contract was a contract of employment or a contract for services was a question of law and therefore under s 136(1) of the 1978 Act the appeal tribunal had jurisdiction to hear the appeal. The appeal tribunal held, as had the industrial tribunal, that there was no overall contract of employment between the parties but further held that each separate contract entered into on the occasion of each engagement was a contract of employment. The employers appealed, contending (i) that whether a contract was a contract of employment or a contract for services was a question of fact and therefore the appeal tribunal had had no jurisdiction to hear the appeal, and (ii) that instead of itself considering whether there were separate contracts of employment the appeal tribunal should have remitted that issue to the industrial tribunal.

Held—(1) (Per Sir John Donaldson MR and Fox LJ) Where an appellate tribunal was limited to hearing an appeal on a point of law it had no jurisdiction to consider a question of mixed law and fact until it had distilled or extracted a question of pure law, since it was not entitled to intervene unless it was satisfied that the tribunal below had misdirected itself in law, and, if the tribunal below did not make any express direction as to the law, the appellate tribunal could only be so satisfied if it was satisfied that no reasonable tribunal, properly directing itself on the relevant questions of law, could have come to the conclusion under appeal; *Edwards (Inspector of Taxes) v Bairstow* [1955] 3 All ER 48 applied.

(2) (Per Sir John Donaldson MR and Fox LJ) Although the formulation of the test of whether a contract was a contract of employment or a contract for services was a pure question of law, the application of the test so formulated to the relevant facts depended so much on the finding and assessment of the relevant facts and the precise quality to be attributed to them that the primary question was one of fact and degree. Accordingly, the appeal tribunal had been wrong to assume jurisdiction on the basis that the issue was a question of law. Furthermore, it was impossible to say that no reasonable tribunal, properly directed, could have reached the conclusion the industrial tribunal had come to and therefore on that basis also the appeal tribunal could not have assumed jurisdiction. It followed (Ackner LJ concurring on the facts) that the industrial tribunal's decision that there was no overall contract of employment between the employers and the applicants was not open to appeal; *Simmons v Heath Laundry Co* [1910] 1 KB 543 followed; *Currie v IRC* [1921] 2 KB 332 applied; dictum of Stephenson LJ in *Young & Woods Ltd v West* [1980] IRLR at 205 considered.

(3) Furthermore (Ackner LJ dissenting), it was apparent on the facts that the industrial tribunal had considered the question whether there were separate contracts of employment between the employers and the applicants, and since there had been no misdirection by the industrial tribunal and its conclusion had not been unreasonable on the facts the applicants had no right of appeal on that issue. Accordingly, the employers' appeal would be allowed and the industrial tribunal's decision would be restored.

Notes

For the nature of a contract of employment and the characteristics of the relationship of employer and employee, see 16 *Halsbury's Laws* (4th edn), paras 501, 520.

For the jurisdiction of the Employment Appeal Tribunal, see 16 *Halsbury's Laws* (4th Edn) (2000 reissue), para 676.

For the Employment Protection (Consolidation) Act 1978 ss 136, 153, see 48 *Halsbury's Statutes* (3rd Edn) 593, 610.

Cases referred to in judgments

Addison v London Philharmonic Orchestra Ltd [1981] ICR 261, EAT.
Ahmet v Trusthouse Forte Catering Ltd (13 January 1983, unreported), EAT.
Airfix Footwear Ltd v Cope [1978] ICR 1210, EAT.
Construction Industry Training Board v Labour Force [1970] 3 All ER 220, DC.
Currie v IRC, Durant v IRC [1921] 2 KB 332, CA.
Edwards (Inspector of Taxes) v Bairstow [1955] 3 All ER 48, [1956] AC 14, 36 TC 207, HL.
Ferguson v John Dawson & Partners (Contractors) Ltd [1976] 3 All ER 817, [1976] 1 WLR 1213, CA.
Global Plant Ltd v Secretary of State for Health and Social Security [1971] 3 All ER 385, [1972] 1 QB 139.
Massey v Crown Life Insurance Co [1978] 2 All ER 576, [1978] 1 WLR 676, CA.
Melon v Hector Powe Ltd [1981] 1 All ER 313, HL.
Morren v Swinton and Pendlebury BC [1965] 2 All ER 349, [1965] 1 WLR 576, DC.
Nethermere (St Neots) Ltd v Gardiner [1983] ICR 319, EAT.
Pioneer Shipping Ltd v BTP Tioxide Ltd, The Nema [1981] 2 All ER 1030, [1982] AC 724, [1981] 2 WLR 292, HL.
Ready Mixed Concrete (South East) Ltd v Minister of Pensions and National Insurance [1968] 1 All ER 433, [1968] 2 QB 497, [1968] 2 WLR 775.
Simmons v Heath Laundry Co [1910] 1 KB 543, CA.
Union of Construction, Allied Trades and Technicians v Brain [1981] ICR 542, CA.
Wiltshire CC v National Association of Teachers in Further and Higher Education [1980] ICR 455, CA.
Woods v WM Car Services (Peterborough) Ltd [1982] ICR 693, EAT.
Young & Woods Ltd v West [1980] IRLR 201, CA.

Appeal and cross-appeal

The applicants, Harry O'Kelly, Thomas M Pearman and Philip Florent (the respondents), who were regular casual workers in the banqueting business carried on by the appellants, Trusthouse Forte plc (the employers), at the Grosvenor House Hotel, applied to an industrial tribunal complaining that the employers unfairly dismissed them from their employment for taking part in trade union activities and applied for interim relief under s 77 of the Employment Protection (Consolidation) Act 1978. An industrial tribunal (chairman Mr G E Heggs) sitting at London Central directed the hearing of a preliminary point, namely whether the respondents were employees who worked under a contract of employment within s 153(1) of the 1978 Act (and thus were entitled to complain of wrongful dismissal and to claim interim relief). By a decision made on 31 March and 11 April 1983 the tribunal decided that the respondents were not employees who worked under a contract of employment within the 1978 Act because they were in business on their own account as independent contractors supplying services, and accordingly the tribunal decided that they were not qualified to claim interim relief under s 77 of the 1978 Act. The respondents appealed to the Employment Appeal Tribunal (Browne-Wilkinson J and Mr T D Anderson and Mrs M L Boyle) which by a judgment given on 11 May 1983 allowed the appeal holding that even though the industrial tribunal were correct in deciding that there was no overall contract regulating the position between the respondents and the employers, nevertheless on each occasion that the respondents worked for the employers they entered into separate contract of service with the employers and accordingly the respondents were employees under contracts of employment within the 1978 Act and were qualified to claim interim relief under s 77. The employers appealed to the Court of Appeal. The grounds of the appeal were (1) that the appeal tribunal wrongly decided to consider for themselves whether the respondents were engaged under separate contracts rather than under an overall contract and ought in the circumstances to have remitted the separate contracts issue to the industrial tribunal. Alternatively, if it was proper for the appeal tribunal to consider the separate contracts issue they wrongly concluded that the separate contracts entered into were contracts of service, rather than for services, and were thus contracts of employment within the 1978 Act. (2) The appeal tribunal was wrong in holding that there was no evidence before the industrial tribunal to justify its findings that it was both parties' view that the relationship between them was not that of employer and employee, and that it was a recognised custom and practice of the catering industry that casual workers were engaged to work under contracts for services. By a respondents' notice the respondents gave notice that on the hearing of the appeal they would contend that the contracts of service found by the appeal tribunal to exist were continuous and not intermittent contracts. They also cross-appealed for an order that there was a continuing contractual obligation on the employers' part to offer them work as and when it was available and on the respondents' part to make themselves available for such work. The grounds of the cross-appeal were that the appeal tribunal wrongly held that on the facts found by the industrial tribunal there was no continuing mutuality of obligation between the parties and ought to have held (a) that economic forces did not negative but supported mutuality of obligation and/or (b) that the relationship of the parties was only or was best explicable as one of continuing mutual obligation.

Alexander Irvine QC and *Timothy Charlton* (instructed by *Linklaters & Paines*) for the employers.
Stephen Sedley QC (instructed by *Tess Gill, Claygate*) for the respondents.

O'Murphy v Hewlett Packard Ltd

EMPLOYMENT TRIBUNAL
M J R GRIFFITHS (CHAIRMAN), A C ALDOUS AND M LESLIE
21 MARCH 2001

Employment—Contract of service—Employment agency hiring out consultant to third party employer—Contracts existing between agency and consultant and agency and third party employer—Third party employer terminating employment of consultant—Consultant claiming unfair dismissal—Nature of legal relationship between consultant and third party employer—Whether consultant employee of third party employer.

O was an IT consultant. He owned and managed CT Ltd for the purposes of the administration of his services. In 1994 an employment agency (the agency) and CT Ltd entered into a contract under which the agency would procure work for O. O was placed with H Ltd. O's contract with the agency included provisions that O would be under the control of H Ltd regarding performance and discipline and confidentiality provisions. The agency's contract with H Ltd, to provide computer personnel, included provisions that agency staff would not be 'deemed to be employees' of H Ltd. O worked as part of a team which included employees of H Ltd; the agency took no part in the working relationship between O and H Ltd. Remuneration was paid through the agency and subject to value added tax (VAT). O's employment was terminated in 2000; he complained of unfair dismissal and applied to the employment tribunal for a decision that he was an employee of H Ltd for the purposes of s 230 of the Employment Rights Act 1996. H Ltd contended that the following facts were relevant to O's working relationship with itself, in addition to the contractual provisions: O was expected to use his own initiative in problem solving; his work was only followed up if problems were not resolved within a set period; his work was not managed on a day to day basis; he received no formal appraisals, holiday pay or sick pay; he was part of a team whose work was of limited duration; his expenses were reimbursed via the agency; his name tag differed from those of employees; he was not given an employee's induction pack, not sent on external courses, did not attend weekly team meetings; he was paid significantly more than employees; H Ltd had a full time employee to co-ordinate contractors; O recorded his time; he had no peripheral benefits; termination of his contract was dealt with by the agency; less management time was spent with him than with employees.

Held—(1) The principles relevant to the issues in the instant case were: (i) that it was for O to prove that he was an employee of H Ltd; (ii) that it was for the tribunal to consider not only the contractual documentation but also the course of conduct between the parties and evidence as to their respective intentions to reach a conclusion as to the overall picture; and (iii) that mutuality of obligation was self-evident from a specific engagement, where it might not be (and was therefore required to be proved) in circumstances of general or global engagements.

(2) Applying those principles to the instant case O would be found to be employed by H Ltd for the following reasons. (i) O was as a matter of fact and contract controlled by H Ltd. The freedom he was given in the work that he undertook was no more than would be expected of an experienced and skilled worker whether contractor or employee. (ii) During the course of each assignment H Ltd undertook to provide work for O and to pay him for that work and O undertook to carry out work assigned to him. Further, there was implied into that contract a mutual obligation of trust and confidence. (iii) H Ltd wanted the personal services of O; it appreciated and required his particular experience and skill; it did not want any contractor provided by the agency. (iv) O worked continuously for H Ltd for a number of years as part of a team and was significantly integrated into the work and staff of H Ltd. His treatment, in terms of the working relationship with H Ltd, was for practical purposes indistinguishable to the treatment given to full time employees of H Ltd. (v) The existence of CT Ltd was no more than for administrative purposes and had no material impact on the relationship between O and either the agency or H Ltd. The only reason for the involvement of the agency, after O had been introduced to H Ltd, was to enable the agency to recover its commission. Further, the agency was the agent of H Ltd and payment by the agent was payment by H Ltd. The fact that VAT was charged was a revenue matter rather than a matter material to the legal relationship between the parties. (vi) The exclusion of sick pay was not a contra-indication of a contract for service. The lack of paid holiday was a contra-indication, but when put in balance against the other factors, was not decisive. (vii) The cumulative effect of the other matters asserted by H Ltd was not sufficient to outweigh the indicators of a contract of service.

Accordingly, O was the employee of H Ltd throughout the period from 1994 to 23 October 2000.

Notes

For categories of workers and criteria for employment, see *Harvey on Industrial Relations and Employment Law* Division A.1.

For the Employment Rights Act 1996 s 230, see ibid, Division Q.

Cases referred to in decision

Abbey Life Assurance Co Ltd v Tansell [2000] IRLR 387, CA.
Carmichael v National Power plc [1999] 4 All ER 897, [1999] 1 WLR 2042, [1999] ICR 1226, [2000] IRLR 43, HL.
Clark v Oxfordshire Health Authority [1998] IRLR 125, CA.
Costain Building & Civil Engineering Ltd v Smith [2000] ICR 215, EAT.
Express and Echo Publications Ltd v Tanton [1999] ICR 693, [1999] IRLR 367, CA.
Hall (*Inspector of Taxes*) *v Lorimer* [1994] 1 All ER 250, [1994] 1 WLR 209, [1994] STC 23, 66 TC 349, [1994] ICR 218, [1994] IRLR 171, CA.
Jarvis and ors v Brentvine Ltd and Esso Petroleum Ltd (unreported) Employment Tribunal.
Johnson Underwood Ltd v Montgomery [2001] EWCA Civ 318, [2001] IRLR 269, CA.
MacFarlane and anor v Glasgow City Council [2001] IRLR 7, EAT.
McMeechan v Secretary of State for Employment [1997] ICR 549, [1997] IRLR 353, CA.
Motorola Ltd v Davidson and Melville Craig Group Ltd [2001] IRLR 4, EAT.
Nethermere (St Neots) Ltd v Taverna and Gardiner [1984] ICR 612, [1984] IRLR 240, CA.
Ready Mixed Concrete (*South East*) *Ltd v Minister of Pensions and National Insurance* [1968] 1 All ER 433, [1968] 2 QB 497.
Serco Ltd v Blair and ors (31 August 1998, unreported) EAT.

Application

M O'Murphy (O) brought a complaint of unfair dismissal against Hewlett Packard Ltd (H Ltd). H Ltd asserted that O was not its employee and was precluded from making the complaint. O applied to the employment tribunal, as a preliminary issue, for a decision as to whether he was an employee of H Ltd as defined by s 230 of the Employment Rights Act 1996.

J Antell for O.
R Pirani (instructed by *Baker & McKenzie*) for H Ltd.

[*Note:* In fact the Employment Appeal Tribunal judgment has now been released and the original decision has been reversed as anticipated (see [2002] IRLR 4 *sub nom Hewlett Packard Ltd v O'Murphy*).]

Propertycare Ltd v Gower and others

EMPLOYMENT APPEAL TRIBUNAL
JUDGE PETER CLARK, MRS MATTHIAS AND MR SPRINGER
14 NOVEMBER 2003

Employment—Contract of employment—Contractual arrangements—Relationship between employer and employee—Mutuality of obligation.

Ten applicants claimed before the employment tribunal that they were employed by P Ltd. The tribunal concluded that the applicants were so employed. In reaching that conclusion the tribunal directed itself that a pre-condition which had to be fulfilled before a contract of employment existed was that there was mutuality of obligation which the tribunal defined as a wage in return for work. P Ltd appealed.

Held—Decided cases showed that mutuality of obligation meant more than a simple obligation on the employer to pay for work done; generally there had to be an obligation on the employer to provide the work and the employee to do the work. In the instant case the employment tribunal had misdirected itself. Nowhere in its reasons was there any finding that there had been an obligation on P Ltd to provide work for the applicants. Its only contractual obligation had been to pay commission on business generated by each applicant. Even assuming that it would be sufficient to make a finding that each applicant had a real expectation that they would receive work, it had made no such finding. Accordingly, the appeal would be allowed and the matter remitted to a fresh tribunal for rehearing.

Notes

For tests for contracts of service, see *Harvey on Industrial Relations and Employment Law* Division A.1.A(4).

Cases referred to in decision

Carmichael v National Power plc [1999] 4 All ER 897, [1999] 1 WLR 2042, [1999] ICR 1226, [2000] IRLR 43, HL.
Clark v Oxfordshire Health Authority [1998] IRLR 125, 41 BMLR 18, CA.
Johnson Underwood Ltd v Montgomery [2001] EWCA Civ 318, [2001] ICR 819, [2001] IRLR 269.
Miriki v General Council of the Bar [2001] EWCA Civ 1973, [2002] ICR 505.
Ready Mixed Concrete (South East) Ltd v Minister of Pensions and National Insurance [1968] 1 All ER 433, [1968] 2 QB 497, [1968] 2 WLR 775.
Stevedoring & Haulage Services v Fuller [2001] EWCA Civ 651, [2001] IRLR 627.

Appeal

Property Care Ltd appealed by a notice dated 28 May 2003 from the decision of the employment tribunal at London (South) (chairman: I M MacInnes) released on 22 April 2003 that T Gower, David McAlpine, and eight other applicants were employees of Property Care Ltd within s 230 of the Employment Rights Act 1996.

J Bowers QC and *Mr Trafford* (instructed by Homelet) for the appellant.
David Berkley QC and *Martin Budworth* (instructed by *Horwich Farrell*, Manchester, and *Edwards Geldard*, Nottingham) for the respondents.

R (on the application of Professional Contractors Group Ltd and others) v Inland Revenue Commissioners

QUEEN'S BENCH DIVISION, ADMINISTRATIVE COURT
BURTON J
13, 14, 15, 16, 19, 20 MARCH, 2 APRIL 2001

Right to peaceful enjoyment of possessions—Deprivation of possessions prohibited except if in public interest—Legislation introduced to counter tax avoidance in area of personal service provision—Whether interference in taxpayer's right to own shares in personal service companies—Convention for the Protection of Human Rights and Fundamental Freedoms 1950, Protocol 1, art 1.

European Communities—Competition—State aid—Personal service companies—Legislation introduced to counter tax avoidance in area of personal service provision—Whether unlawful state aid to companies not affected by legislation—EC Treaty, art 87 EC.

European Communities—Freedom of movement—Principle of non-discrimination—Personal service companies—Legislation introduced to counter tax avoidance in area of personal service provision—Whether unlawful hindrance to freedom of movement for persons, freedom of establishment and freedom to provide services—EC Treaty, arts 39 EC, 43 EC, 49 EC.

In March 1999 the Revenue published a press release (IR35) which outlined proposed changes to the way in which individuals who provided services to clients through 'service companies' were taxed. Service companies were primarily one person companies which charged out the services of that one person (the service contractor) to a client, in return for remuneration paid by that client to the service company. The service contractor received a salary, from which PAYE and employee's national insurance contributions were deducted, and the service company paid the employer's national insurance contributions. Any balance of the remuneration was retained by the service company. The service company could deduct allowable expenses incurred by it against its corporation tax liability, which was charged at the special low rate applicable to small companies. A substantial dividend out of the profit could be paid in due course to the service contractor which would not attract national insurance contributions, and in respect of which income tax would only be payable as and when the dividend was declared. Service companies thus provided a number of fiscal advantages to the service contractors and were particularly common in the information technology sector. In general terms, the legislation introduced as a result of IR35 provided that where (i) a worker provided services to a client through an intermediary company (which was defined as where either (a) the worker alone or with one or more associates had a 'material interest' in the company, or (b) where a payment not taxable under Schedule E was received or receivable by the worker directly from a company, and could reasonably be taken to represent remuneration for services provided by the worker to the client), (ii) those services were deemed to be performed by the worker for the client in an 'employee' capacity (which was to be determined according to the existing common law principles of employment), and (iii) the worker received or was entitled to receive a payment or a benefit which was not taxable under Schedule E, then the worker would be subject to tax and employee's national insurance contributions on the money received from the client on the basis that the remuneration received was deemed to be a salary. The service company would be liable for collection of that tax and national insurance contributions, together with payment of its own employer's national insurance contributions on the deemed salary. Where IR35 applied a service company would no longer be able to set off against its corporation tax liability its general business expenses (except for a 5% permitted deduction) unless those expenses related specifically to a particular provision of services and fell within the limited class of expenses deductible by an employee. The claimants, who represented those who were actually or potentially affected by the legislation introduced by IR35, applied for judicial review contending: (i) that IR35 contravened art 1 of Protocol 1 of the Convention for the Protection of Human Rights and Fundamental Freedoms 1950 because it interfered with the right of a person to enjoy the benefit of a shareholding in a service company by rendering it more expensive and making it uncertain; (ii) that IR35 was incompatible with Community law as the benefit that companies unaffected by IR35 would receive as a result of the imposition of IR35 on service companies constituted an unlawful state aid contrary to art 87 EC of the EC Treaty (which provided that any aid granted by a member state or through state resources which distorted competition should, in so far as it affected trade between member states, be incompatible with the common market), and, further that that state aid had not been notified to the EC Commission as required by art 88 EC; and (iii) that IR35 constituted an unlawful hindrance to the free movement of workers, freedom of establishment and freedom to provide services contrary to arts 39 EC, 43 EC and 49 EC of the EC Treaty respectively. The Revenue contended, inter alia, that any restriction on freedom of movement was justified on the ground that IR35 was necessary to counter tax avoidance.

Held—(1) The right to enjoyment of property was not rendered more expensive by the implementation of IR35. Even if the full amount of a service company's earnings in a given year were subject to IR35, that was not even arguably so severe as to amount to a de facto confiscation of property, to fundamental interference with a person's financial position or to an abuse of the United Kingdom's right to levy taxes. Moreover, the legislation was not uncertain or objectionable in its impact. First, it did not create a new category of law but submitted the service contractors to the same law as they would have been subject to, but for the interposition and/or operation of the service company. Second, applying the common law test of employment to a service contractor did not offend against the concept of certainty. *X v France* (App no 9908/82) (1983) 32 DR 266 and *Svenska Managementgruppen AB v Sweden* (App no 11036/84) (1985) 45 DR 211 considered.

(2) Article 87 EC was not contravened in the instant case for the following reasons. First, IR35 applied to persons in accordance with objective criteria without regard to the location, sector or undertaking in which they might be employed. The reason IR35 only applied to the service companies and service contractors was because they alone were not paying income tax and national insurance contributions on the full amount of the remuneration being received directly or indirectly by the service contractor who did the work. Those companies unaffected by IR35 were already doing so in respect of the equivalent employee. Second, it was a general measure aimed so that as far as possible all those supplying services as an employee rather than as an independent contractor would be paying tax and national insurance contributions accordingly, without reference to the existence of a service company. The measure was seen and intended and had an effect as a tax avoidance measure. Third, it was not an exception to or derogation from a general system, but was intended to ensure compliance with it. It was not limited to any particular sector. For those reasons it followed that IR35, which imposed obligations to pay tax and national insurance contributions on service companies in those cases where in fact the principal was providing services to a client as an employee was not aid to anyone. No one could be identified as the recipient of that aid and looking at it on a broad pragmatic basis in the light of the policy underlying art 87 EC, that was not state aid and consequently did not require to be notified. Dicta of Clarke LJ in *R v Customs and Excise Comrs, ex p Lunn Poly Ltd* [1999] STC 350 at 371 applied.

(3) Any restriction on the exercise of fundamental freedoms guaranteed by the EC Treaty had to be non-discriminatory. It could not discriminate between nationals of different member states, it had to be justified by pressing reasons of public interest, and it had to be proportionate. In the instant case, IR35 was not discriminatory and fulfilled the requirements of proportionality. Moreover, the legislation was justified since its purpose was to counter tax avoidance or diminution of tax revenue. *Gebhard v Consiglio dell'Ordine degli Avvocati e Procuratori di Milano* (Case C-55/94) [1995] ECR I-4165 at 4197–4198, para 37 applied.

The claimants' application would therefore be dismissed.

Notes

For the provision of services through an intermediary, see *Simon's Direct Tax Service* E4.205.

For the right to property guaranteed by the Convention for the Protection of Human Rights and Fundamental Freedoms 1950, see 8(2) *Halsbury's Laws* (4th edn reissue) para 165.

For the meaning of state aid, see 51 *Halsbury's Laws* (4th edn) para 7.03.

For freedom of movement for persons, freedom of establishment and freedom to provide services, see 52 *Halsbury's Laws* (4th edn) 16.01–05.

Article 1 of Protocol 1 to the convention now has effect under the Human Rights Act 1998 and is contained in Pt II of Sch 1 to the Human Rights Act 1998 (see *Simon's Direct Tax Service* Part H1).

For the EC Treaty, arts 39 EC, 43 EC, 49 EC and 87 EC, see OJ C340 10.11.1997.

Cases referred to in judgment

A and ors v National Blood Authority (26 March 2001, unreported), QBD.
Alpine Investments BV v Minister van Financiën (Case C-384/93)[1995] ECR I-1141,[1995] All ER (EC) 543, ECJ.
Arbeitsgemeinschaft Deutscher Rundfunkanstalten (ARD) v PRO Sieben Media AG (Case C-6/98)[1999] ECR I-7599, ECJ.
Bachmann v Belgium (Case C-204/90)[1994] STC 855,[1992] ECR I-249, ECJ.
Belgium v EC Commission (Case C-75/97) [1999] ECR I-3671, ECJ.
Brown v Secretary of State for Scotland (Case 197/86) [1988] ECR 3205, ECJ.
Carmichael v National Power plc [1999] 1 WLR 2042, [1999] 4 All ER 897, HL.
Confederación Española de Transporte de Mercancias v EC Commission (Case T-55/99) (2000) Transcript (Judgment) (Eng), 29 September, CFI.
Customs and Excise Comrs v Schindler (Case C-275/92) [1994] QB 610, [1994] ECR I-1039, [1994] 2 All ER 193, ECJ.
De Gezamenlijke Steenkolenmijnen in Limburg v High Authority of the European Coal and Steel Community (Case 30/59) [1961] ECR 1, ECJ.
Déménagements–Manutention Transport SA (Case C-256/97) [1999] ECR I-3913, ECJ.
Deufil GmbH & Co KG v EC Commission (Case 310/85) [1987] ECR 901, ECJ.
Duff v Minister for Agriculture and Food, Ireland, and A-G (Case C-63/93) [1996] ECR I-569, ECJ.
EC Commission v Belgium (Case C-478/98) [2000] STC 830, ECJ.
EC Commission v France (Case C-270/83) [1986] ECR 273, ECJ.
EC Commission v Italy (Case C-119/92) [1994] ECR I-393, ECJ.
EC Commission v Italy (Case 203/82) [1983] ECR 2525, ECJ.

Ecotrade Srl v Altiforni e Ferriere di Servola SpA (AFS) (Case C-200/97) [1998] ECR I-7907, ECJ.
Elliniki Radiophonia Tileorassi AE v Dimotiki Etariia Pliroforissis (Case C-260/89) [1991] ECR I-2925, [1994] 4 CLMR 540, ECJ.
Express and Echo Publications Ltd v Tanton [1999] ICR 693, CA.
Finanzamt Köln-Altstadt v Schumacker (Case C-279/93) [1995] STC 306, [1996] QB 28, [1998] ECR I-225, [1995] All ER (EC) 319, ECJ.
France v EC Commission (Case C-241/94) [1996] ECR I-4551, ECJ.
Futura Participations SA v Administrations des Contributions (Case C-250/95) [1997] STC 1301, [1997] ECR I-2471, ECJ.
Gebhard v Consiglio dell'Ordine degli Avvocati e Procuratori di Milano (Case C-55/94) [1995] ECR I-4165, [1996] All ER (EC) 189, ECJ.
Imperial Chemical Industries plc v Colmer (Inspector of Taxes)(Case C-264/96) [1998] STC 874, [1999] 1 WLR 108, [1998] All ER (EC) 585, ECJ.
Industrie Aeronautiche e Meccaniche Rinaldo Piaggio SpA v International Factors Italia SpA (Case C-295/97) [1999] ECR I-3735, ECJ.
IRC v Willoughby [1997] STC 995, [1997] 1 WLR 1071, [1997] 4 All ER 65, 70 TC 57, HL.
Italy v EC Commission (Case 173/73) [1974] ECR 709, ECJ.
Italy v EC Commission (Case C-6/97) [1999] ECR I-2981, ECJ.
Kenny v Insurance Officer (Case 1/78) [1978] ECR 1489, ECJ.
Kraus v Land Baden-Württemberg (Case C-19/92) [1993] ECR I-1663, ECJ.
Lehtonen v Fédération Royale Belge des Sociétés de Basket-ball ASBL (FRBSB) (Case C-176/96) (2000) Transcript (Judgment) (Eng), 13 April, ECJ.
Market Investigations Ltd v Minister of Social Security [1969] 2 QB 173, [1968] 3 All ER 732.
Metallgesellschaft Ltd v IRC and A-G (Joined cases C-397/98 and C-410/98) [2001] STC 452, 3 ITLR 385, ECJ.
Montgomery v Johnson Underwood Ltd (9 March 2001, unreported), CA.
National & Provincial Building Society v United Kingdom [1997] STC 1466, 25 EHRR 127, 69 TC 540, ECt HR.
Nethermere (St Neots) Ltd v Gardner [1984] ICR 612, CA.
Openbaar Ministerie of the Netherlands v van Tiggele (Case 82/77) [1978] ECR 25, ECJ.
R v A-G, ex p Imperial Chemical Industries plc (1984) 60 TC 1, CA.
R v Chief Constable of Sussex, ex p International Traders Ferry Ltd [1999] 2 AC 418, [1999] 1 All ER 129, HL.
R v Customs and Excise Comrs, ex p Lunn Poly Ltd [1999] STC 350, CA.
Ready Mixed Concrete (South East) Ltd v Minister of Pensions and National Insurance [1968] 2 QB 497, [1968] 1 All ER 433.
Rewe-Zentral AG v Bundesmonopolverwaltung für Branntwein (Case 120/78) [1979] ECR 649, ECJ.
Säger v Dennemeyer & Co Ltd (Case C-76/90) [1991] ECR I-4221, ECJ.
Skatteministeriet v Bent Vestergaard (Case C-55/98) [1999] ECR I-7641, ECJ.
Sloman Neptun Schiffahrts AG v Seebetriebsrat Bodo Ziesemer der Sloman Neptun Schiffahrts AG (Joined cases C-72/91 and C-73/91) [1993] ECR I-887, ECJ.

Staatssecretaris van Financien v Verkoojien (Case C-35/98) (2000) 2 ITLR 727, ECJ.
Sunday Times v United Kingdom (1979–80) 2 EHRR 245, ECt HR.
Svenska Managementgruppen AB v Sweden (App no 11036/84) (1985) 45 DR 211, ECom HR.
Syndesmos ton en Elladi Touristikon kai Taxidiotikon Grafeion v Ergasias (Case C-398/95) [1997] ECR I-3091, ECJ.
Union Royale Belge des Sociétés de Football Association ASBL v Bosman (Case C-415/93) [1995] ECR I-4921, [1996] All ER (EC) 97, ECJ.
X v France (App no 9908/82) (1983) 32 DR 266, ECom HR.

Application

By form 86A dated 23 June 2000, Professional Contractors Group Ltd, Ruud van Zundert and Square Mile Projects Ltd (the claimants), applied for judicial review of ss 75 and 76 of the Welfare Reform and Pensions Act 1999, as implemented by the Social Security Contributions (Intermediaries) Regulations 2000, SI 2000/727, and of s 60 of and Schedule 12 to the Finance Act 2000 on the grounds that the changes contained in those provisions to the way in which individuals who provided services to clients through service companies contravened art 1 of Protocol 1 of the Convention for the Protection of Human Rights and Fundamental Freedoms 1950 and arts 87 EC, 39 EC, 43 EC and 49 EC of the EC Treaty.

Gerald Barling QC and *Kelyn Bacon* (instructed by *Bond Pearce*) for the claimants.
Richard Plender QC and *Rabinder Singh* (instructed by the *Solicitor of Inland Revenue*) for the Revenue.

Ready Mixed Concrete (South East) Ltd v Minister of Pensions and National Insurance

Minister of Social Security v Greenham Ready Mixed Concrete Ltd and Another

Minister of Social Security v Ready Mixed Concrete (South East) Ltd and Another

QUEEN'S BENCH DIVISION
MACKENNA J
3, 4, 5, 6, 9, 10, 11 OCTOBER, 8 DECEMBER 1967

National Insurance—'Employed person'—Owner drivers employed by manufacturers of concrete to deliver concrete—Whether contracts of carriage with independent contractors or contracts of service.

L had been employed by the applicant company as a yardman batcher in and after 1958. In 1959 the company, which made and sold concrete, introduced a system of delivery by owner drivers. It was the company's policy that the making and selling of concrete should be carried on separately from that of delivering it. A purpose of the owner driver scheme was that it would stimulate efficient cartage and care of the vehicle. In May, 1965, L entered into a new contract with the company for the carriage of concrete. He also entered into a hire-purchase agreement for a lorry with an associated hire-purchase company. The lorry was painted in the concrete company's colours and was adapted to carry their mixing unit. L was to procure an 'A' carriers' licence, was to make the lorry available at all times to the company, and was to use it for no other purpose. He was entitled to employ competent substitute drivers, but if the company were dissatisfied he was to provide another substitute; the company was entitled to require L himself to drive the lorry for the maximum hours permitted by law, save for holiday periods. L was to wear the company's uniform and to carry out all reasonable orders from competent servants of the company, 'as if he were an employee of the company'. L was to maintain both the lorry and the mixing unit, including the making of fair wear and tear renewals at his own expense. He was to pay all running costs, and not to charge the vehicle or mixing unit, which were to be insured by the company. Payment to the owner driver was to be at fixed rates per cubic yard for each radial mile, with provision for minimum annual earnings. L, with other owner drivers, employed and paid a relief driver with the company's consent. Either party could determine the contract by notice, the company having the right to acquire the vehicle. The company gave no instructions to L about the method of driving the trucks from the plant to the place of delivery. The contract contained a declaration that L was an independent contractor. The company in busy seasons also employed employee-drivers at different remuneration. On the question whether L was an 'employed person', viz, employed under a contract of service for the purposes of s 1(2)(*a*) of the National Insurance Act 1965, which provided, so far as material:

> 'For the purposes of this Act, insured persons shall be divided into the following three classes, namely—(*a*) employed persons, that is to say, persons gainfully occupied in employment in Great Britain, being employment under a contract of service; (*b*) self-employed persons, that is to say, persons gainfully occupied in employment in Great Britain who are not employed persons; . . .'

In s 114(1) of the Act of 1965 'contract of service' is defined to mean 'any contract of service or apprenticeship, whether written or oral and whether express or implied'; and 'employment' is defined to include 'any trade, business, profession, office or vocation' and 'employed' is to be construed accordingly except in the expression 'employed persons'. By s 3(1) of the Act of 1965—'subject to the provisions of this Act— . . . (*b*) every employer of an employed person of any description set out in column 1 of Part 2 of Sch 1 to this Act . . . shall be liable to pay weekly contributions in respect of that person at the rate set out in relation to that description . . .'

Held—A contract of service existed if three conditions were fulfilled, and, though one of these was that the servant should be subject to the control of the master to a sufficient degree, for present purposes the important condition was the third, viz, that the provisions of the contract should not be inconsistent with its being a contract of service; in the present case the rights conferred and the duties imposed by L's contract with the company were not such as to make the contract one of service, and his contract was one of carriage, with the consequence that L was not included within the class of employed persons for the purposes of s 1(2)(*a*) of the National Insurance Act 1965.

Queensland Stations Pty v Federal Comr of Taxation ((1945), 70 CLR 539) and opinion of Lord Wright in *Montreal Locomotive Works Ltd v Montreal and A-G for Canada* ([1947] 1 DLR 161) applied.

Notes

As to employed persons for the purposes of national insurance, see 44(2) *Halsbury's Laws* (4th Edn) (1997 reissue) para 32.

As to contracts of service see 16 *Halsbury's Laws* (4th edn) (2000 reissue) para 1 et seq.

Cases referred to in judgment

Amalgamated Engineering Union v Minister of Pensions and National Insurance [1963] 1 All ER 864, [1963] 1 WLR 441, *Digest* (Cont Vol A) 1133, *2632a*.

Bank Voor Handed en Scheepvaart, NV v Slatford [1952] 2 All ER 956, [1953] 1 QB 248, [1954] 2 WLR 867, *revsd* sub nom *Bank Voor Handel en Scheepvaart, NV v Administrator of Hungarian Property*, [1954] 1 All ER 969, [1954] AC 584, [1954] 2 WLR 867, 2 *Digest* (Repl) 269, *614*.

Clarke v Bailieborough Co-operative Agricultural and Dairy Society, Ltd (1913), 47 ILT 113.

Doggett v Waterloo Taxi-Cab Co Ltd [1910] 2 KB 336, 79 LJKB 1085, 102 LT 876, 34 *Digest* (Repl) 37, *127*.

Hardaker v Idle District Council [1895–99] All ER Rep 311, [1896] 1 QB 335, 65 LJQB 363, 74 LT 69, 60 JP 196, 34 *Digest* (Repl) 201, *1416*.

Humberstone v Northern Timber Mills [1949] ALR 985, 79 CLR 389, 34 *Digest* (Repl) 31, *53*.

Montreal Locomotive Works v Montreal and A-G for Canada [1947] 1 DLR 161.

Mooney v Sheehan (1903), 37 ILT 166.

National Labour Relations Board v Nu-Car Carriers (1951), 189 Fed 2nd 756.

O'Donnell v Clare County Council (1912), 47 ILT 41, 6 BWCC 457, 34 *Digest* (Repl) 358, *1480*.

Park v Wilsons & Clyde Coal Co, Haggerty v Wilsons & Clyde Coal Co, 1928 SC 121, *affd*, 1929 SC 38, 34 *Digest* (Repl) 33, *63*.

Queensland Stations Pty v Federal Comr of Taxation (1945), 70 CLR 539.
Short v Henderson Ltd (1946), 115 LJPC 41, 174 LT 417, 34 *Digest* (Repl) 343, *2635*.
US v Silk (1946), 331 US 704.
Zuijus v Wirth Brothers Pty Ltd (1955), 93 CLR 561.

R J Parker QC and *G Slynn* (instructed by *Linklaters & Paines*) for Ready Mixed Concrete (South East) Ltd, Mr Latimer and Mr Bezer.
H A P Fisher QC and *Adrian Hamilton* (instructed by *Mckenna & Co*) for Greenham Ready Mixed Concrete Ltd and Mr King.
Nigel Bridge (instructed by the *Solicitor, Ministry of Social Security*) for the Minister of Social Security, formerly the Minister of Pensions and National Insurance

Reid v North West Ceilings Ltd (trading as Shopspec)

EMPLOYMENT APPEAL TRIBUNAL
RECORDER LANGSTAFF QC, MR D JENKINS AND MR A MANNER
2 APRIL 2001

Employment—Contract of service—Distinction between contract of service and contract for services—Applicant working exclusively for company on number of contracts—Employment tribunal concluding applicant self-employed—Whether tribunal erring in law.

The applicant, R, began working for the respondent company in March 1994. He worked exclusively for the company on a number of contracts as a supervisor. The company provided transport and all equipment save for certain tools expected to be carried by a man of R's skill. He was under the control of the company and not in any way involved in its profits or losses, nor did he negotiate his rate of pay, or provide for a price for the work he was to carry out. He was paid by the hour at a rate prescribed by the company and he was provided with payslips. He paid national insurance on a self-employed basis. There were no specific holiday arrangements, nor was holiday pay given. R took holidays as when he required. Until March 1998 R dealt with his own tax affairs. Prior to that date negotiations had taken place with the company with a view to changing R's status to one which was accepted as that of employee. An employment tribunal determined that R had been self-employed from March 1994 to March 1998 when it was common ground that he became an employee. In consequence, he had an insufficient period of continuous employment to enable him to present a claim of unfair dismissal against the company. R appealed.

Held—On the evidence, the tribunal had failed to indicate the approach it had adopted in reaching the decision that R was self-employed prior to March 1994. If the tribunal had applied the appropriate tests in relation to the degree of control held by the company, whether R was in business on his own account or whether he was 'part and parcel' of the company, it would have come to the inevitable conclusion that R was an employee of the company. He was indistinguishable from workers employed 'on the lump' as opposed to independent contractors. Accordingly, the decision of the tribunal was perverse. The appeal of R would therefore be allowed.

Lee Ting Sang v Chung Chi-Keung [1990] 2 AC 374 and Lane v Shire Roofing Company (Oxford) Ltd [1995] IRLR 493 applied.

Notes

For categories of workers, see *Harvey on Industrial Relations and Employment Law* Division A.1.

For characteristics of the relationship of master and servant, see ibid, Division A.3.

Serco Ltd v Blair and others

EMPLOYMENT APPEAL TRIBUNAL
LORD JOHNSTON, MR G R CARTER AND MR W M SPEIRS
31 AUGUST 1998

Employment—Contract of service—Employment agency hiring out workers to third party employer—Contracts existing between agency and workers and agency and third party employer—Nature of legal relationship between workers and third party employer—Whether created by doctrine of jus quaesitum tertio.

An employment agency in Scotland hired out the services of workers to third-party employers. Two workers on the books of the agency were hired out to S Ltd in 1994. There were two contracts: between the workers and the agency and between the agency and S Ltd. Both workers worked until December 1996 when they were dismissed from their employment. The dismissal instructions emanated from S Ltd to the agency. On a preliminary question the industrial tribunal ruled that the status of the two workers should be categorised as that of employment on the basis that the arrangements between the workers and the agency created by reason of a *jus quaesitum tertio* (literally, 'the third party has acquired a right'; the concept describes the situation where rights are conferred by a contract on a person who is not party to the contract) a legal relationship between the workers and S Ltd which could be categorised on the facts as a contract of employment. S Ltd appealed.

Held—The concept of *jus quaesitum tertio* had a very limited scope in the law of Scotland and certainly did not feature so as to create a contract with mutually binding obligations such as were to be found in a contract of employment, not least because of the very personal nature of such a contract, and the need for mutual trust and confidence as between employer and employee which could not be created by the acts of a third party, even in conjunction with the workers, particularly where the third party (the agency) remained part of the operational scene. The concept of *jus quaesitum tertio* was alien to the concepts involved in employment law and could not be used, in the context of the instant case, to create some form of legal relationship as between the workers and S Ltd. If that approach was wrong, and such a relationship did exist, the tribunal had not directed itself properly in law in categorising such a relationship to be one of employment. The facts found did not support the view that there was sufficient degree of control to enable the workers fairly to be called servants; that they were providing services for remuneration there was no doubt, but they were free as individuals not to accept any particular placement in terms of the contract with the agency, and equally, the control ultimately of employment in the sense of whether they continued, whatever might be the wishes of the actual employer of the services, lay with the agency. Even if the tribunal had been entitled to conclude that the workers had undertaken to provide their own work and skill in return for remuneration and that there was sufficient degree of control to enable the workers fairly to be called servants, it had left out of account completely the intervention of a third party, namely the agency, which had to be a factor inconsistent with a contract of service as between S Ltd and the workers.

S Ltd's appeal would therefore be allowed.

Notes

For *jus quaesitum tertio* (third party rights) see 15 *Stair Memorial Encyclopaedia* para 824.

Cases referred to in judgment

Carmichael v Carmichael's Executrix 1920 SC (HL) 195.
Carmichael v National Power plc [1998] ICR 1167, [1998] IRLR 301, CA; *rvsd* [1999] 4 All ER 897, [1999] 1 WLR 2042, [1999] ICR 1226, [2000] IRLR 43, HL.
Finnie v Glasgow and South Western Rly Co (1855) 2 Macq 177.
Henderson v Stubbs Ltd (1894) 22 R 51.
McMeechan v Secretary of State for Employment [1995] ICR 444, [1995] IRLR 461, EAT; *affd* 1997] ICR 549, [1997] IRLR 353, CA.
Nethermere (St Neots) Ltd v Taverna and Gardiner [1984] ICR 612, [1984] IRLR 240, CA.
Ready Mixed Concrete (South East) Ltd v Minister of Pensions and National Insurance [1968] 1 All ER 433, [1968] 2 QB 497.
Scott Lithgow Ltd v GEC Electrical Projects Ltd 1992 SLT 244, CS.

Appeal

Serco Ltd (S Ltd) appealed from a decision of the industrial tribunal that the status of Matthew Blair and Ian Sampson (the workers), who were workers on the books of NRL Ltd (the agency) and were hired out by the agency to S Ltd, should be categorised as that of employment on the basis that the arrangements or contracts between the workers and the agency created, by reason of a *jus quaesitum tertio*, a legal relationship between the workers and S Ltd which could be categorised on the facts as a contract of employment.

M Mackay (instructed by *Mackay Simon*, Edinburgh) for S Ltd.
Nicola Dandridge (instructed by *Thompsons*, Glasgow) for the workers.
The agency was not represented.

Sidey v Phillips (Inspector of Taxes)

CHANCERY DIVISION
KNOX J
5 DECEMBER 1986

Emoluments from office or employment—Employment—Meaning—Contract of service or contract for services—Taxpayer deriving income from part-time lecturing—Taxpayer's services subject to standard terms and conditions of the education authorities engaging him—Whether contract between taxpayer and education authorities contract of service.

The taxpayer was a barrister who had not practised since 1960. He derived his earned income from writing, examining titles for the Land Registry and part-time lecturing for the Inner London Education Authority and a London polytechnic (the education authorities). For a number of years he was assessed to income tax in respect of his earnings under Sch D. However, in 1976 the inspector of taxes decided that the fees earned by the taxpayer from his lecturing engagements had become considerable and should be assessed under Sch E pursuant to s 181(1) of the Income and Corporation Taxes Act 1970. On appeal against the Sch E assessment before the Special Commissioners the taxpayer adduced oral evidence relating to the types of engagements fulfilled by him. Some of them were for the whole of the academic year, while others were for shorter courses. The heads of departments who interviewed the taxpayer before he entered into those engagements did not place before him formal terms of service but the taxpayer knew that they were not in a position to offer him terms outside the standard terms offered to part-time lecturers by the education authorities. The commissioners found that the standard terms were, by implication, the terms of the contracts between the taxpayer and the education authorities, that those terms pointed inescapably to the establishment of a master and servant relationship, that the lecturing engagements undertaken by the taxpayer were therefore clearly employments and that the taxpayer was properly assessed to tax on his income from that source under Sch E. The taxpayer appealed against the commissioners' determination contending that on the relevant facts found by them the only proper conclusion that they could reach was that the contracts which he had entered into with the education authorities were contracts for services and not contracts of service and accordingly his earnings derived from them were taxable under Sch D.

Held—The taxpayer had not shown either that the commissioners had misdirected themselves in law or that they had reached a conclusion which no tribunal properly instructed could have reached on the basic facts found by them. Accordingly the commissioners' determination that the assessments were properly made under Sch E could not be interfered with. The taxpayer's appeal would therefore be dismissed.

Notes

For scope of charge under Sch E, see *Simon's Direct Tax Service*, Division E4.1.

Cases referred to in judgment

Argent v Minister of Social Security [1968] 1 WLR 1749,[1968] 3 All ER 208.
Currie v IRC [1921] 2 KB 332.
Edwards v Bairstow (Inspector of Taxes) [1956] AC 14, [1955] 3 All ER 48, 36 TC 207, HL
Fall v Hitchen (Inspector of Taxes) [1973] STC 66, [1973] 1 WLR 286, [1973] 1 All ER 368.
Fuge v McClelland (Inspector of Taxes) (1956) 36 TC 571.
Nethermere (St Neots) Ltd v Gardiner [1984] ICR 612, CA.
O'Kelly v Trusthouse Forte plc [1984] QB 90, [1983] 3 All ER 456, CA.
Ready Mixed Concrete (South East) Ltd v Minister of Pensions and National Insurance [1968] 2 QB 497, [1968] 1 All ER 433.
Simmons v Heath Laundry Co [1910] 1 KB 543, CA.
Zuijs v Wirth Bros Pty Ltd (1955) 93 CLR 561.

Case stated

Hugh Richard Sidney appealed by way of case stated from a decision of the Special Commissioners confirming assessments to Sch E as emoluments of employment on income earned from part-time lecturing.

The taxpayer appeared in person.
Alan Moses (instructed by the *Solicitor of Inland Revenue*) for the Crown.

Staples v Secretary of State for Social Services

QUEEN'S BENCH DIVISION (CROWN OFFICE LIST)
GLIDEWELL J
15 MARCH 1985

Employment—Contract for services—Self-employed earners rendering personal service supplied by third person—Self-employed earners working as relief chefs supplied by employment agency—Whether treated as employed earners—Whether subject to supervision, direction or control.

S was the proprietor of an employment agency for chefs. He had, inter alia, two chefs on his books, A and G. S obtained for A and G a number of engagements to work as relief chefs mainly in hotels, but also in restaurants and nursing homes. They were usually in charge of food stocks and supplies and did the ordering. They would fashion their daily menus to make best use of perishable supplies. Pricing of dishes always had to have the approval of management. The terms of their placement by S included a requirement that each would be responsible for paying his own income tax under Schedule D and his own national insurance contributions. The Social Security (Categorisation of Earners) Regulations 1978 (the 1978 Regulations) provided that (subject to certain exceptions) a self-employed earner who fell within a category of employment described in column A of Pt I of Sch 1 to the 1978 Regulations was to be treated as an employed earner for the purposes of national insurance contributions. The categories in column A included, in para 2, persons engaged in employment in which the employed persons rendered or were under obligation to render personal service and were subject to supervision, direction or control, as to the manner of rendering such service and where the person employed was supplied by or through some third person. On S's application the Secretary of State for Social Services determined that A and G when fulfilling the engagements obtained for them by S were self-employed earners within s 2 of the Social Security Act 1975 but fell within para 2 of column A of Sch 1 to the 1978 Regulations. S appealed.

Held—There was inherent in 'supervision, direction or control' that in the event management had the right to control. It was no good being able to supervise somebody if, in the last resort, you could not tell him what to do. The question was: did management have the right to tell G and A not only what job to do but how they should do it? The measure of discretion of a head chef put him in a position akin to that of a person possessing, if not a professional qualification, at least some considerable skill. That being so, he was to be regarded as being a person who in almost every respect was not subject to direction by management as to how he should do his job. The matters relating to the areas which management could control a head chef were largely, if not entirely, matters which went with the description of the job itself or the content of the job itself.

Accordingly, the Secretary of State had erred in law in reaching his conclusion and S's appeal would be allowed.

Notes

For categories of workers: servants and independent contractors, see *Harvey on Industrial Relations and Employment Law* Division A.1.A and C.

Cases referred to in judgment

Edwards (Inspector of Taxes) v Bairstow [1956] AC 14, [1955] 3 All ER 48, 36 TC 207, HL.
Mersey Docks and Harbour Board v Coggins & Griffith (Liverpool) Ltd [1947] AC 1, [1946] 2 All ER 345, HL.
O'Kelly v Trusthouse Forte plc [1984] QB 90, [1983] 3 All ER 456, CA.

Appeal

Mr Staples (S) appealed from the decision of the Secretary of State for Social Services that Mr Armitstead and Mr Gilks, who were chefs de cuisine on the books of S's employment agency, while working as relief chefs through the agency, being self-employed earners rendering personal service supplied through a third person, were subject to supervision, direction or control in their employment and so fell within para 2 of column A of Pt I of Sch 1 to the Social Security (Categorisation of Earners) Regulations 1978.

D Richardson (instructed by *Robbins Olivey & Blake Lapthorn* as agents for *Andrew & Co*, Lincoln) for S.
C Symons (instructed by *the Solicitor, Department of Health and Social Security*) for the Secretary of State.

Stevedoring & Haulage Services Ltd v Fuller and others

COURT OF APPEAL, CIVIL DIVISION
SCHIEMANN, ROBERT WALKER AND TUCKEY LJJ
9 MAY 2001

Employment—Contract of employment—Contractual arrangements—Relationship between employer and employee—Mutuality of obligation expressly negatived—Whether contract of employment implied by conduct.

F and seven others (the applicants) were employed by SHS Ltd as dockers for six years until 1995 when they accepted voluntary redundancy. In January 1996 they were taken on again as casual workers. A letter offering that work made it clear that they would not be employees but would provide their services on 'an ad hoc and casual basis' with 'no obligation on the part of the company to provide such work for you nor for you to accept any work so offered'. They signed and returned copies of that letter together with another document headed 'Temporary terminal operatives' terms and conditions of engagement' which included the following statement: 'You are not an employee of the company; your services being utilised only when mutually agreed, with no obligation by either party other than to honour a specific pre-agreed period of engagement.' From January 1996, the applicants worked for SHS Ltd on many more days than not and did not work for any other employer. They were engaged directly by SHS Ltd and were offered work before other casual workers. A rota system ensured that those who said that they were available for work but were not offered it were rewarded and that those who were offered work for which they were not available were penalised. After working on that basis for three years, the applicants applied to an employment tribunal for written statements of the particulars of their employment, which under s 1 of the Employment Rights Act 1996 were required to be provided to employees. Section 230 of the 1996 Act defined an employee as 'an individual who has entered into, or works under a contract of employment' which is in turn defined as 'a contract of service, whether express or implied and (if it is express) whether oral or in writing'. The tribunal concluded that the applicants were 'employees'. They were not simply working under a series of individual engagements but under an 'overarching' contract of employment. The tribunal found that although the documents containing the terms upon which casual work was offered and accepted expressly negatived mutuality of obligation, terms providing for an 'irreducible minimum of obligation on each side' could be implied from the way in which the parties had conducted themselves. Those implied terms were that SHS Ltd would offer the applicants a reasonable amount of work as and when the work was available, and do so in priority to other casual workers and that, in return, the applicants would make themselves available for work on at least a reasonable number of occasions when work was offered to them. SHS Ltd appealed to the Employment Appeal Tribunal which dismissed its appeal, concluding that the implied terms reflected the reality of the agreement between the parties and that it had been open to the tribunal to find that those terms were not inconsistent with the express terms of the agreement and that it was necessary to imply them to give the agreement business efficacy. SHS Ltd appealed to the Court of Appeal.

Held—Where the terms upon which casual work was offered and accepted expressly negatived mutuality of obligation, there could be no global or overarching contract of employment. The employment tribunal had erred in holding that the applicants in the instant case were working under such a contract, rather than under a series of individual engagements, notwithstanding that the documents setting out the terms under which they were offered and accepted work expressly provided that they were being engaged on an ad hoc and casual basis with no obligation on the company to offer work and no obligation on the applicants to accept it. Terms providing for an irreducible minimum of obligation on each side could not be implied from the way in which the parties had conducted themselves since the inception of the agreement. If there had been no contract, one could not be created by implying terms which watered down the effect of the express terms so as to give it sufficient mutuality of obligation to pass the test necessary for establishing a contract of employment. Moreover, if there had been a contract there was no way in which the terms implied by the employment tribunal could be incorporated into it. Those implied terms flatly contradicted the express terms contained in the documents. A positive implied obligation to offer and accept a reasonable amount of casual work could not be reconciled with express terms that neither party was obliged to offer or accept any casual work. Neither business efficacy nor necessity required the implication of implied terms which were entirely inconsistent with a supposed contract's express terms. Accordingly, the appeal would be allowed.

Notes

For tests for contracts of service, see *Harvey on Industrial Relations and Employment Law* Division A.1.A(4).

Cases referred to in judgment

Carmichael v National Power plc [1999] 4 All ER 897, [1999] 1 WLR 2042, [1999] ICR 1226, [2000] IRLR 43, HL.
Clark v Oxfordshire Health Authority [1998] IRLR 125, 41 BMLR 18, CA.

Appeal

Stevedoring & Haulage Services Ltd (SHS Ltd) appealed from the decision of the Employment Appeal Tribunal dismissing SHS Ltd's appeal from the decision of the employment tribunal that Mr Fuller and seven other applicants were employees of SHS Ltd within s 230 of the Employment Rights Act 1996.

Anthony Higgins (instructed by *Morlings*) for SHS Ltd.
Thomas Linden (instructed by *Pattinson & Brewer*) for the applicants.

Stuncroft Ltd v Havelock

EMPLOYMENT APPEAL TRIBUNAL
JUDGE WILKIE QC, MR HODGKINS AND MRS MARSLAND
12 NOVEMBER 2001

Employment—Contract of service—Whether casual worker under contract of service—Whether mutuality of obligation existing between worker and employer.

H applied to the employment tribunal claiming a redundancy payment from S Ltd. The tribunal made a preliminary decision that H had been an employee of S Ltd, approaching the question of whether there had been a contract of employment by taking into account all the factors and balancing them against one another. Before the tribunal hearing took place, H had written to S Ltd's solicitors, saying: 'Whilst I agree that I was not obliged to accept work from [S Ltd], the work was usually offered to me at a very short notice. I would be called for example on a Friday afternoon before 5 pm with details of a run leaving on Sunday morning and ferry bookings had already been made. During the seven years I worked for [S Ltd] I do not recall an occasion when I refused any work offered and was always flexible and accommodating'. S Ltd appealed, contending that the letter was evidence of want of mutuality of obligation, which was fatal to the existence of a contract of service.

Held—The Court of Appeal had warned employment tribunals against an over-astute exercise in implying mutual obligations where the express documentation did not permit it in cases where consistent behaviour on the part of the parties to the arrangement tempted the tribunal to imply mutual obligations where none existed as a matter of law. Mutuality of obligation was an irreducible minimum in a contract of service and thus a determinative issue. In the instant case, it was not open to the EAT to remit the case to the tribunal for fresh evidence to be given in the light of the very clear and unambiguous statement in H's letter which precluded any possibility of getting round the fact that there had been no mutuality of obligation as between him and S Ltd. The appeal would accordingly be allowed.

Notes

For tests for contracts of service, see *Harvey on Industrial Relations and Employment Law* Division A.1.A(4).

Cases referred to in decision

Carmichael v National Power plc [1999] 4 All ER 897, [1999] 1 WLR 2042, [1999] ICR 1226, [2000] IRLR 43, HL.

Clark v Oxfordshire Health Authority [1998] IRLR 125, 41 BMLR 18, CA.
Nethermere (St Neots) Ltd [1984] IRLR 240, [1984] ICR 612, CA.
Stevedoring & Haulage Services v Fuller [2001] EWCA Civ 651, [2001] IRLR 627.

Appeal

Stuncroft Ltd appealed against the decision of the employment tribunal at Bury St Edmunds on 21 June 2000 that Mr G T Havelock had been its employee within the meaning of s 230 of the Employment Rights Act 1996.

Clive Sheldon (instructed by *Gotelee & Goldsmith*, Ipswich) for Stuncroft Ltd.
Mr Havelock appeared in person.

Synaptek Ltd v Young (Inspector of Taxes)

CHANCERY DIVISION
HART J
27, 28 FEBRUARY, 28 MARCH 2003

National insurance—Earnings of workers supplied by service companies etc—Provision of services through intermediary—Worker establishing personal service company—Company contracting with agency for provision of services to client of agency—Whether company liable for national insurance contributions on payments made by client to agency and then by agency to company—Whether, if arrangements had taken the form of a contract between worker and client, worker would have been regarded as employed in employed earner's employment by the client—Whether question to be determined matter of law—Social Security Contributions (Intermediaries) Regulations 2000, SI 2000/727, reg 6(1)

S personally supplied computer software services through a company he had established in 1990. In 1999 the company entered into a contract with an agency under which S was to provide services for one of the agency's clients. There was no contractual relationship between the company and the client. S duly performed the services for the client. By a notice of decision dated 30 April 2001 the Revenue determined that the company was liable to pay primary and secondary Class 1 national insurance contributions in respect of S's earnings for the services he had performed for the client as reg 6(1) of the Social Security Contributions (Intermediaries) Regulations 2000 applied. The regulations applied where: (a) an individual (the worker) personally performed, or was under an obligation to perform, services for the purposes of a business carried on by another person (the client), (b) the performance of those services by the worker was carried out, not under a contract directly between the client and the worker, but under arrangements involving an intermediary, and (c) the circumstances were such that, had the arrangements taken the form of a contract between the worker and the client, the worker would be regarded for the purposes of Pts I to V of the Social Security Contributions and Benefits Act 1992 as employed in employed earner's employment by the client. The company appealed. The General Commissioners, after considering the relevant authorities to which they had been referred, decided, on balance, that, if there had been a contract between S and the client, it would have been a contract of service with S as an employee. They accordingly dismissed the appeal. The company appealed contending, inter alia, that the question under reg 6(1) necessarily involved a question of law and it was therefore open to the court to substitute its own opinion for the decision of the General Commissioners.

Held—In general the question whether a particular contract was a contract of service or a contract for services was one of mixed fact and law, the evaluation and determination of which was a matter for the fact-finding tribunal. If, however, the question fell to resolved solely by reference to the contents of a written contract, the question was regarded by the court as a question of law. The inquiry which reg 6(1) directed was in the first instance an essentially factual one. It involved identifying, first, what were the 'arrangements involving an intermediary' under which the services were performed, and, secondly, what were the 'circumstances' in the context of which the arrangements had been made and the services performed. The legal hypothesis which then had to be made was that the arrangements had taken the form of a contract between the worker and the client. To the extent that 'the arrangements' were in the particular case to be found only in contractual documentation, it might be true to say that the interpretation of that documentation was a question of law. Even in that case, however, the findings of the fact-finding tribunal would be determinative of the factual matrix in which the interpretative process had to take place, and influential to a greater or lesser degree in enabling the essential character of the arrangements to be identified. Where, on the other hand, the arrangements could not be located solely in contractual documentation, their identification and characterisation was properly to be described as a matter of fact for the fact-finding tribunal. The fact that the tribunal was then asked to hypothesise a contract comprising those arrangements directly between the worker and the client did not, by itself, convert the question of whether the contract was one of service or for services, from being a question of mixed fact and law into a pure question of law. Accordingly, the court was not free to substitute its own opinion for that of the commissioners and could only interfere in the instant case if it concluded that the decision reached by the commissioners was an impossible one on the facts found by them or that they had misdirected themselves in law. As the commissioners' conclusion was clearly a possible one on the evidence before them and as they had not misdirected themselves, the company's appeal would accordingly be dismissed.

Notes

For national insurance contributions on earnings paid through certain personal service companies, see *Simon's National Insurance Contributions Service*, 8.346.

For the Social Security Contributions (Intermediaries) Regulations 2000, SI 2000/727, reg 6(1), see *Simon's National Insurance Contributions Service*, Part III.

Cases referred to in judgment

Carmichael v National Power plc [1999] 1 WLR 2042, [1999] 4 All ER 897, HL.
Clark v Oxfordshire Health Authority [1998] IRLR 125, 41 BMLR 18, CA.
Cooke (Inspector of Taxes) v Blacklaws [1985] STC 1, 58 TC 255.
Davies v Presbyterian Church of Wales [1986] 1 WLR 323, [1986] IRLR 194, [1986] 1 All ER 705, HL.
Davies (Inspector of Taxes) v Braithwaite [1931] 2 KB 628, 18 TC 198.
Express and Echo Publications Ltd v Tanton [1999] IRLR 367, CA.
Fall (Inspector of Taxes) v Hitchen [1973] STC 66, [1973] 1 WLR 286, [1973] 1 All ER 368, 49 TC 433.
F S Consulting Ltd v McCaul (Inspector of Taxes) [2002] STC (SCD) 138.
Hall (Inspector of Taxes) v Lorimer [1994] STC 23, [1994] 1 WLR 209, [1994] 1 All ER 250, 66 TC 349, CA.
Johnson Underwood Ltd v Montgomery [2001] EWCA Civ 318, [2001] IRLR 269.
MacFarlane v Glasgow City Council [2001] IRLR 7, EAT.
Market Investigations Ltd v Minister of Social Security [1969] 2 QB 173, [1968] 3 All ER 732.
McLeod v Hellyer Bros Ltd [1987] 1 WLR 728, CA.
McManus v Griffiths (Inspector of Taxes) [1997] STC 1089, 70 TC 218.
Nethermere (St Neots) Ltd v Taverna and Gardiner [1984] IRLR 240, CA.
O'Kelly v Trusthouse Forte plc [1984] QB 90, [1983] 3 All ER 456, CA.
R (on the application of Professional Contractors Group) v IRC [2001] EWCA Civ 1945, [2002] STC 165, 74 TC 393; *affg* [2001] EWHC Admin 236, [2001] STC 629, 74 TC 393.
Ready Mixed Concrete (South East) Ltd v Minister of Pensions and National Insurance [1968] 2 QB 497, [1968] 1 All ER 433.
Sidey v Phillips (Inspector of Taxes) [1987] STC 87, 59 TC 458.

Cases also cited or referred to in skeleton arguments

Bradley (Inspector of Taxes) v London Electric plc [1996] STC 231.
Consolidated Goldfields plc v IRC; Gold Fields Mining and Industrial Ltd v IRC [1990] STC 357, [1990] 2 All ER 398, 63 TC 333.
Customs and Excise Comrs v Hodges [2000] STC 262.

Edwards (Inspector of Taxes) v Bairstow [1956] AC 14, [1955] 3 All ER 48, 36 TC 207, HL.
English v Emery Reimbold & Strick Ltd; D J & C Withers (Farms) Ltd v Ambic Equipment Ltd; Verrechia (t/a Freightmaster Commercials) v Comr of Police for the Metropolis [2002] EWCA Civ 605, [2002] 3 All ER 385.
Jeffries (Inspector of Taxes) v Stevens [1982] STC 639, 56 TC 134.
Munby v Furlong (Inspector of Taxes) [1977] STC 232, [1977] Ch 359, [1977] 2 All ER 953, 50 TC 491.
Secretary of State for Trade and Industry v Bottrill [1999] ICR 592, [1999] IRLR 326, [2000] 1 All ER 915, CA.
Walls v Sinnett (Inspector of Taxes) [1987] STC 236, 60 TC 150.
Willy Scheiddegger Swiss Typewriting School (London) Ltd v Minister of Social Security (1968) 5 KIR 65.

Appeal by way of case stated

Synaptek Ltd appealed by way of case stated from the decision of the Commissioners for the general purposes of the income tax for the division of South Shields in the county of Tyne and Wear made at a hearing on 27 February 2002 dismissing the company's appeal against a notice of decision of the Revenue dated 30 April 2001 (i) that the circumstances of the arrangements between Gordon Stutchbury and EDS for the performance of services from 1 May 2000 to 29 October 2000 were such that, had they taken the form of a contract between Gordon Stutchbury and EDS, Gordon Stutchbury would be regarded for the purposes of Pts I–V of the Social Security (Contributions and Benefits) Act 1992 as employed in employed earner's employment by EDS; and (ii) that Synaptek Ltd was to be treated as liable to pay primary and secondary Class 1 Contributions in respect of the worker's attributable earnings from that engagement.

Conrad McDonnell (instructed by *Bond Pearce*) for Synaptek Ltd.
Clive Sheldon (instructed by the *Solicitor of Inland Revenue*) for the Crown.

Tilbury Consulting Ltd v Gittins (Inspector of Taxes)

SPECIAL COMMISSIONER: DR A N BRICE
18 JULY, 15 AUGUST 2003

Appeal—Procedure—Witness summons—Appeal concerning the nature of contractual arrangements between worker and client to whom worker's services were supplied by intermediary—Written evidence obtained from client—Revenue applying to Special Commissioner to require attendance of witness from client at hearing of appeal—Taxpayer objecting to issue of summons on ground that it would damage client relationship—Whether issue of summons in interests of justice—Special Commissioners (Jurisdiction and Procedure) Regulations 1994, SI 1994/1811, reg 5.

R, a director of the taxpayer company (T), contracted with T which contracted with an IT company which contracted with a company, F, for the supply to F of IT consultancy services by R. On 7 September 2001 R's representatives contacted the Revenue and asked for an opinion about his status. (If it could be said that R would have been regarded as employed in employed earner's employment by F had the arrangements taken the form of a contract between R and F, then the payments to T would be treated as R's earnings for the purposes of income tax and/or national insurance contributions.) With R's consent, the inspector on 19 February 2002 wrote to Mr B of F for information to establish the exact nature of the terms and conditions which existed in respect of the engagements. On 18 July 2002 Mr B replied in writing to the inspector's twenty-two detailed questions. On 6 August 2002 the inspector wrote to R's representatives to say that she had considered the information supplied by F and was of the opinion that, if there had been a contract between F and R, it would be considered to be a contract of service. Without informing T of her intention so to do the inspector wrote again to Mr B on 6 January 2003 and asked for some further information about the use of a substitute if R had not been available. Mr B replied on 14 January 2003 to give the information requested. The tone of his reply gave the impression that he was displeased to have been troubled again about the matter. T appealed against the inspector's decision regarding R's status. The inspector applied to the Special Commissioner for a summons to be issued pursuant to reg 5 of the Special Commissioners (Jurisdiction and Procedure) Regulations 1994 to Mr B requiring his attendance at the hearing of the appeal to give oral evidence. T objected to the issue of the summons on the ground that one of R's contracts had already been terminated and there was a real risk that the remaining contracts would be terminated if Mr B was summoned to appear at the hearing.

Held—It had been established that it would be desirable, in a case against a decision of the Revenue that payments made to intermediaries such as service companies should be treated as earnings of the worker for the purposes of income tax and national insurance contributions, for evidence to be obtained from both the worker and the client to whom the worker supplied work. Although reg 5 gave the Special Commissioners a discretion as to whether to issue a witness summons, the presumption had to be that an application for such a summons would normally be granted. Regulation 5(11) provided that a person on whom a witness summons had been served might apply to have it set aside and no doubt that would be done if a summons had not been applied for in good faith, or if the witness was unable to give relevant evidence, or if the application were irrelevant, speculative or oppressive. The instant application fell into none of those categories and it was clear that Mr B had relevant evidence to give. Moreover, it was not inevitable that Mr B's oral evidence would repeat the documentary evidence and the documentary evidence might well be expanded and/or clarified by oral evidence. While fully appreciating the commercial risk faced by R, the interests of justice were best served by granting the application for the issue of the witness summons.

Accordingly, a direction was made that when the date of the hearing had been fixed a witness summons would be issued to Mr B of F requiring his attendance at the hearing of the appeal to give oral evidence.

Lime-IT Ltd v Justin (*Officer of the Board of Inland Revenue*) [2003] STC (SCD) 15 applied.

Notes

For the issue of a witness summons by the General or Special Commissioners, see *Simon's Direct Tax Service* A3.518.

For the Special Commissioners (Jurisdiction and Procedure) Regulations 1994, SI 1994/1811, reg 5, see *Simon's Direct Tax Service*, Part H2.

Cases referred to in decision

F S Consulting Ltd v McCaul (*Inspector of Taxes*) [2002] STC (SCD) 138.
Lime-IT Ltd v Justin (*Officer of the Board of Inland Revenue*) [2003] STC (SCD) 15.

Theresa Naylor of Accountax Consulting Ltd for the taxpayer company.
Barry Williams, Inland Revenue Appeals Unit, for the Crown.

Tilbury Consulting Ltd v Gittins (Inspector of Taxes) (No 2)

SPECIAL COMMISSIONER: STEPHEN OLIVER QC
14, 15 OCTOBER, 3 NOVEMBER 2003

National insurance—Earnings of workers supplied by service companies etc—Provision of services through intermediary—Individual establishing personal service company—Company contracting with further company for provision of services to client—Whether company liable for national insurance contributions on payments made by client to further company and then by further company to company—Whether, if arrangements had taken the form of a contract between individual and client, individual would have been regarded as gainfully employed by the client—Social Security Contributions (Intermediaries) Regulations 2000, SI 2000/727, reg 6(1)(c).

T was the controlling shareholder and director of T Ltd. T worked on an information technology (IT) project for F plc and substantially all that work was done at F plc's premises. CW Ltd was under contract with F plc to set up, service and staff that IT project and engaged T Ltd to provide services and make available T's services (with the right, subject to conditions, to provide a replacement). The Revenue considered that reg 6 of the Social Security Contributions (Intermediaries) Regulations 2000 applied and that T was to be treated for national insurance purposes as gainfully employed under a contract of service by F plc. Those regulations applied where (a) an individual (the worker) personally performed, or was under an obligation personally to perform, services for the purposes of a business carried on by another person (the client); (b) the performance of those services by the worker was carried out, not under a contract directly between the client and the worker, but under arrangements involving an intermediary, and (c) the circumstances were such that, had the arrangements taken the form of a contract between the worker and the client, the worker would be regarded as employed in employed earner's employment by the client. T Ltd appealed.

Held—Having regard to the evidence, it was clear that CW Ltd and not F plc had operational control of the project. F plc had engaged CW Ltd to provide its IT services and to set up and operate the project. CW Ltd was engaged as principal and acted personally in the project. It equipped itself with its own specialised personnel to discharge its own obligation to F plc, either by employing them directly or by engaging outside subcontractors, such as the intermediary, T Ltd, which in turn provided T. F plc did not exercise control over the manner in which CW Ltd personnel carried out their duties. To the extent that control was exercisable over the performance of T's services, that lay with CW Ltd. F plc accepted suitable substitutes from CW Ltd and CW Ltd was obliged to accept from T Ltd a suitable substitute for T. At no time was T a part of F plc's business or undertaking. Accordingly, the arrangements involving the intermediary, T Ltd, the circumstances in the context of which the arrangements were made, and the nature of the services performed by T, showed that T would not have been regarded as F plc's employee (making the statutory assumption that he had been contracted to perform services to F plc). Those facts were inconsistent with an employer/employee relationship between F plc and T.

T Ltd's appeal would therefore be allowed.

Notes

For national insurance contributions on earnings paid through certain personal service companies, see *Simon's National Insurance Contributions Service* 8.346.

For the Social Security Contributions (Intermediaries) Regulations 2000, SI 2000/727, reg 6(1)(c), see *Simon's National Insurance Contributions Service*, Part III.

David Smith, of Accountax Consulting Ltd, for T Ltd.
P J Death, Inspector of Taxes, for the Revenue.

Warner Holidays Ltd v Secretary of State for Social Services

QUEEN'S BENCH DIVISION
MCNEILL J
17, 18 NOVEMBER, 21 DECEMBER 1982

Employment—Contract of service—Distinction between contract for services and contract of service—Entertainers engaged for season at holiday camp—Whether employees—Whether performing under contract of service.

W Ltd was the proprietor of a holiday camp. It engaged three entertainers for the holiday season; two of them also did administrative work in the holiday camp. They were provided with full board. Each entertainer was responsible for the content of his own performances, provided that they was suitable for family entertainment. They all had agents, through whom they were engaged by W Ltd. They were paid a fixed sum per week and were responsible for their own income tax and national insurance contributions. The entertainers who were musicians provided their own musical instruments. Their contracts prohibited them from working at other venue during the period of engagement. Each regarded himself as a 'freelance' professional entertainer. W Ltd sought a determination from the Secretary of State for Social Services as to whether the entertainers were employed earners and whether W Ltd was thus liable as a secondary contributor for national insurance purposes. After inquiry the Secretary of State decided that the entertainers were employed earners. W Ltd appealed.

Held—Essentially all the relevant facts had to be looked at in the aggregate, to determine, in the absence of an unambiguous or unequivocal written contract, what it was that the parties intended. It was important to remember that the existence of a contract of service or services was not wholly a matter of private arrangement between the intending contractual parties. Where the community had an interest, as in the instant case, in the collection of contributions for social security purposes, while the intention of the parties as to the nature of the contract they intended was itself important, it was not necessarily conclusive. The parties to a contract of employment could not, by private arrangement, exclude the arrangement public or community obligations. Neither control nor the expressed or purported intention of the parties were of themselves necessarily determinative, each was a factor for consideration. In the instant case the parties purported to express or thought they were expressing themselves in terms indicating the engagement of independent, self-employed entertainers. It was to be noted that no one of the entertainers had at risk any capital (save for his investment in equipment and professional skills) or could improve his financial position in any way by carrying out this engagement more energetically, more competently, or more successfully. There was no question of financial reward above the salary due. Each of the entertainers had bound himself to an engagement which, from the totality of the relevant consideration, was confined to that of service to a master. However hard they strove to achieve the contrary, each, on a proper construction of the contracts into which he entered, entered into contracts of service.

Market Investigations Ltd v Minister of Social Security [1969] 2 QB 173; *Global Plant Ltd v Secretary of State for Health and Social Security* [1972] 1 QB 139 and *Addison v London Philharmonic Orchestra Ltd* [1981] ICR 261 applied.

Accordingly, the appeal would be dismissed.

Notes

For categories of workers: servants and independent contractors, see *Harvey on Industrial Relations and Employment Law* Division A.1.A and C.

For characteristics of the relationship of master and servant, see ibid Division A.3.

Cases referred to in judgment

Addison v London Philharmonic Orchestra Ltd [1981] ICR 261, EAT.
Associated Provincial Picture Houses Ltd v Wednesbury Corp [1948] 1 KB 223, [1947] 2 All ER 680, CA.
BSM (1257) Ltd v Secretary of State for Social Services [1978] ICR 894.
Construction Industry Training Board v Labour Force Ltd [1970] 3 All ER 220, DC.
Edwards (Inspector of Taxes) v Bairstow [1956] AC 14, [1955] 3 All ER 48, 36 TC 207, HL.
Ferguson v John Dawson & Partners (Contractors) Ltd [1976] 3 All ER 817, [1976] 1 WLR 1213, [1976] IRLR 346, CA.
Global Plant Ltd v Secretary of State for Health and Social Security [1971] 3 All ER 385, [1972] 1 QB 139.
Gould v Minister of National Insurance [1951] 1 KB 731, [1951] 1 All ER 368, KBD.
Market Investigations Ltd v Minister of Social Security [1968] 3 All ER 732, [1969] 2 QB 173.
Massey v Crown Life Insurance Co [1978] 2 All ER 576, [1978] 1 WLR 676, [1978] ICR 590, [1978] IRLR 31, CA.
Mersey Docks and Harbour Board v Coggins & Griffith (Liverpool) Ltd [1947] AC 1, [1946] 2 All ER 345, HL.
Midland Sinfonia Concert Society Ltd v Secretary of State for Social Services [1981] ICR 454.
Montreal v Montreal Locomotive Works Ltd [1947] 1 DLR 161, PC.
Morren v Swinton and Pendlebury Borough Council [1965] 2 All ER 349, [1965] 1 WLR 576.
Ready Mixed Concrete (South East) Ltd v Minister of Pensions and National Insurance [1968] 1 All ER 433, [1968] 2 QB 497.

WHPT Housing Association Ltd v Secretary of State for Social Services [1981] ICR 737.
Young & Woods Ltd v West [1980] IRLR 201, CA.

Appeal

Warner Holidays Ltd (the company) appealed from the decision of the Secretary of State for Social Services, pursuant to s 94(3) of the Social Security Act 1975 (the 1975 Act), as to the category for the purposes of the 1975 Act of David Gerard Knight, James Isaac Pinkney and Anthony Keith Fortey (the entertainers) and as to the liability of the company to pay contributions under the 1975 Act in respect of the entertainers.

Eldred Tabachnick QC and *Elizabeth Slade* (instructed by *Bartletts de Reya*) for the company.
John Laws (instructed by *the Solicitor, Department of Health and Social Security*) for the Secretary of State.

W F & R K Swan (Hellenic) Ltd v Secretary of State for Social Services and another appeal

QUEEN'S BENCH DIVISION (CROWN OFFICE LIST)
MCCULLOUGH J
18 JANUARY 1983

Employment—Contract of service—Distinction between contract for services and contract of service—Tour operators—Tour operators engaging couriers to conduct holiday tours and package holidays—Couriers treated as independent contractors—Whether couriers employed under contracts of service.

S and P & M were tour operators. For each tour they engaged a courier. The companies and their couriers regarded their relationship as that of employer and independent contractor. No PAYE deductions were made and the couriers paid class 2 national insurance contributions as self-employed earners. S operated package tours to places of artistic or archaeological interest, usually overseas. Each November potential applicants for the courier positions were sent a list of projected tours and asked to identify those in which they were interested. Three months before the proposed date S would write to the proposed courier and the engagement would be made. Each tour was the subject of a separate offer and acceptance. The couriers were paid a fixed sum per day. They were not entitled to holiday pay or sick pay. They were not included in the company's pension scheme. If a tour was cancelled at short notice the tour manager was not paid. Couriers had to observe S's standing instructions, advise and assemble passengers, take supplies of useful items, keep a great many records, provide information about local details for S's future use, use their initiative in dealing with unforeseen circumstances, including improvising, re-routing, re-timing tours where necessary. Couriers were able to accept work from other tour operators. P & M were package tour operators. They engaged couriers in February, usually by telephone, for specific tours, one at a time. Continuity was not guaranteed. The details of the couriers arrangements with the company were similar to those of S and its couriers. P & M's couriers were expected to provide their own guide books, reference books, stationery, pens and first aid supplies. Each tour operator asked the Secretary of State to determine the true status of two couriers under s 93 of the Social Security Act 1975, submitting that they were self-employed. In each case the Secretary of State decided that the couriers were employed earners. The companies requested a statement of the grounds of the decision and asked the Secretary of State to state a case from which they both appealed. At the hearing a preliminary question arose as to the circumstances in which the court could overturn the Secretary of State's decision.

Held—(1) In the instant case all the relevant facts were before the court. Therefore, the court could, and had to, decide whether it agreed with the views to which the Secretary of State had come about the nature of the contracts. If this exercise led to the opposite conclusion from his, the court had to hold him to have been in error of law and allow the appeals.

(2) When a question of the kind in the instant cases fell for decision all the characteristics of the contractual relationship had to be considered. That was better described as a process of evaluation than one of balancing. The nature of the obligations of the parties to one another had to be determined. That depended on the terms which they expressly agreed and on such further terms as were to be implied. The only relevant intention was that which was to be inferred from the agreed terms. The couriers' right to accept or reject each offer and their freedom to take other work between contracts were not indications of self-employment: they were the consequences of there being a series of contracts. The absence of entitlement to holiday pay and the fact that couriers did not participate in any company pension scheme were no more than the consequences of the short duration of the engagements. The absence of entitlement to sick pay had little, if any, greater significance. Nor was the freedom to earn money on the side during a tour important. The scope for the use of initiative during a tour was no more than the consequence of being at a distance from base. There were ten aspects of the relationships between parties which had been identified which might prove to be of significance in the resolution of questions of the kind in the instant appeals. The first was the degree of control exercised by the employer. The measure of freedom given to a courier working for a tour operator would be much the same whether he was employed or was hiring out his services. It was by no means uncommon for an independent contractor to be required to work to the most detailed specification. Thus while the nature and degree of the control exercised by the tour operators was to be regarded as hav-

ing some significance it was not to be regarded as a factor of major importance. Second, was whether the workers' interest in the performance of their work involved any prospect of profit or loss. This was not a helpful indicator when considering the position of a courier. Whether an independent contractor had the chance of making profits and the risk of incurring losses depended essentially on whether he was running a business of his own and, if so, whether he had an organisation of some sort to maintain. There were many independent contractors who were not in that class. Third, was whether the workers were properly regarded as part and parcel of the employers' organisation. That was of no assistance. Fourth, was whether the workers were carrying on business on their own account or on the employers' account. If the worker in question had a business, the answer to that question would be of value. But its value was to be doubted where the work had nothing that one would ordinarily call a business. Fifth, was whether equipment was provided. Hardly any equipment was required. P & M's couriers provided what little they needed. It was to be inferred that S's couriers used S's equipment. That test was relatively unhelpful. Sixth, seventh and tenth were the incidence of tax and national insurance, the parties' own view of their relationship and what the parties intended, which would be taken together. The parties' own view and what they intended had to be irrelevant except in so far as they were to be deduced from what the parties in fact agreed, which was, in reality, the ultimate question. The express provision that tax and national insurance were to be dealt with on the understanding that the couriers were self-employed was clear prima facie evidence that the intention of the parties, to be deduced from the terms they agreed, was to create a relationship of that kind. There was not a whisper of suspicion that the parties intended to dress up one relationship as if it were another. They were genuine arrangements honourably entered into. Those express terms were to be regarded as the clearest evidence of the nature of their relationship. The eighth test was the traditional structure of the workers' profession and arrangements within it. That was not helpful in the instant appeals. Ninth, was whether the contractual terms were more consistent with a contract of service rather than a contract for services. The most significant were those relating to tax and national insurance. There were also those requiring compliance with instructions and terms about the provision of equipment. The remainder of the terms were as consistent with one type of contract as with the other. The only factor of major significance which pointed to the contracts being of one type rather than the other was the intention of the parties as deduced from the terms which they agreed as to tax and national insurance. That pointed to all the contracts as being contracts for services. There was nothing in any of the terms which was inconsistent with that conclusion.

Dicta of Stephenson L J in *Young and Woods Ltd v West* [1980] IRLR 201 at 205 and of Waterhouse J in *Addison v London Philharmonic Orchestra Society Ltd* [19811 ICR 261 at 271 applied.

The appeals, accordingly, would be allowed.

Notes

For categories of workers: servants and independent contractors, see *Harvey on Industrial Relations and Employment Law* Division A.1.A and C.

For characteristics of the relationship of master and servant, see ibid Division A.3.

Cases referred to in judgment

ACT Construction Ltd v Customs and Excise Comrs [1982] STC 25, [1981] 1 WLR 1542, [1982] 1 All ER 84, HL.

Addison v London Philharmonic Orchestra Ltd [1981] ICR 261, EAT.

Alpine (Double Glazing) Co Ltd v Secretary of State for Social Services (7 April 1982 unreported).

Coates v Modern Methods and Materials Ltd [1983] QB 192, [1982] 3 All ER 946, [1982] ICR 763, [1982] IRLR 318, CA.

Cole Brothers Ltd v Phillips (Inspector of Taxes) [1982] STC 307, [1982] 1 WLR 1450, [1982] 2 All ER 247, 55 TC 188, HL.

Cooper (Inspector of Taxes) v Stubbs [1925] 2 KB 753, 10 TC 29, CA.

Edwards (Inspector of Taxes) v Bairstow [1956] AC 14, [1955] 3 All ER 48, 36 TC 207, HL.

Ferguson v John Dawson & Partners (Contractors) Ltd [1976] 3 All ER 817, [1976] 1 WLR 1213, [1976] IRLR 346, CA.

Global Plant Ltd v Secretary of State for Health and Social Security [1971] 3 All ER 385, [1972] 1 QB 139.

IRC v Scottish & Newcastle Breweries Ltd [1982] STC 296, [1982] 1 WLR 322, [1982] 2 All ER 230, 55 TC 252, HL.

John Perkins (Butchers) Ltd v Secretary of State for Social Services (21 May, 1982 unreported).

Marriott v Oxford and District Co-operative Society Ltd (No 2) [1970] 1 QB 186, [1969] 3 All ER 1126, CA.

Midland Sinfonia Concert Society Ltd v Secretary of State for Social Services [1981] ICR 454.

Morren v Swinton and Pendlebury Borough Council [1965] 2 All ER 349, [1965] 1 WLR 576.

Ready Mixed Concrete (South East) Ltd v Minister of Pensions and National Insurance [1968] 1 All ER 433, [1968] 2 QB 497.

Simmonds v Department of Health and Social Security (8 February, 1982 unreported).

WHPT Housing Association Ltd v Secretary of State for Social Services [1981] ICR 737.

Young & Woods Ltd v West [1980] IRLR 201, CA.

Appeal

W E & R K Swan (Hellenic) Ltd and Page & Moy Ltd (the companies) appealed under s 94(3) of the Social Security Act 1975 from the decisions of the Secretary of State for Social Services that couriers engaged by the companies were employed earners for whom the companies were liable as secondary contributors for national insurance purposes.

A Hamilton QC and *G Kealey* (instructed by *Paisner & Co*, Leicester) for the companies.

S Brown (instructed by *the Solicitor, Secretary of State for Social Services*) for the Secretary of State.

Walls v Sinnett (Inspector of Taxes)

CHANCERY DIVISION
VINELOTT J
12 DECEMBER 1987

Emoluments from office or employment—Employment—Meaning—Contract of service or contract for services—Professional singer in receipt of remuneration for regular teaching work in a college—Whether remuneration emoluments from office or employment.

The taxpayer, a professional singer, lived and worked from his home in Sussex. He was taxed on receipts from his work under Schedule D. However, in 1974 he was appointed to the post of lecturer in music at a technical college in Liverpool. His appointment required him to attend at the college on four days each week of the term; his remuneration from the college was based on a percentage of the annual salary applicable to the position. He was not restricted from carrying on outside work and the college actively encouraged him to do so. No controls were exercised over him by the college concerning the way in which he carried out his teaching duties. At all material times the taxpayer had remuneration from sources other than the college. In 1975 a tax inspector formed the view that the taxpayer should thereafter be assessed in respect of the remuneration from his teaching work under Sch E. The taxpayer appealed to the Special Commissioners against an assessment made for the year 1977–1978 contending that all remuneration received by him fell to be assessed under Sch D. The commissioners dismissed his appeal holding that the taxpayer received his remuneration from the college from carrying out his teaching duties as an employee and was therefore assessable to tax under Sch E. The taxpayer appealed.

Held—The commissioners had before them ample evidence that the taxpayer had a contract of service with the college and it was impossible to say that, on the facts, no body of commissioners properly instructed could have reached the conclusion they did reach. The appeal would therefore be dismissed.

Notes

For what constitutes employment, see *Simon's Direct Tax Service* E4.206. Section 181 of the Income and Corporation Taxes Act 1970 is now s 19 of the Income and Corporation Taxes Act 1988.

For the Income and Corporation Taxes Act 1988 s 19, see ibid part G.

Cases referred to in judgment

Argent v Ministry of Social Security [1968] 3 All ER 208.
R v Brentford General Commissioners, ex p Chan [1986] STC 65.

Case stated

Geoffrey Chapman Walls appealed against a decision of the Special Commissioner upholding an assessment to income tax under Sch E in respect of remuneration earned as a lecturer in music.

The taxpayer appeared in person.
Michael Hart (instructed by the *Solicitor of Inland Revenue*) for the Crown.

WHPT Housing Association Ltd v Secretary of State for Social Services

QUEENS BENCH DIVISION
WEBSTER J
3, 14 APRIL 1981

Employment—Contract of employment—Contract for service or services—Architect accepting work on freelance basis for housing association—Architect required to do work only in office of housing association—Architect working with other architects under supervision of chief architect—Architect paid on hourly basis—Whether housing association liable to pay national insurance contributions in relation to architect—Whether architect employed earner—Social Security Act 1975 s 1, Sch 4.

An architect, L, who had been practising on his own account, applied for a job advertised at a housing association. He was interviewed by the chief architect, H, but not selected for the advertised position. H later offered him work on 'a freelance basis' and L worked for the association from March 1976 to December at an hourly rate of £3. He was not required to keep office hours; on average he worked 28 hours per week. He was required to do his work at the office of the housing association and he worked with other architects, who were employed by the association under the supervision of H. L brought points to H when he required guidance, and on occasion was rebuked by H for the way he carried out his work. He attended office meetings. He was not paid holiday pay or sick pay; he invoiced the association for value added tax. No deducations were made by the association for income tax or national insurance. L applied to the industrial tribunal for a determination of his terms of employment. The tribunal found him to be self-employed. L applied to the Secretary of State for Social Services for a determination as to whether he was employed by the association for the purposes of the Social Security Act 1975 relating to national insurance. The Secretary of State held him to be included in the category of employed earners and the association was therefore liable to pay employers contributions. The association appealed.

Held—The difference between a contract of service and one for services had to reside, essentially in the terms of the principal obligation agreed to be undertaken by the 'employee'. In a contract of service the principal obligation undertaken by the employee was to provide himself to serve; in a contract for services the principal obligation was not to provide himself to serve the employer but his services for the use of the employer. If the terms of the principal obligation agreed to be undertaken was the issue upon which the question depended, then it followed that none of the secondary tests were likely to be directly determinant one way or the other of that question. The tests that had been mentioned in the instant case included the 'label' attached to the contract by the contracting parties, the extent of control by employer over employee and whether the employee was providing or performing the services as a person in business on his own account. Although the fact of whether or not the employee was providing or performing the services as a person engaged in business on his own account was a fact from which it might be possible to draw an inference (sometimes an inescapable inference) as to the nature of the principal obligation undertaken, it was not of itself conclusive of the question, still less so if the terms of the principal obligation were more obviously to be inferred from other facts. The evidence of the association's right to control L were the facts that L worked only in and from the association's offices, that he was expected to attend office meetings, that he worked in the same way as architects on the staff and was told how to do the work and that he was rebuked by H. Most of those facts were perfectly consistent with L, as a self-employed man, joining and being expected to fit in with an existing team of employed architects. Putting on one side the facts found as to the original offer and acceptance the relevant primary facts are that L worked, on average, about 28 hours a week, that he was paid only for the number of hours he worked at an agreed rate, and that L did not in fact work office hours of 9.30am to 5.30pm. The inescapable inference to be drawn from those facts was that L at no time undertook any obligation to present himself for service at the association's premises at any time; that he at no time undertook any obligation even to provide a specific number of hours service and that his principal obligation was to work as an architect during the hours of service which he chose to offer to the association in consideration for which the association agreed to pay him £3 per hour. If that was the principal obligation undertaken by L, as a matter of law, the contract which contained that obligation could only constitute a contract for services. Even if there were an added obligation to provide approximately 28 hours service per week that would not be sufficient to lead to any different conclusion. The original offer and acceptance was to provide services, not service, and there was no evidence that the nature of the contract changed after its inception. The inference to be drawn from the use of the words, 'freelance basis', was that L was 'to be his own boss', that was to say that he did not agree to accept an obligation to 'obey' or be the servant of his employers. The absence of any such obligation would also, as a matter of law, be consistent only with the contract, at its inception, having been a contract for services rather than one of service.There was no evidence that justified a conclusion that the nature of the contract changed at any time after that date.

Notes

For categories of workers: servants and independent contractors, see *Harvey on Industrial Relations and Employment Law* Division A.1.A. and C.

For characteristics of the relationship of master and servant, see ibid, Division A.3.

Cases referred to in judgment

Ferguson v John Dawson &Partners (Contractors) Ltd [1976] 3 All ER 817, [1976] 1 WLR 1213, [1976] IRLR 346, CA.
Global Plant Ltd v Secretary of State for Health and Social Security [1972] 1 QB 139, [1971] 3 All ER 385.
Market Investigations Ltd v Minister of Social Security [1969] 2 QB 173, [1968] 3 All ER 732.
Young &Woods Ltd v West [1980] IRLR 201, CA.

Appeal

WHPTHousing Association Ltd (the housing association) appealed by way of case stated against the decision of the Secretary of State for Social Services given on 30 November 1979 under s 93(1) of the Social Security Act 1975 (the 1975 Act) that Peter Frederick Lowe was included in the category of employed earners for the purposes of the 1975 Act and that the housing association was liable as secondary contributors to pay national insurance contributions in respect of the period he had been associated with the association.

George Newman (instructed by *Trower Still & Keeting*) for the housing association.
Andrew Collins (instructed by the *Treasury Solicitor*) for the Secretary of State.

Wickens v Champion Employment

EMPLOYMENT APPEAL TRIBUNAL
NOLAN J, MR J D ANDERSON AND MRS M L BOYLE
5 OCTOBER 1983

Employment—Contract of service—Distinction between contract for services and contract of service—Applicant employed by employment agency for less than two years—Applicant dismissed by employment agency—Applicant claiming unfair dismissal—Whether applicant able to claim unfair dismissal Whether agency employed more than 20 people—Whether temporary workers on books of agency independent contractors.

W was employed by an employment agency. The agency had 'temporaries' on its books. Its agreement with the temporaries provided that it would provide work when there was a suitable client, but that there might be times when suitable work was not available, that the temporaries were responsible for their own safety at work, that they were to comply with rules in force at each work place, that they would be paid in arrears, not entitled to holiday pay, pension rights, or sick pay, and concluded 'the temporary worker is employed under a contract of services' with the agency. W was dismissed and claimed unfair dismissal. The agency successfully asserted that they employed fewer than 20 employees and that following s 64A of the Employment Protection (Consolidation) Act 1978, which provided that the unfair dismissal provisions did not apply where the period of continuous employment did not exceed two years and the number of employees employed by that employer at any time during that period did not exceed 20, since W had been employed for less than two years, the industrial tribunal had no jurisdiction to hear the claim. W appealed contending: that the temporaries on the books of the agency, of which there were more than 20, were employees of the agency; that control by the employer was not the definitive test of a contract of service; and that there was no evidence that that the temporaries were self-employed—no evidence that they were carrying on businesses of their own.

Held—It was wrong to look at regular and continuing control of the work of the other party to the contract as being necessary or decisive as to the existence, or otherwise, of a contract of service. In the instant case, the contract was not one regulating the relationship on a permanent basis between the agency and the temporaries; it was a document which was entered into afresh each time the temporary worker was assigned to a particular task. No contract of service, properly so called remotely resembled the contract in the instant case. It was quite inconsistent with the normal features of an employment under a contract of service, particularly when its terms were read against the background of the evidence that there was no obligation on the agency to find work or for the temporary to accept a booking made on his or her behalf. The relationship between the agency and the temporaries wholly lacked the elements of continuity and care of the employer for the employee that was associated with a contract of service. Although there was no evidence that the temporaries were carrying on business of their own, that test did not include as a necessary element the question whether the individual carried on a separate business. The decision of the tribunal had not erred in law and the appeal would therefore be dismissed.

Warner Holidays Ltd v Secretary of State for Social Services [1983] ICR 440 considered.

Notes

For exclusions from the right to claim unfair dismissal, see *Harvey on Industrial Relations and Employment Law* Division D1.1.C.

For categories of workers: servants and independent contractors, see ibid, Division A.1.A and C.

For characteristics of the relationship of master and servant, see ibid Division A.3.

Cases referred to in judgment

Ready Mixed Concrete (South East) Ltd v Minister of Pensions and National Insurance [1968] 1 All ER 433, [1968] 2 QB 497.

Warner Holidays Ltd v Secretary of State for Social Services [1983] ICR 440.

Appeal

Miss Wickens appealed against the decision of an industrial tribunal that they had no jurisdiction to hear her claim, against Champion Employment (the agency), for unfair dismissal, in consequence of s 64A of the Employment Protection (Consolidation) Act 1980, since Miss Wickens' period of continuous employment with the agency did not exceed two years and the agency had not, during that period, employed more than 20 employees under contracts of service.

Elizabeth Andrew (instructed by *Robin Thompson & Partners*) for the appellant.

The sole proprietress of the agency, T M Hoodless, appeared in person.

Winter v Westward Television Ltd

EMPLOYMENT APPEAL TRIBUNAL
PHILIPS J (PRESIDENT)
1978

Employment—Contract for services—Individual owning and controlling company—Company contracting with television company for fixed term to provide exclusive services of individual to television company—Television company not renewing contract after expiry of fixed term—Individual claiming unfair dismissal—Whether individual employee of television company.

W was a film and television production executive. He and his wife controlled and beneficially owned a limited company, S Ltd. S Ltd contracted with WTV Ltd to provide the exclusive services of W to WTV Ltd for a term of six months. The contract provided for remuneration to be paid to S Ltd and cl 6 provided that W agreed to acknowledge and abide by the rules and regulations in force as applied to WTV Ltd's staff. At the end of the term WTV Ltd did not renew the contract. W claimed unfair dismissal. The industrial tribunal held that W was not an employee of WTV Ltd. W appealed contending that: (i) since S Ltd was the alter ego of W the separate corporate existence of S Ltd could be ignored; (ii) that the effect of the contract and cl 6 in particular was to transfer the employment of W from S Ltd to WTV Ltd as the whole of the surrounding circumstances were such that there was an additional contract implied between W and WTV Ltd; and (iii) that the substance of the transaction was that W was an employee of WTV Ltd.

Held—There was no justification in the circumstances of the instant case for ignoring the effect of the transaction actually entered into and contained in the contract between S Ltd and WTV Ltd. It was impossible to infer some relationship of employer and employee between W and WTV Ltd; the principal reason being that it was never right to infer a legal relationship when that was inconsistent with what the parties themselves had expressly agreed. The form and substance of the transaction were one and the same. S Ltd and WTV Ltd had entered into a particular transaction of a particular type for a particular purpose.

Accordingly, the industrial tribunal had been correct in concluding that W was not an employee.

Notes

For criteria for employment, see *Harvey on Industrial Relations and Employment Law* Division A.1.

Appeal

Mr Winter (W) brought a complaint of unfair dismissal against Westward Television Ltd (WTV Ltd). WTV Ltd maintained that W had not been its employee since it had contracted with Samian Galleries Ltd, a company controlled and beneficially owned by W and his spouse. The industrial tribunal determined that W was not an employee. W appealed to the Employment Appeal Tribunal.

Yewens (Surveyor of Taxes) v Noakes

COURT OF APPEAL (EXCHEQUER DIVISION)
BRAMWELL, THESIGER AND BAGGALLAY LJJ
1, 6, 16 MARCH 1880

Taxation—Inhabited house duty—House owned by merchant occupied as caretaker by clerk employed by merchant and clerk's family—Whether house chargeable to duty—Whether occupied by 'servant or other person'.

K was a clerk employed by N at a salary of £150 pa. K, with his wife, children and servant occupied a house owned by N. N was assessed to inhabited house duty in relation to the house occupied by K. The relevant statute provided that 'any tenement . . . occupied as a house for the purposes of trade only or as warehouse . . . shall be exempt from inhabited house duties, although a servant or other person may dwell in such tenement . . . for the protection thereof'. N appealed contending that K was only in occupation as a caretaker and the house was used for purpose's of N's trade. The commissioners allowed N's appeal. The surveyor of taxes appealed. The Exchequer Division of the High Court dismissed the appeal. The surveyor appealed to the Court of Appeal.

Held—The appeal would be allowed for the following reasons.

Per Bramwell and Baggally LJJ. The meaning of the expression in the Act was plain; it said 'servant or other person', by which it was to be understood that the 'other person' might not exactly occupy the position of a servant; he might have undertaken the duty of taking care for the proprietor of the building, but not necessarily because he was a servant. A servant was a person subject to the command of his master as to the manner in which he should do his work. The statute meant that the 'other person' employed to take care should be a person who had entered into a contract for that purpose, or who had entered into a contract of service for that purpose. It was impossible to hold that the instant case was within the intention or the spirit or even the words of the Act; it was impossible to say that K was not residing, with his family, in the house.

Per Thesiger and Baggallay LJJ. The legislature, in using the term 'servant' was using that term in the ordinary and popular sense of it, that was to say, not in the sense in which any clerk or manager was called the servant of his employer, or in the sense in which the judges might be said to be servants of the Crown, but in the sense of the ordinary menial or domestic servant. By the words 'other person' was intended some person of the same kind and description as a servant, standing somewhat on the same footing and subject to the same conditions. It was obvious that a clerk with a salary of £150 pa did not come within such words. If he did, where was the construction to stop? The manager of a bank, a foreman with high wages, persons in the position almost of gentlemen, might be put in to take care of premises, and then it might be said that those particular premises were subject to the exemptions contemplated by the Act.

Notes

For characteristics of the relationship of master and servant, see *Harvey on Industrial Relations and Employment Law* Division A.3.

Appeal

The surveyor of taxes appealed against a judgment of the Exchequer Division in favour of C Noakes dismissing the surveyor's appeal by way of case stated from the commissioners for Southwark who had allowed the appeal of C Noakes that he was not liable for inhabited house duty in respect of his houses 11 and 13 Southwark Street, Borough, for the year 1876/77 since they were used solely for trade purposes and occupied only by a caretaker.

Sir H Giffard and *A V Dicey* (instructed by the *Solicitor of Inland Revenue*) for the Crown.

McIntyre QC and *W Graham* (instructed by *Saffery & Huntly)* for Mr Noakes.

Young & Woods Ltd v West

COURT OF APPEAL (CIVIL DIVISION)
STEPHENSON ACKNER LJJ AND SIR DAVID CAIRNS
11 FEBRUARY 1980

Unfair dismissal—Exclusions and qualifications—Meaning of 'employee'—No waiver of rights—Employment Protection (Consolidation) Act 1978 ss 54(1), 153(1)

Mr West worked for the appellants as a skilled sheet metal worker in their factory. When he joined the appellants he was offered alternative methods of payment: either he could become an employee in the ordinary way or he could go on their books as a self-employed person. Mr West chose to be treated as self-employed. No deductions were made from his pay for tax, he was responsible for his own national insurance contributions, he did not receive any holiday pay or sickness benefit from the company. The agreement was entered into with the knowledge of the Inland Revenue, who treated Mr West for tax purposes as self-employed. When Mr West's work was terminated by the appellants, he complained that he had been unfairly dismissed. The company contended that he was not an employee under a contract of service, but that he was self-employed under a contract for services. An industrial tribunal found that Mr West was an employee as defined by the statute and not self-employed as he and the company had agreed that he was. The Employment Appeal Tribunal, by a majority decision, dismissed the company's appeal.

Held—The industrial tribunal and the majority of the Employment Appeal Tribunal had correctly concluded that the respondent was an employee employed under a contract of service, notwithstanding that at his request he had been treated by the appellant employers as self-employed. Since the respondent was an employee within the meaning of the statutory definition, the industrial tribunal had jurisdiction to hear his complaint of unfair dismissal. Where there is an agreement openly made that a person shall be treated by a company as self-employed, it does not follow that he must accept the position and cannot claim compensation for unfair dismissal as if he was an employee. Whether a person is employed or is self-employed is a question of law not a question of fact. The label which the parties choose to use to describe their relationship cannot alter or decide their true relationship, although in deciding what that relationship is, the expression by them of their true intention is relevant, but not conclusive. The legal relationship between the parties must be classified not by appearance but by reality. It is the duty of an industrial tribunal, once a person goes to it and says, 'though I was self-employed, nevertheless I am an employee entitled to enforce my statutory rights', to see whether the label of self-employed is a true description or a false description by looking beneath it to the reality of the facts, and it must be its duty to decide on all the evidence whether the true legal relationship accords with the label or is contradicted by it. In the present case, although it was plain that both parties intended to call the agreement between them a contract for services and not a contract of employment within the Act, the true legal relationship of the parties was not that of a self-employed agent working independently of the company. Applying the test suggested by Mr Justice Cooke in *Market Investigations Ltd v Minister of Social Security*—'Is the person who has engaged himself to perform these services performing them as a person in business on his own account?'—it would be impossible to regard the respondent as a person in business on his own account. The facts found by the industrial tribunal—that apart from being paid his wages without deductions and not being entitled to holiday or sick pay or to have the benefit of the disciplinary procedure, there was no difference at all between the working conditions applicable to the respondent and those applicable to the workers who were subject to PAYE—were strong enough to satisfy the respondent's burden to show that the label was a false label and that, though the mutual intention of the parties was to call the work services under a contract for services, nevertheless it was in reality service rendered under a contract of service. Unlike *Massey v Crown Life Insurance Co* [1978] IRLR 31, there was no such ambiguity in the relationship between the respondent and the company as could make their declared intention as to what it should be decisive of it. Nor could it be held, as contended on behalf of the appellants, that though a party cannot alter the true relationship, if the parties genuinely and expressly intend to establish a person as self-employed then he cannot make an unfair dismissal claim as an employee. In such circumstances, the parties can resile from the position which they have deliberately and openly chosen to take up. To reach any other conclusion would be to pre-suppose some kind of estoppel against invoking the statute which would, in effect, permit the parties to contract out of the Act and to deprive a person who works as an employee within the definition of the Act under a contract of service of the benefits which the statute confers upon him. There would be dangers of employers anxious to escape from their statutory liabilities pressing persons whom they intend to employ to take up that employment on the terms that it shall be called a contract for services with a self-employed person. Accordingly the appeal would be dismissed.

Obiter dicta

There was no reason to assume that as a result of the decision in the present case the respondent would have both the fiscal advantages of the self-employed which are denied to an employee and the statutory rights which are available to an employee but denied to the self-employed. Since the true legal position was that the respondent was an employee, the Inland Revenue has a statutory duty to reclaim tax deductions which were granted to him as self-employed.

Notes

For categories of workers, see *Harvey on Industrial Relations and Employment Law* Division A.1.

For characteristics of the relationship between master and servant, see ibid, Division A.3.

Mr N R L Clifford (instructed by *Messrs Thomas Cooper & Stibbard*) for Young & Woods Ltd.
Mr West appeared in person.

APPENDIX 7

Tax Bulletin 45 extract

February 2000. IR Tax Bulletin Issue 45
Provision of personal services through intermediaries

Would the worker have been an employee if engaged directly by the client?

A broad outline of the new rules was given in a press release dated 23 September 1999. They are intended to apply where a worker supplies his or her services to a client through an intermediary such as a service company or partnership. One of the central questions in deciding whether the new rules apply to an engagement is to establish whether the worker would have been an employee of the client if engaged directly. This article addresses this issue in detail. More details of the proposals can be found on the Inland Revenue website at www.inlandrevenue.gov.uk/ir35.

The approach to be adopted

Whether a worker would have been an employee if engaged directly by the client depends on a range of factors, set out in this article. But the final decision is not reached by adding up the number of factors pointing towards employment and comparing that result with the number pointing towards self-employment. The Courts have specifically rejected that approach. In *Hall v Lorimer* Mummery J made the following comment which was quoted with approval by Nolan LJ in the Court of Appeal:

> 'In order to decide whether a person carries on business on his own account it is necessary to consider many different aspects of that person's work activity. This is not a mechanical exercise of running through a checklist to see whether they are present in, or absent from, a given situation . . . It is a matter of evaluation of the overall effect, which is not necessarily the same as the sum total of all the individual details. Not all details are of equal weight or importance

in any given situation. The details may also vary in importance from one situation to another.'

When the detailed facts have been established the right approach is to stand back and look at the picture as a whole, to see if the overall effect is that of a person in business on his own account or a person working as an employee in somebody else's business. If the evidence is evenly balanced the intention of the parties may then decide the issue (*Massey v Crown Life Insurance Co*).

Establishing the facts

In deciding whether a worker would have been an employee if engaged directly by the client it is firstly necessary to establish the terms and conditions of the engagement. In a simple case involving one intermediary (eg where a worker works through a service company) these will normally be established mainly from the contract between the client and the intermediary. It is that contract that will usually reflect the terms that would have applied had the worker been engaged directly by the client. The contract may be written, oral or implied—or a mixture of all three.

Having established the terms and conditions it is then necessary to consider any surrounding facts that may be relevant—eg whether the worker has other clients and a business organisation. In this context other contracts the company has under which the worker's services are supplied and any business organisation of the company which is relevant to the supply of the worker's services will be taken into account as relevant surrounding facts.

Deciding employment status

There is no statutory definition of 'employment'. However, the question of employment status has come before the Courts on numerous occasions. The approach taken by the Courts has been to identify factors which help to determine if a particular contract is a 'contract of service' (employment) or a 'contract for services' (self-employment). Relevant factors are:

Control

A worker will not be an employee unless there is a right to exercise 'control' over the worker. This may be a right to control 'what' work is done, 'where' or 'when' it is done or 'how' it is done. Actual control of this sort is not necessary—it the right of control that is important.

Where a client has the right to determine 'how' the work is done this is a strong pointer to employment. But it is not an essential feature of employment—many 'experts' who are employees are not necessarily subject to such control (for example, ship's captain, consultant brain surgeon, etc).

Equally, a right to determine 'what' work is carried out is a strong pointer to employment. It will normally be a feature whenever a client needs a worker to undertake whatever tasks are required at any particular time or where the worker is required to work as part of a co-ordinated team.

A working relationship which involves no control at all is unlikely to be an employment (*Ready Mixed Concrete (South East) Ltd v Minister of Pensions and National Insurance* [1968] 2 QB 497).

The right to get a substitute or helper to do the job

Personal service is an essential element of a contract of employment. A person who has the freedom to choose whether to do the job himself or hire somebody else to do it for him, or who can hire someone else to provide substantial help is probably self-employed (*Australian Mutual Provident Society v Chaplin* (1978) 18 ALR 385 and *Express and Echo Publications Ltd v Tanton* [1999] IRLR 367). However, this must be viewed in the context of the arrangements overall. For example, a worker may choose to pay a helper to take phone messages and deal with invoicing and general book-keeping work for the intermediary. But this would not be directly relevant when considering an engagement where the worker is engaged to lay bricks for a client.

Provision of equipment

A self-employed contractor generally provides whatever equipment is needed to do the job (though in many trades, such as carpentry, it is common for employees, as well as self-employed workers, to provide their own hand tools). The provision of significant equipment (and/or materials) which are fundamental to the engagement is of particular importance. For example, where an IT consultant is engaged to undertake a specific piece of work and must work exclusively at home using the worker's own computer equipment that will be a strong pointer to self-employment. But where a worker is provided with office space and computer equipment that points to employment. The fact that a worker might occasionally choose to do some of the work at home using his or her own computer does not change that (many employees do just that). (*Ready Mixed Concrete (South East) Ltd v Minister of Pensions and National Insurance*).

Financial risk

An individual who risks his own money by, for example, buying assets needed for the job and bearing their running costs and paying for overheads and large quantities of materials, is almost certainly self-employed. Financial risk could also take the form of quoting a fixed price for a job, with the consequent risk of bearing the additional costs if the job overruns. Another example of a financial risk is where a skilled worker incurs significant amounts of expenditure on training to provide himself with a skill which he uses in subsequent engagements. This can be treated in the same way as investment in equipment to be used in a trade, as a pointer to self-employment, if there is a real risk that the investment would not be recovered from income from future engagements (*Market Investigations Ltd v Minister of Social Security* [1969] 2 QB 173).

Basis of payment

Employees tend to be paid a fixed wage or salary by the week or month and often qualify for additional payments such as overtime, long service bonus or profit share. Independent contractors, on the other hand, tend to be paid a fixed sum for a particular job. Payment 'by the piece' (where the worker is paid according to the amount of work actually done) or by commission can be a feature of both employment and self-employment.

Opportunity to profit from sound management

A person whose profit or loss depends on his capacity to reduce overheads and organise his work effectively may well be self-employed (*Market Investigations Ltd v Minister of Social Security*). People who are paid by the job will often be in this position.

Part and parcel of the organisation

Establishing whether a person becomes 'part and parcel' of a client's organisation can be a useful indicator in some situations. For example, someone taken on to manage a client's staff will normally be seen as part and parcel of the client's organisation and is likely to be an employee.

Right of dismissal

A right to terminate an engagement by giving notice of a specified length is a common feature of employment. It is less common in a contract for services, which usually ends only on completion of the task, or if the terms of the contract are breached.

Employee benefits

Employees are often entitled to sick pay, holiday pay, pensions, expenses and so on. However, the absence of those features does not necessarily mean that the worker is self-employed—especially in the case of short-term engagements where such payments would not normally feature.

Length of engagement

Long periods working for one engager may be typical of an employment but are not conclusive. It is still necessary to consider all the terms and conditions of each engagement. Regular working for the same engager may indicate that there is a single and continuing contract of employment (*Nethermere (St Neots) Ltd v Gardiner* [1984] ICR 612). Where an engagement is covered by a series of short contracts, or an initial short contract subsequently extended for a longer period, it is the length of the engagement that is relevant, rather than the length of each contract.

Personal factors

In deciding a person's employment status it may sometimes be necessary to take into account factors which are personal to the worker and which have little to do with the terms of the particular engagement being considered. For example, if a skilled worker works for a number of clients throughout the year and has a business-like approach to obtaining his engagements (perhaps involving expenditure on office accommodation, office equipment, etc) this will point towards self-employment (*Hall v Lorimer* (1993) 66 TC 349). Personal factors will usually carry less weight in the case of an unskilled worker, where other factors such as the high level of control exercised by the contractor are likely to be conclusive of employment.

Intention

It is the reality of the relationship that matters. It is not enough to call a person 'self-employed' if all the terms and conditions of the engagement point towards employment. However, if other factors are neutral the intention of the parties will then be the decisive factor in deciding employment status (*Massey v Crown Life Insurance Co* [1978] ICR 590).

Revenue guidance

In most cases the question of whether a worker would have been an employee of the client if engaged directly will be obvious from a careful consideration of the terms and conditions of the engagement and the surrounding facts. However, where a worker is in doubt about whether an engagement would have been employment or self-employment then he may ask for an opinion from the Inland Revenue. Full details of how to contact us can be found on our website at www.inlandrevenue.gov.uk/ir35. In such cases a copy of the relevant contract setting out the full terms and conditions of the engagement will have to be provided, together with details of any fact that he considers relevant to the status position. An opinion will only be given on signed contracts and not on draft agreements.

The terms of contracts used by service company workers who obtain engagements through agencies tend to be of a standard form. Such contracts typically require the worker to work on the client's premises, use the client's equipment, work standard hours, be paid at an hourly rate and be subject to a high level of control. In such cases, the opinion of the IR about the engagement is likely to be that it would be employment.

Where a worker is engaged on this type of contract for a period of one month or more, and cannot demonstrate a recent history of work including engagements which have the characteristics of self-employment (see the third example below) then we will say that the engagement would have been employment and therefore be covered by the new rules. Where the contract is for less than a month, then, although the engagement may still have been one of employment, the status position will be considered on a case by case basis.

Examples

The examples which follow illustrate the process for deciding whether an engagement is employment or self-employment. These examples are purely illustrative. They do not indicate the IR's view of the employment status of particular groups of workers. The role of the IR is to provide advice and guidance about the employment status resulting from a given set of circumstances, not to impose any particular status. The terms and conditions of any engagement are entirely a matter for the parties involved.

EXAMPLE 1—GORDON—AN IT CONTRACTOR WORKING THROUGH HIS OWN SERVICE COMPANY

FACTS	COMMENTS
Job description/control	
Client is a large retail concern. The contract was obtained through an agency. The terms and conditions of the engagement are set out in the contracts between the client and the agency and the agency and Gordon's company.	The fact that the engagement has been obtained through an agency has no bearing on whether Gordon would have been an employee or not.
Gordon works as part of a support team for the client's payroll system. The team leader (another IT contractor) tells Gordon what work he is to carry out at any particular time (eg help-desk work, specific maintenance tasks, etc).	

FACTS	COMMENTS
Job description/control—cont	
The client has the right to tell Gordon 'how' the work should be carried out—although in practice such control is not normally necessary. Gordon must work a regular forty-hour week on the client's premises.	The extensive right of control that exists here is a very strong pointer to employment. The more important features are the client's ability to shift Gordon from task to task and to specify how the work should be done—but in addition the client can control where and when the work is carried out.
Payment basis/risk	
Gordon's company is paid an hourly rate for Gordon's services. Any extra hours worked (by mutual agreement) are paid at 1.5 times the normal hourly rate. The client makes payment monthly following submission of an invoice by the agency. Gordon's service company invoices the agency.	The company is paid an hourly rate for Gordon's services and the only financial risk comes from invoicing. There is no opportunity to profit from sound management of the work covered by the contract. Overall this points to employment.
Holiday pay/sick pay	
No sick pay or holiday pay paid under the terms of the inter-company contract.	The engagement runs for six months and holiday pay/sick pay might be expected had there been a direct engagement. But both parties see the actual company/client contract as a contract for services and this is probably why no such payments are made. A minor pointer to self-employment.
Length of contract and personal factors	
The contract is for six months.	
Gordon uses a computer, telephone, fax, etc at home to seek and negotiate contracts for his company. Gordon has worked through his company for two other clients in the last two and a half years—one for three months and one for two years. Prior to that he was a direct employee of another engager.	Gordon's company has a limited 'business organisation' consisting of an office and associated equipment at his home. This is a pointer to self-employment—but not an overly important one in the context of a six-month contract of this sort.

FACTS	COMMENTS
Other factors	
The company is contracted to supply Gordon to do the work personally. All equipment and materials are supplied by the client.	Both point to employment.
Neither side can terminate the contract early.	Neutral factor (no right to terminate is common in engagements of this length—whether employment or self-employment).
There is no restriction imposed by the contract that prevents either Gordon or his company providing services to others during the engagement.	Mild pointer towards self-employment.
Both parties never intended Gordon to be an employee of the client.	Pointer to self-employment, but will only be relevant if the other factors are neutral.

Overall picture

The engagement is fairly long term and there is an extensive right of control over Gordon. He must carry out the services personally. The client provides equipment and accommodation and there is no significant financial risk to the company.

The only pointers to self-employment are the minimal financial risk (from invoicing), the ability to work for others (again, a minor point) and the existence of a business organisation/work for other clients.

Standing back from the detail therefore the engagement is one which would have been an employment had it been direct between Gordon and the client. The common intention for self-employment does not alter that. Whilst it would have proved decisive in a 'borderline' situation a review of other factors points strongly to employment here. The new rules would apply to the engagement.

EXAMPLE 2—HENRY—A CONSULTANT ENGINEER WORKING THROUGH HIS OWN SERVICE COMPANY

FACTS	COMMENTS
Job description/control	
Client is a large manufacturing company. Under a previous contract Henry has undertaken a broad review of a 15 year old production line and established that significant improvements could be made to the line to increase productivity. Under the current contract Henry is to produce a further report with detailed and costed proposals on the improvements and how they might be carried out with minimum disruption to production.	A specific task has been agreed and the client cannot shift the worker to another task. Henry has the major say over how the work is carried out and when. The clients does have some right to ongoing control over the work in that regular reports are required and changes in Henry's proposals can be sought.
Henry has a free hand over how his work is carried out and when (although there is a deadline of three months for completion). However, Henry is required to keep the client fully informed about progress and the client can require Henry to modify proposals if any aspect seems unsuitable to them.	Overall, control is limited.
Payment basis/risk/opportunity to profit	
Henry is paid £70 an hour but there is a ceiling of 300 hours on the work. If Henry takes longer than this he will only be paid extra if unforeseen difficulties arise or the client insists on unreasonable changes. If the work takes less than 300 hours Henry is only paid for the hours worked.	Henry is being paid an hourly rate and there is no real prospect of his making a loss. Nevertheless he is subject to a ceiling and must complete the work in the time allowed for otherwise he will have to finish the work in his own time without further payment. This is a mild pointer to self-employment.
Holiday pay/sick pay	
No sick pay or holiday pay paid under the terms of the inter-company contract.	Pointer to self-employment.

FACTS	COMMENTS
Length of contract and personal factors	
The contract has a deadline of 3 months.	
Henry has worked through his company as an engineer for many years and it is accepted that the company is 'in business'. The company has had many engagements similar to the current one and is generally engaged to provide an 'expert' service by clients with little engineering expertise.	The company has a business organisation and many different clients. This is a significant pointer to self-employment.
Henry has an office and computer at home which he uses for work extensively.	
Equipment	
Henry visits the client's factory regularly to examine the production line and processes. The only significant equipment he uses is his own computer (to prepare the report). 70% of the work is done in his office.	Significant and fundamental equipment is provided by the company as is office accommodation. This points to self-employment.
Other factors	
Engagement cannot be terminated 'early' other than following a breach of contract.	Neutral factor (no right to terminate is common in engagements of this length—whether employment or self-employment).
There is no restriction imposed by the contract that prevents either Henry or his company providing services to others during the engagement.	Mild pointer towards self-employment.
Both parties intend that the company is engaged to carry out the work and that Henry is not an employee of the client.	Pointer to self-employment, but will only be relevant if the other factors are neutral.

Overall picture

Henry is a skilled worker who has been engaged to carry out a specific task and control over him is limited. He is paid based on an hourly rate but there is an over-riding limit within which the work agreed must be completed. There is a contract deadline of three months and the company has many other clients. Some important equipment is supplied by the company and the work is mainly carried out away from the client's premises.

Henry would have been self-employed if engaged directly by the client and the new rules will not apply. Even if the contract had been expected to last for a longer period—say, nine months—the other factors would still have led to a conclusion of self-employment.

EXAMPLE 3—CHARLOTTE—AN IT CONSULTANT WORKING THROUGH HER OWN SERVICE COMPANY

FACTS	COMMENTS
Job description/control	
Charlotte's client for this engagement is a software company. She has been engaged for her programming skills to work on a specific project as part of a team developing a new piece of software. She works to the client's project manager who allocates particular sub-programs to Charlotte that she writes. The client expects the project to last for around three months. The manager specifies the way in which the sub-program is to be structured and can require changes to be made to make the work fit in with other parts of the program as it is developed, to rectify overall design faults, etc. Charlotte works a set number of hours but actual working times are flexible in line with the company's flexi-time arrangements for its employees. She is required to work at the client's premises.	There is an extensive right of control over Charlotte. The more important features are the client's ability to shift Charlotte from task to task and to specify how the work should be done. In addition the client can control to some extent where and when the work is carried out. But control is not total. Charlotte is engaged to work on a specific project so cannot be told to work on something completely different—and she cannot be required to work elsewhere. Overall, this is a strong pointer to employment.
Payment basis/risk/sick pay/holiday pay	
Charlotte is paid £3,600 every four weeks in return for working a 40-hour week. Extra payments are made at the equivalent hourly rate for any additional hours agreed.	It is the arrangements between the service company and the client that are important here. The company is paid the equivalent of a salary—with overtime payments—but no sick pay

FACTS	COMMENTS
Payment basis/risk/sick pay/holiday pay—cont	
Payment is made 14 days after the company has invoiced the client. No sick pay or holiday pay is paid; under the contract Charlotte has with her company she is paid an on-going, but much lower, salary which includes provision for holiday pay and sick pay.	or holiday pay. Although the invoicing arrangements result in a small financial risk this is minor. Overall there is no significant financial risk and no opportunity to profit from sound management of the task. This points to employment.
Length of contract and personal factors	
The contract is for 12 weeks—but there is provision for an extension if the project over-runs and all parties agree to the extension.	
Charlotte does some work for another client at weekends and has worked for various clients in the past—always through her company and often through employment agencies. Her contracts have usually lasted for between one and three months. Most have been similar to this one but some have involved her in specific tasks for a fixed fee using her own equipment and working at home.	Charlotte and her company have a 'business organisation'—including an office and associated equipment based at Charlotte's home. She has a variety of clients and all her contracts have been fairly short term.
Charlotte has an office at home and a computer and other office equipment that is used for some of her other work. These contribute to her company's business organisation—which she uses to obtain work, keep records, prepare invoices, etc.	This is a strong pointer to self-employment.
Other factors	
The company is contracted to supply Charlotte to do the work personally. All equipment is supplied by the client.	Both point to employment.
The engagement cannot be terminated 'early' other than following a breach of contract.	Neutral factor (no right to terminate is common in engagements of this length—whether employment or self-employment).

FACTS	COMMENTS
Other factors—cont	
There is no restriction imposed by the contract that prevents either Charlotte or her company providing services to others during the engagement.	Pointer to self-employment.
All parties intended that the company/client engagement would be self-employment.	Pointer to self-employment, but will only be relevant if the other factors are neutral.

Overall picture

This is a borderline case. On balance, given all the facts, Charlotte would have been self-employed had she been engaged directly by the client. The new rules will not apply to the engagement.

The following point towards self-employment:

- Existing business and a variety of different engagements, some of which would clearly count as self-employed if she had been engaged directly by her client.
- Overall business organisation (office and equipment at home, business like approach to obtaining engagements and carrying them out, etc). Charlotte would clearly be regarded as being 'in business on her own account' for those engagements where she carried out of a specific task for a fixed fee using her own accommodation and equipment.
- Risk from invoicing.
- The lack of an exclusivity clause.

Other factors point to employment:

- There is fairly extensive control over Charlotte. The client can dictate 'what' work is carried out on the project and 'how' the work is done. But control is not total. Charlotte cannot be directed to work on another project or undertake some quite different work. Nor is there control in other areas (eg she subject to the clients normal staff rules/disciplinary procedures).
- There is virtually no financial risk in the engagement and no opportunity to profit from sound management of the task.
- Charlotte must carry out the work herself.
- All equipment and accommodation is provided by the client.

What can then have more significance is the extent to which the individual is dependant upon, or independent of, a particular paymaster for the financial exploitation of his or her talents (see *Hall v Lorimer*). The fact that Charlotte's company is also engaged in contracts which involve carrying out a specific task for a fixed fee, using her own equipment, suggests that it is a genuine business and neither she nor her company rely on a single client for the exploitation of her talents. These factors balance the control and other employment factors that exist in this particular context and put the matter near the borderline where the mutual intention for self-employment becomes decisive.

However, the overall picture would have been rather different had the engagement been longer. For example, had the engagement been for twelve months the 'personal factors' would have been far less significant and the employment pointers would have predominated. Just because a person has an established business does not automatically make them self-employed for all engagements (see *Fall v Hitchin* ((1972) 49 TC 433)—also referred to in *Hall v Lorimer*). Also, if she had not also had contracts of a type which would clearly have fallen within the definition of self-employment, employment pointers would have dominated and the contract at issue would have been one of employment. The same could apply to shorter contracts.

Index